AF342416

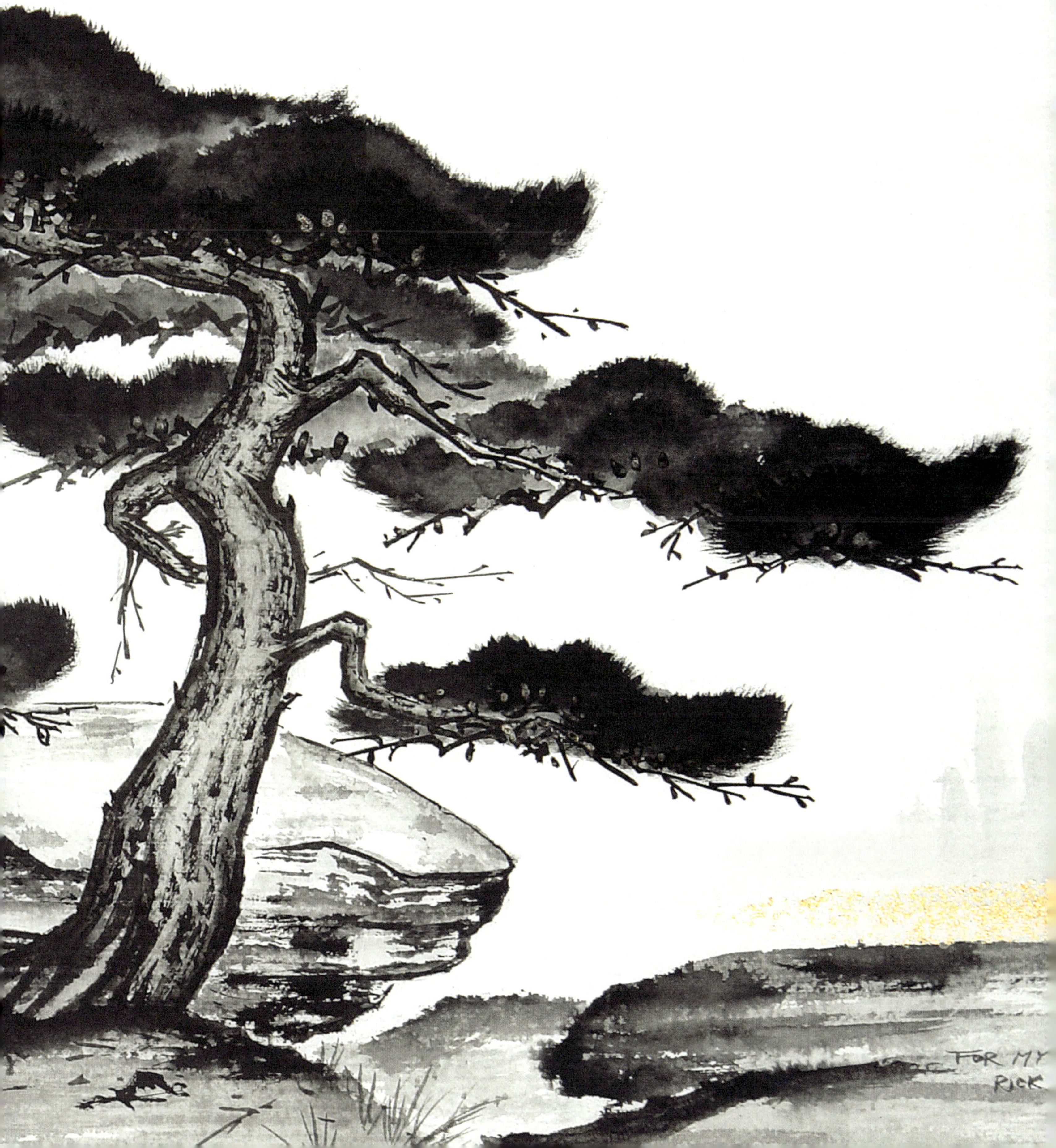

FOR MY
RICK

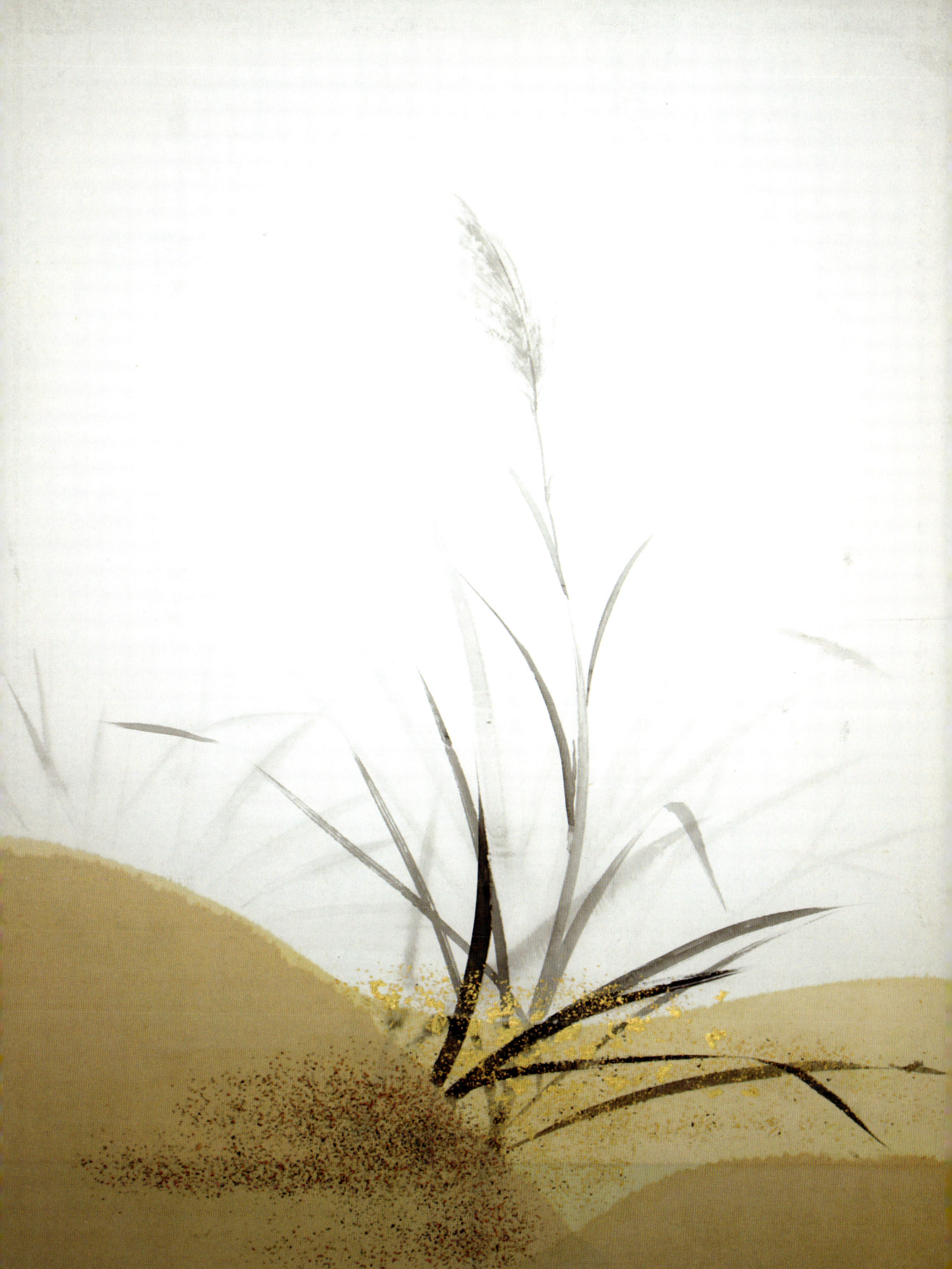

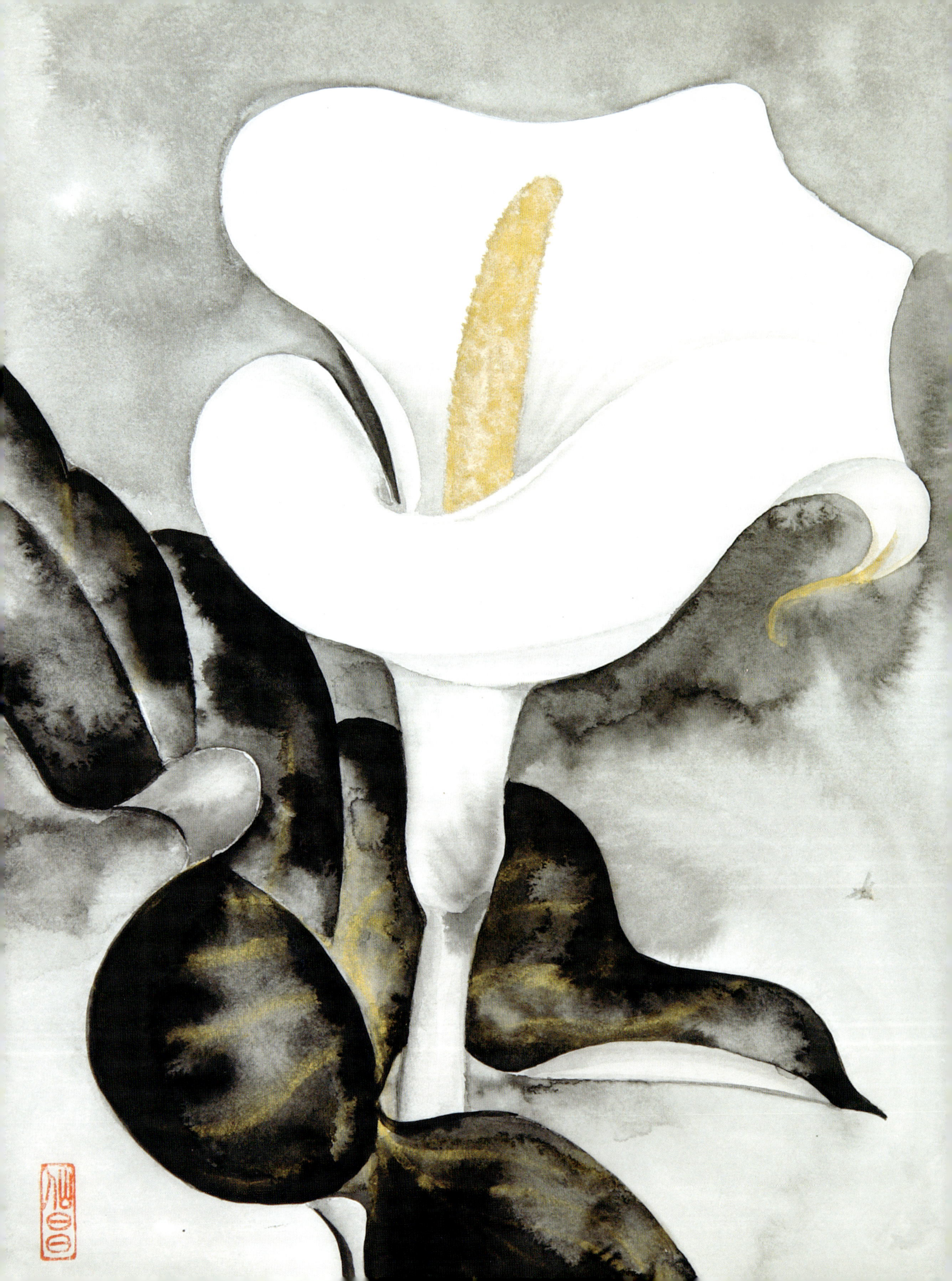

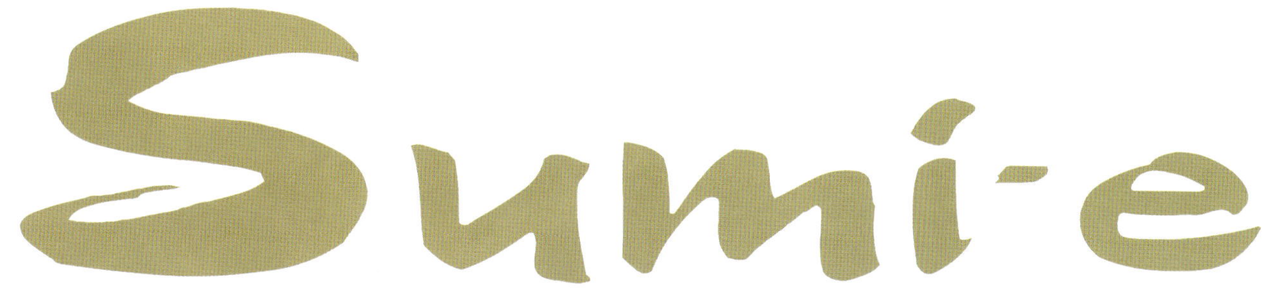

Sumi-e

THE ART OF JAPANESE INK PAINTING

SHOZO SATO

TUTTLE PUBLISHING
Tokyo · Rutland, Vermont · Singapore

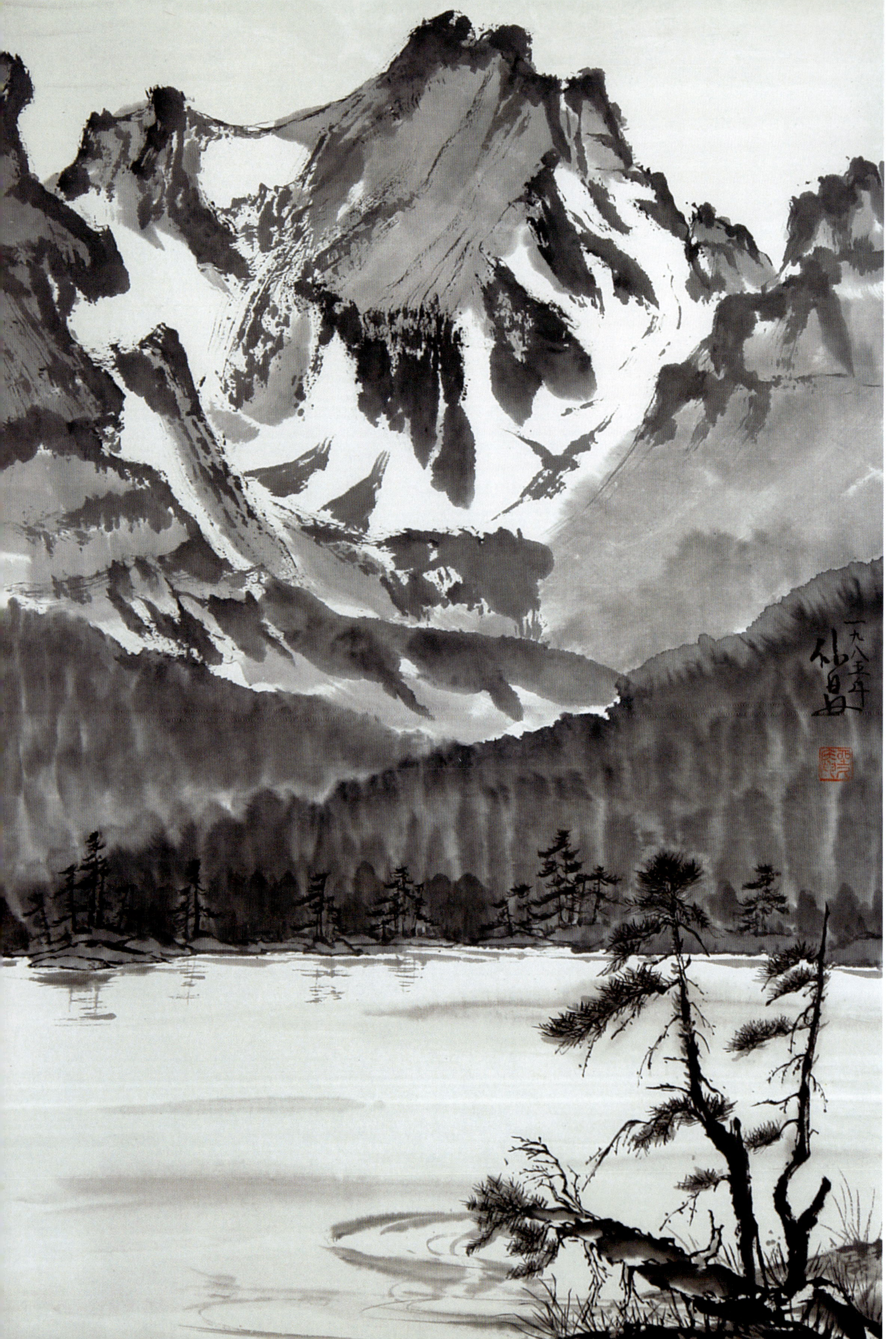

Contents

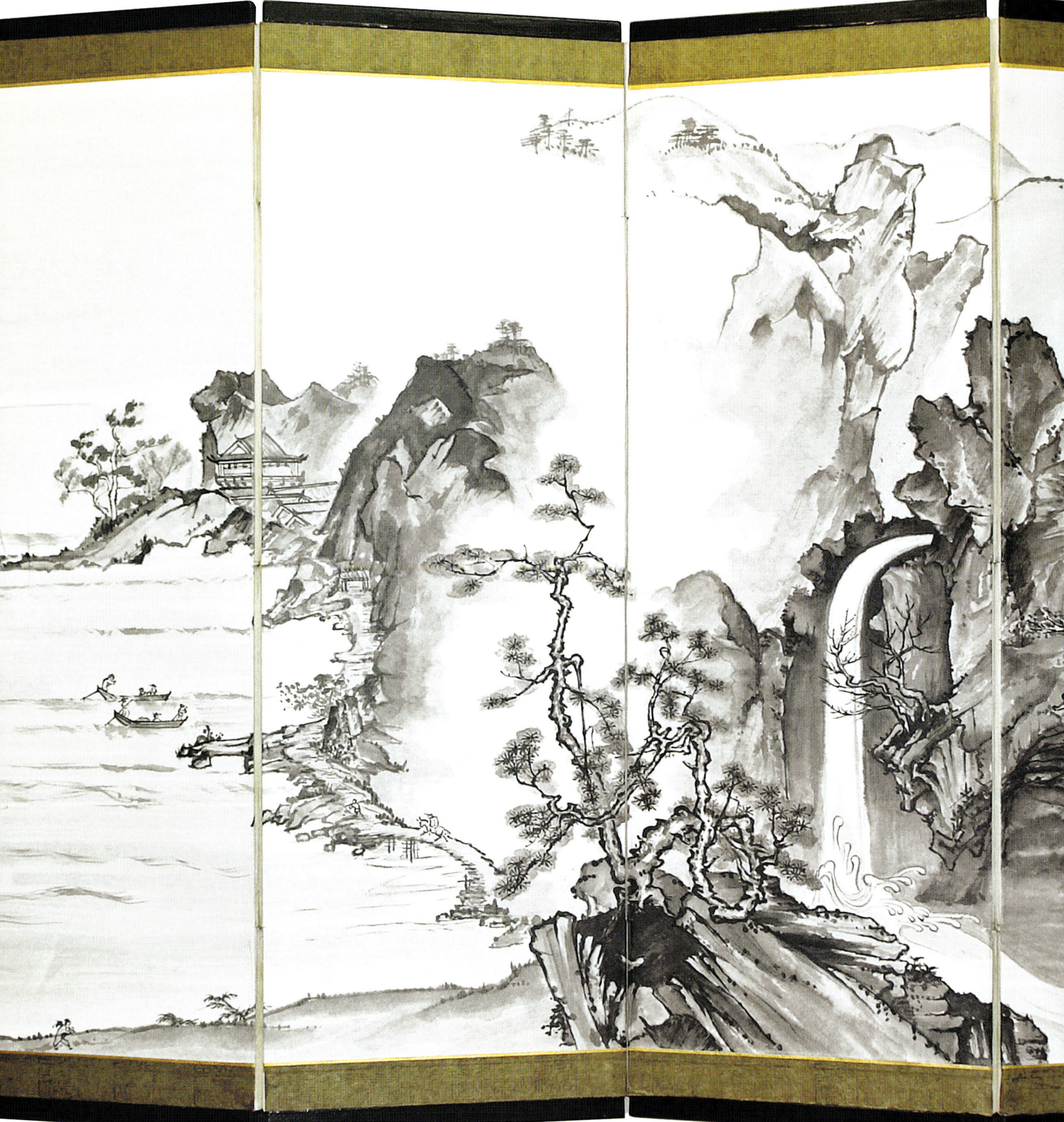

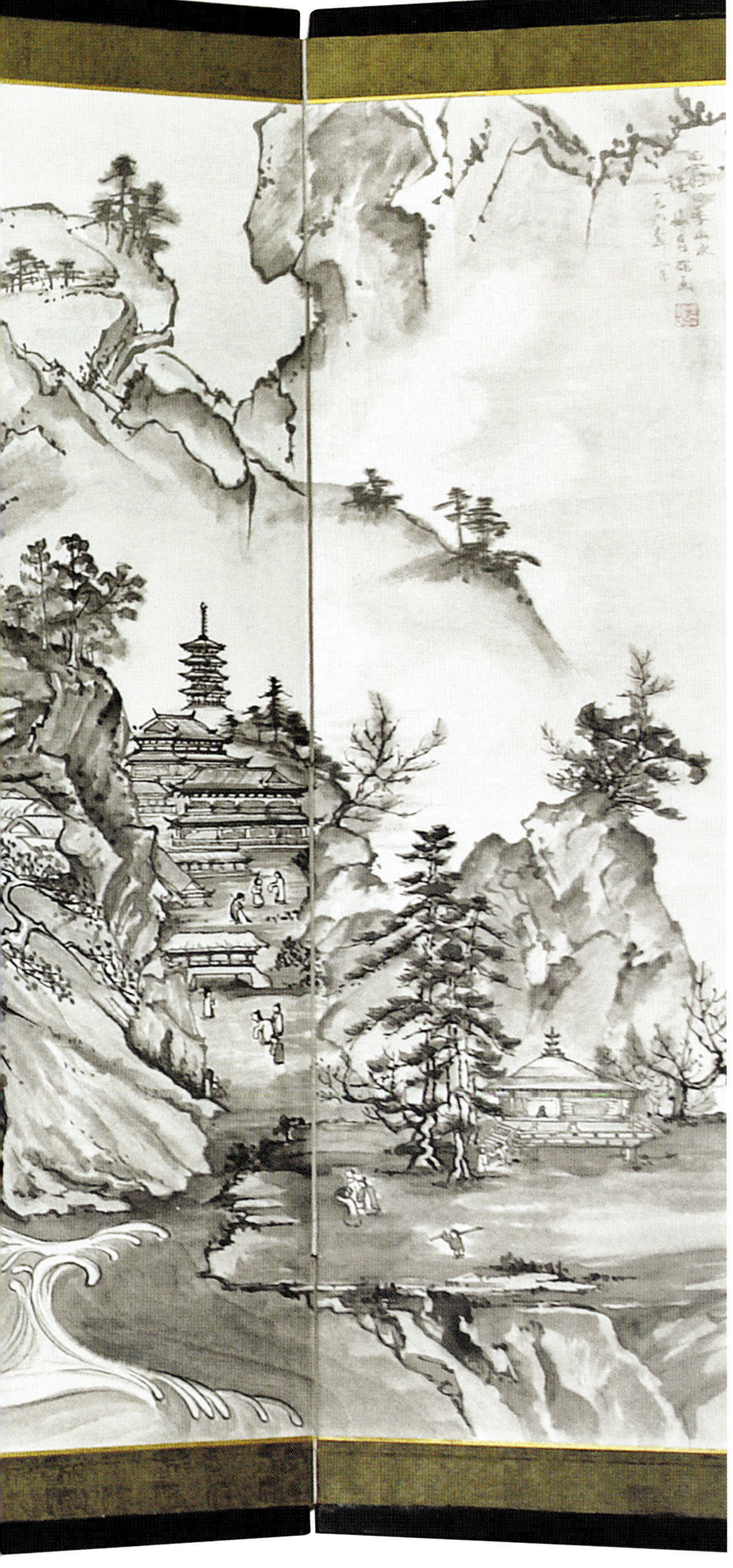

Preface

Years ago, when I was still a young art student in Japan, a Zen master once asked me: "What is the core function of art for you?" I pondered over this koan for some weeks. Then I replied to him, "It is vitamin C for the soul." He asked me to elaborate, and I explained that humans require vitamin C to maintain good health, but too much is simply wasted, that is, expelled from your body; likewise, art brings energy to your soul, however, too much can lead to decadence.

No matter how you as an individual may answer that question about art's function, artwork should express a universal reality, whether tranquility or agitation. The goal of the Japanese arts through the ages has been to create a sense of tranquility and peace. This applies to the art of monochrome, commonly known as sumi-e.

Den sho 伝承 (*den* = oral; *sho* = tradition or handing down) is the traditional oral way of passing down technical information, in all forms of art, to each successive generation. This book was written with the intention of translating this longstanding Asian teaching method from its oral form to the written page. It is difficult to offer a *den sho*–like, "one to one" teaching experience through a book. But I hope that some form of this practice's power will be conveyed even through the written word, as I pass along the experience I received from my own mentor years ago in the art of sumi-e.

Den sho means that the mentor, in addition to giving oral instruction, will often literally take the hand of the student and guide him or her. This close contact in instruction also leads the mentor to convey over time a philosophy of art and a way of life to the student; thus, this approach to creating art of course reaches beyond the commercialization of the art form. In fact, a tenet of the teaching of the fine arts at the university level in Japan is that students are not allowed to enter their work in competitions or display them in galleries, simply because if a painting is sold, the thinking goes, a young student's mind will be set on the style and subject matter of the work rather than its meaning, and the student will lose his or her own intrinsic creative spirit.

In this book, my hope is that while the "how to" has been shown in step-by-step fashion, some of my deeper experience will also be conveyed through the words and images. In my classes at university and professional levels, and now with you here in these pages, it has been my mission to pass my experience on together with the philosophical and technical aspects of the art of sumi-e.

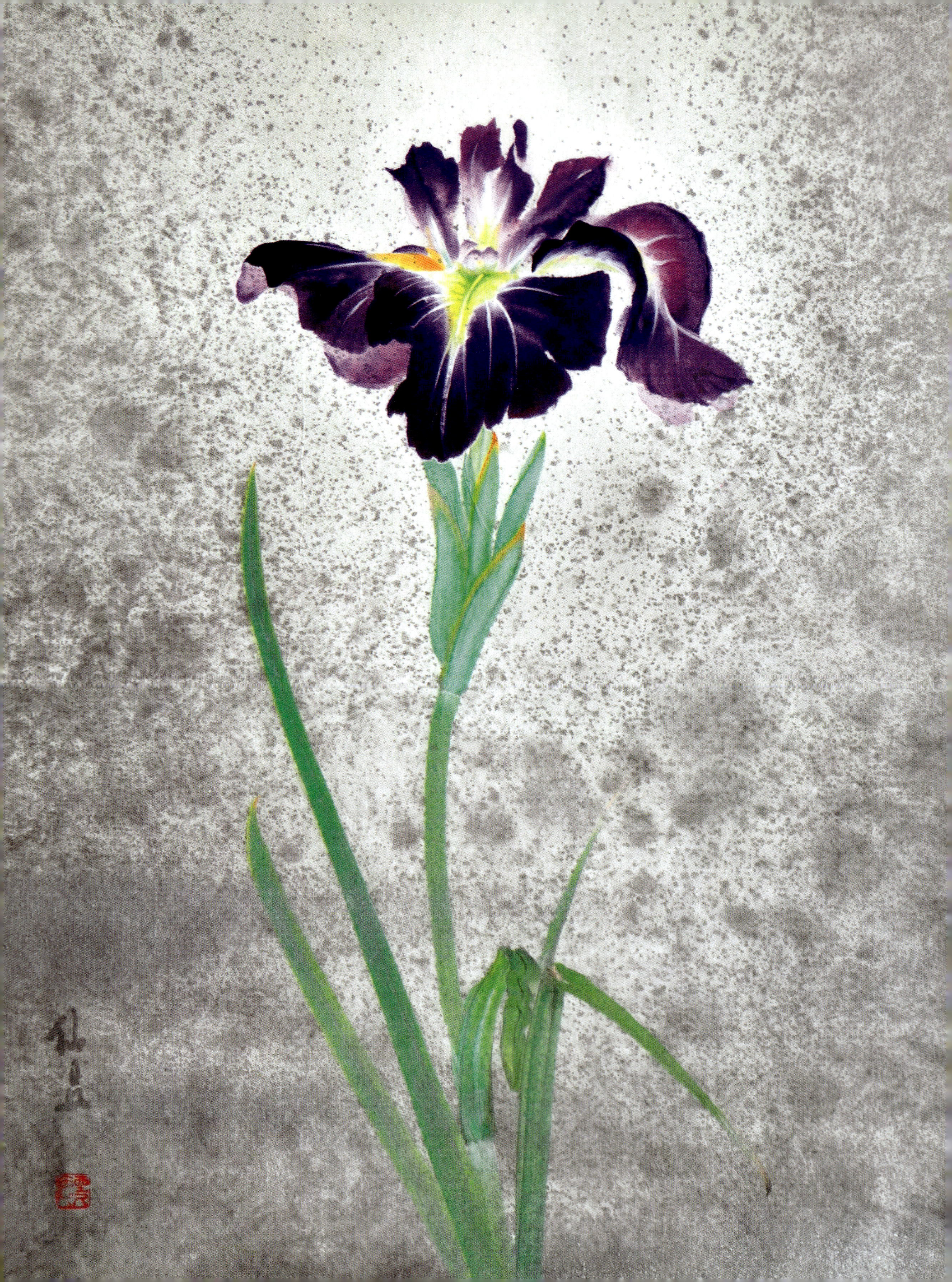

Suiboku-ga and Sumi-e

Sumi-e is commonly described as art done in monochrome, with the use of sumi ink and handmade paper. *Sumi-e* means "black ink painting" (*sumi* = black ink; *e* = painting). The ideogram 墨 which is read *sumi* in Japanese can also be read as *boku* in Chinese, and as is true of most Asian art and culture, the roots of Japanese painting are found in China.

The early stages of monochrome art became a recognized genre during the ninth century in China, and *suiboku-ga* (*sui* = water; *boku* = sumi ink; *ga* = painting) was gradually disseminated throughout the Far East. These paintings were usually done on silk. Later, when handmade paper became readily available, the spreading of sumi ink upon that new, absorbent surface created another, different form of monochrome painting which has a more direct spiritual connection with the artist: sumi-e.

I have elected to make a definitive distinction between suiboku-ga and sumi-e styles of ink painting, because technically speaking, suiboku-ga, which was developed from the "outline" painting done on sized silk, came *before* the art that is produced with minimized strokes in sumi ink—sumi-e. Internationally, and especially in the U.S., all monochrome art that uses sumi ink has been called sumi-e. Very little has been written about suiboku-ga in most English-language texts, and in most publications on the subject the terms *sumi-e* and *suiboku-ga* are used interchangeably.

But being aware of their differences helps you to see that there are "two sides to the coin" in monochrome art, and helps you to recognize how philosophy is an essential underpinning to this art. As well, a brief look at their contrasts offers a glimpse of the rich history that ink painting has absorbed and reflects today.

Suiboku-ga is based upon the Chinese word *sui un sho ga* (*sui* = water; *un* = spreading in gradation; *sho* = distinct representation, *ga* = painting). Since the word *suiboku-ga* contains the additional concept of "water," it has more complexity in contrast to the simpler word *sumi-e*.

Suiboku-ga is commonly painted in greater detail with overlapping brush strokes, and in addition, it may be large in size. Obviously, the literal definitions of the words mean that if a work contains great detail with many brush strokes in black ink, it can also correctly be termed sumi-e or boku-ga; but suiboku-ga would be a more formalized terminology for this type of work.On the other hand, paintings which are produced with minimal strokes are the ones I prefer to call sumi-e.

Paintings have been important to humankind from ancient times. Long before it would reach across the water to Japan, the influential Northern Sung style of paintings had its beginning in China during the first and second centuries of the Han Dynasty (221 BC–AD 221). In the Han Dynasty black ink was used for creating "white paintings": an outline of sumi ink was drawn, then filled in with brilliant colors to create multicolored paintings. Eventually, white paintings without pigments added became recognized as a new genre of art. Then, during the Northern Sung period (960–1126), brush strokes in sumi began to be used within the outlines, instead of color, to further enhance the subject. The overall impression of these paintings was grand but somber, and carried a hint of oppressiveness. Northern Sung styles continued to prevail during the subsequent Southern Sung period (1127–1279) but new methods were also being introduced. Artists began to use the brush sideways to produce a gradient of different tones in sumi ink, which offered in another way to render the subject, often without using outlines. These were the foundations which led to the developing of paintings done solely in sumi ink.

The major contributions to Chinese painting as we know it today began with the Northern and Southern Sung periods, and continued through the dynasties of the Yuan (1280–1368), the Ming (1368–1644), and the Ching (1644–1912). The imperial courts of each of these dynasties established a system where court-appointed masters in painting produced artwork expressly for the emperor and other royalty. These master artists were given ornamental belts and studios within the royal compound and they proudly displayed their belts to show rank. However, individual rulers promoted their own cultural heritages (be they Han, Mongolian, or Manchurian) via their master artists' brushes, and also influenced the nature and subject of the artworks, leaving little creativity to the artists. For example, if the Emperor built a summer palace, he might request that the artist make paintings suggesting coolness for the walls and doorways. The artist's job was to visualize what the emperor wished and then carry it out. To do this it was necessary for the artists to have thorough knowl-

Left: This shobu iris was painted using traditional Japanese pigments, with sumi in the background pattern. Chapter 5 explores this technique further.

edge in style and techniques, but the original ideas and the artistic sensibility belonged to the patrons. Even so, during this long period of the court-appointed artist system, artwork did not remain static and the artistic approach to paintings did continue to change.

Throughout the long history of China, the work of scholars, government officials, wealthy landowners and other members of the educated classes included the transcribing of documents and the writing of literature. These gentlemen of letters were accustomed to using brush and ink on paper when recording documents or writing poetry. They did not have professional training in painting techniques but especially during the Southern Sung dynasty, as a hobby, many began to add simplified artwork to their poetry; it was natural enough, since they were so familiar with the use of a brush. Thus began the merging of poetry with artwork.

Generally speaking, the literati did not use the rigid outline technique in these simplified paintings but began to use the brush in innovative ways. Artwork by the court-appointed artists was often criticized as lacking in vitality and as being stagnant; the literati, on the other hand, were using their own creative ideas, and their spontaneous and energized methods in painting were a refreshing change. Their simplified but sometimes bold use of the brush would often capture the spirit of the subject, and could convey a wide range of expression, from dynamic power to elegance and tranquility. This is the art style that I term sumi-e.

Zen Buddhist monks from China introduced the Northern Sung style of paintings to Japan during the Muromachi period in the fourteenth century. These works reflected the oppressive grandeur that was so characteristic of the Northern Sung. During the fifteenth century, as the monks brought the newer, more flexible styles of Southern Sung and Yuan to Japan, new trends in artistic expression began there.

This was also a time when other great changes were taking place in Japan and the warrior classes came to power. With the advent of the Tokugawa Shogunate system of government in 1603, a new era of social stability emerged in the nation and there was now time to cultivate the arts. Zen Buddhism exerted a powerful influence on the warrior classes who no longer were required to spend time in endless territorial or civil wars. A newly developed pastime for these upper classes was *chado*, tea ceremony, which influenced Japanese arts of all kinds toward greater elegance and refinement.

During this same period in China under the Ming and Ching dynasties, in place of the black ink outlines, a new style of art emerged using vibrant and opulent colors. Limited by the court-appointed artists system, this art too reached a point of stagnation. But when the Ching Dynasty came into power, the emperor promoted literary education as well as suiboku-ga in the style of the Southern Sung. As a consequence art reached a high point in refinement, both in craftsmanship and artistic expression.

However, the literati throughout these periods refused to be caught up in the trends and fashions of the times and retained their belief that paintings should capture the spirit (not all the physical details) of the object or theme. From their viewpoint, intricate paintings with minute details were merely an "explanation"; they did not convey the spirit of the subject. Compared to the art's beginnings based in Northern Sung style, the brush strokes were now reduced in number and simplified and were often combined with poetry. This style of painting, whether done by the Chinese literati (*wen jen*) or the Japanese literati (*bunjin)*, suggested the subject, rather than describing its details. Importantly, the *bunjin* artists also recognized the importance of active empty space: the viewer was stimulated to become a participator in the painting. This active empty space is an important component of the style.

Also during the Ming and Ching dynasties, another style of color painting was developed that adapted some sumi-e brush handling techniques. Unlike the sumi-e approach where several tones of sumi were applied to the bristles of one brush to create a gradation, this time, color pigments were applied to the bristles to create a gradient blend of colors. Often black ink was also incorporated as part of the painting. This technique is still commonly seen in contemporary Chinese paintings.

Even this very brief history of the emergence of painting with sumi (black ink) shows us that in both suiboku-ga and sumi-e, and even in paintings using color, the focus of the art of ink painting since its inception has been on the quality of the line; this is what captures the form. In the art of the West, the focus is generally more on color to develop the form.

As we move on to the details and process of creating ink paintings, we will look at and create paintings of both kinds, in order to understand suiboku-ga and sumi-e more deeply.

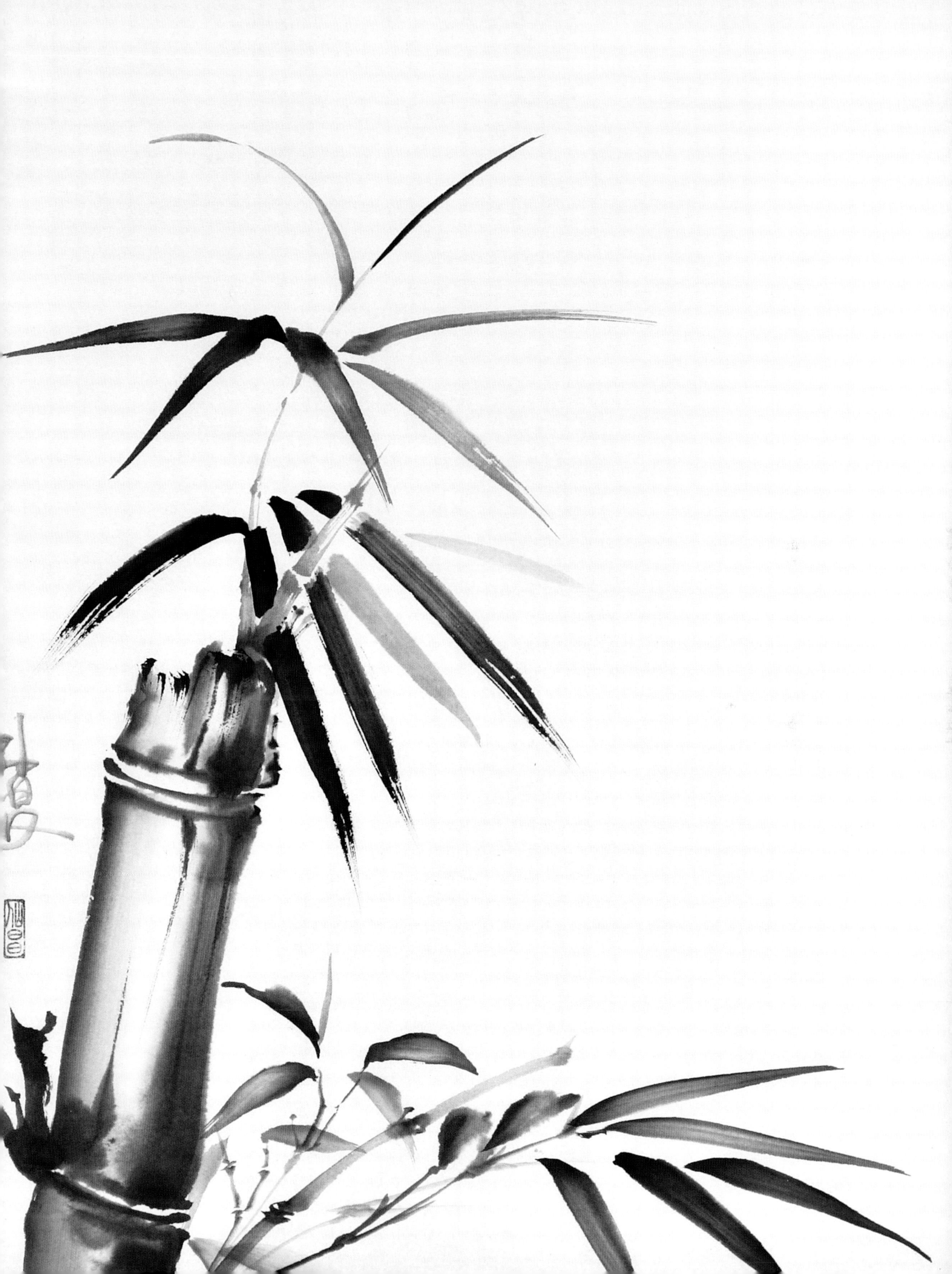

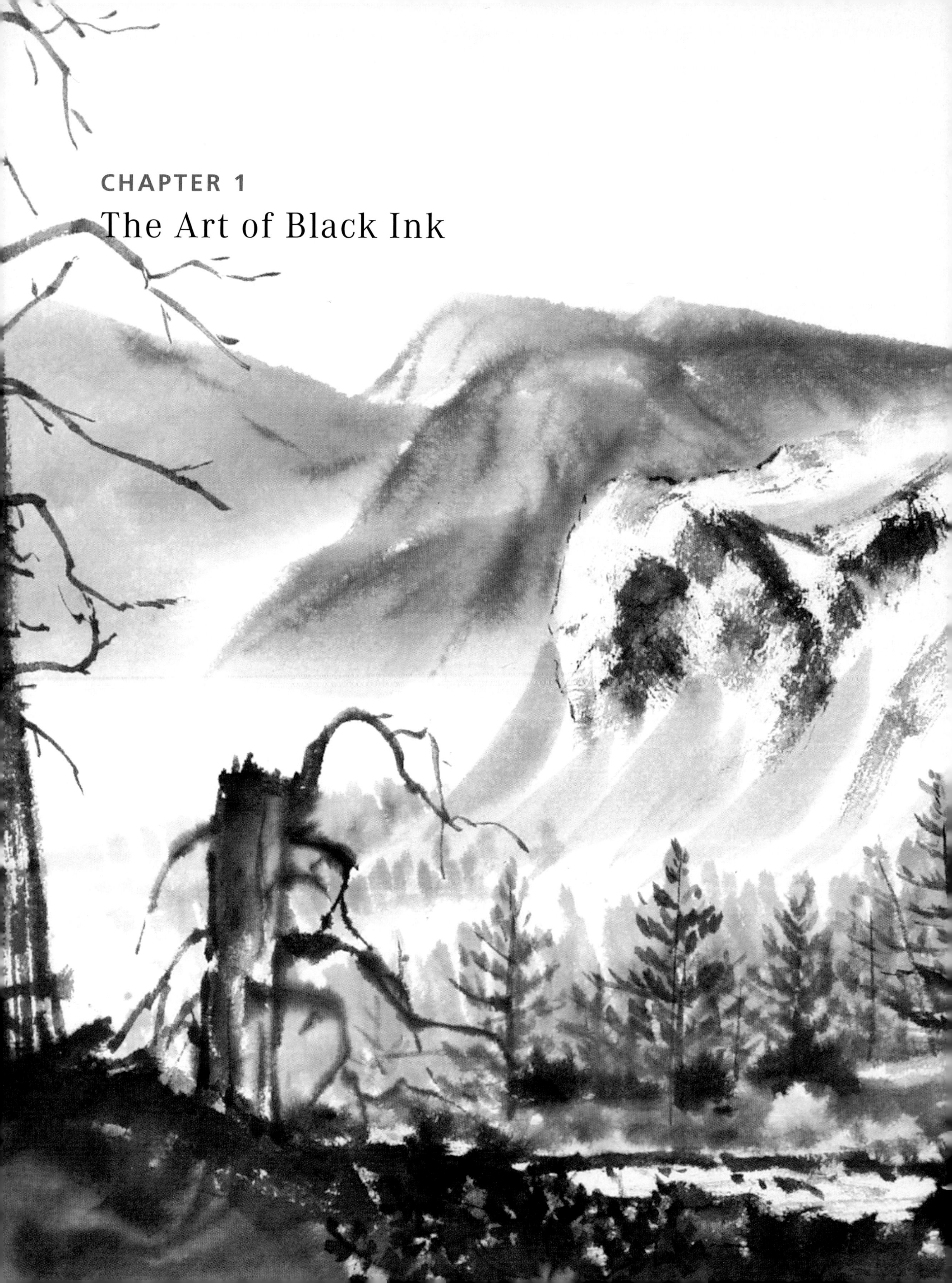

The Art of Black Ink

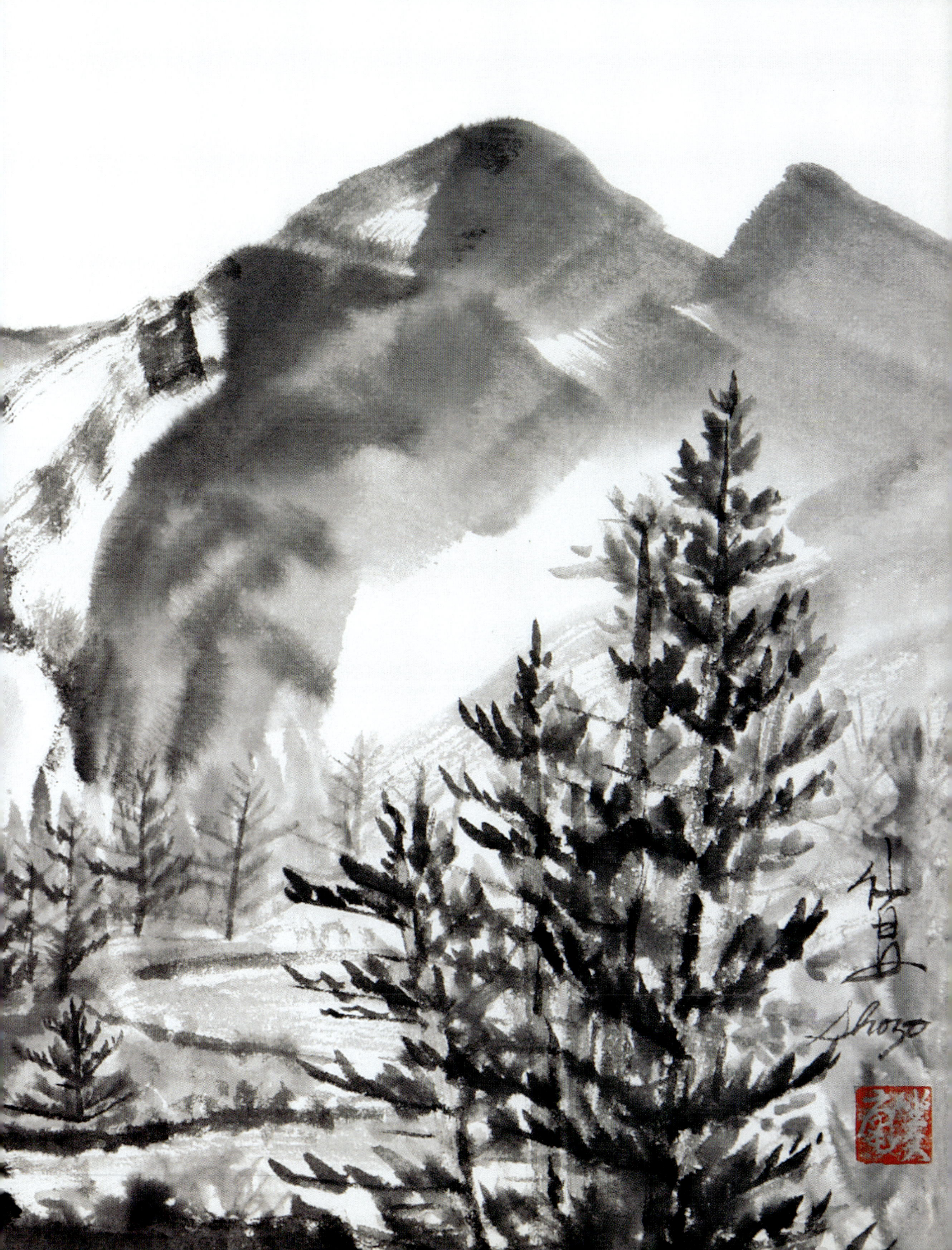

The Relationship between Calligraphy and Painting

Among the historical differences between European-based cultures and the Far East is the method and tools of writing, so important for communication and keeping records. From the earliest times, a brush was used for writing in China and this practice continues today in many areas of Asia. The use of the brush as a tool in both writing and painting makes it difficult to draw a clear demarcation between them; there is an overlap between the utilitarian and the fine arts.

As we learned earlier, during the periods in history when China was ruled by emperors, among the populace were very well educated landlords and priests who were accustomed to dealing with brush, ink and paper every day. During their daily activities of copying sutras or writing documents for the government, they would take a break from their work to enjoy composing poetry and often would add a simple paintings to their work. Whether one would call it writing or painting, these works by the literati gradually became recognized as a genre of art. In Japanese their work is called *bunjin-ga* (*bun* = letter, *jin* = person, *ga* = painting).

It has been recorded that the earliest Chinese paper appeared around 206 B.C. during the Han Dynasty. It is generally supposed that the fibers from various plants woven for clothing, such as varieties of flax, were also used for making of paper. Archaeological finds in remote Chinese provinces include paper made from flax. Eventually fibers from other plants began to be used. As papermaking developed from the primitive to the sophisticated, the making of sumi ink from soot was also perfected. As the availability of paper became widespread and brushes of various types and sizes were developed, both writing and painting undoubtedly became more commonplace. In the Far Eastern countries down through the ages, all documents and other written forms of communication required sumi ink and brush, until European cultural influences brought new ways to write. Today, the world over, the convenience of ballpoint pens, fountain pens and pencils makes them a daily necessity. And computer-generated text—e-mails and such—has taken over much writing.

Yet, writing with a brush continues today. In contemporary Japan, every first grader in school learns to write with a brush in a special class reserved for calligraphy. In contrast to pens and pencils, the use of a brush, whether for calligraphy or painting, carries with it established methods and rules both historically and traditionally developed. The various types of brushes and the effect they leave on the various kinds of paper are of paramount importance. The amount of ink the brush can hold must be controlled and the effects created when painting lines, from wide to narrow, in tones from dark to light, requires knowledge, skill and experience. When one is taught as a child, this may become routine, but when an adult is confronted with brush, ink and paper for the first time, it can be a daunting challenge.

Learning some basic lessons from writing can help you.

The brush is used in a similar way for both calligraphy and painting, and I feel that learning the use of brush through calligraphy brings better understanding of the basic qualities of lines for a painting. Therefore, I consider this a very important first step.

When writing with a ballpoint pen, one moves the tip continuously across the paper, but when writing with a brush, one often lifts it up and then down as it moves across the paper in order to create a line which narrows or widens. When writing with a brush, the movement will be a combination of right to left *and* up and down. This simple movement appears to be easy, yet it is difficult to master. Here are some helpful ways to learn and embody the key principles and to make a physical connection with sumi-e.

KNOWING THE DIFFERENCE BETWEEN A PEN AND A BRUSH: ENERGY

To understand the difference between the use of a brush and a ballpoint pen, let us first turn to the ideogram *dai* ("great," "big").

- Use your pointing finger as an imaginative brush, and trace the character on the next page. Beginning on the left end of the horizontal line, give your finger a little pressure, then relax the pressure and move on to the right.
- When you come to the end of the stroke, repeat a similar pressure but in addition bring your fingertip back a bit on the line, then lift your finger up. (This horizontal line alone is the ideogram for the number "one." You have already written a word!)
- The next stroke to trace begins at the top and moves to the left bottom. Give a slight pressure at the beginning and move down with a slight curvature, then gently release your finger from the paper. Your fingernail should be last to leave the paper.
- The next stroke begins near the joint of the horizontal and upright lines. Make contact with the paper with your fingernail first, then as you move your finger to right bottom, the ball of the finger should make contact with the paper and give pressure. Gradually release the pressure so that your fingernail is the last to leave the paper.

Now you have experienced the writing of the ideogram of "great." This simple exercise shows how different the use of a

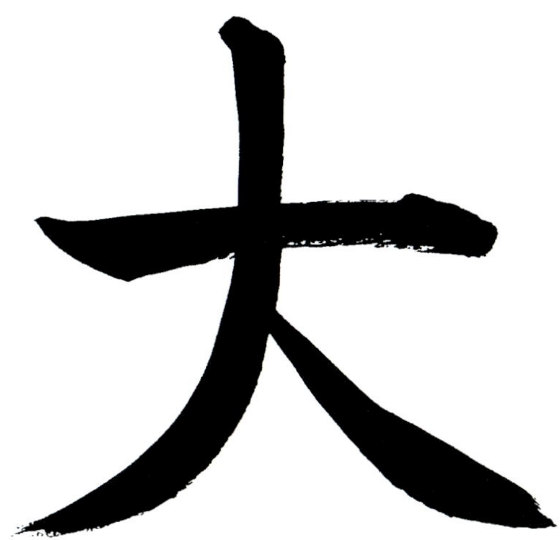

Above: **This ideogram is** *dai,* **or "great." Following the exercise steps in the text, trace over it with your index finger to better understand the intrinsic nature of brushwork.**

brush is from a ballpoint pen or pencil. Energy is a key difference. In the instructive text here, "pressure with the fingers" is used as a convenient way to explain the process but in reality, these "pressures" should be internalized *chi* or *ki,* energy which is centered in the lower abdomen to form a unity of body and spirit. The pressure of the ball of your finger should be accompanied with your inner energy. In the yin-yang balance of energy, this energy is considered "yang." When pressure is reduced while the finger is moving to the right in the first stroke of *dai* the energy becomes "yin," but the increased ending pressure is again "yang." We can say, with only slight exaggeration, that the energy balance among "yang-yin-yang" has been experienced in this one line. This is the uniqueness of the use of black ink with a brush.

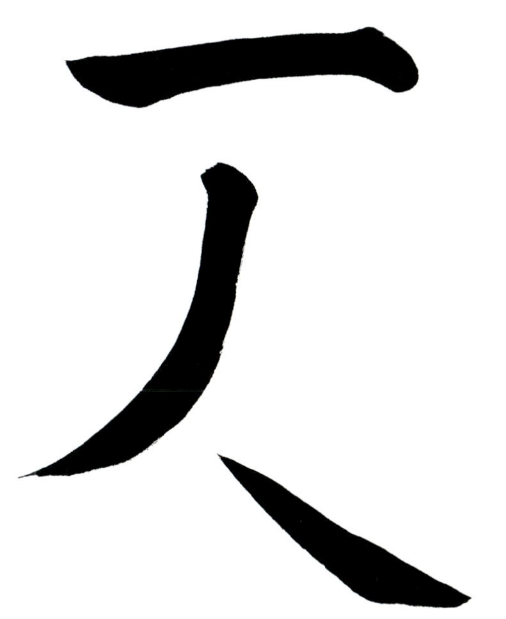

Above: **The individual lines for the ideogram of** *dai.*

Now try the exercise again, this time tracing not the character *dai* but its separated, individual strokes, focusing on each one. Follow the lines with your fingertips once more, this time focusing on your inner energy while your finger moves along the lines. The actual use of the brush with ink will feel different than this, of course. Nevertheless, this will help you to become aware of your inner energy.

PRACTICING WITH *EI*, *DAI* AND *WA*

Ei: Eternity—The Eight Strokes

There are eight basic strokes from which all of the kanji ideograms in Chinese, Korean and Japanese are formed (as written in the formal style). There is a character which includes all eight of these basic strokes, so practicing it is useful for beginners. This is the word *ei* which means "to prolong" and can be translated as "eternity."

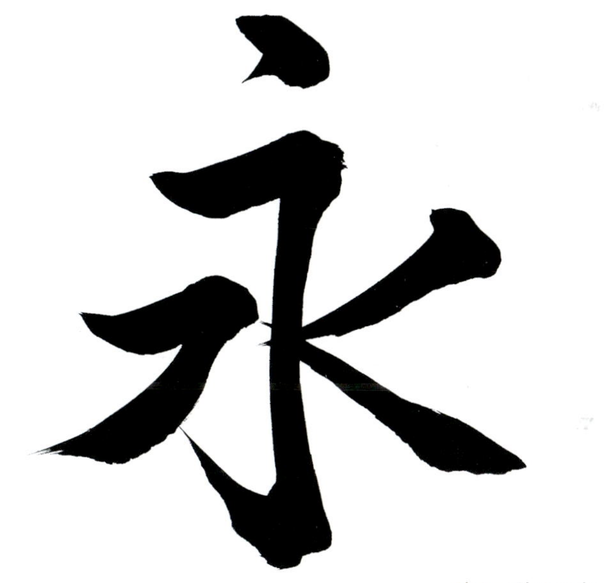

Above: *Ei:* **Eternity**

To develop an understanding of the eight strokes, use your pointing finger as a brush to trace the strokes. Follow the directional lines shown in red on the next page. Feel the up and down pressure of movements across the paper. This should help to give you a feel for the visual effect you plan to create.

These brush strokes that are used to create all the other ideograms are also the basic strokes for creating a painting. For instance, Stroke 2 or Stroke 5 can be immediately used for a bamboo stalk, and Stroke 6 and Stroke 8 are essentially the shape of the leaves of bamboo.

When you do write this ideogram with a brush, some of the lines such as 2, 3, and 4 are actually formed as a single continuous line.

The movement of the energy and active empty space are the fundamental aspects in visual art and have been crystallized in this single ideogram. This is a clear illustration that the art of calligraphy is the foundation of the art of black ink.

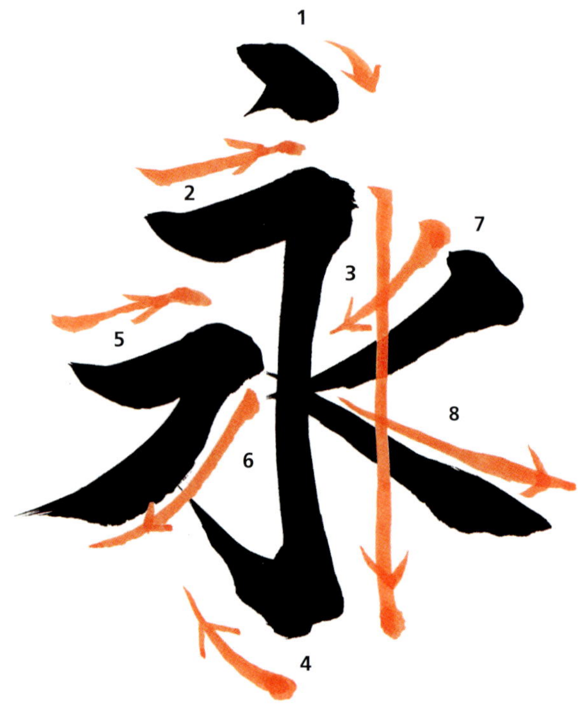

Stroke 1 To create the "dot," the brush should be placed lightly on the paper. The little pointed mark on the left indicates where the brush is lifted and moved on to the next stroke.

Stroke 2 The movement of the brush is directed to the right, as the red arrow shows. Notice, this line is very different from one created by a ball-point pen which is an even line from beginning to end! Substantial pressure should be given to the beginning and ending of the stroke. Give greater pressure down on the paper as you begin; then relax your fingers as you move right; but when reaching the end, increase pressure and give a slight bounce; then change the direction of the brush 90 degrees while the brush is still in contact with the paper for the downward movement coming next.

Stroke 3 In the process of changing the direction of the brush, notice how a bone-joint form is created. As Stroke 3 moves downward, relax your finger pressure and lift the brush up, then move down with pressure to the end of the line.

For **Stroke 4**, the brush is turned 45 degrees and moves to the left. It is lifted up to create the point. (Again notice the bone joint effect.) Note that Strokes 2, 3 and 4 are one continuous line.

Stroke 5 is similar to Stroke 2. At the end of the Stroke 5, turn the brush 45 degrees to the left and move down for Stroke 6.

Stroke 6 In this case, the transition between 5 and 6 is much smoother without added pressure. Compare the joint line between 2 and 3 with that between 5 and 6. This 5–6 joint will not result in a bone joint. Note that the 5–6 line does not touch the midpoint of 3 and is framed by the space of line 2–3–4. This is because 5 and 6 are thicker lines and the space is needed to create more active empty space. In the process of moving down for Stroke 6, lift the brush up slightly then down (more pressure), and finally the brush is gently lifted up. The tip is the last to leave the paper. Lift the brush, then move in a clockwise circle in the air to begin Stroke 7.

Stroke 7's head is created with the definite "landing position" of the brush. As the brush moves down toward the left, it is lifted gently but the tip remains in contact with the paper. While the brush is in the air, your arm should be in clockwise movement and moving down for Stroke 8.

The line for **Stroke 8** should begin with the tip of the brush. Gradually press down to the halfway point of the bristles, giving maximum pressure. Then gently lift the brush to create the end point.

Dai: Great or Big—Strokes for Painting

Dai is a simple ideogram containing three strokes. Let's look at them again (see the facing page):

1. the **A** stroke is wide to wide;
2. the **B** stroke is wide to narrow; and
3. the **C** stroke is narrow-wide-narrow.

The strokes in this ideogram can be immediately transformed into the fundamental strokes for a bamboo painting.

Similar to the previous example of the eight-stroke ideogram *ei,* here the **A** stroke's beginning and ending are given additional emphasis with pressure, while the center part is more relaxed: wide...to wide. If you create a series of consecutive A strokes, you will recognize a bamboo stalk in horizontal position. Draw them in an upright fashion, and you will successfully create a stalk of bamboo.

The joint lines of the bamboo stalk are exactly the same stroke—stroke A—but are much smaller. Each stroke has a definite beginning and ending with a slight curvature in the center.

Below that, notice how the same composition of lines, but much finer and smaller, creates bamboo sub-branches.

The **B and C** strokes can be used to paint leaves of bamboo. The B stroke, wide at the beginning, forms a leaf that is coming toward you.

Thus the ideogram *dai* has the required fundamental lines for painting bamboo. Look at *Morning Breeze* on page 130, one example of a bamboo painting.

You should recognize that from one basic stroke with the brush, combined with an artist's understanding of the function and quality of line, variations can be used to create a painting.

These brush strokes are characteristic of *kan-ga,* Japanese paintings which were influenced by Chinese calligraphy and painting. After he returned from China, the "saint of suiboku-ga" Sesshu (see page 20) used these brush strokes in almost all of his paintings of trees and rocks in outline form. The Kano School, the major school appointed by the Shogunate, also used this *kan-ga* technique in their paintings.

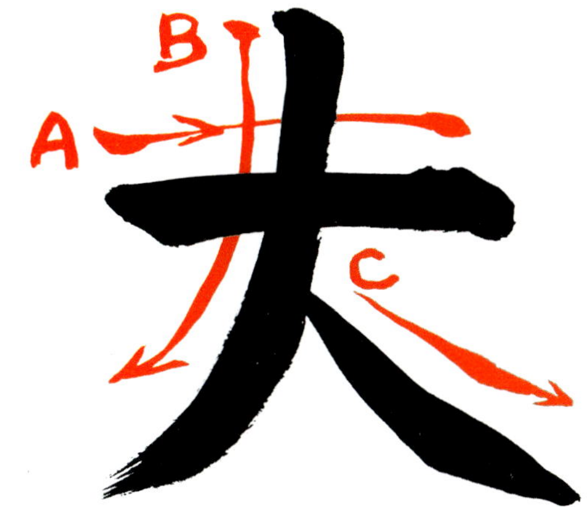

Dai: Great or big

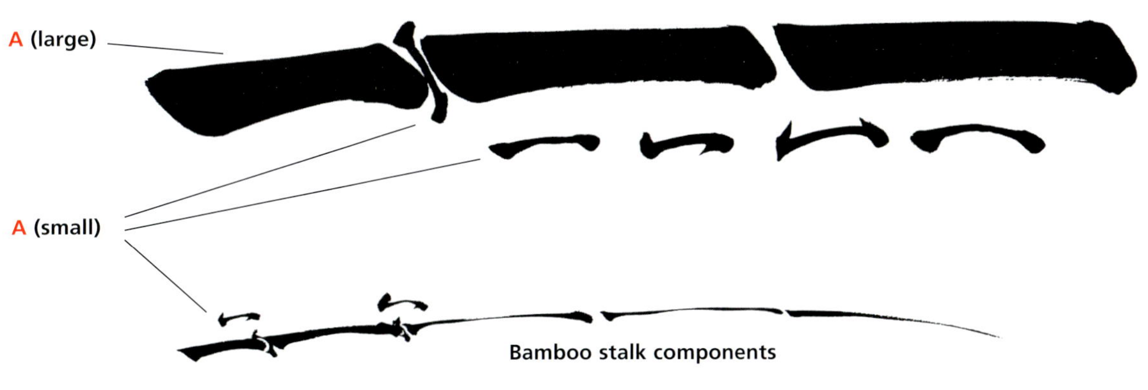

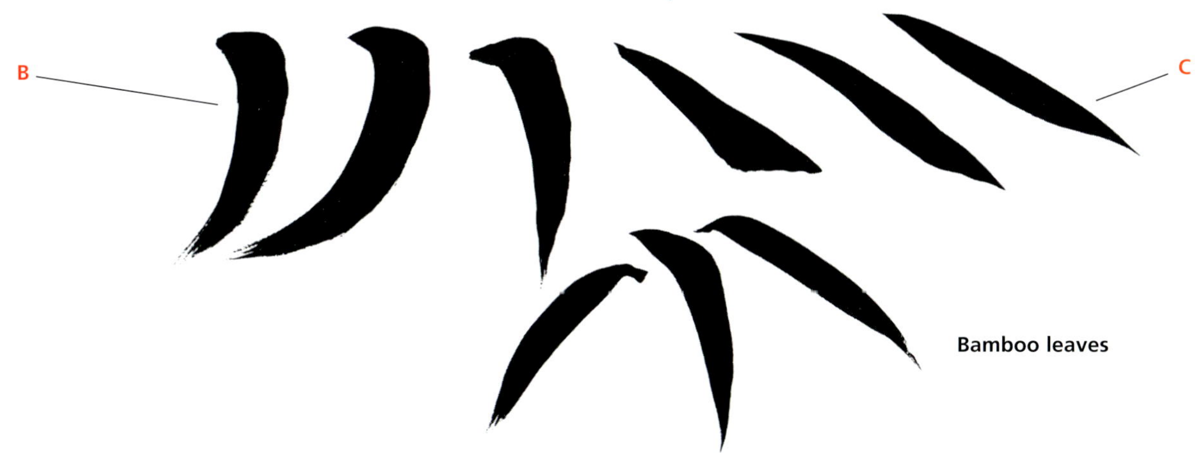

Wa: Harmony—The Three Styles

We can learn another helpful introductory lesson from writing the character for "harmony," *wa,* in the three different styles: *kaisho* (formal), *gyosho* (semi-formal) and *sosho* (informal). It is possible to write these three styles using one type of brush. However, because the styles are so different—from the rigidity of formal writing to the flowing lines of informal writing—professionals and beginners alike find it much easier to use a proper brush for each category. We will discuss brushes in greater detail in Chapter 2, but some information is impor-tant to understand now because the use of each brush is directly related to the making of variations and quality in lines.

For writing ideograms in the formal style, called *kaisho,* the best brush is made with coarse hair. The power required in writing formal ideograms necessitates a stronger and springier quality for the brush, which is generally made from the weasel-sable type of hair. This "springy" aspect contributes to forming the definite beginnings and endings that the formal style may require.

The semi-formal style of writing, *gyosho*, requires an extreme balance while moving from wide to narrow and back to a wide line again. Generally speaking, in this style one continuous motion is used to complete the ideogram; the word *gyo* means "motion," in this sense "without definite stops" as each stroke continues to the next. The brush for writing in semi-formal style has whiskers of small mammals such as a weasel or rabbit in the center of the bristle to create a springy effect, with soft sheep hair on the outer edge surrounding that core.

The informal writing style is known in common Japanese terminology as *sosho*: the "grass style" of writing. In this most simplified style of writing, a very soft brush is customarily used and all of the lines flow together in one ideogram; moreover, each word in a sentence continuously flows on into the next one. In Western cursive writing the letters of a word are connected, but in grass writing all of the words are also connected. In the example here, *wa* was completed as a single unified line. To make the one continuous line with effects that are wide to narrow, wet to dry, the brush that is used must be composed solely of soft sheep hair with bristles that are longer than in most brushes.

The spirit of ink is called *bokki* (*boku* = ink ; *ki* = spirit, energy). Again, it is essential when working in ink to focus your energy and transfer it to the page. It is not uncommon when viewing ink works to find examples where a person may have executed his calligraphy with *bokki* but his signature may not show the same dynamic vibrancy because the spirit of *bokki* was relaxed and the concentrated power was dissipated.

If a person is exposed to masterpieces and if the mind and spirit are pure and open, a mysterious power and force can be felt. When I was young and just entering my teens, my Japanese painting mentor would take me to a museum in Kyoto to contemplate great masterpieces. These experiences faded in my memory as I grew older. But in the 1970s while I was deeply engrossed in teaching sumi-e at the University of Illinois, scientists in Japan, by using an electron microscope with a magnification of 50,000 times, discovered that in the ink of some of the sumi-e works by great masters, the carbon particles show distinct patterns depending upon the energy expended at the moment the strokes were executed. (In English, a good summary of this study is found in *Zen and The Art of Calligraphy* by Omori Sogen and Terayama Katsujo, translated by John Stevens [Routledge & Kegan Paul, London], 1983.)

Simply stated, if it has been painted with *chi*, a line created in sumi ink (which is made up of carbon particles) shows a particular alignment of electrons, compared to the alignment of electrons in lines not painted with *chi*. Stick ink which is ground on a grinding stone must be used for this interesting alignment of carbon particles to occur. During the process of grinding the ink stick, the friction activates the electrons. When a person loads a brush with freshly ground ink and has the proper physical and mental preparation, that energy affects the electrons in the ink. The line created in calligraphy can record the energy of the artist. This "recording" of the electrons' alignment will last for many centuries.

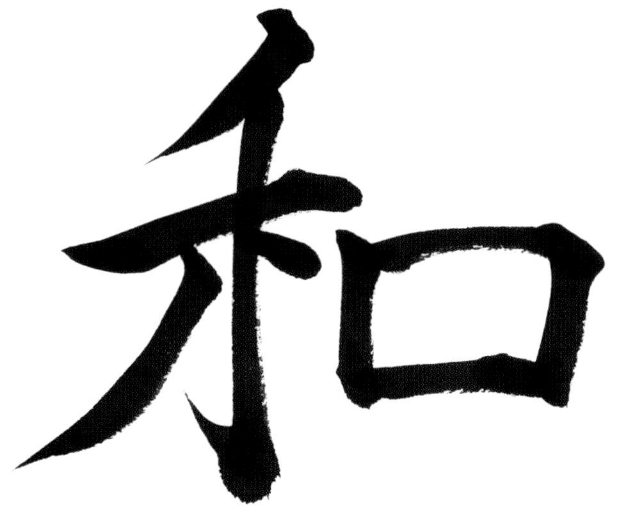

Wa in *kaisho* style

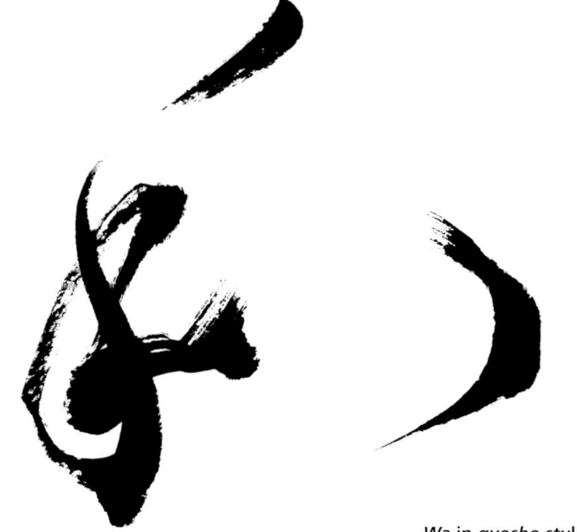

Wa in *gyosho* style

Wa in *sosho* style

Similar to being equipped with "antennae," some artists, Zen priests, and other people with acute sensitivity are able to sense and respond to these unseen electron alignments. A common comment used to describe this sensing of traces of energy is, "I am moved by that work." It is only recently that this scientific information was documented. But great artists of past generations seemed to intuitively understand that this dynamic energy or force had an effect on their work. Students were taught to open up their senses and receptivity so that they could "tune in" to these great works of art when viewing them.

Today science continues to be used to better quantify and qualify the energy in other ways. A new training system was developed in Japan for younger students to help teach how to recreate the energy of *chi* or *ki*. Sensors are attached to various parts of the body to measure brain waves and the physical state of the body. By seeing the changes made visible on a monitor, a student can more immediately understand how controlled breathing and concentration used as physical preparation can bring about a meditative condition, a state of *chi* or *ki*.

A famous Zen saying states, "The way of art is the way of the Buddha." This basically means that at birth the mind is innocent and pure but as the years go by, our minds accumulate desires and trivia of all kinds. Zen meditation purports to remove those countless interferences, bringing one back to a clean slate, so that one is ready to face the world again. In any creative act, when a person is totally focused on that process or performance with heart, mind and soul, it is similar to the Buddhist *zazen* process; the mind is completely cleared of extraneous thoughts. This is the wonder: that over the ages, ink particles can convey artistic impact with depth and feeling when created in such a state.

Right: In this calligraphy by Zakyu-an Sensho, notice the *nijimi* effect (*nijimi* = ink spreads beyond the original lines) of the beginning brush "dot" in the first (top) ideogram. When arriving at the third ideogram, the brush movement is somewhat slower so that the paper will absorb the remaining ink. The brush is then reloaded with ink and writing is resumed with the fourth ideogram, "Buddha." Note that the second and fifth ideograms are the same word and mean "way." In the art of calligraphy when writing in semi-formal style, it is common practice to vary the visual image if the same word should appear in the same phrase. Word for word, a direct translation of this would be "Art way is Buddha's way."

LEARNING FROM CLASSIC MASTERPIECES

One vast change in our society since the beginning of the twenty-first century is how very tight security has become. These safeguards apply to transportation, mail of all kinds, even e-mail; and to many buildings, including museums. When you enter a museum in most countries, you will go through security and your bag will be searched, or you may even be asked to check it. But there was a time in the past when it was a common sight at museums to see art students, with a complete set of equipment such as oil paints, setting up an easel in front of a well-known painting and proceeding to make a copy as a study in the craft of a particular artist.

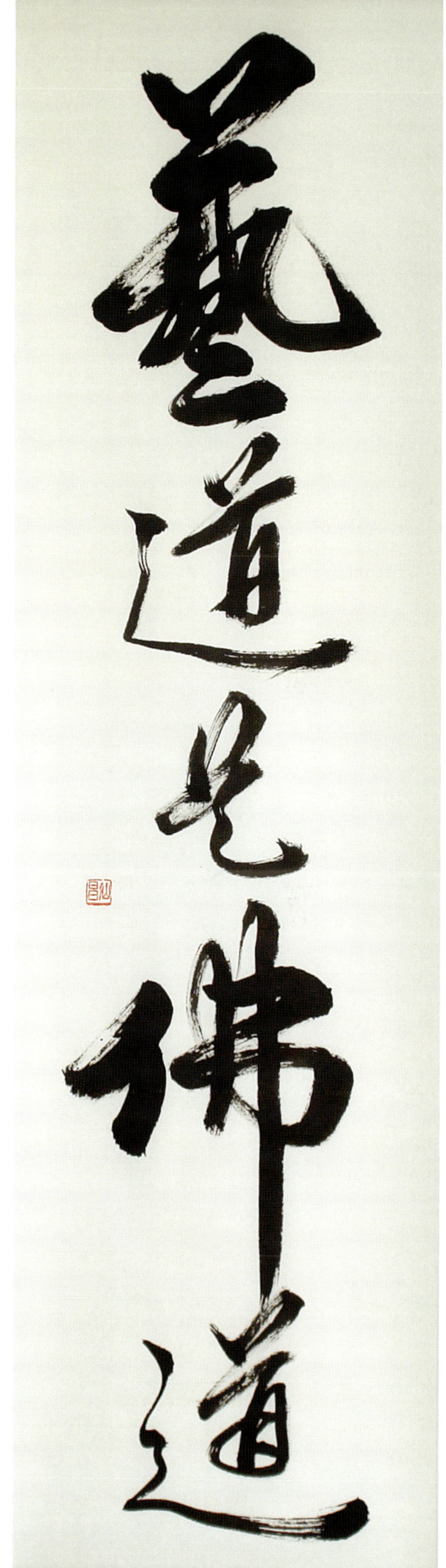

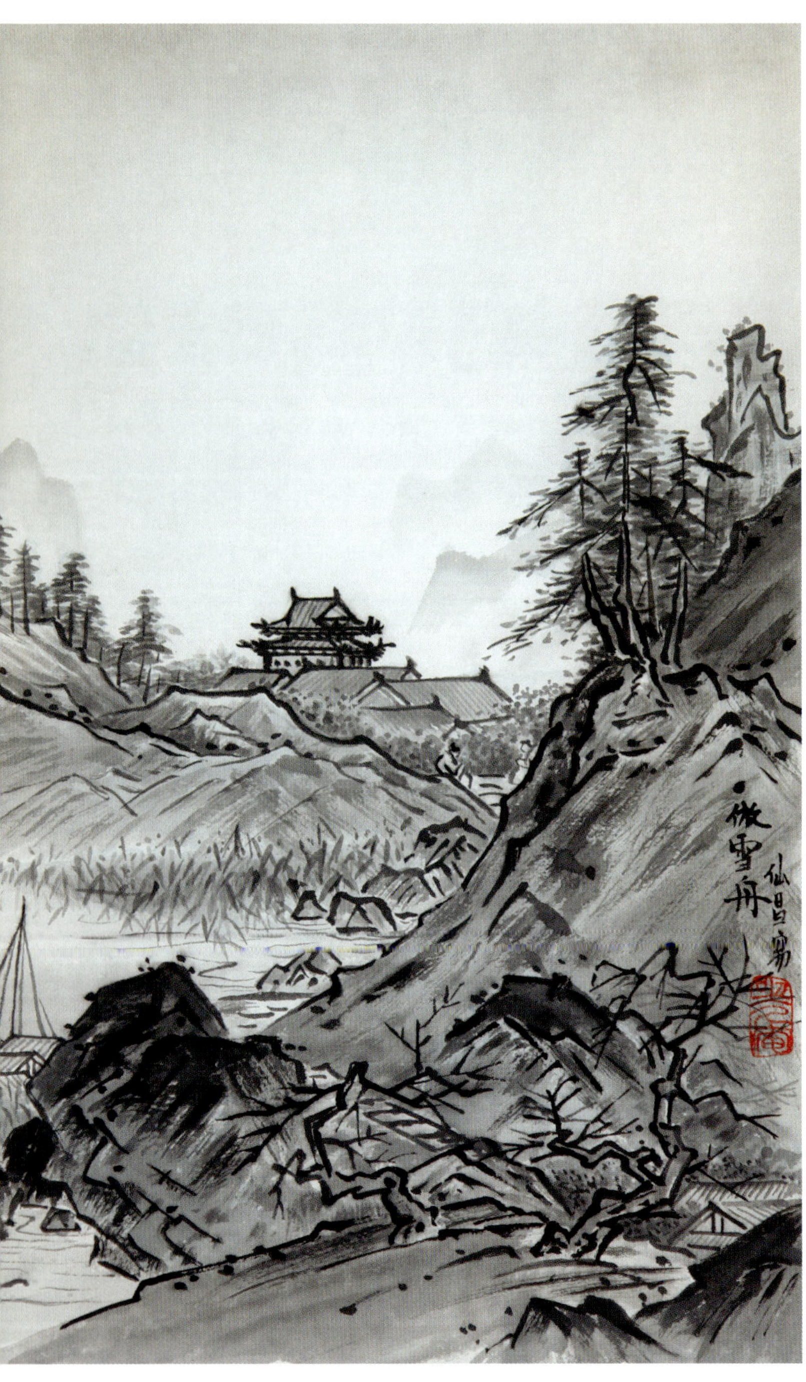

This practice of copying has been used in art education for ages. Although copying masterpieces in a museum today has become a near impossibility, on the other hand because printing techniques today have become so technically advanced, one can easily obtain remarkable-quality reproductions for copying and studying at home.

But copying correctly may not be as simple as it sounds. As an art student when I was young, I experienced such copying studies in Tokyo. And in the late 1980s, I traveled to China to study and compare the Chinese methods in art education with my own approach at the university level. While there, I attended the Zhejiang National Academy of Fine Arts in Hangzou. There the professor of painting in charge of instructing "visiting students" gave me his work of a sumi-e landscape to copy. I set about to faithfully copy his work and awaited his return to the studio for his critique. He told me, "You have copied the work well and the paintings look so much alike. However, your method of copying is not correct." Unsure of his methods and wishes, I had taken his recommendation to "copy" as meaning to reproduce an identical version of his work.

But when artwork is to be reproduced for the painter's education, the first task is to study the brush techniques. These details in brush strokes should be studied and then internalized. Secondly, when recreating a work of art, a personal quality of the student or copier should remain.

As a professor in fine arts in universities in the United States, I have not used copying as a teaching tool. However, during one of my intense summer sumi-e workshops, we did focus on making copies of two masterpieces, in this case works by Sesshu. Toyo Sesshu (1420–1506) has often been called the "saint of suiboku-ga." Sesshu traveled to China in 1467 to study techniques and styles of the Sung to Ming dynasties. These works are in the style of the Northern Sung paintings which were very popular in China during that time. Upon his return to Japan, Sesshu blended what he had learned in China with methods and techniques he developed on his own, and crystallized these into his own style. Many great masterpieces of his work in both Chinese and Japanese landscapes still remain today.

This pair, landscape scenes of autumn and winter, are replicas of Japanese National Treasures. The images shown here are my own copy pieces.

Sesshu often used light transparent hues over his suiboku-ga, which we also used for the autumn scene in our workshop reproductions. In addition, to add a sense of patina, I used tea which had been steeped overnight, in some cases diluting it with water for a lighter stain. This method of using tea is common when recreating ancient masterpieces. (Counterfeiters and forgers of old artworks also use this technique.)

In my copy of the winter landscape, the snow is enhanced by leaving more whiteness of the paper visible, especially on the trees.

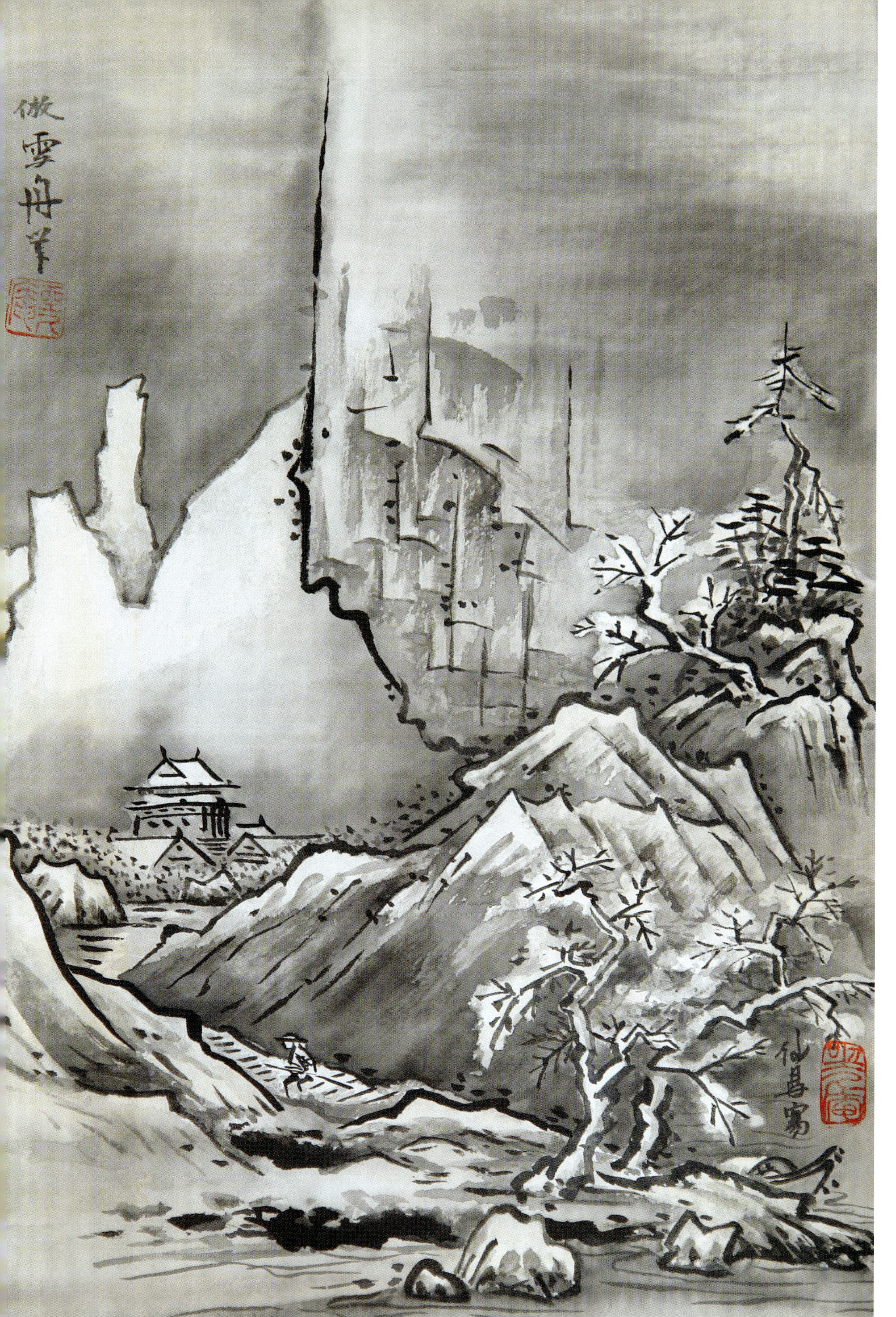
倣雪舟筆
仙昌寫

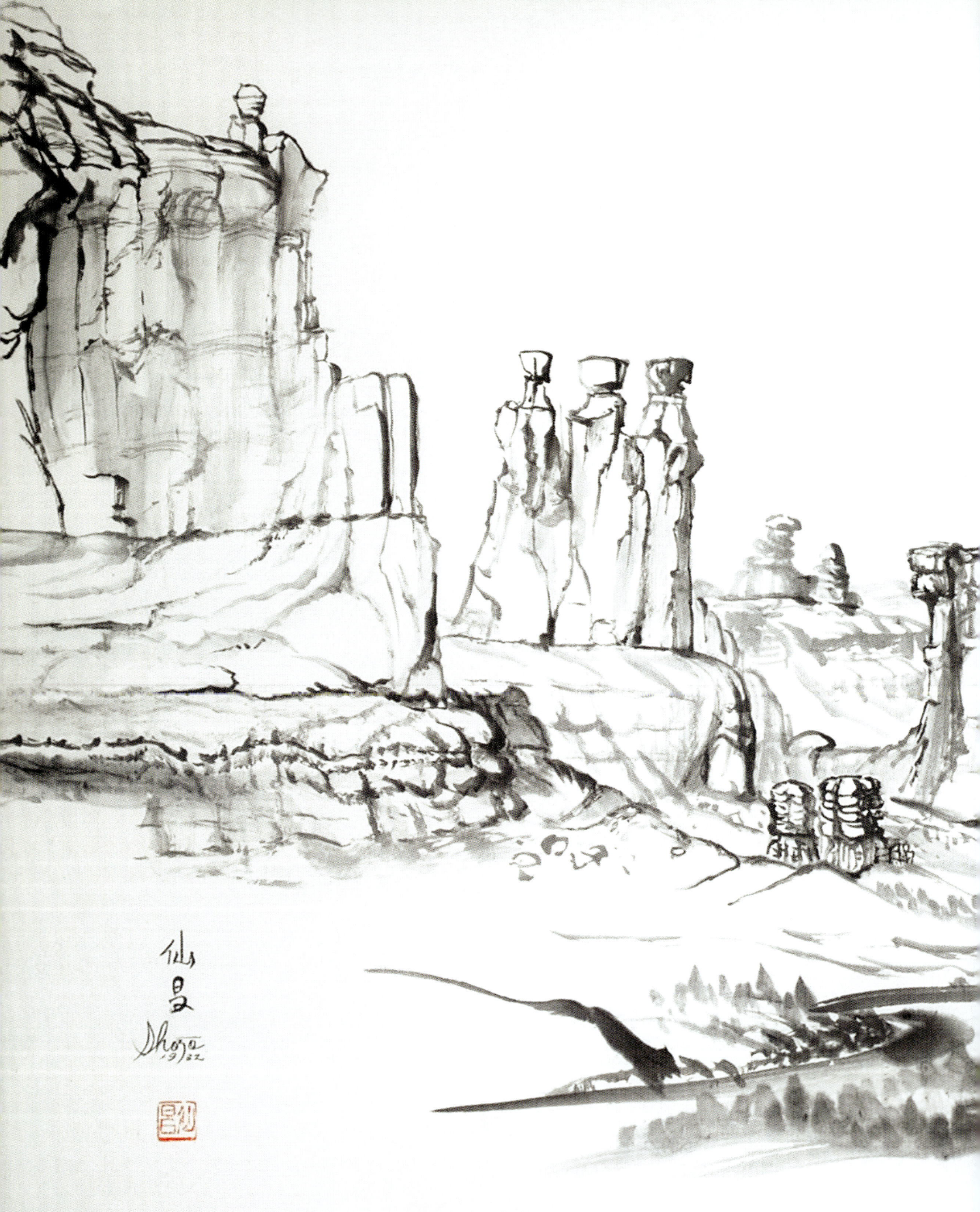

Four Treasures in the Studio

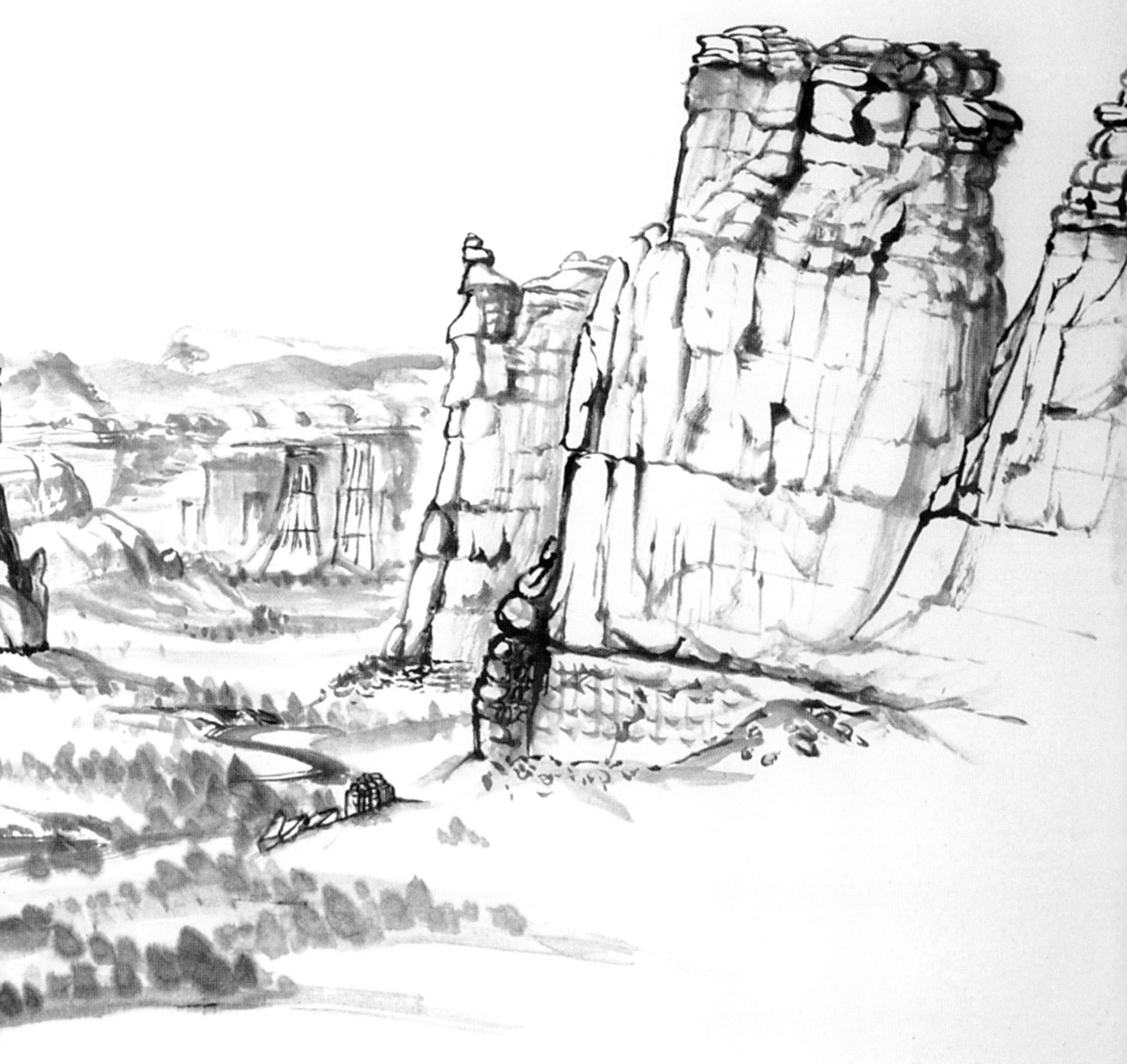

These objects can range from simple utilitarian pieces to highly decorated pieces which themselves become art. In more recent times these craft pieces have become items of interest for antique collectors. In their travels to China for study, Buddhist monks brought the four treasures of equipment back to Japan. Especially during the Edo Period in Japan when the arts and crafts flourished, artists and calligraphers reverently collected these Chinese objects. In juxtaposition, the Zen philosophical influence on writers and painters was that the studio reflect minimalism and simplicity instead of highly decorated antique objects. A Zen-oriented artist endeavors to develop a refined spiritual element in his work which an over-decorated studio will not inspire.

BRUSHES: TYPES, EFFECTS AND CARE

A saying in Japan over the centuries has been "Kobo does not choose a type of brush." This maxim is used to teach young students of art that it is not the expensive tool that matters, but having a true desire for study. Kobo Daishi (774–835 A.D.), also known as Kukai, was a famous Buddhist priest who traveled to China and studied Chinese Buddhism. However, maxims aside, historical documents reveal that Kobo himself, while tutoring the emperor in calligraphy, remarked that the choice of brush was very important depending upon whether one is writing in formal, semi-formal, or informal "grass" style. Besides his accomplishments as a priest, including establishing the Shingon Namikkyo Sect of Buddhism, Kukai was very versatile in talent and is still considered one of the three all-time best calligraphers of Japan. Later the emperor bestowed the title of *Daishi* ("great master") on him. Throughout the ages he has been considered one of the "saints" of calligraphy. Another Japanese proverb that references him is "even Kobo Daishi makes mistakes with a brush," indicating that no perfect human being exists.

The student of sumi-e must recognize the various types of brushes and how they are constructed. If you purchase those mass-produced inexpensive brushes, you will become disenchanted because the brush will not perform as expected. A disillusioned person will eventually give up on training. For this reason, even a beginner should start with a quality (and more expensive) brush as an investment. Such a brush will last for several decades. After the basics of brush usage and techniques have been mastered, a creative artist can produce work without the use of a brush but instead with fingertips, a long beard, a sponge or even rolled-up or crushed paper. All of these can function to create a painting or work in calligraphy. But the brush is where to begin.

Types of Brush Hair

Brushes for calligraphy and sumi-e are constructed from the hairs and whiskers of weasels, squirrels, martens/sable, raccoons, wild boars, horses, sheep, cats and humans. The specific use for the brush will determine the kinds of hair

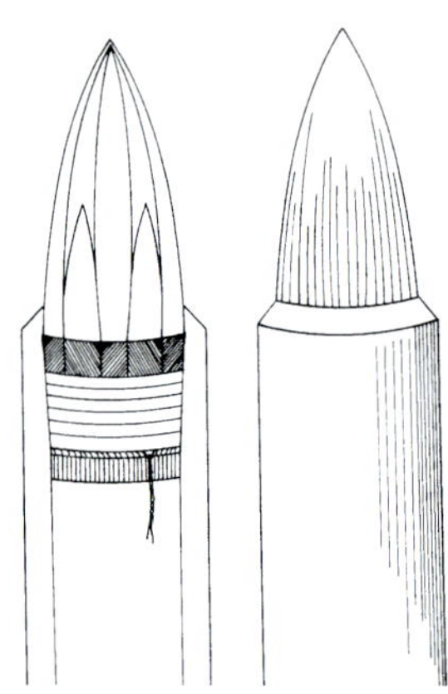

A front view (right) and cross-section view (left) of a sumi-e brush. The cross-section view shows where the hairs have been glued, bound and wrapped tightly with string before being anchored in the brush's stem.

and/or whiskers used and the location of these various hairs within the bristle. The knowledge required for the blending of the hairs in specific brushes takes years of apprenticeship, training and creativity on the part of the brush maker. To know whether to take the hair from the tail, body or whiskers and how to create a skillful combination is the work of a master craftsman. Some artists have been known to have had very personal brushes crafted from human hair, with hairs lovingly gathered from the artist's child for example. Today it is becoming increasingly difficult for brush makers to obtain hairs and whiskers from wild animals, so a wide variety of domestic animals' hair, such as horse, is used. In addition to the horse's mane and tail, all its other hairs from soft to coarse are used and 90% of most brushes today are made of horse hair.

Once when I was in Beijing, I was shopping for a large mountain horse hair brush. The brush shown at right came in a large beautiful box covered with cloth brocade. Written on the cover of the box was "this is a sacred mountain horse hair brush." Once I had my new purchase back home in my studio, I set to work with great expectations. The bristles were heavily glued and it took considerable effort to loosen them (a process

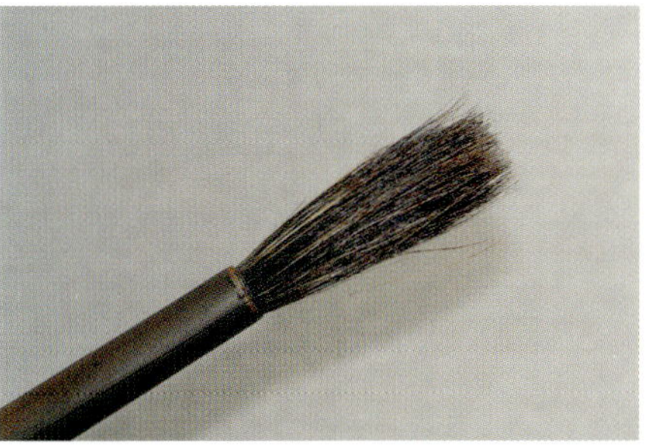

This is a typical example of the brush commonly known as a mountain horse hair brush. It is composed of hairs from the tail and mane of a horse, combined with wild boar hairs.

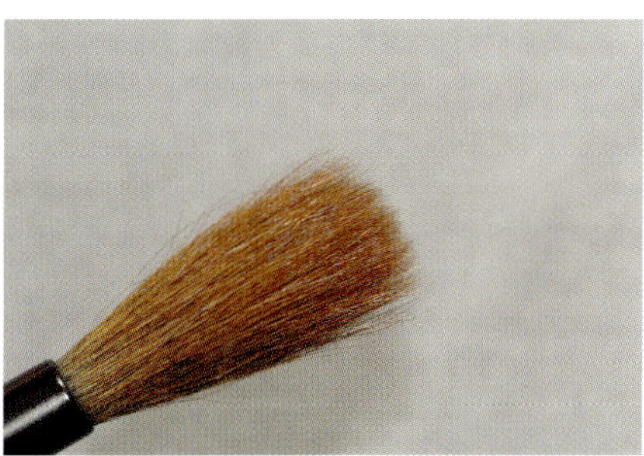

This brush is in the mid-range for resiliency (or "spring") in the bristles. The bristles of this example are made of weasel hair, but squirrel and sable hair are also used for this type of brush.

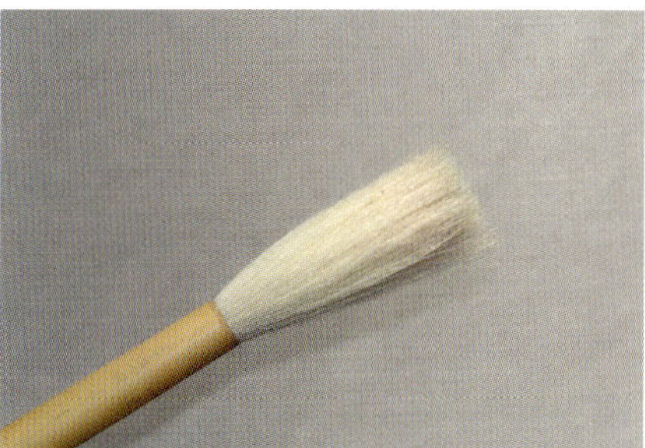

This brush is made from soft sheep or rabbit hair. Depending upon how the brush will be used, even a sheep hair brush may include the coarse white hair of a horse in the center.

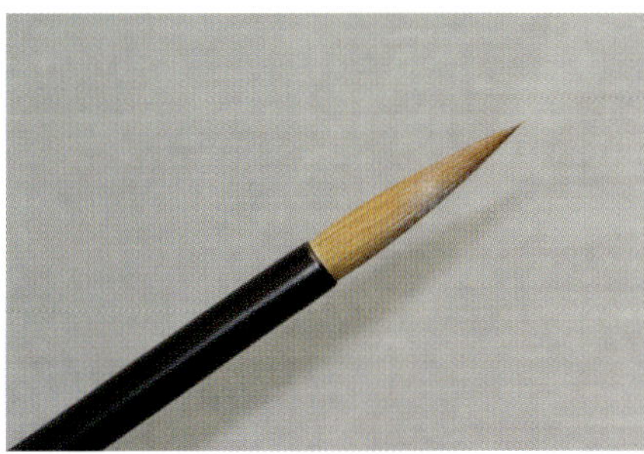

This brush is used for calligraphy or painting. Weasel hair is used for the bristles, but the very center contains whiskers of small mammals. When you paint bamboo leaves, for example, the whiskers help to bring the bristles back to a point to make the leaf tip.

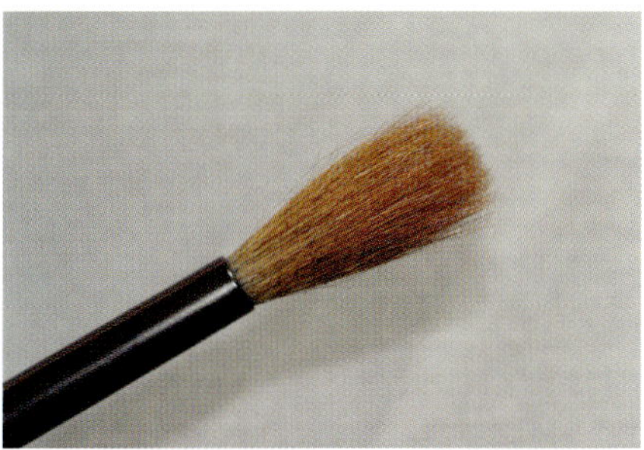

Brushes are sold with the bristles starched together. This is the same brush shown in the photo at left, now viewed after the bristles have been loosened.

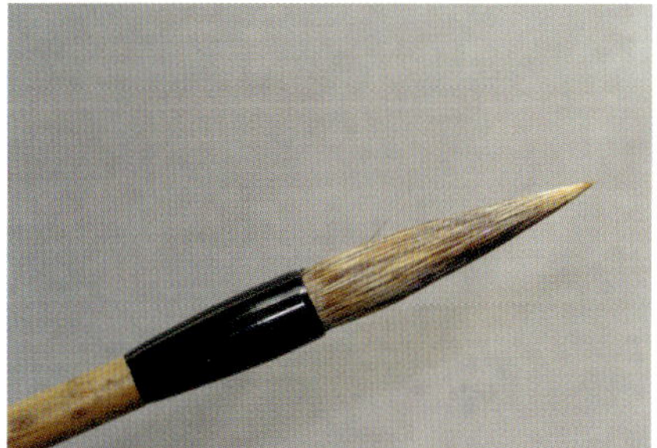

This brush is similar to a mountain horse hair brush, but its bristles are of raccoon hair.

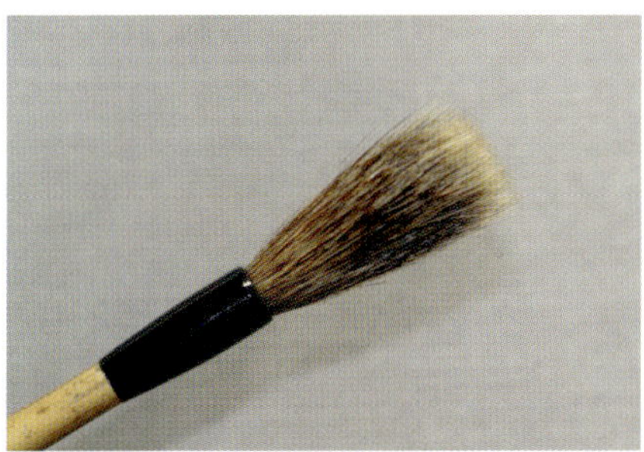

The same raccoon-hair brush seen at above right, after the bristles have been loosened.

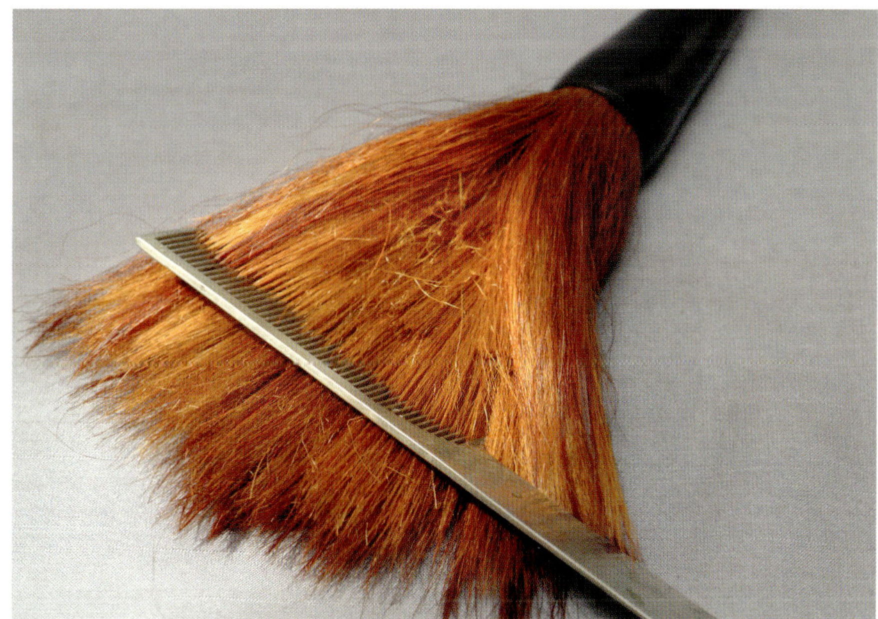

This brush is not a mountain horse hair brush after all: horse hair is used only on the very outer skirt, and the inside of the brush is made up of plant fibers. The metal comb shown here is made especially for the care of brushes.

you will learn on the next pages). Finally when about a third of the brush was relaxed, I dipped it in sumi ink and tested it. Strangely, after the ink dried, there was a red outline around the black ink. Somewhat mystified, I again worked to loosen the bristles and washed out more glue. The water became red and even more peculiarly, the red intensified as I continued to wash the bristles with frequent changes of water. When the brush was dried again, I discovered that horse hair was only on the very outer skirt and that the inside of the brush was made up of plant fibers. Moreover the center fibers were cut, as you can see in the photo on page 25.

It is difficult to assess the quality of brushes that are constructed of an assortment of hairs and that also vary in thickness simply by looking at the finished product. Quality brushes usually use natural hair with natural point. Some manufacturers will use a technique that abrades the cut hair to a point like natural hairs. Some manufacturers may just use longer hairs cut short in a blunt cut in the center. If the cut hair is not properly abraded to a point like a natural strand is, the brush will not come to a point when used.

During my study trip to China, I stopped at a brush specialist's shop. I picked out a few brushes and then the shopkeeper brought out another brush, suggesting that it was an inexpensive but good quality brush. I told him that if it was indeed a good brush and inexpensive, then it would be ideal for my classes so I would likely plan to buy a quantity of them. I then added that I would pay for the one brush, but first wished to open it up to see the hairs inside. The shopkeeper whisked the brush away, and gave me another brush which was several times more expensive. The first brush must have been mass-produced with cut hairs in the center which he did not wish to expose.

In a quality brush specialist's shop, within each category of brushes on display, one brush is already loosened so you can see the composition and hair combination of the bristles. Shopkeepers may also suggest that you test the brush you're considering; this may be done by using water, which turns black on a chemically treated gray paper. This will help you determine which brush you should purchase. Quality brushes are expensive, often exceeding more than several hundred dollars, but the investment is well worth it and provides use and enjoyment for many years to come.

For a practitioner of sumi-e, having a few quality brushes should be sufficient. Among them should be a large and a small *choryu* brush; a large and a small **mountain horse hair** brush; a wide flat brush, called a *hake;* and/or a *ren-pitsu* brush (these consist of small brushes lined up and joined together to make a wide flat brush). Artists have a tendency, when traveling, to automatically stop into art supply stores and often they end up buying brushes as souvenirs. These brushes, when used, can give unexpected pleasure, but they may also end up simply overfilling your drawers.

Brushes are given various names by the companies that produce them or the specialty shops that sell them. There are some brushes that carry the same name consistently regardless of the company which produces or sells them, whether in China or Japan. Choryu, the long "flowing" brush, is one

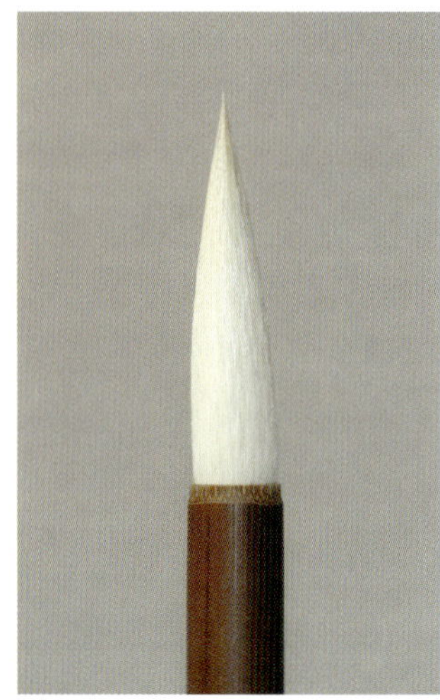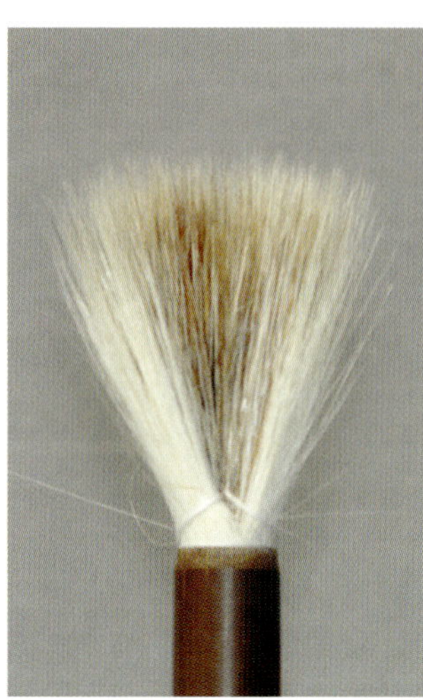

Left: **White sheep hairs form the outer layer of the choryu brush.**
Right: **The choryu brush with its bristles tied open to reveal the several types of hairs that compose its center.**

example. This brush is made for sumi-e artists. If you possess only one brush, this is the brush to have whether you are a beginner or a professional sumi-e artist. The outer skirt of the choryu brush is sheep hair, wrapped around coarser hairs inside. By opening up the brush, you can see that the inside hairs of the bristle are composed of very coarse hair, like whiskers, along with other types hairs ranging from medium hard to medium soft, carefully placed to give greater flexibility so that the brush can also be used for painting bamboo or pampas grass leaves. Each time you complete the painting of a leaf, the tip of the bristle returns to a straight point.

The flexibility and resilience of the choryu brush is important. Brushes constructed solely of sheep hairs will not spring back so are difficult to use sideways, but when the choryu brush is used sideways, the bristles will not spread and will be easier to manipulate. By holding the brush at the perpendicular, either very thin or very wide lines can be drawn. *Choryu* means "long flowing stream," and perhaps the name was chosen because once ink is applied, long lines can be painted with this brush.

The mountain horse hair brush is made of very coarse hairs. Originally these hairs came from a type of Asian deer, but today the mountain horse hair brush is composed of horse hair combined with bear or other coarse bristles. It is used mainly for the dry brush techniques (see page 57); its coarse bristles give lines unique qualities, and allow you to create multiple line types with one continous stroke of the brush.

Menso brushes come in a variety of sizes to meet special needs. A small menso brush is ideal for painting human hair, strand by strand, or eyebrows one hair by one. The slimmest of these brushes is composed of only five or six whiskers. The eyebrows of the Noh masks used in Japanese drama and also those of Japanese dolls are painted on with this type of brush. Because these brushes are extremely slim, the slender "head" is first inserted into a small bamboo tube, stabilized and then set in the second handle. It looks, in fact, like a brush with a double handle.

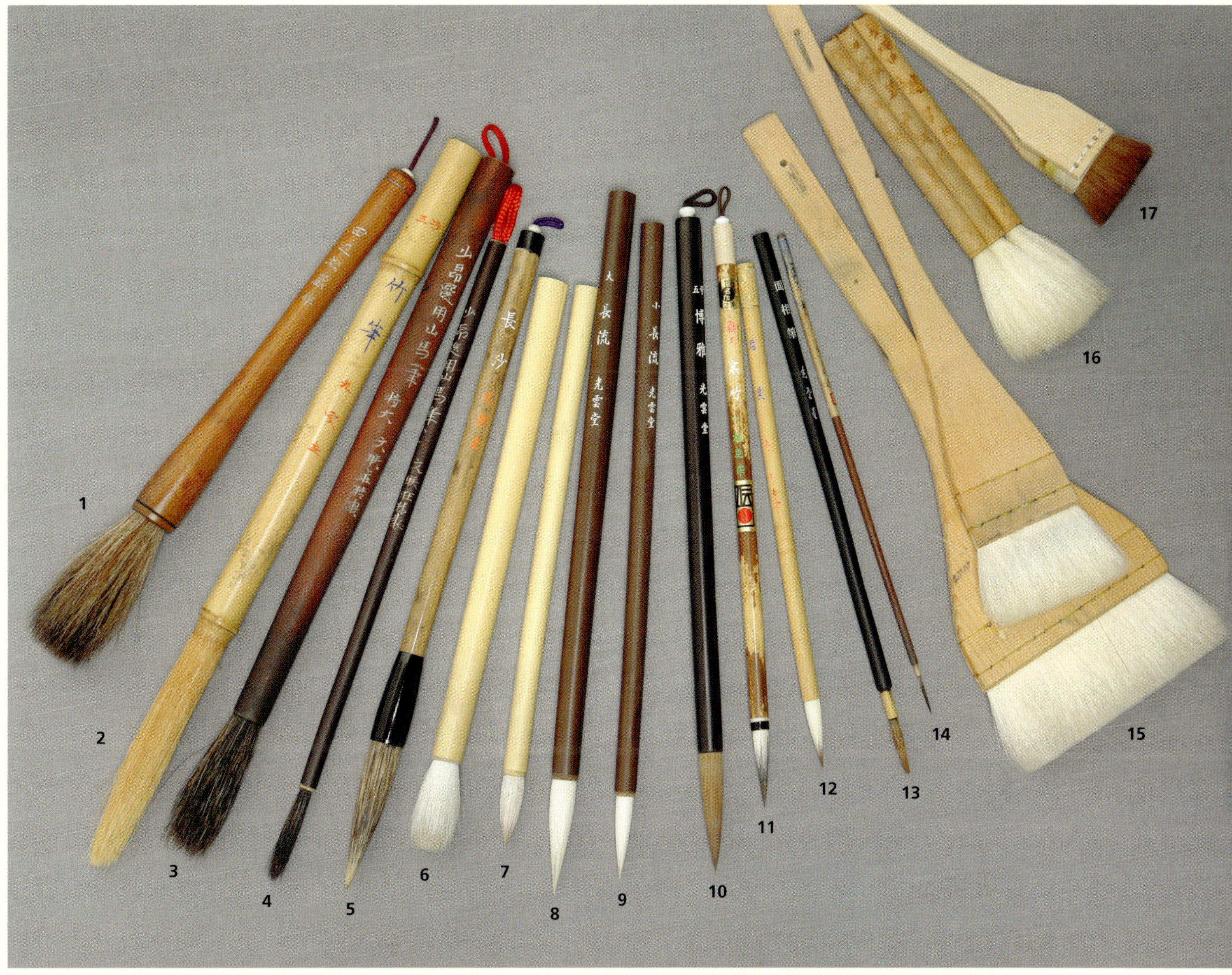

Brush #1 is for formal to semi-formal calligraphy, however, in hair composition, it is primarily coarse, so I often use it as a large mountain horse hair brush, because the bristles are resilient and springy, useful for painting large forms such as rocks and mountains.

Brush #2 has bristles of bamboo fibers which are the extension of the bamboo handle. These brushes continue to be made with the same method used since ancient times; one end of the bamboo stalk is softened by soaking, then pounded with a small wooden mallet to separate it into fibers. This brush is used for certain effects in calligraphy. I also use it as another mountain horse hair brush.

Brushes #3 & #4 are mountain horse hair brushes with hairs taken from the mane and tail. The coarseness of the hair allows the creation of unique qualities in lines. In addition, when it is used sideways, multiple textures can be created which makes it an effective brush in creating the rough surface of rocks, etc.

Brush #5 has bristles made from coarse raccoon hair, so it has some resilience and flexibility. I use this brush for calligraphy and landscape painting.

Brushes #6 & #7 have bristles made from soft sheep hair. These brushes are good for adding a color wash or for painting flower petals.

Brushes #8 & #9 are large and small *choryu* brushes: These brushes are made for sumi-e.

Brush #10 has bristles made of weasel hairs and is used for calligraphy and sumi-e.

Brushes #11 & #12 are used in sumi-e for making outlines, and for adding signatures or other formal-style writing at small sizes.

Brushes #13 & #14 are *menso* brushes; their bristles are made from small mammal whiskers and are used to create extremely fine lines.

Brush #15 is called *ita hake* (*ita* = board; *hake* = flat brush) in Japan. These large or small brushes are used for wetting the paper with water or to smooth the paper out. They are also often used to produce a gradation in ink tone.

Brush #16 is called a *renpitsu* and is used in ways similar to Brush #15. Renpitsu brushes can be found in many variations, with differences in the number of brushes connected for width. Holes are drilled through the handles and the brushes are held together with a thin piece of bamboo. You can divide a wide renpitsu brush to the desired width by cutting the skewer that holds the brushes together. The major difference between the *hake* (#15) and the renpitsu is that the renpitsu has more density in the amount of hair, and therefore it can hold more ink. For instance, with one application of ink, you can make a series of sections in a bamboo stalk without running out of ink. See techniques on page 126.

Brush #17 is made for stenciling and painting designs on kimono fabrics. However, it is very effective in making gradations from dark to light. There are times when a brush which is not made specifically for calligraphy or painting can be used creatively to produce unique effects. I may add different tones of ink to the bristles of this brush to create leaves on distant trees, or when I need to create graduated tones of ink.

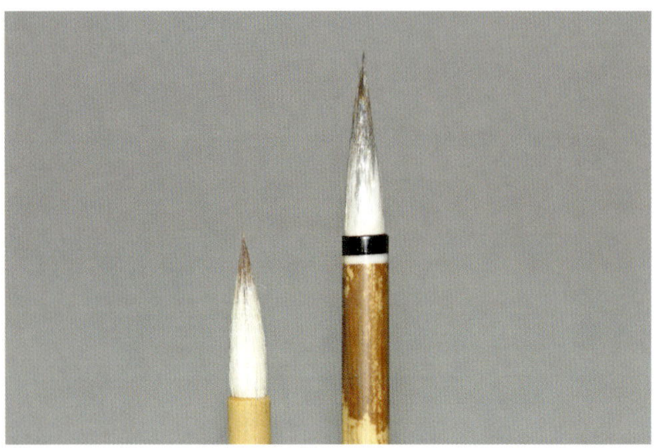

These brushes are made to use in "formal" style calligraphy and as an out-line brush for suiboku-ga. White sheep hair forms the outer skirt and the center is composed of whiskers and other hairs which are flexible, yet strong. (Actual brush head size, larger brush: L = 3cm/1.25", D = 7mm/0.25". Smaller brush: L = 2.7cm/1.0625", D = 7mm/0.25")

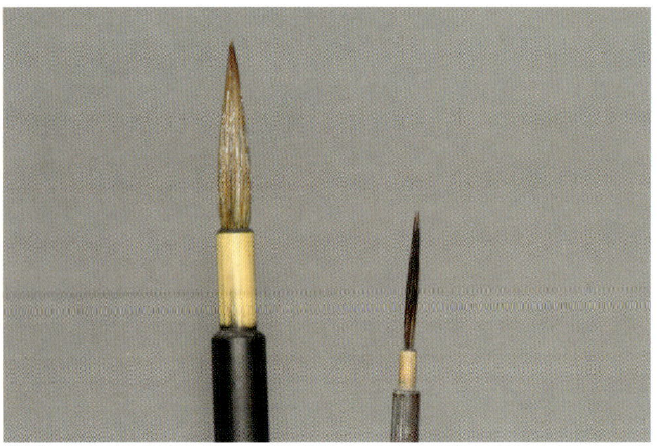

Menso brushes come in a variety of sizes. The menso has many uses and so is a convenient brush to have. (Actual brush head size, larger brush: L = 2.5cm/1", D = 4mm/0.125". Smaller brush: L = 6cm/2.375", D = 1mm/0.03")

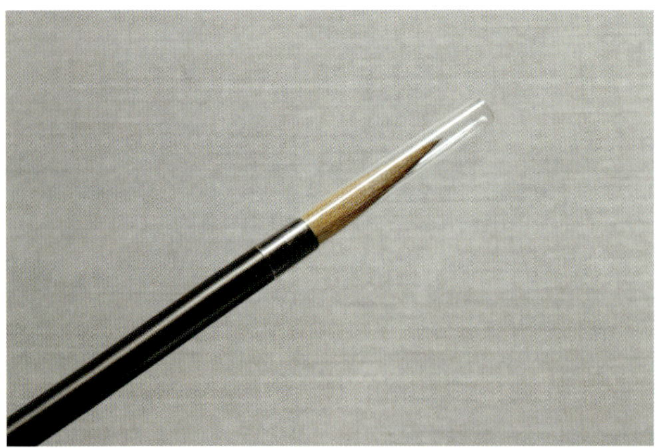

Brushes in art supply stores are usually covered with a clear plastic tube which serves expressly to protect the tip when the brush is being handled during its journey from the manufacturer to wholesalers to retailers. Once the hairs of the brush have been loosened, the bristle will not go back into the cap and you have no further use for it. When the bristles are wet and form a point, if you put the cap back on, moisture cannot escape and often fungus will start to grow; eventually the hair will begin to fall out.

How to Loosen the Brush's Bristles

When you purchase a new brush its bristles are starched to hold them together. But for use in sumi-e, the bristles must be loosened.

It is extremely important that the brush is not dipped in water to loosen the bristles. If you dip the brush in water to loosen it, the starch will be revitalized and the brush will become "gooey." The moisture will be drawn into the center of the brush and it will take a long time to get it out.

The proper process for loosening a brush's bristles is shown on the facing page.

How to Care for the Brush

Artists who have worked in oil, acrylic paints or watercolors are accustomed to using brushes with bristles compressed in metal. Often these brushes are left in water or cleaning fluids for a long period of time. It is highly important for a person who is instead using brushes of the Far East to understand how they are produced and the care they require. Animal glue, which is used to stabilize the bristles in the handle, is very much like gelatin and will eventually dissolve in water. If a brush for sumi-e is left in water over a period of time, the bristles will fall out.

Each time you use a brush, moisten it first with cold water to bring life back to each hair.

The care of a brush after you have finished using it is very important also. Carefully wash out all of the ink. You may use a gentle soap to assist in this process. (Special soaps have been created expressly for brushes.) Never use warm to hot water; that will dissolve the brush's animal glue and eventually the bristles will fall out.

Special care must be given to washing the base of the bristles. Otherwise, after years of use, the accumulated ink dries around the individual hairs at the base and the brush will not form a point again. The best policy is to never let ink collect at the base of the bristles. Press, squeeze and gently twist several times, then extract the moisture with a paper towel by pressing very firmly at the base of the brush. If traces of ink come out on the paper towel, wash the brush again.

The correct drying process is to place the wet brush on a cloth and gently squeeze; then move the brush to another part of the cloth and brush down to comb the bristles into a point. *Do not pull the bristles away from the handle.* If as you are pressing down you were to continue pulling the brush through the cloth, your incorrect drying process would eventually make the hair fall out of the brush.

There is a special comb available that helps to remove the accumulated ink at a brush's base as you wash it. Big brushes are especially vulnerable to ink buildup, and the individual hairs can also become entangled during the process of washing, making the brush bulge out. Use the comb during washing and again after the brush is dry.

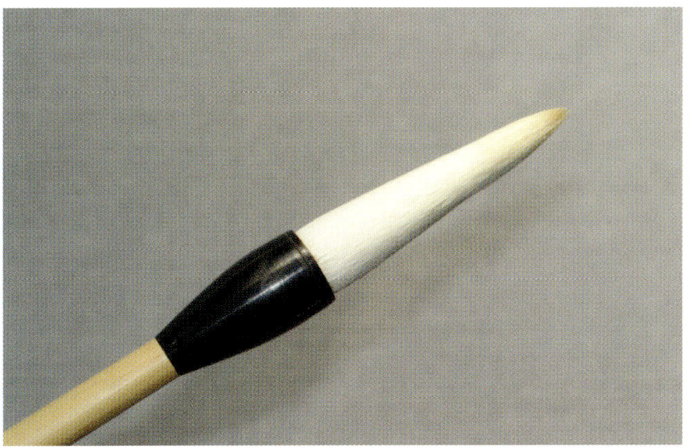

A sheep hair brush.

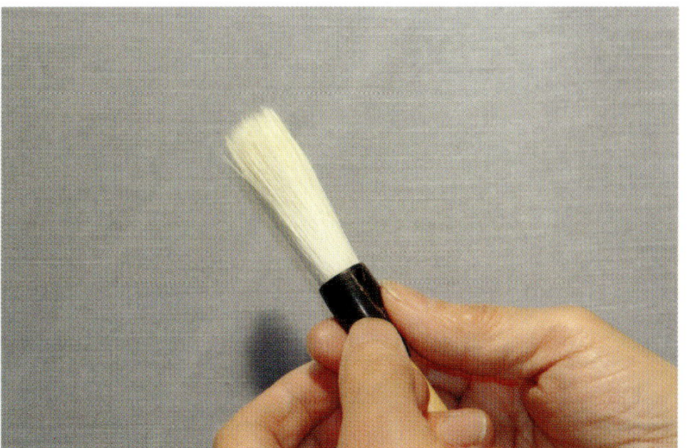

The same brush after the bristles have been loosened. Depending on how the brush will be used, even a sheep hair brush may have the coarse white hair of a horse in the center.

HOW TO LOOSEN THE BRUSH'S BRISTLES

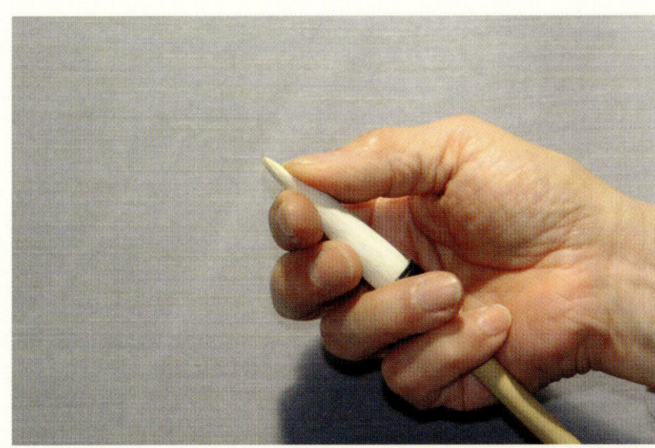

1. Hold the brush in your hand; the tip of the bristles should be between your thumb and index finger. Press the tip gently between them, then release. Rotate the brush.

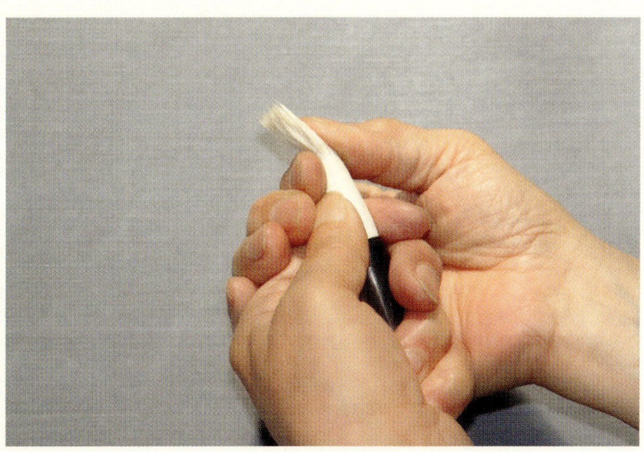

2. Repeat the press-and-release of your fingertips as you continue to rotate the brush. Move down, gradually loosening each section of the brush head.

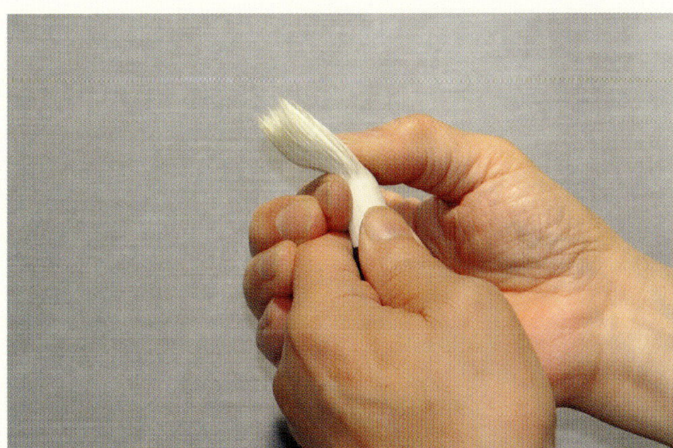

3. It takes several minutes to completely free the hairs. Here, about half of the bristles have been loosened. Be patient. I recall an incident where a student did not heed directions and tried to loosen the whole head by forcefully bending the bristles, and the unit came out of the handle.

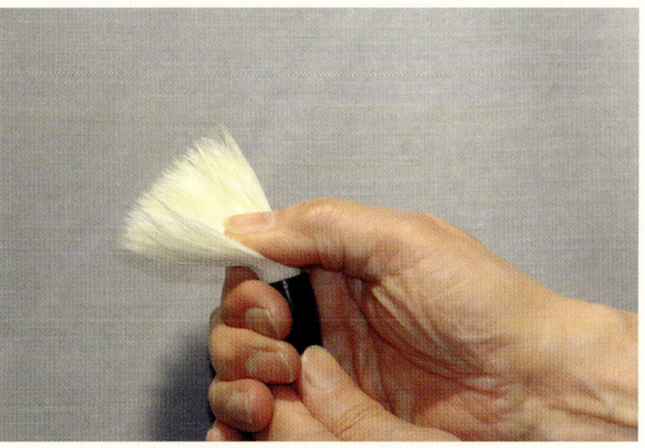

4. Finally the entire brush has been loosened. Next, dip the brush in water and swish it around to wash out the starch. The water will turn milky. Repeat, changing the water several times. Each time you take the brush out of the water, remove as much water as you can by pressing the bristles on a cloth or paper towel. Your new brush is now ready to use.

Brush Hangers

Many different types of brush hangers are available in art supply shops. Depending upon their style, they hold various sizes and lengths of brushes. They are an ideal way to store brushes because moisture on the bristles will drip down and evaporate.

The example below is a standard brush hanger. These have either hooks or pegs on both sides for hanging brushes. Some brushes have a string loop already attached to the end of the handle; if the brush does not come with a string loop for hanging, you can easily put one on yourself.

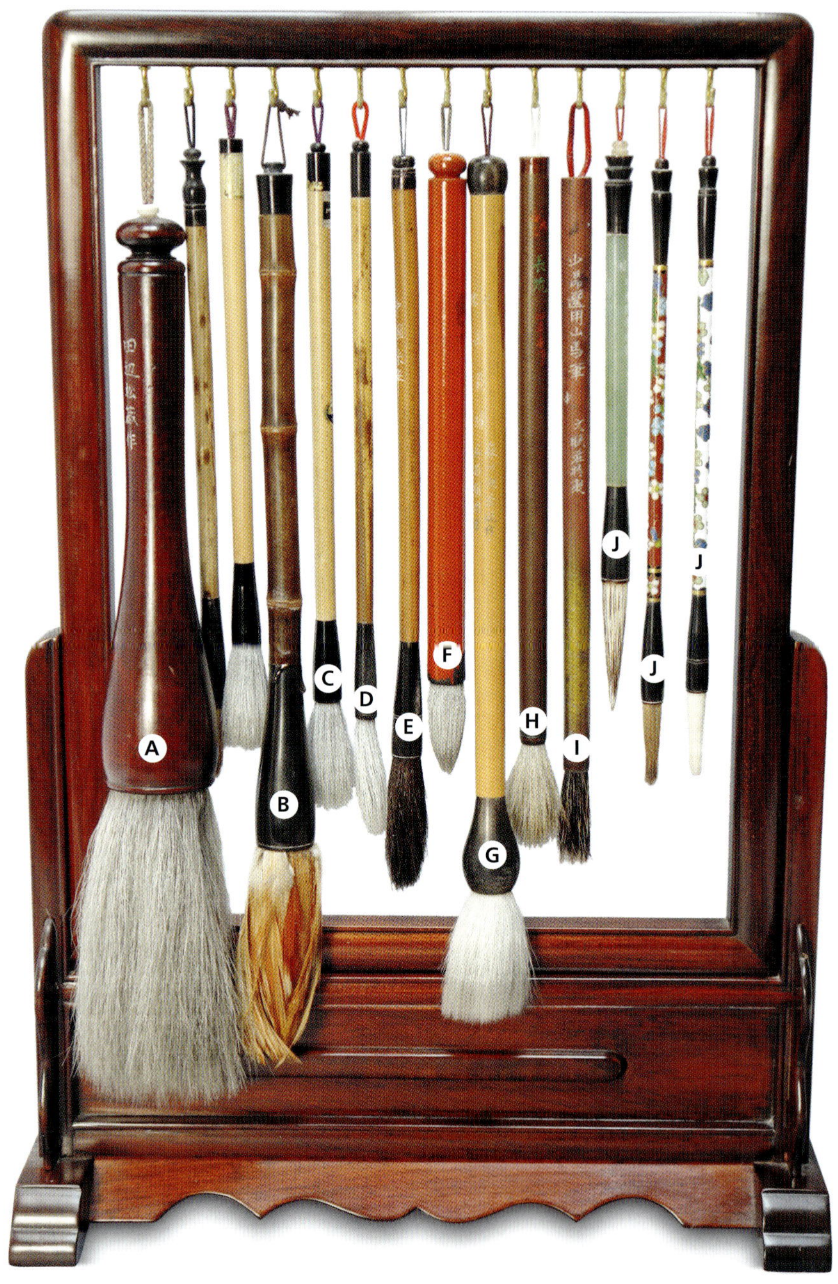

A. This large brush is composed of coarse white horse hairs, and its springy and flexible traits make it well suited for writing large calligraphy.

B. This brush has a bamboo handle with joints, and its head is composed of bird feathers, preferred by some contemporary calligraphers.

C. The white hairs of this brush have a springy effect that can be used for many different purposes.

D. The long sheep hairs make this brush good for semi-formal to informal calligraphy.

E. This brush is composed of long horse hairs.

F. This red lacquer brush of sheep hair has whiskers in the center; there-fore, it is used for large ideograms but also works well for semi-formal calligraphy.

G. This brush has a long handle and the thick short white hair of sheep. It is convenient for painting flower petals, for example.

H. The versatile choryu brush.

I. A mountain horse hair brush, for which there are many uses.

J. The three beautiful brushes on the far right were purchased during a visit to China. The red cloisonné probably has weasel type hair. The one with the green stone handle is most likely raccoon hair. (That the green is jade is just wishful thinking!)

PAPER: THE FOUNDATION

Sometime around 2,000 years ago, archaelogical evidence has shown, hemp and linen fibers from old rags and the plants themselves were used to make paper in China. Before that time silk had been used as the writing surface; silk served the purpose well because in its original state, it is very stiff due to the glue-like substance the worm puts on the threads. Thin slats of bamboo strung together were also used to write upon. Before the time of paper and silk, archaeological findings show that clay tablets were used for writing and keeping documents. A wet cloth was placed upon the tablet to keep the clay moistened until the writing was completed. The tablet was then dried and fired. The earliest writing was words chiseled on stone or bone. Of course, far from China, in ancient Egypt, it is well known that Egyptians developed papyrus more than 5,000 years ago.

The hemp fiber paper produced in ancient China was exported on the Silk Road to the Middle East. Around the Persian Gulf, hemp and fibers from mulberry trees were made into paper. The first known paper factory was established in Baghdad in 793 A.D. Until then, Europeans had been dependent upon parchment which was made from animal skins. Papermaking was introduced and transported to Europe from the Middle East.

By this time, the papermaking process had been brought by Buddhist monks to Korea and Japan. By 780 A.D. the Japanese had perfected the system of papermaking and it is recorded that they produced 233 types of paper. Japanese paper is still handmade today using the traditional methods. A major difference between western papers and Japanese papers is in the length of the fibers. Western paper is generally made from plant fibers which have been crushed and ground into pulp. In Japanese paper, the natural strength of the fibers is honored and the fibers are blended and interwoven like felt. It is for this reason that even thin handmade paper maintains some durability when given moisture.

Japanese papers are mainly produced from *kozo* (a type of mulberry); *mitsumata* (*Daphne* genus); and *gampi* (another species of the *Daphne* genus). Gampi is said to be insect resistant. It also the most durable in terms of the time it will last, so it is one of the most popular types. Ink will not spread out on these smooth white papers, so they are considered the best papers for calligraphy and painting.

Among the many varieties of paper made in China, a very popular one for calligraphy and painting is made from fibers of rice straw. It is an absorbent type of paper, and the various wet to dry effects of the brush can be obtained easily. *Toshi* is another Chinese paper that has been produced since the Han Dynasty; it consists of bamboo fibers. Papers made from bamboo fibers are termed *Shuan* papers. Other papers commonly found in most Chinese art supply shops in the U.S. are Taiwan cotton and Taiwan linen. These papers are very durable when wet, as is Chinese *pi* paper (*pi* means "skin" or "leather"). *Giao li* is an inexpensive sized paper that is good for calligraphy or sumi-e. *Jen ho* paper is relatively thick and absorbent.

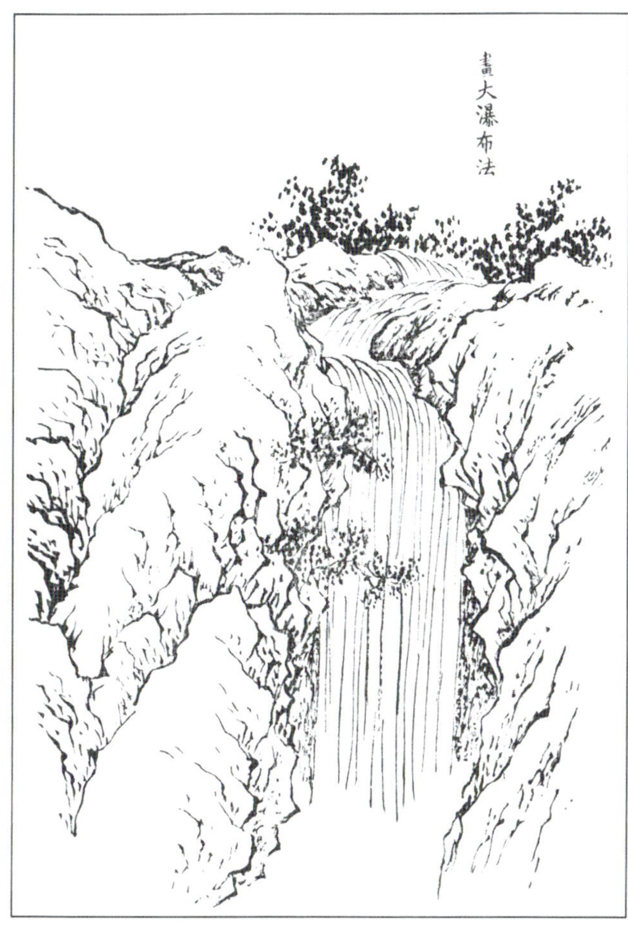

Among the specialized papers made for sumi-e, some have finely processed clay added into them to enhance the light ink tones. (Contemporary magazines which carry fine photographs in color, such as fashion magazines, also use paper which has clay in it.)

Handmade papers are expensive. But in Japan, Korea and China, the same materials are also treated in a similar process but via machine rather than by hand, so good manufactured papers are also an option. My suggestion is that you check the Internet, focusing on Asian papers, to begin to understand the range of papers available. In choosing paper, your main concern should be what goals you have in mind for your art. Then decide whether absorbent or sized paper will best serve your purposes.

Paper is absorbent (think of paper towels), and a drop of water will instantly be soaked up. Sized paper, in contrast, is treated to be more resistant and water does not permeate it as easily, which makes it similar to watercolor paper. (It is possible to create sized paper from absorbent paper by painting it with liquid "dosa" as a sizing agent. See "How to Size Paper," page 189.) The major difference between the two is that sized sumi-e paper is much thinner than watercolor paper.

This thinness of paper is important to consider together with the manner in which you plan to display your sumi-e work. Most contemporary sumi-e artists will frame their work in a western-style picture frame, in which case the thickness of the paper really does not matter. But if the work is to be displayed in the traditional manner, that is, as a hanging scroll, it will be rolled rather tightly for storage, and therefore should be done on thin paper. If a painting on thick paper is mounted as a scroll, when it is unrolled, cracks may appear across the painting especially during the dry seasons.

If there are art supply stores which carry Chinese or Japanese papers within your traveling distance, when visiting them you can determine which papers are sized and unsized by simply adding a small amount of moisture to the corner of a sample of the paper. The result can be seen instantly: If the moisture leaves a gray mark, it is absorbent unsized paper. If the moisture does not leave a mark, it is sized paper.

My personal preference is to use the sized *torinoko* paper which is used for making *fusuma* (sliding doors) in Japan, because it comes in large sizes. It is thick and is very suitable for framing in Western fashion. This paper is available as both handmade and machine-made, from Japanese art supply stores; Chinese art supply stores do not carry it. *Torinoko* or "child of bird" (*tori* = bird, *no* = of, *ko* = child) can be translated as an egg, which has a smooth and durable surface, and is slightly cream colored, an apt description for this paper. Torinoko is made from gampi fibers, thus it is strong and the smooth surface makes it easier to paint on. It is considered to be the "king of handmade paper."

Papers which work well for calligraphy and painting, both handmade and machine-made, are numerous, so it is impossible to comprehensively list company and brand names here. Once you have determined the type of work you wish to produce, you should select the *type* of paper that is appropriate to use: absorbent or non-absorbent (sized) paper; thin but strong paper; thick heavy paper, and so on. All varieties are available. Today, most art supplies stores carry various sizes of tablets with paper especially made for sumi-e. For practice purposes, inexpensive thin paper is sufficient. For good results I recommend thicker sumi-e paper and quality sumi ink.

Characteristic of the plant fibers from which they are made, papers for sumi-e and calligraphy will expand when given moisture, and will shrink when dry. This uneven shrinkage causes an unwanted wavy and bumpy surface on your painting. Most professional frame shops do not have the knowledge and expertise to stretch the paper smooth again, but you can learn to do it yourself; the techniques to stretch and dry these wrinkled papers to smoothness again are taught in Chapter 7.

BLACK INK: VARIATIONS IN TONE

In ancient times China developed a method of making permanent ink out of soot. Sumi is an achromatic ink which neither reflects nor transmits light. It is so permanent that if you get it on your clothes by accident and do not notice it immediately, it is almost impossible to wash it out.

Consider how, after many washings, an item of black clothing's color fades. The faded black will now have either a brown tone or a bluish tone. Sumi ink shows the same characteristic: when the ink is thinned it will have a brownish or a bluish tone. The highest quality sumi ink will have a pure gray tone.

The carbon for sumi ink comes from three sources. Rapeseed oil, when burned, produces soot that is so fine that it has in-depth blackness. Pine sap, when burned, produces soot which has a quality of transparency, and the tone of ink when thinned ranges from light black to bluish gray. Industrial oils are used to produce inexpensive sumi that has a brown tone.

Companies that produce sumi have used the same process for many centuries. Many small chambers are built, each holding small receptacles for the oil or sap, each of which contains a wick. These are lit and smoke eventually deposits soot on the walls of the chambers. When a certain thickness accumulates, it is collected. The soot is then mixed with *nikawa* (animal skin glue) and kneaded until it reaches the consistency of bread dough and is shiny black like coal. Small pieces of this material are then pressed into molds of various forms and sizes, depending upon a company's specifications. The sticks of sumi are then carefully removed from the molds and placed in ashes to dry slowly and naturally so that they will not crack or split. After the sumi sticks are completely dried, they are removed from the ashes and polished according to company standards. Then they may be gilded or decorated, and labeled. Along with the company's name, each ink stick's container will note the ink's tone, such as blue.

The ink may also be left to mature for years after it is made into a stick; it is believed that sumi ink improves with age. Consequently, old Chinese sumi ink sticks are quite expensive. Ink sticks which are very old, perhaps even several hundred years old, may begin to crumble as the adhesive becomes very old. The ink stick is simply pulverized again and reformed with fresh glue.

The Japanese learned to produce sumi ink by the Chinese method. Today, sumi manufacturers in Japan are creating new methods and now many innovations are available. Traditionally nikawa was used but today contemporary chemicals are used to make an acrylic glue. You will still find the traditional stick form of sumi, but in addition, liquid ink is available in varying degrees of density which makes it convenient to use for practice.

For some time now, there has been a growing interest in sumi-e and in both Chinese and Japanese calligraphy worldwide. This has resulted in a wider assortment of sumi ink in both jet black and blue tones being available. Some companies have become so exacting that the degree of blue tone may be designated in numbers. Others produce ink in many varied tones, so you may also find sumi with a hint of a purplish hue; or jet black with a nice warm feel; or sticks that appear grayish blue. Brown tone ink is fine for practice but a better quality ink tone should be used for your serious work.

An aphorism states "sumi is black and yet it is not black," which means that black ink in a painting suggests many things including the whole spectrum of colors. A serious sumi-e artist should explore and experiment with these new products and use the sumi ink that provides the best results for his or her creative expression.

Soot (*susu*) is carbon and is a good conductor of electricity, including that found in human energy. Therefore, the brush and sumi ink can provide an imperceptible power and energy to the finished work.

A sumi-e artist should be prepared to use two sets of grinding stones and brush washing containers: one for blue tone and one for regular black ink.

Ink Sticks

Ink sticks vary greatly in price. One stick can cost as much as several hundred dollars while inexpensive ones can be purchased for a few dollars. It is difficult to judge the quality of an ink stick by appearance because any ink stick can be given visual opulence. Ask the shopkeeper for the tone of the ink in addition to the price. Blue tone inks are expensive, and the brown tones are the inexpensive ones.

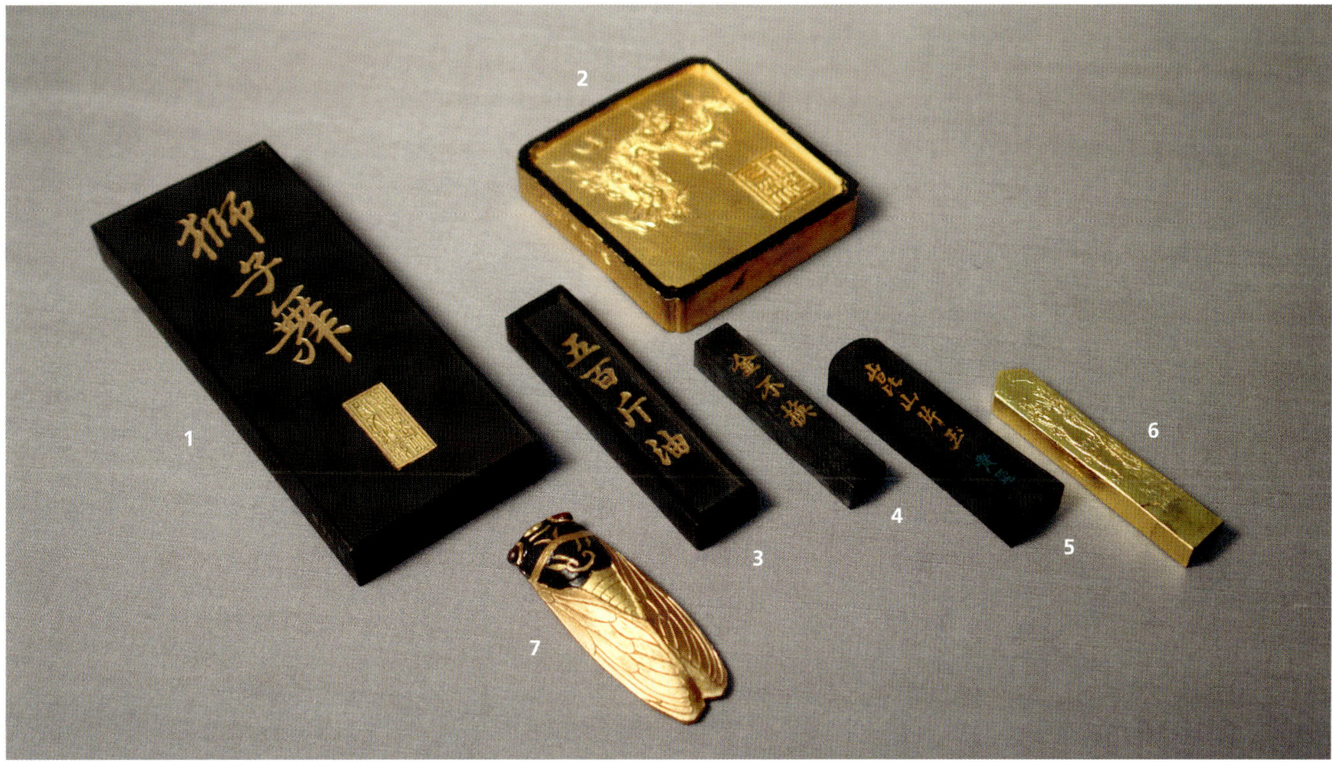

Different types of ink sticks.

1. **A l**arge square block of ink. The ideogram in gold relief states the brand name: "Lion Dance." Since the Han Dynasty and through the centuries, many famous calligraphers and painters have enjoyed using ink produced by this company. This ink stick is encased in a brocaded box and comes from a district in China known as a good sumi producing region. (Measurements: length 14.5 cm/5.5", width 6cm/2.25", thickness 1cm/0.4")
2. This gorgeous ink stick has a dragon embossed in gold relief; the back side has a tiger. It was produced by Genrindo. (Measurements: length 8cm/3.125", width 7.5cm/3.625", thickness 1cm/0.4")
3. The ideograms in gold state the brand, "500kg of Oil"; this is a Chinese ink stick.
4. This ink stick was produced in China. The gold ideograms state the brand, literally "This Cannot Be Exchanged for Money." (Measurements: length 6.5cm/2.5", width 1.2cm/0.5", thickness 8mm/3.125")
5. This is a Japanese blue tone sumi ink stick produced by Genrindo Company. It is the same size as #3.
6. This blue-toned black ink stick is covered with gold leaf. Its box offers a 200-year-long history of its medicinal qualities, stating that its original purpose was as medicine. It contains eight different types of Chinese medicines which counteract or neutralize poisons. It will also reduce inflammation and detoxify. It checks bleeding and so forth. Yet one can also use it as blue tone sumi ink for calligraphy and painting! It is imported by a well known Japanese company which produces sumi ink. (Measurements: length 7.5cm/3", width 3cm/1.25", thickness 7mm/0.25")
7. An ink stick in the shape of a cicada, produced in China.

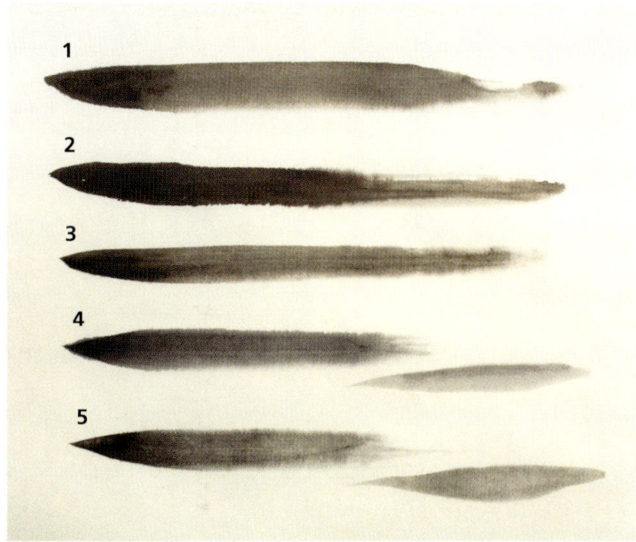

The brush strokes 1 through 5 are from ink that came from the ink sticks of the same number.

Brush strokes from **ink sticks 1, 2, 3** produce a rich condensed black. Note, however, that the diluted lighter ink at the strokes' end shows a somewhat brownish tone. When the literati and other suiboku-ga artists started using light ink, then the quality of the ink they used had to go beyond simple jet blackness. Especially for sumi paintings, the sense of very light coolness produced by blue tone ink was considered a valuable effect within the category of black ink. Unfortunately photo reproductions cannot fully capture the effects of light ink, but **ink sticks 4 and 5** are blue tone ink and blue can be sensed in the gradient.

As these samples show, the ink sticks deliver different effects on paper.

Sumi ink was used for traditional calligraphy, an art form where a complete Zen statement or poem was written. When used in this manner, the blackness of the ink is the important characteristic. When the literati and other sumi-e artists began to use lighter ink tones in their work, then the quality of the ink they used became important because their art expressions needed to surpass a uniform jet blackness. A gradient in tone of ink was necessary to convey subject, form and color. Especially in sumi paintings, the sense of very light coolness produced by the blue tones of ink was considered a valuable effect within the category of black ink.

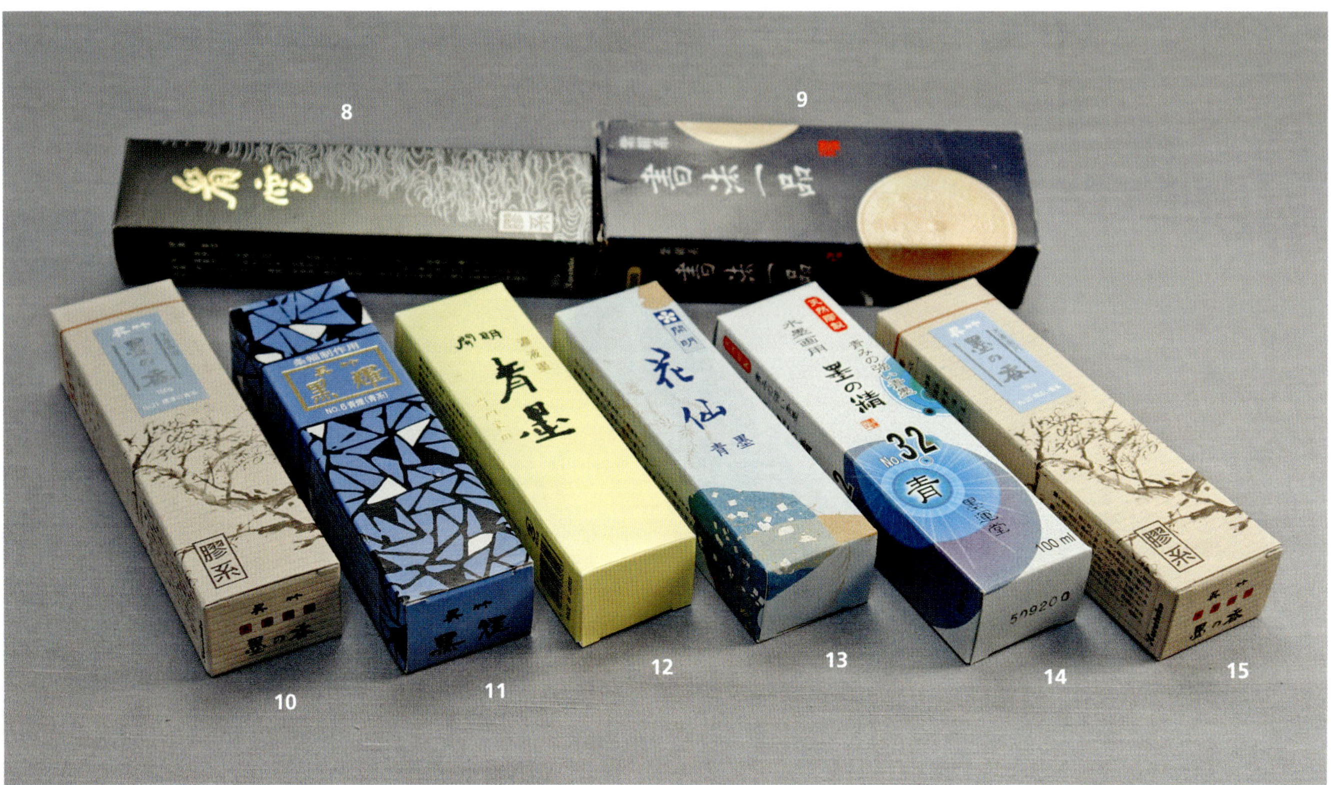

A variety of liquid inks

Here we can see the tones of ink produced by the various ink sticks shown above.

The sample liquid inks **#8 and #9** are sold specifically for calligraphy purposes, thus their goal is a richness of jet black. However, the boxes offer a bit more detail: #8 indicates on the lower right that it contains nikawa (animal skin glue), and #9 states that it has a purplish blue hue category.

Samples #10 through #15 are different blue tone inks made by different companies. This is just one small portion of the range that is available for purchase. **#10 and #15** are made by the same company, Gochiku Sumi. Both boxes indicate at left bottom the nikawa category. They also list a number scale rating the degree of bluishness; a number 21 rating is "standard blue", number 20 is lighter blue, and so on.

#11 is also made by Gochiku Sumi, and is categorized as a number 6 blue tone. **#12** is a blue tone ink by Kaimei Co. meant especially for creating light ink effect. **#14** is produced by Bokuundo Co. and the box indicates to dilute it at a 20-to-1 ratio for a light blue effect. The label also states that this is a natural nikawa blue tone ink for suiboku-ga with a number 32 degree of blueness.

As these samples show, the above liquid inks' effects differ as well.

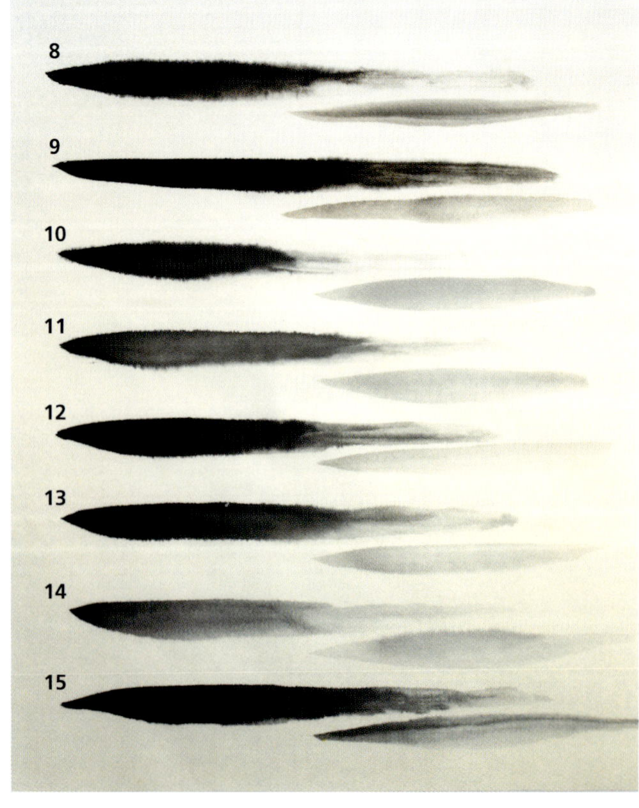

SUZURI: THE STONE FOR GRINDING INK

When you visit specialty stores selling Asian painting and writing equipment, you will find a remarkable collection of grinding stones. They come in different shapes, ornamentation, color and price. Most of these are natural slabs of stone from different quarries that are famed for producing beautiful stones, and suzuri are typically named after the quarry district they come from. For instance, the *Tankei suzuri* is made from a smooth, purplish stone from Tankei (Duanqi) in the southern Chinese province of Guangdong, considered one of the best sources. There are dozens of quarries and districts offering a dazzling array of suzuri.

The most basic suzuri shape is a rectangle, carved to create a gradual incline for the plain or flat section where the ink stick is ground. At the far end, there is a small deeper section to hold water, which is commonly called the "ocean." To use the suzuri, you place some water in the "ocean" (filling it only approximately halfway) and hold the ink stick perpendicular to the suzuri. Move it slowly and smoothly back and forth against the surface. After some time, the ground ink is then pushed into the "ocean" and more water is brought up. With great patience, continue this grinding activity until the necessary darkness of ink is obtained. In the classroom, we take advantage of the grinding time by using it for meditation.

Because grinding ink is time consuming, many artists buy liquid ink for their everyday practice needs. When the time comes to paint a work, if you are using premixed liquid ink it should be poured into the ink stone and, with an ink stick of the same tone, it should be ground to activate the electrical energy discussed in Chapter 1.

If the surface of a suzuri is too smooth, grinding ink will take a much longer time. The best way to examine the quality of the suzuri is to check whether the surface that will serve as the grinding plain shows the cross grain of the stone.

Suzuri made from clay, ceramics and cast iron also have a long history. There are different sizes of suzuri for your needs, ranging up to about 25cm by 25 cm (10 by 10 inches).

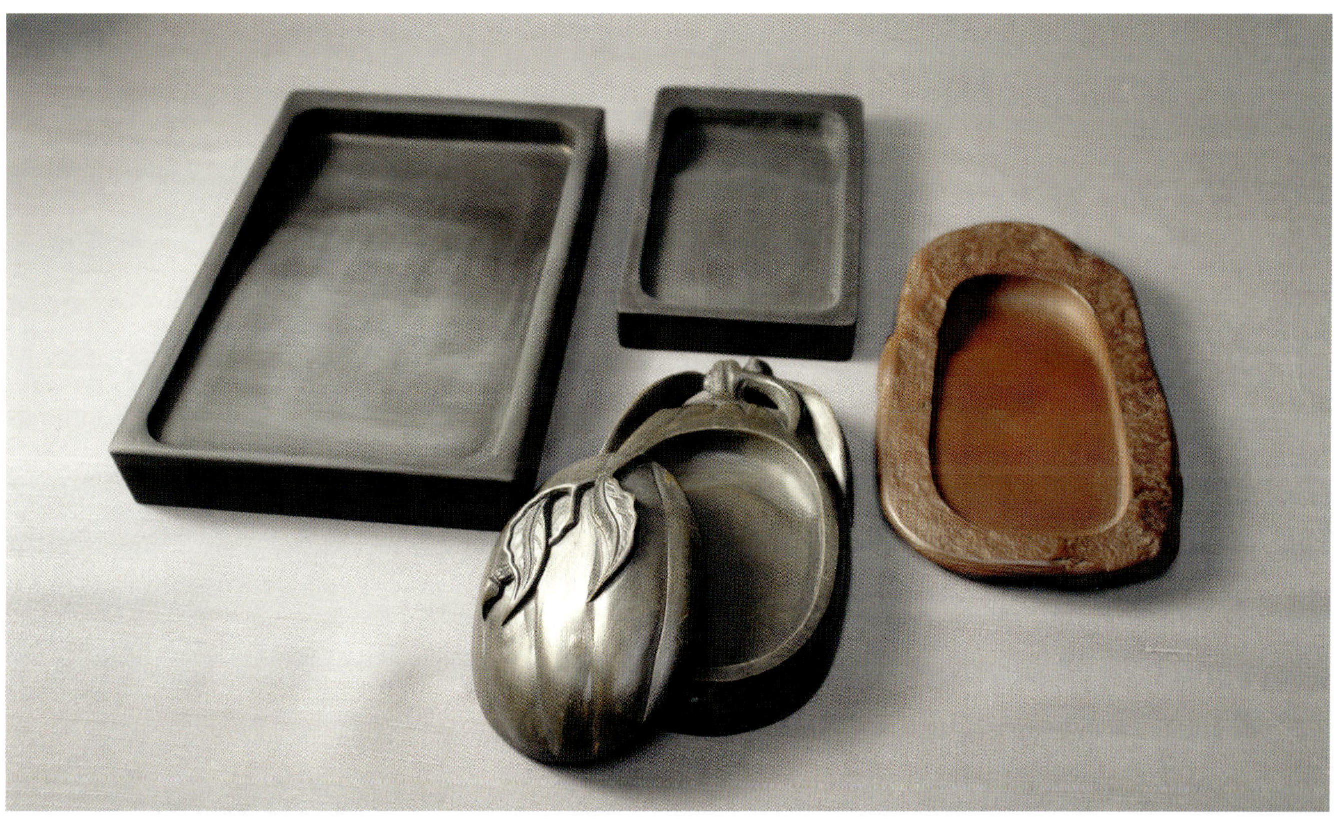

Different types of suzuri.

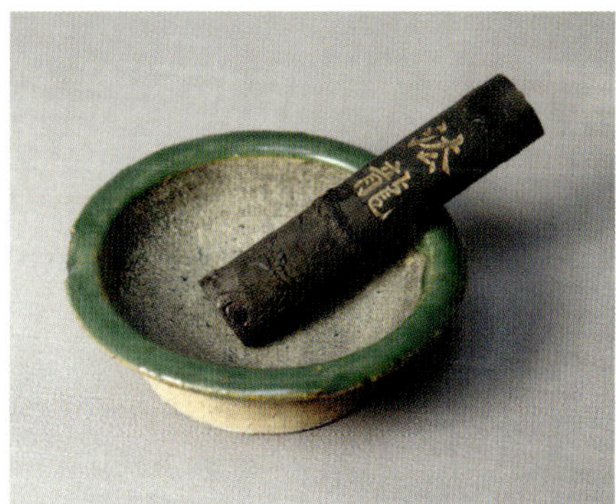

This suzuri is the mortar-and-pestle type.

A close-up view of the surface of a high-quality suzuri.

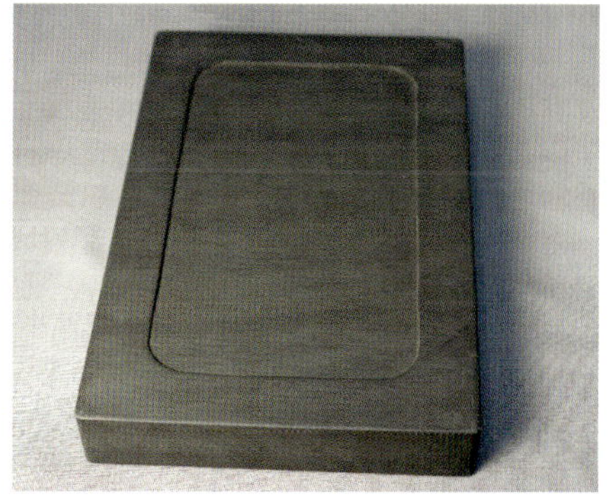

A high-quality suzuri which shows a pattern of striations.

OTHER STUDIO TOOLS

Brush Stands

Ceramic brush stands come in a variety of sizes and shapes
and it is easy to find appropriate containers of this sort to
hold brushes. It is also easy to locate the brush you wish to
use in such a stand. However, it is important to remember
that a wet brush placed in a container bristles-up is not advis-
able. Moisture in the bristles will collect at the base where
the hairs are tied together and fixed in place with a special
glue. If the base of the brush is kept damp for a considerable
length of time, two things may happen: the adhesive material
may dissolve, or fungus may begin forming at the base. Either
one will cause the bristles to fall out. It is best to let the
brush dry completely before it is placed in a brush stand.

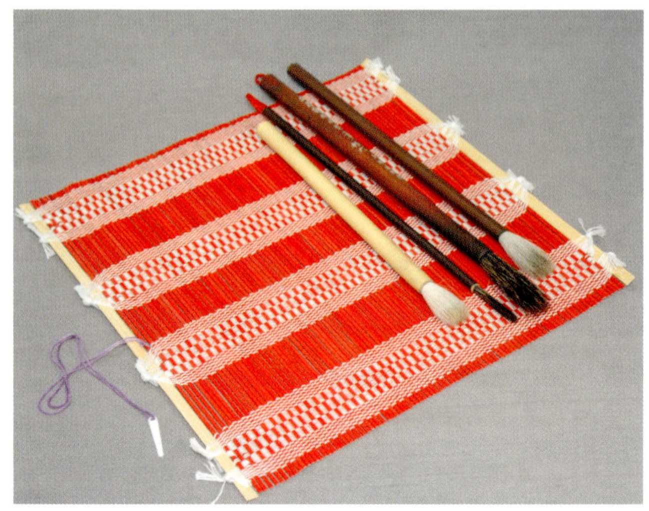

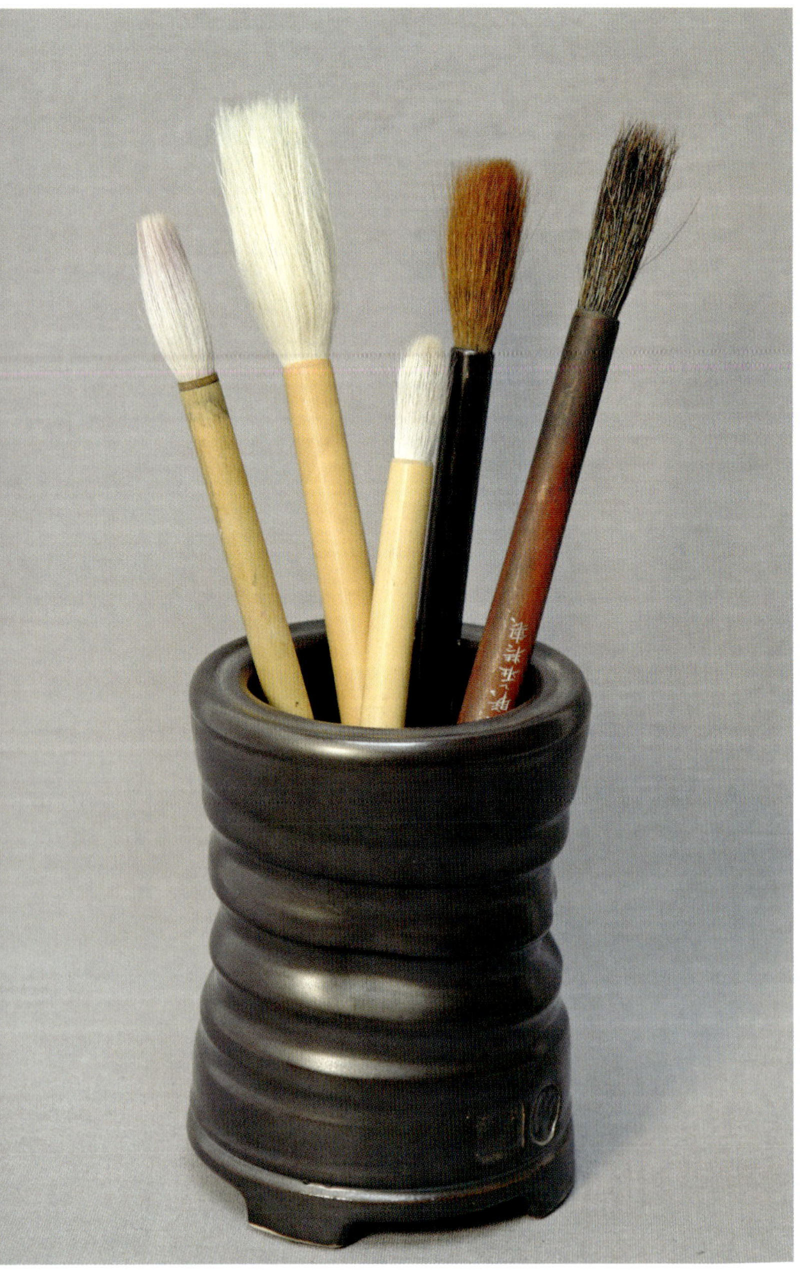

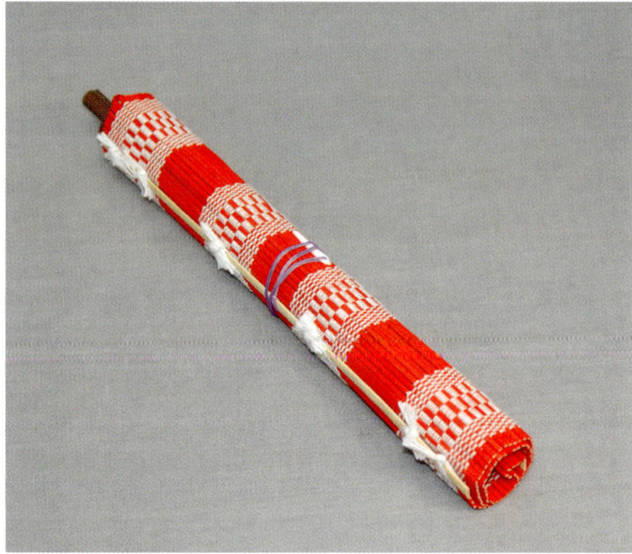

Bamboo Mat Brush Holders

When brushes are taken from your studio for painting at
another site, or even just taken from the brush hanger or
brush stand to be stored in your drawer, this type of mat is
very useful. The very nature of the mat is that it has flexibility
in one direction with rigidity and strength in the other to protect the bristles.

Many different colors, designs and sizes are available. If
you cannot find one in an art supply store, you can find similar mats, meant for rolling sushi, in Japanese supermarkets. A
cord to hold the mat in a roll is a recommended convenience.
Air circulation within these mats is good.

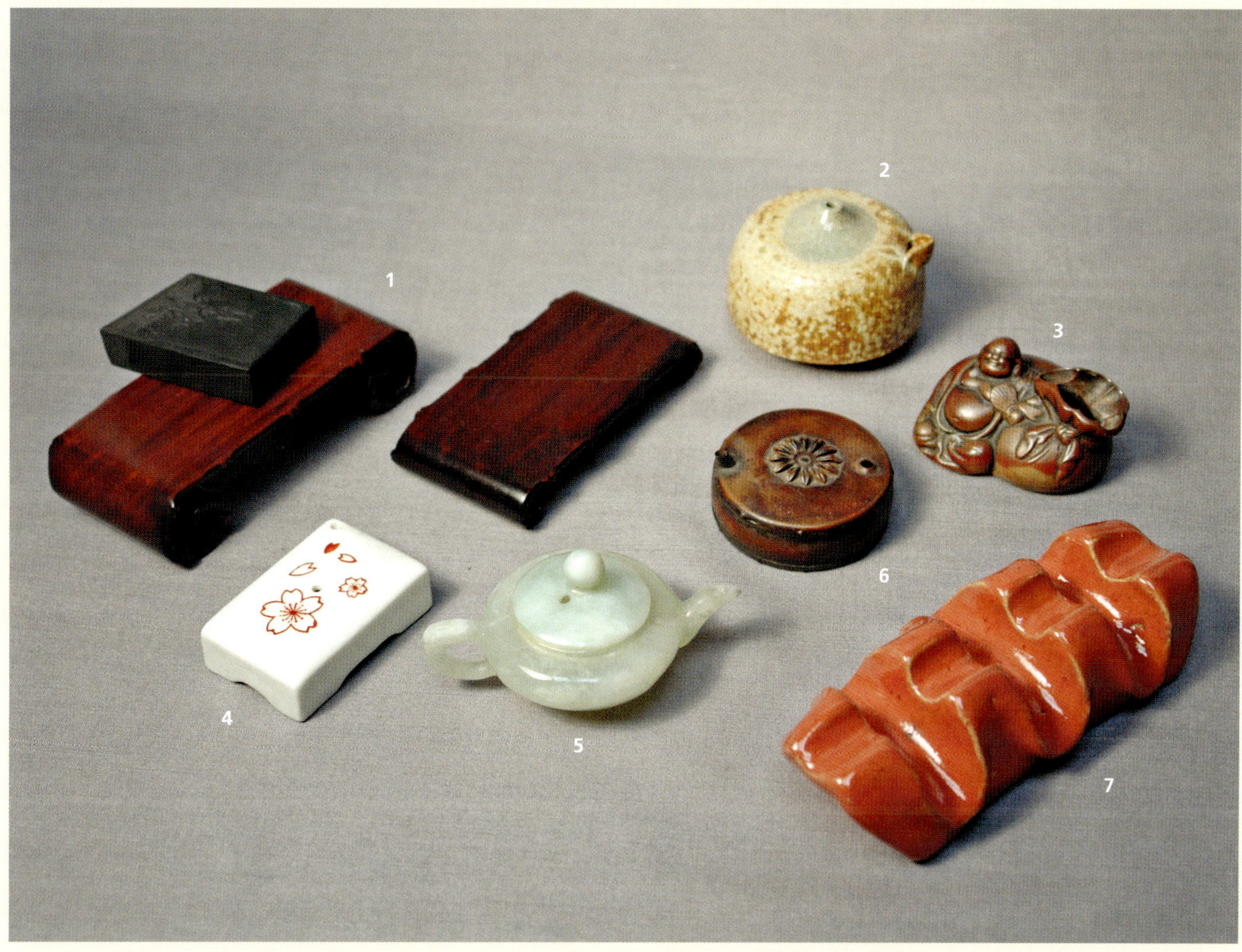

After the sumi ink stick has been used, the wet end should not touch the table. An artist in sumi-e should develop the following procedures as a habit. The moment after the ink stick is used, blot it on a paper towel or cloth, and wipe off the wet surface and all the sides. If you do not dry the ink stick off, eventually moisture will seep in and cracks will begin to develop, and a portion may break off. Next, place your ink stick in a safe place to dry; an ink plate or rest is one option.

During the grinding of an ink stick, often water must be added. The *suiteki* (*sui* = water, *teki* = dropper), similar to a tiny teapot, is used for this. These utensils will provide water, drop by drop, for grinding even small amounts of ink.

1. After the ink stick has been used, the wet end should never touch the table. Small trays like these are handy for safely resting your wet ink sticks.
2. When grinding an ink stick, often water must be added in small amounts. This stoneware *suiteki* has a small air hole to allow for pouring, and a spout.
3. At first glance this Hotei (one of the Seven Happy Gods) looks like bronze, but it is stoneware. The bag opens up for pouring water. It is a humorous and well-made piece.
4. This porcelain suiteki has two small holes, one for water and one for air. Suiteki of this category should be submerged in water to fill them.
5. This miniature teapot is carved from green stone and was purchased during my travels in China. It has a removable lid for adding water. Note that most of the time, small suiteki will be sufficient for artists working in sumi-e and suiboku-ga. However, when you do large sized work, all the equipment should also be large and functional.
6. This bronze suiteki also has a spout, along with the small hole for air.
7. This brush rest was made by a friend who works in ceramic art.

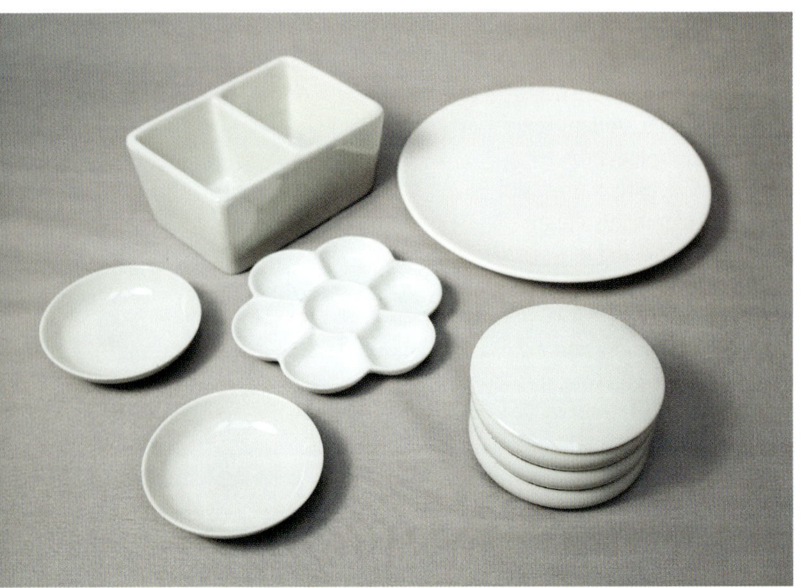

A variety of ink plates, for mixing sumi and water to create different intensities of black.

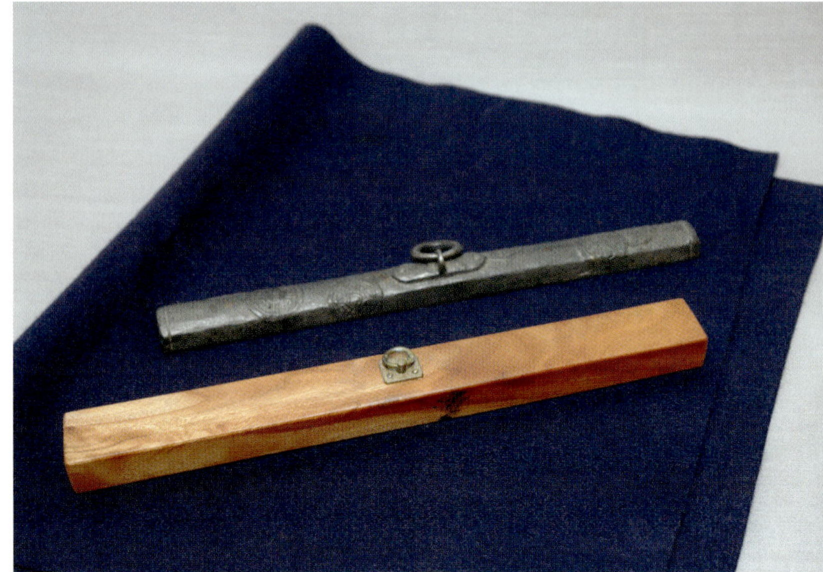

A protective woolen mat and two paper weights. The upper weight is cast iron, and the lower one is wood with a lead bar inserted inside to provide weight.

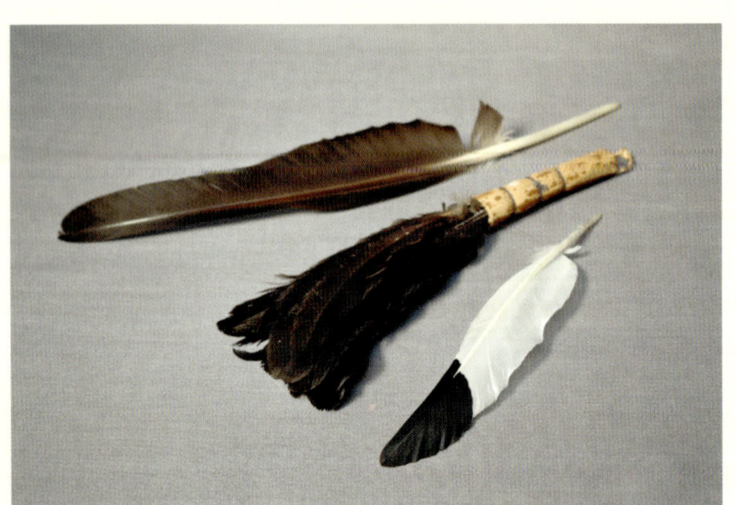

FEATHER DUSTERS

During sketching or while doing creative artwork, it is convenient to have feather dusters. I have been using the duster shown in the center for over 60 years.

Obviously erasing is not possible when you are working with ink and brush. When one must erase during the making of preliminary planning sketches, using a pencil would mean that eraser marks would impact your paper's integrity. So charcoals are best for sketches, because you can erase using a feather. The feather is useful for removing charcoal dust that accumulates on the page, and it can also erase a line completely if you choose. If you cannot find one to purchase in art shops, any other type of feather will do just as well. One or two will be sufficient.

Protective Mats and Paper Weights

Sumi-e or calligraphy artists generally use thin paper through which the ink seeps. This seepage will leave black marks on the table underneath. So the mat provides protection for the table, but also, better results can be achieved in the art when a felt mat or some similar substitute is placed on the work surface. This is because of the miniscule space created between the paper and the cloth, which allows room for the ink to expand. If you used old newspapers instead of such a cloth, the ink would seep through your sumi-e paper and make direct contact with the newsprint which in turn prevents the ink from expanding.

My personal preference is to use a thick tightly woven fabric of wool which is quite smooth. The popular inexpensive fleece fabric is similar to wool in some ways but it is too soft and lacks the firmness needed for your brush strokes. I like to use a lighter color of cloth than black or dark blue. When wet with light ink, the paper becomes semitransparent, and a dark color under it will interfere with seeing the true tone of ink. If the mat is wool, one can wash off the ink marks after use. For over forty years, I have used a woven wool mat of light purple which I have washed many times. It is convenient to have several mats ranging in size from small to large.

When you work with thick paper it is usually easy enough to hold it in place by hand, but often sumi-e paper is very thin. A paper weight is necessary to hold thin paper in place. Depending upon the size of the work, a weight on the top and the bottom of the paper may be required. Sometimes it may be necessary to use weights on both sides as well. It is important in sumi-e to use weights that have a flat, even bottom. Often I see fist-sized stones used as paper weights, but that is a mistake because of the cushioning effect of a mat beneath the paper; the paper surface will be pressed out of shape by the uneven weight.

SEALS

In Japan, seals are nationally registered and are sometimes more important than a signature. In Chapter 1 we discussed the traditional Asian practice of making study copies of masterpieces. In these cases, the student will copy the original artist's name as it appears on the art. This act of copying original artists' signatures is accepted in the world of art. However, you are not allowed to copy the seal. If the art student puts down humbly the phrase "copy of study…" then that student's own name can be signed on the work also.

As a general rule when a seal is carved, the ideogram for the surname is done in white with a red background, and the given name is done in red with a white background.

In traditional arts such as calligraphy, suiboku-ga and sumi-e, when a student reaches a certain level in proficiency, in lieu of a diploma the teacher or mentor will bestow upon the student an artistic name called a *gago* (*ga* = grace, *go* = title). A gago is commonly composed of one ideogram from the teacher's name and one ideogram from the student's given name. Today in contemporary artistic activities, many professional artists use their own names instead. In my case, when I was young I was given a gago, but after I reached the level of tea master I began to use my tea ceremony title as my gago.

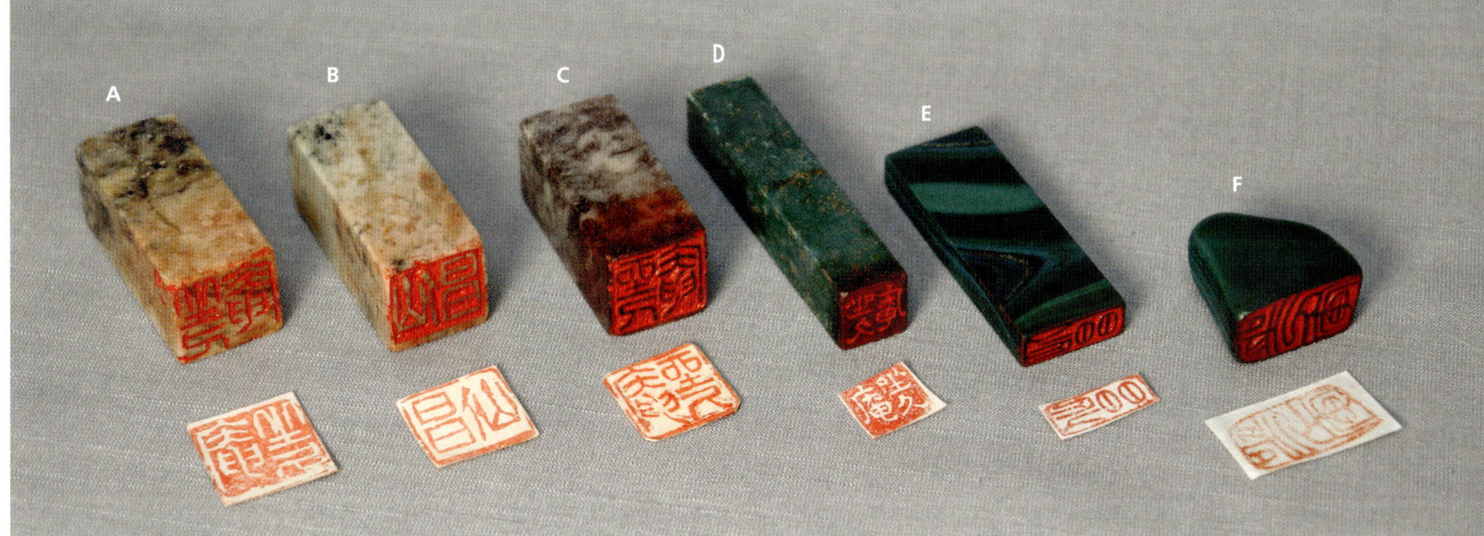

The seal on the far left **(A)** is in an ancient writing style that is especially reserved for use on seals. It shows my artist surname, "Zakyu-an" (*za* = seated, *kyu* = long, *an* = hut). The **(B)** seal reads "Sensho" (*sen* = sage, a name bestowed on me by my teacher; *sho* is taken from "Shozo"). The decision of which seal to use on a particular work depends not only upon size, but also on other factors. In some cases, perhaps the red background of a seal such as (A) would be too strong for the work, so a seal with a white background is selected instead. It is a good idea to have seals in several sizes and shapes, and with both red and white backgrounds, to use as your official stamps. On **(C)**, the red lines of my surname are slightly smaller than those of the (A) seal so more white space is shown. **(D)** is a green jade-like stone which shows my surname as a white ideogram on red, and it is one quarter the size of (A). The **(E)** seal is a red ideogram of my given name carved on a slender oblong piece of malachite. The seal made with an irregularly shaped piece of malachite, **(F)**, uses red lines for my surname.

Stamp Pads

Stamp pads in Japanese are called *shuniku* (*shu* = vermillion, *niku* = meat, signifying red). Traditionally, the vermillion pigment was mixed with natural plant lacquers then used to paint palaces, shrines and temples a brilliant red. This is why many Chinese buildings from the past are red. The pigment ranges between red and orange, so those variations in color allow you a choice. Colors vary from red, to orange red, to a red that is almost brown. Using a dark red gives the effect of an ancient work. The most important characteristic for the stamp pad's pigment is that it be insoluble in water. In recent years the vermillion pigment is being manufactured with chemicals that replicate the original natural earth materials.

In making seal stamp pads, the vermillion pigment is mixed with oil and soft sheep hair, then placed in different types of containers. If, after many years of use, the stamp becomes light, mix the contents of the stamp pad well using a

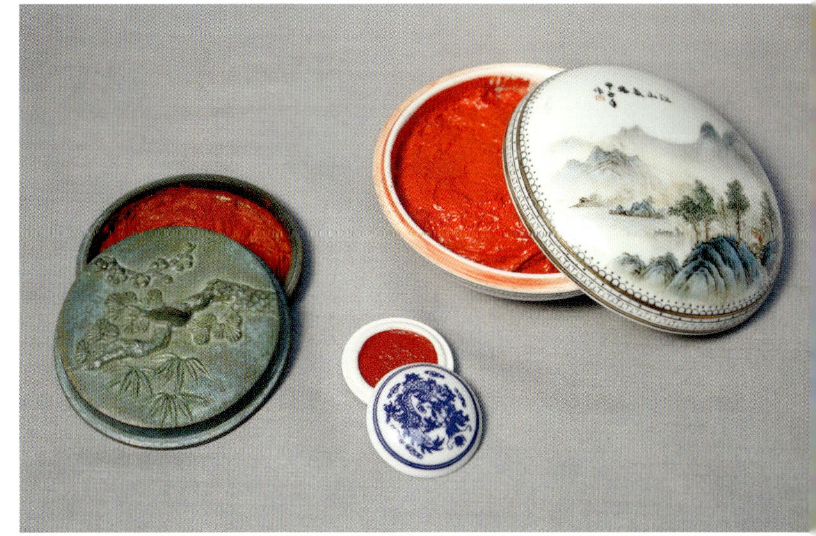

small flat instrument with a square head, to reactivate the vermillion color. When new some stamp pads may be a little oily; in that case, after placing the seal on the stamp pad, be sure to stamp it on some waste paper to reduce the excess oil. This process may have to be repeated several times in order to protect your work from the damage of oil spreading into it.

Also test the stamp on another paper first to achieve the shade you wish. If you desire a deep vermillion color on your work's seal, the first or second imprint will achieve that. If a more subtle red is right for a particular work, you may need to stamp the sample paper several times before reaching the desired lightness.

Once a seal is stamped on your work, it is permanent. Remember not to touch your work for two or three days while the seal dries. After stamping, place a protective paper beneath and above the seal to protect it from being smeared.

Using the T-Square to Add a Seal

When adding your signature and seal stamp to your finished work, it is artistically important to place them where they do not detract from your painting. Find the space that is not active empty space. Since the seal is red in color, on monochrome it will jump out; thus the choice of size and choice of red line or white line become important. Depending upon the size and manner of work, it may not be appropriate to place both your surname and given name on the same painting. You should prepare samples of your collection of seals, printed and cut to size. These paper sample seals can be moved around on your work to help you determine where to place your actual seal.

Cushion the area where you wish to place your seal with about ten sheets of paper. The seal will not come out well if stamped over a hard surface.

When you find the right location for your seal, leave the sample seal in place and use the T-square to adjust it to the correct angle. Line up the T-square so that the perpendicular and horizontal lines parallel your work's edges.

Once the T-square is set, remove the sample seal; press your seal down on the stamp pad and ink it well, and place it in the correct position in the T-square. Then give pressure to the top, then to the bottom, then to the left and the right of the seal. A benefit of using the T-square is that just in case you are not satisfied with the way the seal looks with the first stamp—for example if one corner is darker or lighter—it is easy to go back and stamp the seal again to even the print out. Without the T-square it is virtually impossible to return the seal stone to the exact spot. It is an important standard practice to examine the stamped seal very carefully; you remove the T-square only after you are completely satisfied with the result.

Usually the T-square is made of wood or plastic, with its bars' width matching the standard seal size. If you wish to place two seals on your work (such as your surname and your given name), this allows you to do so without moving the T-square, simply by placing the second seal in the other angle of it. The spacing will automatically be correct. The standard custom is to leave a one-seal-sized space between the two seals, and your signature is placed one seal-sized space above the top seal. From top to bottom, follow the pattern of: signature - space - surname seal - space - given name seal. After using your seals, be sure to carefully wipe off the ink.

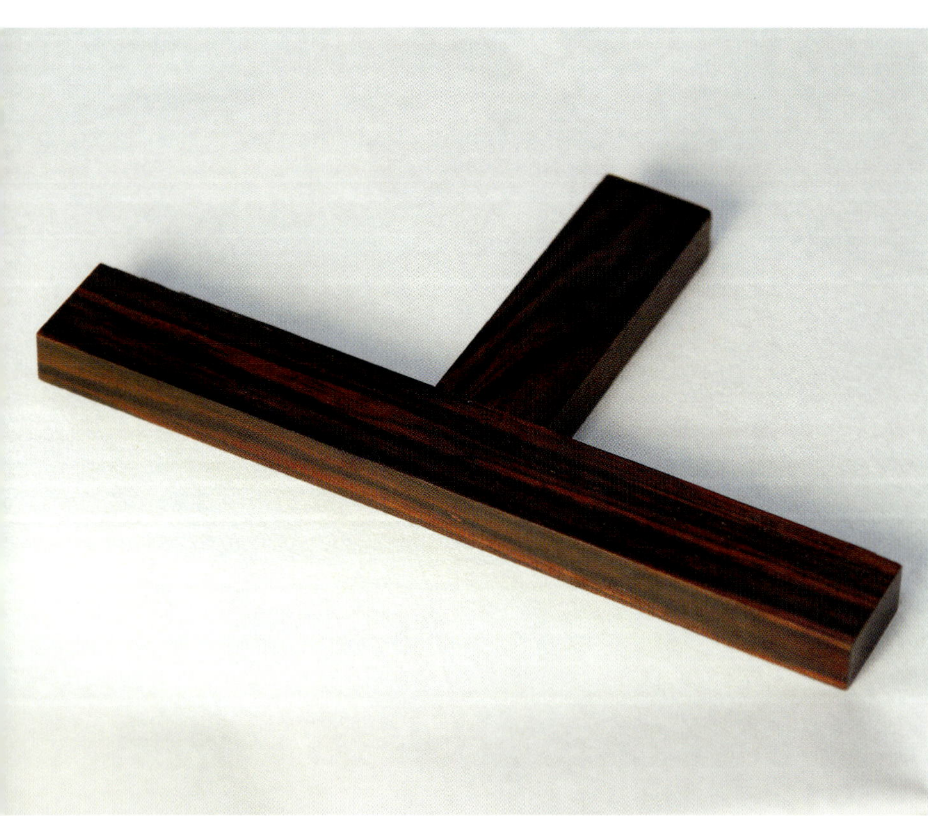

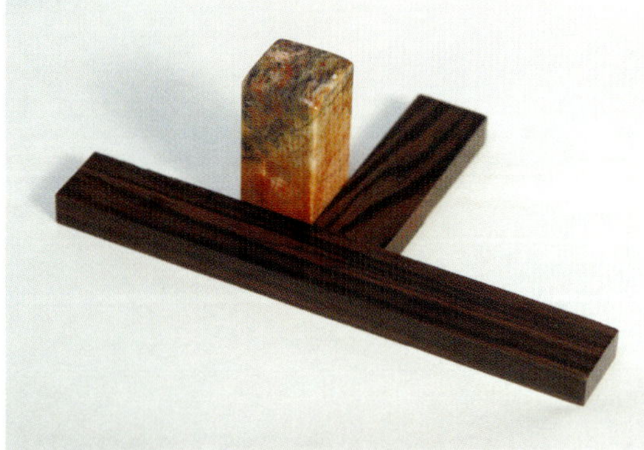

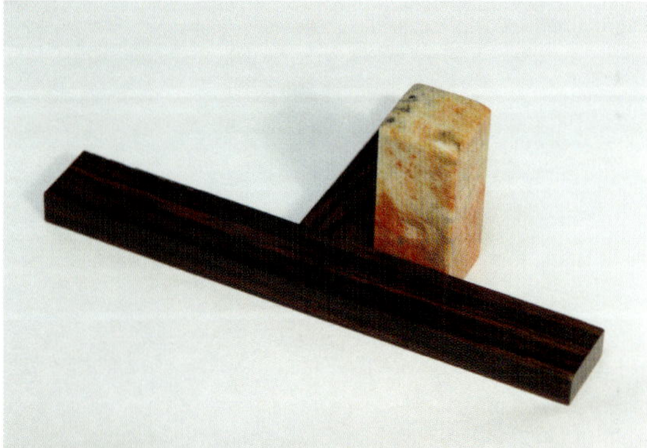

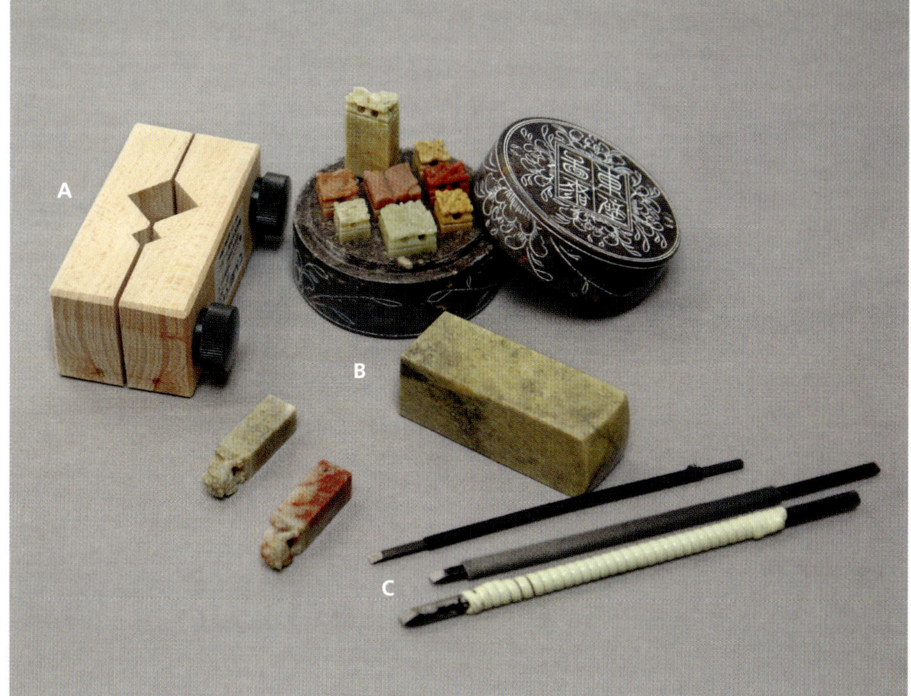

A. A wooden vise is a good way to hold your seal in place as you carve. (If you hold the stone in one hand while you carve with the other, there is greater danger that the knife will slip and cause you injury.) Another method is to tape the stone firmly in place on the edge of the table.

B. The circular stone container holds different kinds and sizes of soapstone seals. Farther below it are two more with "Fu dogs" carved on top. Another common carving motif for seal stones is the Chinese zodiac.

C. Here are various sizes of inexpensive seal carving knives made from square steel rods. The handles are wrapped with cord to create texture for a better grip and to provide more maneuverability.

Make Your Own Seal

Carving your own seal is not difficult, but it does require great patience. That said, you will receive much pleasure from using a seal of your own design that you have carved by yourself.

Seal stones may look like marble or granite in appearance because the stone varies in color and pattern, but they are all made of soapstone. These stones can be purchased in supply shops specializing in Japanese or Chinese art. Make sure also to purchase a special carving knife for the seal.

After you select your soapstone, place it face down on paper and draw an outline of it. Within that outline, draw the desired design for the seal: your name or initials, or perhaps your zodiac sign or another symbol. When the sketch is completed, reverse the page to see the image front to back, and copy that design onto the surface of the soapstone. Often the area where you wish to carve the design may be uneven or rough. In that case, use sandpaper of #400 or higher to make the stone's surface smooth. If you make a mistake in the process of carving, simply sand it down.

Easiest to make is a white line seal. This means that you carve the design down into the soapstone. The carving depth should be about 1mm. If you wish to make a red line seal, you must carve the background away leaving the design raised.

From time to time, lightly touch your seal to the ink pad to see where the carving needs to be readjusted. Remember, to obtain the proper printing effect, you should cushion the paper you are stamping with a pad of about ten sheets of paper.

Step 1. Once you have selected your seal stone, draw several outlines of the base on paper.

Step 2. Draw in your design within the space. Your design may be based upon the initials of your name, a flower, your pet, etc.

Step 3. Often you will find that the carving surface of the soapstone is not smooth. You can sand it smooth with sandpaper (#400 or finer). If in the process of carving you make a mistake, you can simply grind the stone back to its original smoothness.

Step 4. The simplest seal stamp to make is one that prints white lines on red. If you are using letters, remember that your design must be reversed. During the process of carving, check your progress frequently with test stamps to determine whether you wish to make a wider or deeper cut.

Step 5. If you wish your stamp to print red lines against a white background, generally the design is framed in a red outline. To provide imperfect beauty, you may deliberately create a break in the line for more space. These are artistic decisions.

It is highly important that you are aware of the dangers and take proper care. A slip of the knife can cause a cut or puncture wound.

Above: These examples of seals were carved by students in my sumi-e class at the University of Illinois, and have been enlarged to show the details. The actual seals were carved on stones which were 1.9cm/0.75" square. The student who carved the swimming trunks and sandals was a graduate student from Hawaii so his carving was a very personal statement.

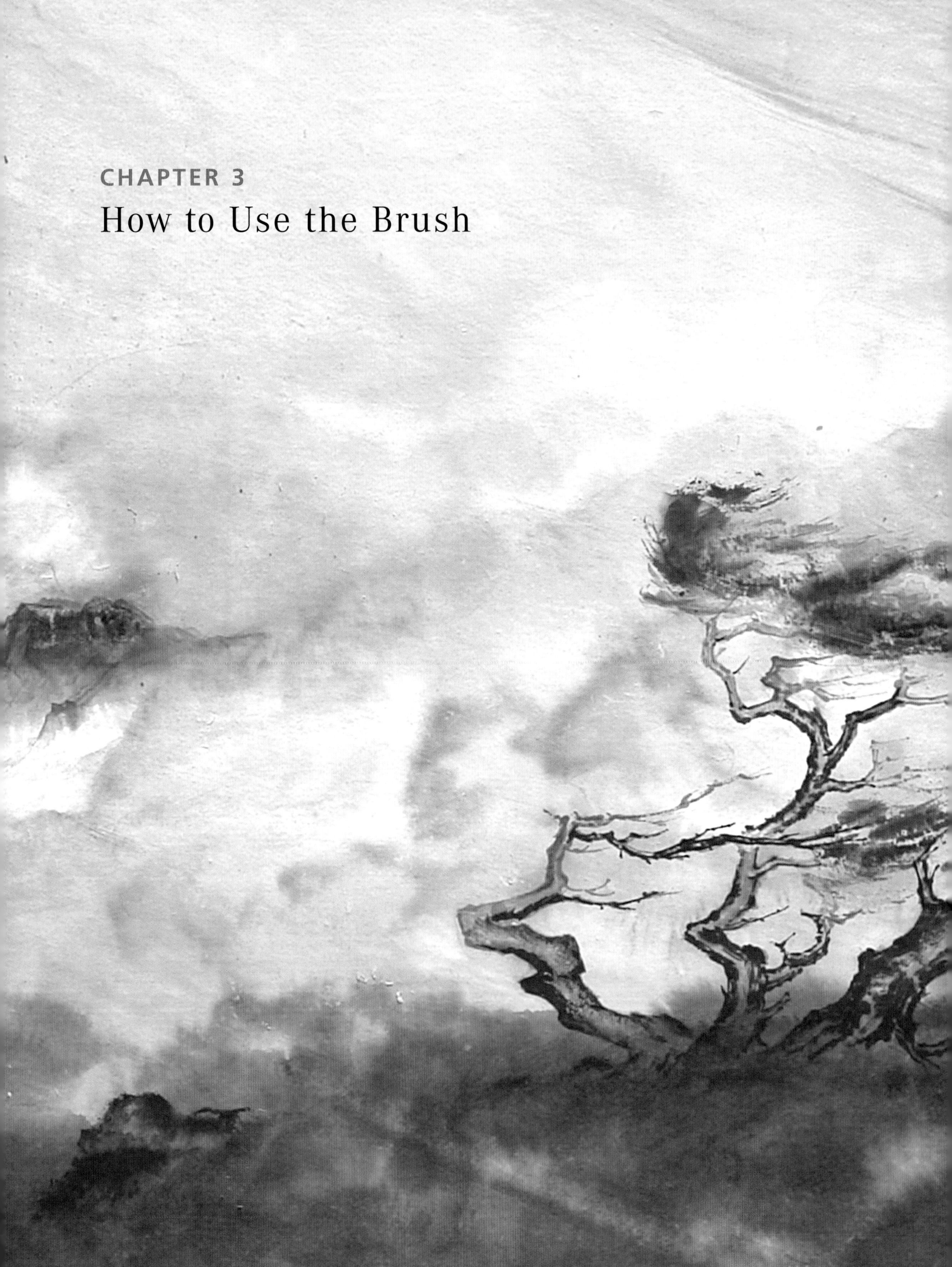

CHAPTER 3

How to Use the Brush

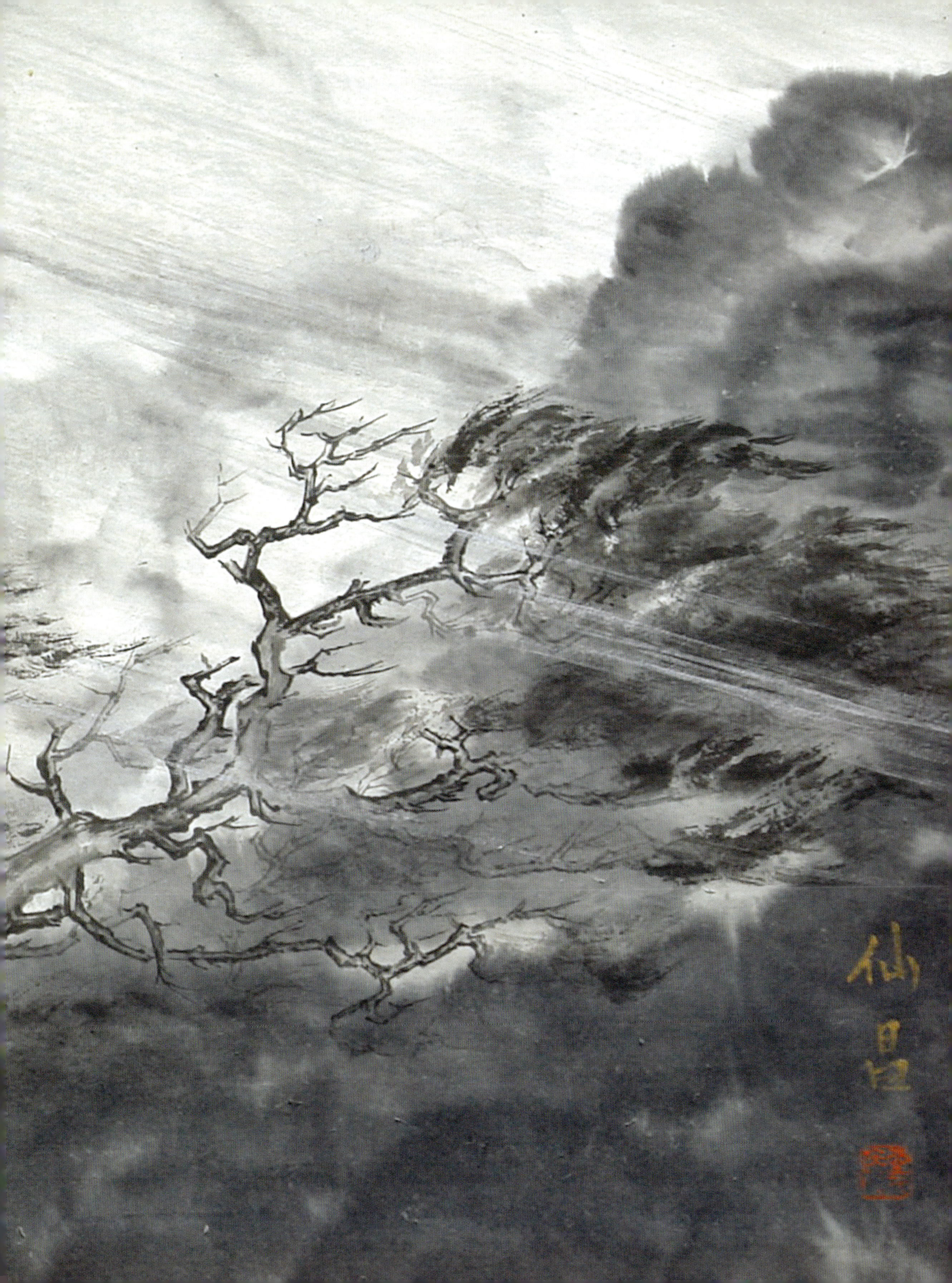

Basic Brush Use

A brush is handled different ways for different purposes. The artists and literati in China developed a system over the centuries for how to effectively handle a brush, and the same system is used today. In calligraphy, the brush must be exactingly held perpendicular to the paper.

There are certain overall positions of fingers, arm and posture which will enable a person to hold the brush in that way, and those positions also apply for sumi-e and suiboku-ga, especially when you are creating strong to supple wide or narrow lines. However, when it comes to painting, especially in sumi-e style, it is common to hold the brush at a 45-degree angle so that the bristles will have maximum contact with the paper from the tip of bristle to the base. Therefore, each artist must create his own rules and very original ways on how to utilize the brush for bringing about the effects desired.

We will begin with a careful look at a few of the standard methods of holding the brush upright and at a perpendicular. Then we will learn the positions and movements for controlling the brush correctly as you create different kinds of strokes. Set up your workspace, and prepare your brush, paper, and ink. Then follow along with the below photos, and refer to the DVD as well. While looking at the photos, pay attention to the grid lines of the shoji screen in the background; they help you to see the angle and position changes from photo to photo.

Holding the Brush at a Perpendicular

For all of these methods, the elbow should be raised to a horizontal position throughout. When I became a student as a young boy under a strict teacher, he placed a ceramic saucer on my elbow to ensure that I held my arm up in the correct position. (Under the Chinese system, water is put in the saucer!) Notice how this position is very different from holding a ballpoint pen.

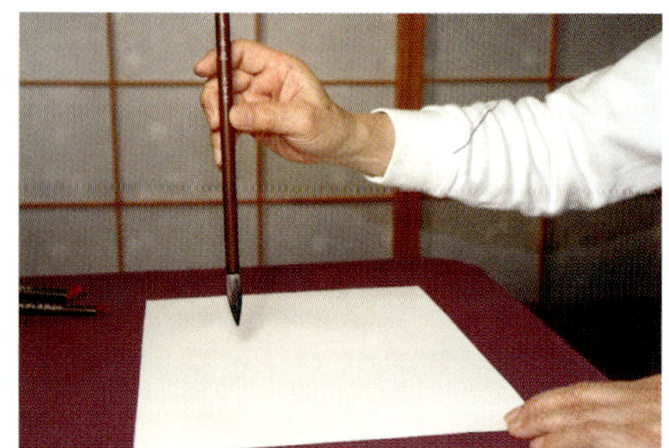

METHOD 1. Hold the handle of the brush lightly yet securely in your hand, with primarily the thumb and middle and ring fingers providing the support.

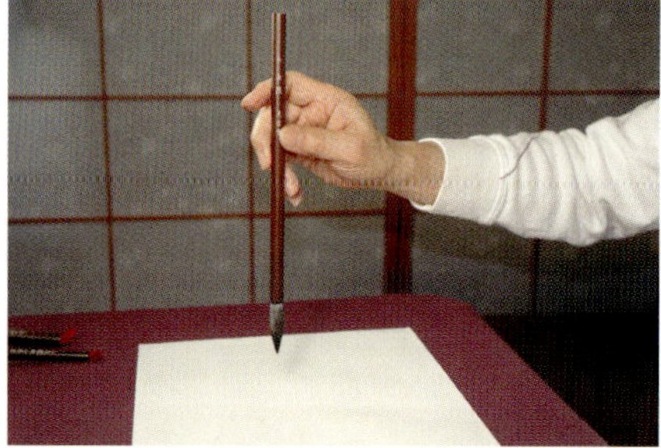

METHOD 2. The ring finger placed firmly at the back of the handle will provide more stability.

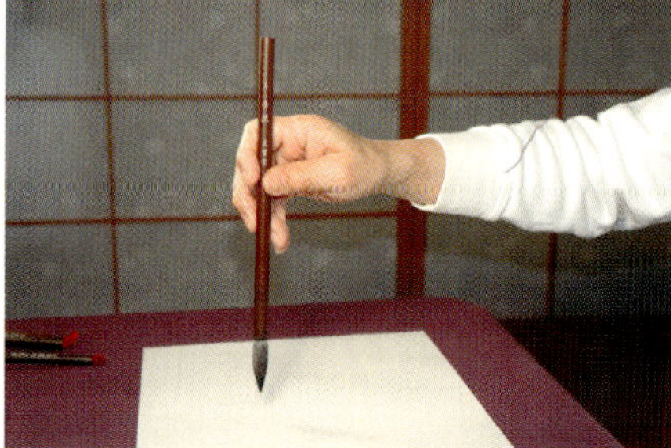

METHOD 3. Here all the fingers, with the exception of the little finger, support the handle of the brush. This gives greater stability when you are manipulating it.

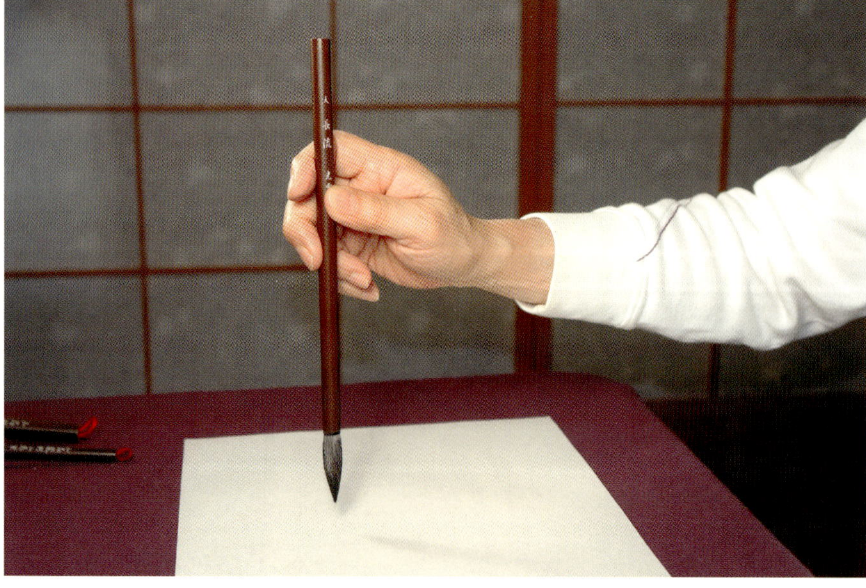

METHOD 4. Now even the little finger is used for securely holding the handle.

Arm and Wrist Movement: Narrow-Wide-Narrow Line

Now we move on to arm and wrist movement. This demonstration shows not only your arm but also the wrist movement required for a certain line to be created.

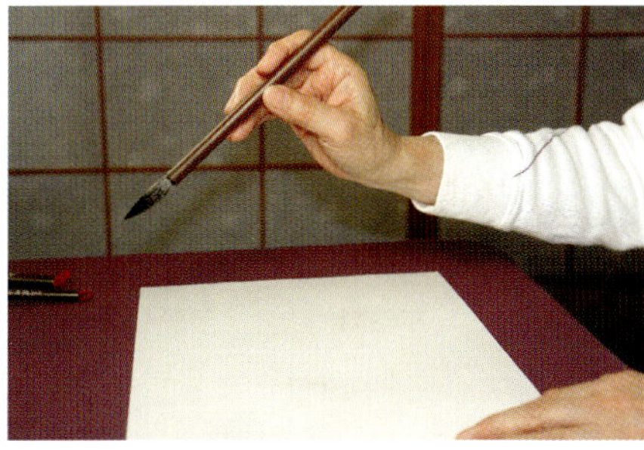

1. The wrist bone serves as an "axis of a wheel" or pivot and remains stationary as the hand moves around it. The brush is lifted, hand above wrist.

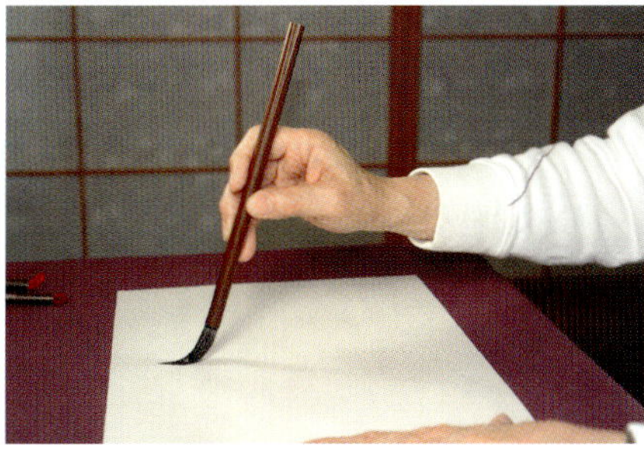

2. The tips of the bristles now make contact with the paper.

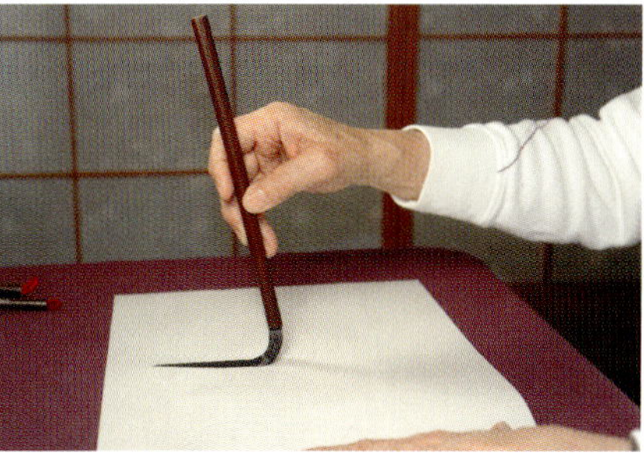

3. The hand is turning down below the wrist bone as the line is extended.

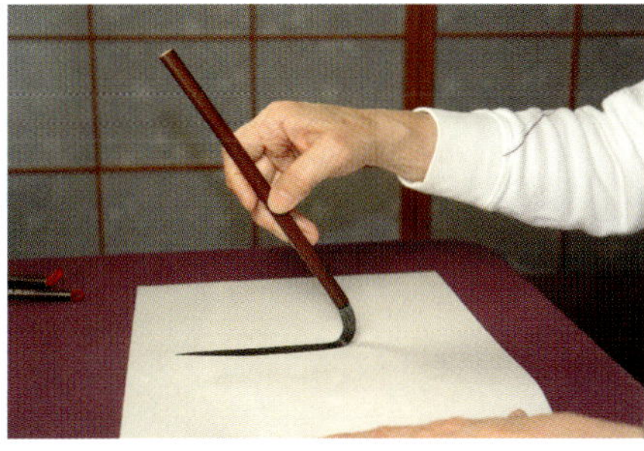

4. Fingers and brush are now lower than the wrist with the brush under the wrist. The drawing of a narrow-wide-narrow stroke is now completed.

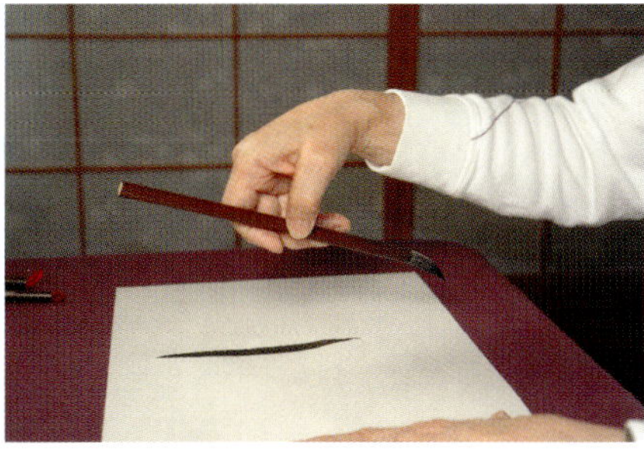

5. The hand is now under the wrist bone. Take note of the grid of the shoji screen in the background, as a marker to judge the arm position.

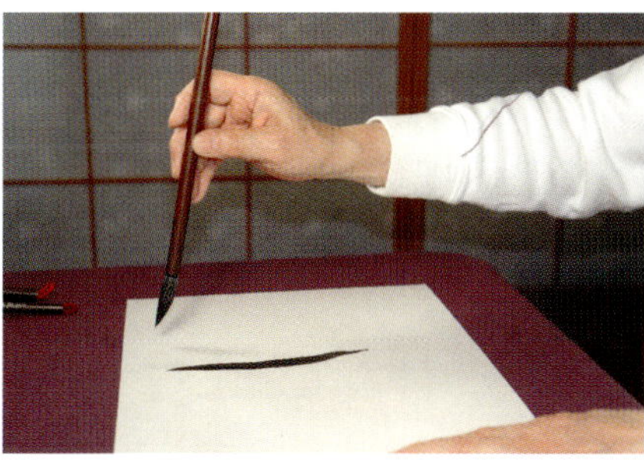

6. This narrow-wide-narrow line is a combination of moving the entire arm in synchronization with the wrist and finger movement.

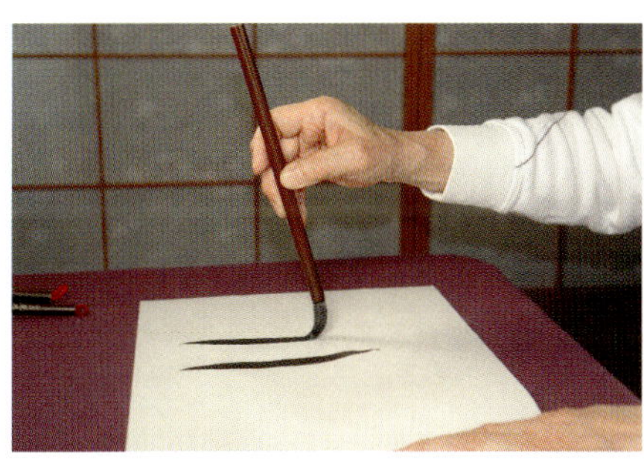

7. The narrow to wide portion of the line: Notice the hand moving downward. Again, check the shoji screen in the background.

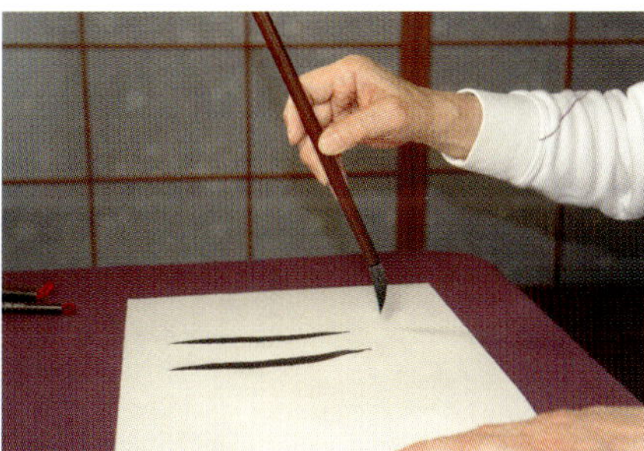

8. Completion of the narrow-wide-narrow line: with movement of the arm and hand in unison, gently lift the brush up.

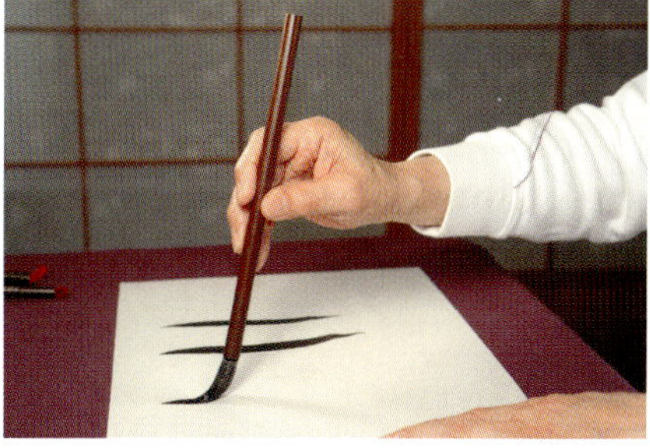

These 3 photos show how *not* to use the brush. The result will be an unsuccessful narrow-wide-narrow line. Compare the background grid between this photo and the next: incorrect motion.

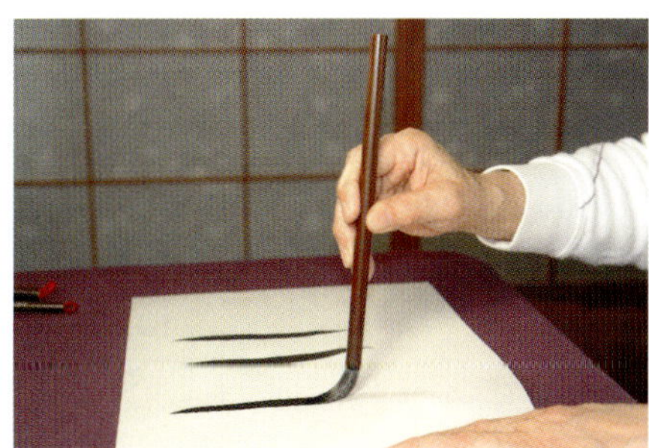

How *not* to use the brush, continued: It is incorrect to draw narrow-to-wide lines by moving the arm toward the body with a slight movement of tilting the brush.

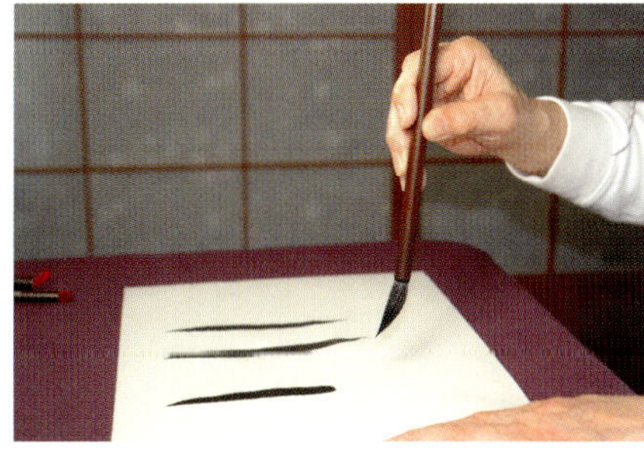

How not to use the brush, continued: The line is drawn without turning the wrist downward and without paying attention to the tip of the brush—which should be brought under the wrist without use of fingers, as was demonstrated in Steps 6–8 above. Look at the next photo, at right: its left-most stroke is the resulting unsuccessful line.

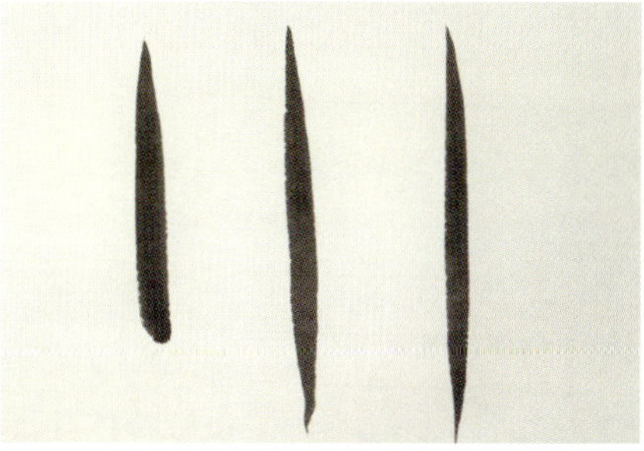

It is easy to see the differences in the painted line depending upon arm, hand and finger movements. *The right-hand line*, a successful narrow-wide-narrow line, was created with proper use of the entire, coordinated arm/hand/finger movement (Steps 1–8 above). Notice the *center line's* wiggle in the bottom tip; this never happened when I was young, but with age and arthritis, using the wrist as a pivot sometimes causes bone joints to protest.

Directional Lines

After you understand how to control brush movements by controlling the wrist and finger tip movements, the next challenge is to make the same stroke in eight different directions.

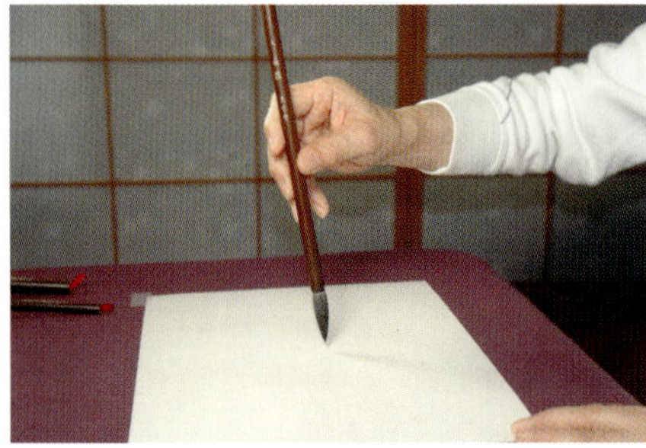

1. A narrow-wide-narrow stroke will be created by beginning at the center of the paper and moving up.

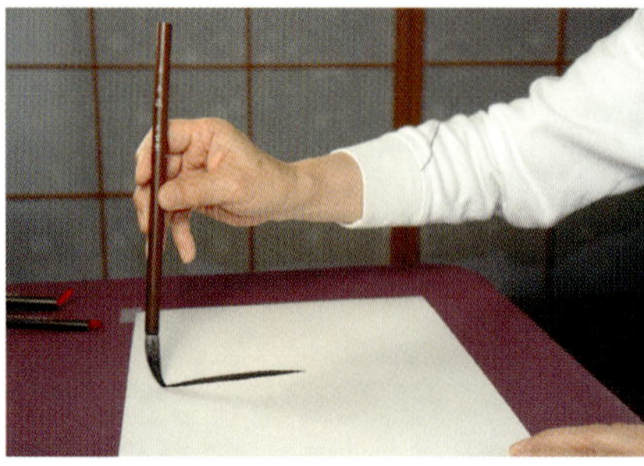

2. A successful narrow-wide-narrow line has been created.

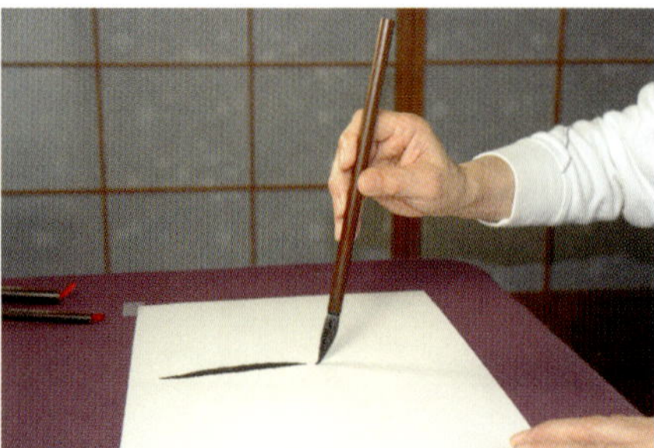

3. Starting again from the center of the paper, prepare to make a downward stroke.

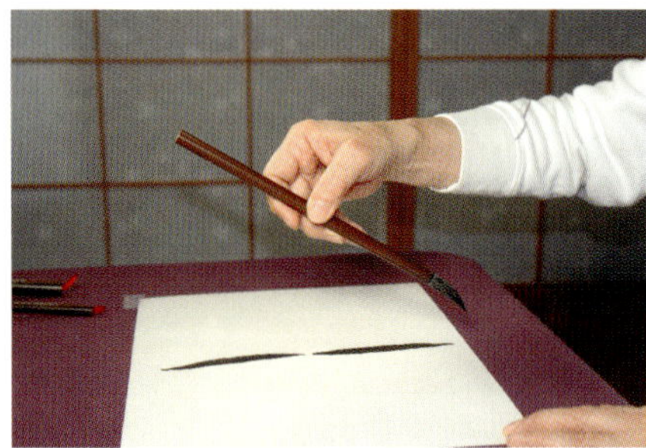

4. A downward stroke has now been created. Be aware that the wrist pivots when forming this line.

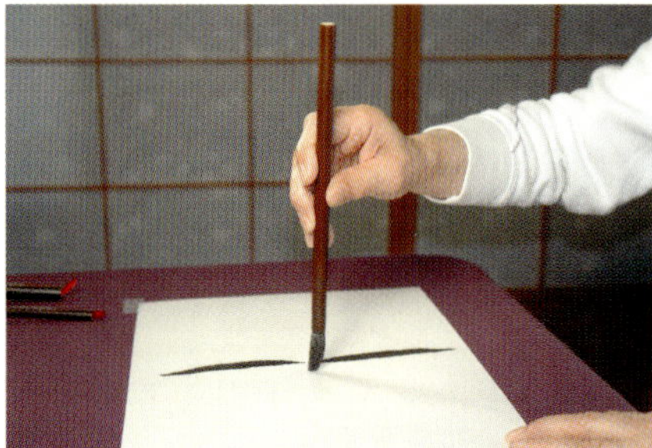

5. From the center move to the left.

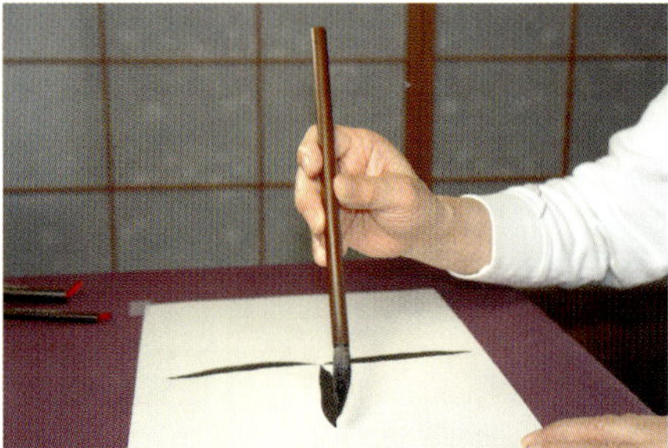

6. Complete the line...

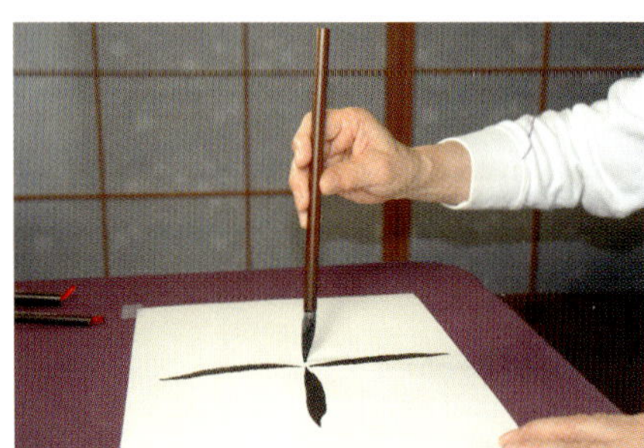

7. Then move back to the center.

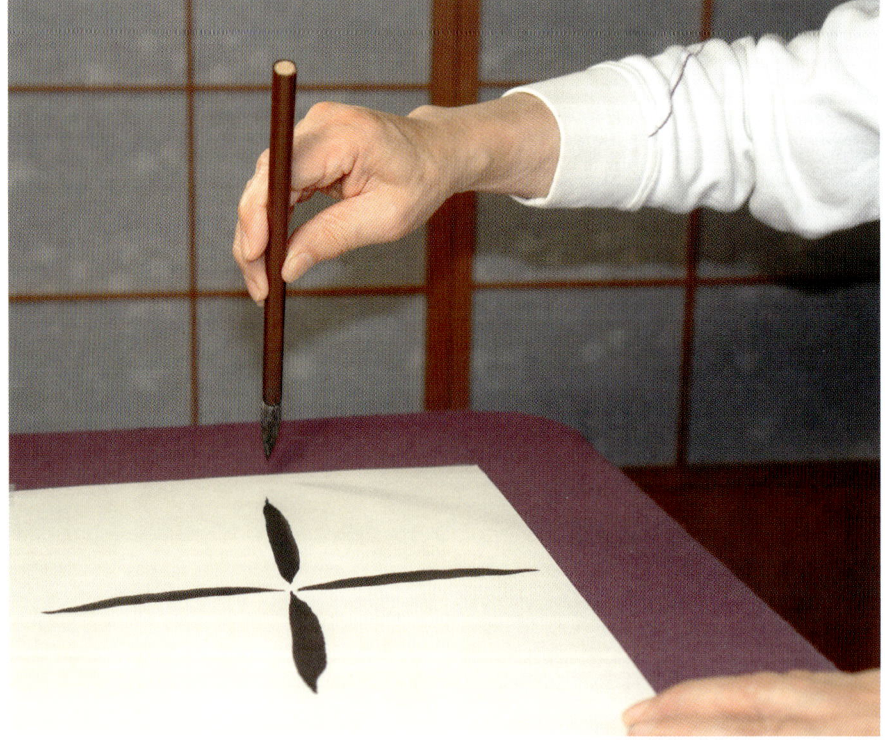

8. From the center now move to the left. Complete that fourth line, then move back to the center.

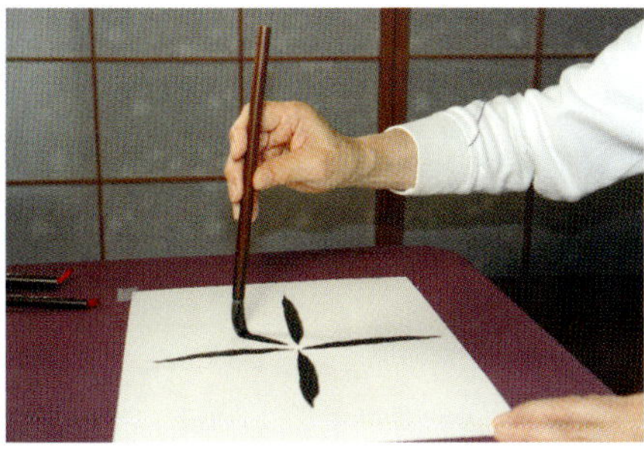

9. From the center, move diagonally to the right 45 degrees to paint the next line.

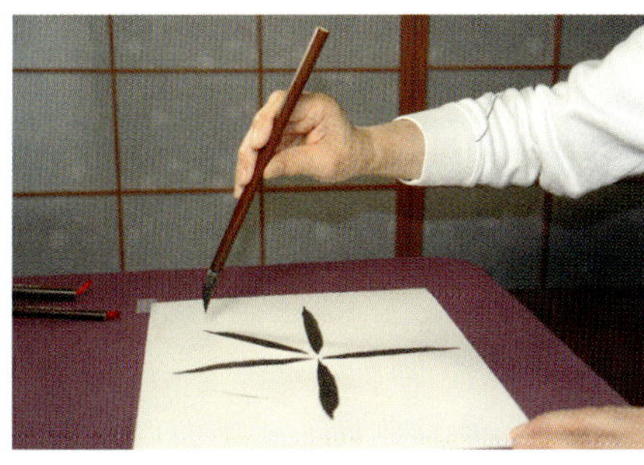

10. Keep your attention focused on the correct, unified movements of your fingers, hand and arm.

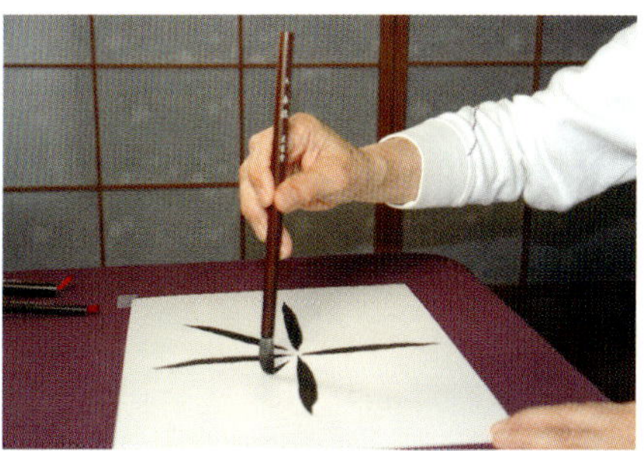

11. Again from the center, move up and to the left 45 degrees.

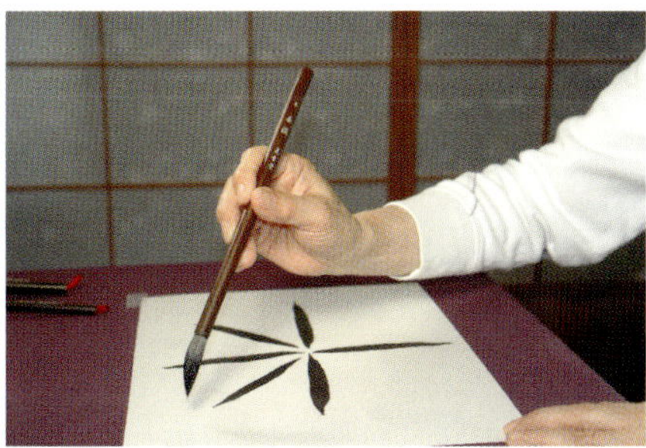

12. The sixth stroke is now complete.

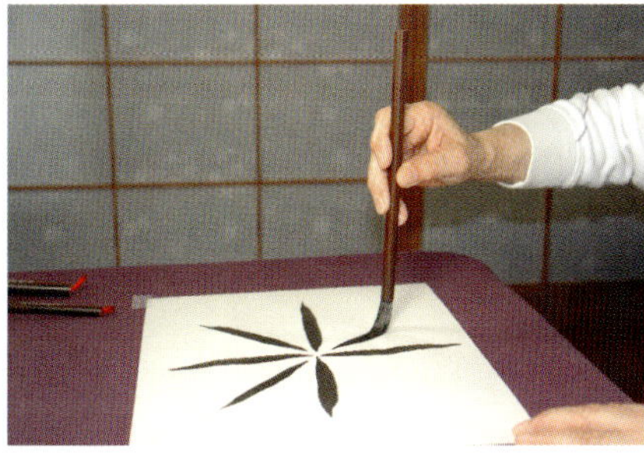

13. From the center, move to the right and down 45 degrees.

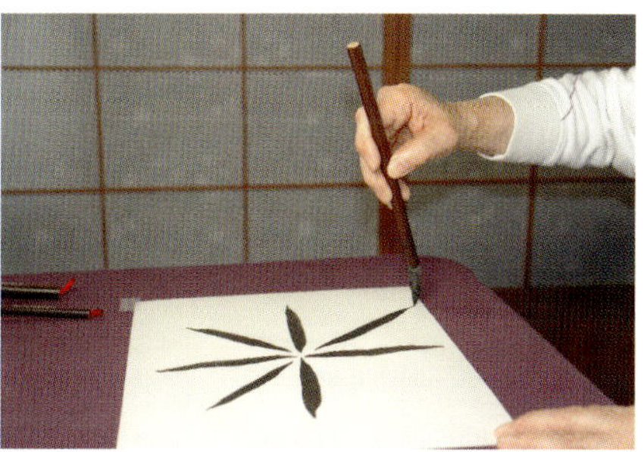

14. Seven strokes are now complete.

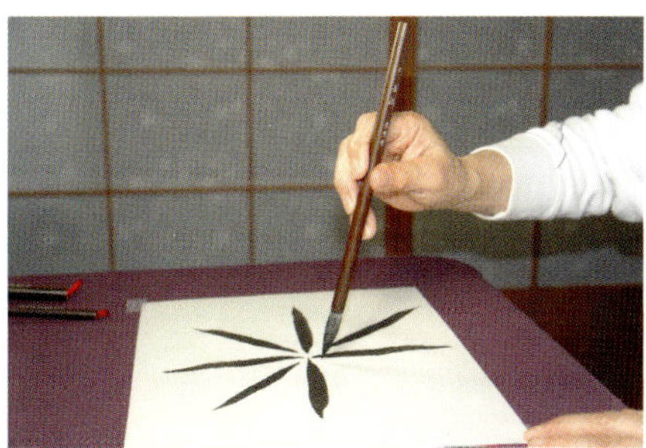

15. The final stroke is from the center to the left lower portion of the paper.

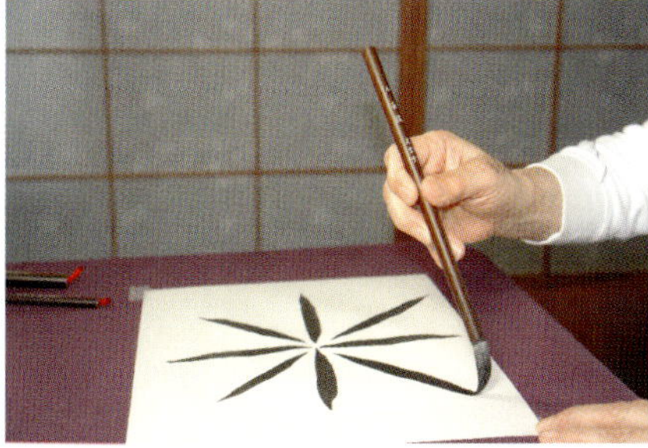

16. Remember to turn your wrist to bring the brush tip below it.

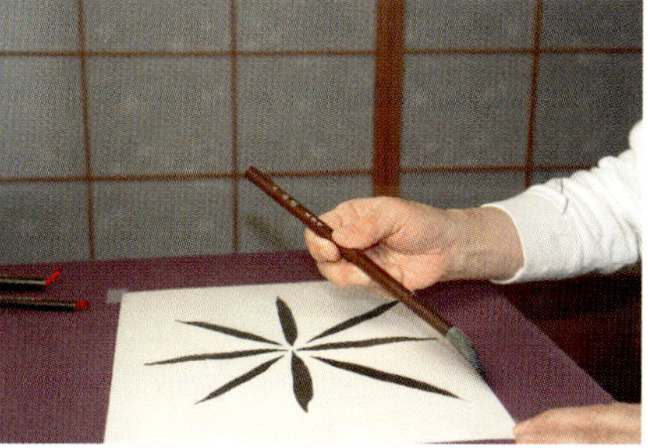

17. The final motion is of the arm and hand in unison, gently lifting the brush up.

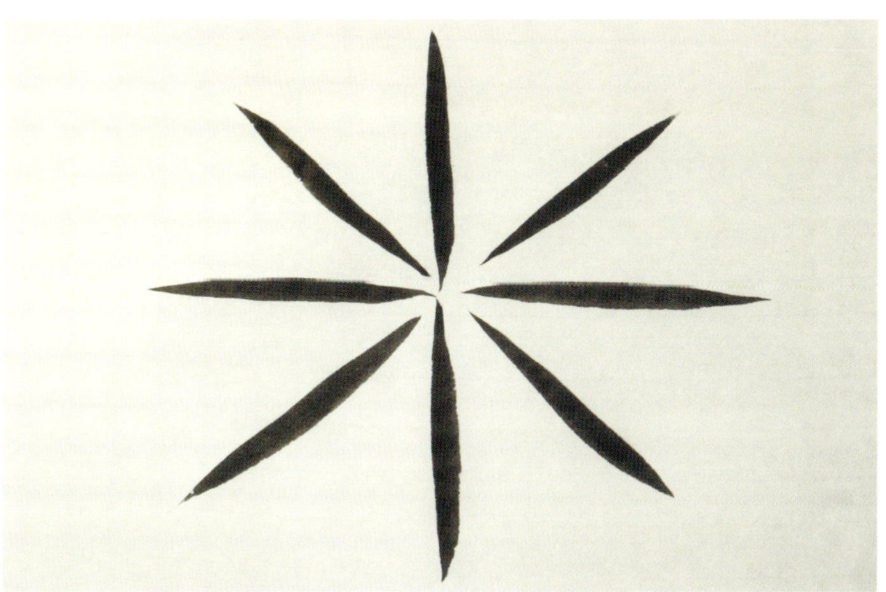

Here we see the completion of the radiating strokes. *The brush is a sacred tool for the painter* and can be compared to a samurai sword. If an artist can master control of the movements in every direction, he or she will become capable of creating lines that reflect greater strength, grace and beauty.

After the successful practice in drawing narrow-wide-narrow lines in different directions, we will now experiment with drawing curving lines similar to those we'd use for Chinese orchids.

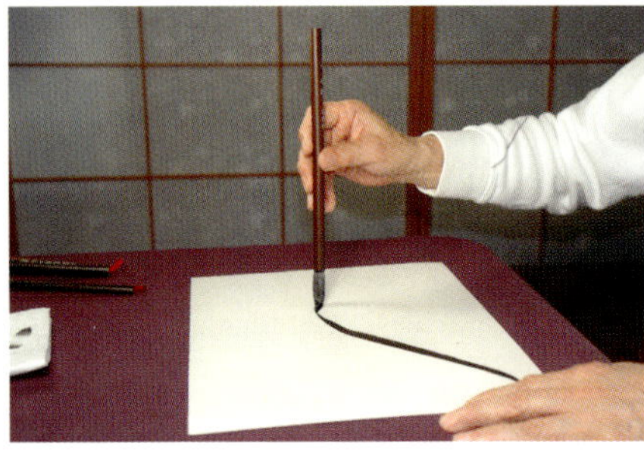

1. From the left bottom of the paper, move diagonally toward the right top with a narrow-wide-narrow line. At the narrowing, lift the brush tip up and curve, to show a twist in the leaf.

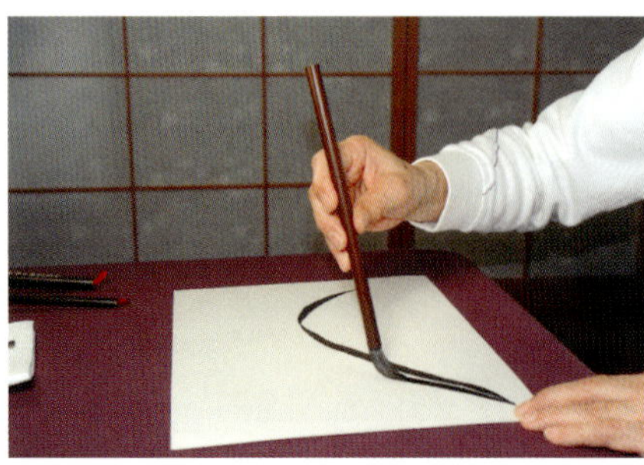

2. The second leaf will be straighter. Begin at the base of the orchid...

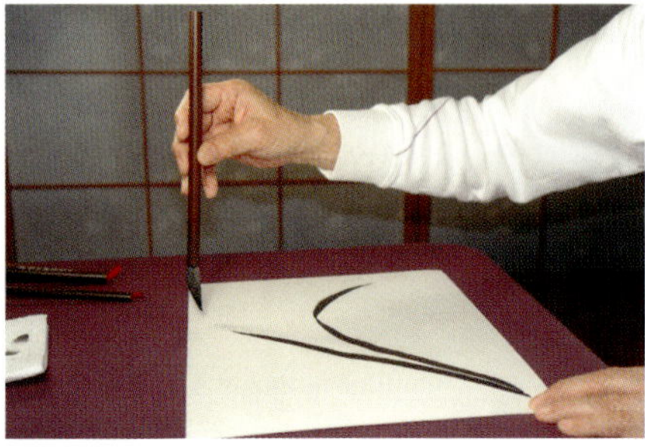

3. ...and make a long version of a narrow-wide-narrow line.

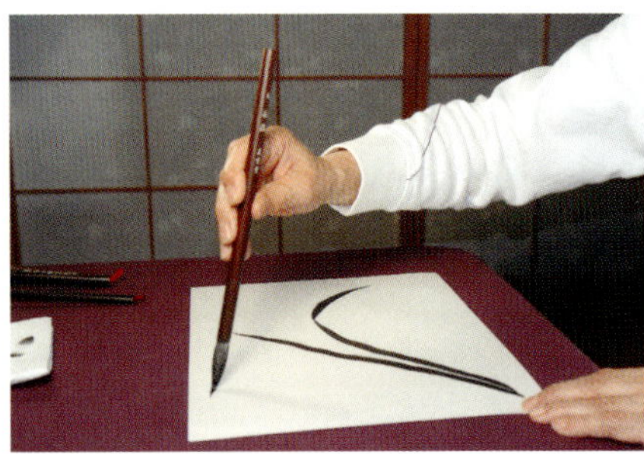

4. Beginning at the left top, make a curved narrow-wide-narrow line in the shape of a nearly-new moon.

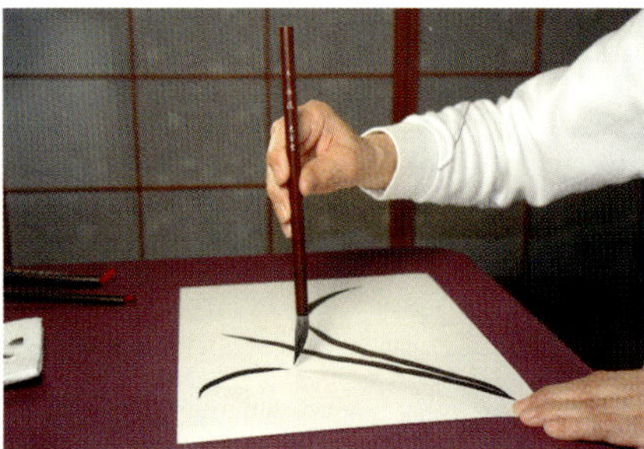

5. The "new moon" line has been successfully completed; now continue with a longer version of the narrow wide line to the base of the orchid.

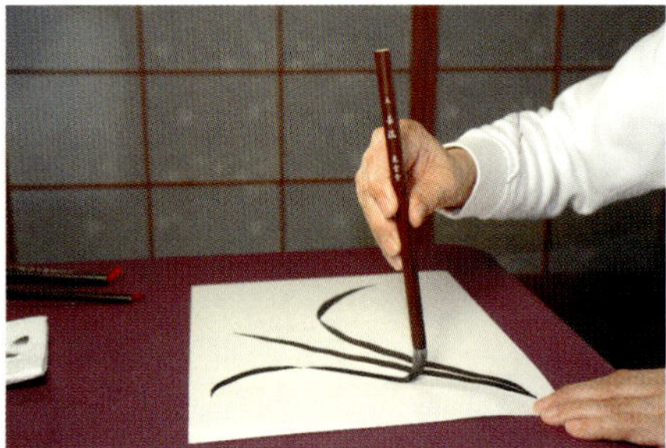

6. Complete the line.

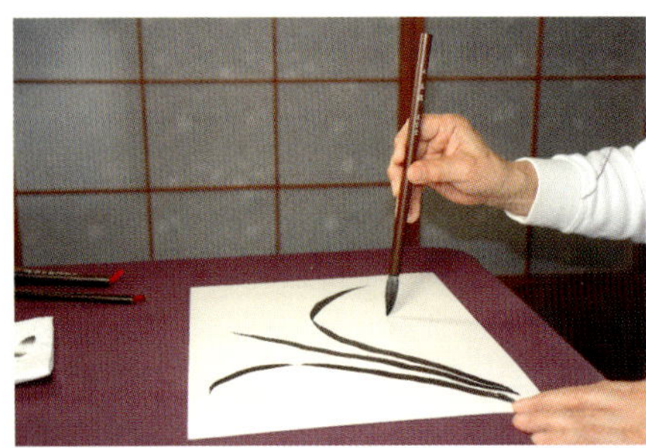

7. This time from the right, move your brush toward the left in a narrow to wide stroke.

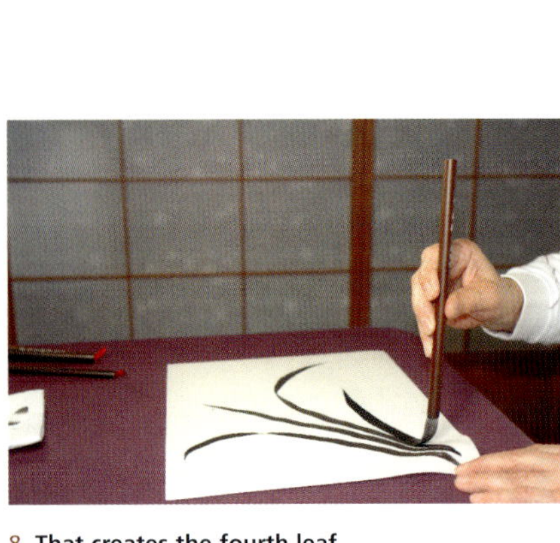

8. That creates the fourth leaf.

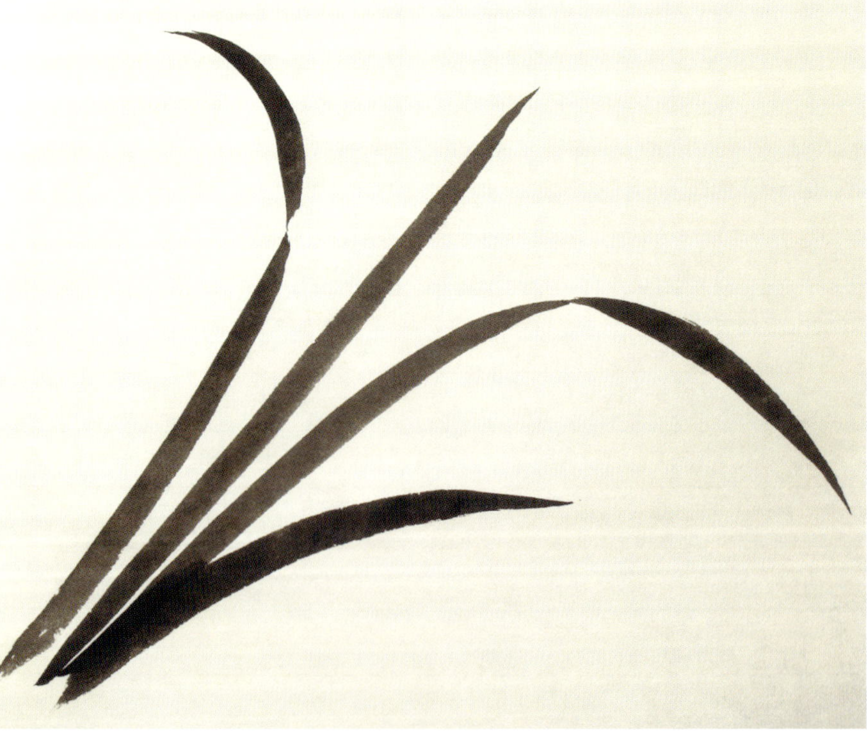

This exercise in curved lines is a first step in practicing brush movements for painting Chinese orchids or any other plant with long leaves, and you can also transform it to practice making twisted bamboo leaves. More lines should be added to complete the composition. A large choryu brush was used for this exercise; the combination of hairs in a choryu brush makes it ideal for painting these types of lines.

This exercise is helpful in improving your level of brush control. Focus on the maximum use of your tool in synchronization with your fingers, wrist and arm. Note that the handle of the brush in the photos below shows the word "Choryu"; the location of that word will help you to monitor the turning of the brush. The word will always face outward.

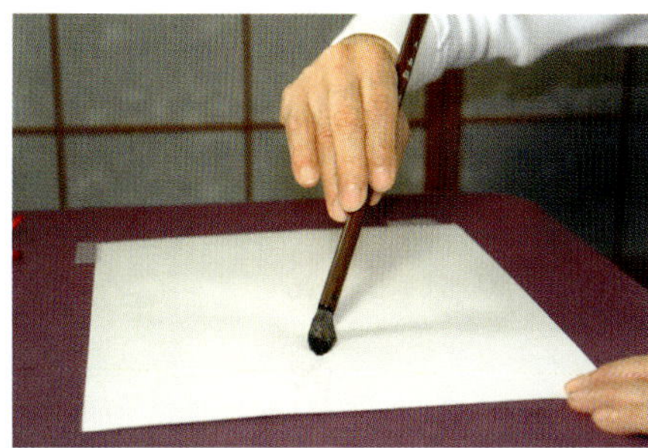

1. The elbow must be held up and maintained on that level for the duration of the line.

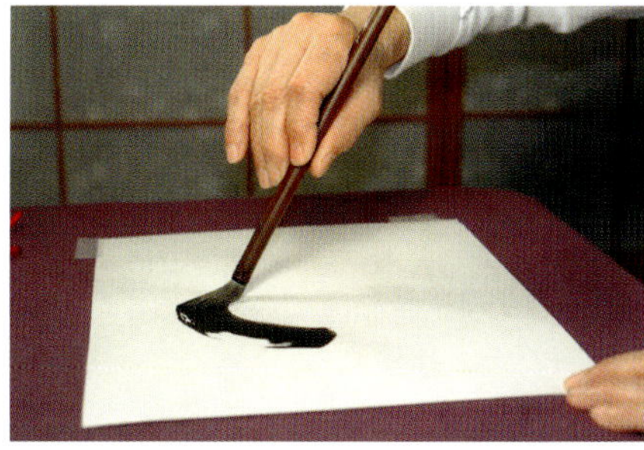

2. As the circular line is a quarter of a circle complete, the elbow must still remain high, but the fingers move away from your body. Be aware of the relationship between the index finger and thumb.

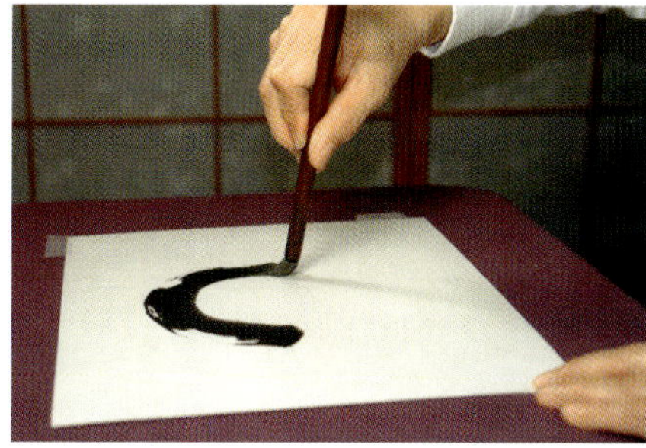

3. A half circle is now completed: notice the position of the thumb. In the first photo you did not see the thumb but now the thumb comes to the left.

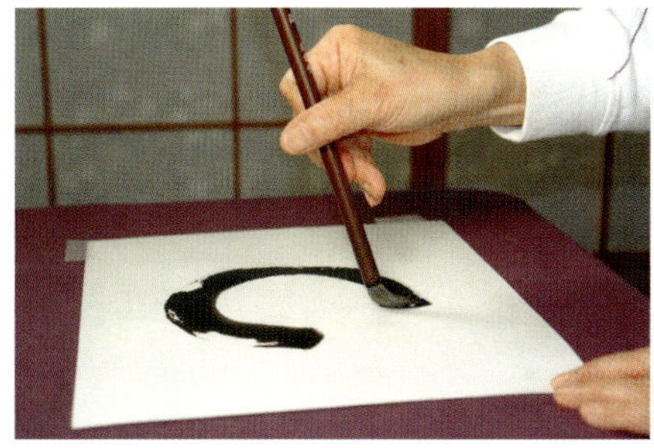

4. The circle is three quarters complete. The thumb is now in full view: this means that the brush has been rotated by the index finger and thumb. In addition, proper pressure of bristles against the paper has been maintained.

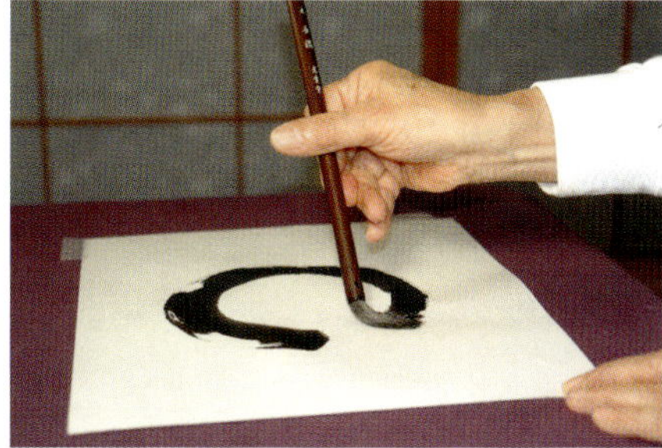

5. The wrist and arm comes toward your body. The circle is almost completed. Note the position of fingers and thumb in relation to the palm.

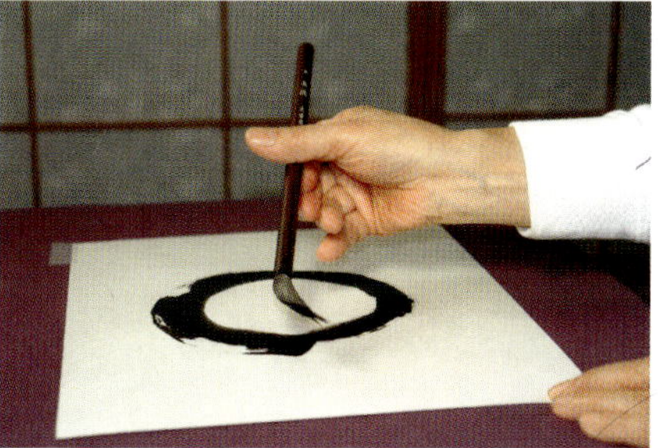

6. The circle is completed. The ideogram on the brush can be seen in the same place as when you started. This means the tip of the brush, like the hands of a clock, faces out during the entire process. This exercise involves maximum use of the fingers in working with the brush.

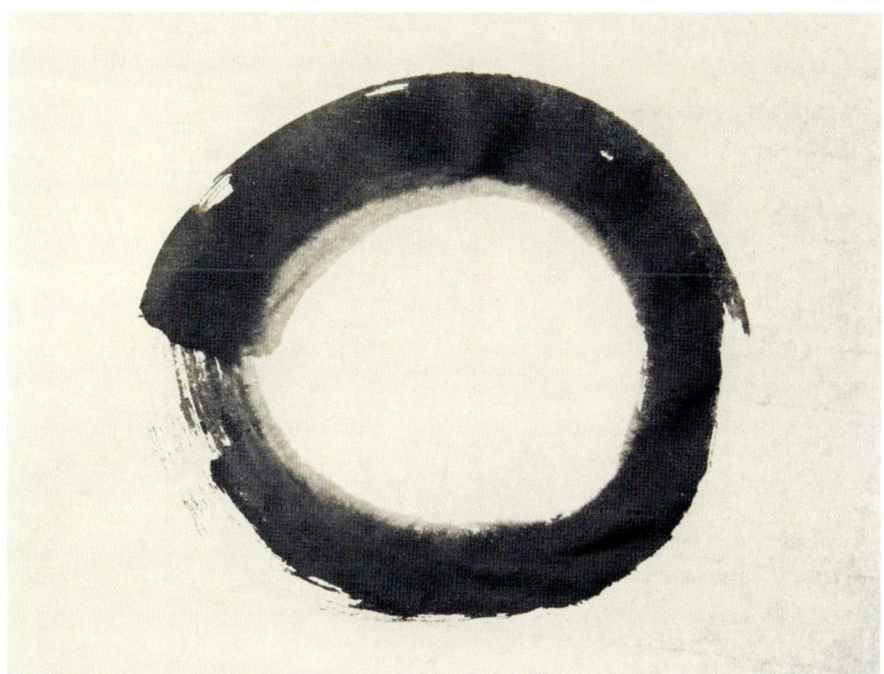

When you practice making a circular line, apply ink to the entire bristle length, with dark ink from midpoint to the tip and light ink from midpoint to the base. When the circle is painted, dark ink is on the outer rim and light ink remains on the inner portion. Often this circle is compared to an *enso*, a Zen circle. The *enso* represents the symbolic statement for Zen monks which means "Subject and object become as one. You and the universe become one." For sumi-e artists, the goal in making this circle should be for the body, mind and spirit to become as one during this creative act.

Making Circles of Various Sizes

Using the same steps we learned for the circle, practice with different sizes. Experiment with various tones of ink. When making circles, remember to apply ink to the entire bristle length: darker ink from midpoint to tip, and lighter ink from midpoint to base.

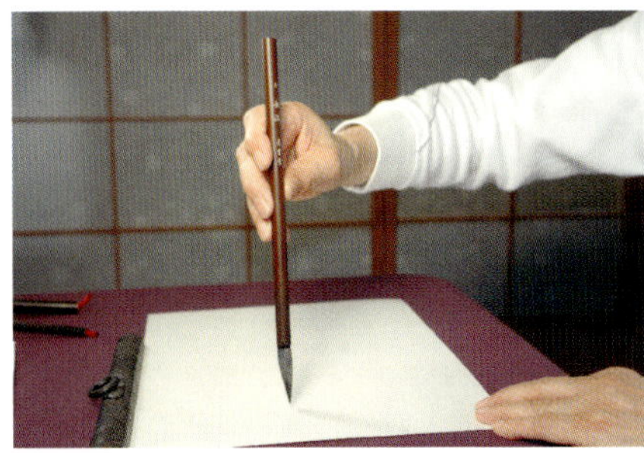

1. Smaller circles can be useful in painting small circular objects such as grapes.

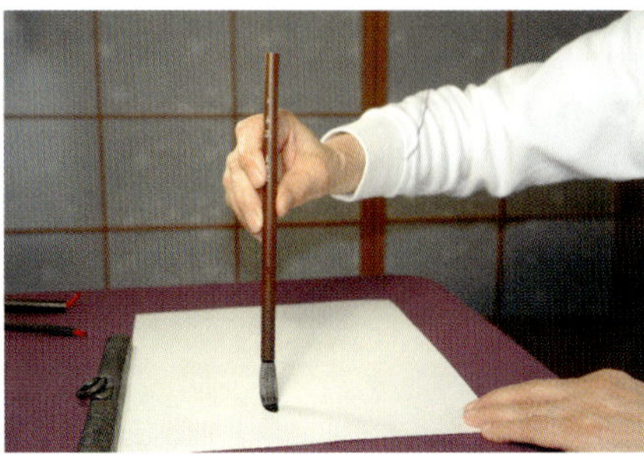

2. These small circles can be created by simply turning the brush with the finger tips.

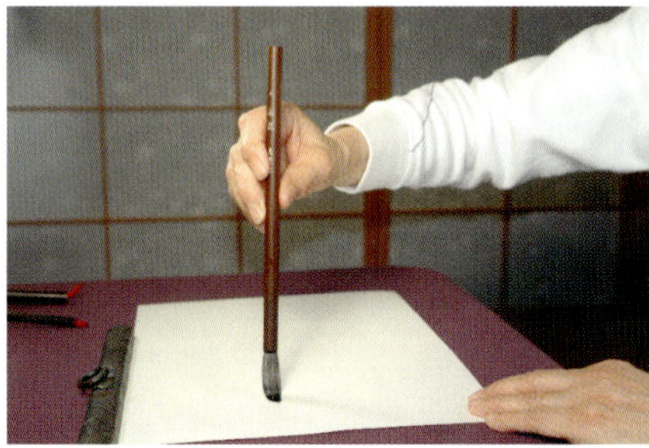

3. The motions are the same as for larger circles.

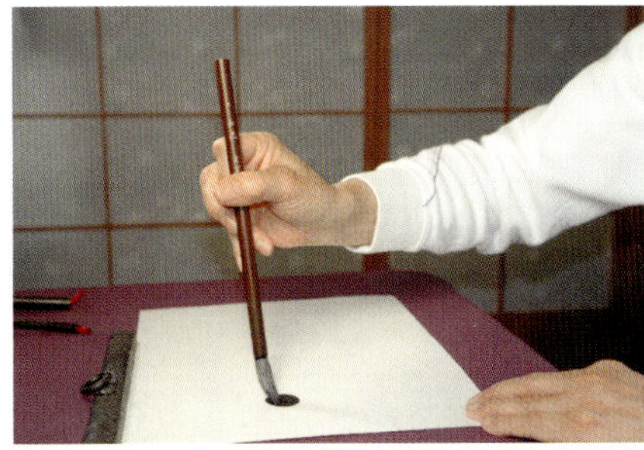

4. Note the position of fingers and thumb in relation to the palm.

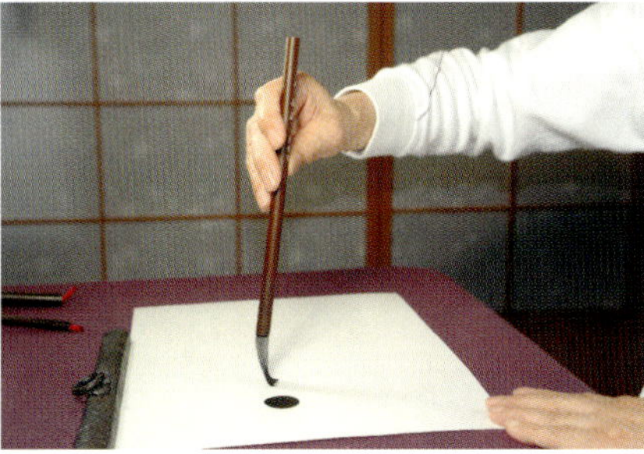

5. Now a slightly larger circle is created with a white space in its center. Apply lighter ink to the bristles and then darker ink at the tip.

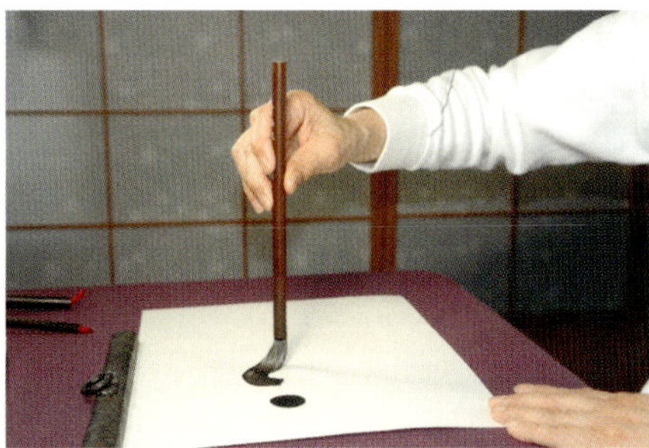

6. This time the brush will be rotated with the finger tips as previously but at the same time the arm will simultaneously move in a small circle.

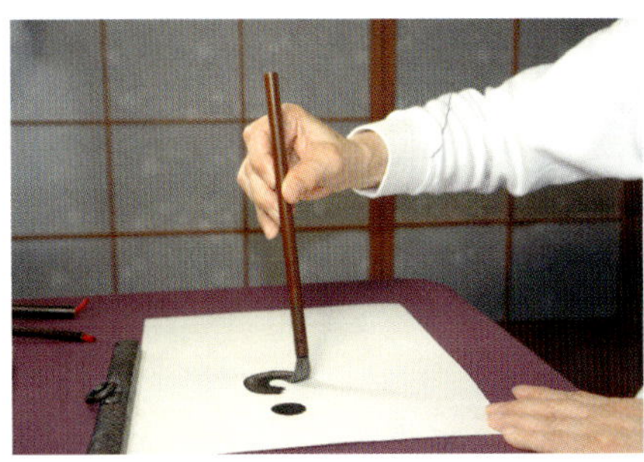

7. Continue the circular movement...

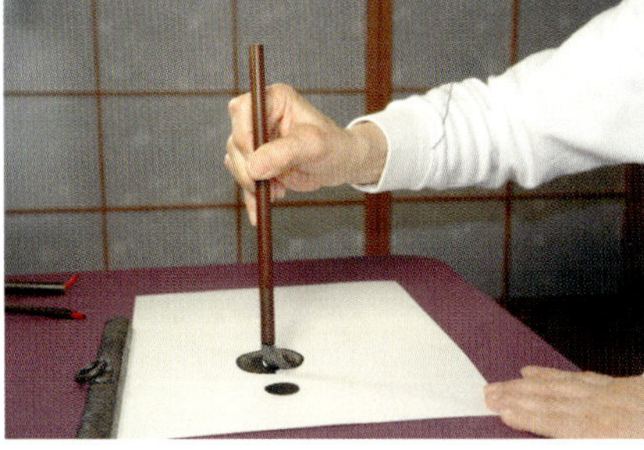

8. ...keeping your fingers, hand, and arm working together.

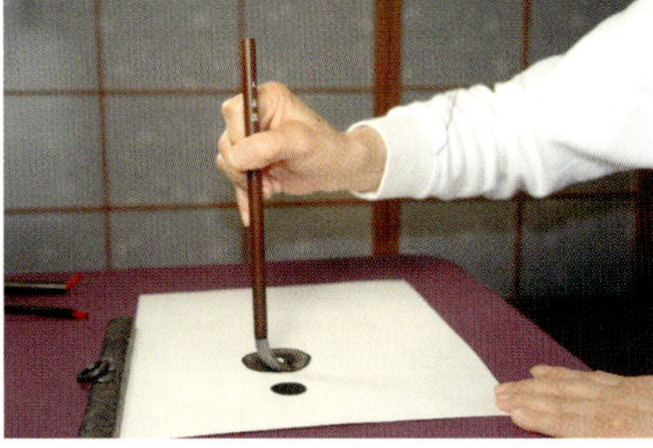

9. You can check your painted circle's lighter and darker areas to detect if there may be parts of the circle-painting process that you need to work on further, to achieve smooth and consistent form.

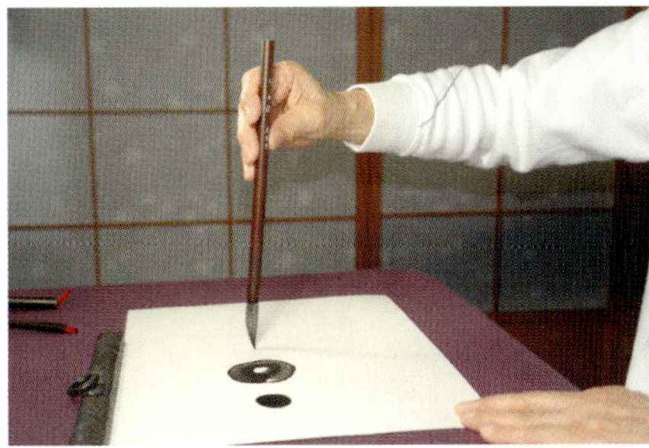

10. The mid-sized circle is completed.

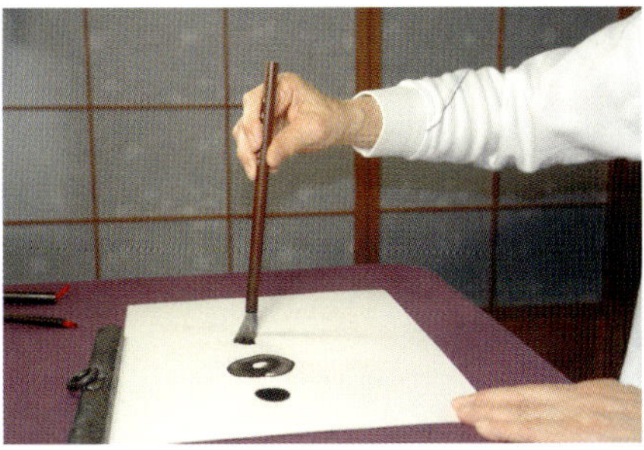

11. The next circle is created with the same application of ink: lighter ink on the lower half of the bristles and dark ink on the tip.

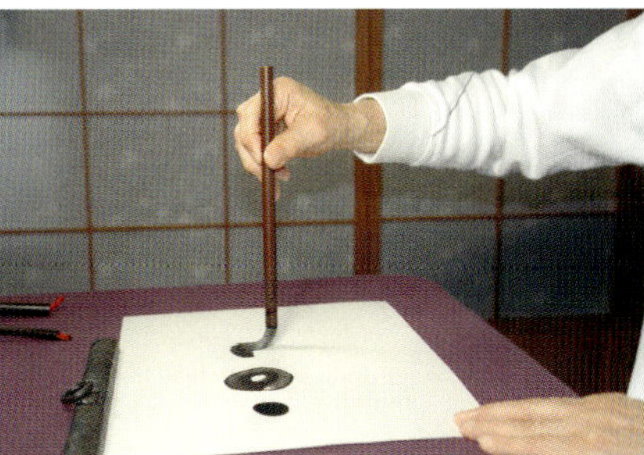

12. Focus on carefully directing your fingers' energy in conjunction with the brush handle and head.

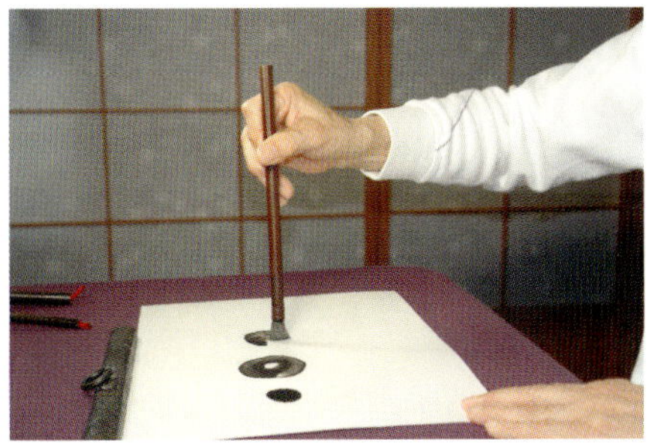

13. The third circle will not include a white center.

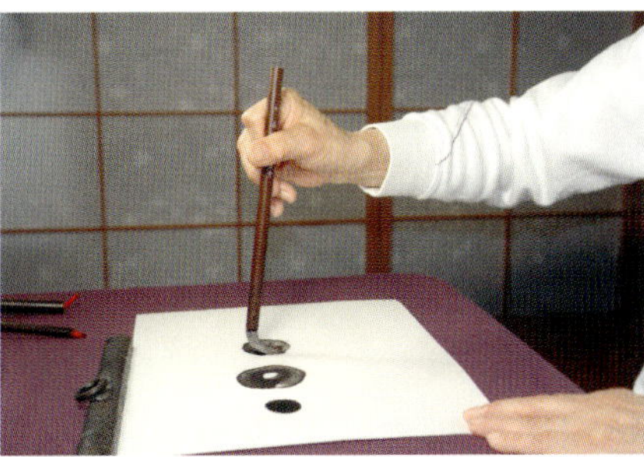

14. A grouping of circles similar to the third one could easily serve as a cluster of grapes, for example.

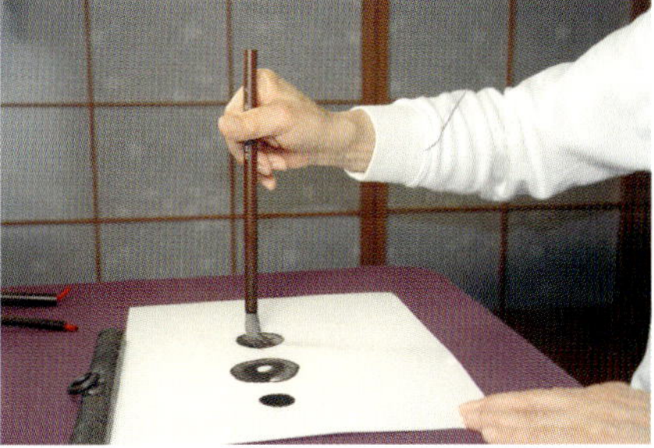

15. By mastering making of circles in a variety of ink tones you can create many images, from fruits to suns.

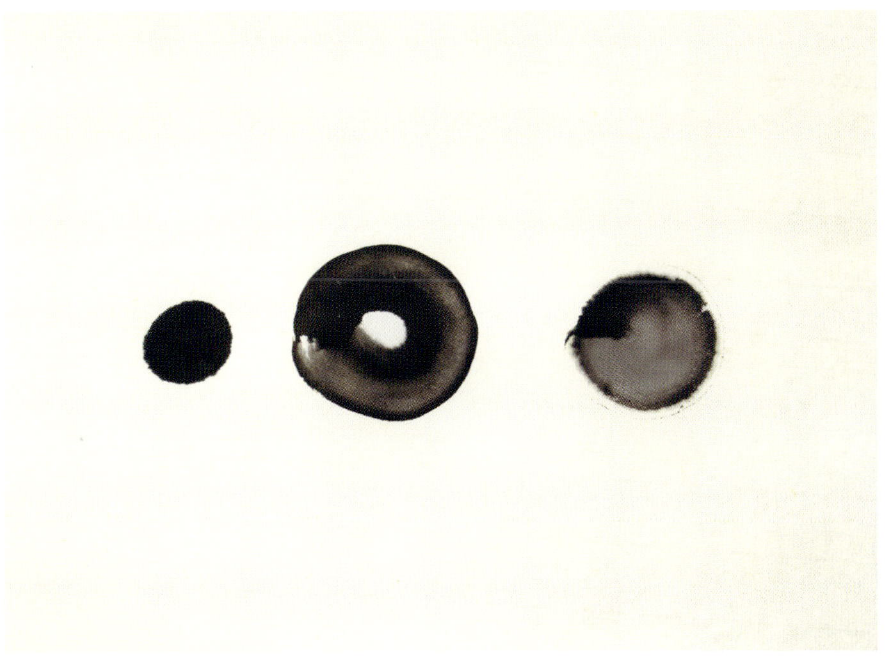

A closer look at the resulting circles. The basic circle can be modified in many ways to paint different circular forms.

Horizontal Use of the Brush

In this technique, the brush is held in a completely different way compared to the previous exercises in order to move it sideways. The result will be a distant mountain peak. Begin with a clean brush, and apply light ink from the base to about two-thirds of the way up the bristles. Apply dark ink to the remaining portion, all the way to the tip.

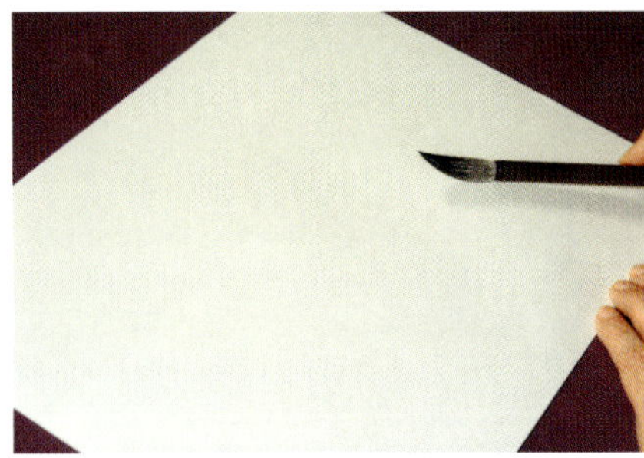

1. As you see, the bristle curves up at the tip. Beginning from the far right of the paper, move up toward to the left.

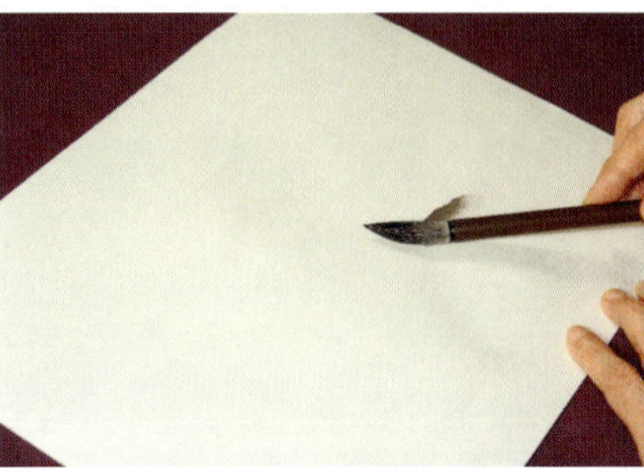

2. The lower portion of the brush bristles, loaded with the light ink, comes in contact with the paper. As the brush gradually moves to the left, begin to increase the pressure against the paper. The darker and lighter ink tones begin to blend.

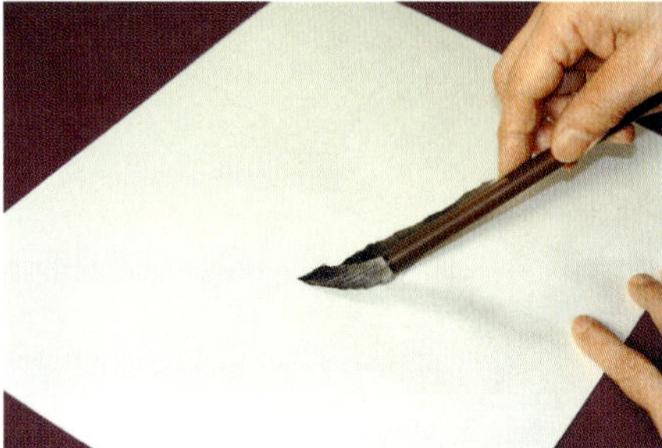

3. Move the curved bristles down and the tip will begin to come in contact with the paper as you move to the left. The bristles must be in full contact with the paper as you reach the portion that will be the summit of the mountain.

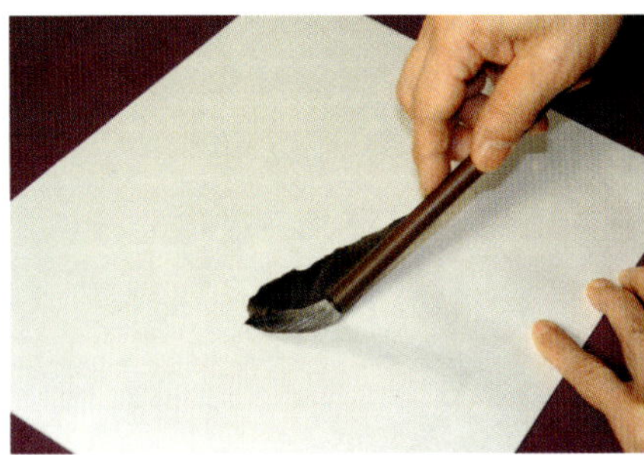

4. Still moving left, gradually come down from the summit. Give pressure to the brush's base.

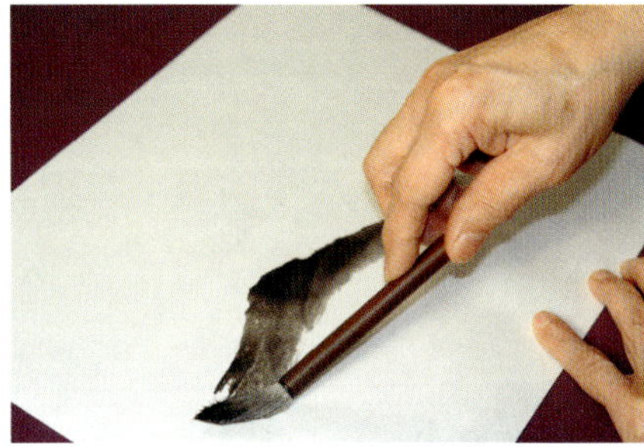

5. In this example, the end of the stroke creates an unexpected pocket of white.

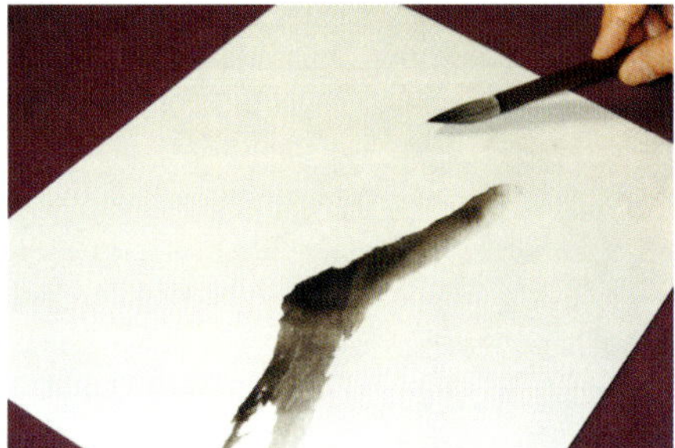

6. Simply use the tip of your brush to outline the missing portion of the mountain slope's line. Another more distant peak is next.

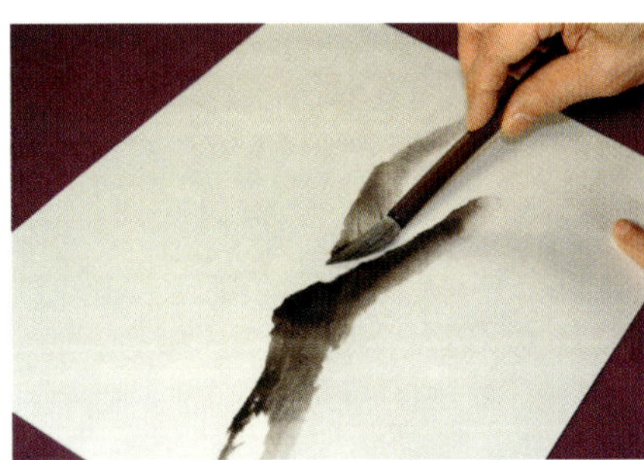

7. Wash the bristles and load lighter ink onto your brush. Add a touch of dark ink to the tip. On a plate, tap the brush lightly several times to blend the ink from dark to light within the bristles. Create a second mountain peak at the right side.

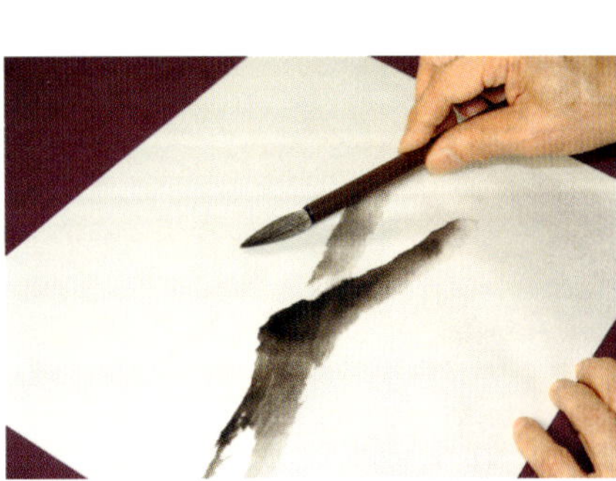

8. Again wash the brush and apply lighter ink. Proceed to create a third distant peak.

This exercise offers helpful practice in holding the brush horizontally, and in experimenting with creative effects from the use of different tones of ink applied to the bristles. On the right bottom corner, a brush mark demonstrates that gradient effect.

Wide Strokes

This exercise teaches the technique for creating a line of maximum width with a brush that is ordinary in size.

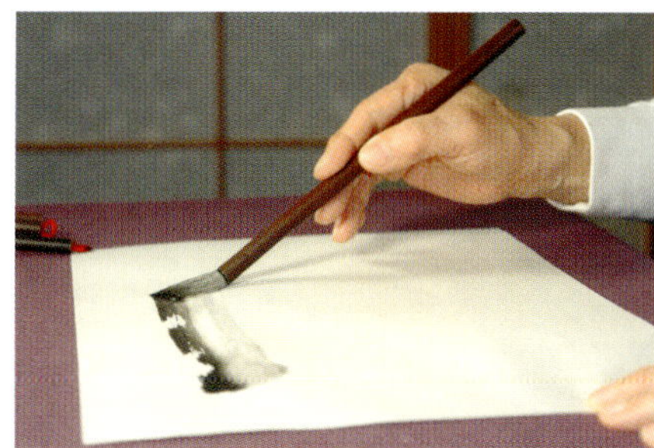

1. This example shows how a beginner in sumi-e attempts to maximize the width of a line by pushing down too hard on the base of the brush. Consequently the tip of the brush then lifts up and a maximum width is not achieved.

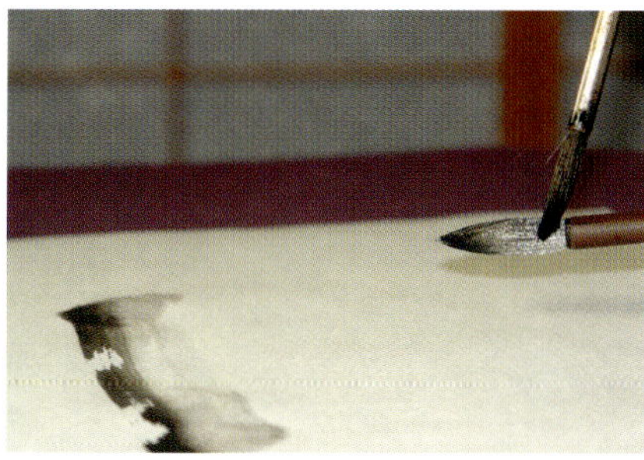

2. For a more successful approach in creating a wide line such as a bamboo stalk, wash the brush, apply light ink to the bristles, add dark ink to the tip and with a separate small brush apply dark ink to the base of the bristles.

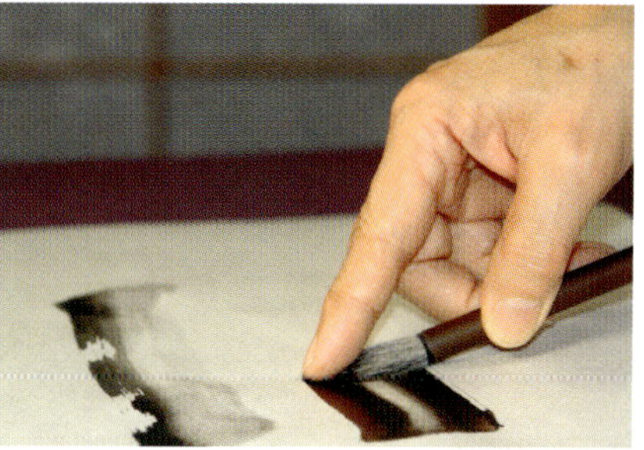

3. The brush should be positioned so that the dark ink at the base of the bristles is facing down on the paper. Hold the brush horizontally as in the photo, with your pointing finger on the tip to make sure it is in contact with the paper

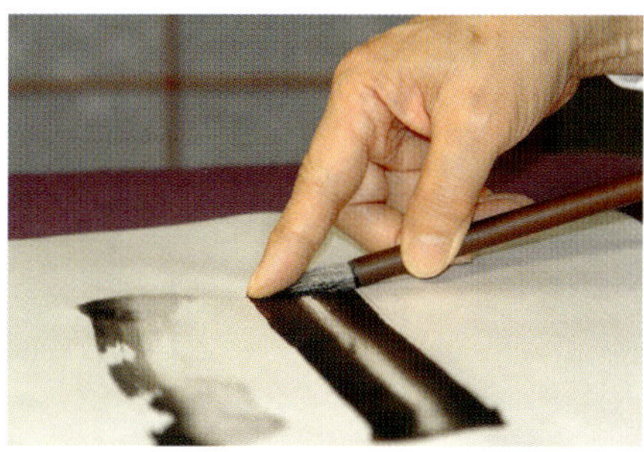

4. A successful wide-to-wide stroke with highlights and shadows. Now experiment with different widths and ink effects in wide-to-wide lines. Try wide lines with the brush held as normal, without the added pressure from your finger tip.

The lines on the left resemble a stalk of bamboo painted in light ink. To the left of that stalk is a brush mark showing the tone of ink that was used on the brush.

The center stalk reflects highlights and shadows. The brush mark next to it shows the dark-light-dark ink loading that was used on the brush.

The far right stalk results from a gradient of dark to light. To its right, a brush mark shows the ink gradient that was used on the brush.

In painting with colors, the lighter portions are generally in the foreground. However, in black ink paintings, dark ink will be seen as the foreground and light ink will appear as the background. In this example showing three stalks of bamboo, the center stalk is in the foreground, the stalk on the right is in the mid ground, and the stalk at far left is the farthest away.

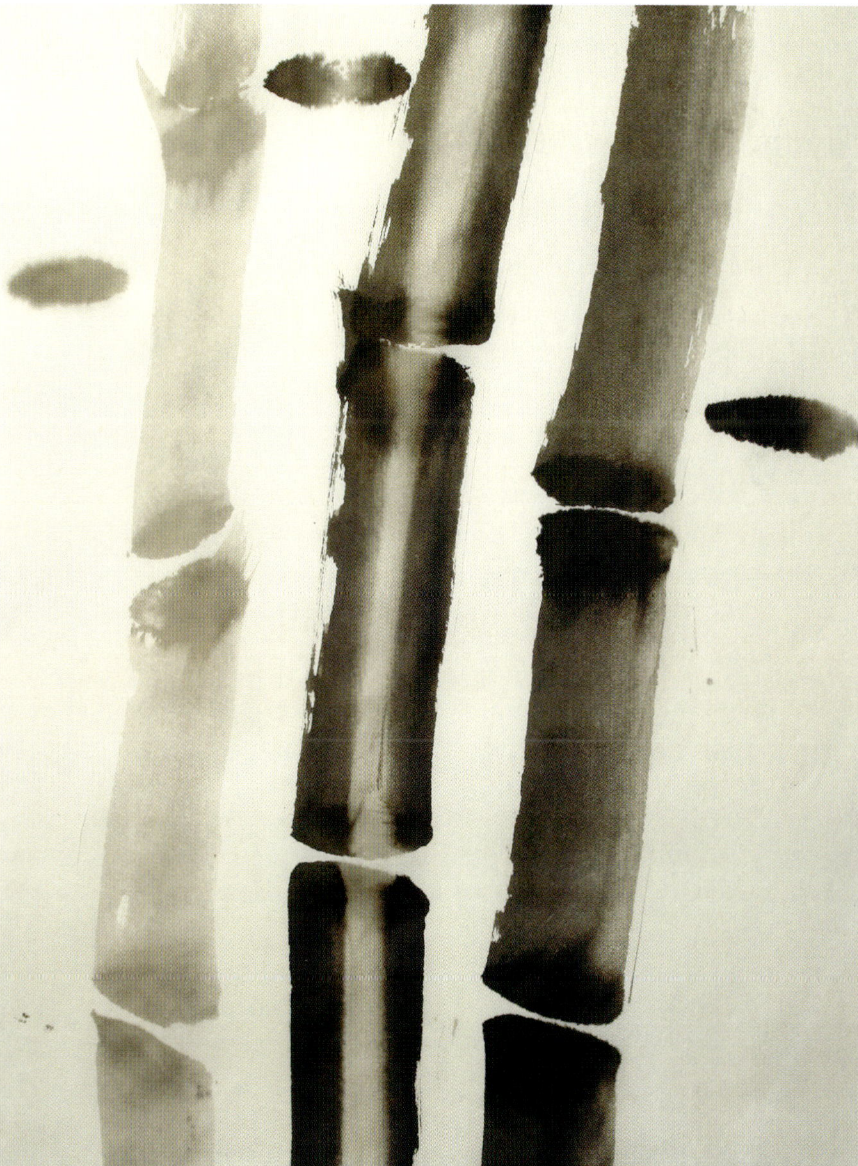

Pressing with Vibration: The Stamping Technique

The stamping technique does not use a line in motion. On a clean brush, apply medium dark ink to two-thirds of the bristle length. At the tip, apply dark ink. On the surface of a plate, wriggle the bristles so that the ink is blended to create a gradient tone.

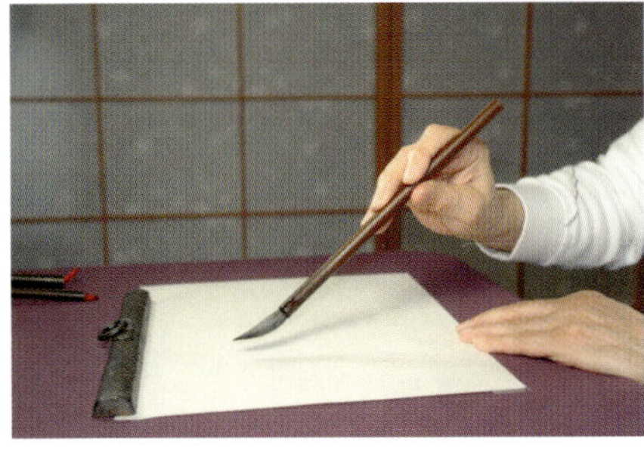

1. Bring the bristles of your brush to a point again; then hold the brush as shown in the photo and press down.

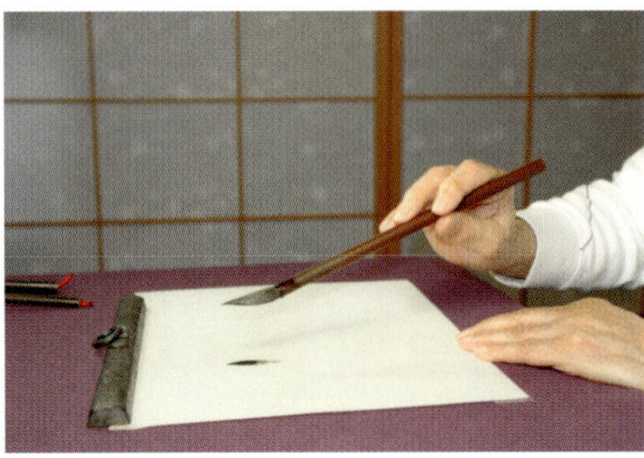

2. The first "stamp" is completed.

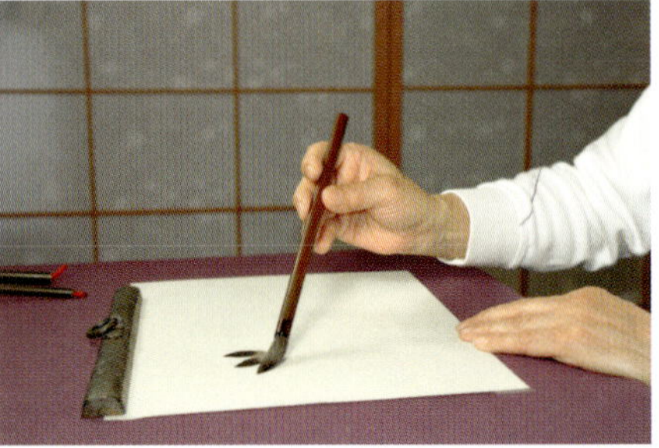

3. Repeat this same stamping process in a circle as if you were painting flower petals.

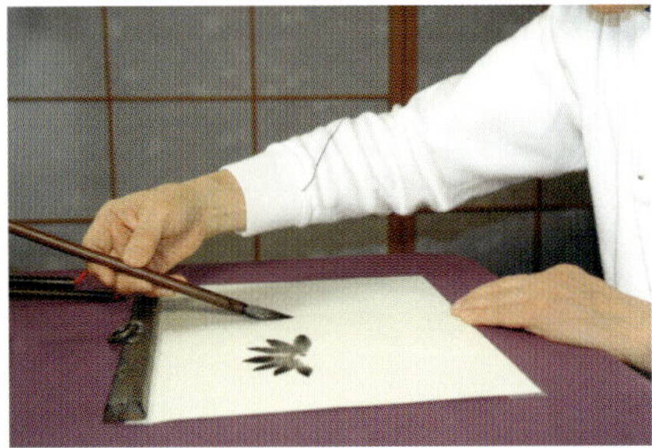

4. Begin a new group of strokes, but first, reverse the application of ink on the bristles: Wash the brush well, then apply medium ink to the top two thirds of the bristles, and add dark ink with another small brush to the base of the bristles.

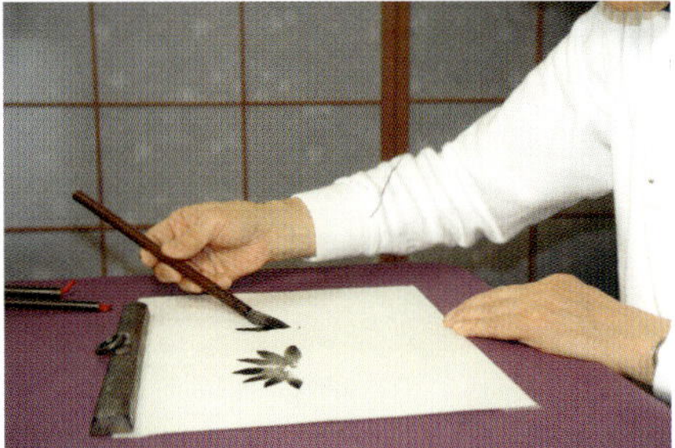

5. Repeat the stamping process, this time stamping from the center out.

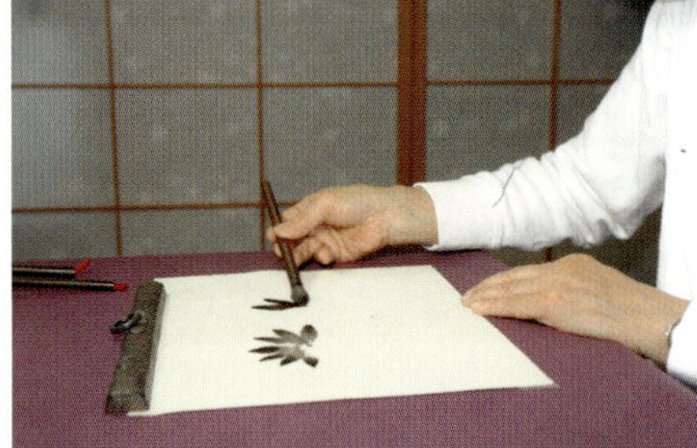

6. This is a fun technique. You can adjust the application of ink to make many creative variations.

SPECIAL EFFECTS

The Nijimi Effect: Plum Blossoms

The *nijimi* effect means that ink spreads beyond the original brush lines. The stamping technique will work very well on absorbent types of paper, where the nijimi effect can be easily seen.

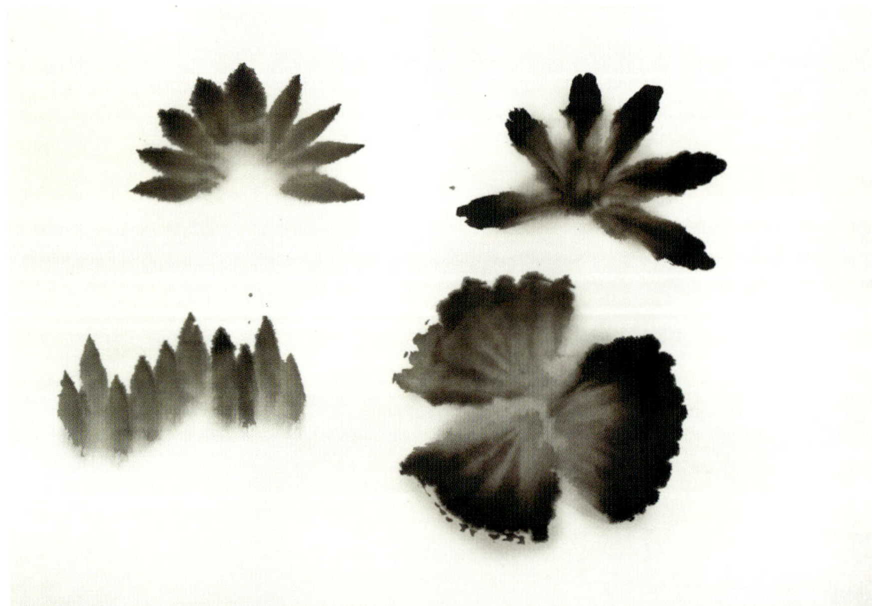

Top left: The result of the stamping technique in steps #1–#3.
Top right: Petals where the ink has been loaded in reverse.
Bottom left: A distant grove of trees created by stamping horizontally in an irregular line.
Bottom right: Stamping can be used to create wider petals such as those of poppies or carnations, as well as broad leaves like grape leaves.

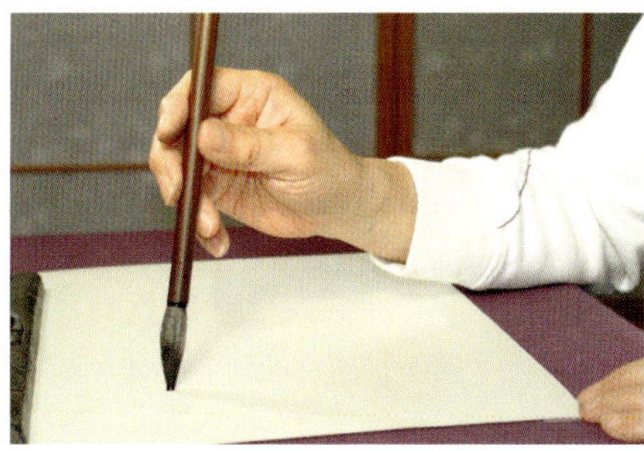

1. Apply light ink on the full length of the bristles. Touch the tip of the brush to the paper. The size of the dot you create will depend upon the duration of time you touch the paper. The longer the brush remains in contact with the paper, the more bleed, and the larger the dot will become.

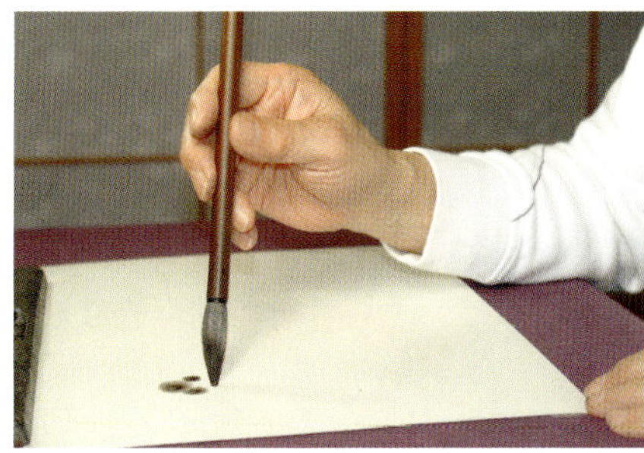

2. Try the technique to create pink plum blossoms in traditional form. After making a large dot on the top, move slightly lower and add medium size dots on the left and right, then a smaller dot at the lowest point.

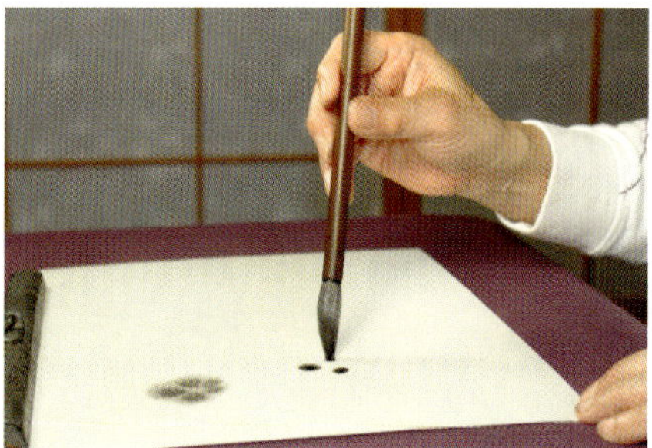

3. Next, create a dark pink half-opened flowering plum blossom, with three dots.

Splash Technique

Another type of dot is formed by using the splash technique. This is another "fun" approach, but, as with any technique, this requires practice if you wish to obtain the desired effect.

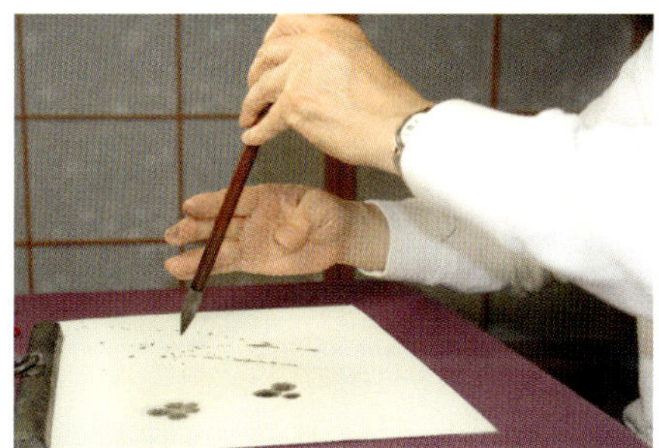

You can hit the brush handle with your hand to create the splash, or you can swing the brush in a certain way. Once you have mastered and can control the technique, if you wish to add a gust of wind or sudden rain to a bamboo painting at the last minute, for example, a few splashes can be quite effective. (On the other hand, you may also ruin the whole painting.) A good way to practice is to use plain water on the brush and experiment on a concrete floor. Use various types of brushes and see what effects they create. Eventually you will begin to understand how much force and swing you should use for the desired effect.

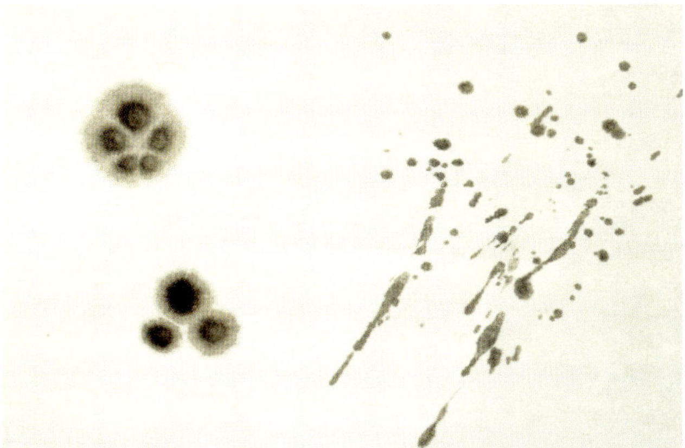

Example results of the dot technique (left side of the paper) and splash technique (right side of the paper). In the five dots at top left (the plum blossom), the brush was loaded with a full amount of light ink; notice the nijimi effect. The lower three dots (the half-opened blossom) were created with a lesser amount of dark ink on the bristles, so the nijimi effect is not as pronounced.

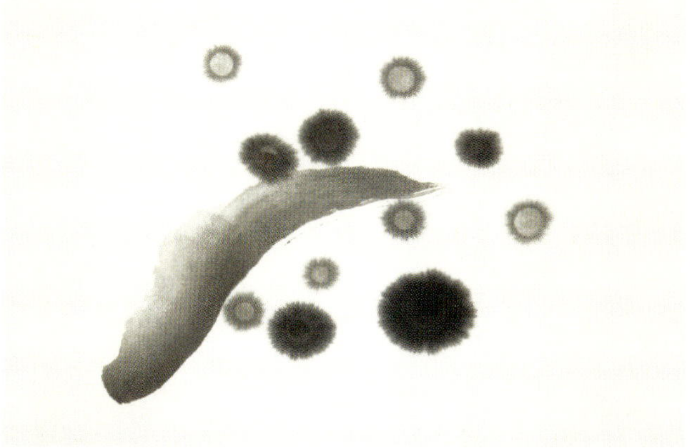

Notice the dots with pale centers. Light ink was used for these. When the ink was dropped onto the paper the ink formed a darker circle on the outer rim while water remained primarily in the center. A darker ink was used to create the darker circles, and each dot retained a more consistent tone even within its center. However, the nijimi effect can clearly be seen as radiating lines extended beyond the rim of the circle.

The results of the nijimi effect are impacted by the paper's absorbency, and also by the brand of the ink and the amount of ink in the water. The example image at left is on triple thickness absorbent paper from Japan. The example image above is on double thickness absorbent paper from China. In a sense, thicker paper will allow the nijimi effect to expand more. As we can see, each paper exhibits individual characteristics, like human faces.

Mist and Fog: Three Techniques

The choice of method to create mistiness or fogginess depends upon the skill of the artist. Adroitness in use of the brush is important, but today, many other convenient tools are also available. Here are three techniques.

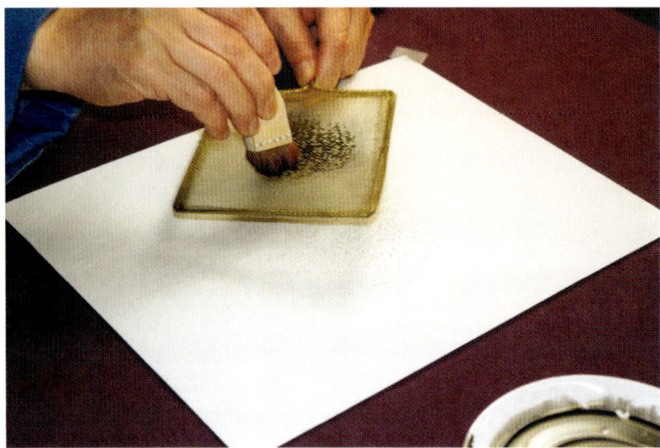

This brass screen with a handle, used together with the short hair brush called a *hake*, is an inventive way to create a fine spray.

The result of this fine spray, on dry paper. After you understand the effects which can be created on dry paper, then experiment on pre-moistened paper. The individual fine dots will not be seen.

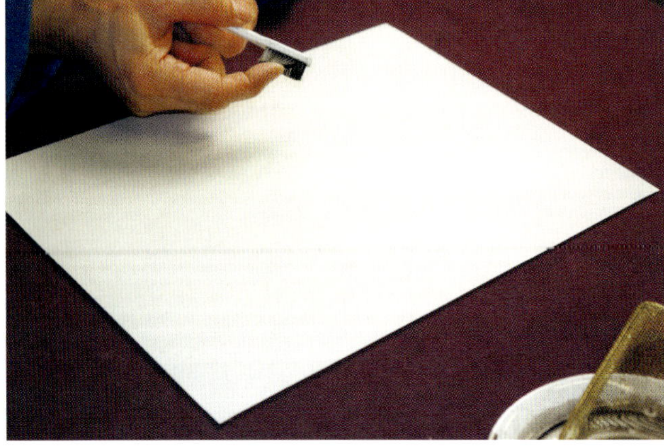

An old toothbrush is used to spray ink. Apply ink only on the surface of the bristles, and with your finger, abrade the surface of the brush to get a fine mist.

The result is a fine but uneven cluster of dots, compared to using a screen and *hake* brush.

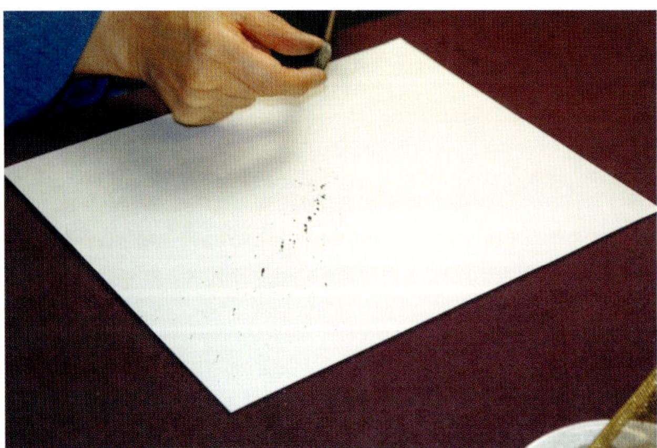

Using a brush you can create a similar treatment. After applying ink on the tip, soak out the excess on a paper towel. Then with an abrading or scratching motion, pluck the tip of the brush.

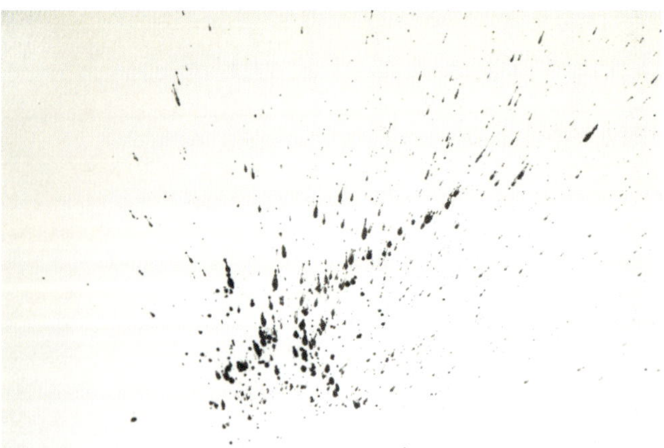

Because of the uneven length of the hairs on the brush, the dots become more directional, which can be a useful technique for the splashing of fish or waves.

Dry Brush Techniques

Brush strokes with a sense of texture add an enriching dimension, and painting with a dry brush is a way to create them. This technique is exciting because one must be constantly be aware of the random location of each bristle tip and how it can be used to create a certain type of line with its effects. A mountain horse brush, composed of coarse hair, is most effective for this technique; a choryu brush will work as well. The amount of ink on the bristles should be minimal so that the bristles will spread out. When the bristles are spread apart, many possibilities open up as you decide which of the bristles to use to create the desired effects. Often, my explanation to my students is to think of the brush as the legs of an octopus. All eight legs each have their own mission.

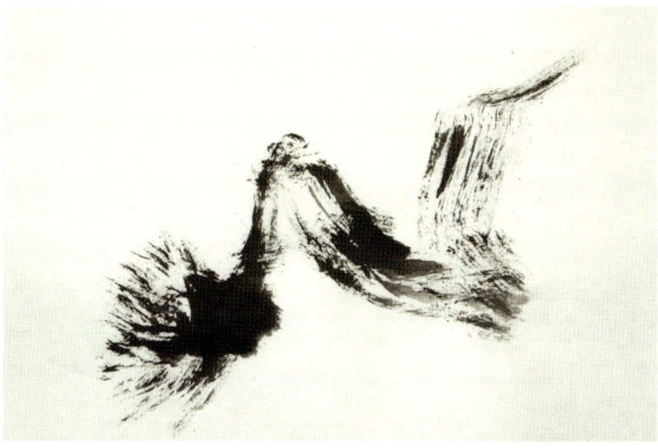

Beginning from the left, let the open brush simply land on the paper. Then lift it up with only the tips touching the paper. Turning the bristles sideways, move up; at the crest of the lines, come down using the full width of the bristles. Turn the brush again using the full width; and at the top, once more move sideways for the narrow ending of the stroke. This is a very different approach in comparison to the usual sumi-e brush strokes.

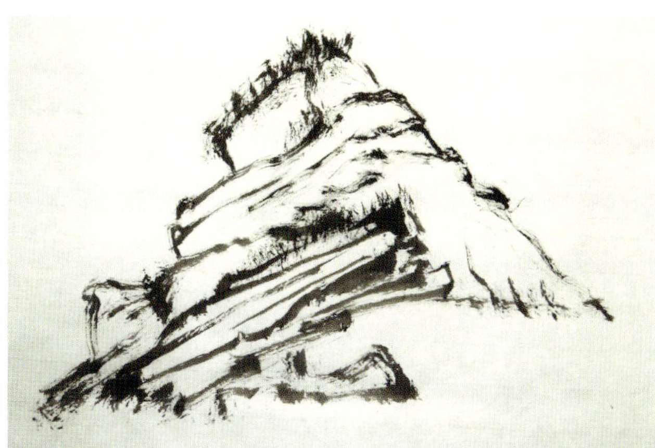

Beginning on the lower right side and moving upward, use one tip of the open dry brush bristles to make the ragged outline stroke. At the midway point, turn the bristles and use some of the other bristles (or "octopus legs") to create the layered effect of the slope.This quick sketch is an example of how one can use the dry brush effect to create multiple lines of dramatic irregularity such as you might find in rocks or mountains. (See page 74, *After the First Snow*.)

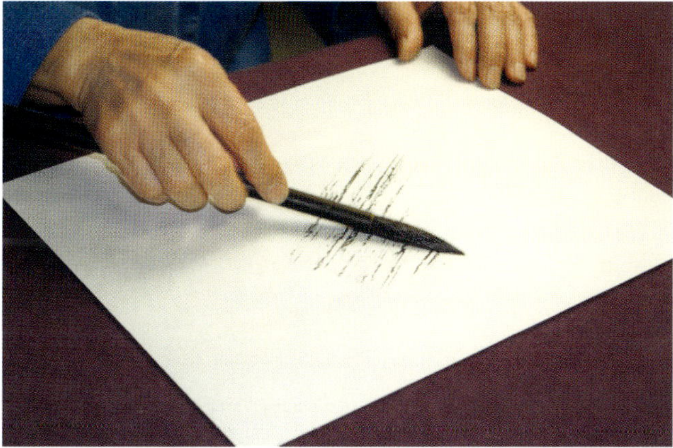

After ink is applied to the bristles of a mountain horse brush, soak up the excess ink in the brush using a paper towel. Then using the full length of the bristles, move the brush in a light sliding motion to create small dots and irregular lines.

A close-up view of the textured lines this creates. This technique is useful for painting rain showers.

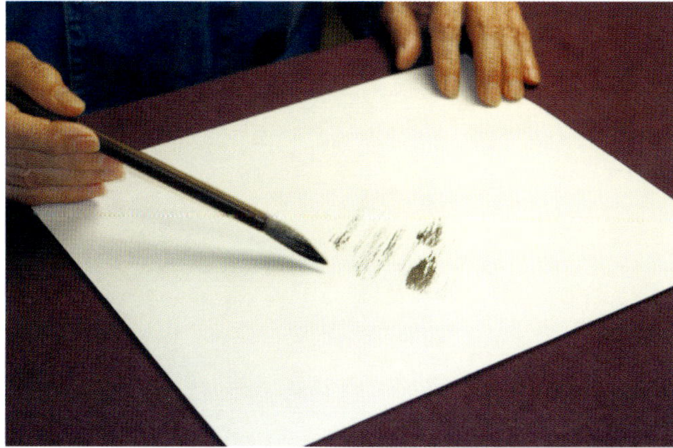

The traditional Chinese manuals use the term "big ax cuts" in describing how to create texture for rocks or craggy mountain surfaces. This "ax cut" effect, from thin to wide, can be created with a dry choryu brush.

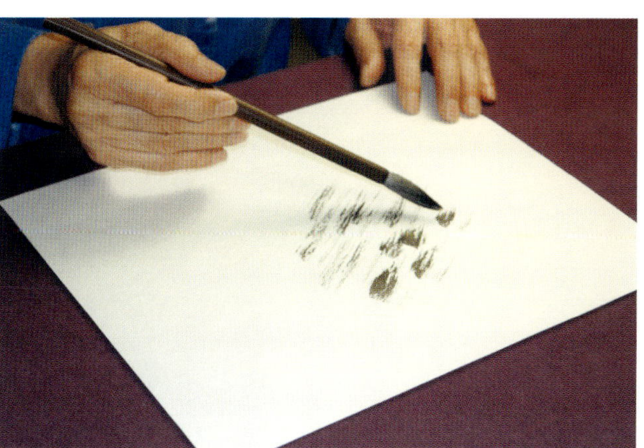

Smaller ax strokes are created.

White Out Techniques

When creating a painting in black ink, a challenge faces the artist if one of the main subjects is white, like snow, white caps of waves, or white water in a stream. If an artist succeeds in creating such a painting, this of course provides great satisfaction. Today, though, many different methods to assist in achieving this are available and are widely used. Watercolor artists use a resist substance in liquid form, which is commonly available at art supply stores. However, the paper used for sumi-e is very thin and becomes semi-transparent when wet, so it requires different techniques from those used by watercolor artists. Milk has commonly been used to reject black ink. (The fat molecules are the key, so skim milk will not work.) More recently, in Japan, sumi ink producers have created a "white out" substance in powder form.

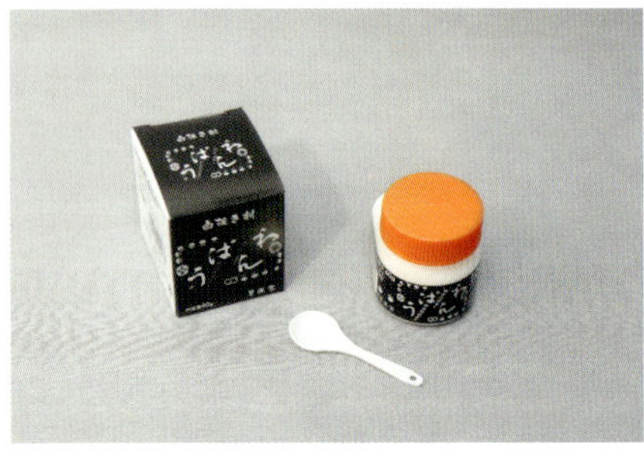

1. The outer box (the name of the producing company is Boku Undo Co. Ltd.), the container of white out substance, and a measuring spoon.

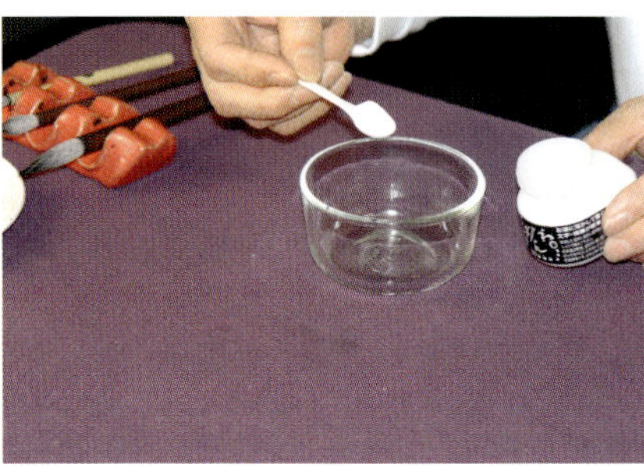

2. One level scoop of white powder is dissolved in 15 scoops of warm water. This becomes a milky liquid.

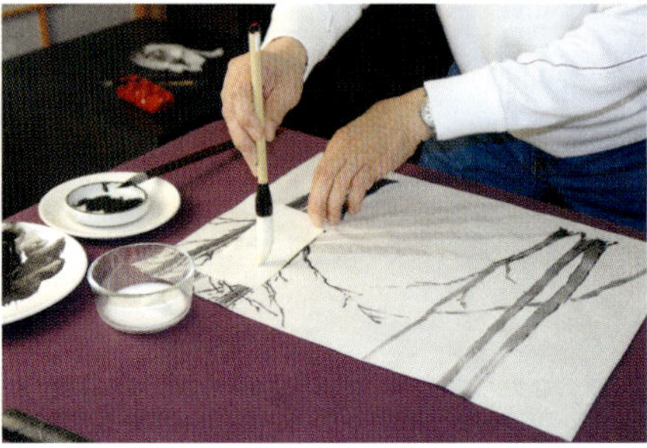

3. In this forest scene, rays of sunlight stream through the darkness of the woods. To protect areas where white out solution is not wanted, cover them with water-resistant or waxed paper.

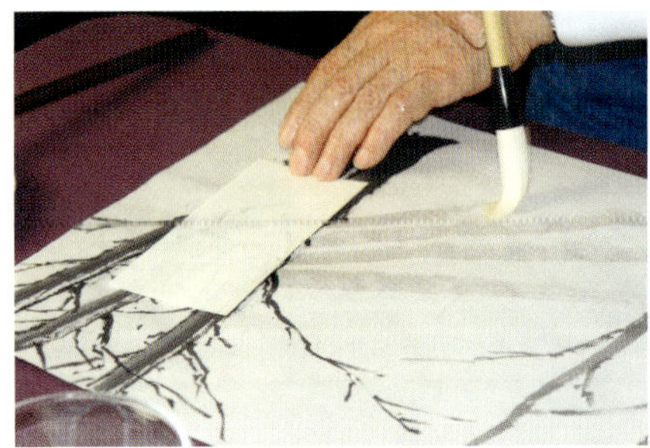

4. Rays of sunlight are painted with white out.

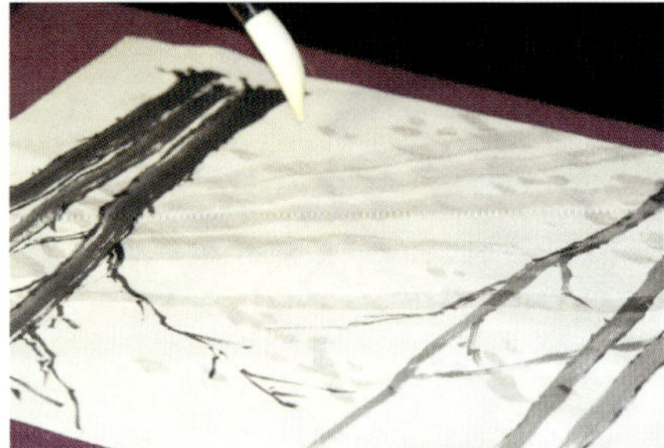

5. Wherever the impression of light is needed, apply white out.

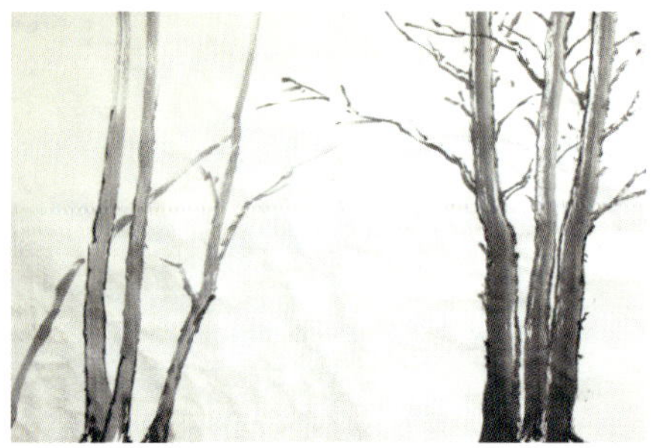

6. After the white out is applied, the paper must be completely dried. The drying will cause the paper to have wavy convolutions.

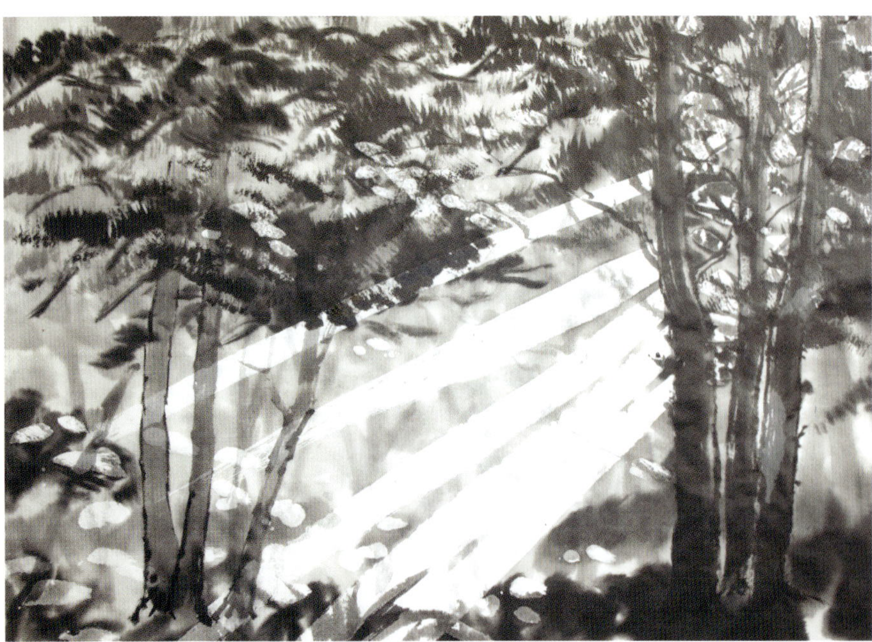

7. Next, paint in the surrounding deep forest. Notice that where lighter ink was painted over the areas of paper treated with white out substance, the resist was successful and the ink does not show. With darker ink some ink cover may sometimes occur. I have not used this chemical white out method in my own paintings as of yet because it is a fairly recent product. However, you might like to explore its possibilities and experiment with the effects that can be produced.

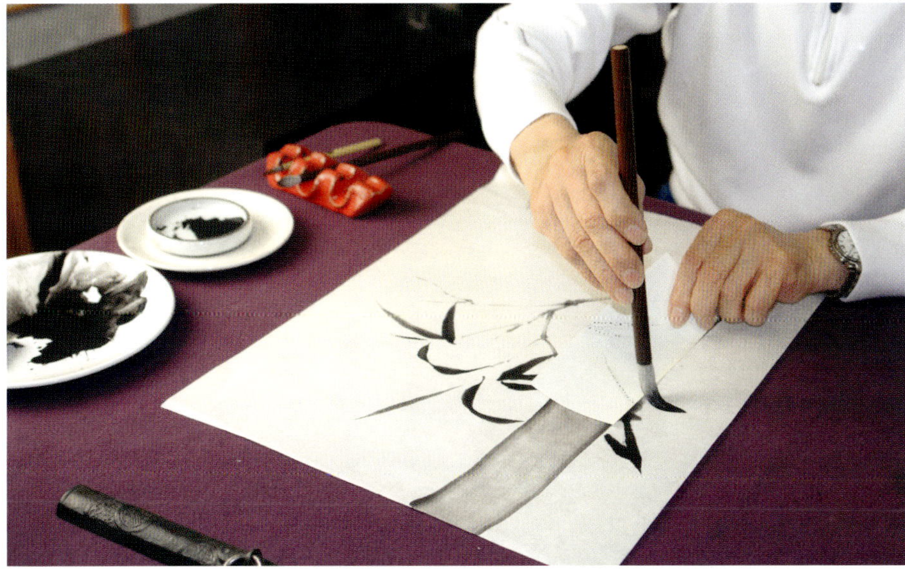

There are more traditional techniques to use, as well. For example, if you wish to paint bamboo leaves protruding out from behind the bamboo culm, cover the culm with water-resistant paper then paint the leaf over it.

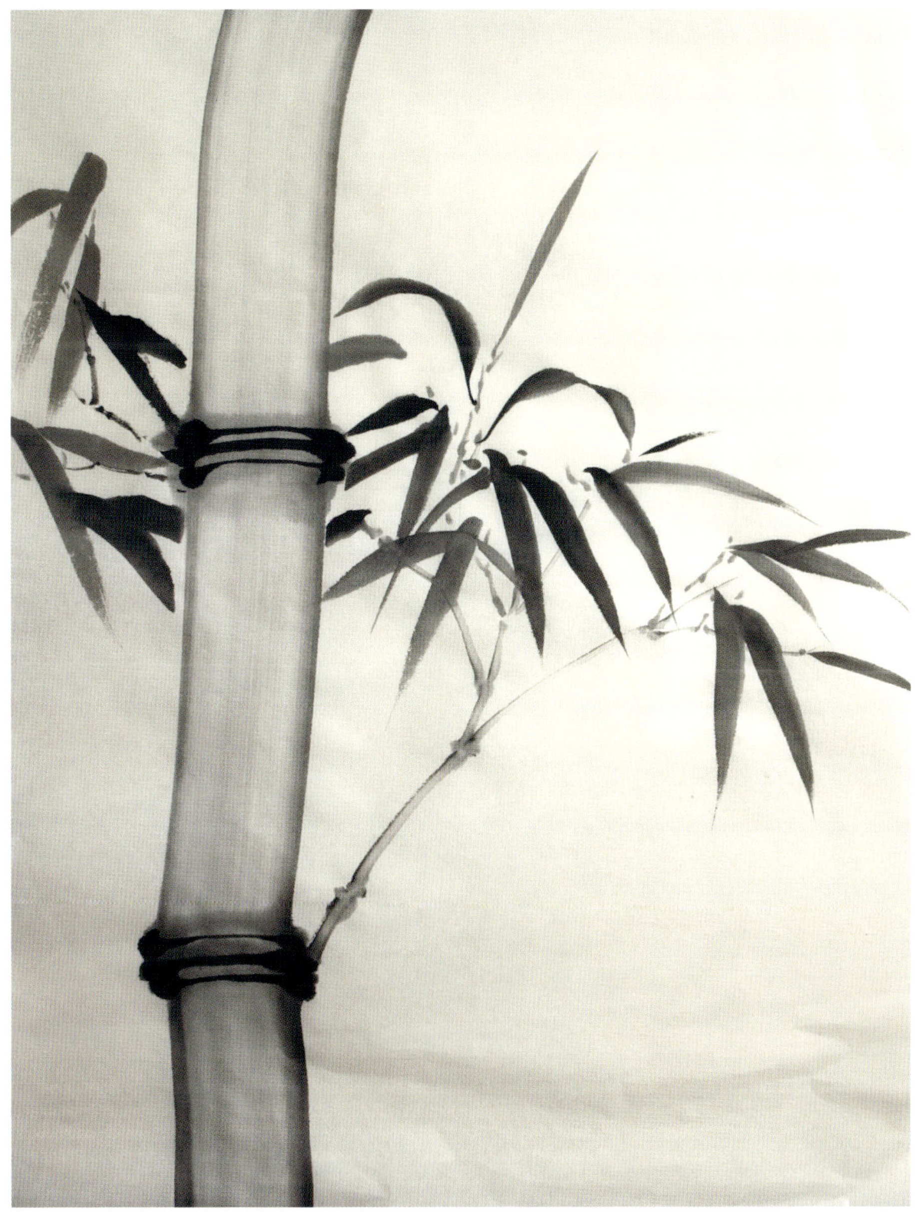

Notice the leaves appearing behind the culm without overlapping it. This same concept of creating "white out" areas can be applied by cutting a shape from water-resistant paper, such as a bird, and using it on the work in a reverse-stencil sort of way, to result in a lighter bird flying against the background of a darker sky. In a scene depicting a forest, trees such as white-barked birches can be covered with cutouts and their surroundings can then be painted in. These are just a few hints. Creative artists will find their own way.

Wrinkled Paper Technique

Paper for sumi-e is flexible and thin, unlike the canvases used for oils and acrylics or the paper used for watercolors. This difference opens up the possibilities for certain effects. Wrinkling or crinkling up the paper is becoming an acknowledged technique for sumi-e. The technique serves as a good reminder of how certain challenges an artist must overcome will sometimes add unexpected and wonderful effects. The accidental lines serve to spark the creative imagination.

When I was in China at the Zhejiang Academy for the Arts, I visited the studio of a well known Chinese calligrapher, Wan Dong Ling (he painted the calligraphy in the painting *After the First Snow,* page 74). I was interested in purchasing some of his calligraphy so he invited me to his studio. He then proceeded to cover the entire floor with crushed newspaper and next he spread a large sheet of sumi paper on top, so that it was "floating" on the crushed paper without the stability of a table or desk. In a standing position, with a long-handled brush, he began to write his calligraphy. The instability and unevenness of the paper created a positive effect on his work, which contained lines about "the wind blowing my sash." He said, "I thought you might like to see how I create calligraphy." This was a lesson for me: to be able to make the uneven surface part of the overall process.

When using the wrinkled paper technique in sumi-e, the artist will be ruled by the unexpected folds and lines, but still should form the crinkles holding in mind an idea of the finished work. For example, if you wish to create a painting of cliffs along the seacoast, you would crush the paper in a way that reflects similar forms. Below, the wrinkled paper technique is used to create the famous Pali Cliff on Oahu Island in Hawaii. After the lines are added in Step 4, you must use a hair dryer to dry the fresh ink. Next stretch the paper out using the mizubari or ura uchi technique (see Chapter 7) so that it is completely flat. The paper must be dry before you continue on with Step 5. The contrast you create in Step 5, between the sharp lines formed by following the crinkled paper folds and the softer lines of the shaded areas and vegetation, is key to the success of the technique.

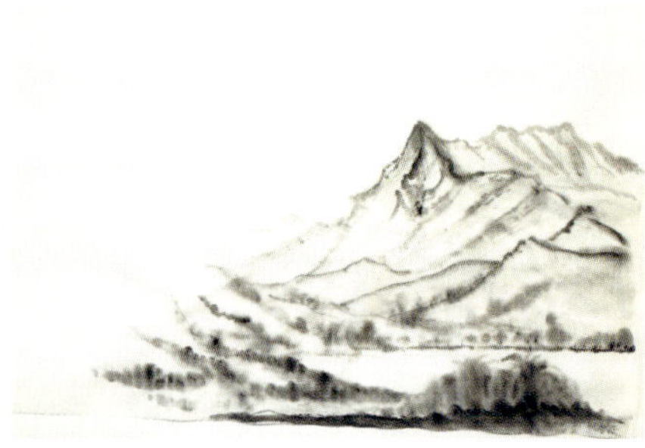

1. Paint in the right side's background mountains with a brush. Leave space at the left for Pali Cliff.

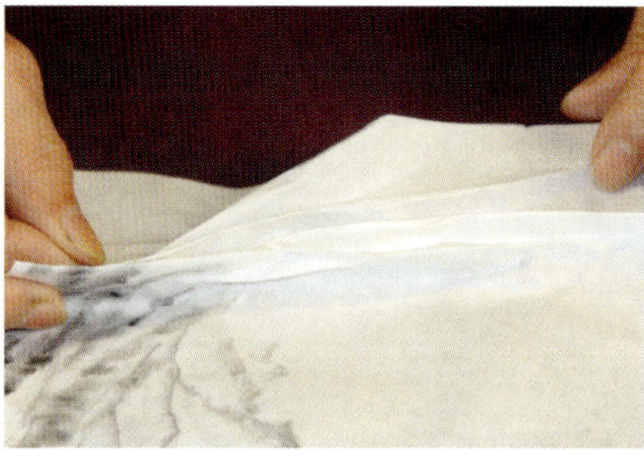

2. Fold, crease and crinkle the left side of the paper to "form" the sharp upright cliff.

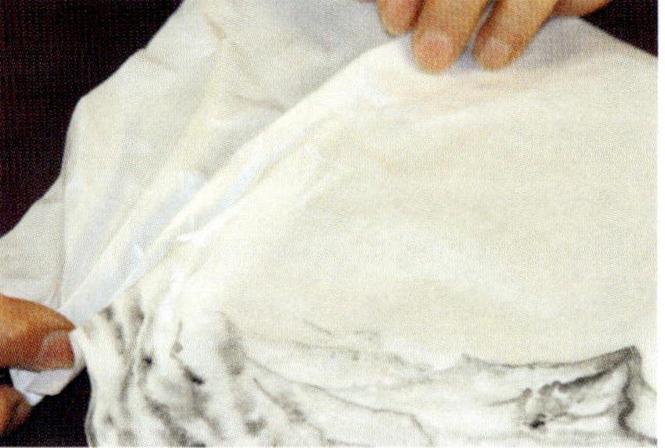

3. Note how the wrinkles and folds are done to connect with the form of the painting's subject.

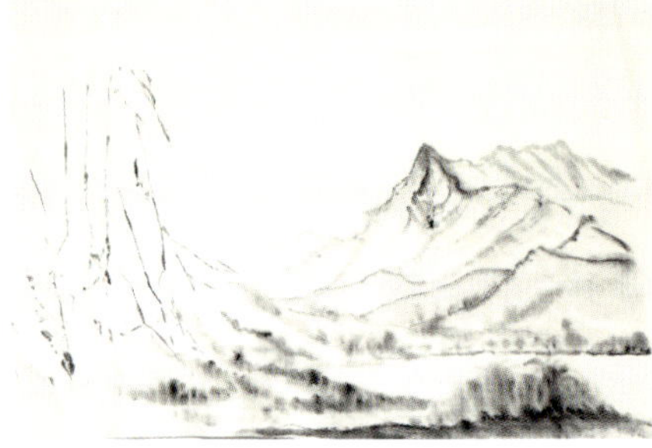

4. Open the paper again, to a semi-flat state, and use a brush sideways to create certain lines for Pali Cliff. The "accidental" lines of the folds join in. Dry.

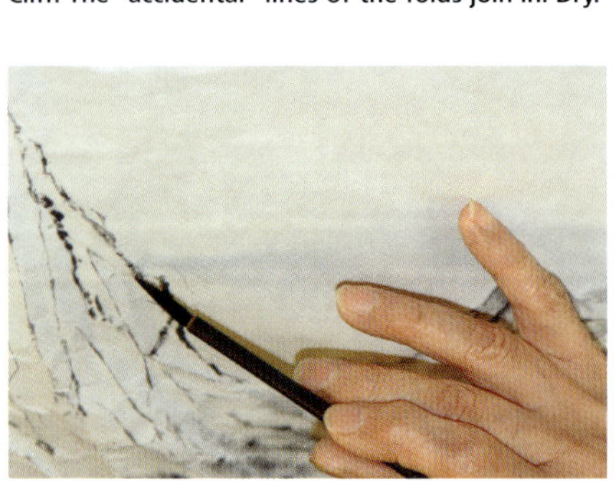

5. Now, with a small mountain horse brush, begin creating the cliffs by connecting line to line. Then lightly use a brush sideways on the crushed paper to create the rugged, irregular lines. Finally, use an upright brush to create the shaded areas.

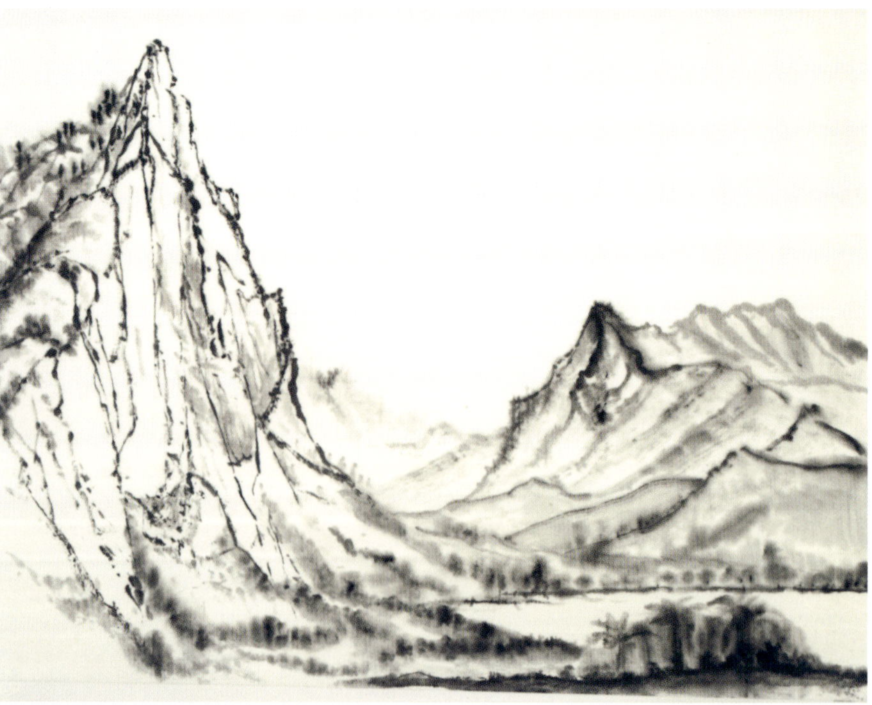

6. After the cliff portion of the painting is completed, add the distant mountain peaks to its right, and finish the back side of the cliff. Above is the completed *Pali Cliff.* Notice that accidental jagged lines are honored if they do not destroy the total effect. The back side of the peak is somewhat gentler with vegetation to show contrast with the dramatically sharp drop in this volcanic peak. The face of the cliff is given some shading and vegetation in strategic places. (See Chapter 7, "The Traditional *Hyogu* Technique," to see how this painting was mounted and framed.)

Application of Gold or Silver Leaf and Dust

Traditional architecture in Japan, primarily castles, palaces and large residences, featured large interior wall spaces, sliding doors and folding screens; murals and paintings using gold and silver were often used to ornament them. These large residences could be dark, even during the daylight hours, so when affordable, gold or silver used on the walls or in paintings would also often serve to reflect the light of oil lamps and candles. Silver had the tendency to tarnish, so gold was the coveted choice. Techniques were developed to incorporate gold leaves in many of the fine arts, and even in monochrome painting, gold and silver leaves were often used. This continues today in sumi-e.

Gold leaves are created from gold nuggets which have been pounded to a very thin layer. To achieve the desired thinness, these are placed in handmade papers and layered in stacks. Then, mechanically, the stack is pounded to form the thin even layers. Eventually the gold leaf is made so thin that if held up to light, you can see through it. When the pounding is completed, the excess gold leaf that hangs out around the edges is cut off and collected. It is sold as another form of gold for painting, *kiri mawashi* (*kiri* = cut; *mawashi* = round). Gold used to denote the reflection of sunlight, or other metals used as mist, serve as "artistic punctuation" with careful placement.

The following pages show the basic techniques for applying leaf and dust. After the glue is completely dry on your work, remove the excess gold (or whatever metal you are using) leaf or dust using a soft wide hake brush. Save the excess for future use.

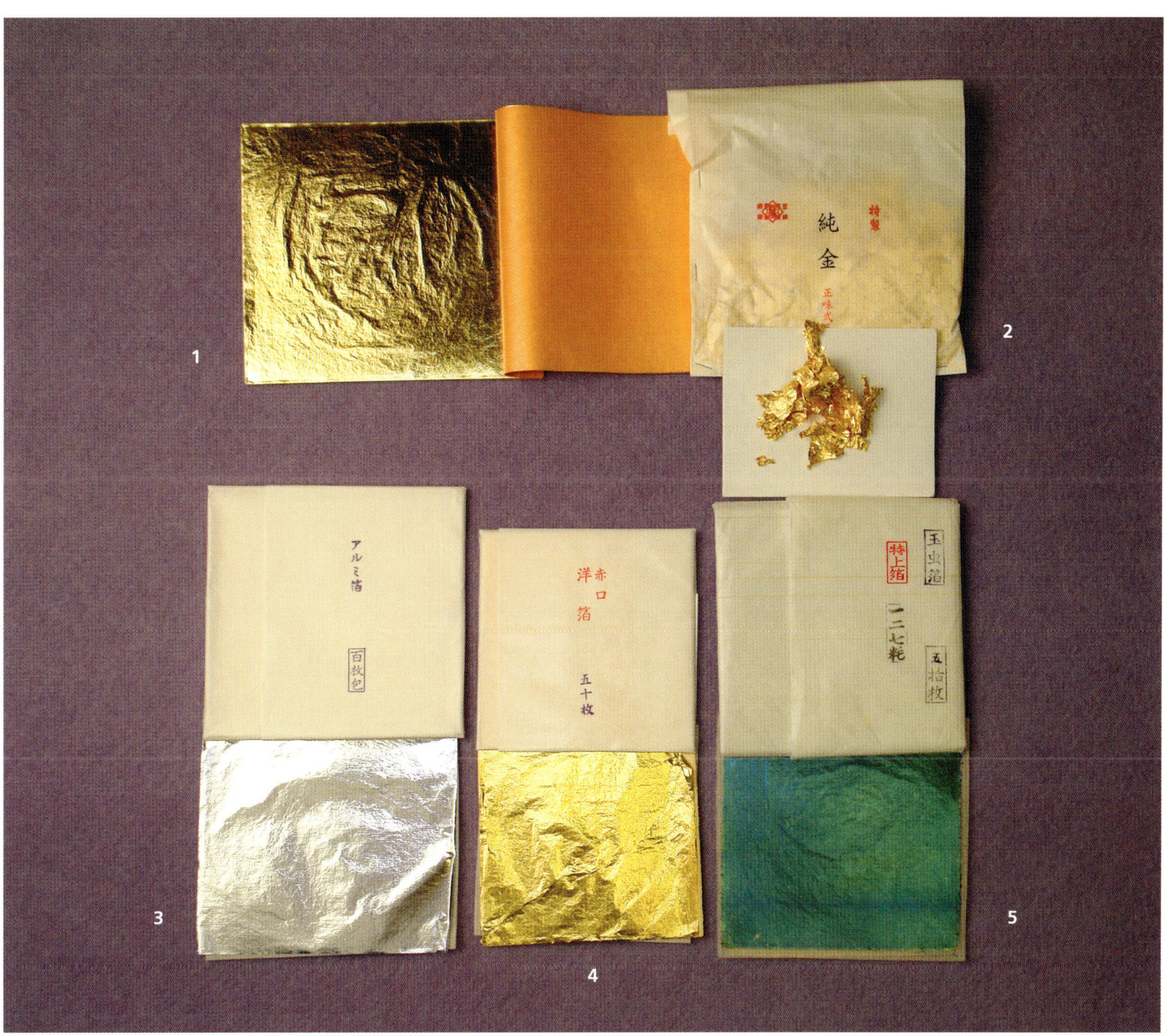

1. A booklet of simulated gold made in Italy. This material is reasonable in price and is commonly used. It must be shellacked to maintain its gold color over a period of time.
2. This envelope states that its contents are pure gold. As the sample on the square paper shows, the kira mawashi gold has the appearance of crushed paper.
3. Aluminum leaf in a silver tone. Since silver tarnishes easily, aluminum is a popular substitute. Under very special circumstances, platinum sheets can be custom ordered. Platinum leaf was used in some paintings created for the Imperial Palace of Japan.
4. This bright-hued gold has retained its color after some 50 years.
5. This especially beautiful contemporary creation is made of chemically treated aluminum. It is called period color because it resembles aged silver; although the limitations of photography make it appear greenish here, the sheet reflects a collage of iridescent colors.

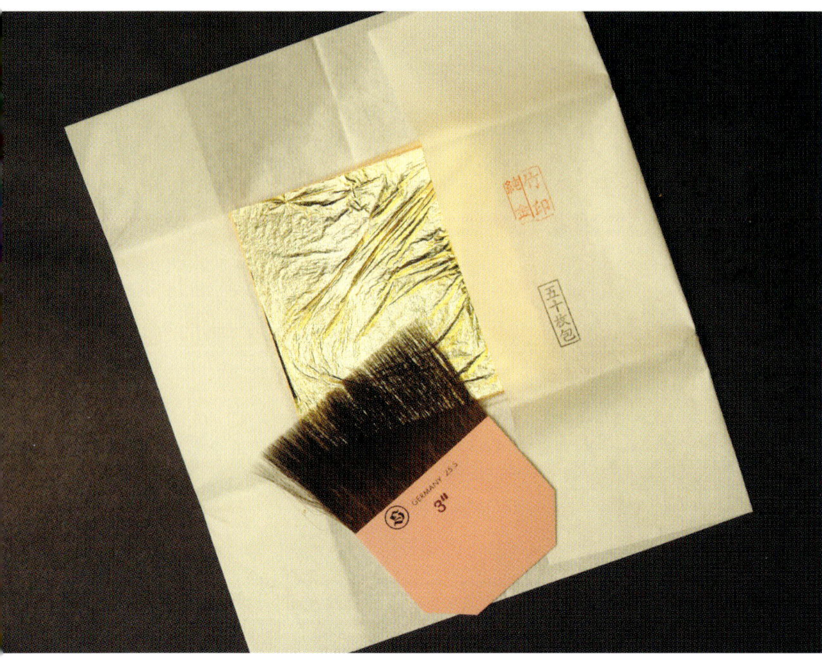

A package of pure gold leaf. The brush's long hairs are used to brush the leaf flat; its hairs are so soft that if you touch the brush to your palm you will not feel it.

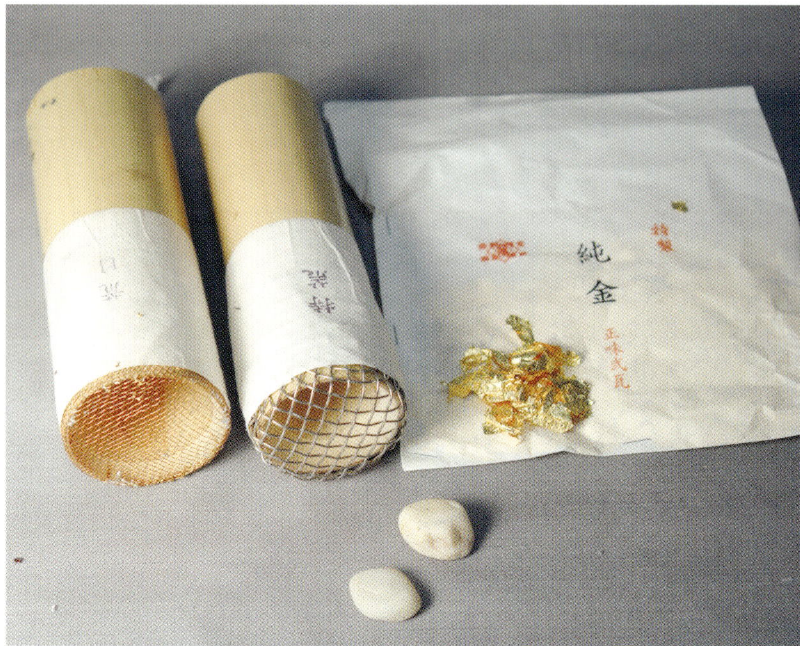

These tubes are tools used for applying gold flakes to traditional Japanese paintings. The size of the mesh chosen depends upon the purpose and effect desired. The gold shown is *kiri mawashi*, the excess gold that is cut off the sheet edges during the gold leaf manufacturing process. These fine gold leaf pieces are placed in the tube, a small stone is added, and the tube is shaken and agitated so that the stone breaks the leaf into very small pieces that sprinkle onto the painting.

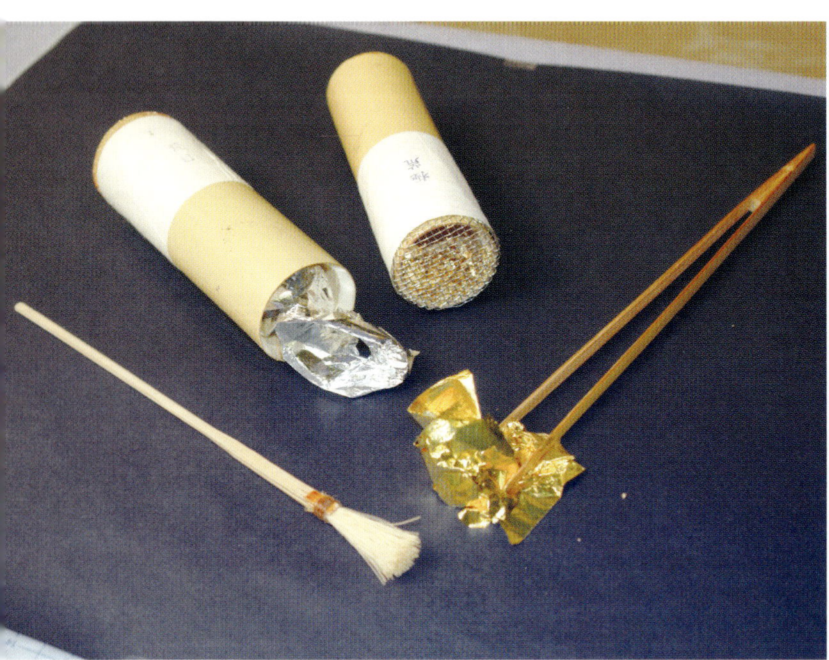

Gold leaves, whatever the brand, are impossible to handle with the fingers so special bamboo tweezers must be used. If you should wish to have small square pieces, crush the leaf and insert it into the tube as shown at the left side of the photo. In place of a round pebble, the specially crafted horse hair brush is used to push gold pieces through the screen. This method allows you precision in the amount and placement of the gold.

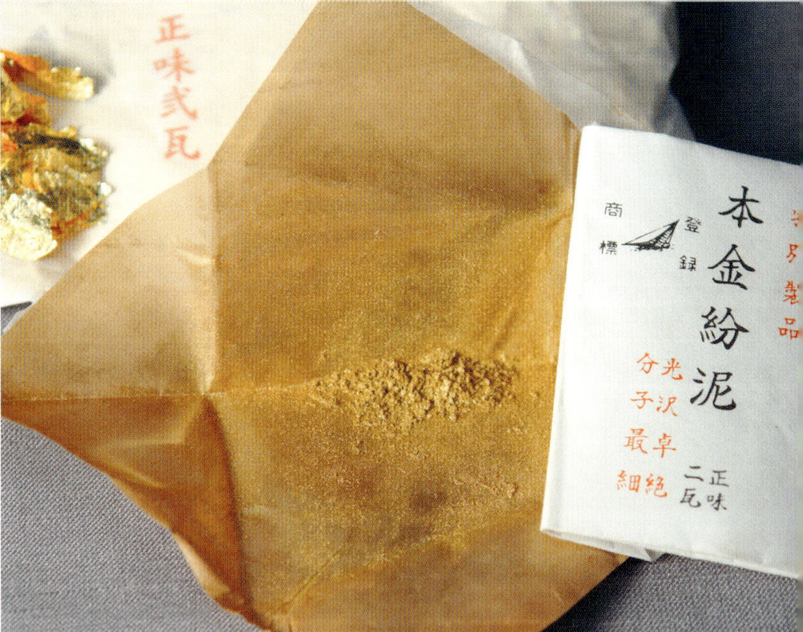

There are two types of gold powder and pigment available for purchase. The type of powdered gold shown here is mixed with nikawa (animal-based glue) and applied like paint. When dry, the painted surface will have a shiny gold effect. The other type of gold powder creates a matte finish.

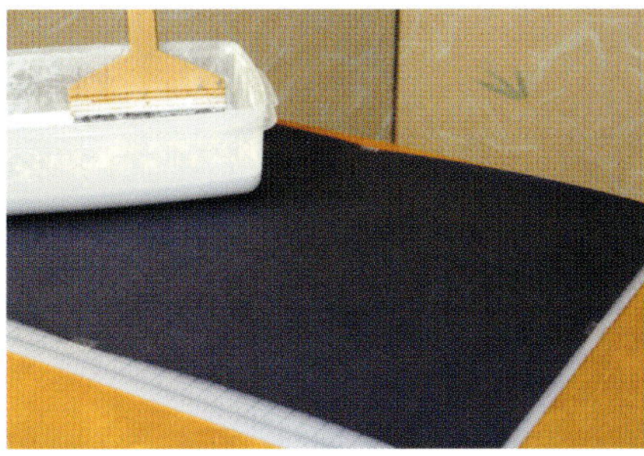

1. This dark blue torinoko paper works well to demonstrate because the application of glue and its effects can be clearly seen. At left is a plastic container of glue and a *hake* brush. In order for the gold leaf to remain on the paper or cloth, the glue used must sustain its viscosity for a period of time.

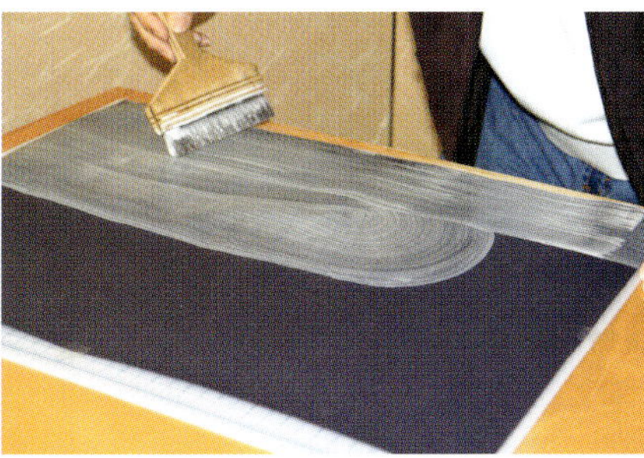

2. If the glue is too thin it will soak into the paper and lose its adhesive power. For small areas, white PVAC-based household glue will work. Here, wallpaper glue is painted on in the pattern of a cloud common in Japanese decorative painting.

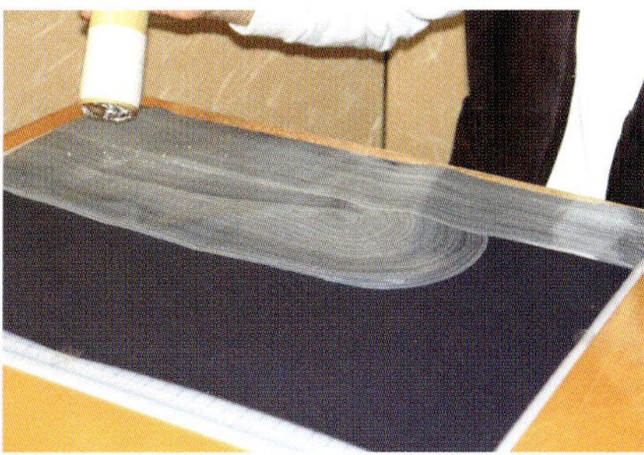

3. Aluminum flakes are sprinkled on by pushing them through the mesh.

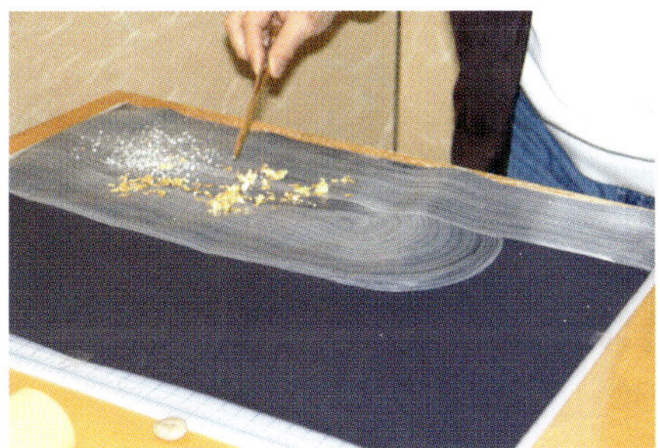

4. Now crumpled gold leaf is placed on the designated area with the bamboo tweezers.

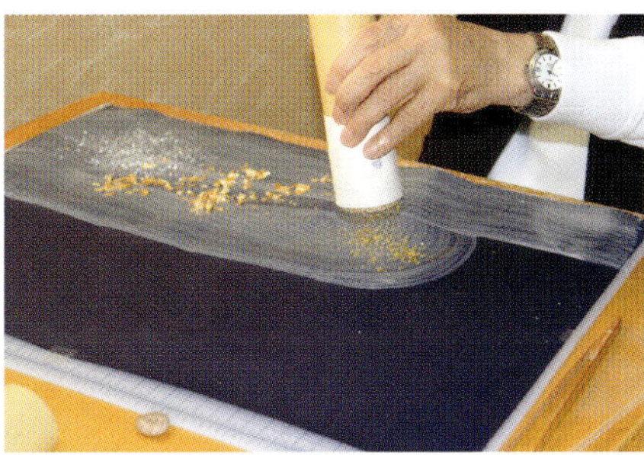

5. Gold leaf is dusted on the surface by agitating the tube.

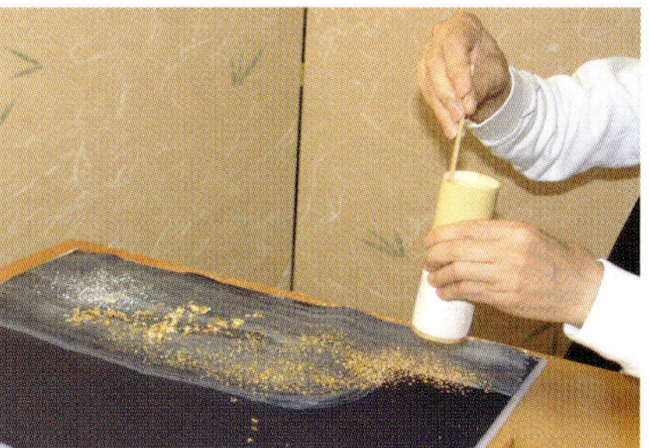

6. With a long-handled coarse hair brush, gold flakes are pushed through the screen.

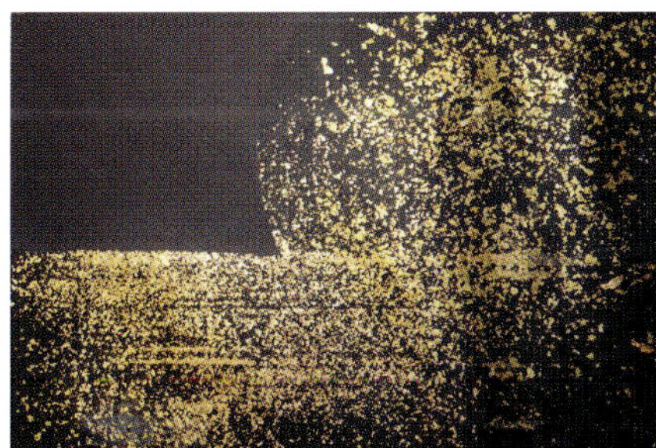

Notice that, running through the center of this example, the gold dust's edge forms a sharp horizontal line. The glue was still viscous along this edge when the dust was applied, but below it the glue dried out while I was working, and less dust adhered. Depending upon what you wish to obtain, apply the proper amount of glue or you may be disappointed with the effect.

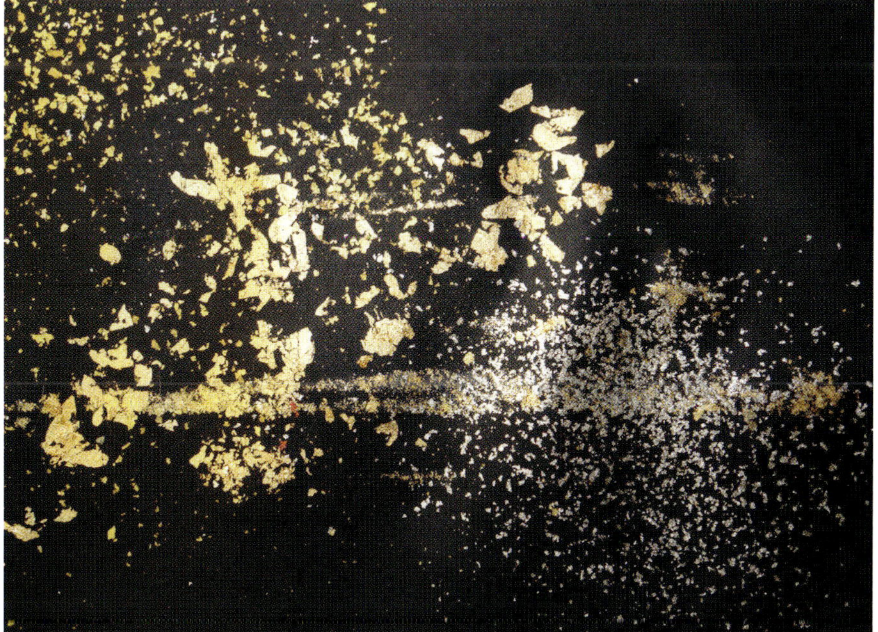

This close-up shows the irregular shapes and random effects you can obtain by dropping the *kiri mawashi* flakes on the wet glue. In some cases, these gold pieces are cut into different sizes or thin strips and are painstakingly put in place individually with tweezers. In museums you may see Japanese paintings that show gold applied in such a manner.

Landscape Painting Techniques

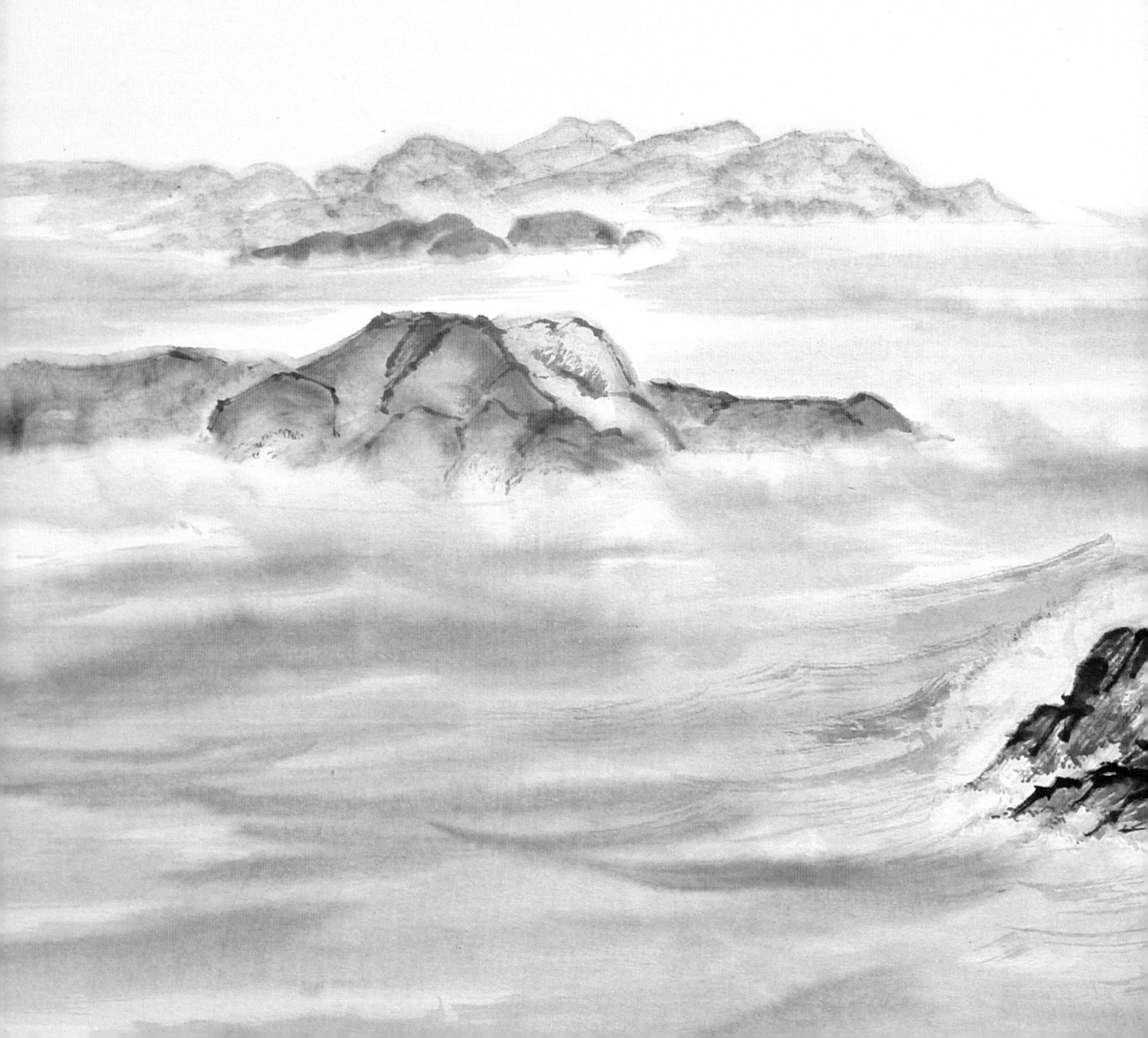

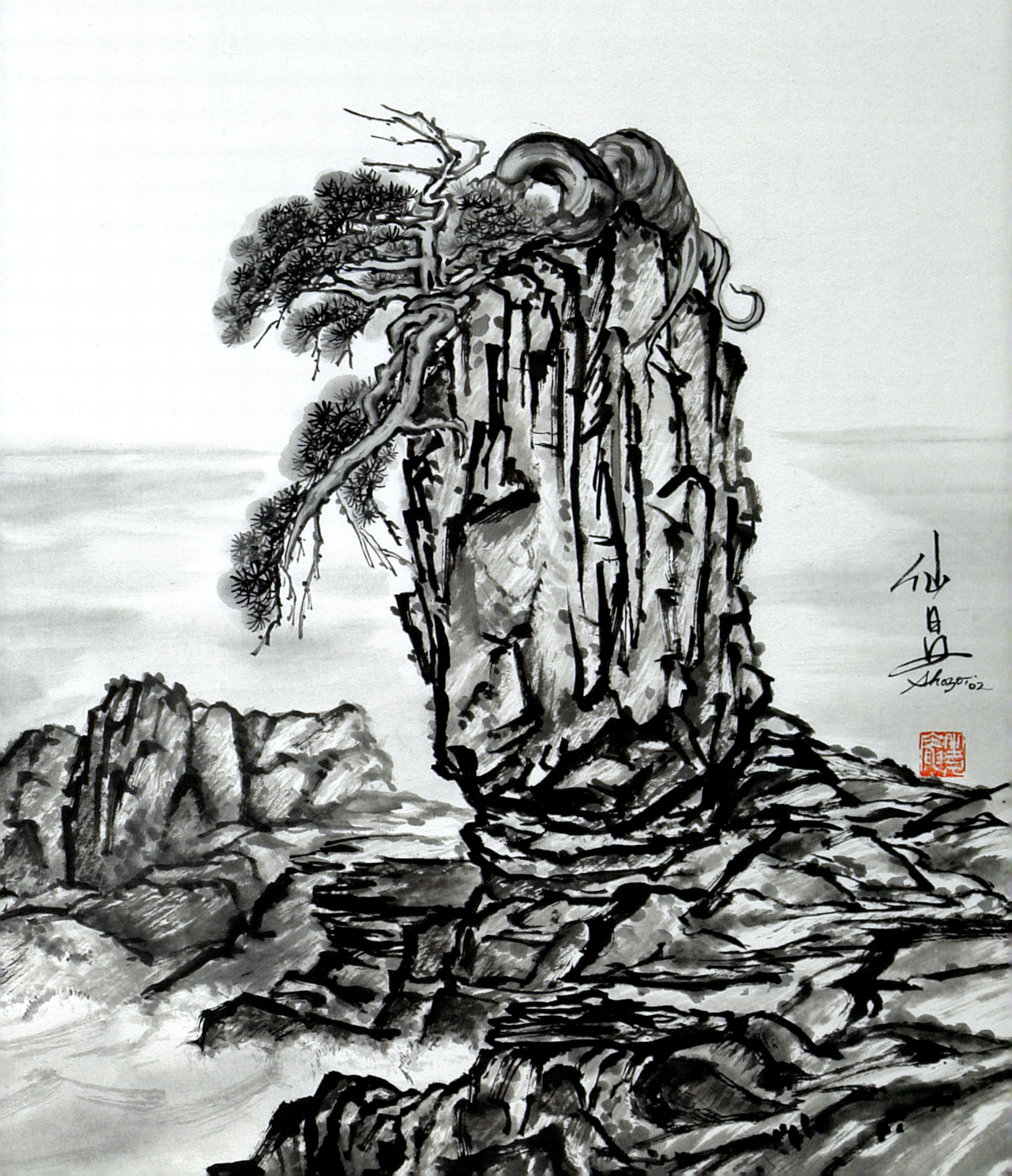

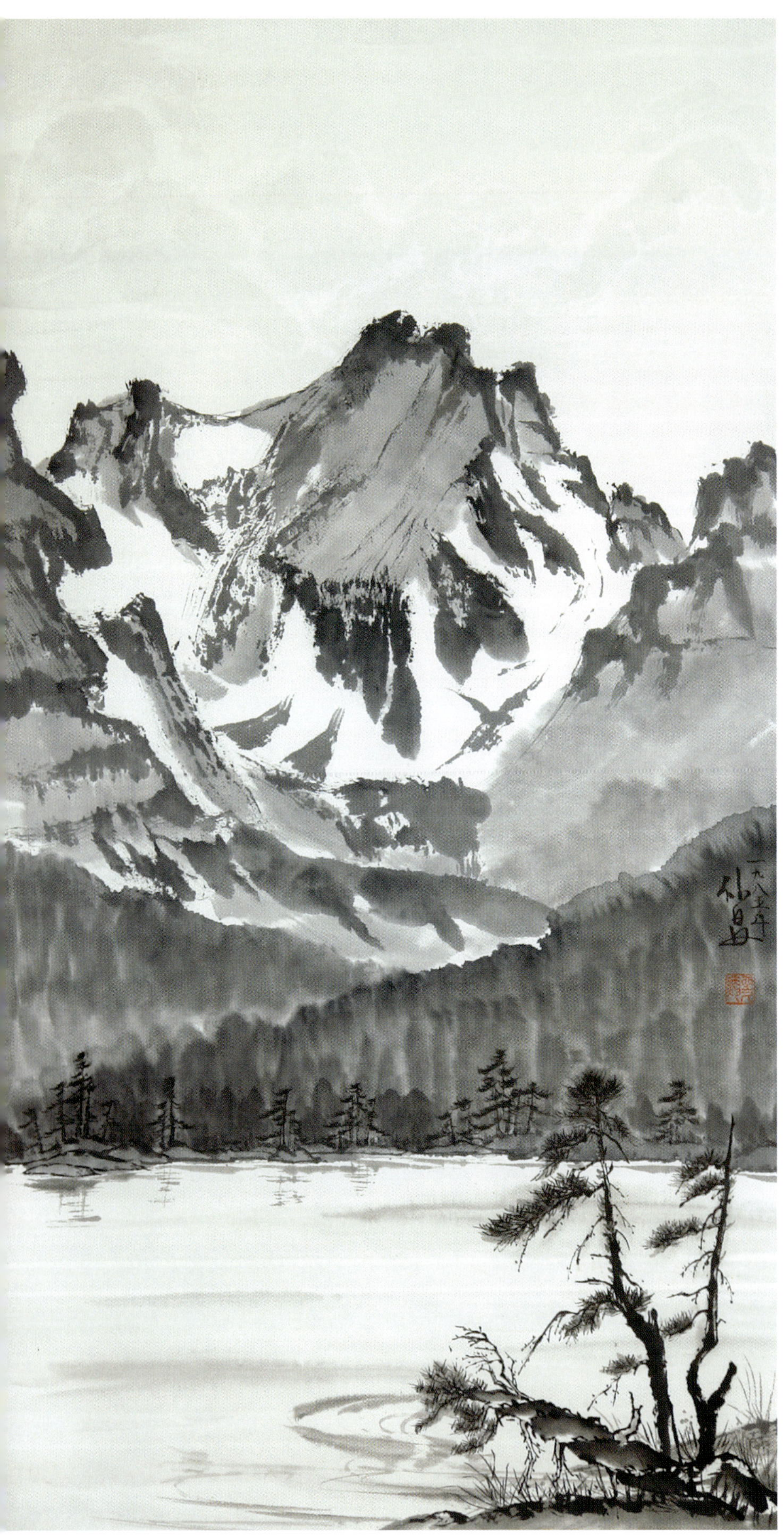

1. Indian Peaks

Size: L = 39.5"/100.5 cm x W 20.5"/52cm
Paper: Sized
Sumi Ink: Standard
Category: Suiboku-ga

The inspiration for this painting came from a visit to the Indian Peaks Wilderness Area in the Colorado Rockies where a rugged summit towers over Long Lake. Long ago glaciers carved and shaped the mountains with steep ravines and crevices, where snowfields remain throughout the summer. This was a setting of much grandeur, but my strongest memories are of the thousands of mosquitoes buzzing around. My wife patiently fanned them away with a spare sketch pad while I made my sketch.

This painting is large in size and is in the category of suiboku-ga. After about 90% of the painting had been completed, the foreground appeared to need some focus so I put in an aged pine tree which would increase depth in perception and enhance the height of the distant summit. In the process, the top of the pine blended into the distant spruce-fir forest so I used the sticky side of transparent tape to lift out the paper fibers surrounding the tree top. This technique created a clear demarcation between the tree top and the distant forest.

This painting was mounted as a traditional hanging scroll by a superb craftsman, the late Mr. Keitaro Aoki of Keiundo Co. in Asakusa, Japan, a descendant of a long line of scroll mounting craftsmen. Craftsmen of this caliber take months, even years when mounting a scroll. Before the final mounting on silk brocade, the artwork will be exposed to various atmospheric conditions from high to low humidity, and will be wetted and then slowly dried many times. With this kind of treatment, the scroll will always hang flat and straight. (It is possible to have scrolls mounted in a short period of time, but they will have side edges that curve inward when hung.) Scrolls are a convenient way to keep paintings because after they are rolled they take so little space for storage, and they are easy to transport. The box for this scroll is made of paulownia wood and is 25"/63.5cm long with a width and height of 4"/10cm.

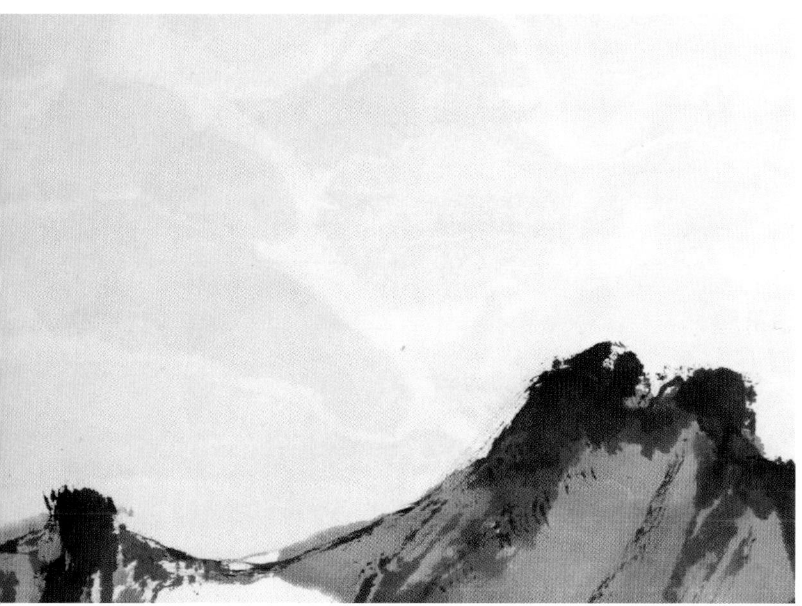

In traditional sumi landscapes the sky is usually not painted. But in this work, to enhance the whiteness of the remaining snow, light gray ink has been applied for the sky. This type of absorbent paper will show every overlapping stroke (because moisture forms a barrier for additional marks), hence, the faint white outlines hint of summer clouds. To successfully carry this technique out, your brush movements should be swift, made before the previous stroke dries out. Look back at the painting as a whole; notice how the light gray sky combined with the dark ink outlining the rugged outcrops of rocks augments the whiteness of the snow.

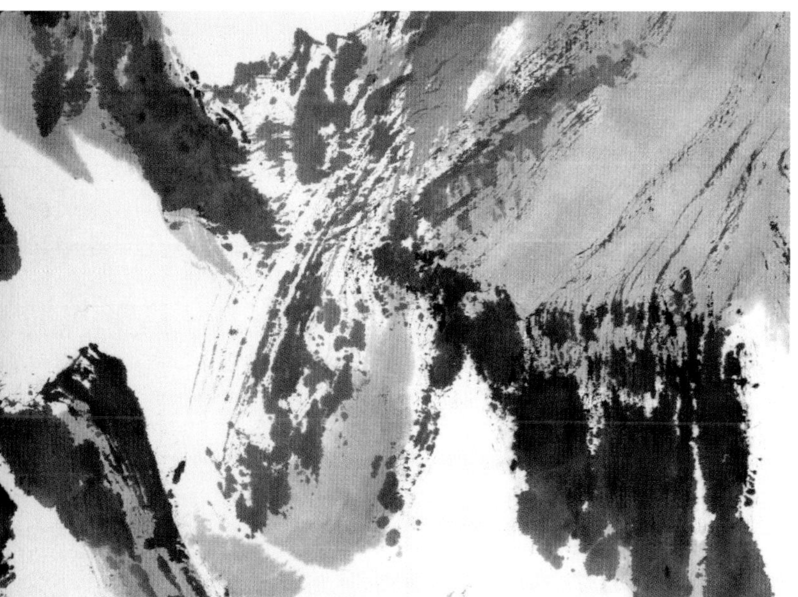

Painters working in oils, acrylics, and watercolors use color combinations and contrasts to communicate. Sumi-e and suiboku-ga artists must instead depend upon textures and tone to create their expressions in monochrome. So artists in this medium should be constantly aware of how their contrasting brush strokes, from gentle to rugged, can convey powerful expression.

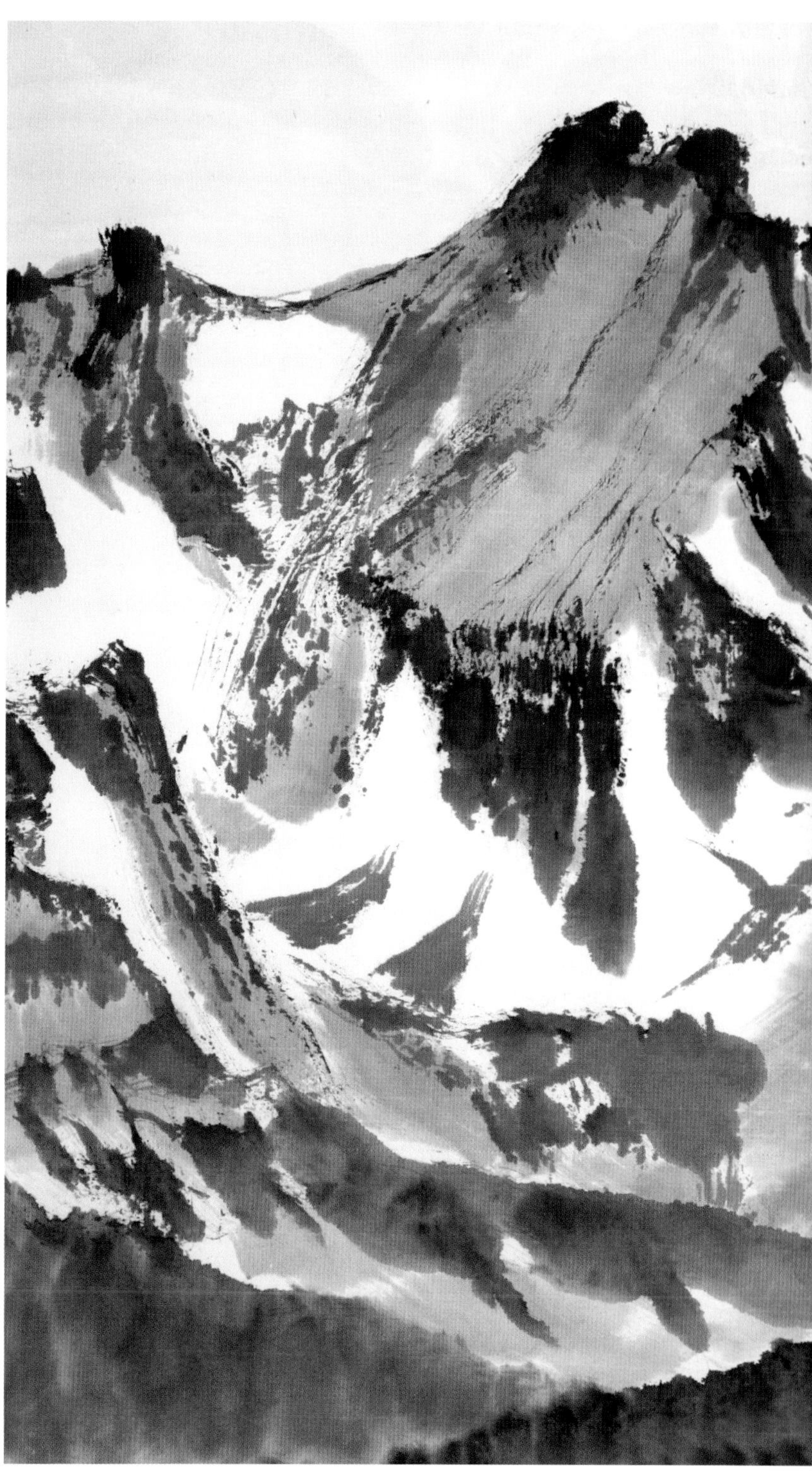

The rocky summit is created with a mountain horse brush using darker ink to form the outlines of the summit. I often point the brush tip up and push upward forcefully in creating the rocky points. By doing so, the coarse hairs of the brush spread out, creating a texture that gives the feeling of the rough and rocky scree.

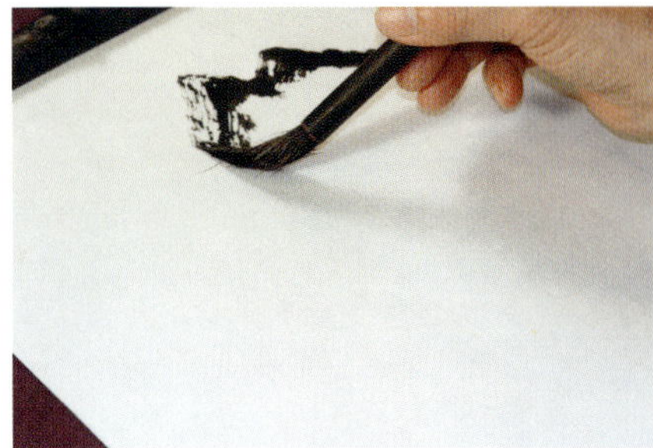

1. After forming the first peak, the brush is again pushed up to form the second peak.

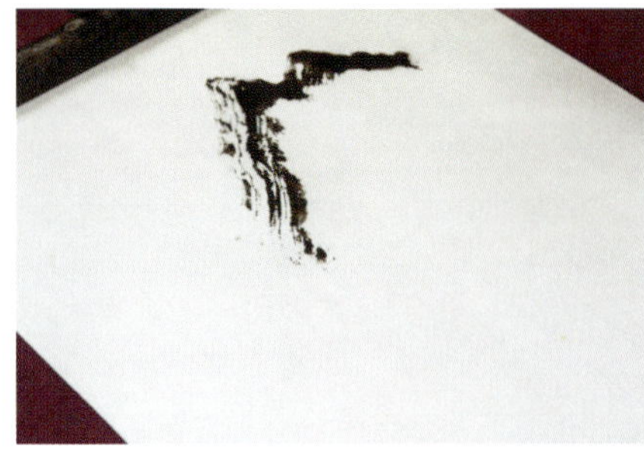

2. Multiple ragged lines are formed for the craggy peaks.

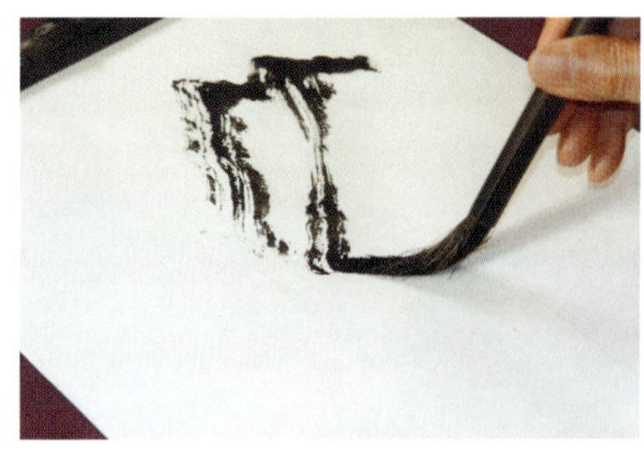

3. Add additional lines in the same manner. Notice that the brush is at a 45 degree angle in relation to the paper.

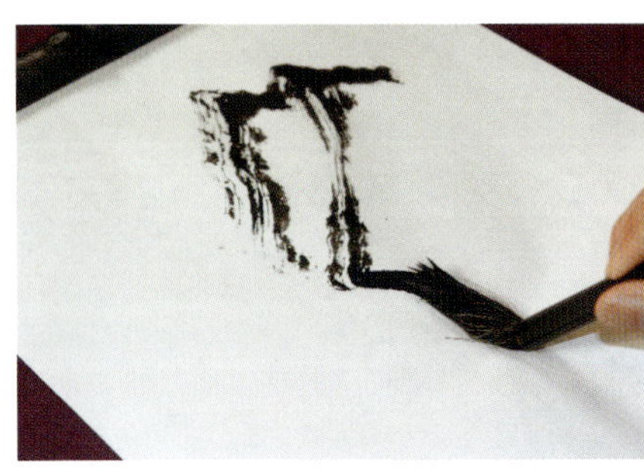

4. This photo and the next two show the painting of the cliff and ravine. Prepare the brush with water at the base and dark ink on the tip.

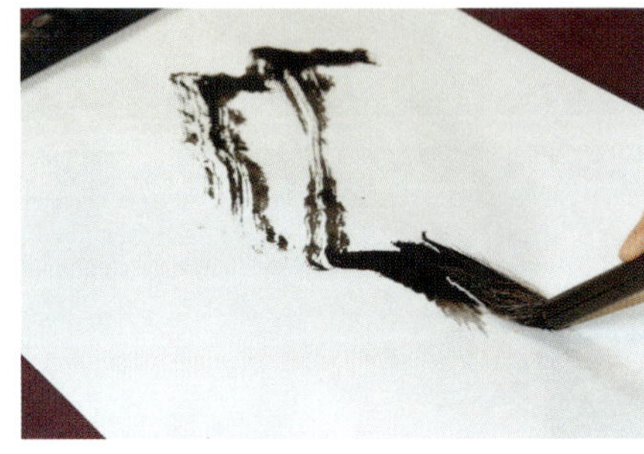

5. Press the base of the brush against the paper, so that water will soak into the paper to create variations from dark to light. Additional water can be applied to the brush's base with another brush to further enhance variations in ink tone.

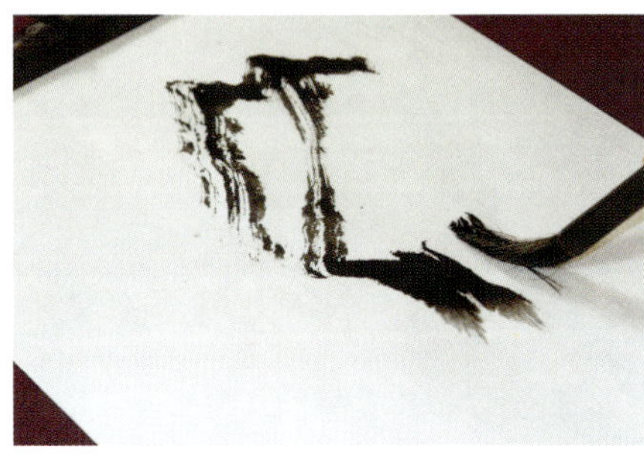

6. The cliff is nearly completed. Notice the gradient in ink tones. At this point, water can be applied with a small brush to the areas of light ink tones to create further variations in them.

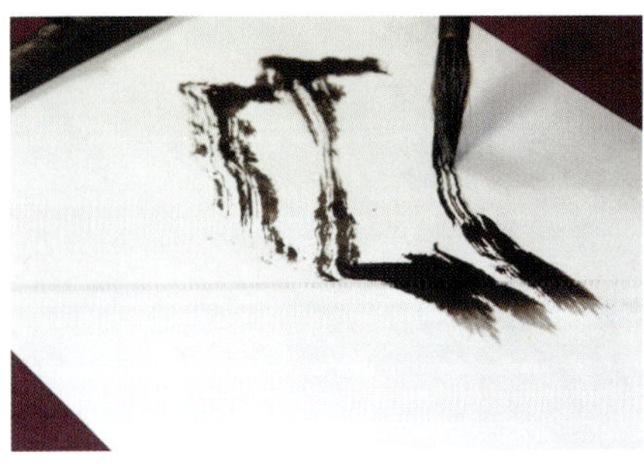

7. Separate the bristles at the tip of the brush and move upright to give texture to the slopes.

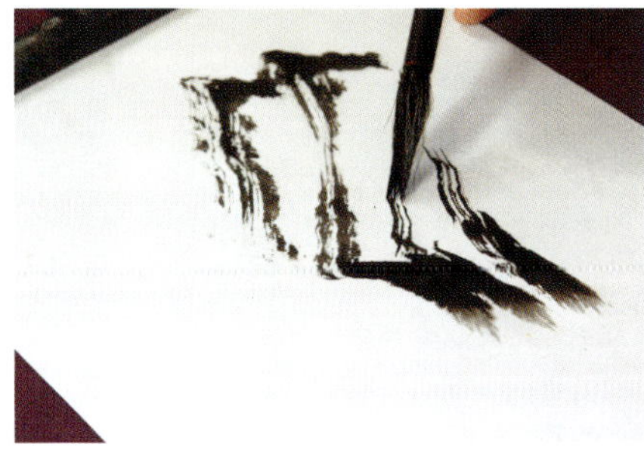

8. Continue with additional slopes.

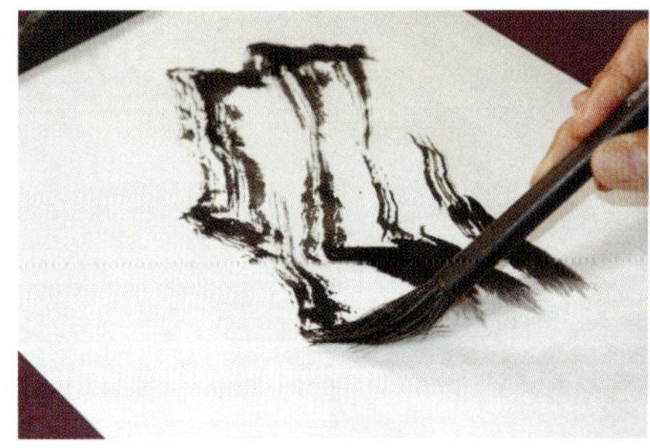

9. Continue adding lines for slopes.

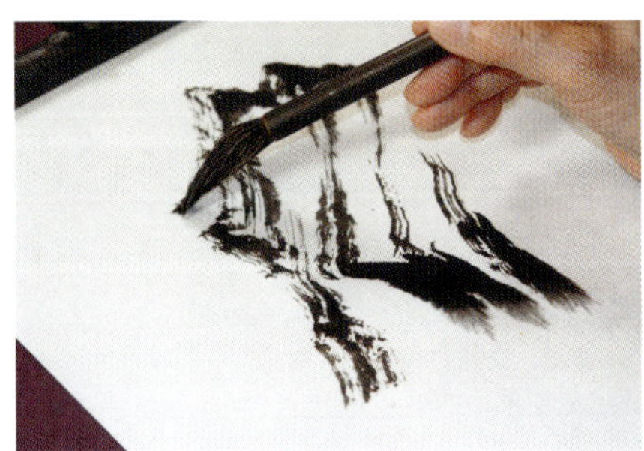

10. Create the secondary peaks around the snowfields.

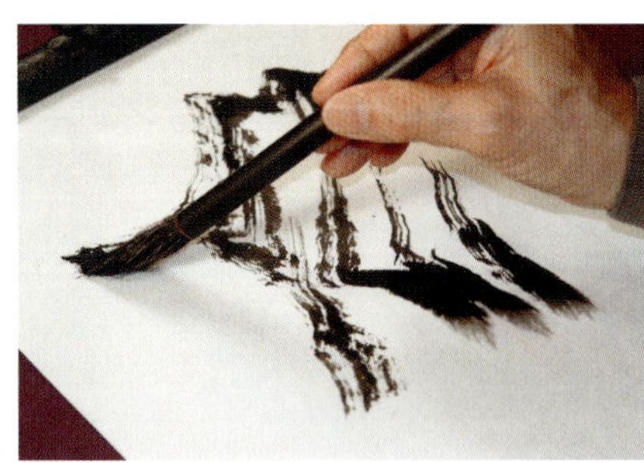

11. The direction of the brush is changed and comes downward.

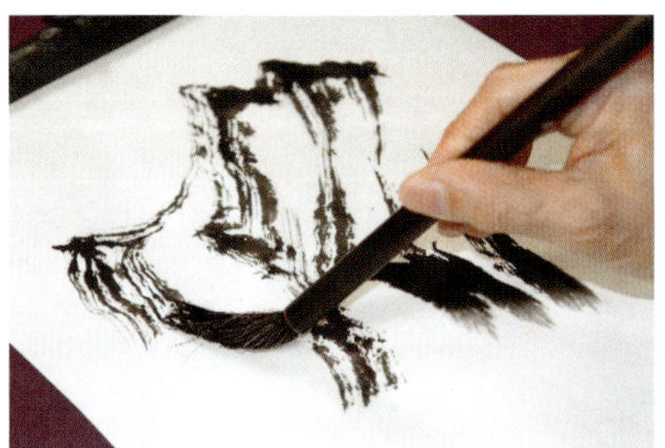

12. The tip of the brush is pointed up to get the multiple line effect.

13. Shade the rocky slope with light ink. Then, outline snowfields. In these samples, the shading was carried out with the mountain horse hair brush. One can use a regular choryu brush instead, but it would give an effect of even tones.

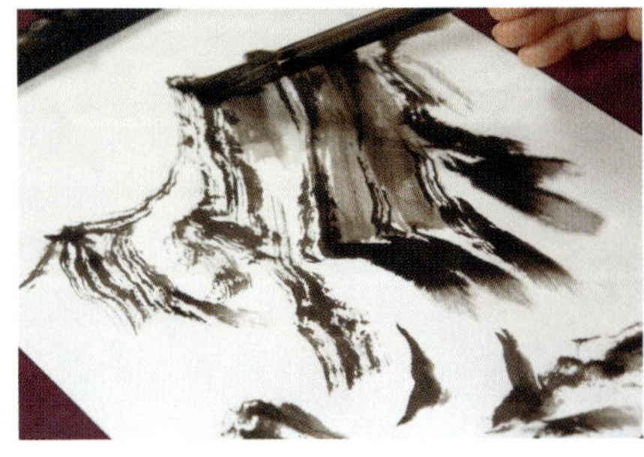

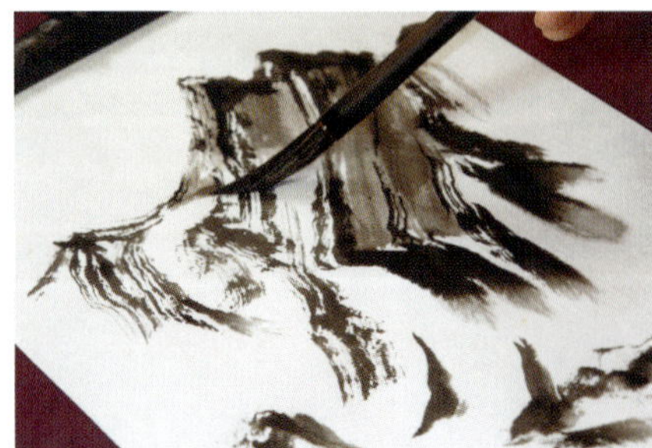

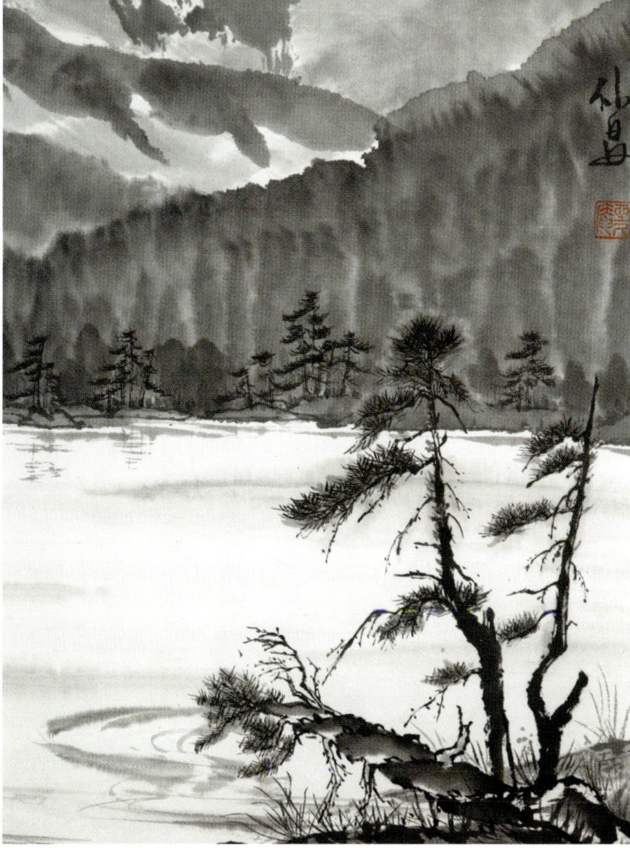

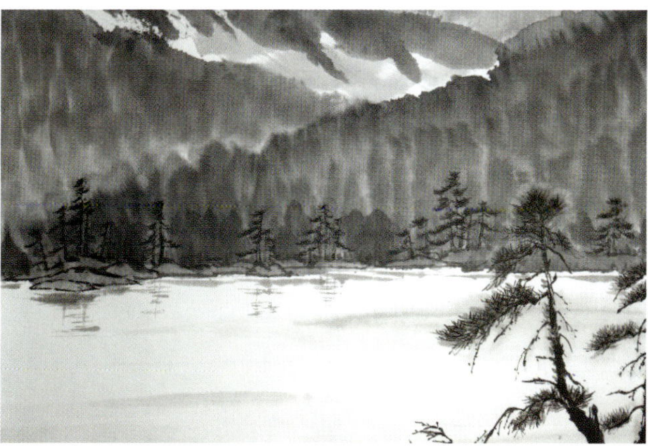

14. When examining the painting after I thought it was completed, I felt a need to insert some depth and drama to the painting so I added the aged pines in the foreground, with one fallen tree dipping in the lake and creating ripples to show movement on the water surface. I felt that the grasses, ripples and aged trees would add a poetic element and complement the grandeur of the distant mountaintop.

15. The forest at the base of the mountains was created by using the stamping technique (see below). However, because it was an afterthought, the foreground tree's top blended into the spruce-fir forest so I used my secret technique (see page 66) to make a clear demarcation around it.

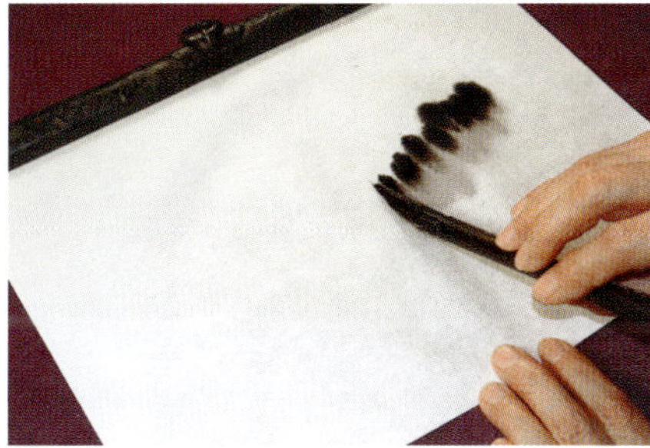

This is a common technique for creating the effect of a distant forest or grove of trees.

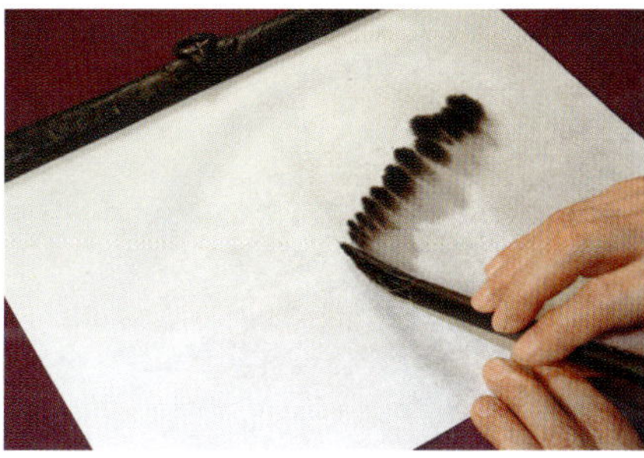

Apply ink along the bristles with dark ink at the tip, light ink in the middle and water at the base. Press down from the tip of the brush to the base.

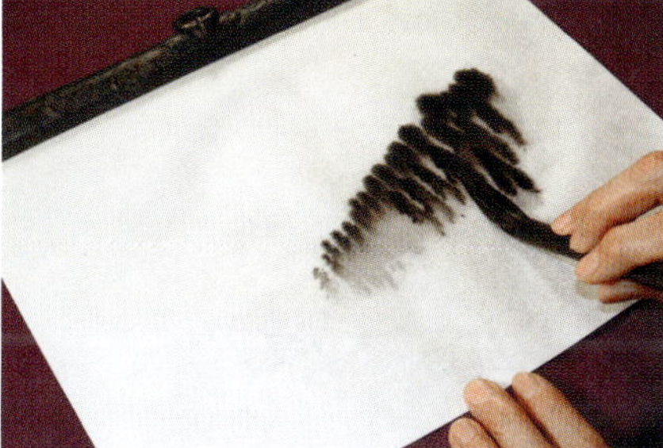

After the outline of the grove or forest has been created, continue to provide density as shown. By adding strokes, density emerges.

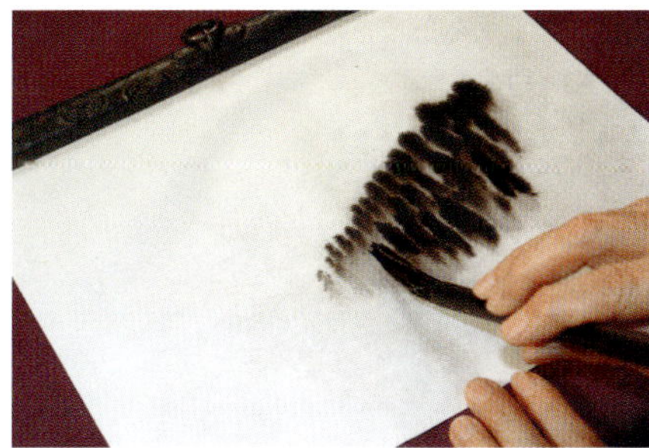

Continue to add trees with the stamping technique until you reach the desired size of your forest.

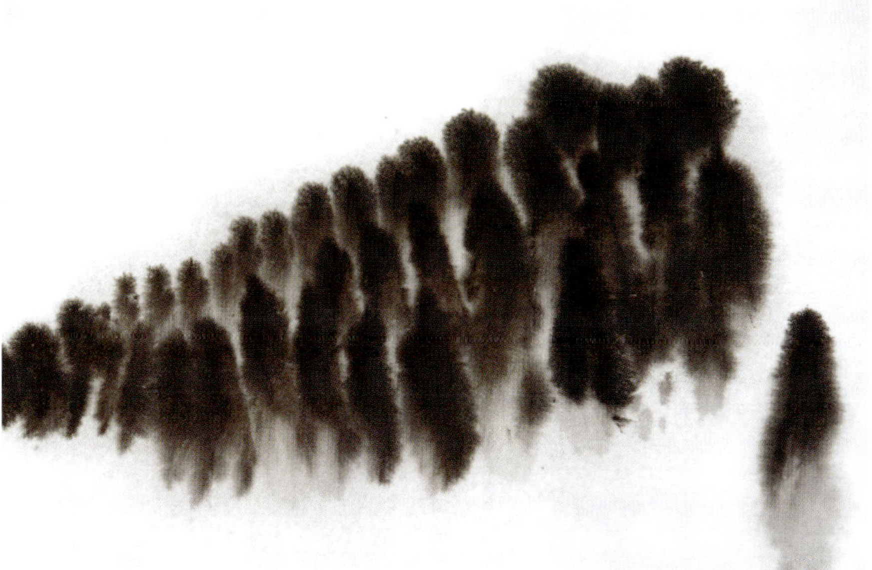

A closer view. (At the far right corner there is a sample dark-to-light brush mark, standing alone; for details about the stamping technique, see page 54.)

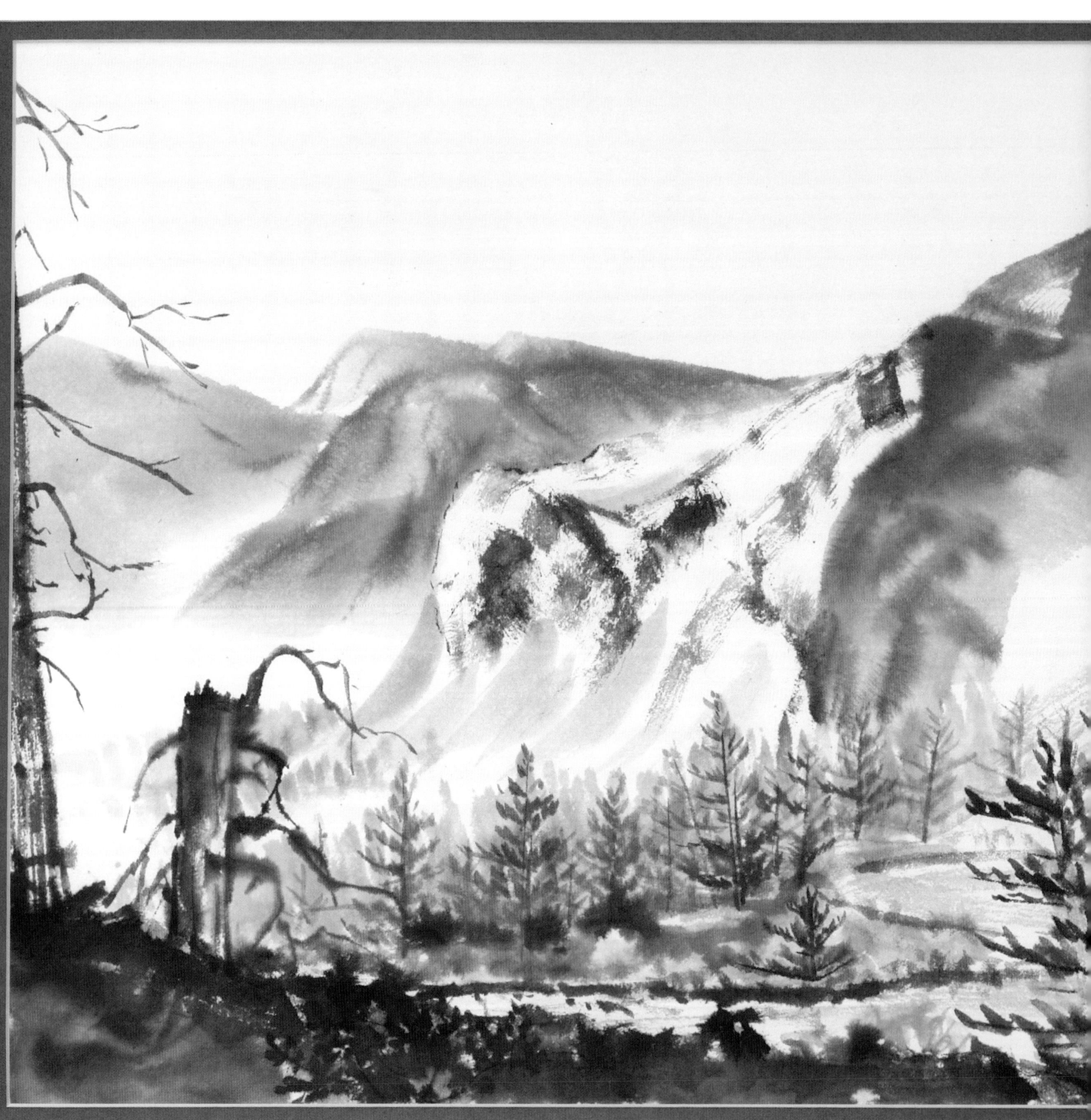

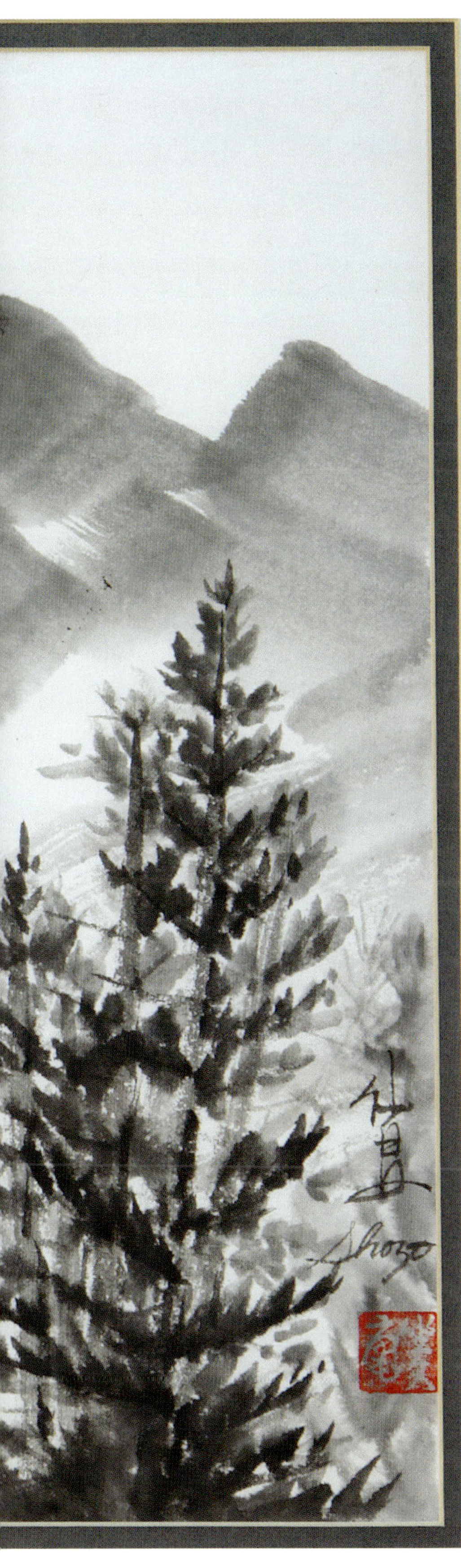

2. Collegiate Peaks

Size: H = 15.25"/39cm x W = 20.5"/52cm
Paper: Gasen shi (unsized paper)
Sumi Ink: Standard
Category: Sumi-e

In comparison to some of the more rugged glacier-carved mountains so often portrayed in photographs, the Collegiate Peaks, located in the central Rocky Mountains of Colorado, have a gentler formation as the terrain slopes down from the summit. All the same, these Collegiate Peaks are still in the Rocky Mountain chain: they also feature rocky outcroppings with jagged cliffs and steep ravines. It was my endeavor in this sumi-e painting to show the contrasts from the gentle to the rugged.

In rendering the slope of the peaks as they reached the summit, the brush was used sideways as demonstrated in the following pages. Then, using a dry brush with darker ink, holding it upright, I painted the rugged cliffs, the foreground trees, and distant groves. You can see how contrasts in technique produce more clarity in the texture of the cliffs, trees, and groves, as opposed to the surface of the gentler slopes. This painting is in the sumi-e category.

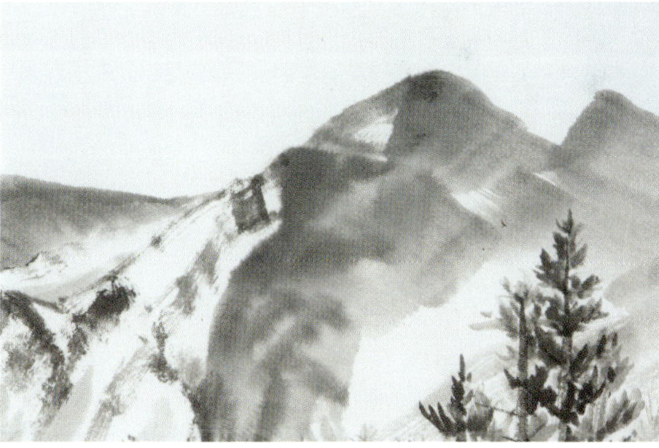

The typical *bokkotsu* technique was used for the mountain peak: in other words, no use of outlines. Additional strokes were used to add the dark and light areas. Different tones of ink are first applied on the bristles and then the variations can be created. This technique is one of the basic skills necessary in mastering the art of sumi-e.

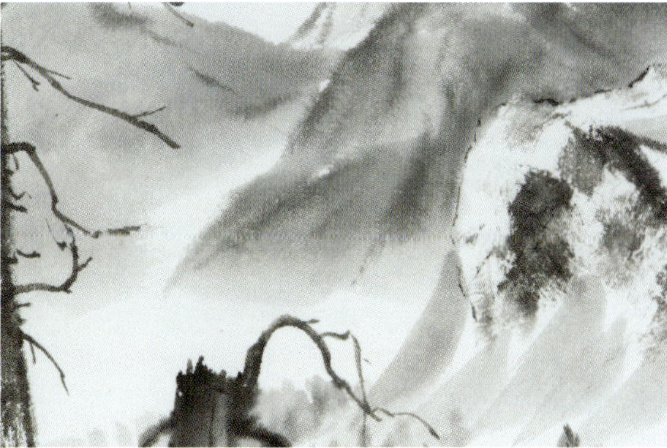

Light ink is added in a gradient so that the white spaces suggest fog or the cold misty air. On the other hand, in the above photo, distinct breaks were used to show the whiteness of the remaining snow. Within this light ink surface of the summit and slope, while the paper was still wet, slightly darker ink on the tip of the brush was used to suggest the rocky ravine on the slope. Dark ink was used to show the rugged rocky outcrops. A semi-dry brush held upright was used to add the rough texture of the rocky crags.

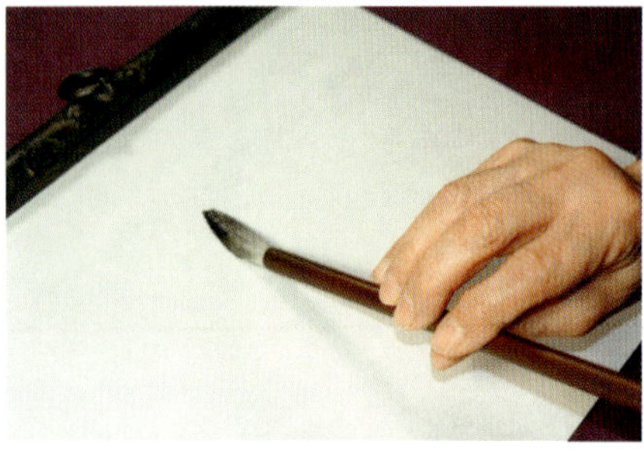

1. For the bokkotsu style, dip the brush in water, then add lighter ink to the middle and darker ink on the tip. Hold the brush sideways, with the brush handle lower than 45 degrees.

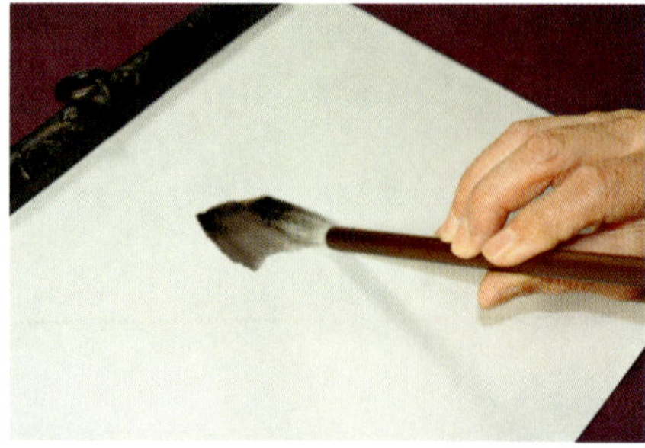

2. Slowly move the brush to the lower right, keeping the total length of the bristles in contact with the paper.

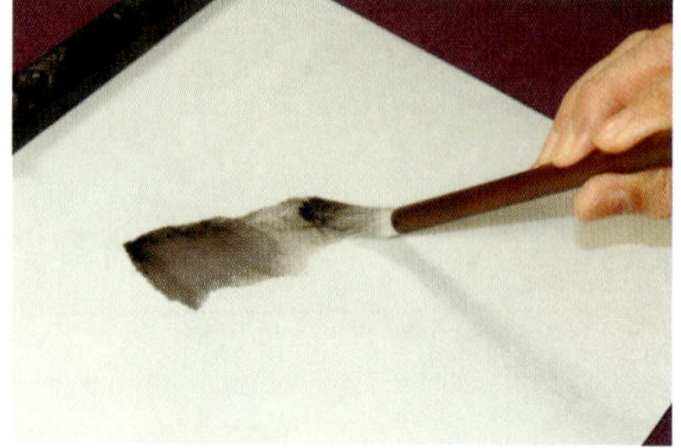

3. Complete the right-hand side of the peak.

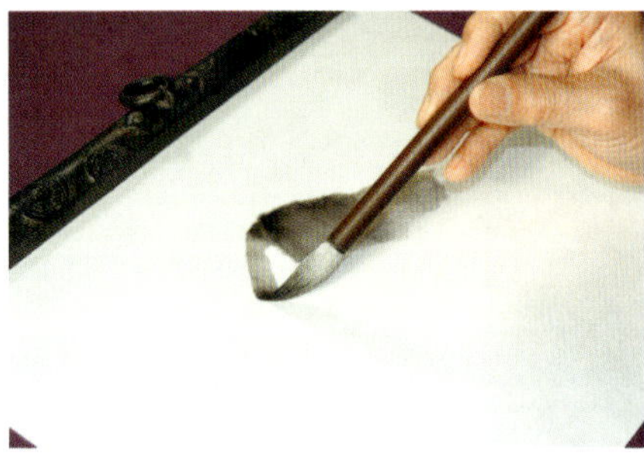

4. Wash the brush then apply lighter ink to finish the left side of the peak.

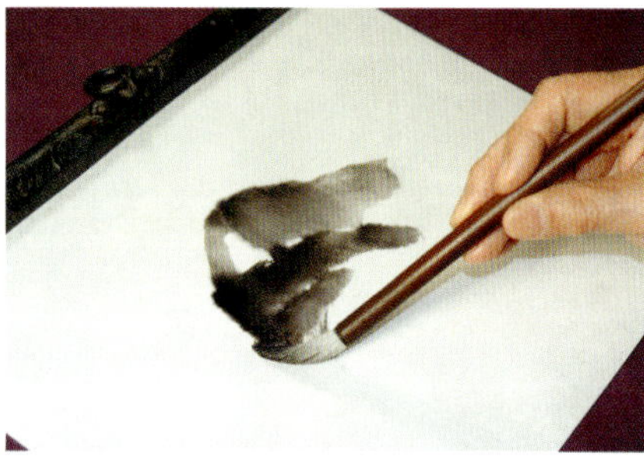

5. While the paper is still wet apply darker ink to the tip of the brush and create a secondary peak on the side.

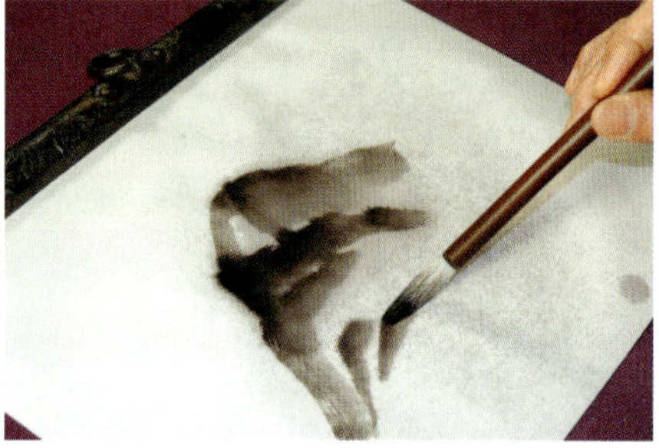

6. The second peak is finished with a ravine.

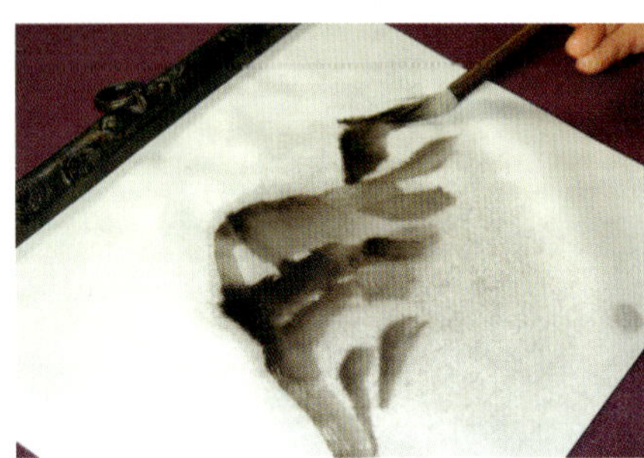

7. An additional peak is added on the right-hand side.

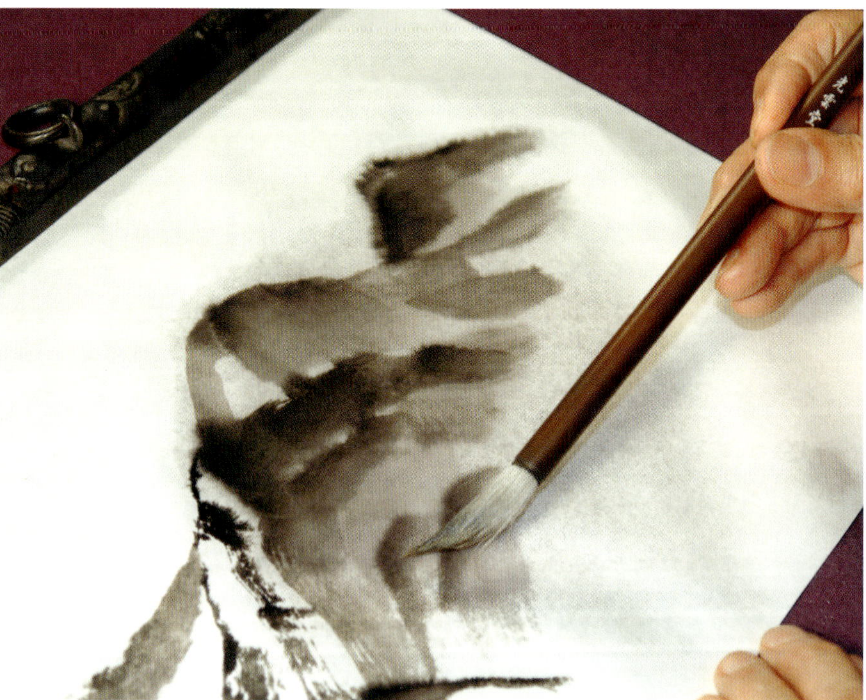

8. The brush is washed and then darker ink is added to a drier brush to complete the slope outline where the snowfields and rocky outcrops begin.

9. Continue shading on the side of the secondary peak. In sumi-e, depending upon the effect you wish to create, commonly either a very wet brush can be used sideways or a drier brush can be used upright to produce texture.

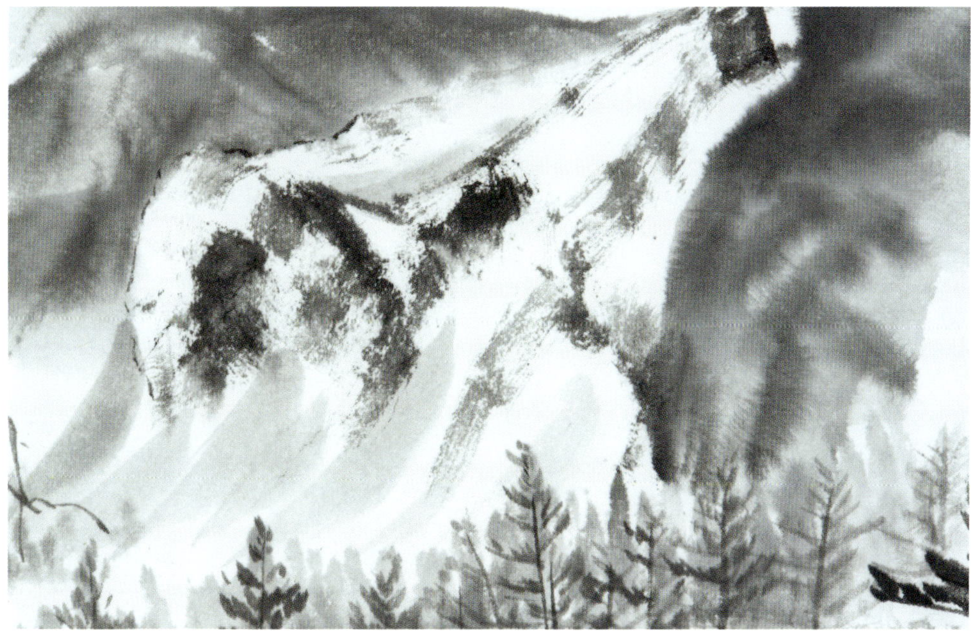

10. After painting the rocky outcropping, wash the brush. By this time, the water will be light gray, a good color for shading in the sloping surface of the snow.

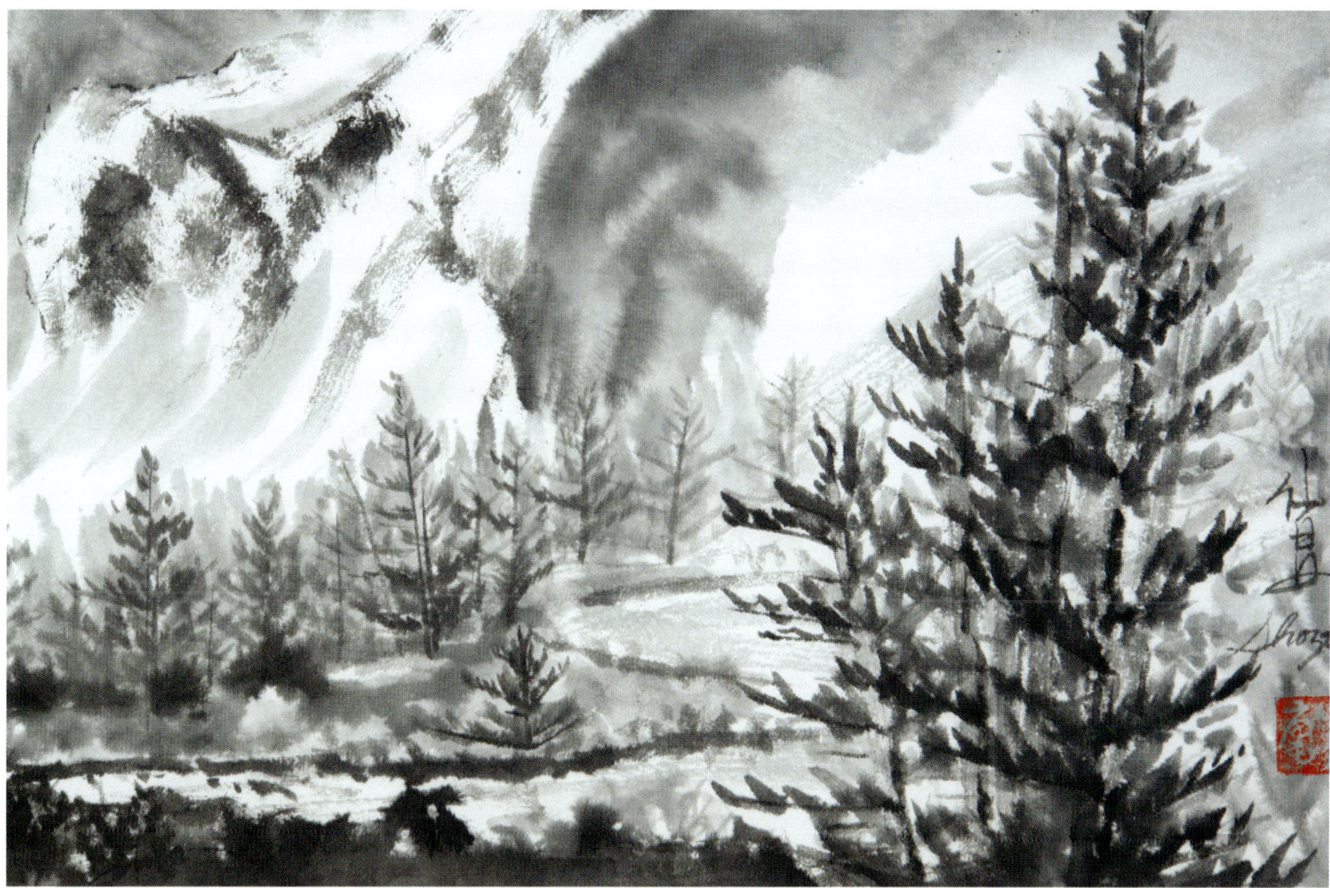

When painting trees, I usually begin with the foreground trees, then move on to the background trees. By controlling the tone of ink, perspective can be obtained with darker ink in foreground and ink becoming increasingly lighter toward the more distant trees. The path is exaggerated by adding small plants along the S-shaped curve; this adds perspective.

3. After the First Snow

Size: H = 55"/140cm x W = 17.25"/44cm
Paper: Sized
Sumi Ink: Standard
Category: Suiboku-ga

This work was painted while I was visiting in China, but it was composed from sketches made on site of a waterfall in the rugged Uncompahgre Mountains of Colorado the year before. The new-fallen snow in early autumn covered the high peaks and yet, the snowmelt from the lower elevations enhanced the volume of the flow in the waterfall, while late summer sub-alpine flowers were still in bloom along the river banks. We were traveling by Jeep with friends toward the glacier-carved Uncompahgre Peak which soars upward some 14,000 feet. After an exhilarating tour, we stopped by the waterfall for lunch and rest. Inspired by the grandeur of the scenery, I made a few sketches.

This painting was to be mounted as a traditional hanging scroll so I used the wisdom of the classic *Mustard Seed Garden Manual*, first published in China in 1679, as a guide in composition; it states that "whenever a stream and/or waterfall are in the painting, an indication of the source should be clearly suggested."

To provide contrast in the whiteness of the waterfall, dark ink was used to create the foreground rocks as a frame. Dark ink was also used for the spruce trees but at mid-ground, ink tones were lighter to give the effect of sunlight, depth and a sense of distance. Then the viewer's eye is carried on to the tree line that follows the "zigzag" of the stream's ravine, to its source at the snowfields. Ancient Chinese landscape works used this schema to create an instant journey through the painting.

To assist in this work's mental journey, a more realistic style in technique was used, with the addition of greater detail. One can imagine beginning at the waterfall, moving through the forest and hiking along the river bank upwards to the rugged glacial carved peak.

The text was done by the expert Chinese calligrapher Wan Dong Ling (my visit to his studio is described on page 60). The four main ideograms may be translated as "Fresh snow, opening of new season." The smaller calligraphy lines read, "Painted by Shozo Sato, 1988, October. Wan Dong Ling gave text to this painting."

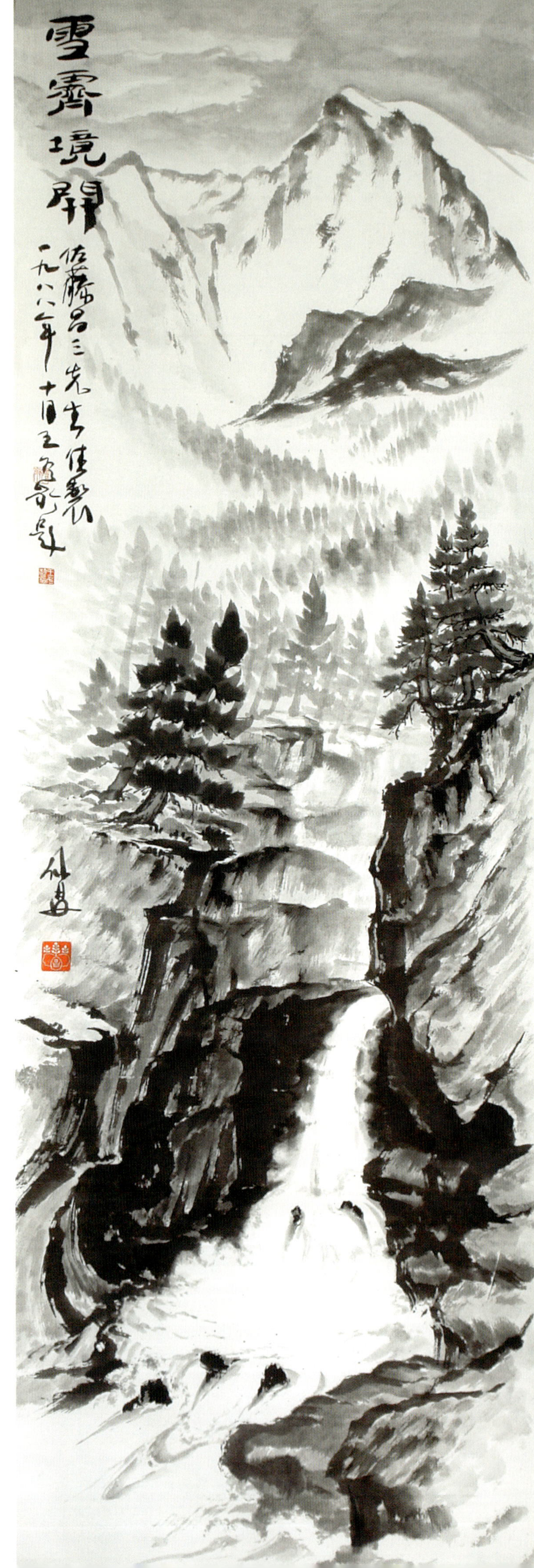

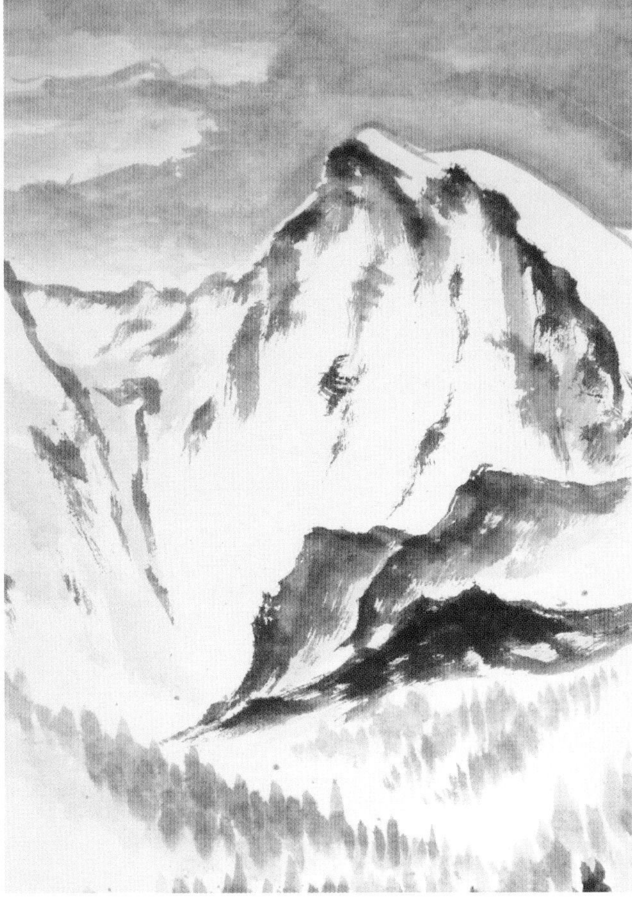

To highlight the freshness of the snow, the snow clouds in the sky were made a bit darker.

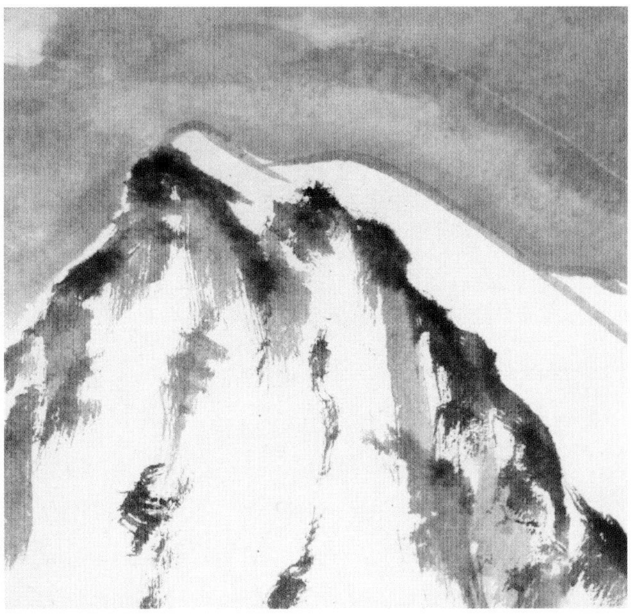

The rugged glacial cirque is reinforced with the use of darker ink to emphasize the precipitous glacial carving of the peak.

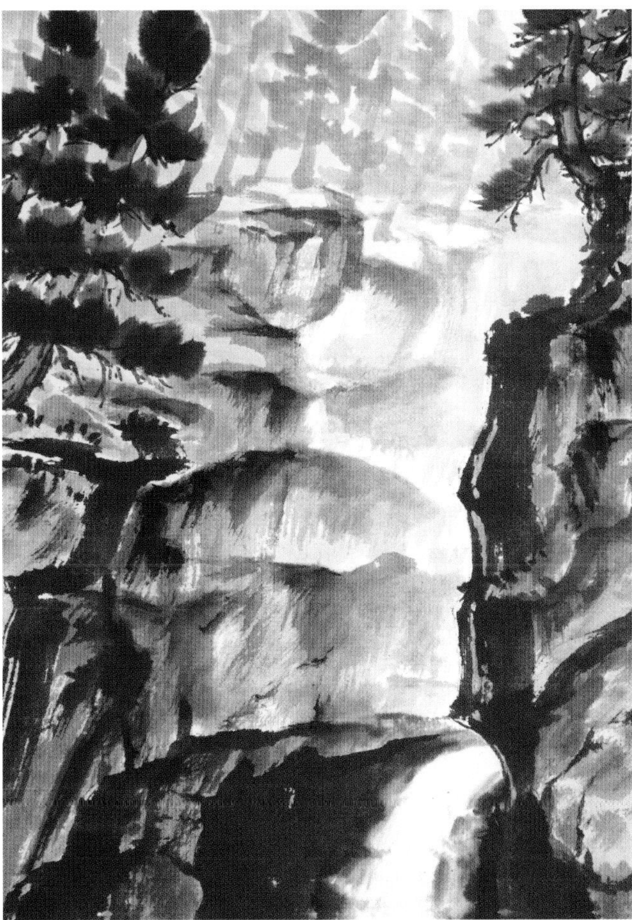

Forests grow along the mountain's sides and along the gorges. To create texture and depth for the gorge, I began with dark ink and moved on to using lighter ink in gradation which eventually faded into very light ink to show depth and the effect of the sunlight. A dry brush should be used to create texture and contrast for the rocks and for hints of mist from the splashing water.

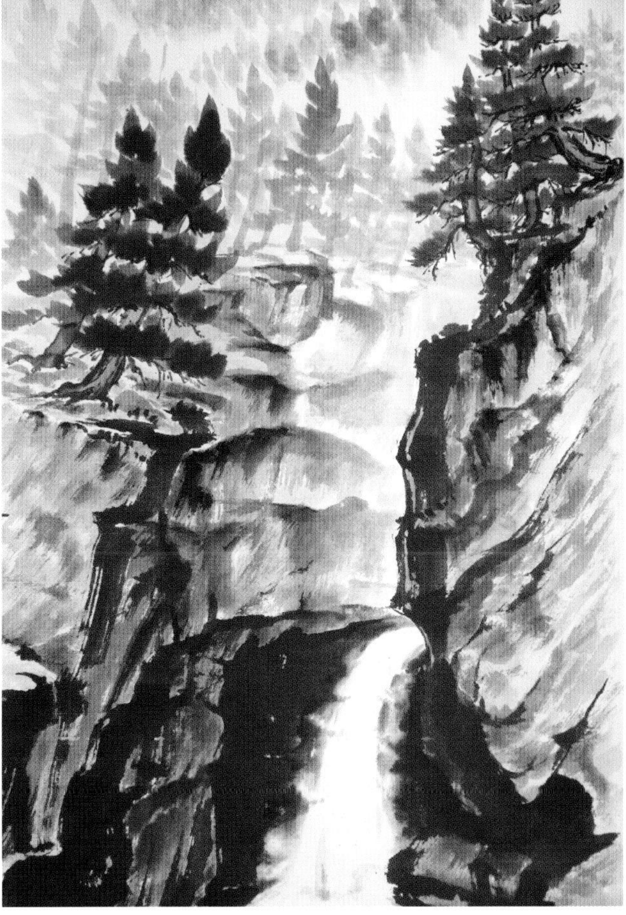

To express this water's tremendous force in a painting, begin by using very light ink. In dots, not lines, outline the movement of the water. Then gradually begin to sculpt out the fall's outline. When you watch a young child creating images with crayons, notice that while drawing, for instance, a jet plane, he or she literally becomes the jet and (if allowed) will "roar" with the jet as he or she draws. The same approach should be taken in painting a waterfall; one must literally become the waterfall.

4. Murmuring Surf

Size: H = 40.5"/103cm x W = 20"/50cm
Paper: Unsized, pre-mounted on a board
Sumi Ink: Blue tone
Category: Suiboku-ga

Along a rugged sea coast, it is not unusual to see a few trees growing on rocky outcrops which protrude from the ocean to form small islands. Depending upon the time of day, the weather and the season, such scenes can be a poetic and deeply moving spiritual experience. A gentle rain under misty conditions with muted colors, when the seas are tranquil, makes them classic subjects for sumi-e and suiboku paintings.

My intention in this work was to have light coming out from behind the rock to create the sense that sunlight would soon break out through the veil. This light also strengthens and enhances the presence of the rock. One can sense the muted sounds of the waves which helps add to a sense of tranquility.

To paint this type of work requires patience. The gentle rain is created by repeated brush strokes in upright lines. This is a typical suiboku-ga approach in creating a painting: Instead of a few minimal strokes to capture the image, as in sumi-e, suiboku-ga uses multiple strokes and a longer duration of time to complete the work.

In this painting, the rain clouds on the upper part of the painting were created by using a *tarashi komi* technique with light ink and water. In the tarashi komi technique, apply light ink and then immediately, using a separate brush which is loaded only with water, add a drop of water to the surface so that ink is pushed by the water. When dry the outlines appear like natural cloud formations. The tarashi komi technique is very useful for creating certain effects.

This work is unusual in that it does not use the standard and rhythmical sumi-e brush strokes rendered with strength; the total atmosphere is one of a sense of tranquility in misty haziness.

The final touch is the swift movement in the outline of the waves: with dark ink, a calligraphy-like line imbues the painting with unexpected vitality and accent.

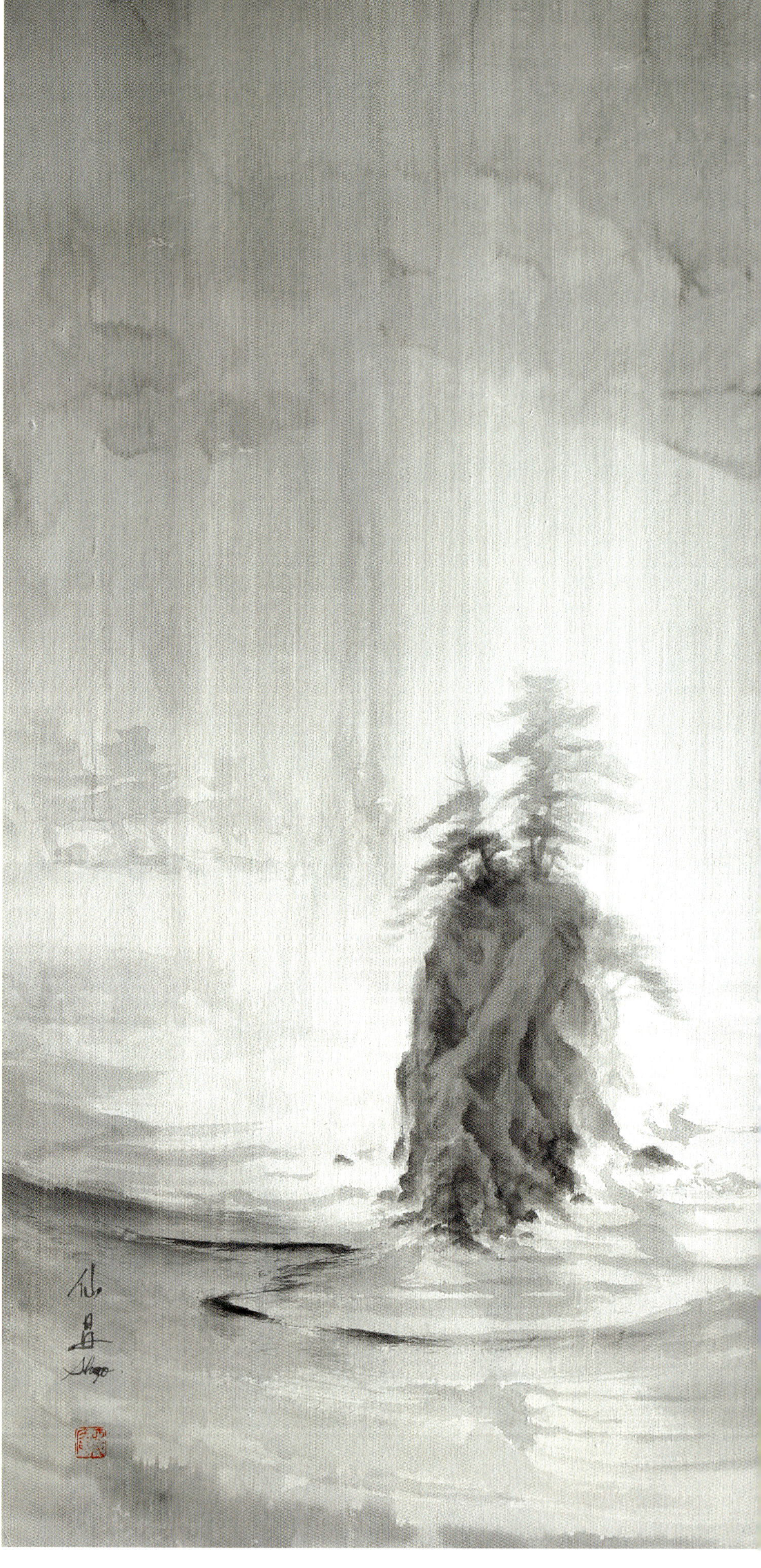

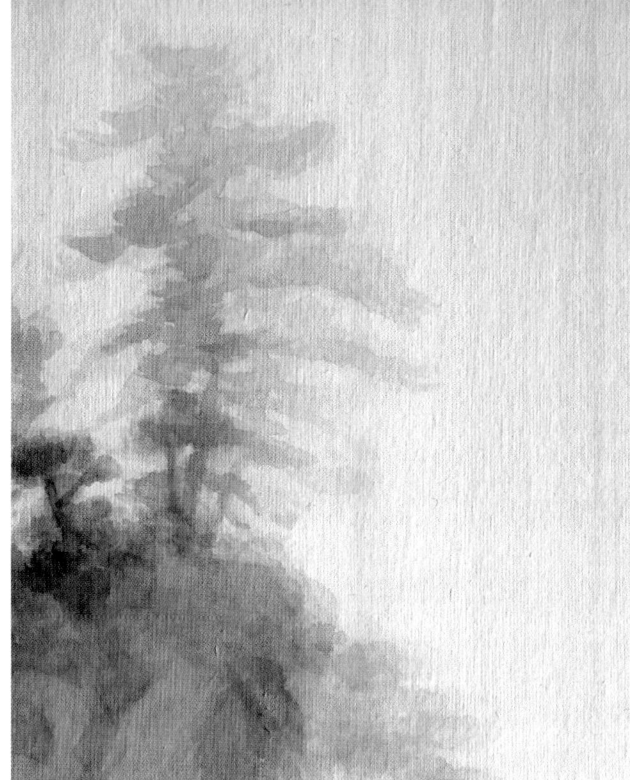

Rain clouds were painted with a *renpitsu* brush (see Chapter 2) loaded with light ink. The brush should be in contact with the paper at a 45-degree angle. It is moved left to right to paint the cloud formation. Immediately, with a separate brush loaded with water, add drops of water in the center of the cloud formations. Do not move the paper. In the drying process, the darker ink is pushed out to form the cloud patterns. Then the up-and-down of the misty rain is applied with a renpitsu, because the bristles are flat, and multiple fine lines can be created. A painting like this one requires the use of much water and light ink. Consequently, if the paper is not stabilized it will become uneven and wavy when dry. So I usually mount the paper onto a board first. Use acid free or handmade paper, and glue two or three layers on birch plywood which has been given a water-resistant finish. Foamcore can be used instead of plywood.

When painting misty or light rain it is important to hold the brush completely perpendicular to the paper, with bristles spread apart. A minute amount of light ink should be on the brush as it moves from the top to bottom. With each stroke, wait until the stroke lines are completely dry before applying the next stroke. Otherwise individual lines will merge and the painting will become flat. A hair dryer will help to speed up the process. Careful attention should be given to the tone of ink for each stroke and artistic judgment should be exercised for the number of strokes to apply to create depth in the rainfall. To suggest that sunlight will soon break through the clouds from behind the rock, use light gray ink to create dots to outline the trees and rock. Gradually intensify the tone of ink to a darker gray to create the texture of the rocks. When using absorbent paper, once ink is applied it is difficult to make readjustments; therefore, increase to darker ink tones very carefully.

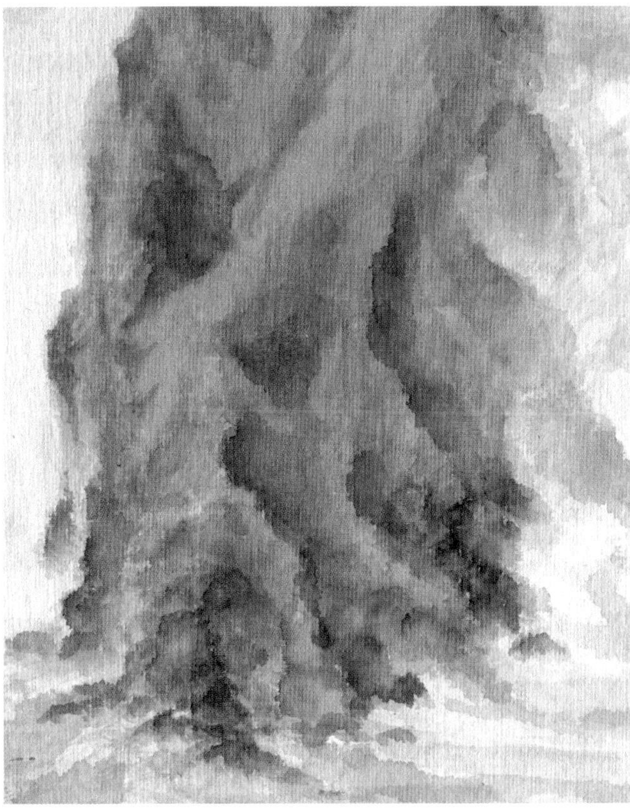

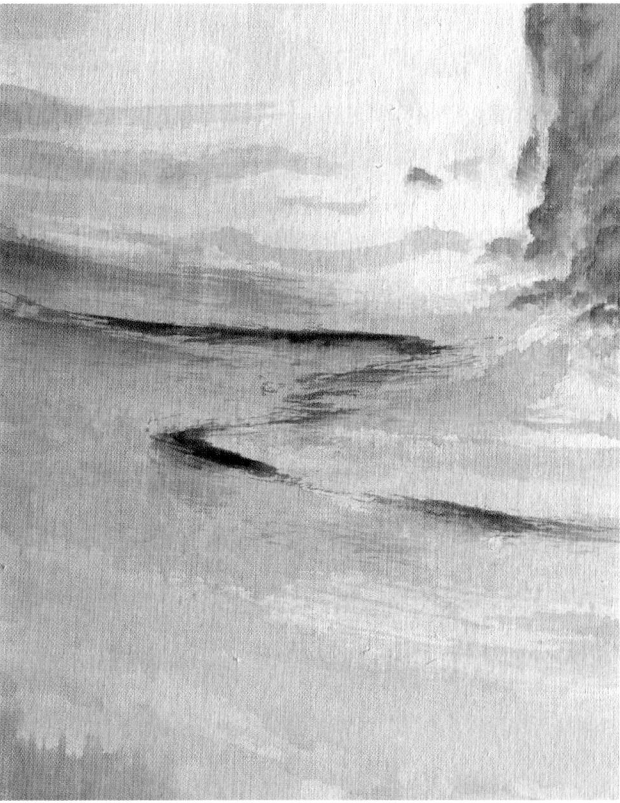

This close-up view of the rock shows in detail how a sense of texture for the rock is created. Similar to a digital image's pixels, dot-like movements are used. This way of using dots in various tones of ink to create the "three-dimensionality" of the rock is not a traditional technique; the standard style uses outlines. It will take time to complete this work. Throughout, remember to remoisten your work so that dark tone of the ink remains accurate.

The final touch is the outlining of the water in swift lines like a piece of calligraphy in "grass writing" style. The following is my "tip" to you: When mounting the paper onto the board, I applied the glue using the glue brush in an up-and-down motion that created undetectable ridges, which became functional after the paper was dry. This preparation created a strong directional sense to the strokes.

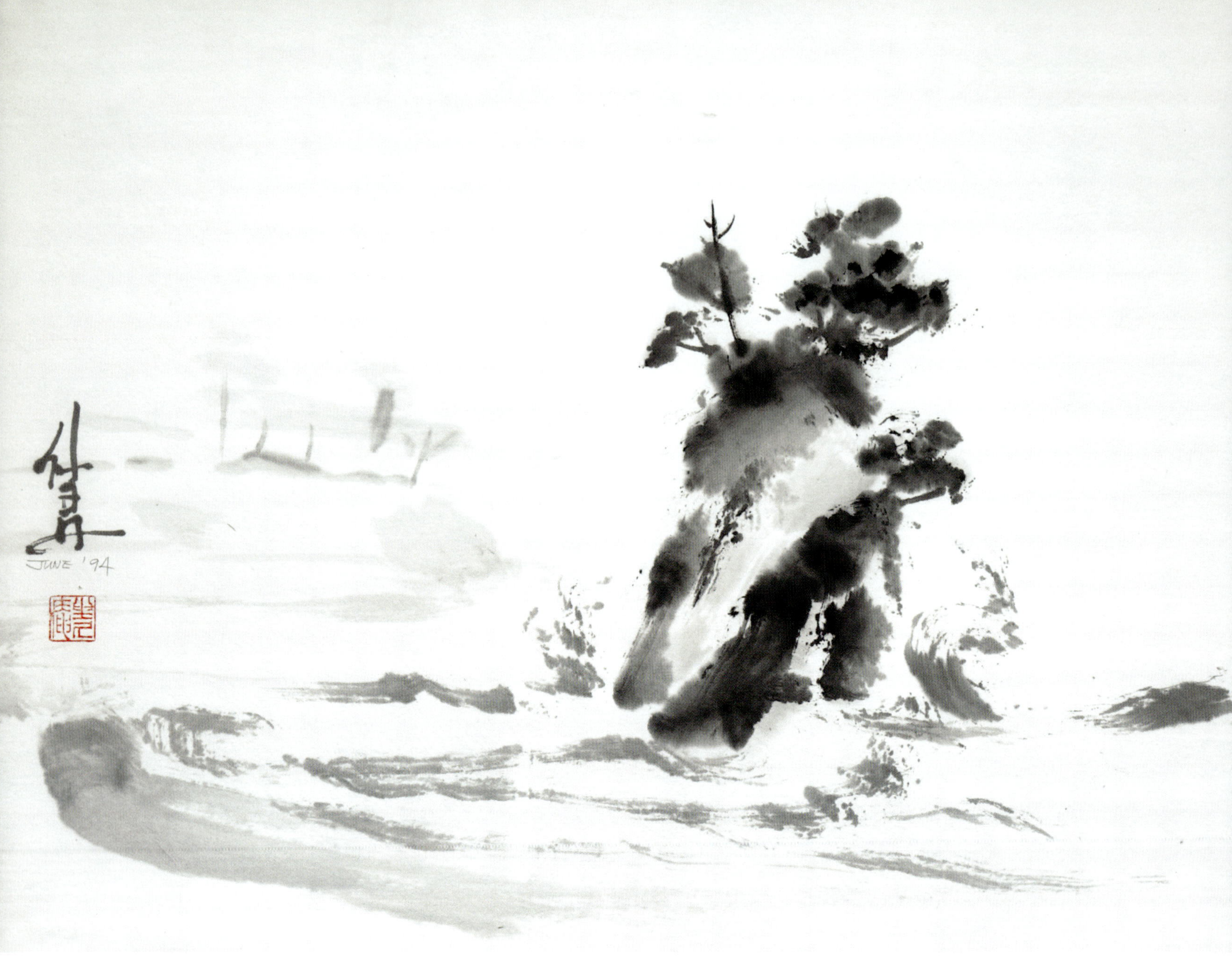

5. Islet with a Pine Tree

Size: H = 12.25"/31.5cm x W = 17"/43cm
Paper: Unsized
Sumi Ink: Blue tone
Category: Sumi-e

After the previous suiboku-ga painting, *Murmuring Surf*, had been completed, in my mind the details of the scene were still very vivid. This remembered image was transferred to a work in sumi-e with simplified and minimal brush strokes. In this painting, the brush is used in quite an active way in comparison to the previous painting. The waves, which were totally tranquil in the previous painting, are lively here. These two paintings are good examples for comparing the suiboku-ga category and the sumi-e category. Both use the same materials, yet the techniques separate the two into totally different categories of painting.

This work took about five minutes or less to paint and the previous required a few weeks of dedicated effort to complete. Once the image was deeply ingrained in my system, I did not have to rely on sample sketches or photos; so this was a direct expression from my creative spirit, without the need to think about how best to control the brush and ink.

The treasure of sumi-e artists is that after many decades of constantly pursuing and practicing the painting methods, the nature of a theme or object, the technique, the kinds of brush strokes to use, all these elements are accumulated and stored in the mind. Whether it is for flowers, trees, landscapes, or water surfaces ranging from rivers to oceans, the painting vocabulary is installed within one's memory system.

Often I am asked during sumi-e demonstrations how I can paint so swiftly without having a visual image to refer to, such as a photograph or sketch. I am asked, "Is it so easy to paint something in sumi-e?" My answer is that it has taken over fifty years to develop a memory system which carries the essential technical information about a subject, a system that can now be accessed to bring that subject to life on paper with black ink. From years of experience, the sumi-e artist learns that once you draw a line, it cannot be readjusted or eliminated. And after years of experience and practice in creating certain subjects, the image that you have installed in your memory system can be brought to life in sumi-e again almost instantly.

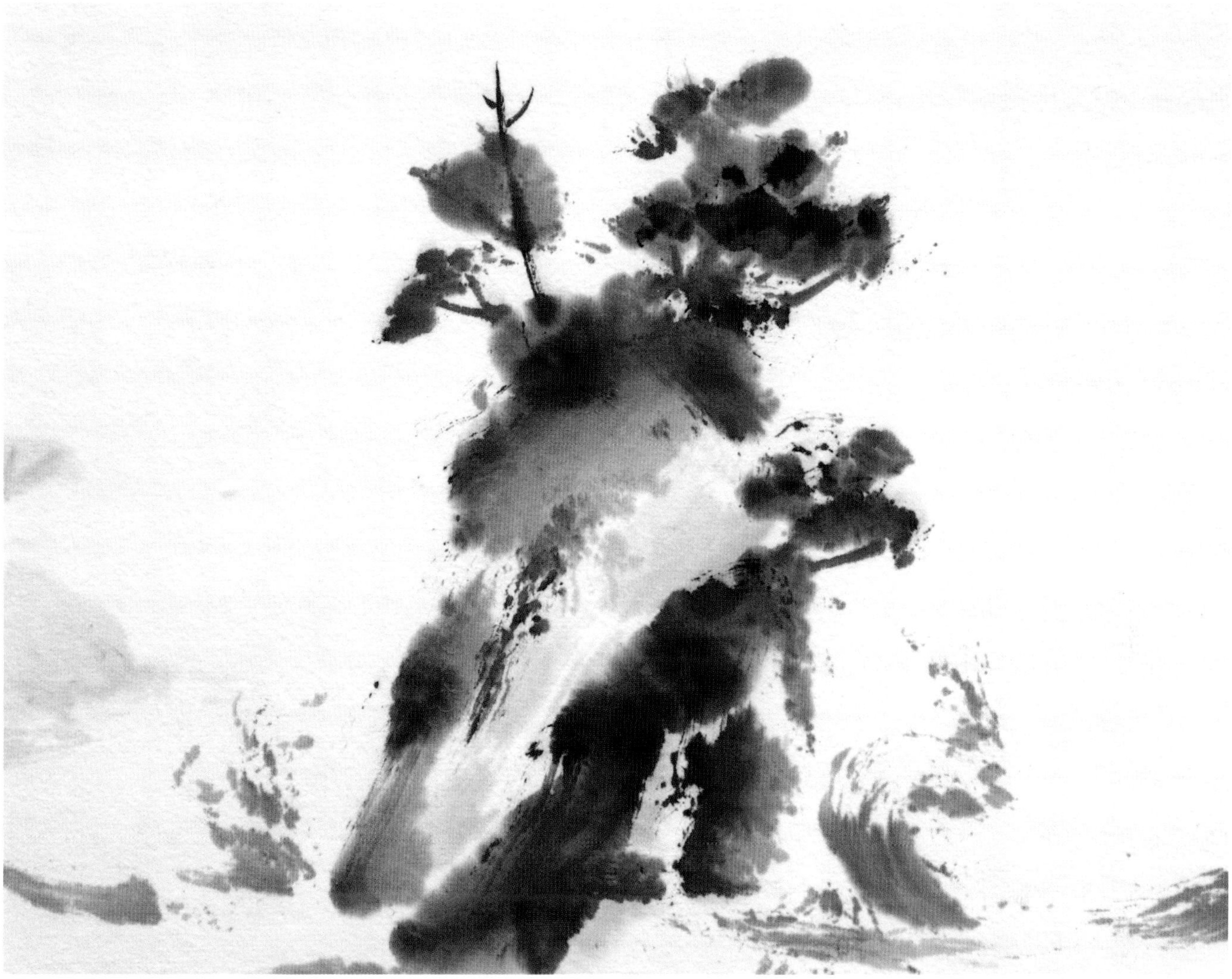

The brush is prepared with the basic three tones of ink: dark ink on the tip, medium ink at mid-point, light ink at base. Then use the brush sideways to complete the background rock and the the foreground rock outline. Next, almost as if you are dropping the ink, add pine needles. Then remove moisture from the brush and with the tip, apply dark ink to suggest the trunk and branches.

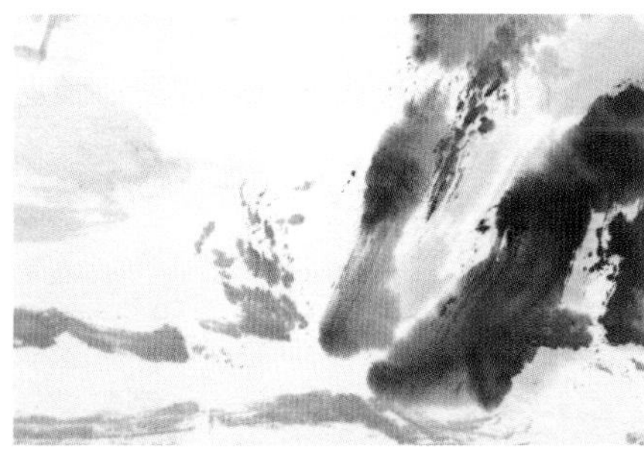

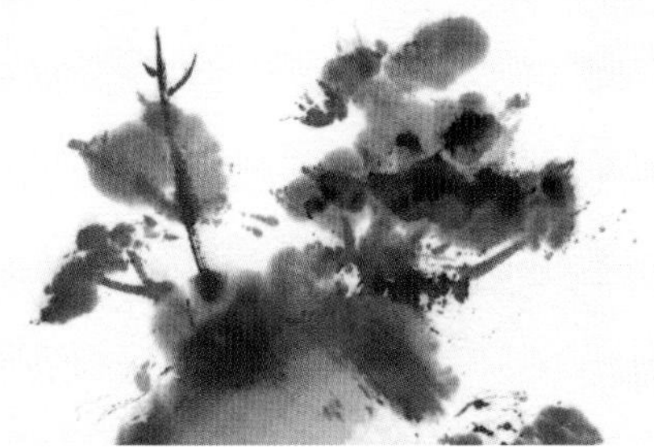

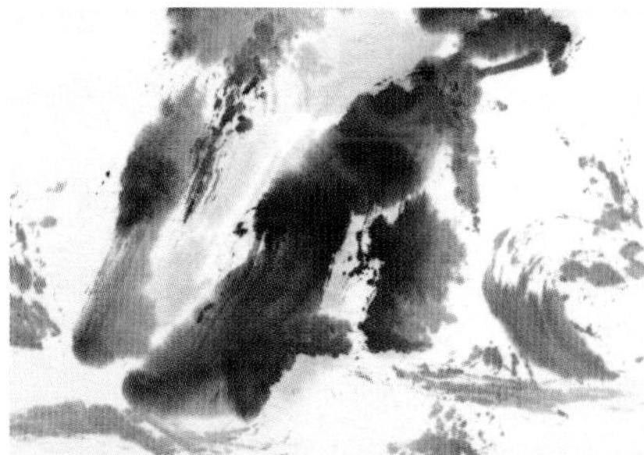

The foreground rock outline is darker and the background rock is lighter, which helps to create a three dimensional sense. After the painted surface has become semi-dry, separate the bristles of a dry brush and use it to add the feel of texture in the rocks with dark ink. If the paper is still too wet from the previous strokes, the ink will spread and the textured effect will be lost.

To create a sense of color in the pine needles, after you have applied groups of dark ink, immediately apply lighter ink to blend the groupings. This adds depth and coloration. To the lower part of the tree and on the rock surface, apply light ink to suggest the growth of vegetation.

To add a sense that light is breaking through, the sky is left clear; use semi-dark ink with brush held upright to form the waves. Then using only the brush tip add a few dots where necessary to enhance the sense of splashing waves. Finally, with lighter ink, paint foreground waves and seashore, and with light ink paint the background headland.

6. Navarro River in Moonlight

Size: H = 36"/91cm x W = 20"/56.5cm
Paper: Sized paper, pre-mounted on a board
Sumi Ink: Blue tone
Category: Suiboku-ga

Northern California, well known for its fog and mistiness, provides scenes which are optimal for suiboku-ga. This scene, the estuary of a river flowing into the Pacific Ocean, is densely forested with redwoods and displays very little contrast during the day, so it is not an especially inspiring scene for a painting. But after a rainy day, with mist and fog drifting through the forest and surface of the water, suddenly it transforms into an ideal subject for a monochrome painting.

One evening, while driving through the forest, I saw the breathtaking beauty of the mist along the river under a full moon. Here was the challenge that has been faced by sumi-e artists throughout the centuries: how to use black ink to express the moonlight in mist—in all of its whiteness and softness.

To paint this subject matter on highly absorbent paper is an impossibility. I used sized paper stretched on a board, because this type of painting requires the use of water, applied time and time again, so stability is needed.

Since very light ink will be used, it is best to make an actual-size sketch on a separate piece of paper (see page 38 for more information about sketching with charcoal), then transfer it to the mounted sized paper. Begin with the use of very light gray ink and the smallest brush you have. The individual heights of the trees were marked with dots.

In Japanese aesthetics, a full moon is beautiful to see but in its perfection is not especially poetic. Adding a few drifting clouds across its face makes it more bucolically pleasing and gives it what is commonly called imperfect beauty.

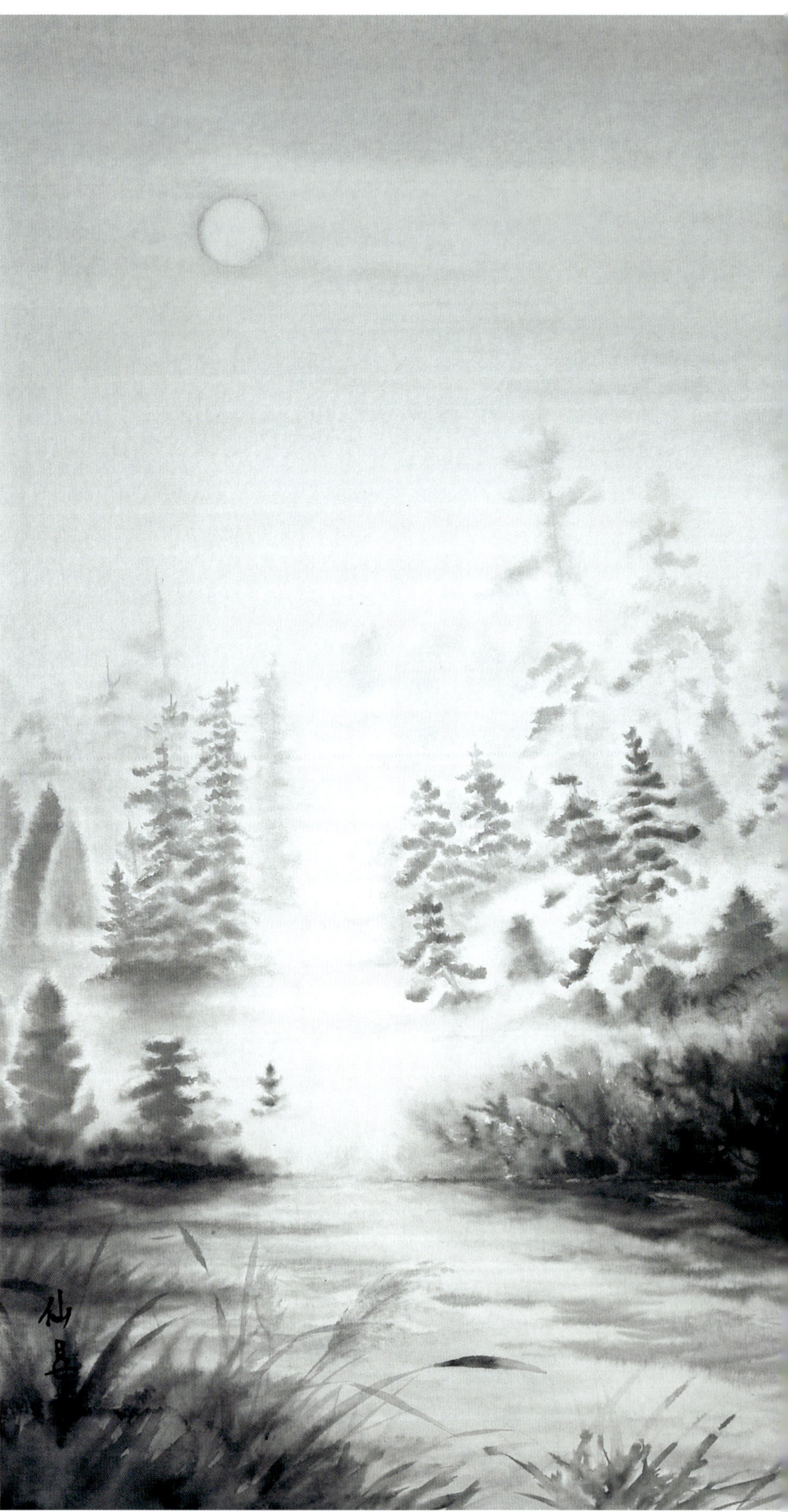

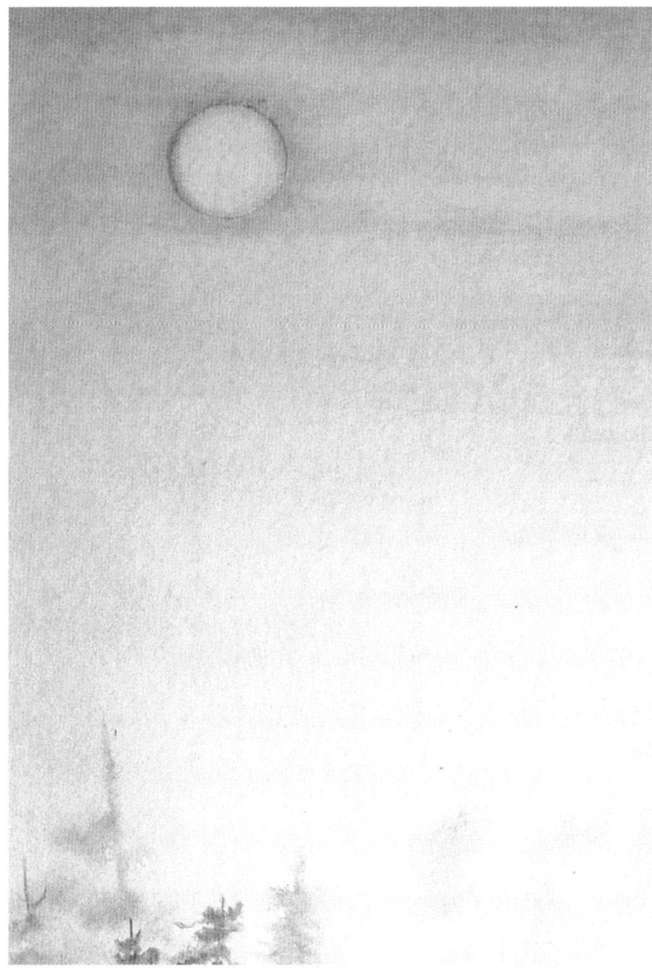

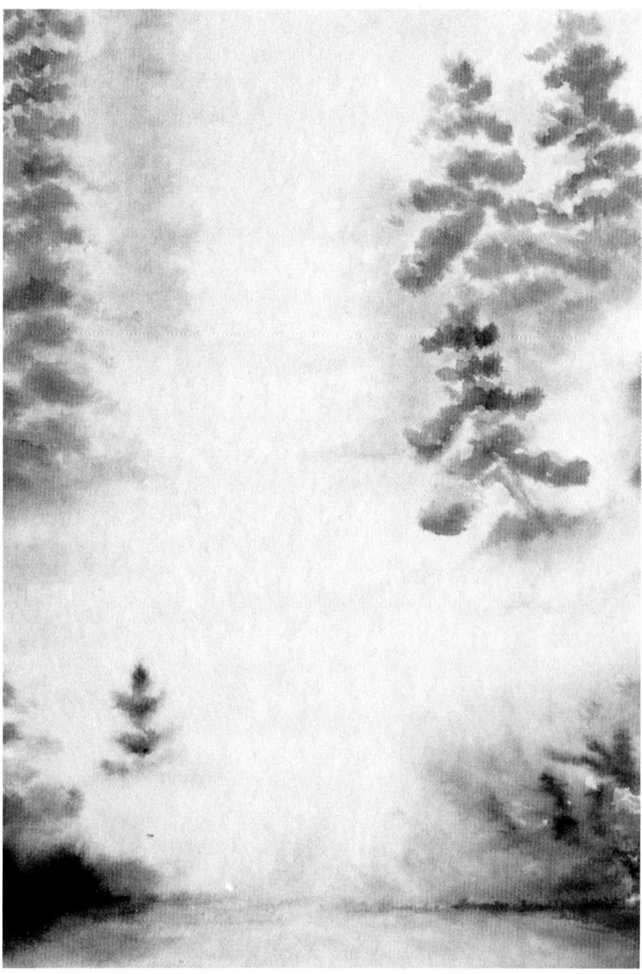

A moon shape was cut out of water-resistant paper and placed at the precise position where I wanted the moon; then with the lightest gray ink I outlined the circle. Gradually the width of the outline was increased, and with another brush loaded with water I blended the outline's edge into the sky. At the same time the excess light gray ink is extended horizontally to the left and right to create the stratified layers of clouds. During this process it is important to add moisture to the paper, so that the light gray horizontal strokes will not also show harsh and unwanted lines.

In painting the trees, begin with the lightest tones of ink and gradually add darker ink toward the center of the tree. Leave open the spaces where the trees overlap. The effect of the moonlight upon the mist and fog must be well coordinated with the direction of the moonlight. You are dealing with 1) mist that is reflecting the moonlight onto the outlines of the trees in the moonlight; and 2) the glistening effect of the mist through the trees and on the river. Close to the ground, the effect of the heavy rising mist is created.

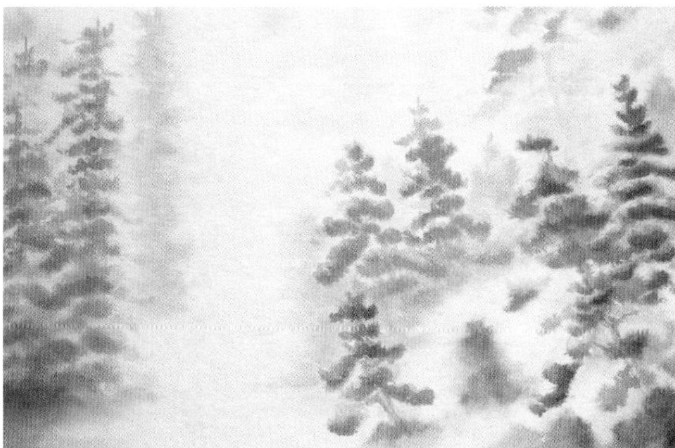

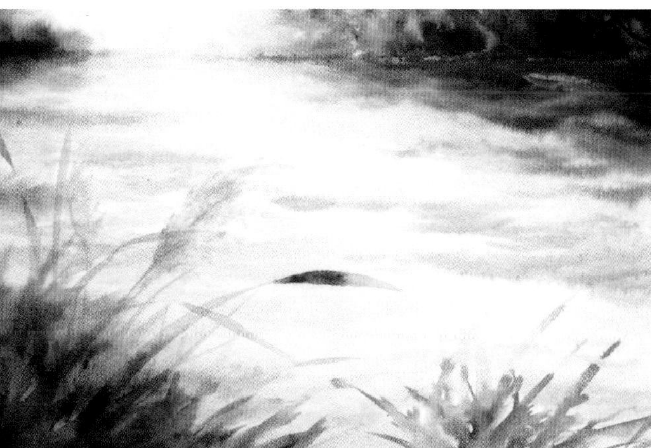

When painting a tree, regardless of the circumstances, pay attention to the movement of the branches and the direction and height of the tree relative to the other trees. Most importantly, the artist must be aware of the rhythm the tree branches create. In this type of painting, it is best to prepare at least two extra brushes: one for water, and the other to be kept reasonably dry to soak up excess water. This allows you to have better control over the amount of ink used in the painting.

The foreground of this painting focuses on the surface of the running river. While it may be a misty night, there are still reflections of moonlight on the water. The surface has, though, a different appearance due to the soft mist. So the activeness of the running water is expressed by the ripples, but is much softer than a normal daytime view. At the end, foreground grasses were added. I felt the need for a "punctuation" somewhere in the center so the twisted blade of grass was used to create an additional sense of depth.

7. Pine Breeze in the Moonlight

Size: H = 16.5"/41.5cm x W = 17"/43cm
Paper: Sized
Sumi Ink: Standard
Category: Sumi-e

Quite opposite from *Navarro River in the Moonlight*, which was painted using the concepts of suiboku-ga, this work is in the minimized and simplified techniques of sumi-e. They were employed here to capture another kind of scene of pine trees and wave action under bright moonlight.

The previous painting reflects a central pattern in composition. This composition, though, uses a right-side pattern. The diagram below shows how triangular composition works.

The use of triangular composition greatly influenced the theory of composition in Japanese and Chinese art (not only for painting, but also for other arts like flower arrangement). It was originally developed in the east in religious art; the paintings focused on religious figures and consisted of three separate images which, when placed together, related to each other to compose a triptych. The central pattern was of some religious figure—clearly the dominant figure—accompanied at its sides by two attendant figures.

This traditional form for a triptych in composition was eventually secularized, and can also be applied to the composition for a single painting. Notice how *Pine Breeze in the Moonlight*, following the right-side pattern, has a wide active empty space to its left. That active empty space would serve to give emphasis to a central painting, if three works were displayed together.

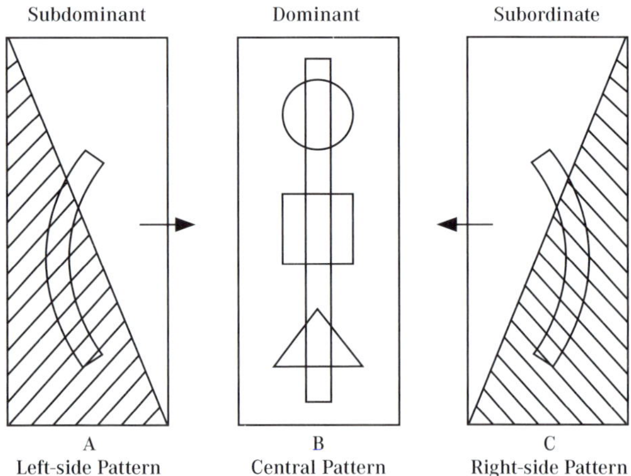

The triangular composition scheme can be used for a single work of art, or for a triptych. When painting using either the left- or right-side pattern, ensure that the composition incorporates the space to transform it into an active empty space, which is an essential aspect of sumi-e.

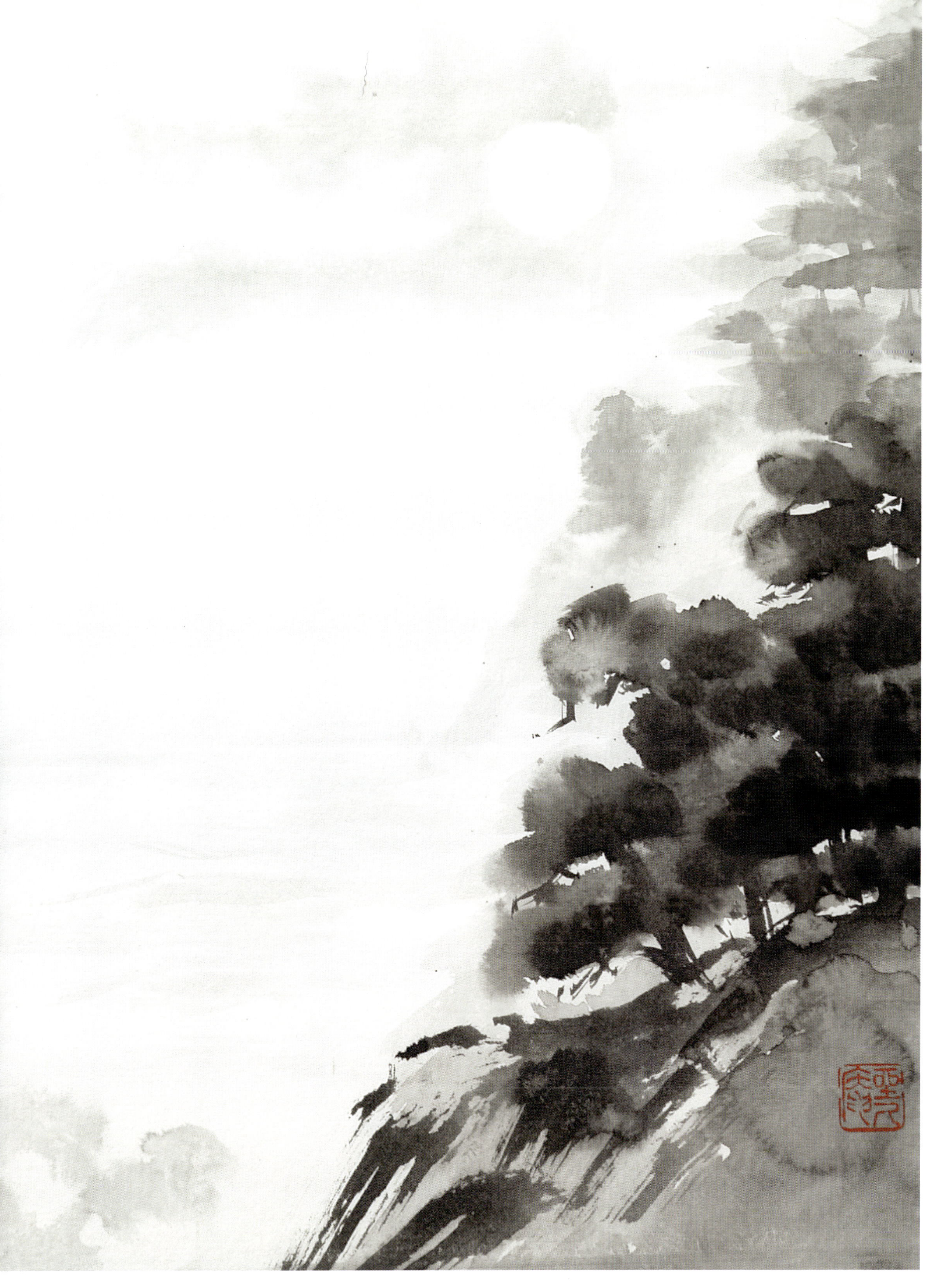

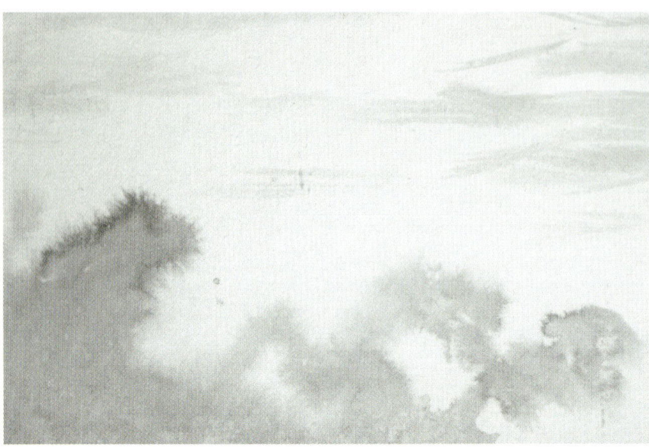

After the outline of the moon has been created with light ink, quickly add moisture around the moon and across the space of the sky. Then apply light ink to create light clouds around the moon, emphasizing its whiteness. While the light gray ink for the clouds is still wet, take a dry brush (bristles open and spread out) and guide the light gray to the desired formation of the clouds. It is important to do this while the surface is still wet, thus eliminating definite brush marks from the clouds.

Splashing waves against the rocks are handled with the same treatment as the clouds. First pre-moisten the surface of the paper with water, then use light ink on the brush to create the activeness of the waves. In this case, you need to show the formation of the waves, so do not use the additional dry brush technique to disperse that brushwork; the lines are necessary to show wave action. Although light ink has been used, in the process of drying, the ink particles will begin to move to the outer edges of the strokes to create the natural outline of crashing waves.

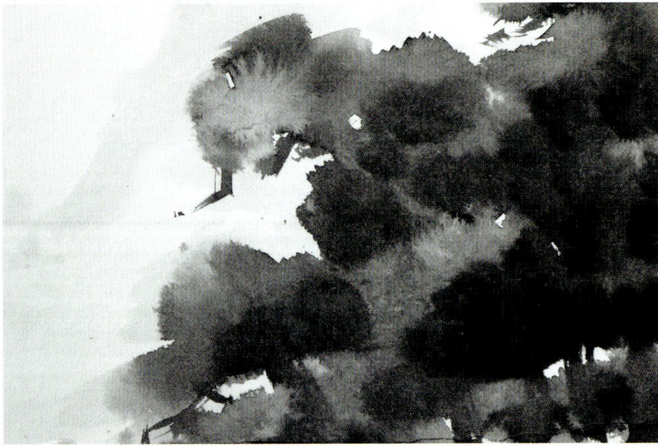

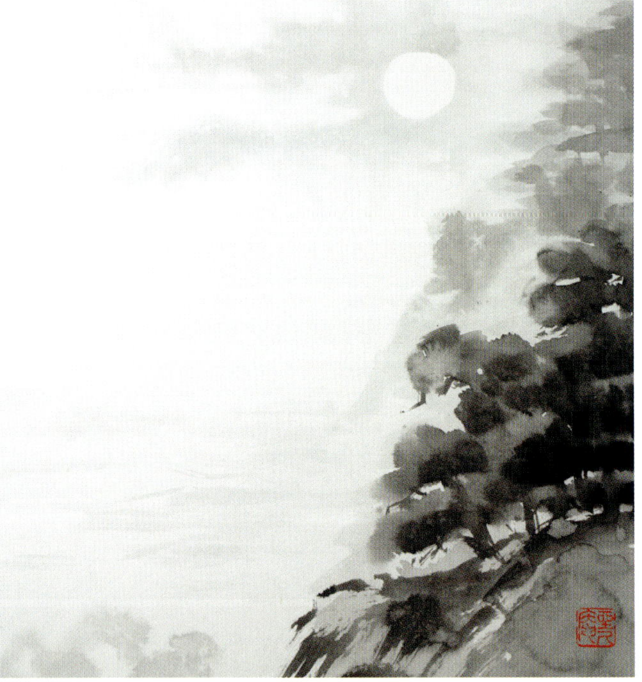

When painting pine needles, first apply light ink and then immediately use darker ink to create shadow effects in the moonlight. It is important to maintain moisture on the surface of the paper so that the two tones of the ink will blend naturally. In this painting, I dropped clear water on one of the top branches to give the effect of glistening pine needles, a common technique called tarashi komi.

After the paper has dried, use darker ink to suggest tree trunks and branches. Dark ink is also used to outline the cliff reflected in the moonlight. For this, the use of forceful strokes with a dry brush is important to keep this painting from becoming mundane. This one section of activity, in dark ink, gives energy to the open space and creates a yin-yang contrast.

Right: This work, *Moon and Clouds*, was painted on white torinoko paper to assist in enhancing the sense of moonlight. The white clouds are the dominating subject, the moon is subdominant, and the trees and surface of Lake Michigan are subordinate. Near the top of the clouds, notice the dark irregular outline; this is the honored tarashi komi effect, but here it should have been avoided. In a painting of clouds in thunder and lightning, perhaps drama would be appropriate, but in this tranquil painting under moonlight, the softness of the floating clouds should ideally not have definite outlines.

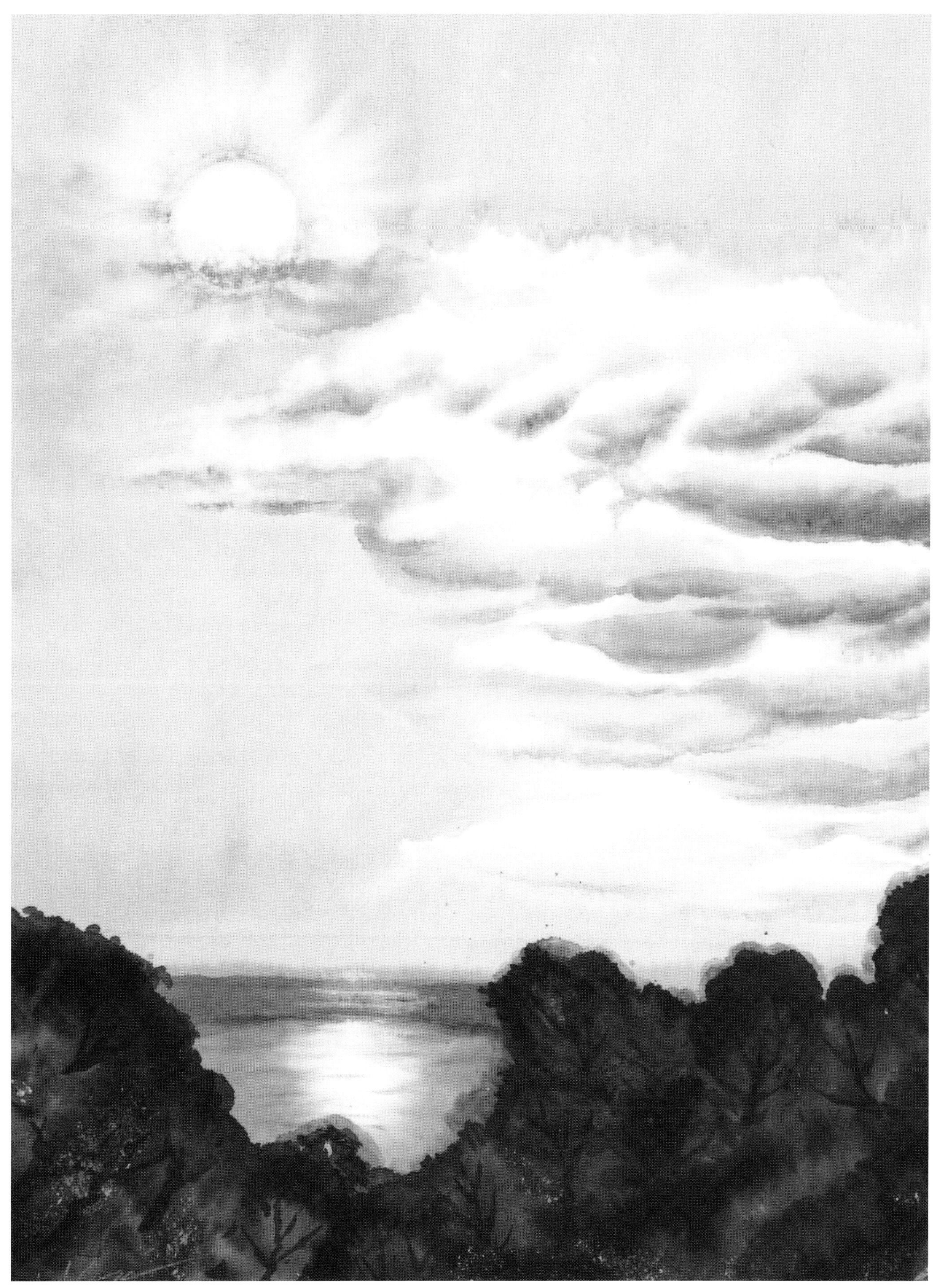

8. Dragon Pine

Size: H = 24"/61cm x W = 40"/102cm
Paper: Unsized
Sumi Ink: Blue tone and standard
Category: Suiboku-ga

Forces of nature over the centuries have carved and created
rocks and trees into shapes and forms beyond imagination.
This is the drama of nature, the theme which has inspired
and provided the base for my paintings.

There is a small cove in Northern California that shelters
one lone rock protruding from the base of the rugged shore-
line and on the top is a gnarled and twisted pine tree with
roots lodged in the crevices of the rock. It appears to have
been there for centuries. While this cove is somewhat sheltered, the storms of the Pacific can produce tremendous
forces at times, hence the stunning double twist or corkscrew
in the trunk of the tree. Yet the tree roots clung on with tenacity, and even today the pine's branches display the vitality of
life by continuing to produce new growth in its needles.

In my imagination the tree resembled a dragon about to
take flight. The side facing the Pacific shows only tree roots
clinging onto the rocks, but the sheltered side facing the cliffs
shows branches verdant with pine needles. Artistic license
was taken and I dramatized the position of the base of the
tree on the upright rock.

I used black ink with a brown tone for the rocks and black
ink with a blue tone for the tree. Blue tone ink was also used
for the distant rocks. In composition, the rock and tree are
dominant, the mid-ground rocks are subdominant and the distant rocks are the subordinate subjects. Like the previous
painting *Pine Breeze in the Moonlight,* this painting also follows a right-side pattern.

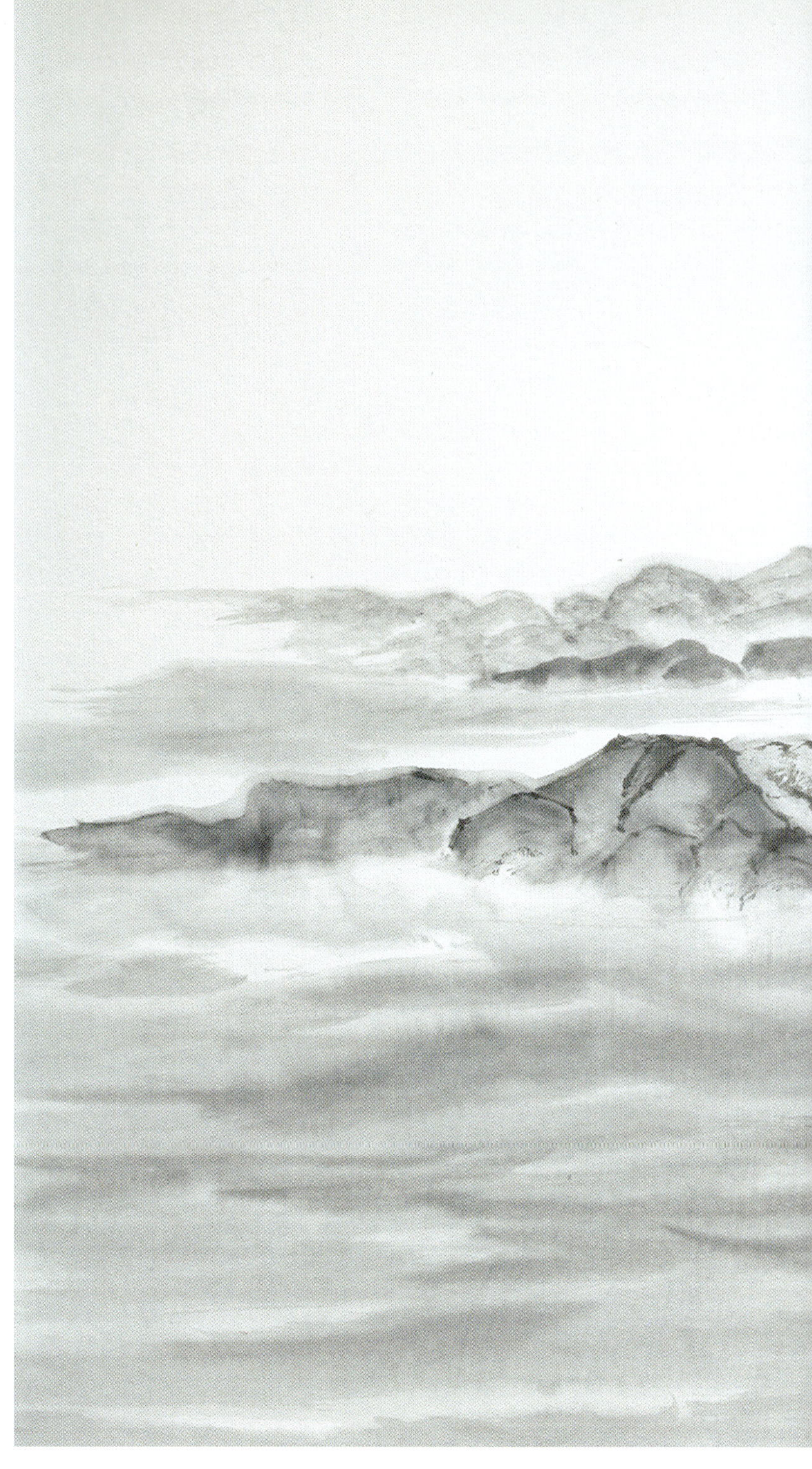

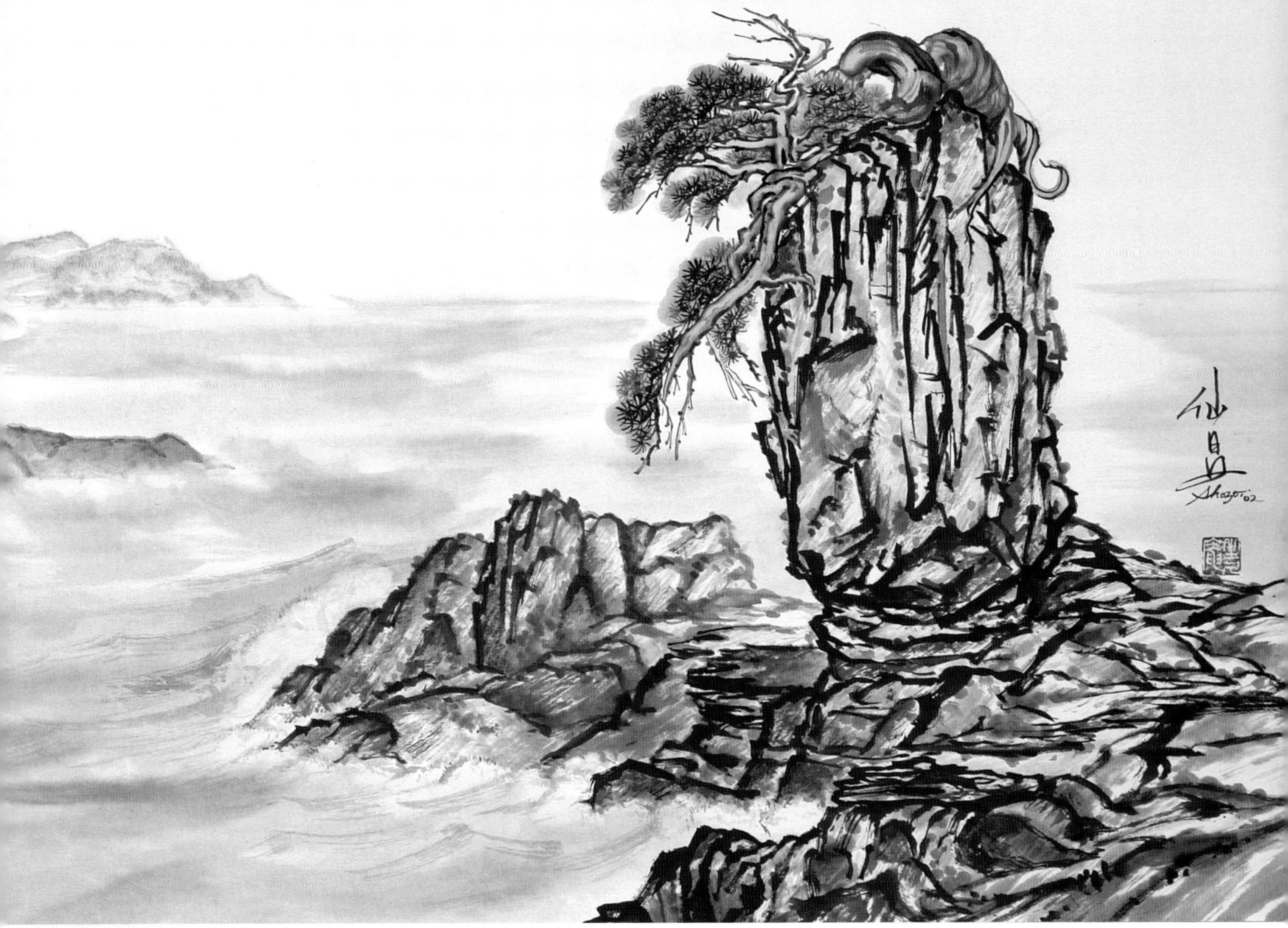

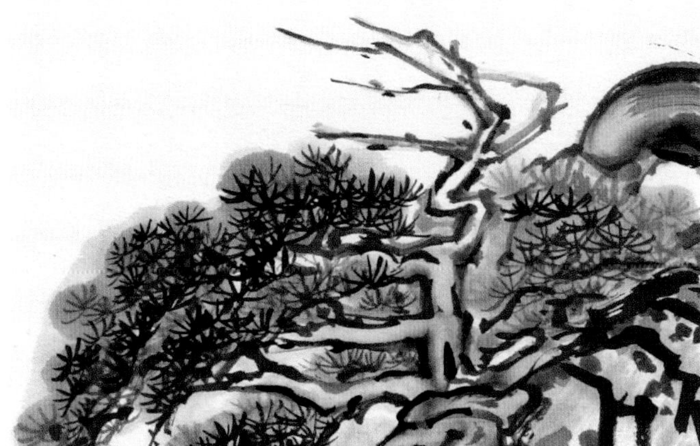

One dead branch sticks up from the pine tree to dramatize and exaggerate the years of hardship in survival. The pine tree and needles were painted in the traditional method (see Chapter 5), with the needles painted one by one. Then lighter ink was applied to give the sense of density.

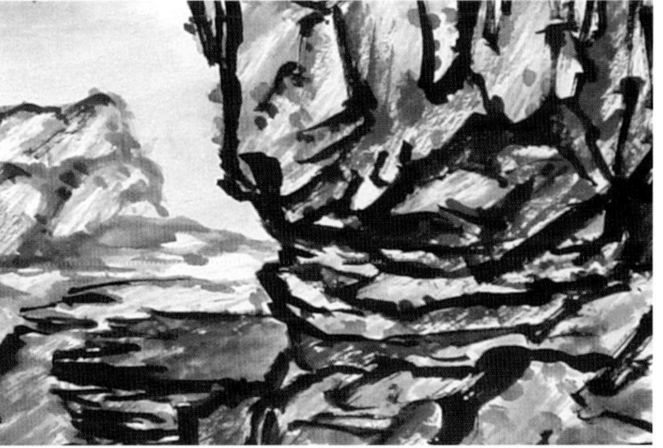

To roughen the surfaces of the rocks, a drier brush with brown tone ink was used to create the multiple fine lines which follow the main line brush movements to give texture.

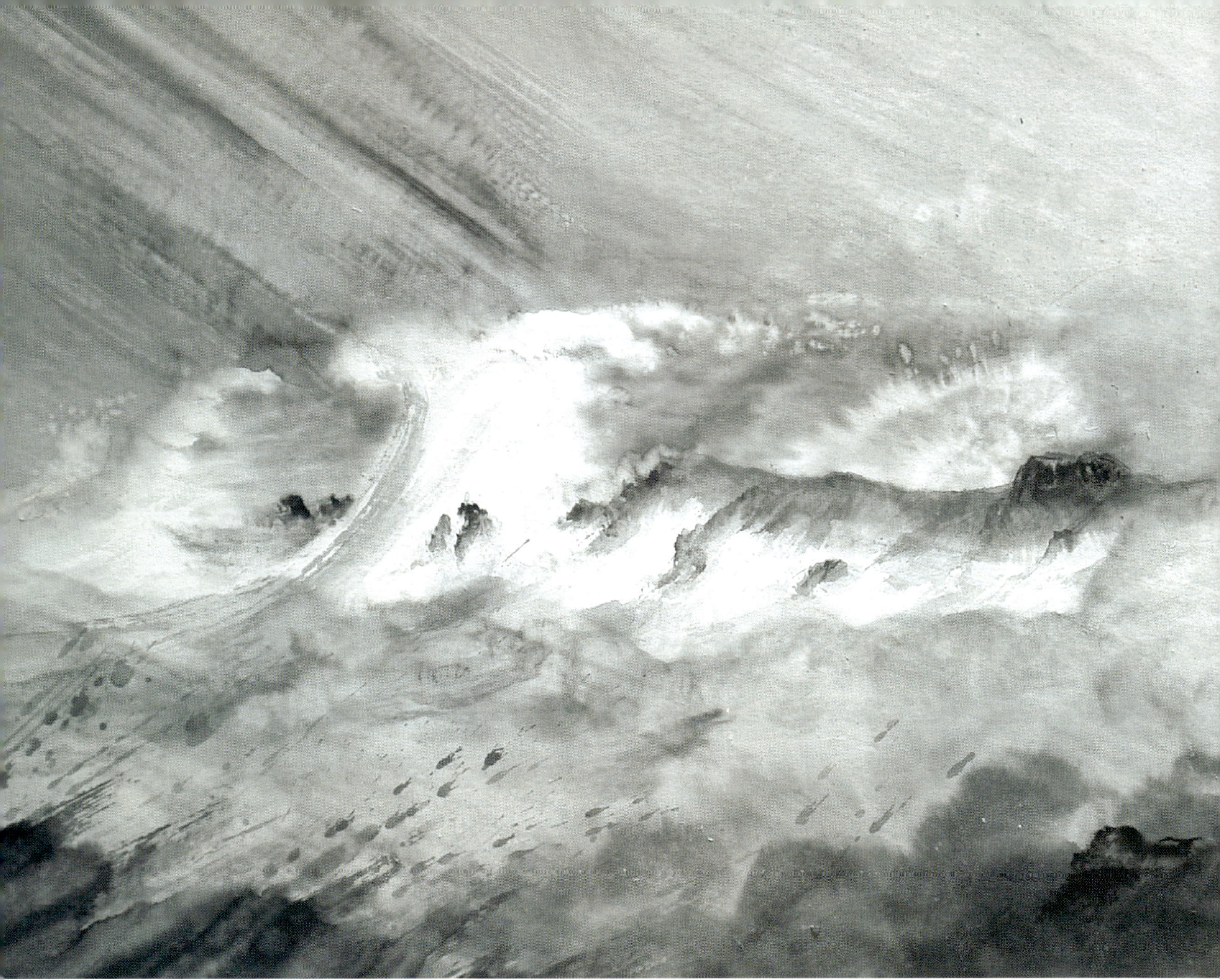

9. Fury of the Pacific

Size: H = 19"/48cm x W = 50"/127cm
Paper: Sized; pre-mounted on a board
Sumi Ink: Blue tone and standard, and silver pigment
Category: Suiboku-ga

The creative process for artists comes through many different avenues. One common situation is that an artist has a certain image in mind and, according with that image, gradually accumulates sketches and then eventually uses this information to develop a composition for a painting. Step by step, while the artist uses carefully-judging eyes, the composition of the painting begins to grow.

The contrasting situation is that the artist's mind is so possessed with images and situations that, without prior preparation or sketches or compositions, he or she "dives" into the creative process. This work, *Fury of the Pacific,* fits the latter category. I was almost in a state of frenzy as I made this painting. In this work, the use of the brush as a tool in the traditional ways was minimal and I was completely in sync with this tree standing against the powerful wind, leaves straining, the occasional view of rocks seen when the water crashed against any object in the way.

It required enormous inner energy to create this painting of hurricane force winds. If a stranger had entered the studio while I was working, I would, no doubt, have appeared to be insane. This is a once in a lifetime creative experience.

During 1994 on the coast where I live, there was a great Pacific storm. Close to the beachfront, trees appeared to almost take flight as I attempted to sketch against the power of the wind. My endeavor in this painting was to portray the great forces of nature through the immediacy of sumi ink.

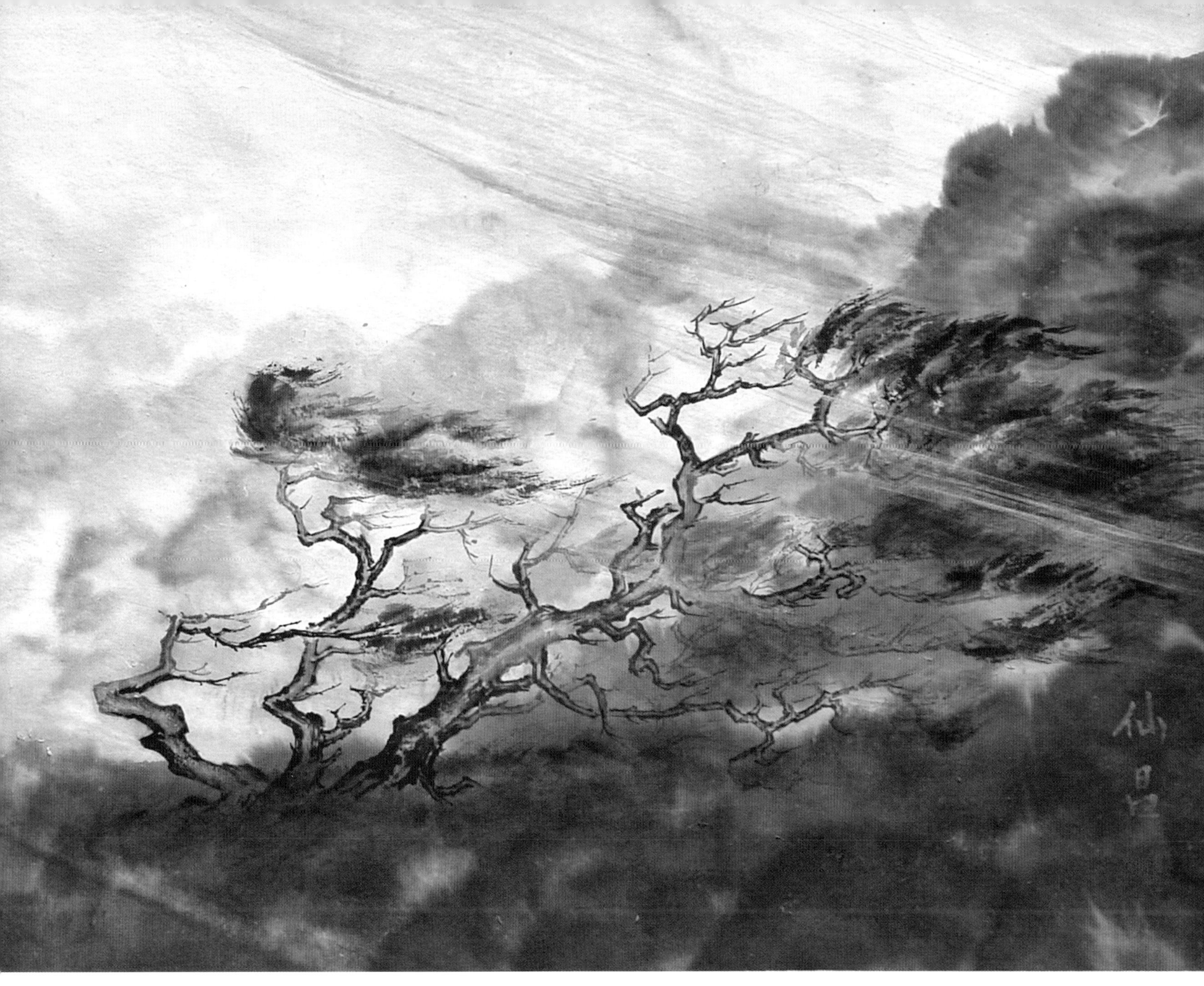

Powerful brush strokes were made directional to show the gale force of the wind and rain. Other parts of the painting, such as wave action, were mainly created using the tarashi komi technique in maximum effect.

After I had finished painting the left-hand side's wave patterns, I moved on to add the trees that were forcefully bent by the wind. Then the related headland "terra firma" and the rocks were completed. But when I stepped back and re-examined the painting, I became aware that the painting was divided into two parts: wave activity to the left and tree activity to the right. I had overlooked my basic principle in composition, that of dominant, subdominant and subordinate elements. A few days later, I decided to add the very obvious black rock in the center to bridge the left and right. Along with adding that black area, I enhanced and enlarged the leaves on the branches, which helps make them look as if they would be blown off.

These additions brought balance to the painting. Thus, the right-hand side's trees and ground are the dominant subject, the left-hand side's wave movement is subdominant and the rock in the center is subordinate.

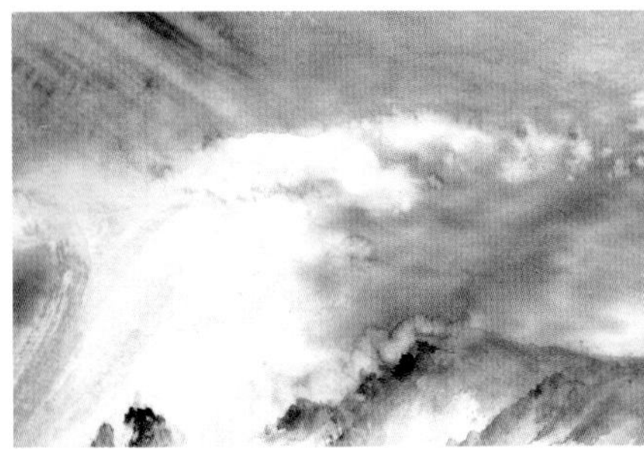

To confine and secure the outline of the crashing waves' whitecaps, first very light ink was used to dot the outline. Then, I prepared one brush with water and one with light ink. With these two brushes held in the same hand (like chopsticks), I tattooed the water and ink alternately onto the paper. Contact was first made using the ink brush, then a tap of the water brush immediately followed to spread and push out the ink to create whiteness. During this stage it is also important to guide the whiteness in the proper direction. The enlargement at right allows you to see the result. After the waves were basically completed, the necessary outlines were added to them.

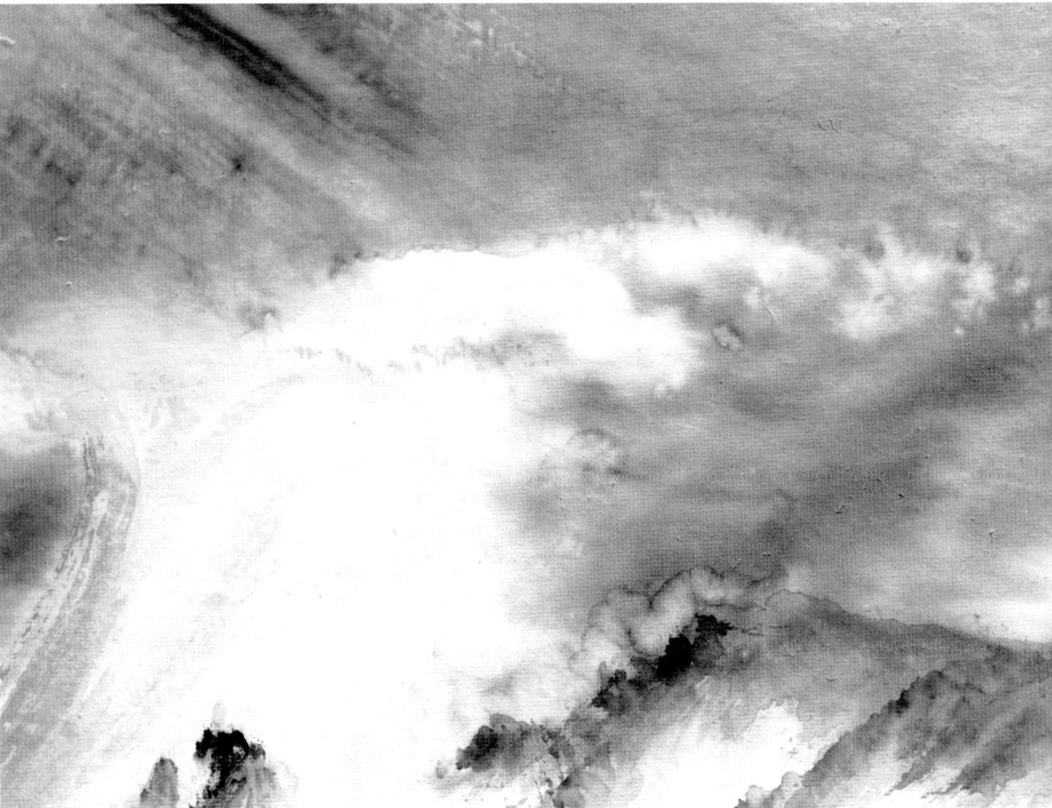

The result of the unorthodox brush use: water and light ink blended to express frenzied creative energy.

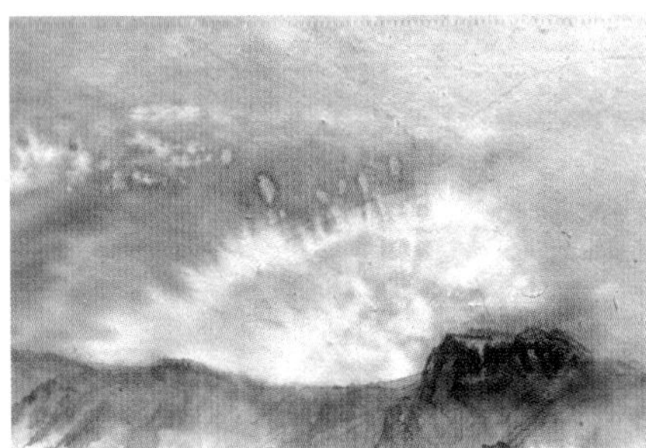

Splashing waves are almost impossible to paint with a brush. To create this effect, I loaded a large brush with water and another brush with light ink and they were used simultaneously for a splash technique (see page 55), in a manner almost as if the brushes were colliding with the surface of the paper. The force of spraying water pushed the light ink to the outer edges. I then immediately used a hair dryer with maximum force to stabilize the ink at those edges, before it seeped back into the white. Once the surface dries, touch-ups cannot be made. Therefore, during this splash technique you literally hold your breath and move with coordinated speed. You must pay attention to the moisture content on the paper. If necessary, before the surface of the paper completely dries, you may go back with light ink to enhance the effects desired, and then dry the section.

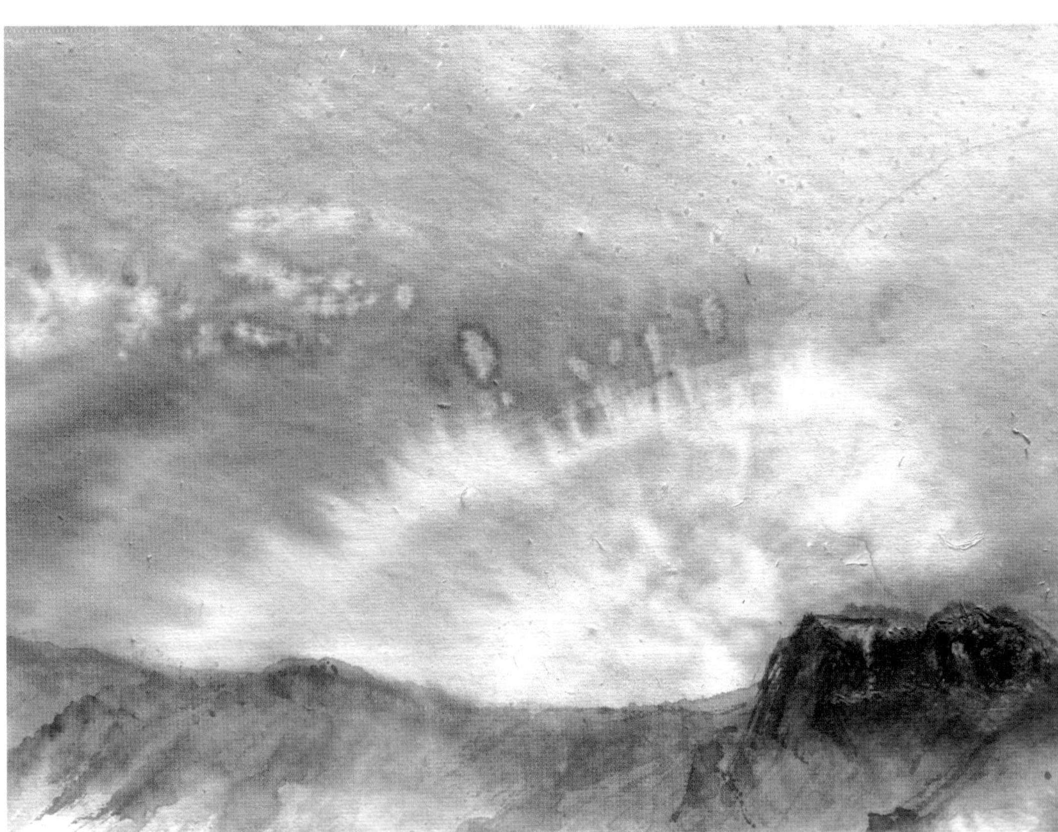

Here the result of the splash technique used for the waves can be seen in more detail.

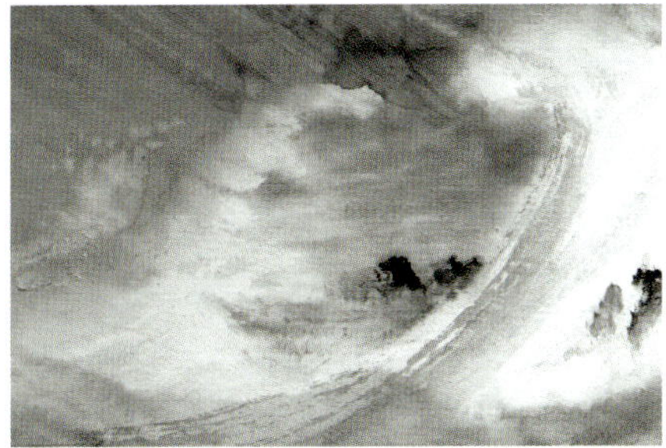

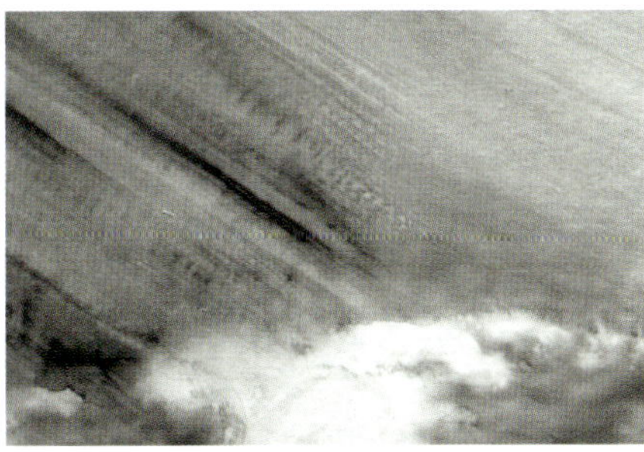

 After most of the painting's sections were completed, I used a brush to refine certain areas. Here, beginning at the center bottom of the wave, I moved my brush upward with a swift stroke to enhance the force of the wave. Above: The wild gale force winds created an unforgettable sound. To recreate it, I vibrated my brush as I executed the lines showing the rain and wind.

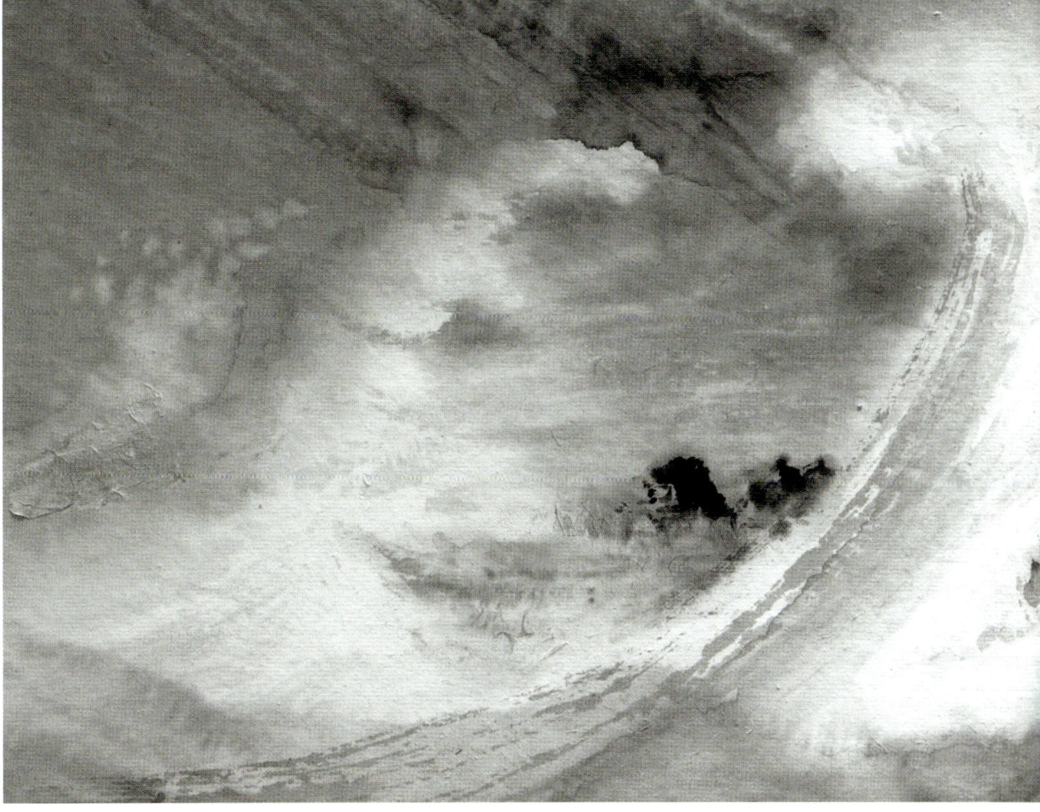

Here is a closer view of the wave stroke that was added to enhance the three-dimensionality.

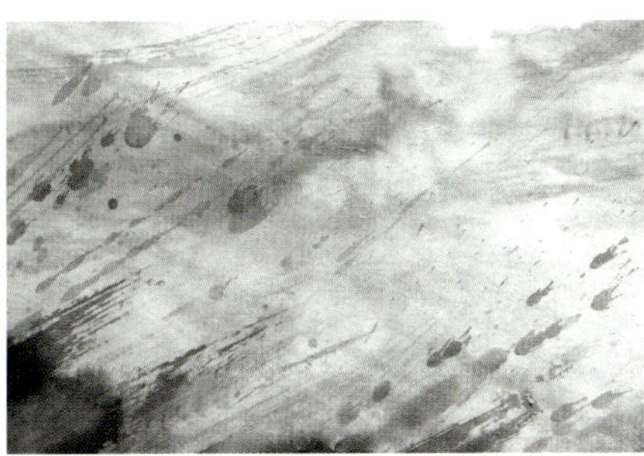

Splashing ink with a brush is a common technique with many variations (see Chapter 3). In this painting, to intensify the brush strokes' force, the splash technique was carried out with a mountain horse hair brush.

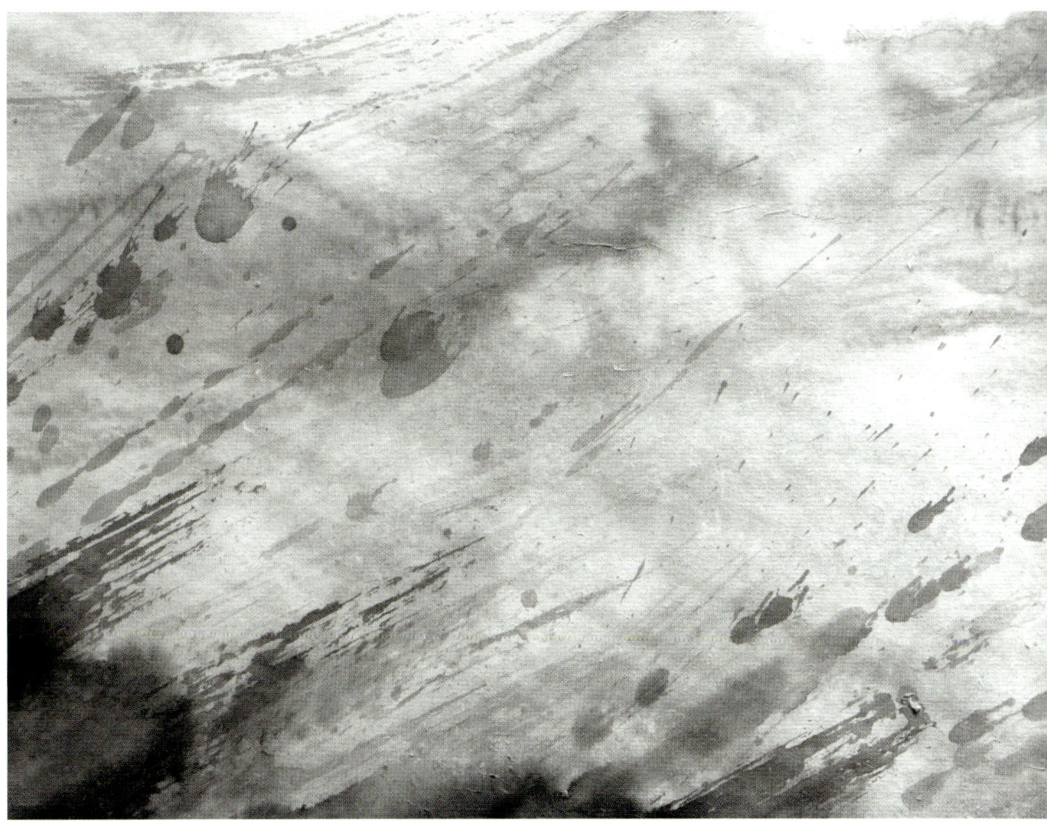

The splash technique adds energy to the painted strokes.

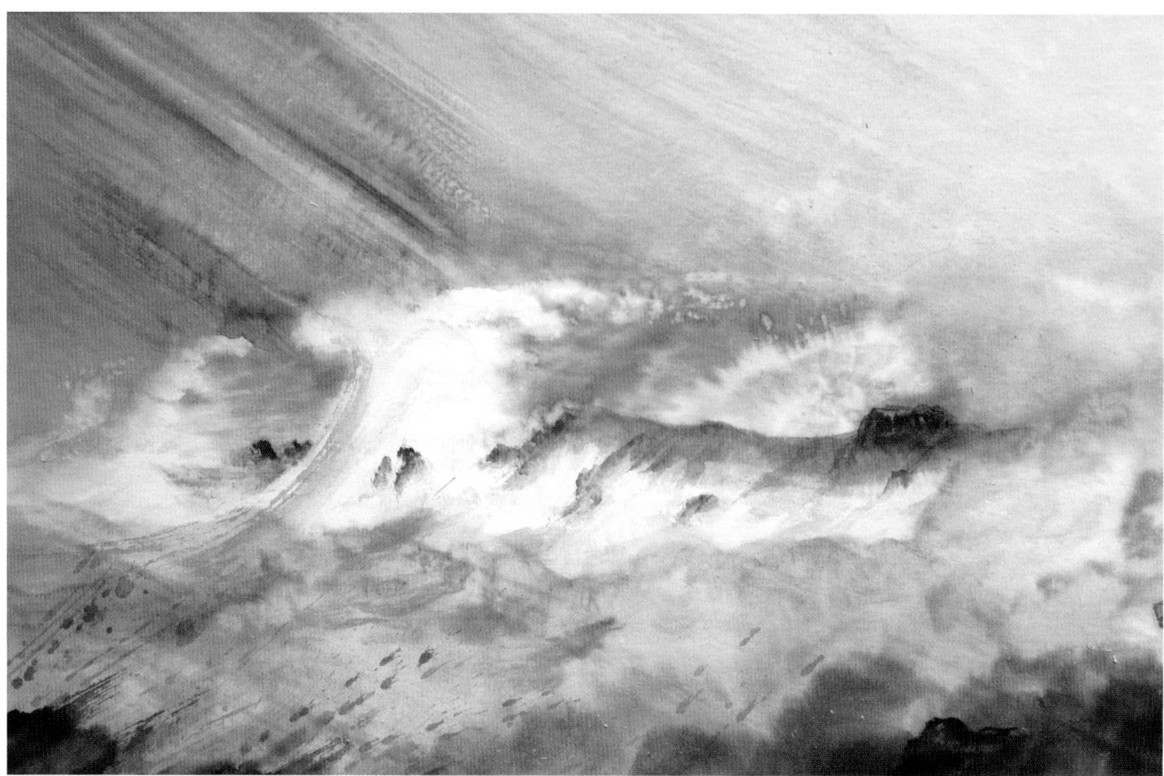

It is difficult to create the violent and turbulent wave energy underneath the surface of the ocean in a painting. The power of sumi painting is that the immediate energy or *chi* of the artist (see pages 18–19) can be transferred onto paper.

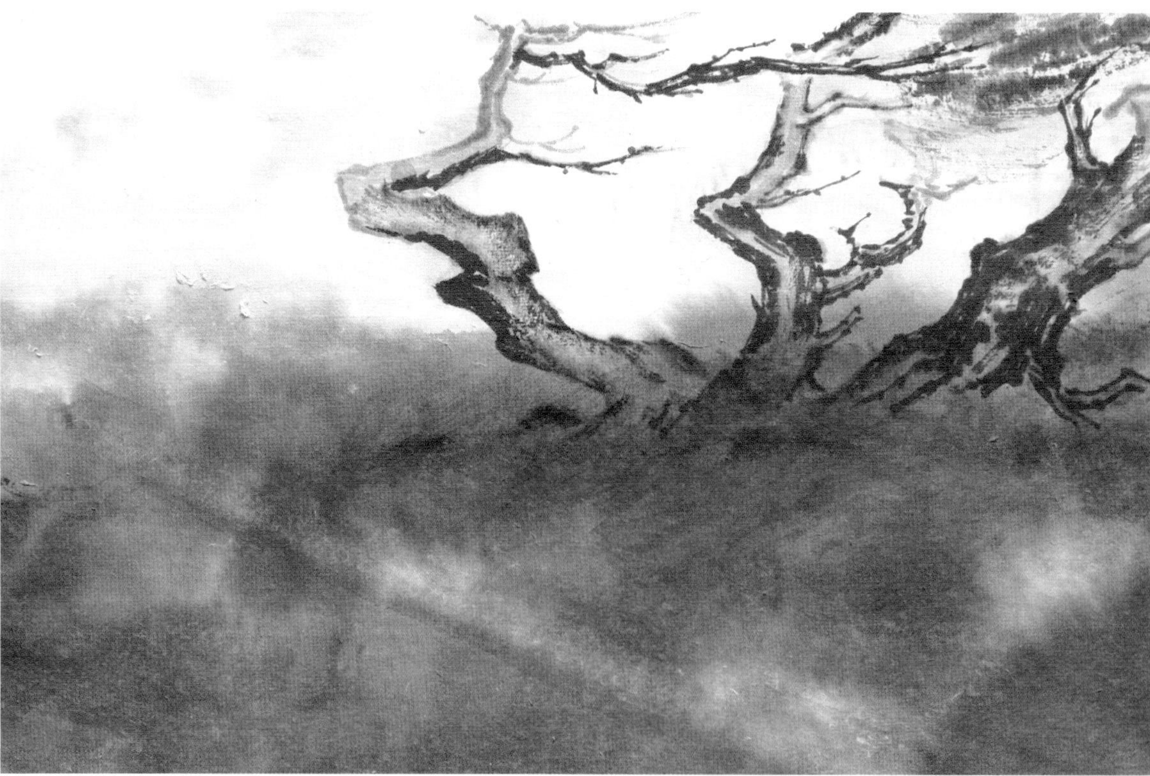

The trees of the headlands have been shaped by years of storms coming in from the west and have grown into unique shapes. In this painting the forms were highly exaggerated to show the painfully bent branches. They were drawn using the traditional outline technique.

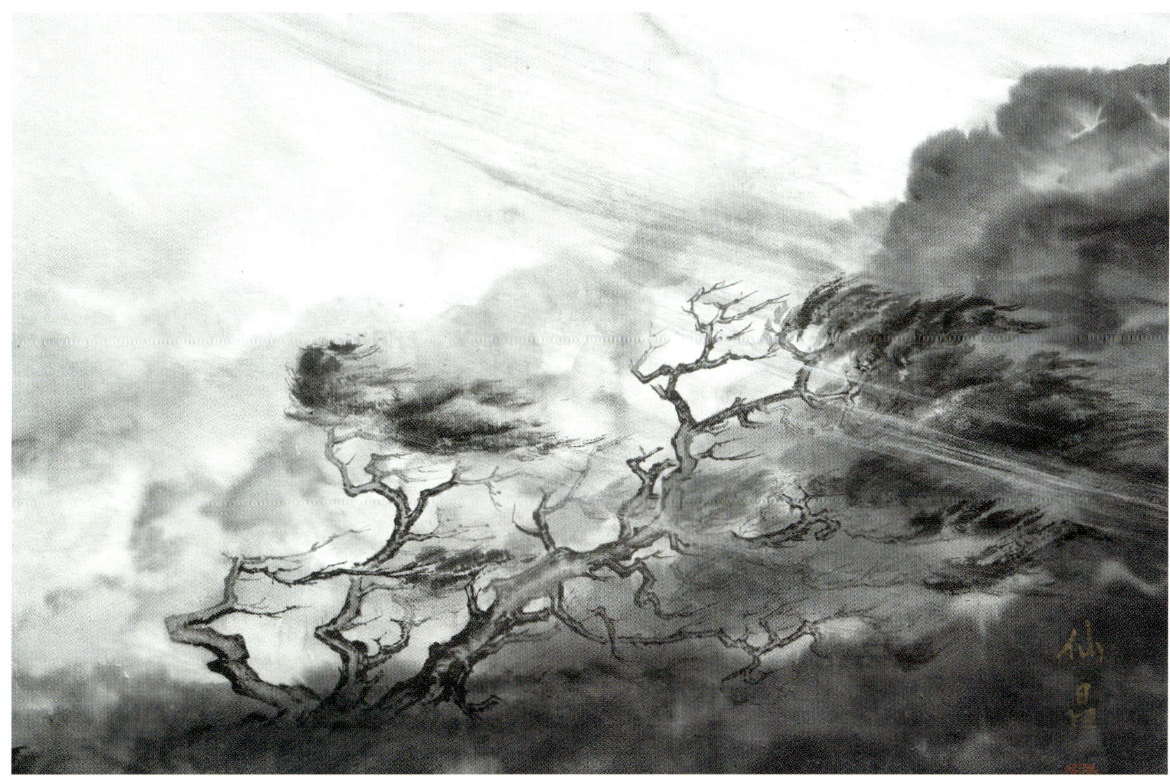

First I created the tree trunks and branches with light ink then went back with darker ink to outline and give shading and texture to the trunks. With each stroke, I was hoping to capture the intense feeling of pain which such force can cause. Using a mountain horse brush with dark ink on the tip I added the leaves blowing in the direction of the raging wind.

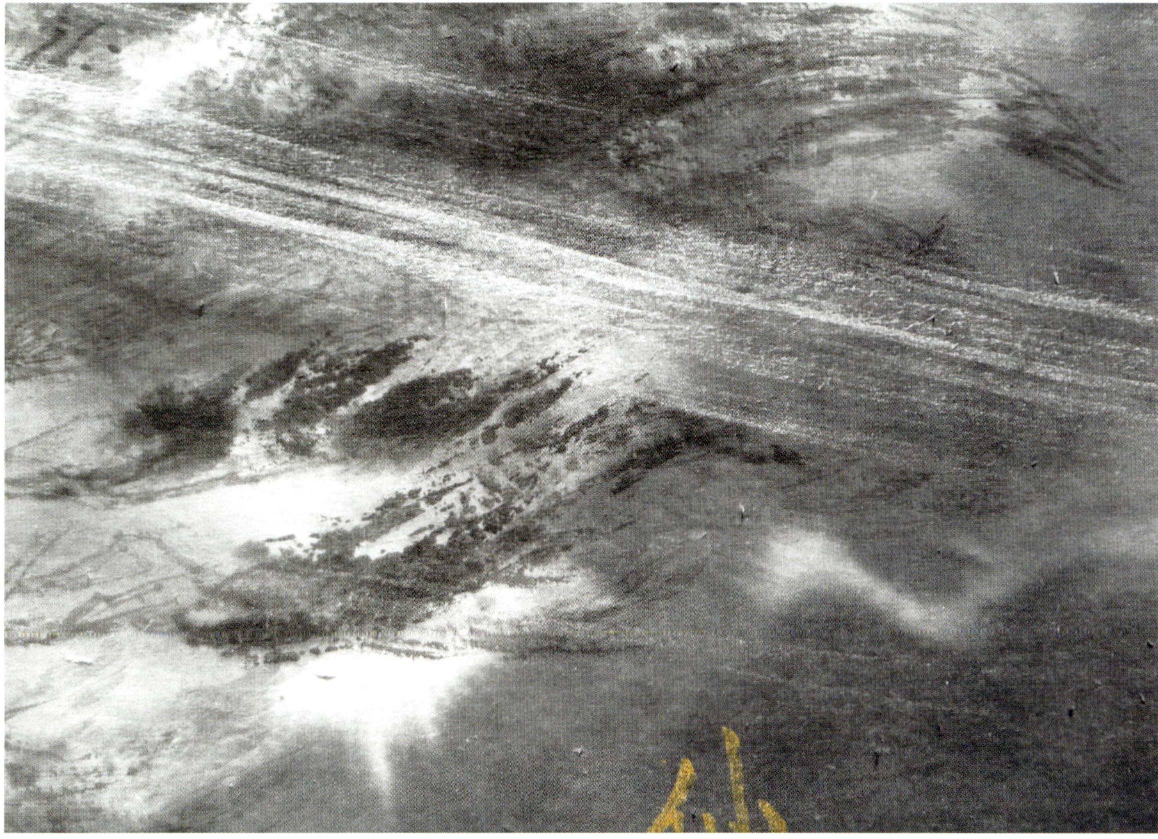

The final touch—adding the force of rain and wind—was impossible to paint over the dark ink section but very much needed. Therefore, using a mountain horse brush, I applied Japanese silver pigment over the dark ink. Traditionally, both gold and silver leaf or pigments are permitted in suiboku-ga.

10. Arches National Park

Size: H = 27"/69cm x W = 39.25"/100cm
Paper: Unsized, pre-mounted on a board
Sumi Ink: Blue tone
Category: Suiboku-ga

The history of suiboku-ga shows that deviant shapes in nature have been the subject of many a masterpiece, from mountain peaks half concealed with clouds, to the unusual towerlike mountains of Guilin, China. When the focus is moved away from Asia, toward for instance the continent of North America, other kinds of exotic shapes can be found.

The desert southwest of the United States is filled with strange and colorful rock formations, and during the 1980s I was privileged to spend a few months on a sketching tour to some of these remote and exotic places. Growing up in Japan, I had never experienced grandeurs of nature like this, other than the ones shown through the eyes of Hollywood of course. I sketched from morning to evening, marveling at the shapes and colors sculpted by natural forces. Places such as Canyonlands, Canyon de Chelly, and Arches National Park may be familiar sights to many readers of this book. For me they were a novel experience.

Arches National Park was done using the outline technique. Whenever the outline technique is employed in a painting, one must be aware of the effect of every line. Each individual line must lend some meaning to the image, must add an expression that defines the subject, such as depth, the flatness of a surface, the roundedness of it, and so forth. Therefore, most especially during work on outline paintings, with each brush stroke a part of your body and soul must be poured into the painting. The tip of the brush serves only as the channel. During such a creative process, it is as if through the brush's bamboo handle your creative energy and blood pours out. This is a dramatic metaphor but sumi-e and suiboku-ga artists who work with sumi ink and brush should maintain this level of intensity and concentration.

For this work, the brush was held upright for drawing fine lines, but it was also used sideways to provide the shadow effects. This is a vast country so to create that sense, the wide open spaces of sky were left above the distant cliffs. I enhanced the winding roadway with diminutive shrubs growing along-side, to give balance to the composition and to create the effect of distance and space.

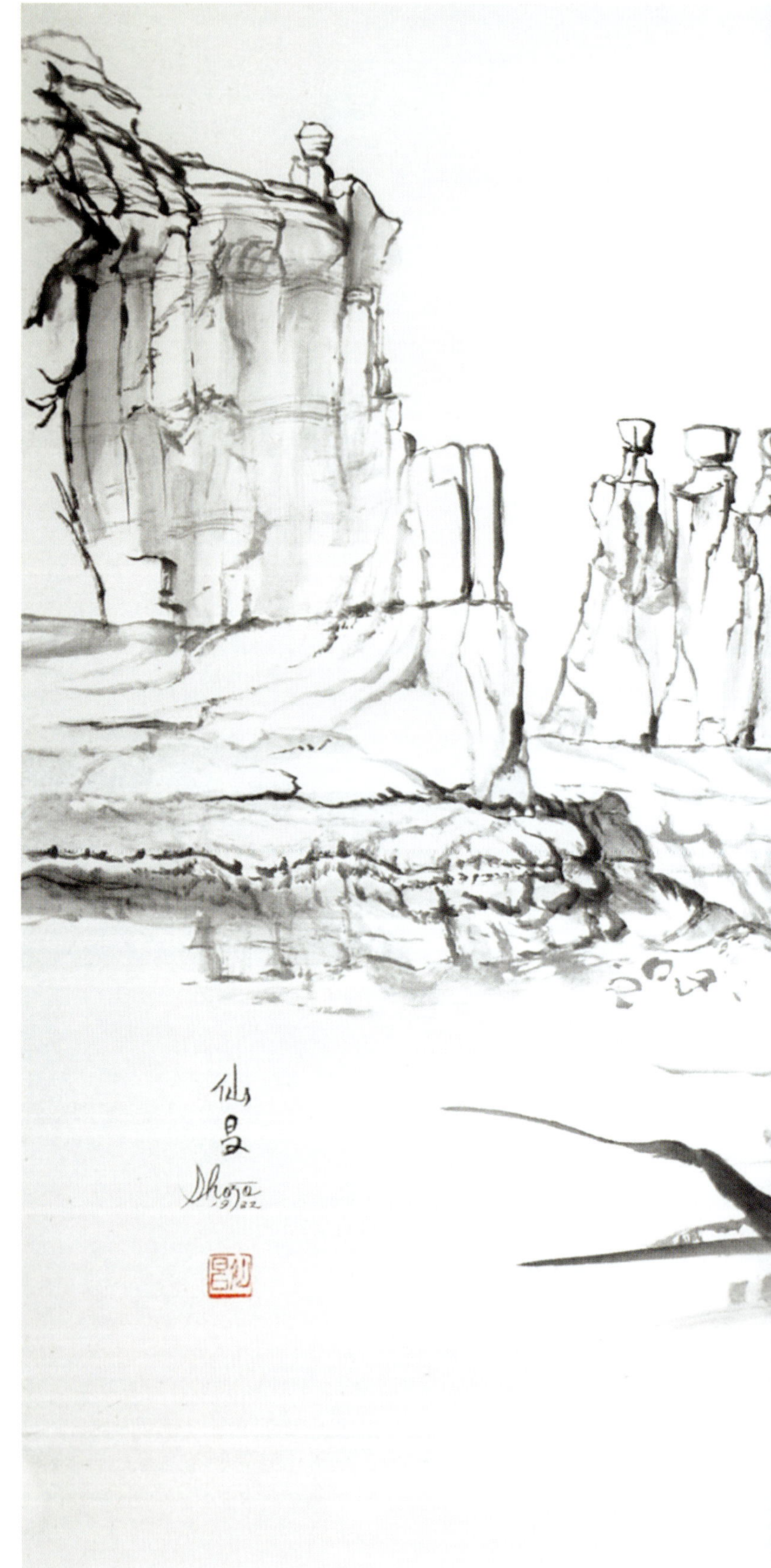

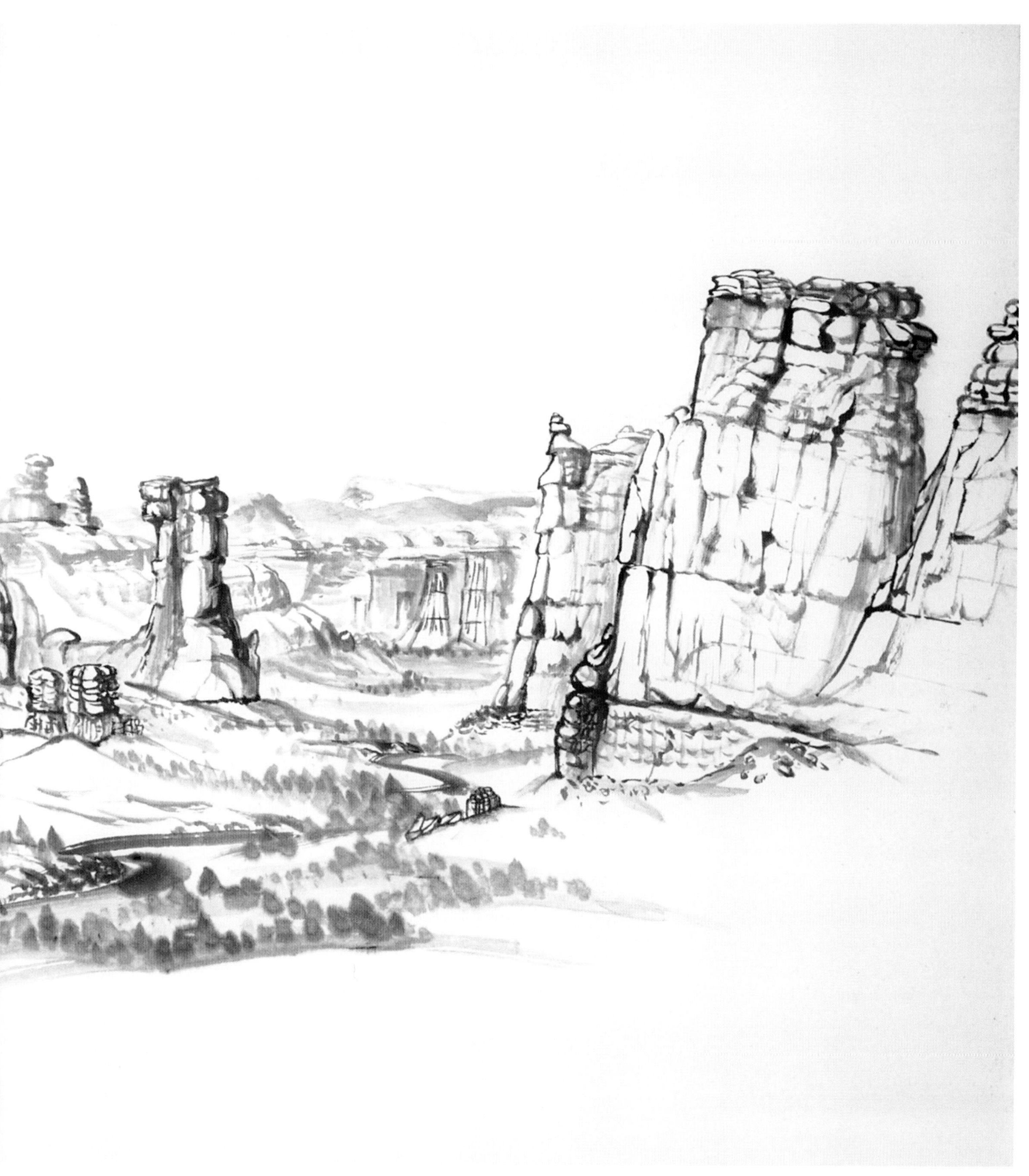

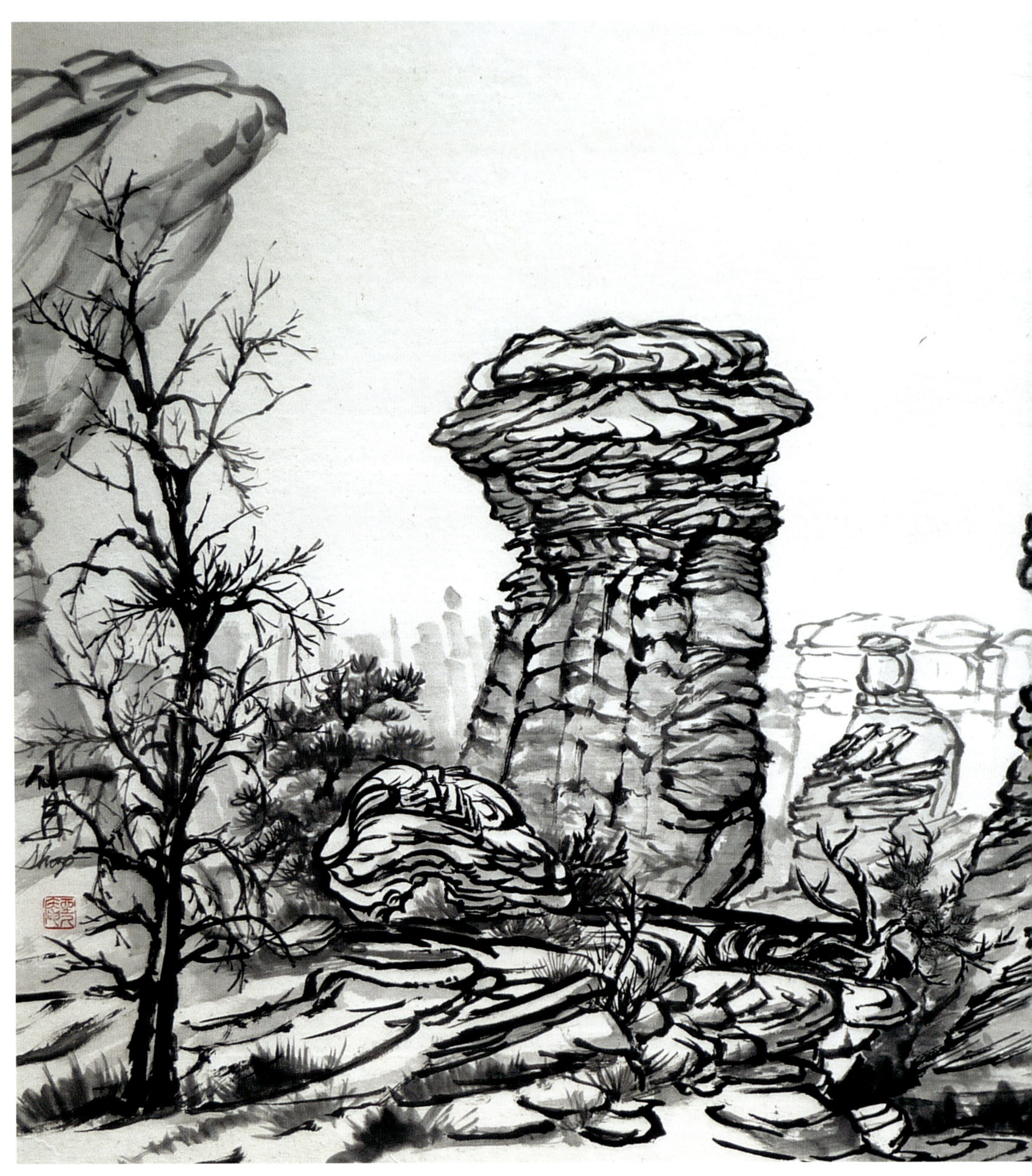

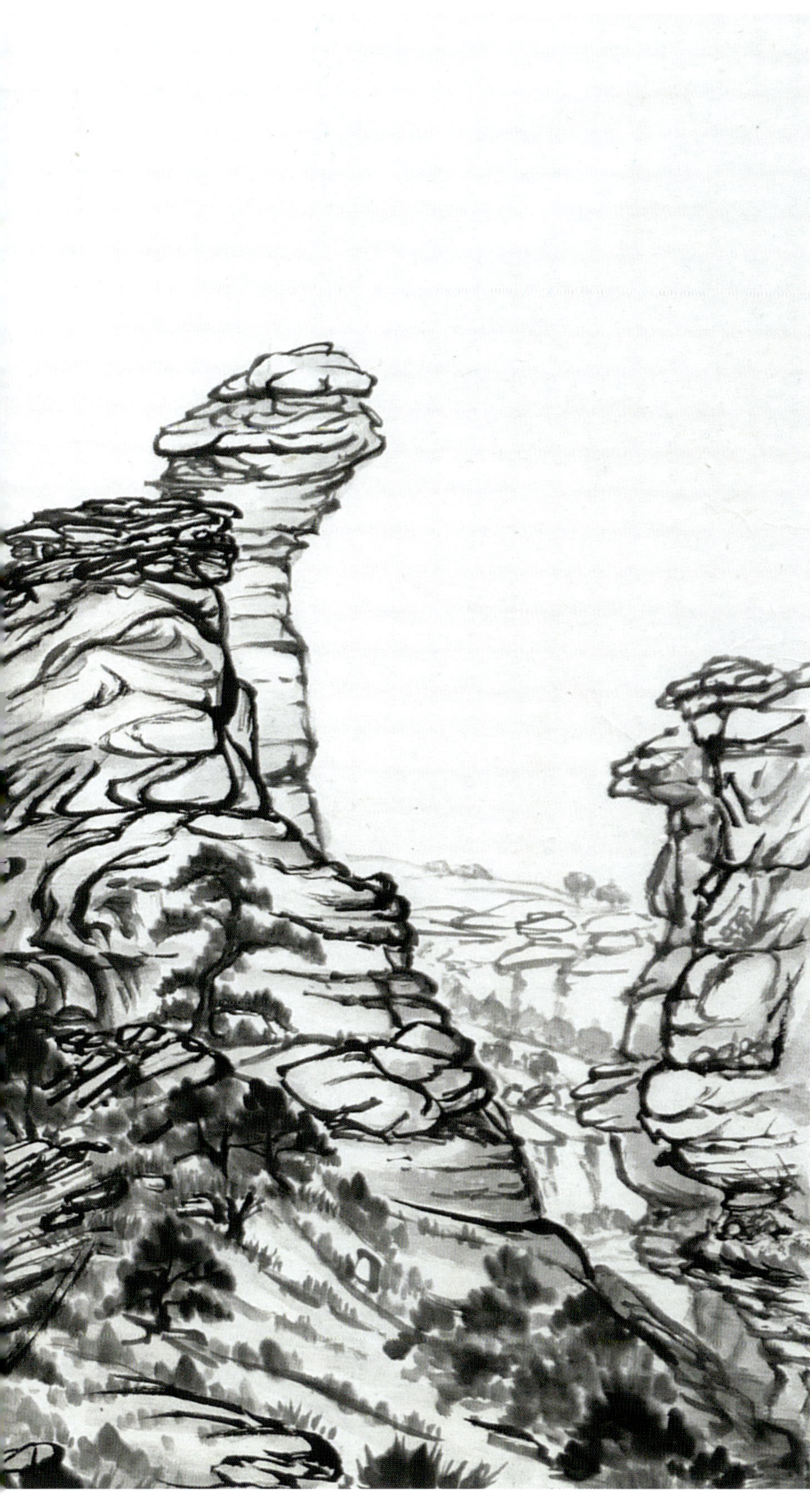

11. Canyonlands: Anasazi Towers

Size: H = 26.5"/67cm x W = 54"/136cm
Paper: Unsized
Sumi Ink: Blue tone
Category: Suiboku-ga

One can drive across hundreds of miles of flat semi-arid desert in the Southwest along the interstate highway, then turn off a side road to Canyonlands National Park and suddenly be greeted with remarkable structures carved by the natural elements over timeless ages. These panoramic and incredible sights are something to behold. That natural erosion created formations with such artistry is nearly beyond belief. Standing among them, all sense of time dissipates.

To capture this grand and rather surrealistic scene in sumi was a challenge. I camped out in my van for a week, working with my sumi lines to describe the details, hoping that I could capture something of the spirit of the place.

Notice the sandstone layers of the main tower of this composition; they were a maze of seemingly jumbled lines. As I was painting each line in them, my mind was continually wandering back through the geologic history these layers contained.

Surprisingly, the tenacity of life in such an inhospitable setting is evident: it is possible to find vegetation such as trees and bushes in this land of rock and bright sunshine. Including it adds a note of contrast to the image.

Compare the line quality used for the rocky tower, in contrast to that used for the dead tree, and then the lines used for the living tree. Each of these forms requires a completely different brush technique.

12. Monument Valley

Size: H = 27"/69cm x W = 39.5"/98cm
Paper: Unsized
Sumi Ink: Standard
Category: Suiboku-ga

The vast open sky and sand colored desert in a natural valley with a formation of many towers is a wonder. It is said that some of the early Spanish explorers once thought these were the remains of a great civilization. At first glance this barren area appears to belong to another planet; yet upon scrutiny, there are grasses and shrubs growing next to ancient looking weathered wood. Life and death do coexist in the desert.

A brush pointed upright was used for creating the details of the upright towers. The brush was used sideways, in a 45-degree angle, for the surface of the sand hills.

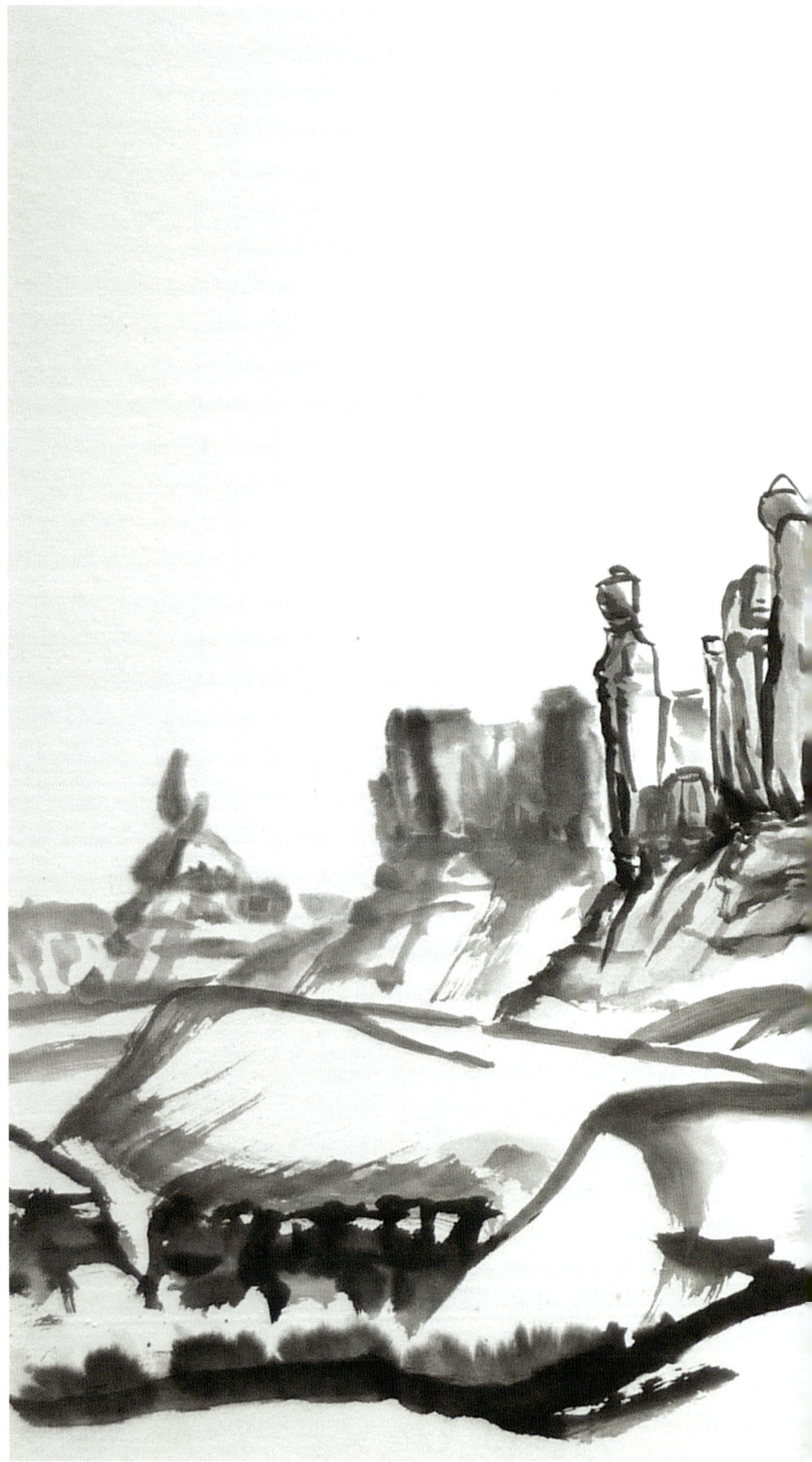

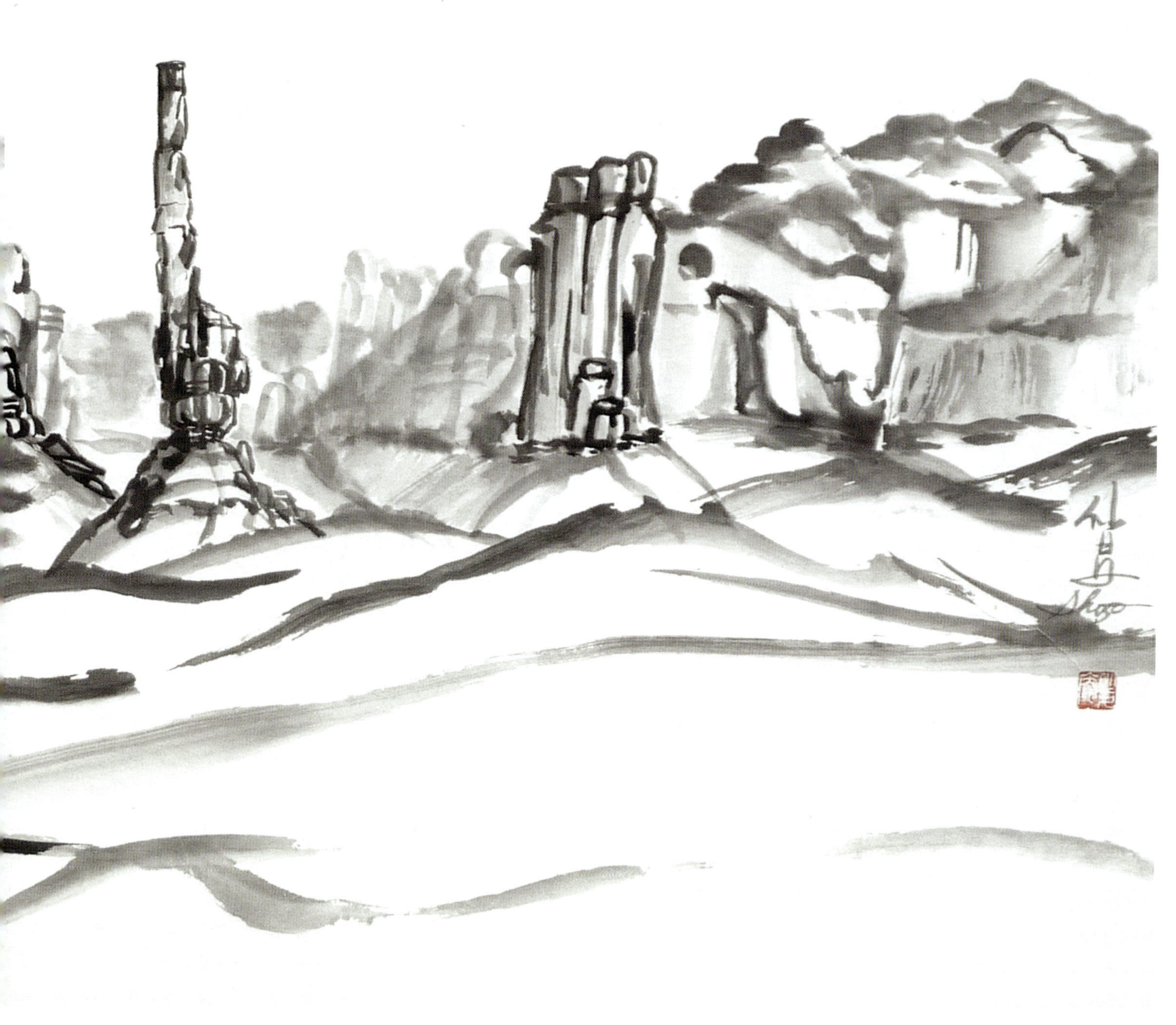

13. Chillon Castle on Lake Geneva

Size: H = 27"/69cm x W = 30.5"/77cm
Paper: Unsized
Sumi Ink: Blue tone and standard
Category: Suiboku-ga (tarashi komi)

"Lake Lehman lies by Chillon's walls, / A thousand feet in depth below" wrote Lord Byron in his poem "The Prisoner of Chillon." The waves constantly lap along the castle walls, and this creates a mysterious ambience. This painting of the castle takes a realistic approach, but the rising mist from the lake and the black clouds behind the castle are my additions to add a sense of Chillon Castle's legendary atmosphere.

The angular man-made structure is in direct contrast to the softness of the natural elements of rising mist and dark trees. To create the surface of the rooftops and stone structure of the castle, a drier brush is used sideways to give the texture of aged stone.

Details on the castle—the flat and even stone walls, the many small windows facing downward—were faithfully recorded to show their contrast to the massive structure of the walls. The upper part of the castle was completed first, then dried to stabilize the ink before moisture was given to the lower part of the painting in preparation for the tarashi komi technique used next for the mist and trees.

In this situation, for the tarashi komi technique I used two brushes, holding them like chopsticks: one for light ink and one for water. At the base of the castle, water was applied first, then light ink so that the light ink would keep moving to create the effect of rising mist. To create the effect of rolling fog, circles in light gray were painted, then water was added to blend and push the ink out. When the rolling mist forms the size and shapes you desire, use the hair dryer to stabilize the pattern. Otherwise, the ink will keep on spreading and you will lose the forms you wish to capture.

The total time for creating this mist was only a few minutes. However, the mist is created by the ink and water expanding and blending and the key is to know how to control it. Once it is dried in undesirable formation or tone of ink, it is almost impossible to touch up.

Trees were created in a similar way, with the water this time used to create lighter tones so that lines for tree trunks and branches could be added. With this tarashi komi technique, we see that there are two different effects which can be created: the mist on the left-hand side is much lighter and softer and conveys a feeling of rising. In contrast, the right-hand side's tree is more dense and massive with branches hanging down.

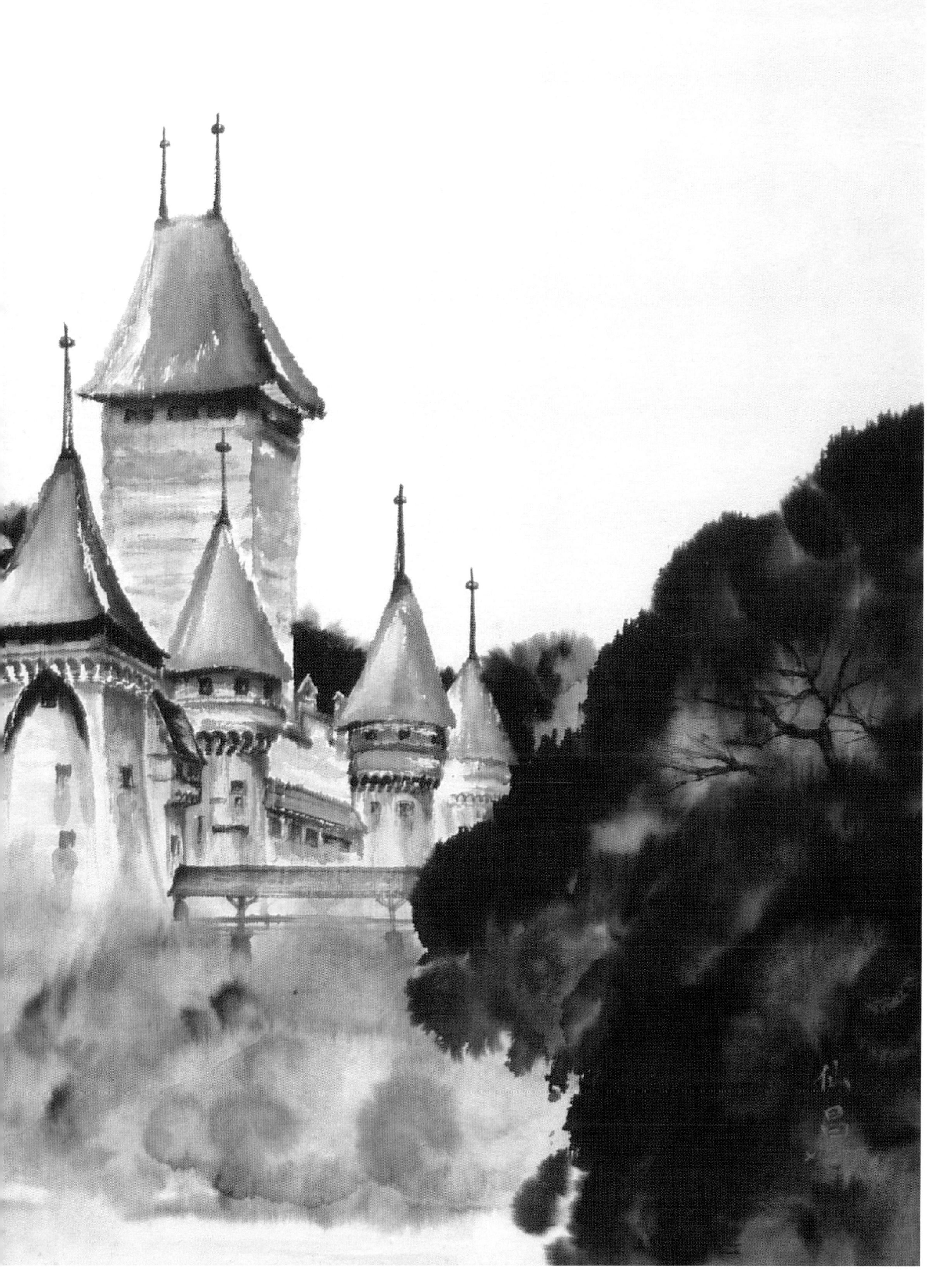

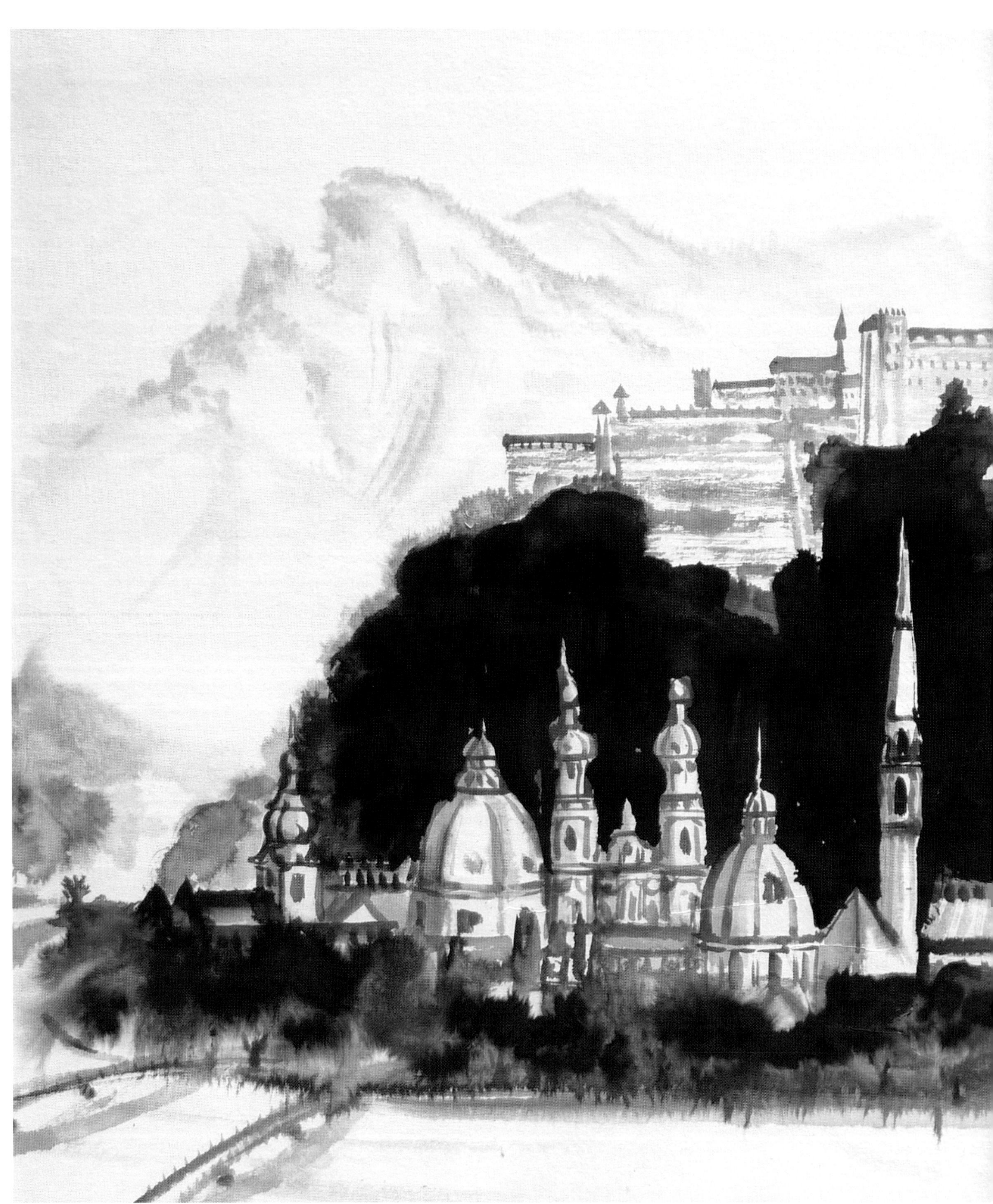

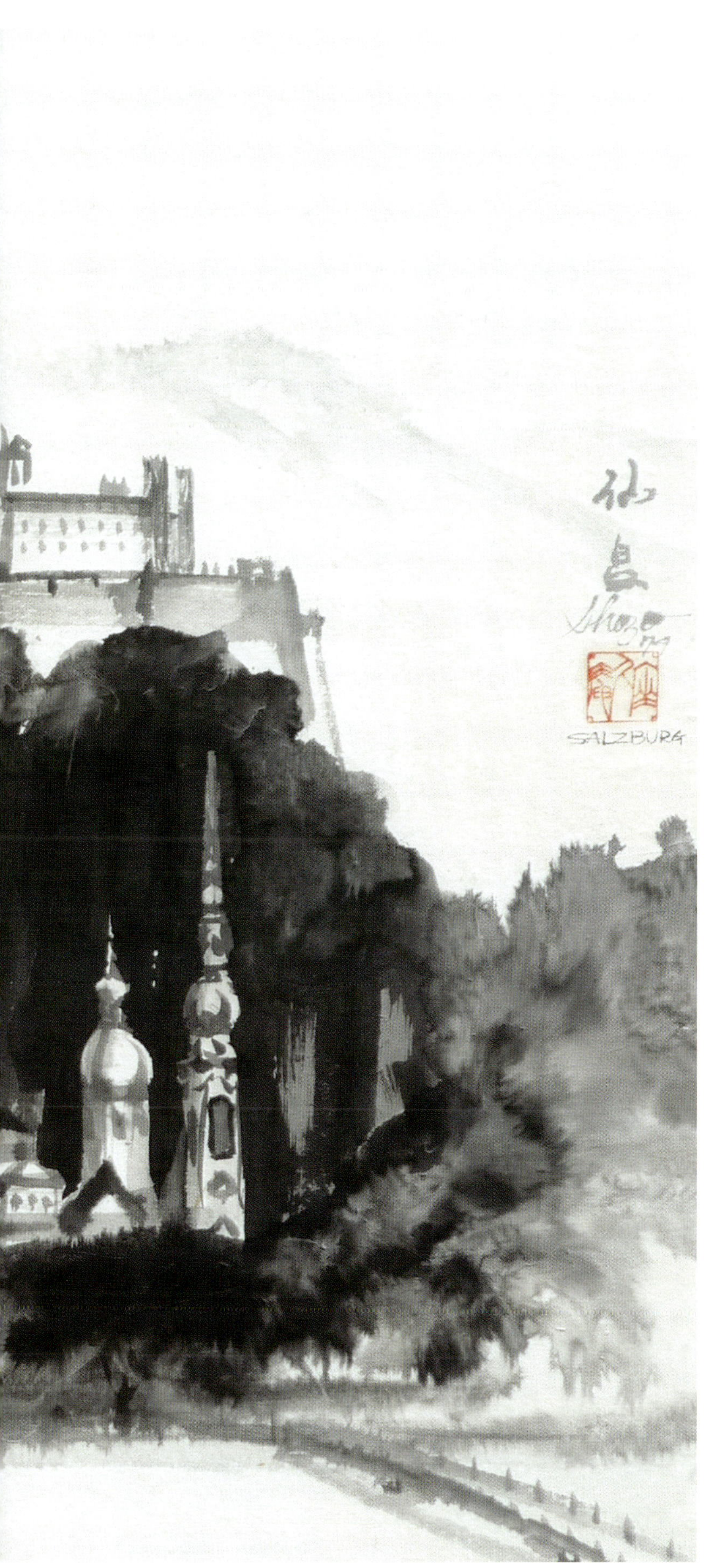

14. Salzburg Castle and Bishop's Residence

Size: H = 27"/68cm x W = 35.5"/91cm
Paper: Unsized
Sumi Ink: Blue tone
Category: Suiboku-ga

The city of Salzburg, nestled in the Tyrolean Alps of Austria, is internationally known for its acclaimed annual Mozart Festival. It is also the setting for the perennially popular musical, *The Sound of Music*. This picturesque city is both an inspiration and challenge for a painter.

Set in the verdant green of the Austrian Alps is the massive fortress of a castle built on a hill, and below it are the imposing domes of the Bishop's Residence Castle along with many church bell towers. Both castles look down upon the Salzburg river with its wide flood plain planted with willow trees.

To create the trees along the river and on the slopes separating the two castles, the tarashi komi technique was used to its maximum to help express the contrast between the geometric structures of the castle and the surrounding natural elements.

Along the river, the "weeping" willows' branches and the bridges were not painted in detail but were merely suggested so they would not detract from the dominating subjects of the Bishop's Residence and the church towers, nor from the subdominant castle on the hill.

To "secure" the outlines of the towers from the seeping ink of tarashi komi, I first used very dark ink to paint around the white space of the towers. Ink has an adhesive in it and once it is completely dry (a hair dryer comes in handy), it will act as a barrier so that additional moisture or ink will not seep in. You will notice that the spire on the left dome got lost because the ink was not completely dried.

In the background, in light ink, the high peaks of the Alps are shown. At the lower right-hand side, very active tarashi komi is used to suggest the forest beyond.

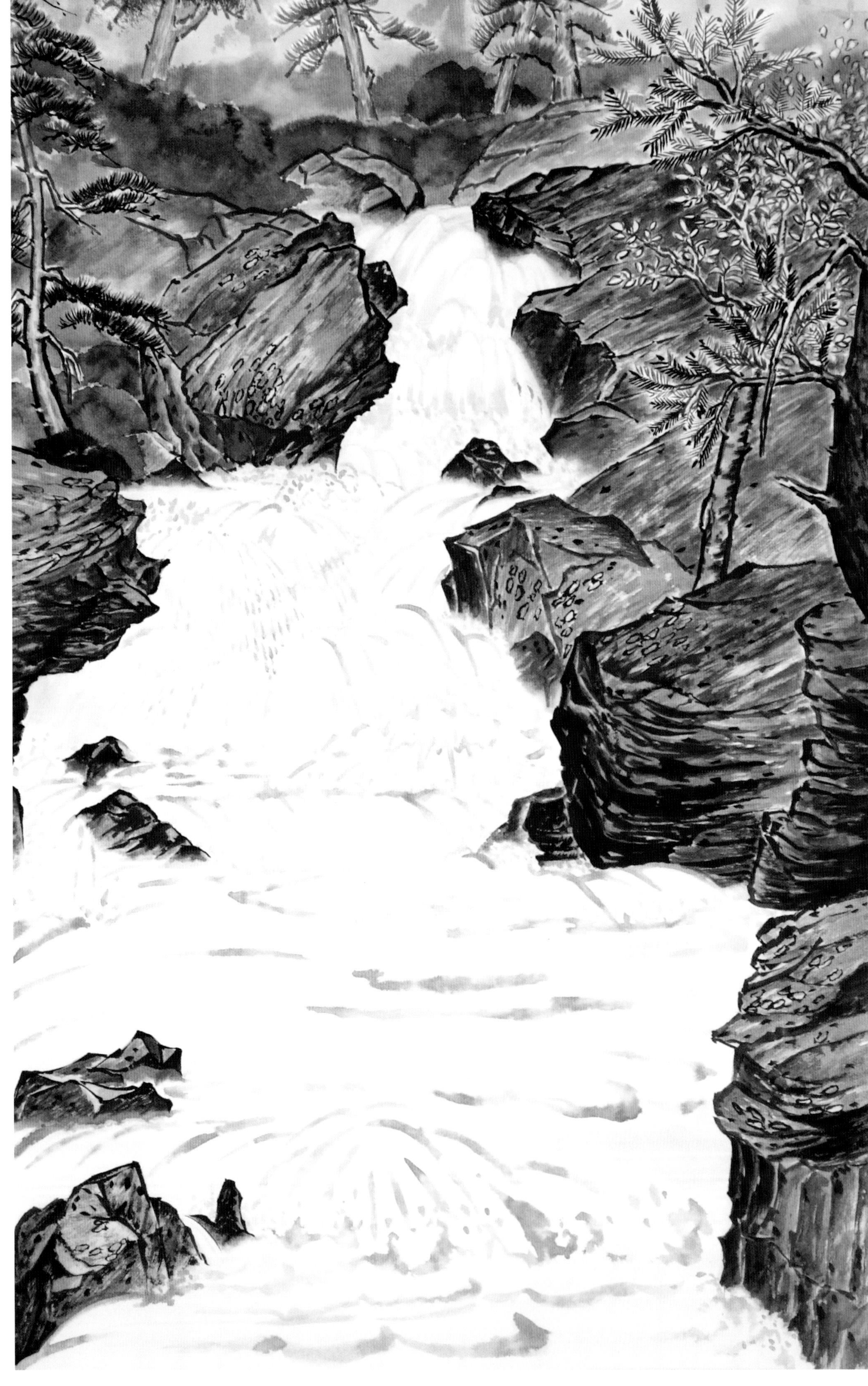

15. Mountain Cascades in Suiboku-ga

Size: H = 30"/76.5cm x W = 20"/51cm
Paper: Sized
Sumi Ink: Blue tone and standard
Category: Suiboku-ga

The turbulent cascades of water in a rushing mountain stream are captured here using a stylization technique unique to the Japanese arts. It combines the exaggerated methods of the rich and decorative paintings of the Rimpa School with the outline techniques of suiboku-ga, to capture the detailed forms in water movement.

Stylization and some exaggeration are necessary elements in making successful suiboku-ga and sumi-e. In both forms, the simple whiteness of the untouched paper leaves the viewer to complete the scene in his or her imagination. The viewer thus becomes personally involved in the painting. This suggestiveness is the key to sumi art. However, in this suiboku-ga painting, the tumbling force of water is the main subject, so the sense of turbulent motion and direction is suggested by lines in light ink to show direction and formation in the torrents of water falling down over the rocks.

Each time ink is applied in an overlapping stroke, the surface of the paper must be dried. This technique would be difficult to achieve on ordinary sumi-e paper; *Mountain Cascades in Suiboku-ga* was painted on thick torinoko paper which is sized. As always, selecting the right type of paper is very important based on the subject and method of your painting.

This scene was sketched on site, then re-created in the studio. There were many more trees, shrubs and grasses at the actual site, but because the painting's focus was to be on running water and rock formations, I chose to reduce those plants to a minimum. During the sketching many elements came to my notice, such as the rocks at this site being very dark from the wetness of the splashing water, and the fact that each section of the cascade had its own harmonious activity, joining to form a sort of symphony with pools of calmness interjected.

The following pages show the process and progress of translating this to paper and sumi. The final challenge was to re-balance the texture of activity in the rock formations with the activeness of the water.

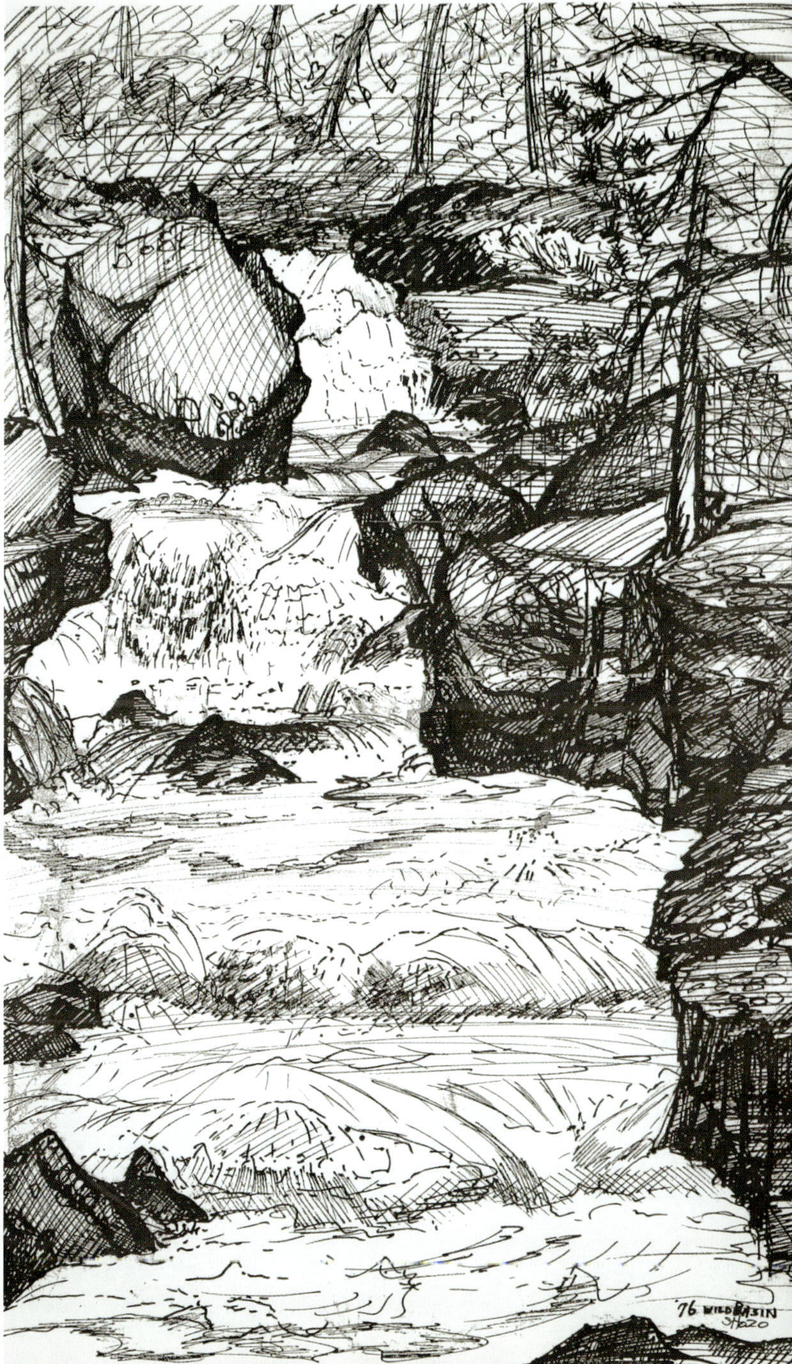

Right: Without basic practice in sketching, you will find that when you attempt sumi-e, the brush movement does not capture the forms you intend. Your sketchpad and pen or pencil are essential to your fundamental training in ink painting. This is one of my sketches, done decades ago in felt-tip marker; it served as a reminder to me of how water tumbles in cascades down the rocky slope of a mountainside.

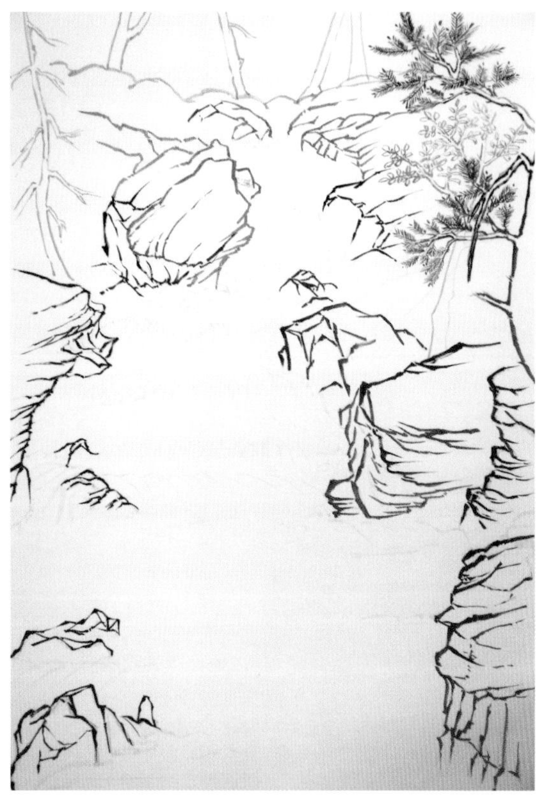

1. Torinoko paper was stretched and glued on a board. Now, with light ink, the outline positions of the rock formations are put in.

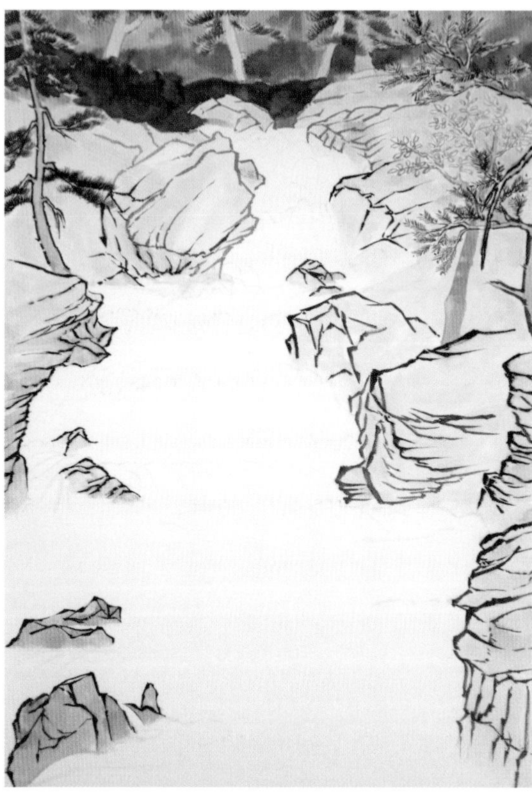

2. Using light ink, the surface of the rocks is slightly darkened. In the far background darker ink is used for the vegetation to define the beginning of the cascades.

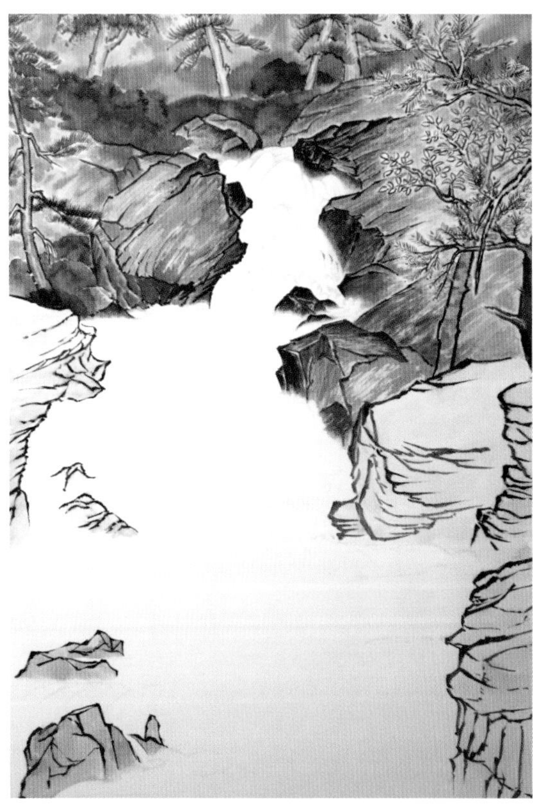

3. Working from the top of the painting, gradually three-dimensionality is added to the surface of the rocks, especially where lichens and mosses are growing. Special attention is given to places where running water tends to splash against rocks.

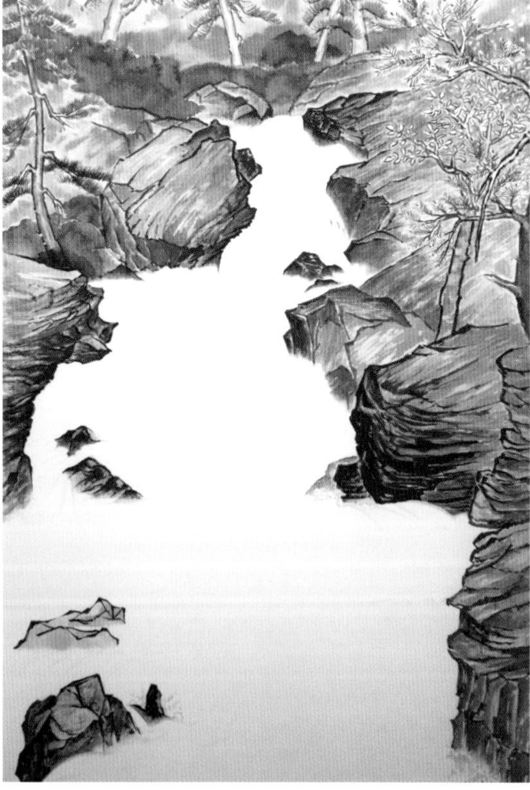

4. Dark ink is used to create a frame of rocks to surround the water. Then a thin brush loaded with very light ink is used to begin creating the movement of water at each level.

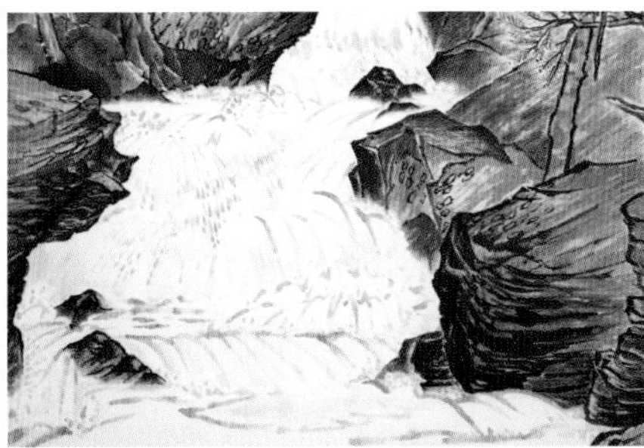

The formation of rocks underneath water creates the distinct movement as the currents collide and splash. The tumbling and converging as it plunges downstream lends the running water its poetry and music.

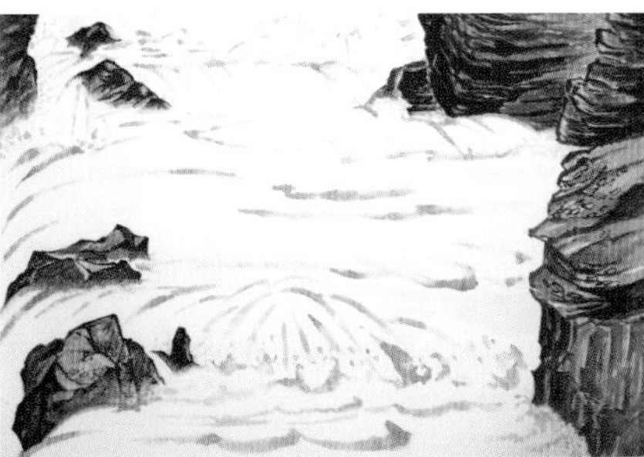

The sound of a mountain stream, a very special thundering "symphony," is abstracted into a visual reality in light ink. Water cascades down over the rocks and when reaching a level place it forms small pools of temporary calm.

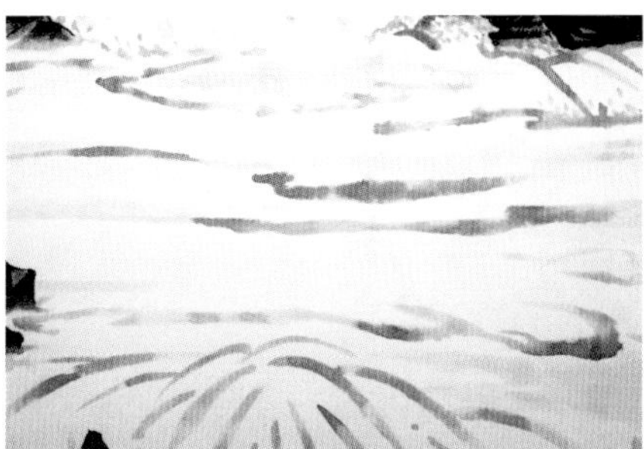

To catch the movement of eddies in the pool, I used the tarashi komi technique: first each line of an eddy was painted with light ink, then before it dried, I applied a drop of dark ink on the wet surface of the line to emphasize the effect.

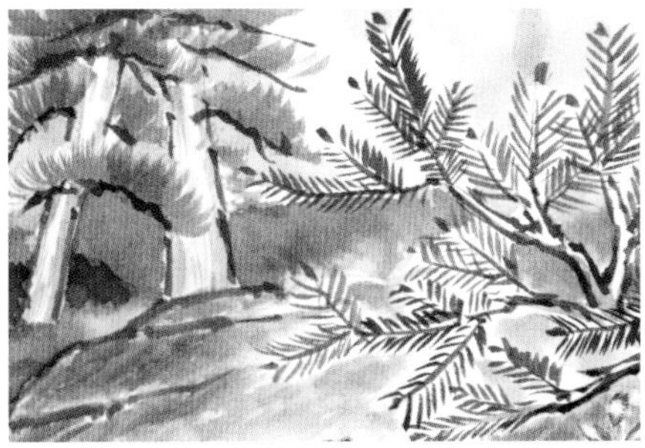

When the outlines of tree trunks, branches, leaves or needles are painted in, certain areas must be left white, such as the bodies of the tree trunks. But by accident or mistake, sometimes the white areas might end up with ink. When this happens, you can use tape to gently lift out the fibers of the accidentally-inked paper to lighten the area. Because tori-noko paper is thick, its surface can take this treatment. Lifting out fibers will leave a rough surface, so use your fingernail or some other hard-surfaced object to smooth over the spot.

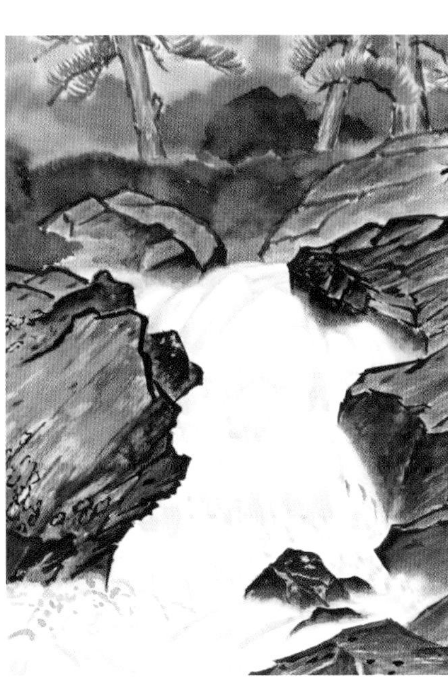

After I completed the painting and re-examined the total effect and results, I felt that the texture of the individual rocks was competing with the movement of the water, so I added contrast.

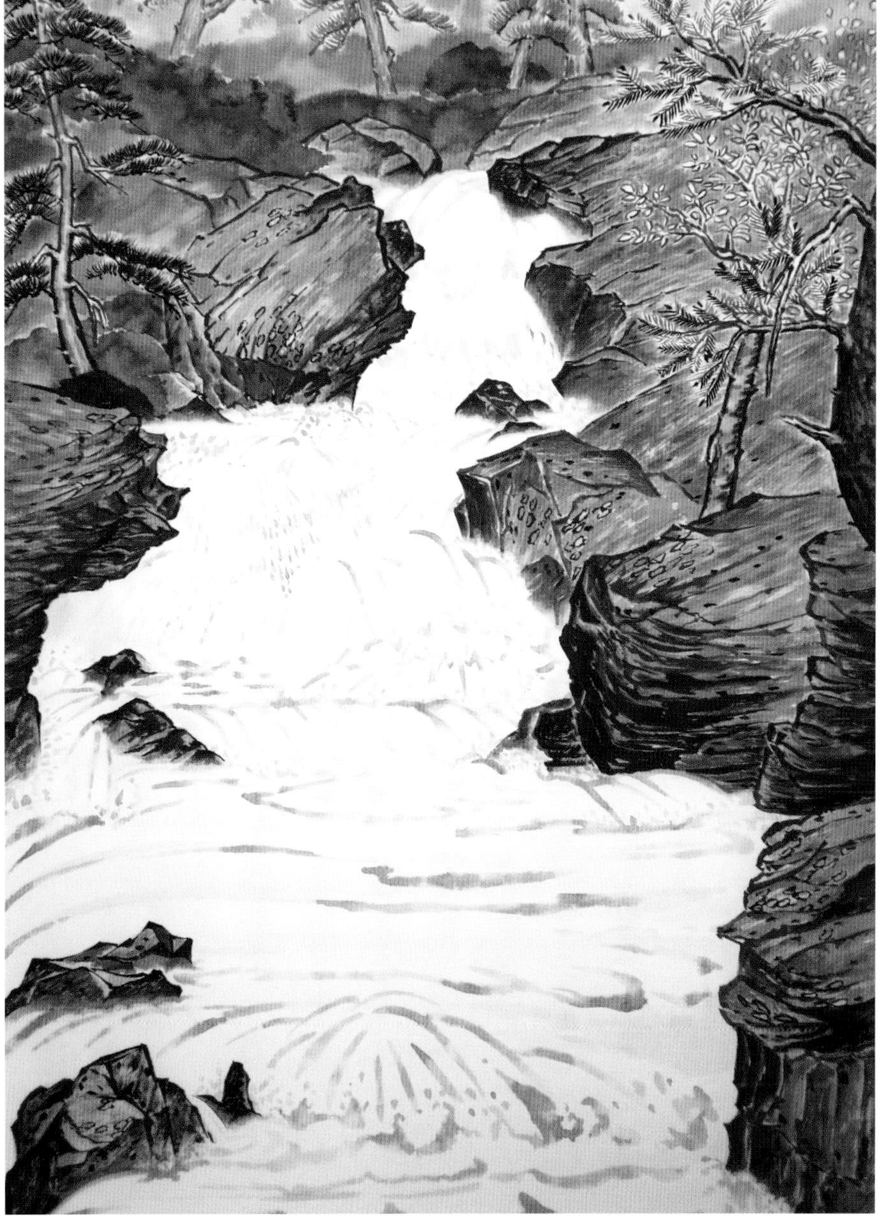

In order to help the water stand out as the dominant subject, I toned down the rocks by making them darker: the contrast with the white surface of running water is now greater. Refer to page 104 to see this in more detail. When such touch-up work is required, the paper surface must be re-moistened. Depending upon the dryness or wetness, the sense of depth in the sumi changes.

16. Mountain Cascades in Sumi-e

Size: H = 25"/89cm x W = 18.75"/48cm
Paper: Unsized
Sumi Ink: Blue tone and standard
Category: Sumi-e

After completing the previous painting of
Mountain Cascades in suiboku-ga, I used
the same sketch to paint the cascades
again with the use of minimal strokes.

The paper was not pre-mounted and
was highly absorbent, so it was impossible to add or retouch a stroke. Each
stroke was a final expression so the
energy of brush strokes is more readily
sensed. Brush strokes in suiboku-ga and
in sumi-e both require great energy, but
that is more easily discerned in sumi-e.

While it is in the sumi-e category,
because creating the rock formations
entailed more detail I used the standard
brown tone sumi ink for the rocks and
blue tone sumi ink for the water. The bristles of the brush were somewhat flattened
to form the flow of the water, with the
attempt to recapture the sense of movement in direction and force of water in a
single stroke.

Historically, combining standard
brown tone and blue tone sumi inks was
not done in the same painting. However,
as sumi-e has become an international
art in contemporary times, I sometimes
use these combinations to enhance a
sense of color.

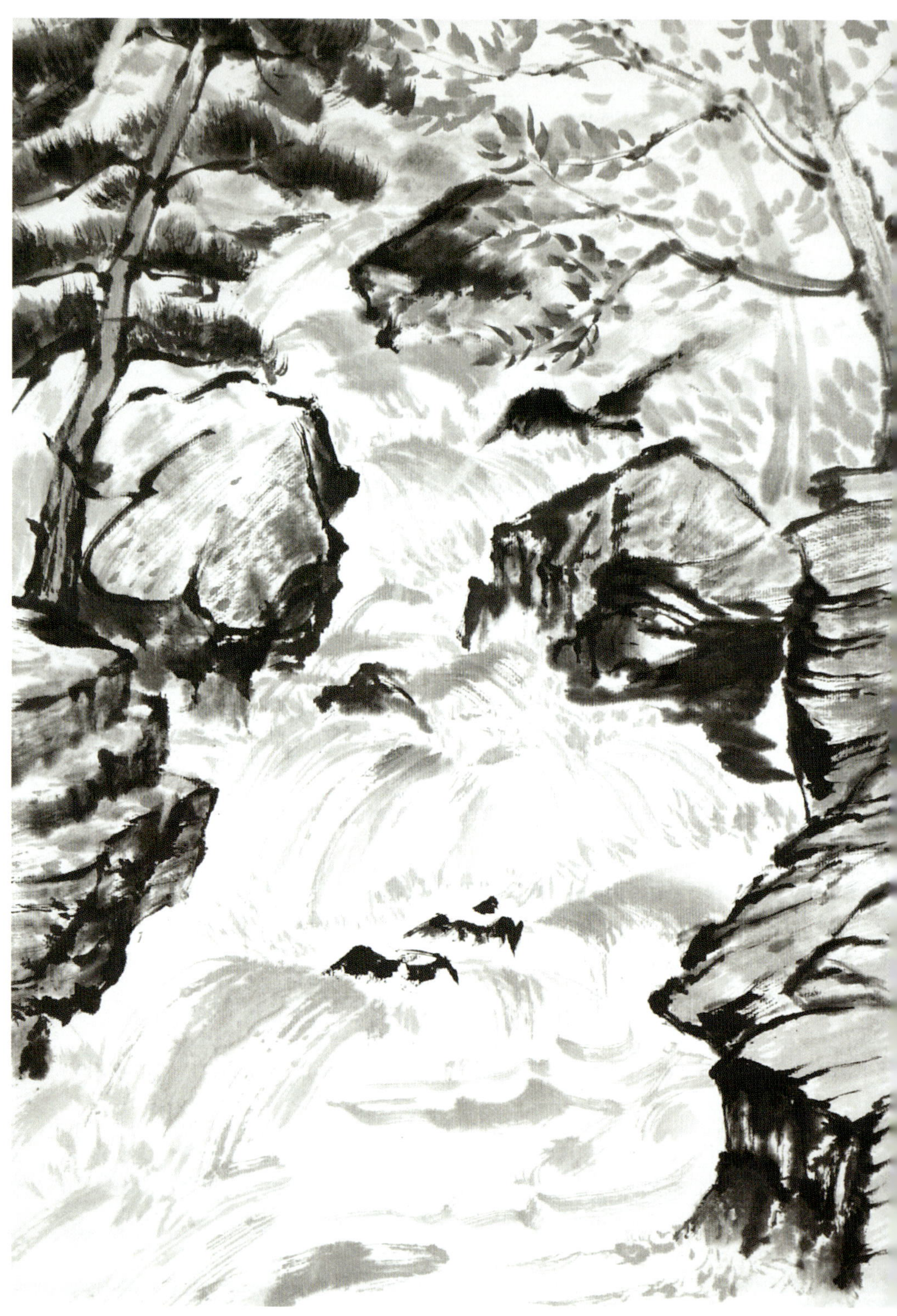

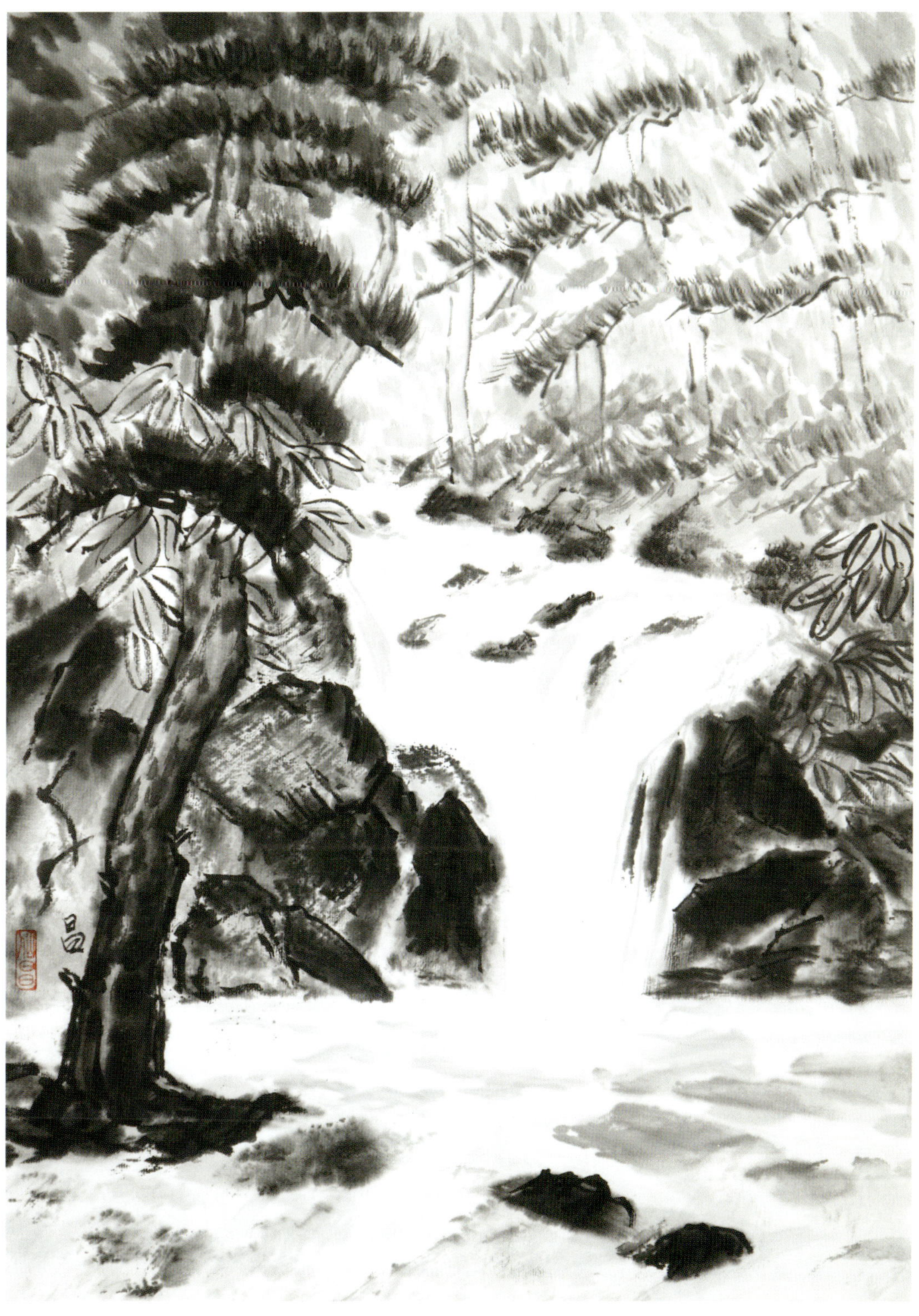

This sumi-e painting also captures cascades. It is done on unsized handmade paper, and like the facing image, it uses blue tone ink to accent the running water.

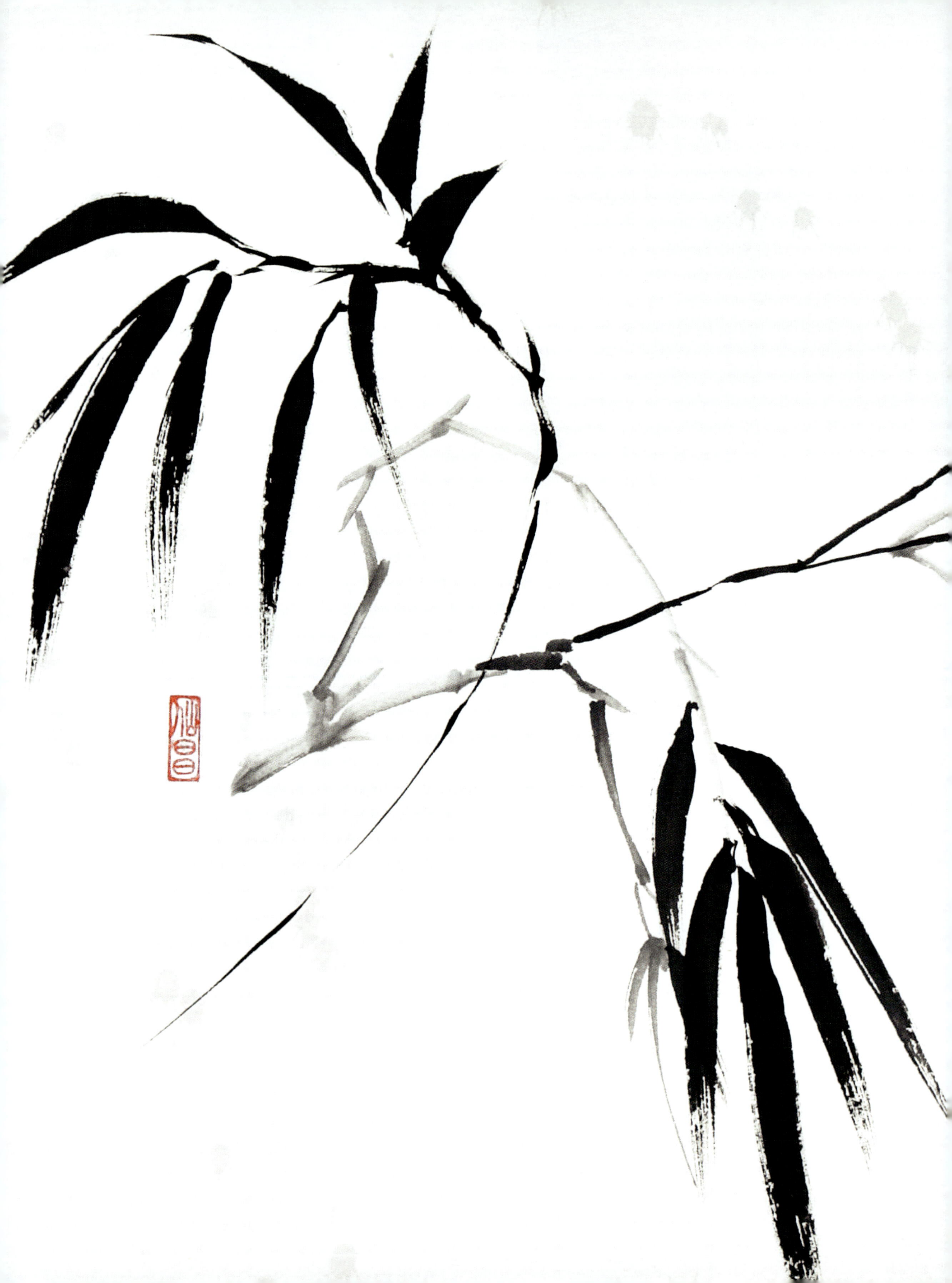

CHAPTER 5

Trees, Bamboo, Flowers and Grasses

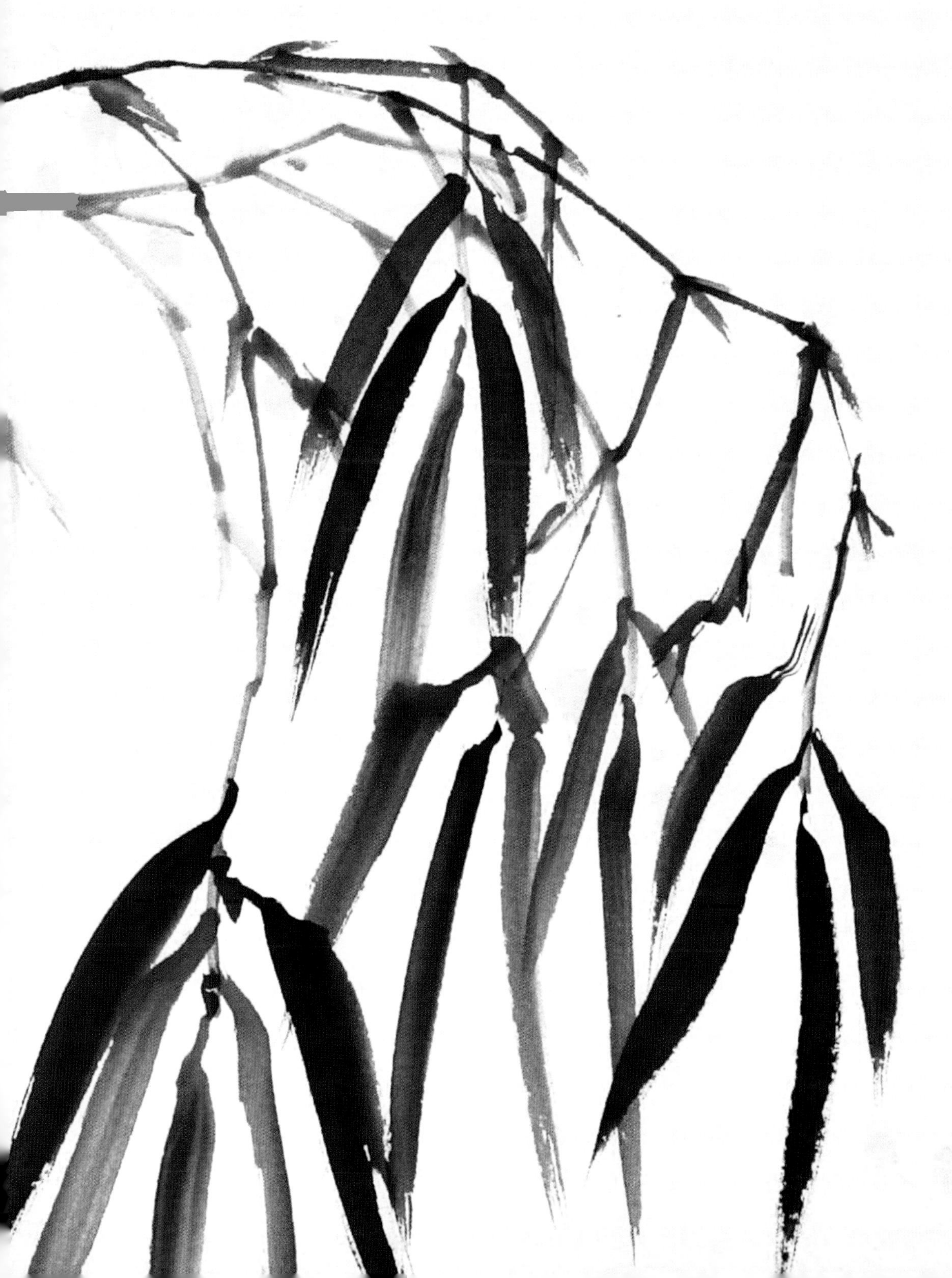

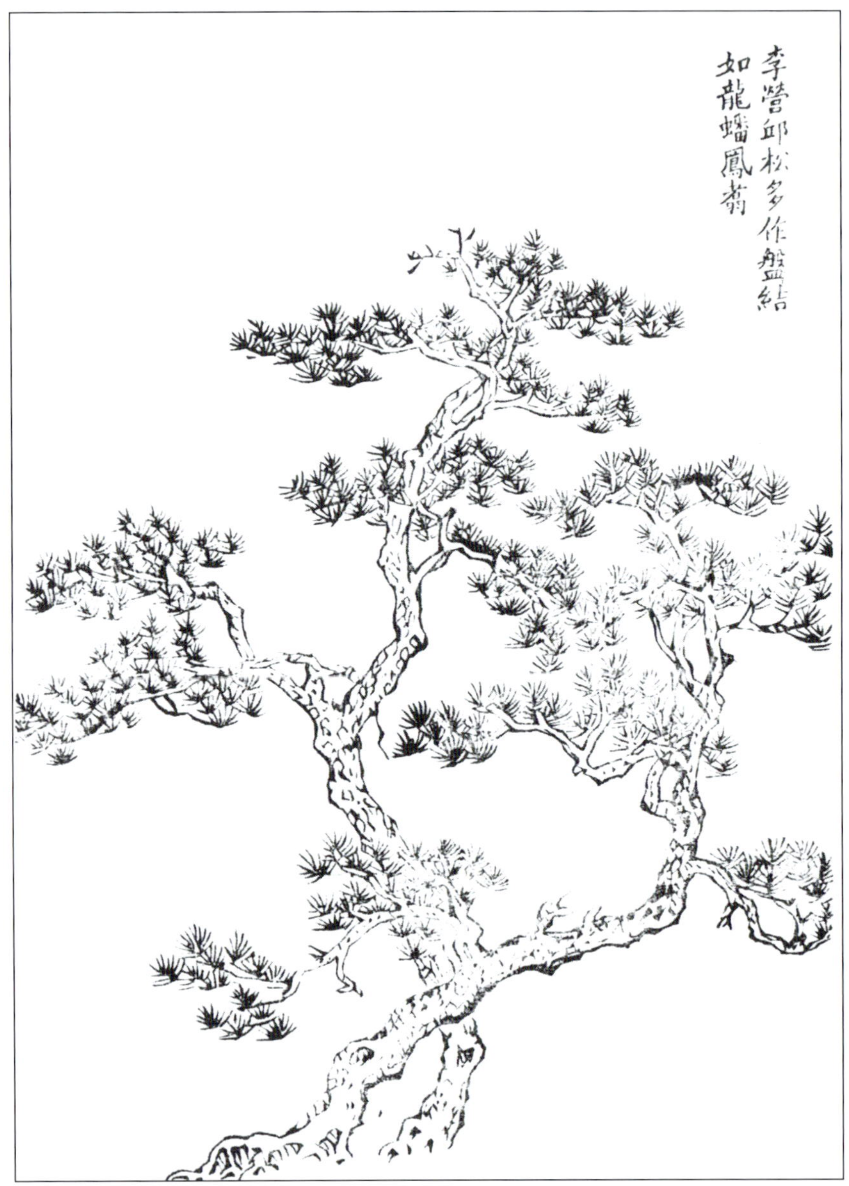

The caption on this page from the *Mustard Seed Garden Manual* reads "Li (Ch'eng) Ying-ch'iu painted pines with the sinuosity of a coiled dragon or a soaring phoenix."

The countries in the Far East have also long revered three plants as symbols that have philosophic significance. In the *Mustard Seed Garden Manual,* these are referred to as the "Three Princes." The **pine** is the "prince" of the evergreens. It is symbolic of unchanging happiness and longevity, because in most species pines are long-lived and have endured under the harshest conditions.

The **flowering plum** is the "prince" of the flowering trees; it is symbolic of bravery since it is the first to bloom in very early spring, and while the form of its flower is simple, its fragrance can travel for miles. (Some species of plum in the West do not have fragrance, but the flowering plums in Japan are very fragrant.)

Bamboo is the "prince" of the grasses, and it symbolically represents endurance and flexibility. When the wind blows, the bamboo bends along with it and when laden with snow or ice, it can bend down and touch the ground, but when the snow or ice melts and drops away it will spring back to its original form.

Generations of great masters have used these subjects in their masterpieces. Uniquely some of the artists have dedicated their creative life solely to painting one or two subjects. For example, it may be the flowering plum an artist focuses on, studying it and painting it under very different conditions, modes, styles and at varied sizes.

The techniques for painting these three plants are also used as teaching tools for mastering brush strokes in sumi ink. Along with the "Three Princes," we will also focus on works that feature some other traditional subjects: lilies, iris and grasses.

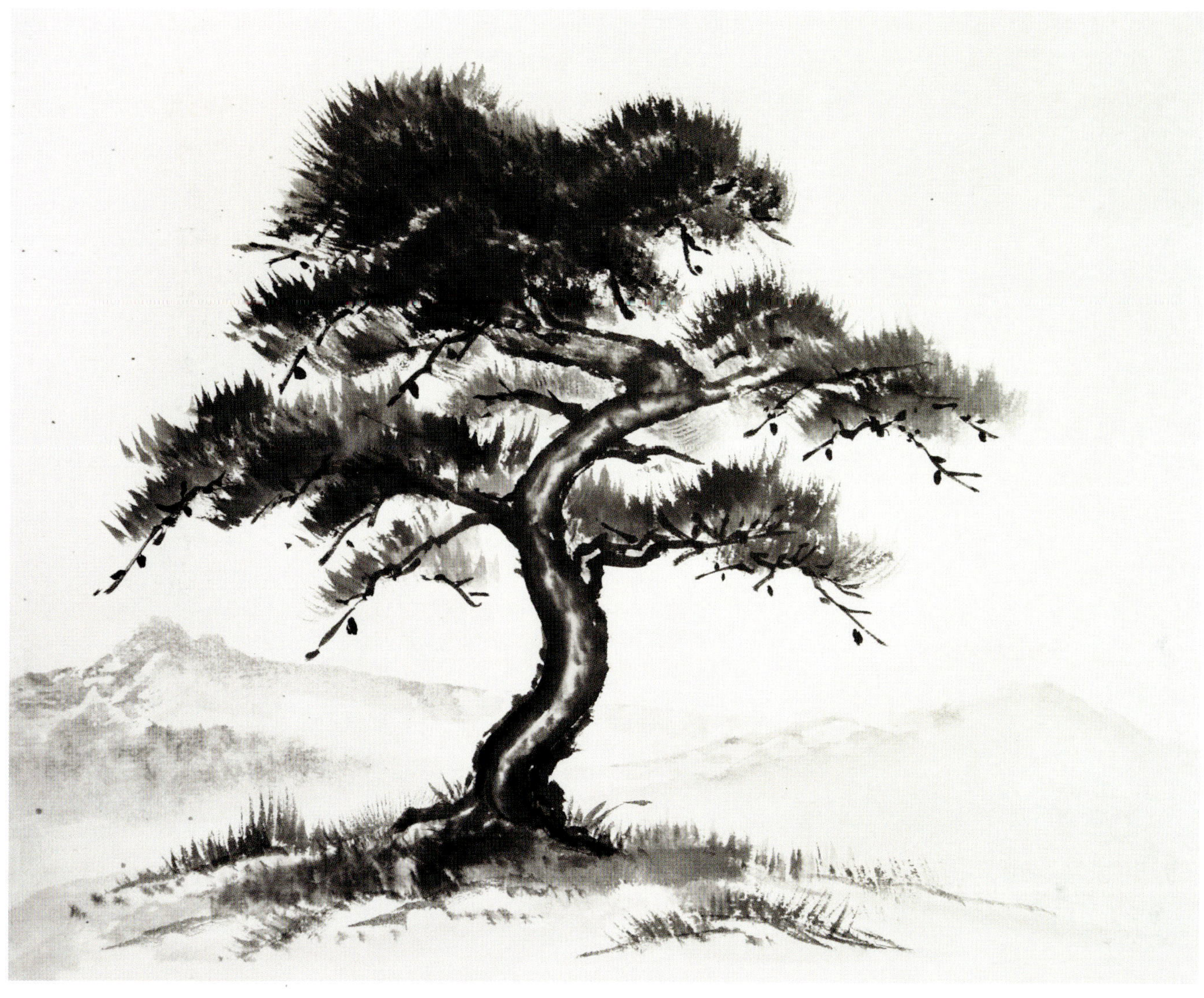

Painting Trees

In "The Book of Trees," one section of the *Mustard Seed Garden Manual,* there are pages containing examples of various master artists' trees (an example is on the facing page). Also covered in detail is advice on how to paint a single tree, how to paint groups of two to three trees, and how to paint entire groves of trees.

There are pages on how to paint leaves, the outlining techniques to be used on each leaf, the different formations and leaf groupings that should be on different branches, and so forth. It is easy to see how one's entire life could be spent on ink painting.

Because trees are so essential to the composition of landscapes in suiboku-ga or sumi-e, there is indeed much to learn about them. Since it is the "prince of the evergreens," the pine is a suitable place to begin.

On the next pages are the techniques for painting trunk, branches, needles and other details for a basic style of pine tree. The method described for needles is a standard one that is useful to have in your repertoire. When I am painting a pine tree, the method with which I paint the pine needles depends upon whether I am working in suiboku-ga or sumi-e style. Sometimes, I do paint them individually.

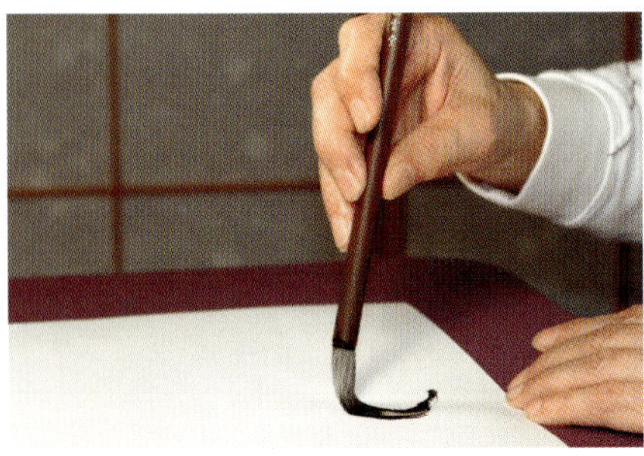

1. To prepare the brush, put dark ink on both ends of the bristles, and light ink in the center area. While holding the brush upright, flatten the bristles. From the right begin the base of the tree; keep the bristles spread in full contact with the paper, and move upward to create the trunk.

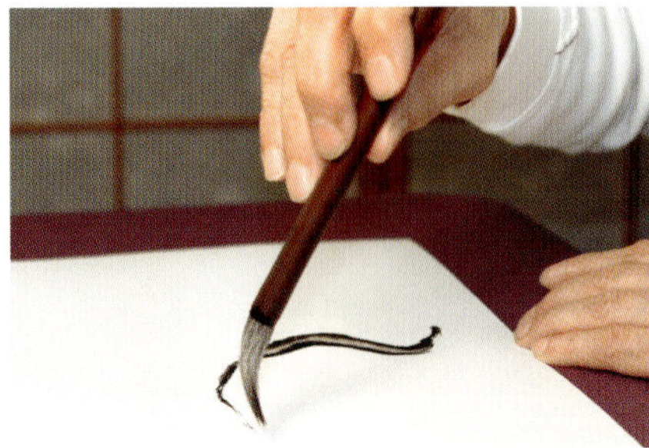

2. Turn the brush sideways to create the first branch, ending with a narrow-wide-narrow line. Then readjust the tips of the brush's bristles and spread them open again.

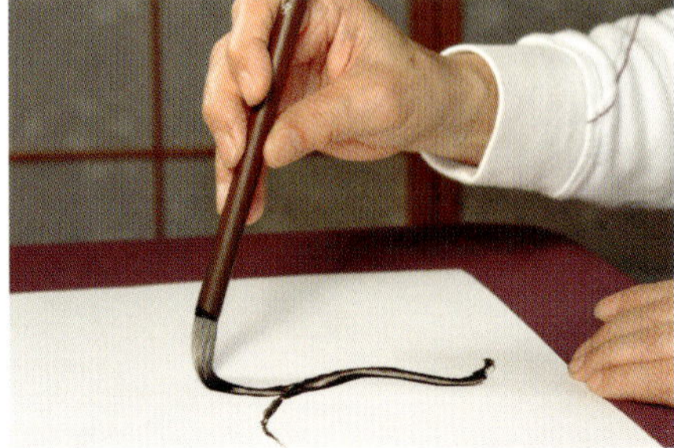

3. Continue to paint the main trunk, gradually moving up, then turning the brush sideways to create another branch to the right. Again readjust the brush as previously to work on the rest of the main trunk.

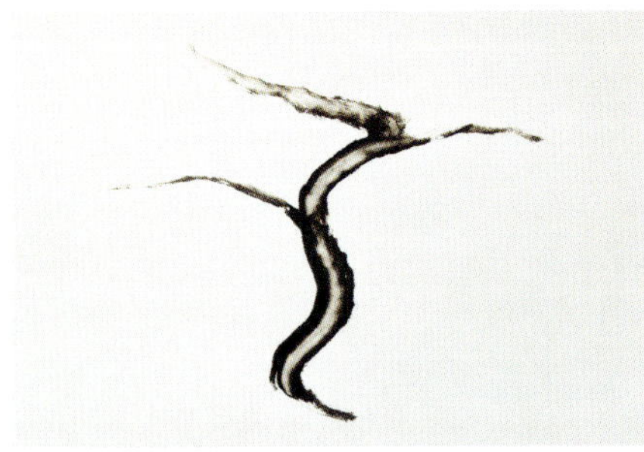

4. Proceed to the left. Whether the pine tree has a straight or twisted trunk, you can use this same method to create any form you wish.

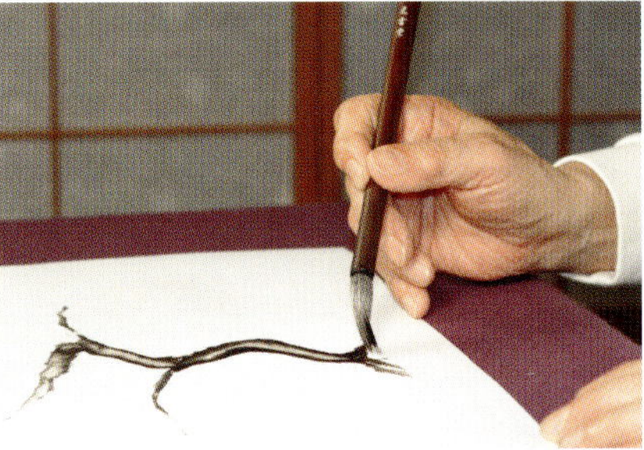

5. It is important that the base of the tree with its extension of the roots be recognized. Add the base and the suggestion of the exposed roots.

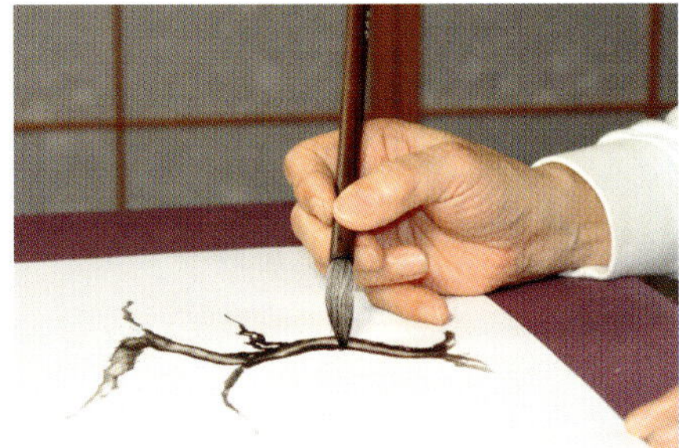

6. Next begin adding small accents to give the roughness of pine bark to the tree trunk.

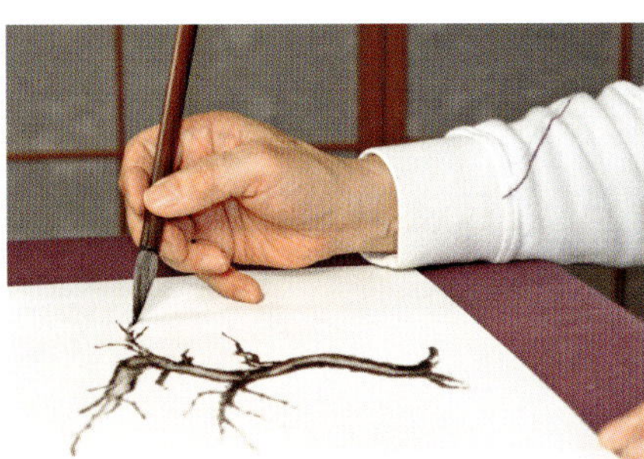

7. Expand the number of branches to give the tree form.

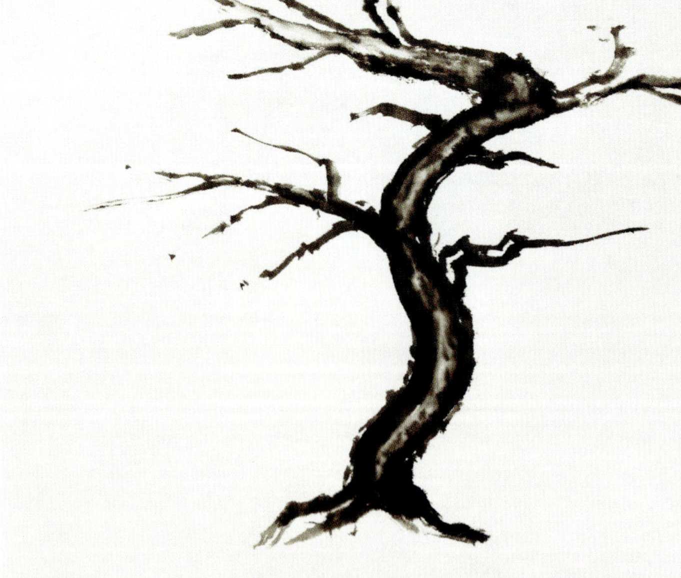

8. The brush should be reasonably dry and spread out flat, as shown here.

9. Remember that the branches of evergreens must be created to look as though they can adequately carry the weight of the needle groups they'll support. The lower branches usually grow sideways, often sloping down. At the very top the younger branches grow upright. At this point you may choose to readjust the width of the tree's trunk by adding lines, as this image reflects.

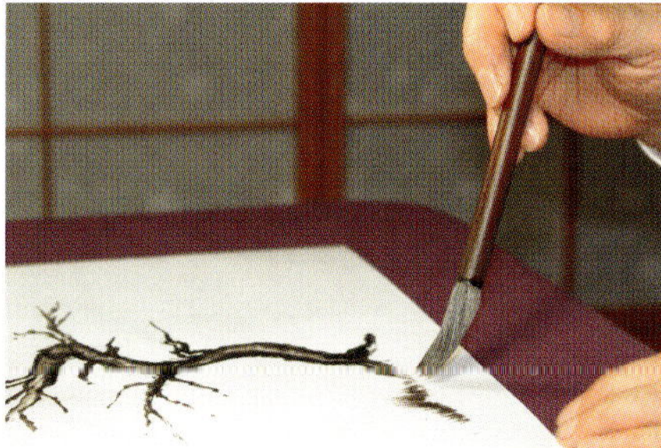

10. Use the multiple tips of the brush to create forbs and grasses. Then begin painting pine tree needles in groups. A common practice is to first use lighter ink; then flatten out the brush and remove excess ink; last, add darker ink to the tips.

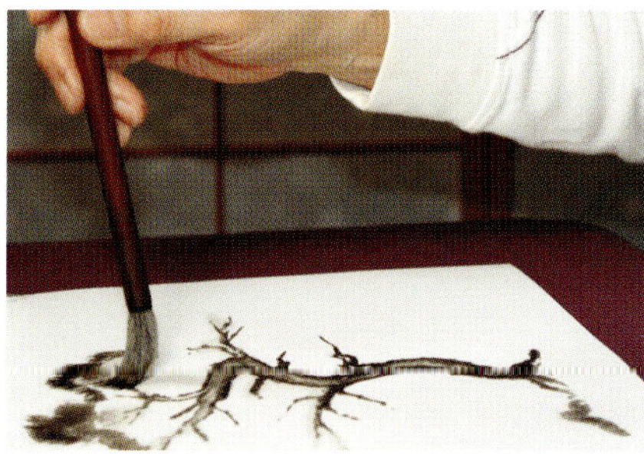

11. Then begin with darker ink for the second grouping. Using this method you will create the foreground groups in darker ink first, and as the ink is used, lighter background groups will automatically follow.

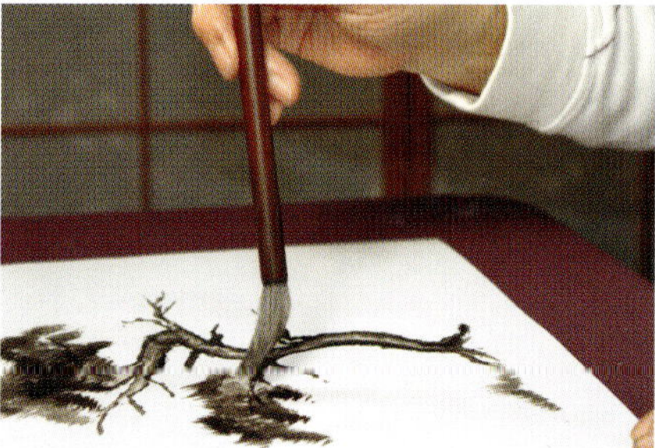

12. In this method of painting pine needles, at the center of the group the brush simply comes down straight. On either side of the group, turn the brush slightly toward the center of the group so that the multiple lines will form a fan shape.

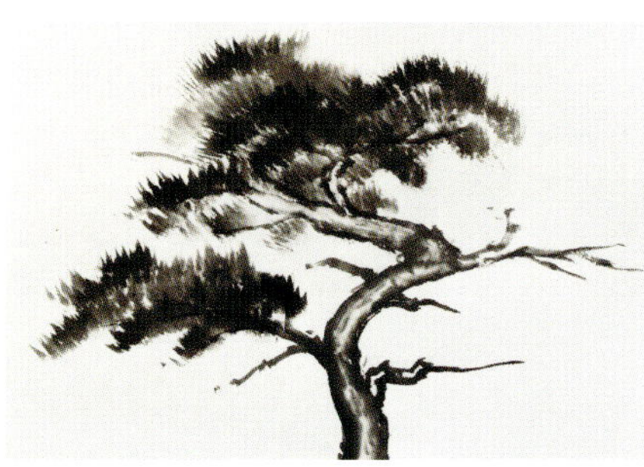

13. You will notice that the needle groupings form the shape of an opened fan. Overlapping with slight difference in tone of ink will give a sense of density.

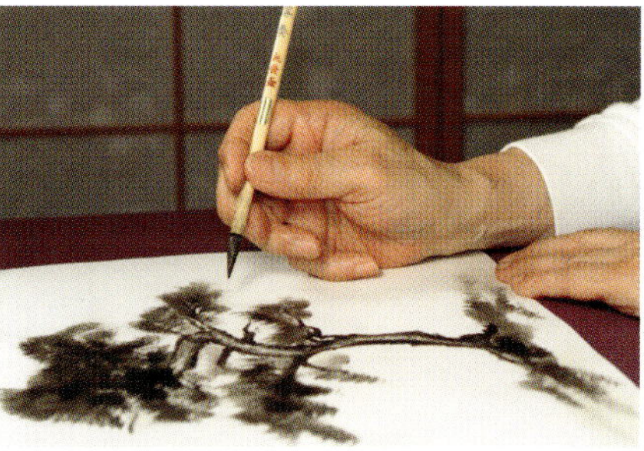

14. After completing the pine needles, double check the composition to see if there is a balance in the dominant, subdominant and subordinate relationship. Use a similar brush to add more groundcover, then change to a smaller brush to add details.

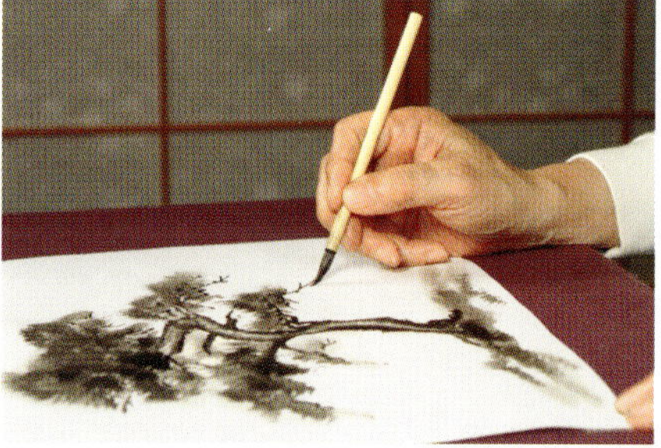

15. Many aged evergreens, especially pines, have old branches without needles, sometimes with pine cones. With the smaller brush, reasonably dry, add jagged lines in dark ink to create these aged branches.

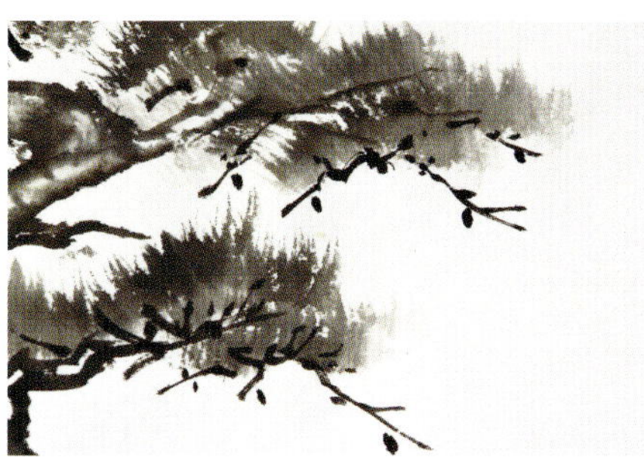

16. Dots on the bare twig branches are the attached pine cones.

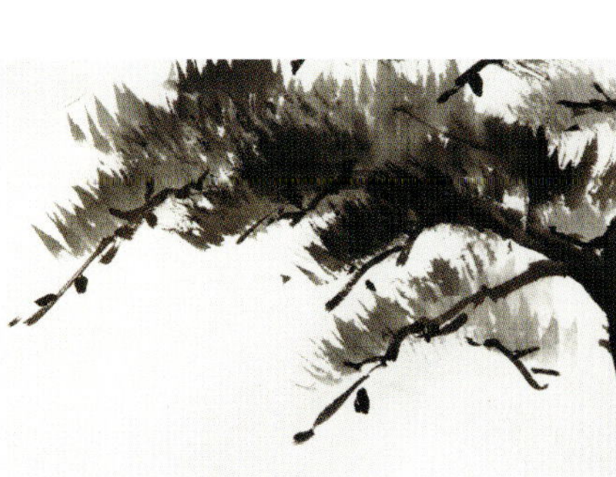

17. Pay close attention to each grouping of pine needles. Using different tones of ink helps to distinguish the various masses.

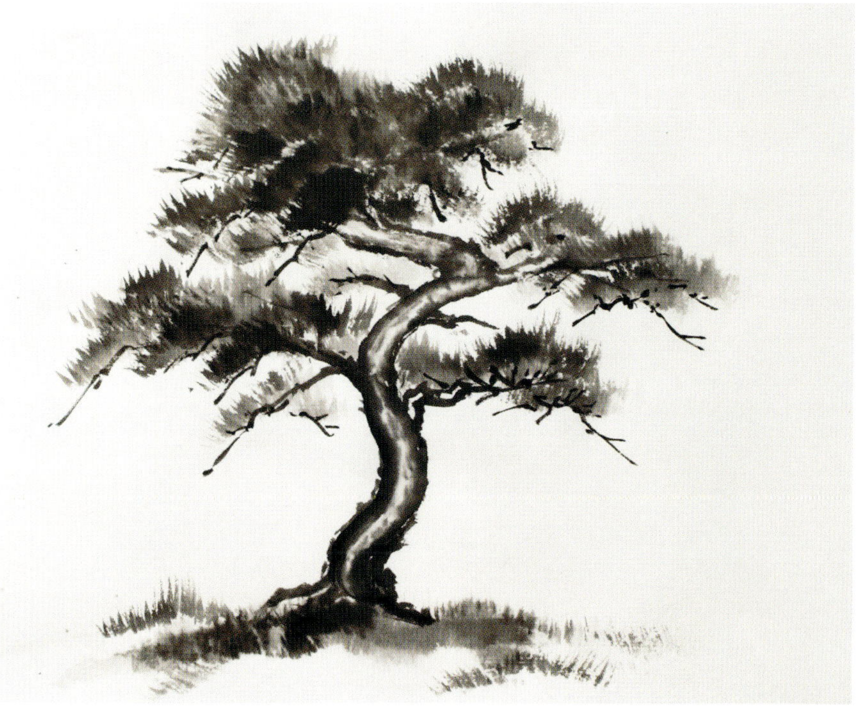

18. The results of this quick method of painting a pine tree. The top groupings of pine needles are dominant; lower groups to the left, right and back are subdominant; and the branch at the midpoint of the tree trunk on the right is subordinate.

PAINTING TREES WITH A UNIQUE BRUSH

A common practice among artists is to create one's own custom brushes for special needs. For example, it may be useful at some point to adjust an inexpensive watercolor brush by cutting the tips of the bristles with scissors to make them uneven, for painting distant leaves in various tones of ink. Here are a few ways of painting trees with special (or specialized) brushes and techniques.

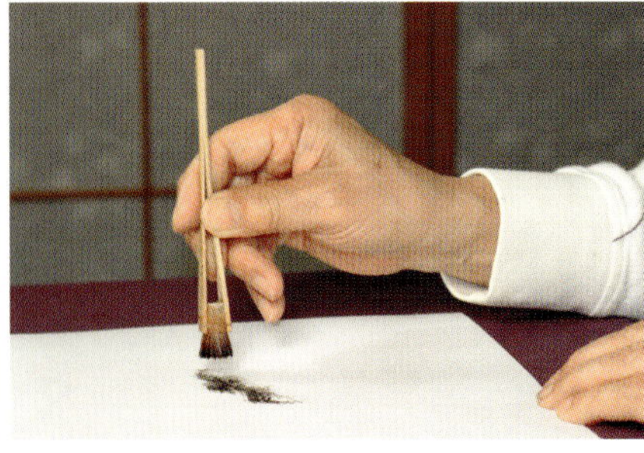

1. This brush is normally used for fabric and textile painting. It works well to make strokes from dark to light in a smooth manner. Apply lighter ink on one end of the tips and darker ink on the other.

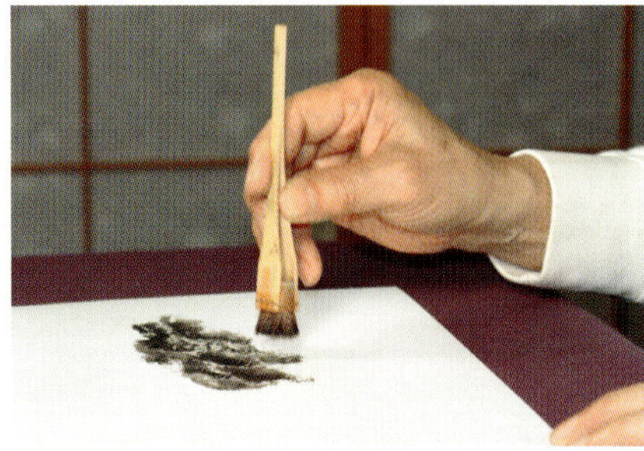

2. Then with a stamping technique you can easily create the effect of groups of leaves. By moving the brush in a slight curvature during each stamping, you can give the tops a rounded curve.

3. This is the result. This technique can be used to create a distant grove of trees on the slopes of a peak or on hillsides.

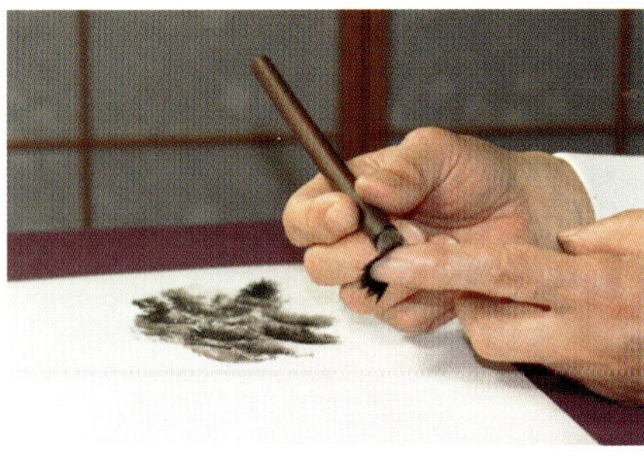

4. A common sumi-e brush such as a choryu brush can be used too. Apply a minimum amount of ink to the tips of an almost dry brush. Open the bristles and spread them apart in a slight curvature.

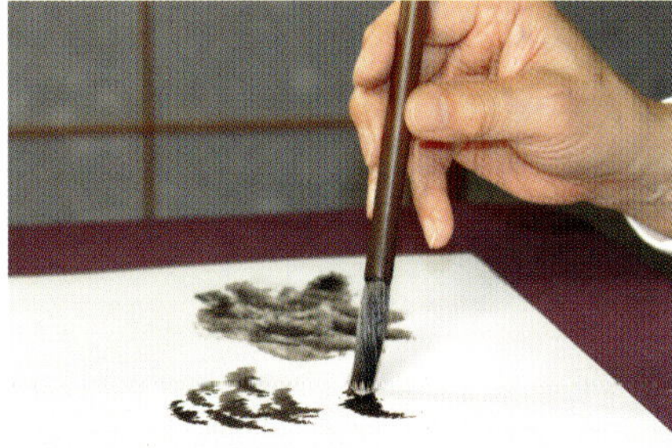

5. Using the brush in the same way as above, instead of painting, stamp out the shape.

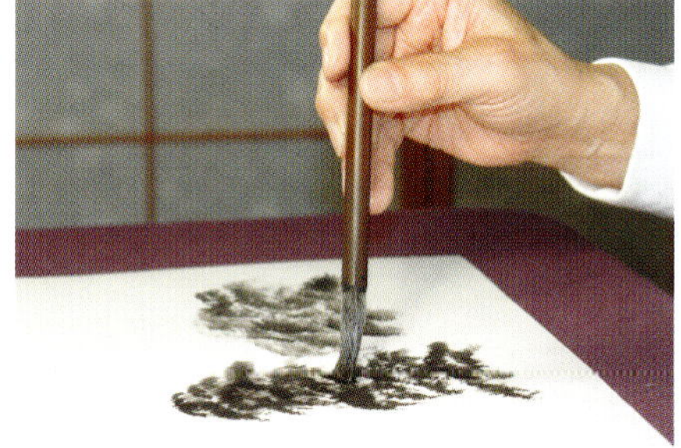

6. Move the brush left to right to extend the pattern. After you have done the desired amount of branches in darker ink, use a lighter ink to fill in the central part, giving a sense of density.

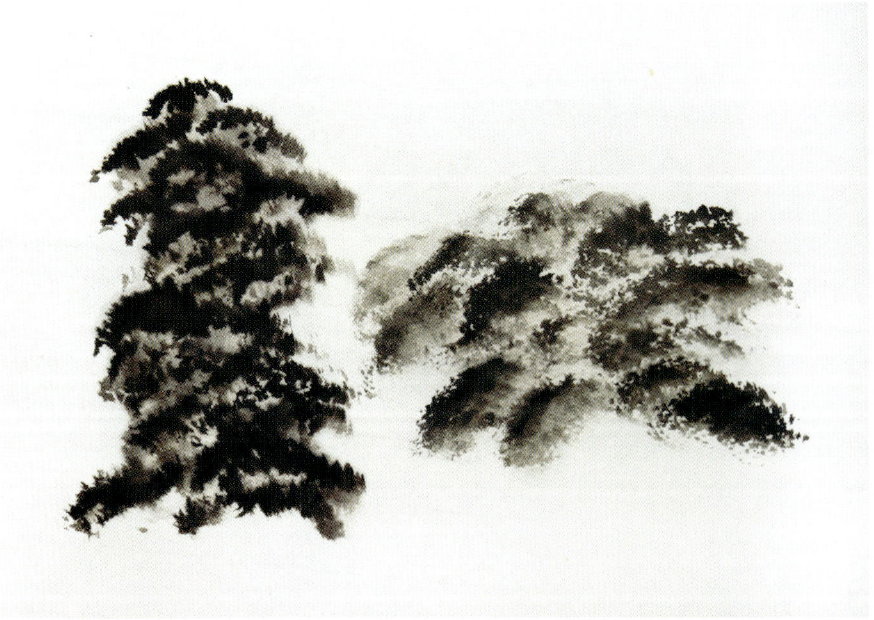

7. Although they were employed in the same way, these two different brushes offer two different results. This can be helpful when creating the leaves of several species of trees, for example.

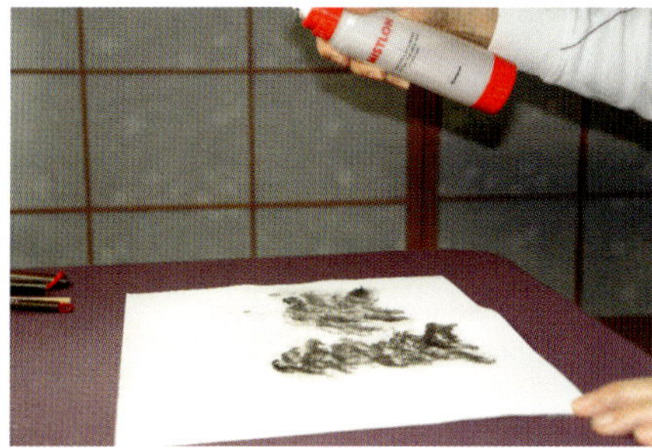

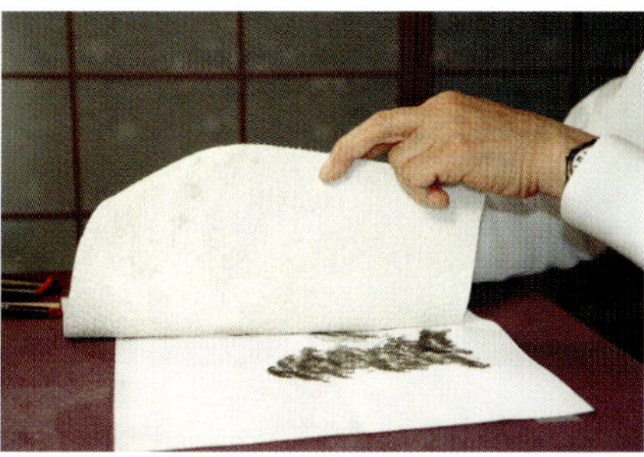

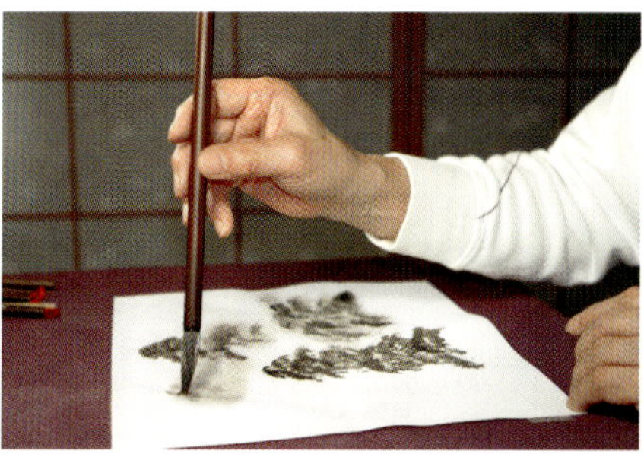

8. In case you wish to create distant tree leaves in a misty atmosphere, after the ink is completely dry, gently mist water over the painting with a handheld sprayer.

9. With a paper towel, soak up the excess moisture from the painting.

10. Now repeat the same technique used in Steps 1–6 to paint more leaves with either darker or lighter ink. Whichever tone of ink you use, the added moisture on the paper will cause spread.

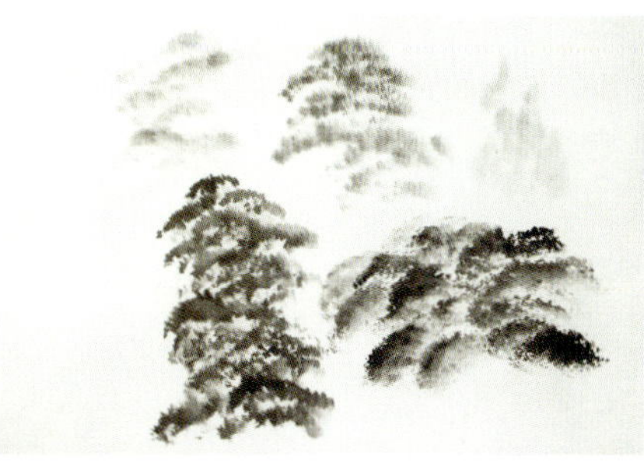

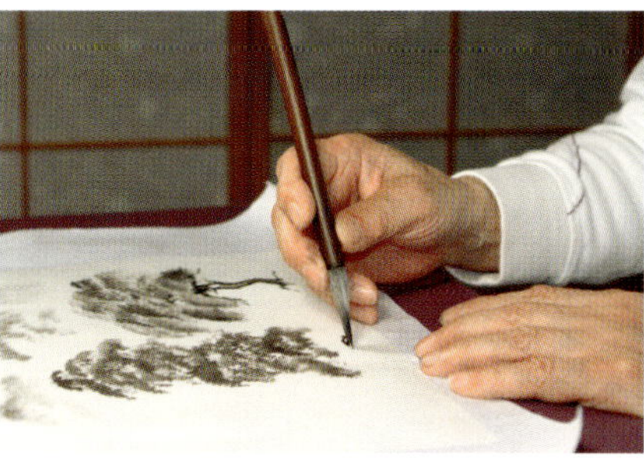

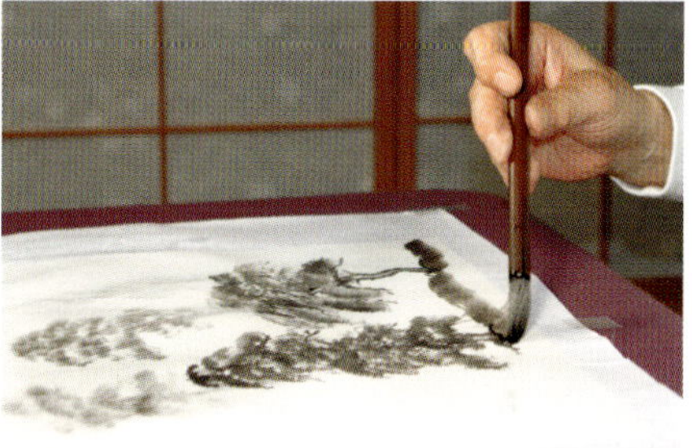

11. Compare the crisp groups of tree leaves on the lower two examples with the misty effect of the three upper trees.

12. After the sprayed section is dry, create tree trunks for the groups of leaves in the foreground.

13. After completing the trunk, branches and base of the tree, add the ground cover.

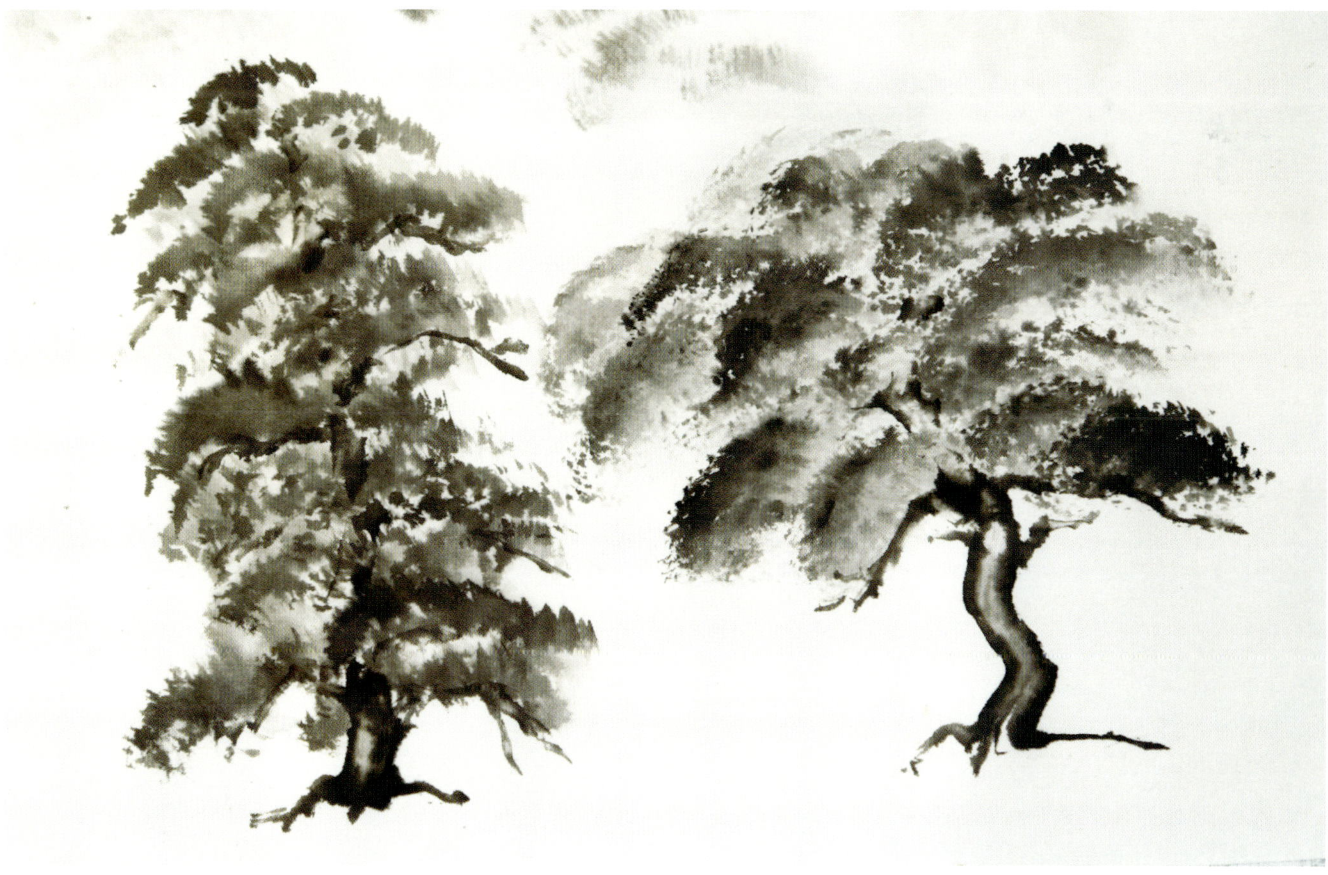

14. Here is the completed, simplified version of a tree. It is important to study nature: although you may think an evergreen is an evergreen, the various species differ widely—pines are quite unlike spruce or hemlocks. Also study the tree you plan to paint in relation to the other objects around it and in the background. Whether it's in high mountain terrain, meadows or along the sea coast, you should place a tree within its proper environment.

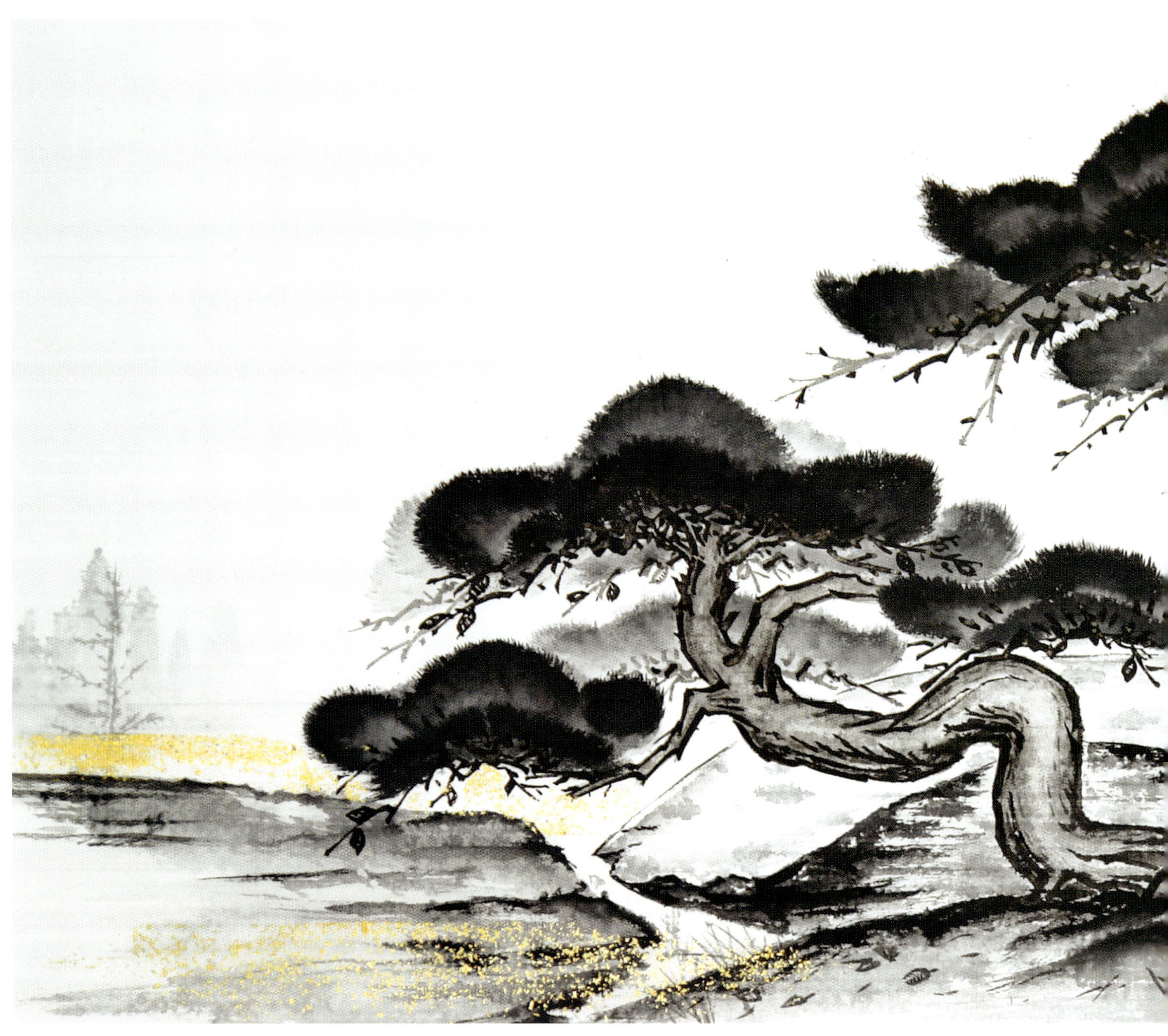

1. Two Pines

Size: H = 19.75"/50cm x W = 43.75"/110 cm
Paper: Sized and pre-mounted on a board
Sumi Ink: Standard with gold dust
Category: Suiboku-ga

This pine tree combination was found in the Rockies of Colorado. I was amazed to discover that these two pines were joined at the roots and in their combined power over many years of growth were able to push up a great boulder. This was a revealing study on how plants in nature brave harsh conditions and perform unexpected feats.

It also fits with the tradition of ink painting. From the earliest times in the history of ink painting, Chinese masters have selected elements of nature such as a tree, a mountain or rocks and used these to make a statement about human

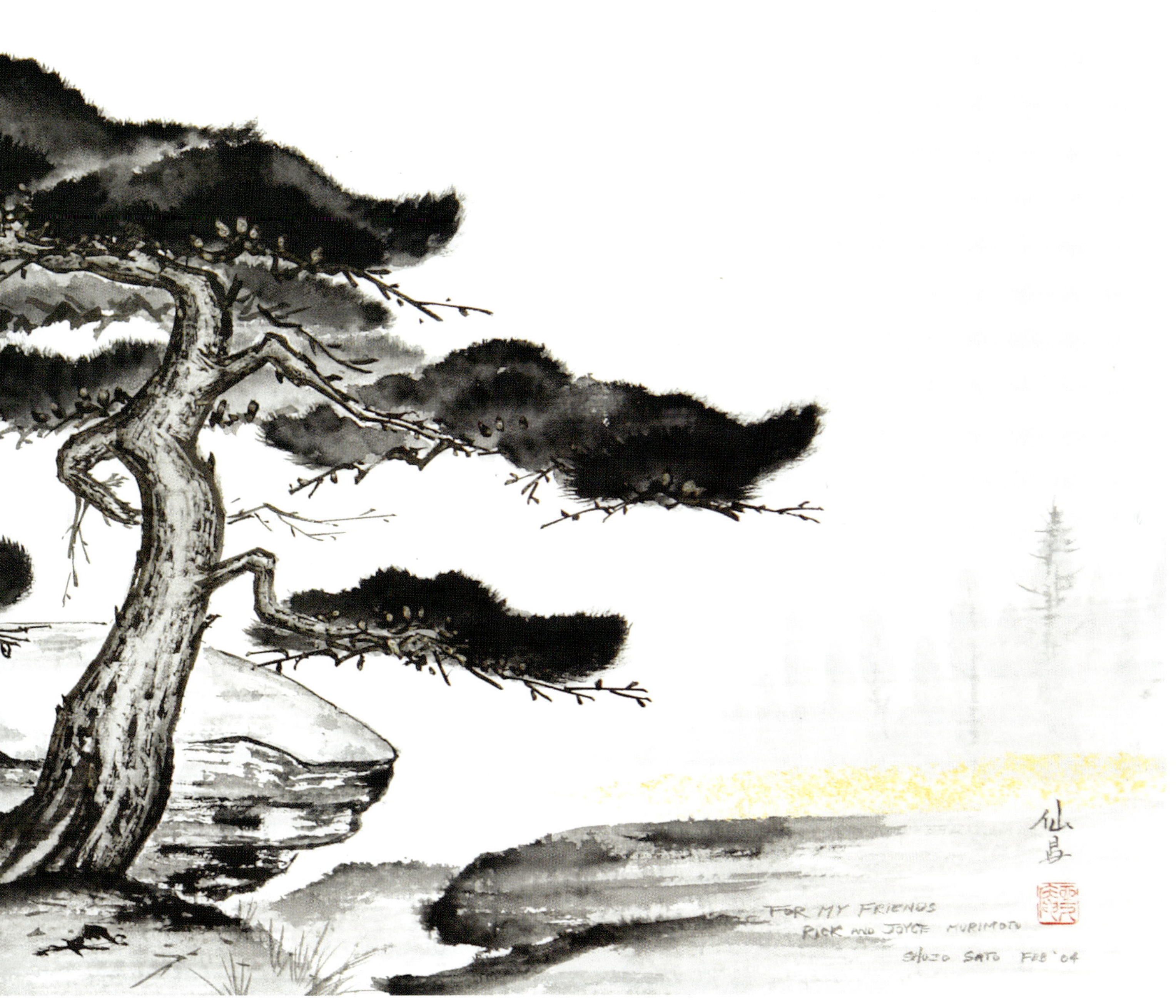

character. What appears to be a painting of a pine tree in the foreground combined with a waterfall in the background, for instance, may be a philosophic statement concerning the passage of time in life.

Likewise, in this simple landscape is a message that two together, with their combined energy, can lift a monumental weight over time even while facing the sometimes brutal conditions that nature wields.

Collection of Dr. and Mrs. Richard Morimoto.

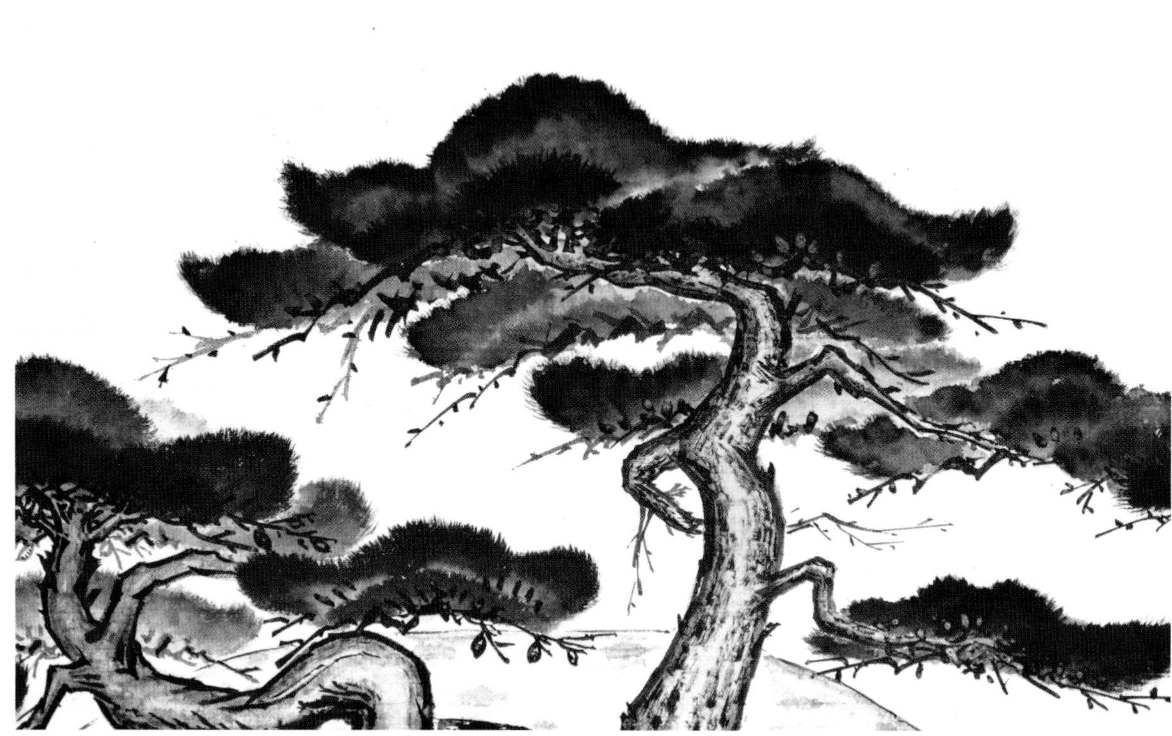

The taller pine tree was painted to symbolically show strength and masculinity. Its needle groupings were given more mass, and by adding some branches with pine cones, the tree gained a more realistic touch. When painting plants that have many branches with needles or leaves, you should always remember to maintain a rhythmical balance in the composition.

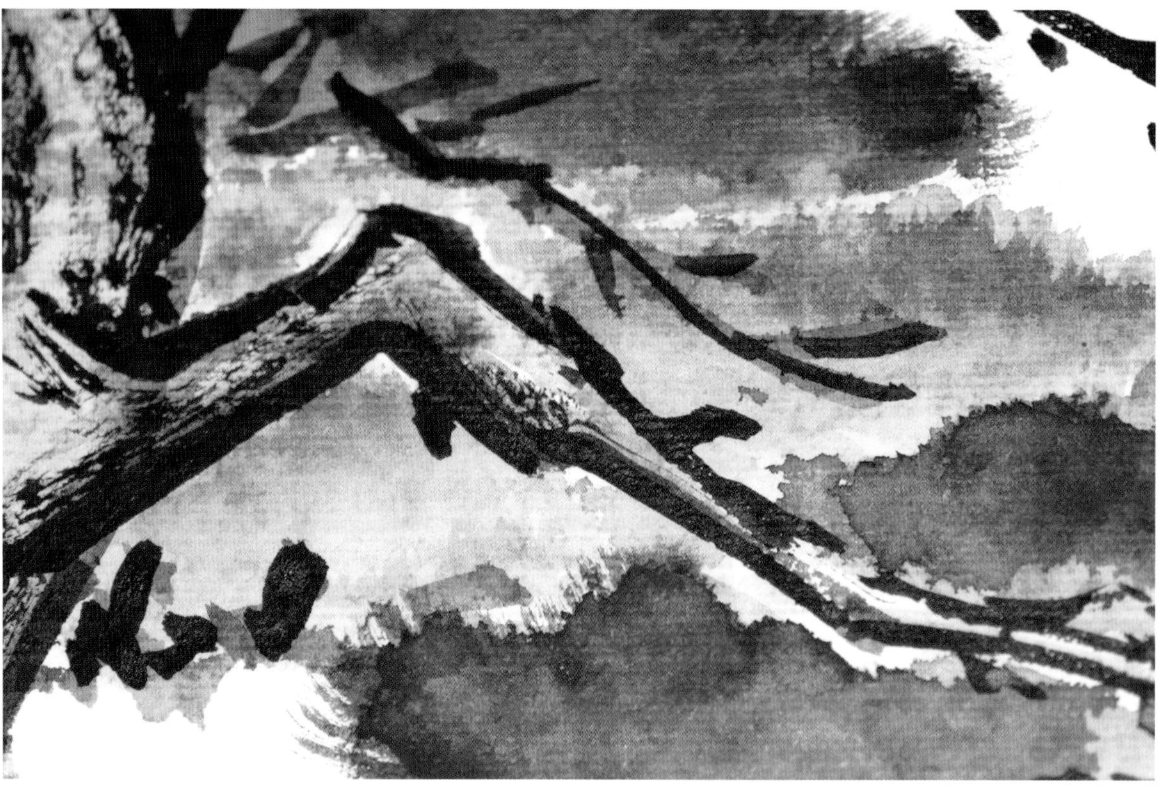

It is quite common to use the outline technique in black ink painting, especially in suiboku-ga. While painting this outline for the branch, the artist must use inner energy to result in lines that have the strength to carry the heavy load of needles. In this section of the background, the massive grouping of needles is done in the tarashi komi technique, without the painting of the individual needles. After the ink is almost dry, use a mountain horse hair brush without ink to extend that area in the manner of pine needles growing out.

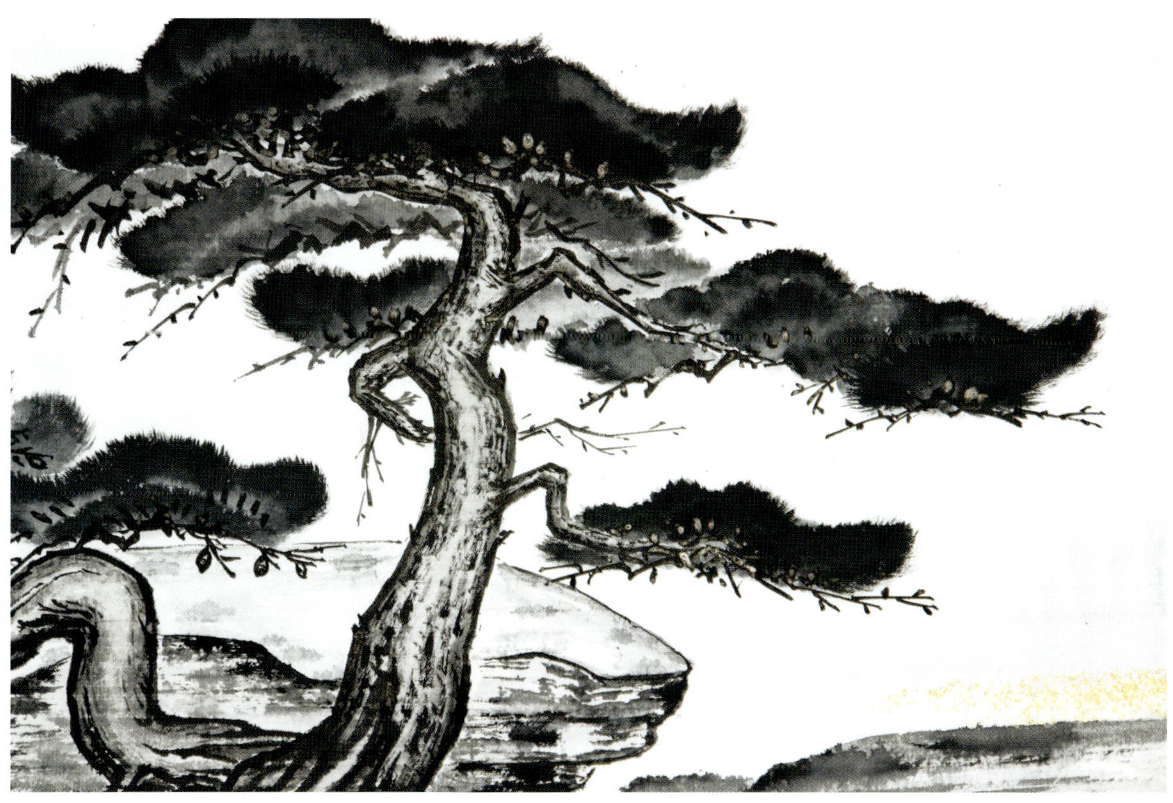

Notice the horizontal composition of the pine branches with boulder behind, and the differences in texture between the tree's trunk and the boulder.

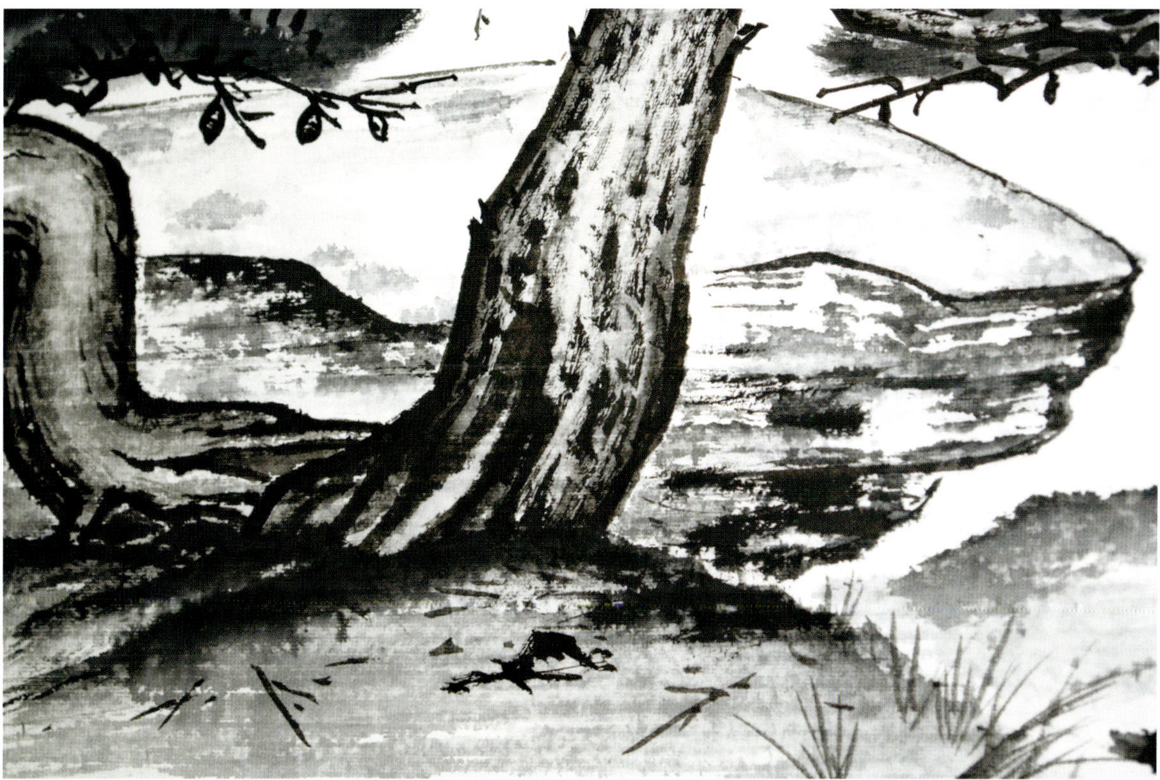

In creating the texture of the boulder, I used a dry brush. The bristles were held horizontally (see Chapter 3). The two trees' barks were painted to intentionally show a difference. The taller tree is more textured and rough, signifying *yang,* while the accompanying tree has bark which is smoother, symbolically representing *yin.*

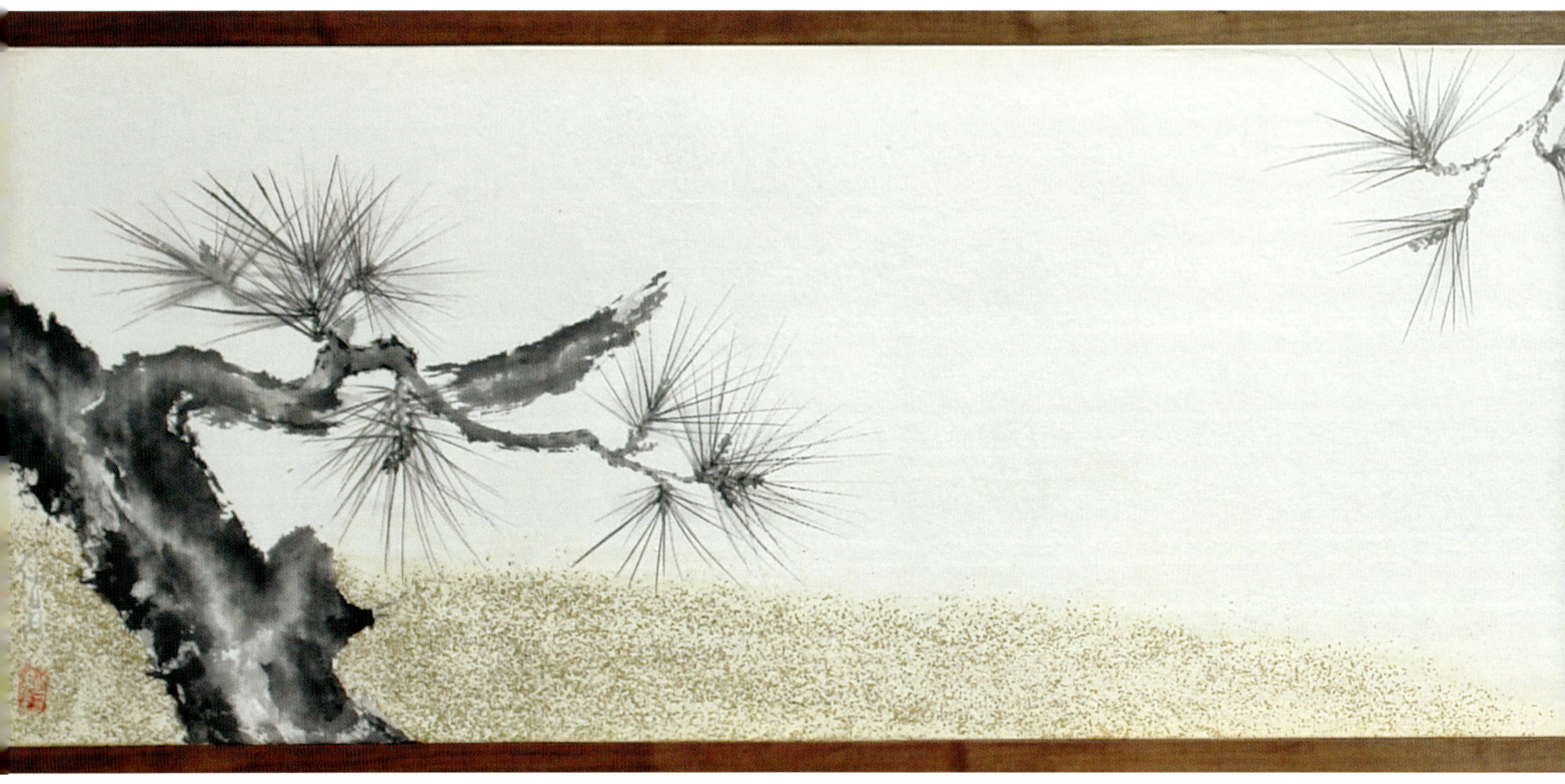

2. Pine Breeze: Screen for the Tea Ceremony

Size: H = 15"/38cm x W = 71.5"/182cm
Paper: Sized
Sumi Ink: Standard with gold dust
Category: Suiboku-ga

The traditional way of life for the Japanese has incorporated many categories of the arts into daily living. Tea ceremony is the epitome of this. In fact, it has been said that the tea ceremony aesthetic represents a crystallization of the best of the Japanese traditional arts. For centuries, tea masters dedicated themselves to selecting tea ceremony articles which met certain criteria in craftsmanship. This keen scrutiny and selection among the common crafts, such as ceramics, has led to the upgrading of the craft arts into fine arts in Japan, and now they receive international recognition.

Sumi art plays a role in the tea ceremony as well. The Japanese tea room includes an alcove called a *tokonoma*, created specifically to display calligraphy or a painting in black ink. Folding screens were created to identify the special space in the room where tea equipment is set up. These folding screens are often painted in sumi-e or may display calligraphy of a Zen statement or poetry. The subject of the painting or hanging scroll often denotes the season, and in Japan there are four distinct seasons. Therefore, connoisseurs collect specific tea ceremony utensils and tools to enhance each season.

An important part of the tea ceremony is that all of the senses are involved. Tea rooms are mostly quiet, but the

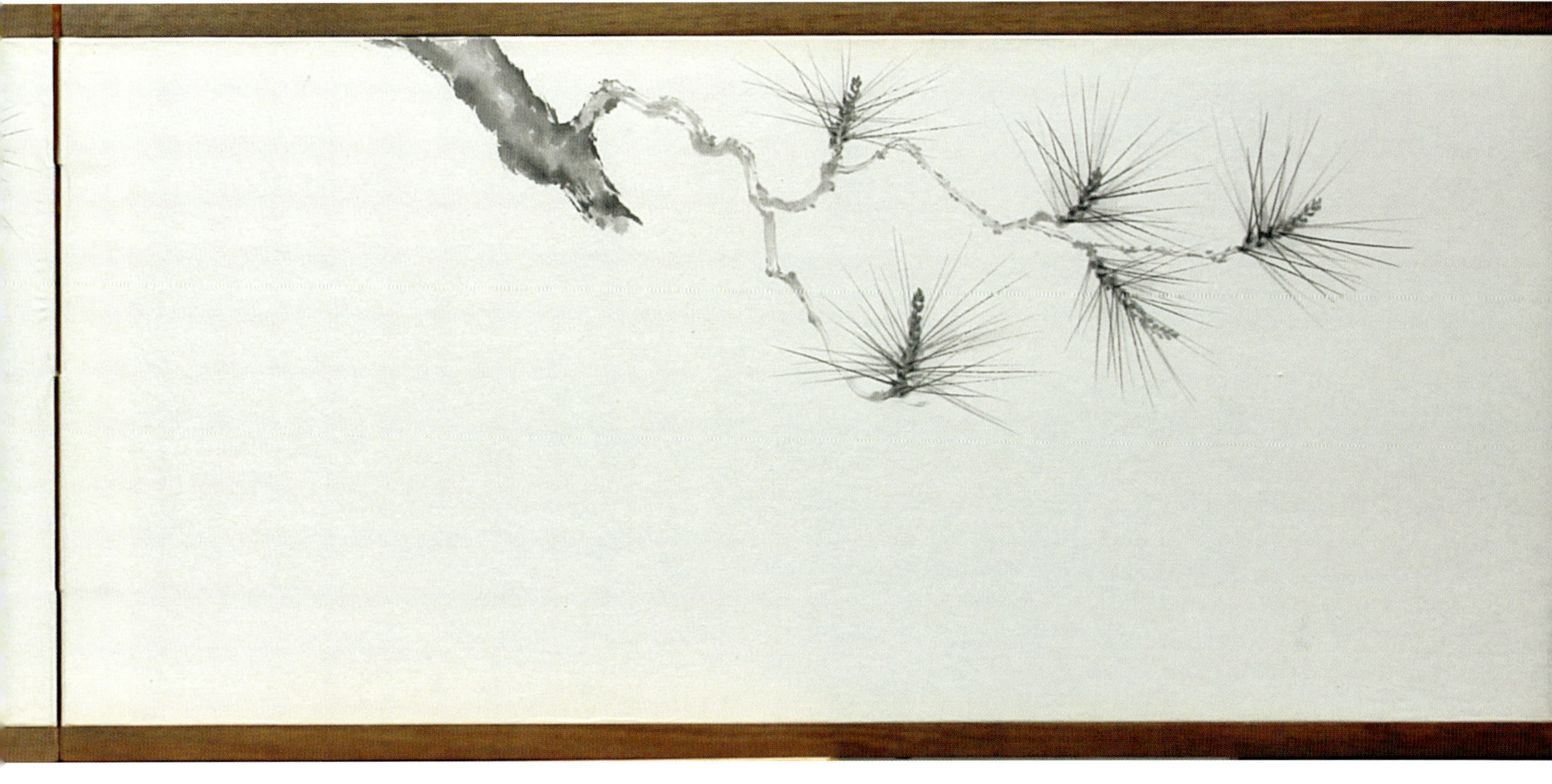

sound of the water simmering in the cast iron kettle (the *kama*) is an enjoyable sound and is commonly called "pine breeze." In order to create this unique and pleasurable sound from the rising temperature of hot water, craftsmen who make the kama place an additional three pieces of metal at the bottom of the kama during the casting process. How this is carried out is a special craft secret. As the water temperature rises, hot water causes these pieces to begin vibrating. Accordingly, a kettle's value is determined by the quality of the sound produced, just as in a musical instrument.

This screen depicts a literal "pine breeze" by reflecting the romanticized sound of a gentle breeze in the forest, providing an atmosphere of tranquility and harmony. The tree trunk is the dominating subject on the left panel; the small branch at the top of the left panel is subordinate and the right panel branch is subdominant. The active empty space on both of the panels gives the composition balance.

The screen is folded in a 90-degree angle when it is in use, and designates the area in the tea room where the tea equipment sits. Meant for use in the summer, it prevents heat from reaching the guests.

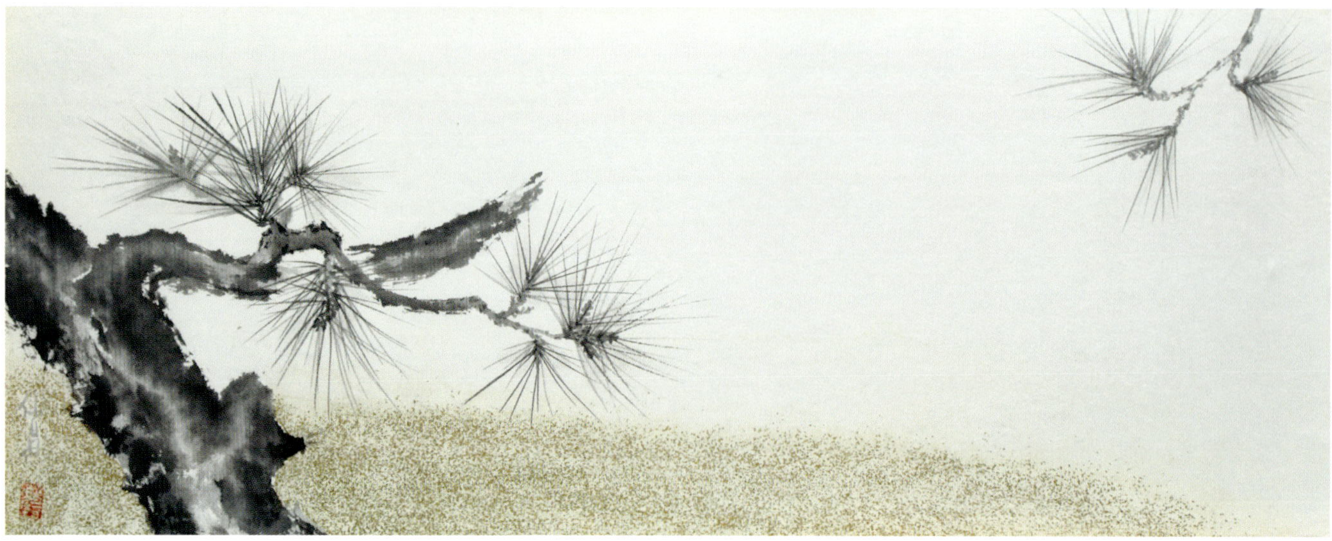

Because this painting will be viewed up close when in use as a tea ceremony screen, on this left-hand side of the panel, the pine trunk and branches with needles are painted quite realistically. The rough thick trunk is done with a drier brush, and is created in a similar way to painting bamboo culms (see Chapter 3, page 53). Apply dark ink at the base and tip of the bristles, with very light ink at the midsection. The excess ink should be soaked up from the brush using a paper towel. To paint the secondary branch extending to the right, wash and reapply ink to the brush and as you move to the right, at the halfway point of the branch, leave a space then complete the broken end of the branch. At that juncture of space, create the sweeping sub-branch with pine needles. Before the ink dries out, using dark ink on the tip of the brush, give "definition" to certain parts of the branches. It is important to make these darker lines while the paper is still wet. The dark ink at the base of pine needles in groups of 2, 3 or 5 marks the source of energy for the needles: use a small brush to make these dots. Then with the thinnest long-bristled brush in your collection, paint each pine needle from the base to the tip. Each line should have lifelike energy. After completing a group of pine needles, shade the lower part of the needles with very light ink supply a certain sense of density to each group. It is important to use darker ink for foreground pine needles and lighter ink for the background pine needles. When the tree is completed, apply gold dust (see page 61 for techniques).

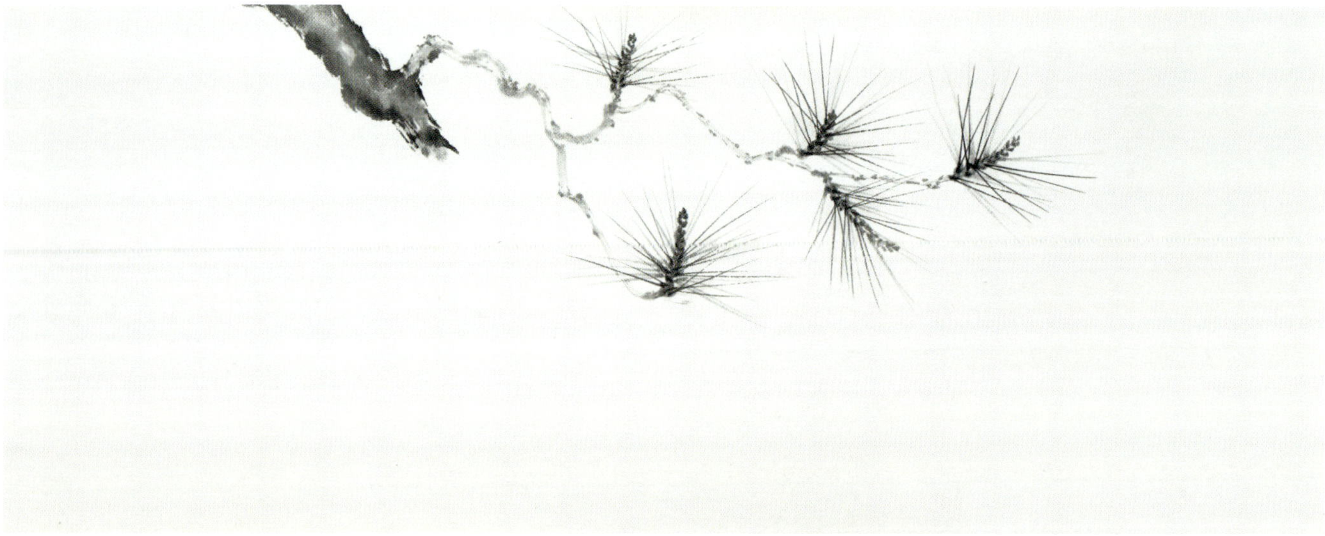

While the left-hand panel shows the foreground, the right-hand panel is meant to give the sense of height and a distant feeling. Use lighter ink to create these branches. The individual groupings of pine needles are painted to create different rhythms. On the bracts, add dark ink as dots to balance the left and right sides of the composition.

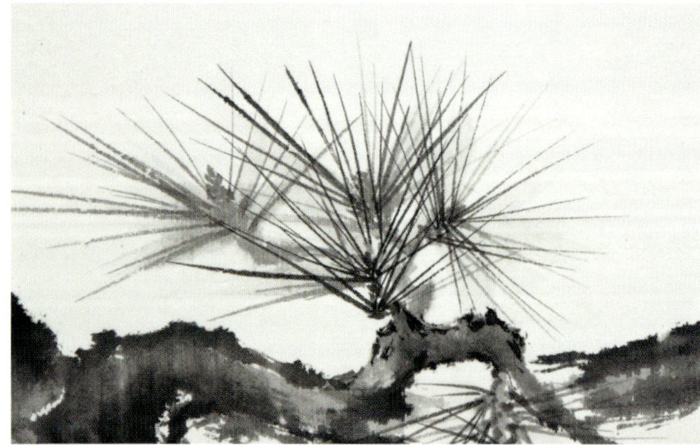

In black ink painting, dark ink shows strength: from a perspective point of view, dark ink comes forward and light ink moves toward the back. With careful application using different tones of ink, perspective can be achieved.

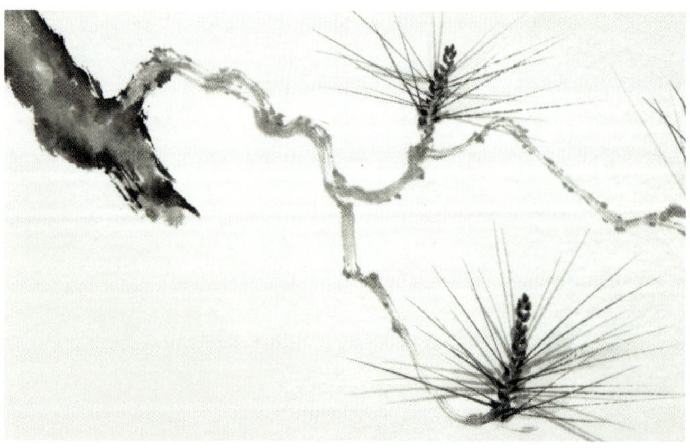

The right-hand panel's groupings of pine needles are much less dense. Therefore, the bracts are made slightly longer. The active empty space on both of the panels provides balance to the composition.

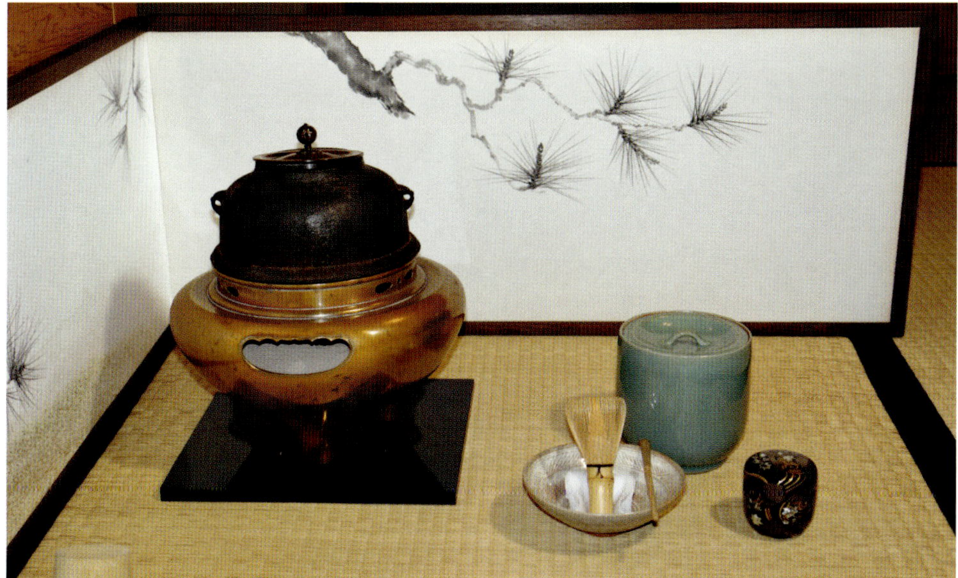

In a tea ceremony room the folding screen serves as a backdrop for the tea equipment, set up in summer style. This is the view that faces the host. From this vantage point, one can see the use of active empty space in the painting. The cast bronze brazier and cast iron *kama* are placed underneath the large pine branch. Notice that the utensils reflect the groupings of pine needles in the painting: Five groups of pine needles complement the five groupings of tea utensils (including the waste water bowl with dipper, partially shown at far left).

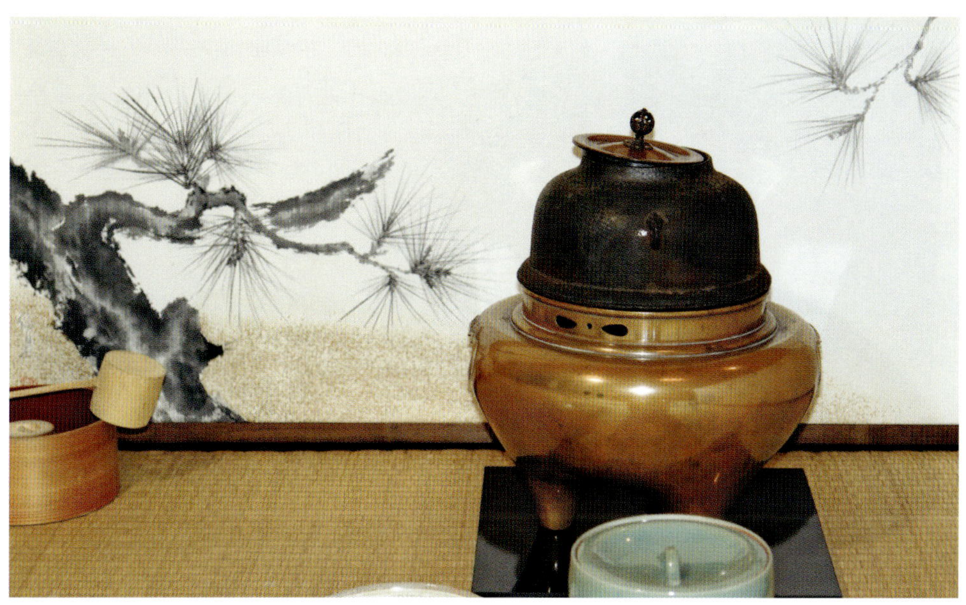

The large empty space on the left panel was intentionally created for the *kama* (cast iron kettle). Underneath the tree trunk is space for the dipper and waste water container. The gold dust complements the bronze brazier.

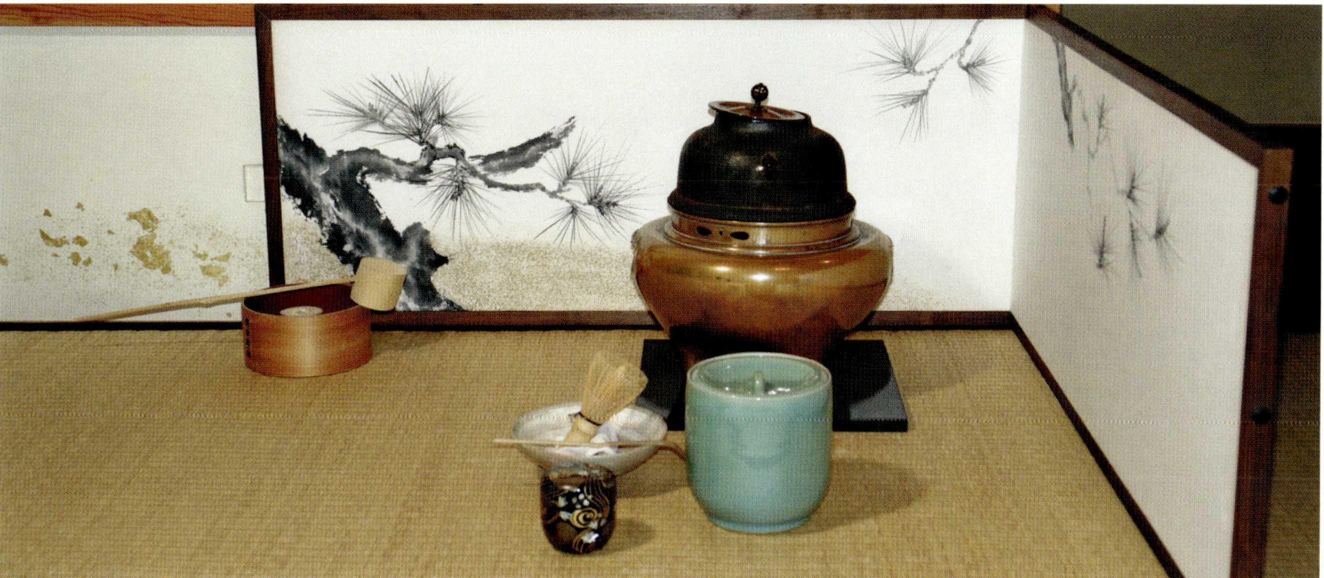

This is the overall view which the guests will see while seated in the tea room. The equipment for tea now becomes a part of the painting on the folding screen. The concept of dominant, subdominant and subordinate is a useful arrangement in all kinds of design organization. On a smaller scale, the celadon water jar has mass so it forms a group in the foreground with the water jar as dominant, the tea bowl as subdominant and the black lacquer tea caddy as subordinate. When the host is seated in front of the guests, a larger group in composition is formed. This concept of composition can be used to bring art into your everyday life in many ways.

Painting Bamboo

My experience in teaching university classes, especially in the Midwest, has been that most of the students have never seen a living bamboo plant, much less bamboo growing in groves! Therefore, in class their compositions of leaves have no life and look more like wet socks hanging on a clothesline. The beginning of a bamboo stalk should convey the outward-pushing energy of growth and it follows that the leaves should share that same lifelike feeling.

Since painting bamboo requires wide-to-wide strokes for the culm (or stalk) and sub-branches, and narrow-wide-narrow strokes for the leaves, along with perhaps a few wide-to-narrow strokes for certain branch sections, it is a relatively easy subject for beginners in sumi-e. Along with learning to master three basic strokes, students can learn basic elements of composition: how many leaves to use for a mass, how to recognize active empty space, and so forth. At the same time, what appears to be a simple subject is one which a serious artist may spend a lifetime painting. Growth patterns, climatic conditions . . . the variations and possibilities to be captured in sumi are endless.

There are over three hundred species of bamboo. Some species have many short sub-branches of about a foot (0.3m) long, while other bamboo species can grow to a height of over twenty feet (6m), with sub-branches as long as five feet (1.5m). This wide variation in nature means that you can paint your bamboo freely depending only upon your composition needs.

Bamboo can grow very quickly, sometimes as much as two to three feet a night. To show this energy that emanates from the joints, each brush stroke for the culm should be forceful and smooth at the beginning and the end.

It is your choice as the artist whether the culm sections will be painted as successive strokes, or as a single brush stroke beginning at the bottom and going up all the way, skip-ping brief spaces to create the individual joints. The artist may begin at the bottom segment's top joint and move the brush downward to the bottom, then from the second joint move upward to paint each higher segment of the culm. The direction choice also depends upon the type of paper you are using. If the paper is very thin, it is difficult to work from the bottom up because the bristles will catch the edge of the paper.

In the painting of bamboo on the facing page, you will notice that the culm on the right has highlight and shadows all incorporated in one stroke. (See Chapter 3 for this basic technique.) The bamboo culm on the left is without highlight and shadows. Depending upon the application of ink, however, when the brush is moved swiftly, often you find these white sections left in your strokes. This is a desirable effect; do not go back and paint them black. Accept this highlight as an accidental gift. If your brush is overloaded with ink it will not happen, so use a dry brush. On unsized paper this effect will happen more naturally but on sized paper you may have to use a drier brush.

If you decide to compose piano music using only the black keys, you work within the limitation of those five keys. Likewise, when you paint bamboo, you use only a few kinds of strokes. The comparison between music and bamboo painting is a simple one, but it is true that while being composed of very few elements, bamboo expresses many themes and moods.

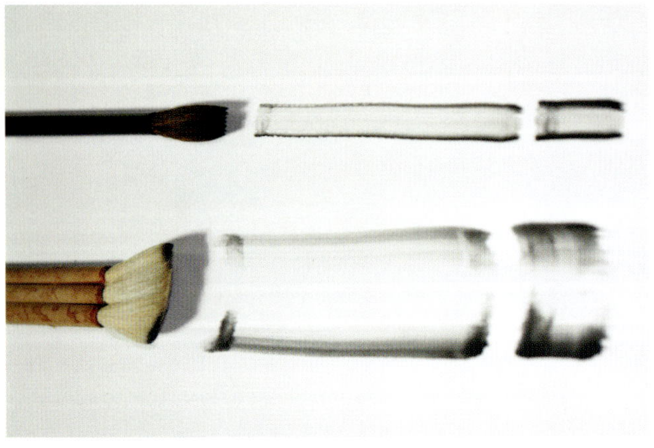

To create a wide bamboo culm with highlight and shadows the renpitsu brush, shown at bottom, will work very well. When you use a standard sumi brush, as shown at top, flatten the bristle tips, then apply dark ink at the sides to create a highlight and shadow effect. In the white spaces shown between the individual culm strokes, you will add small wide-to-wide lines to complete the joints (see pages 16–17).

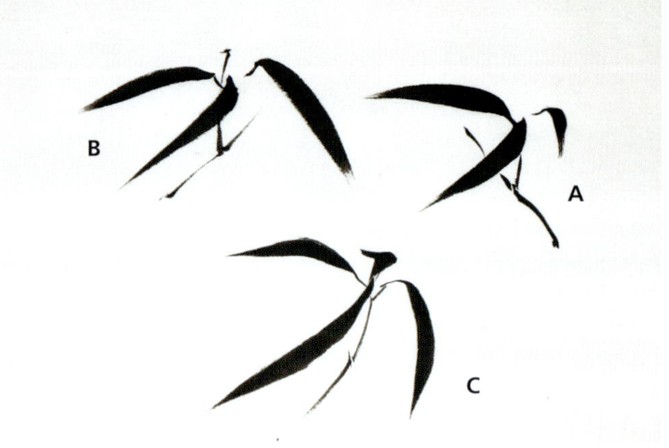

Leaves grouped in various numbers and formations are given names in the *Mustard Seed Garden Manual*. These examples often show how closely the classic Chinese teaching methods for painting relate to the use of a brush in writing ideograms. In **A**, the form of two bamboo leaves together resembles the "tail of a swallow in flight." **B** shows three leaves in a pattern resembling the Chinese or Japanese ideogram *kai* which means "supporting." **C**'s leaf formation is like the sudden "take-off of geese in flight."

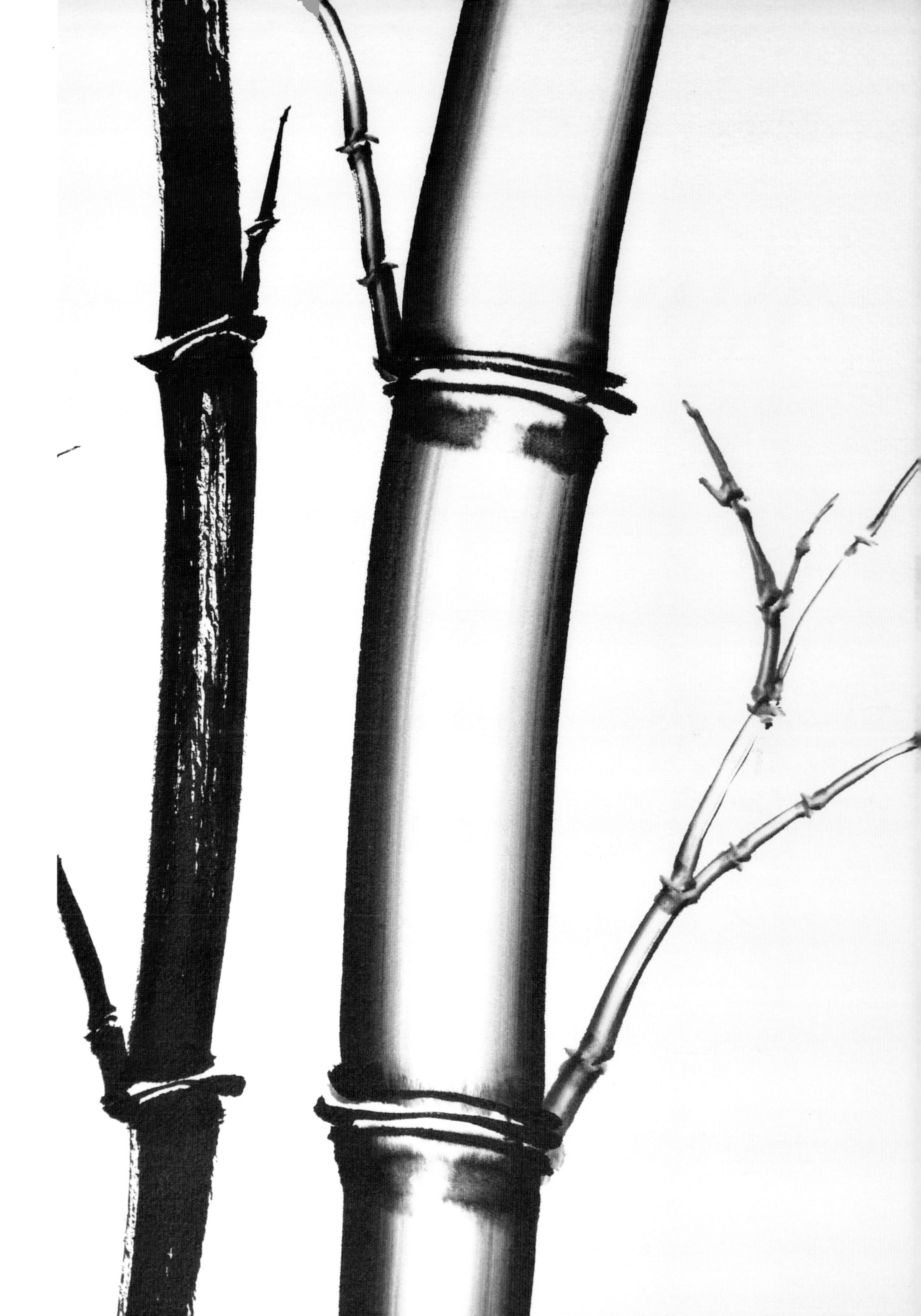

PAINTING BAMBOO LEAVES

This will give you practice using the wrist and fingertips to make the bottom leaf point in a precise form. It may be done with wrist movement, or the entire arm may go up for the final point. (Review page 45 to see how wrist action is used for this stroke.) Success also depends upon the type of paper you use. For example, newsprint as practice paper is useful for getting familiar with forming the strokes. But because its fiber content will not show the fine variations you will be exploring below in Row 2, you should use sumi-e paper for these.

Row 1: To paint the top row of leaves apply dark ink on the brush and beginning at the far left, paint a continuous line of leaves. As you reach the far right, notice the effects as the ink begins to run out.

Row 2: Wash the brush, remove the excess water, then apply light ink on the bristles with dark ink on the tip. Beginning at the left, paint a bamboo leaf; examine the slight variation in tone of ink that this gives the leaf.
For the next leaf in Row 2: Wash the brush, apply lighter ink and remove excess moisture on a paper towel. Touch the point in dark ink. Hold the brush completely upright and paint a leaf. The dark ink spreads to create the veins.
For the third leaf in Row 2: Use the same application of ink as for the previous leaf. Begin as usual but as you move the brush down the leaf, move the tip along the lower edge of leaf to create the darker edge.
Far the rightmost leaf in Row 2: Use the same application of ink, but this time gradually turn the tip to the upper edge to create the darker edge.

Row 3: Practice making a variety of bamboo leaves by applying ink in a similar range of methods.

Practice painting bamboo leaves growing in different directions. At the center top is a young bamboo leaf still formed in a roll. The leaves to its left and right are semi-opened, and the following leaves are bent leaves. The bent leaves are, in essence, two short leaves put together: create a short leaf, lift the brush, then begin another short leaf. The key to painting a bent leaf successfully is that the underside should show a continuous arc.

Practice making bamboo leaves in groups. Whenever you paint three leaves in a group, begin with the center leaf. Then add the left and right leaves. If you have a brush such as a choryu which is ideal for bamboo leaves, as you complete the leaf the bristles will automatically return to a point.

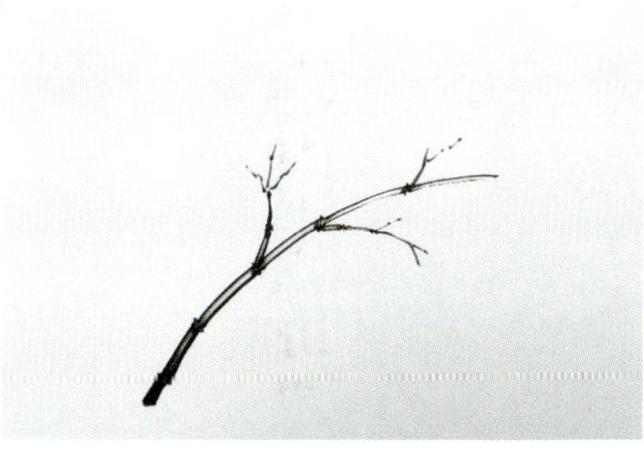

1. First, paint a sub-branch. (Because the leaves' placement is crucial to the composition, once you are accustomed to painting bamboo, you can paint the leaves first, then insert branches at the end.)

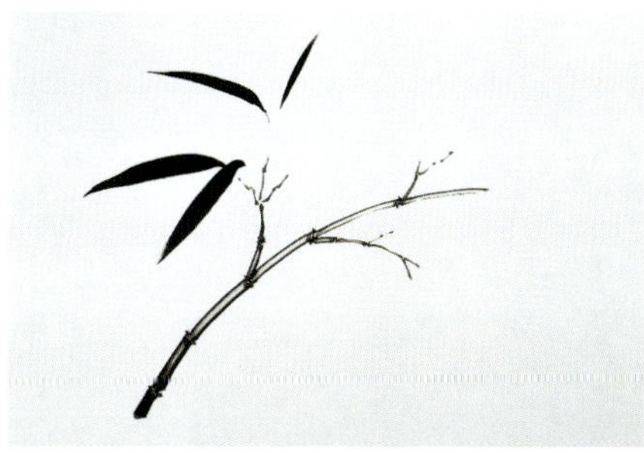

2. A common mistake is to connect every leaf with the branch. Instead, paint leaves with a space between them and the branch so that you are not limited if you wish to expand your composition.

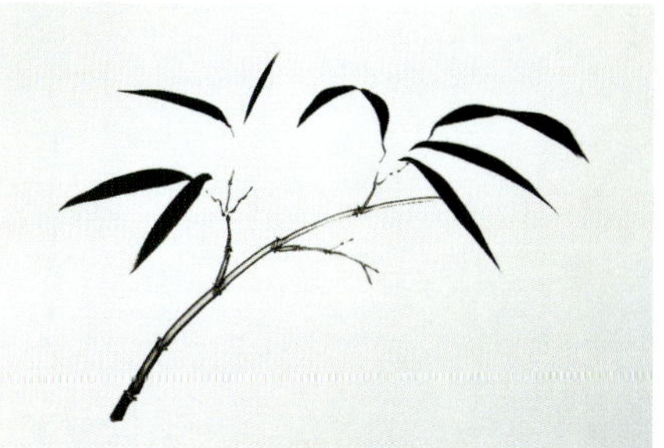

3. Now four more leaves have been painted on the right side.

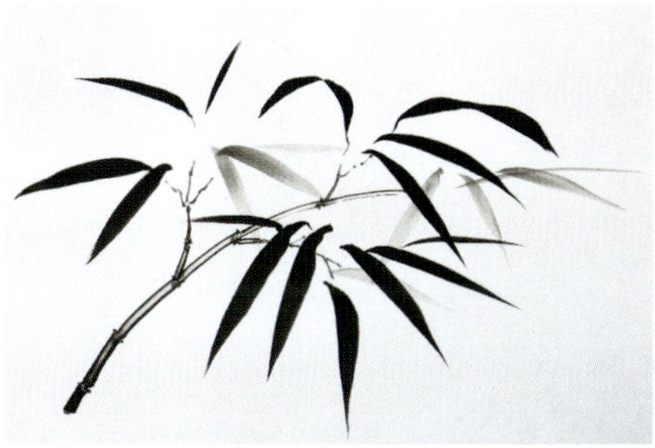

4. Four leaves and then three leaves have been painted in.

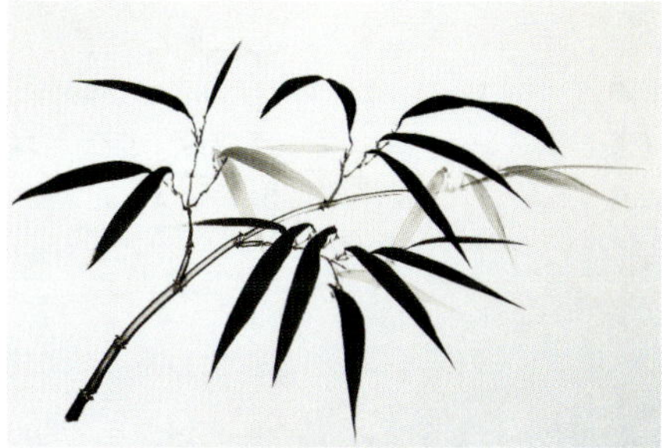

5. Paint the background leaves in lighter ink.

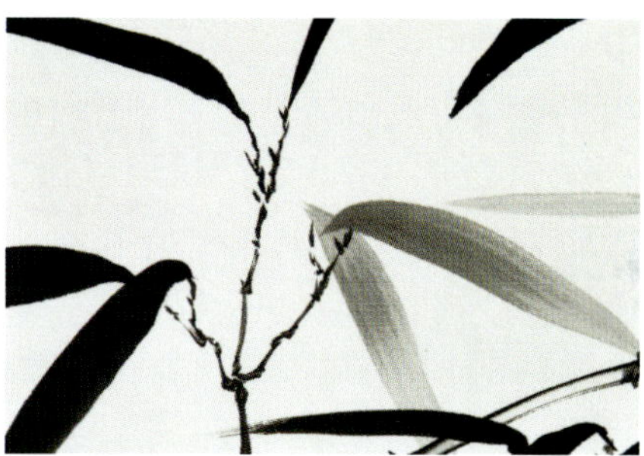

6. Notice how the narrow stems connect the leaves to the sub-branch.

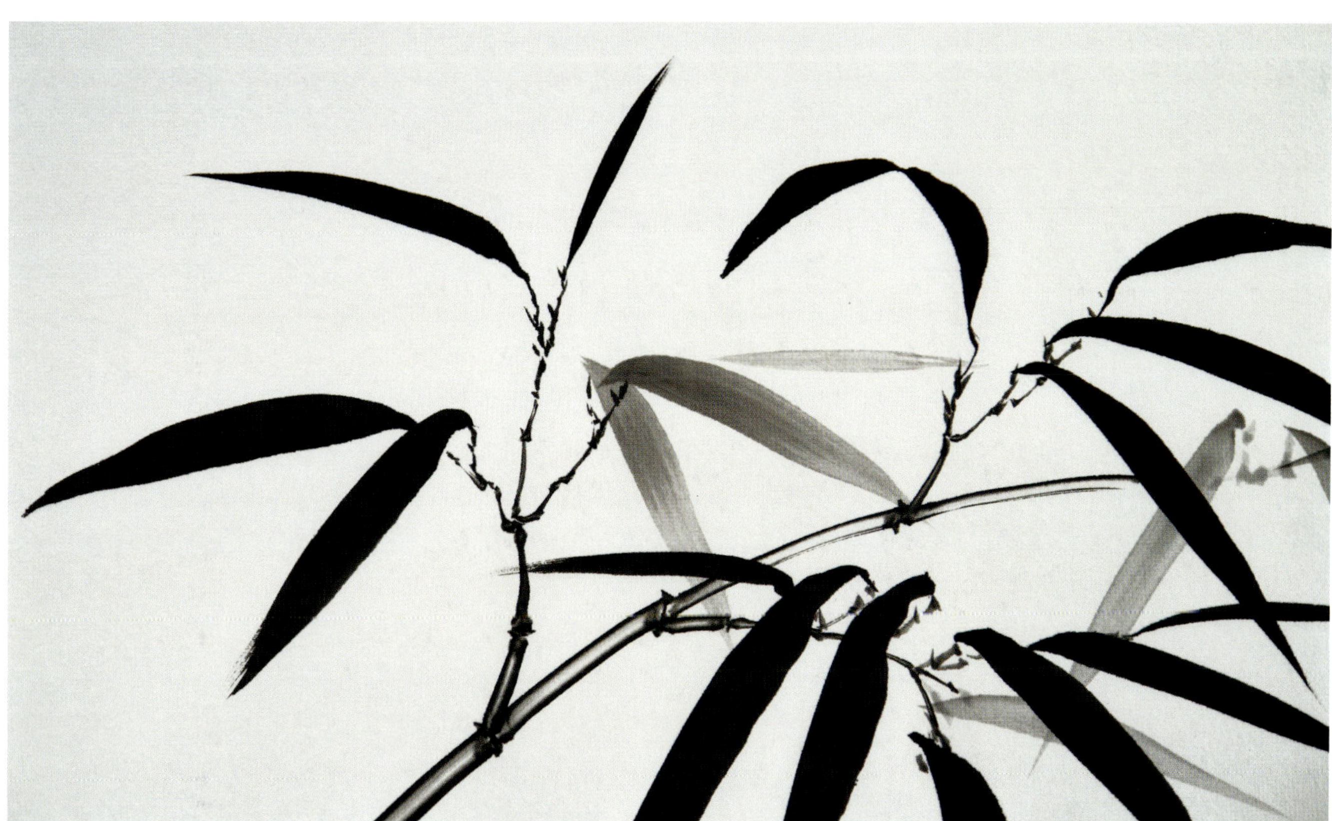

7. Individual leaves are now securely connected to the branches. Remember, however, that your creation is not meant to be a detailed botanical study of bamboo. This is sumi-e, which uses the art of suggestion. What is important is that you have successfully suggested that this is bamboo, along with conveying the larger message you wish to state through the painting. The artistic message is the essence, rather than realistic detail.

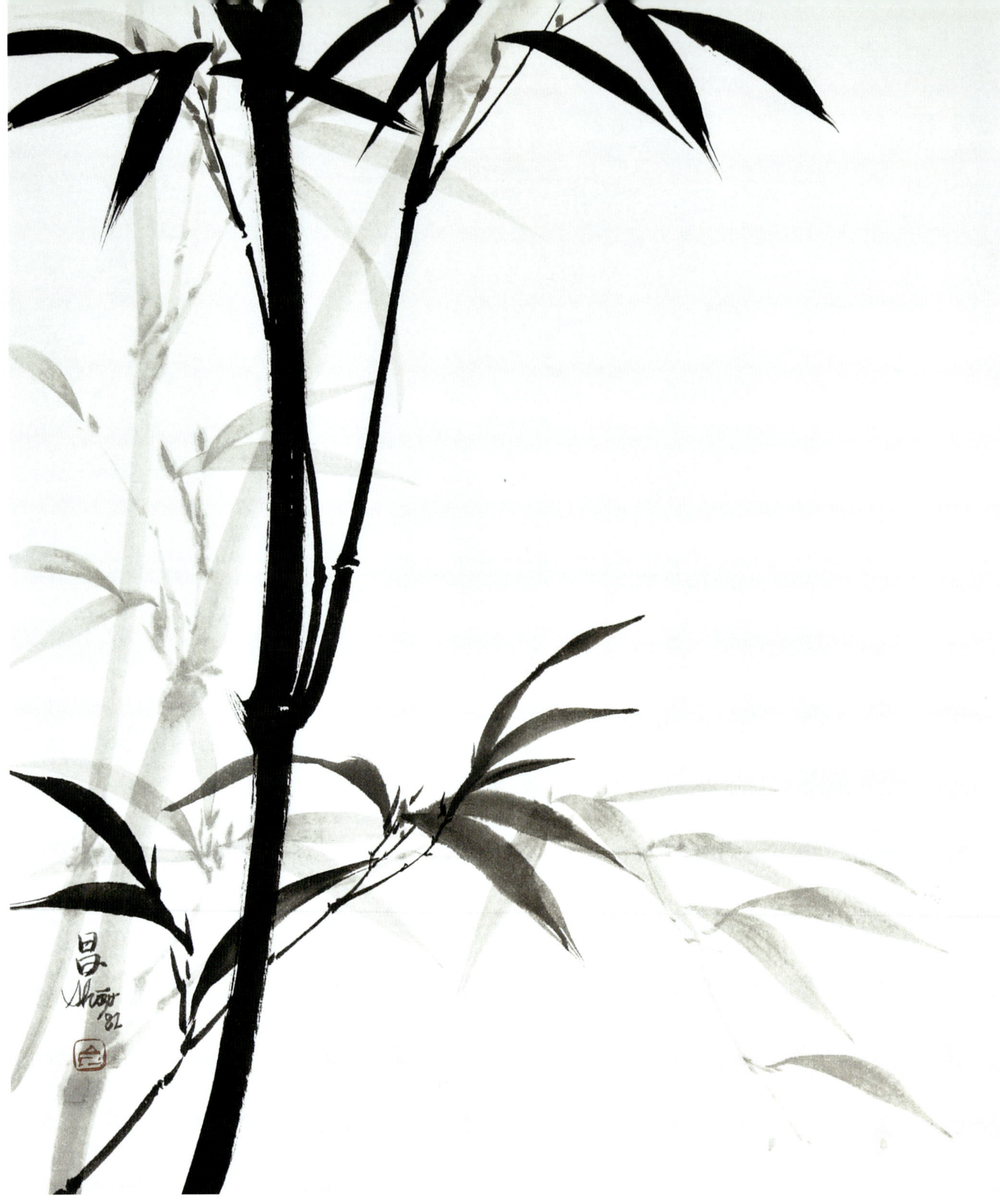

1. Morning Breeze

Size: H = 17.75"/45cm x W = 14.75"/38 cm
Paper: Shikishi board, unsized
Sumi Ink: Standard
Category: Sumi-e

Morning Breeze is a simple composition with a stalk of bamboo in dark ink going straight up and another stalk of bamboo at an angle behind in light ink.

The background branch of bamboo on the lower right, painted in light ink, gives a sense of morning light, provides balance and enhances the active empty space.

Shikishi board is paper (either sized or unsized) pre-mounted on a board. It comes in various sizes, and is convenient for displaying in contemporary-style picture frames (see page 179).

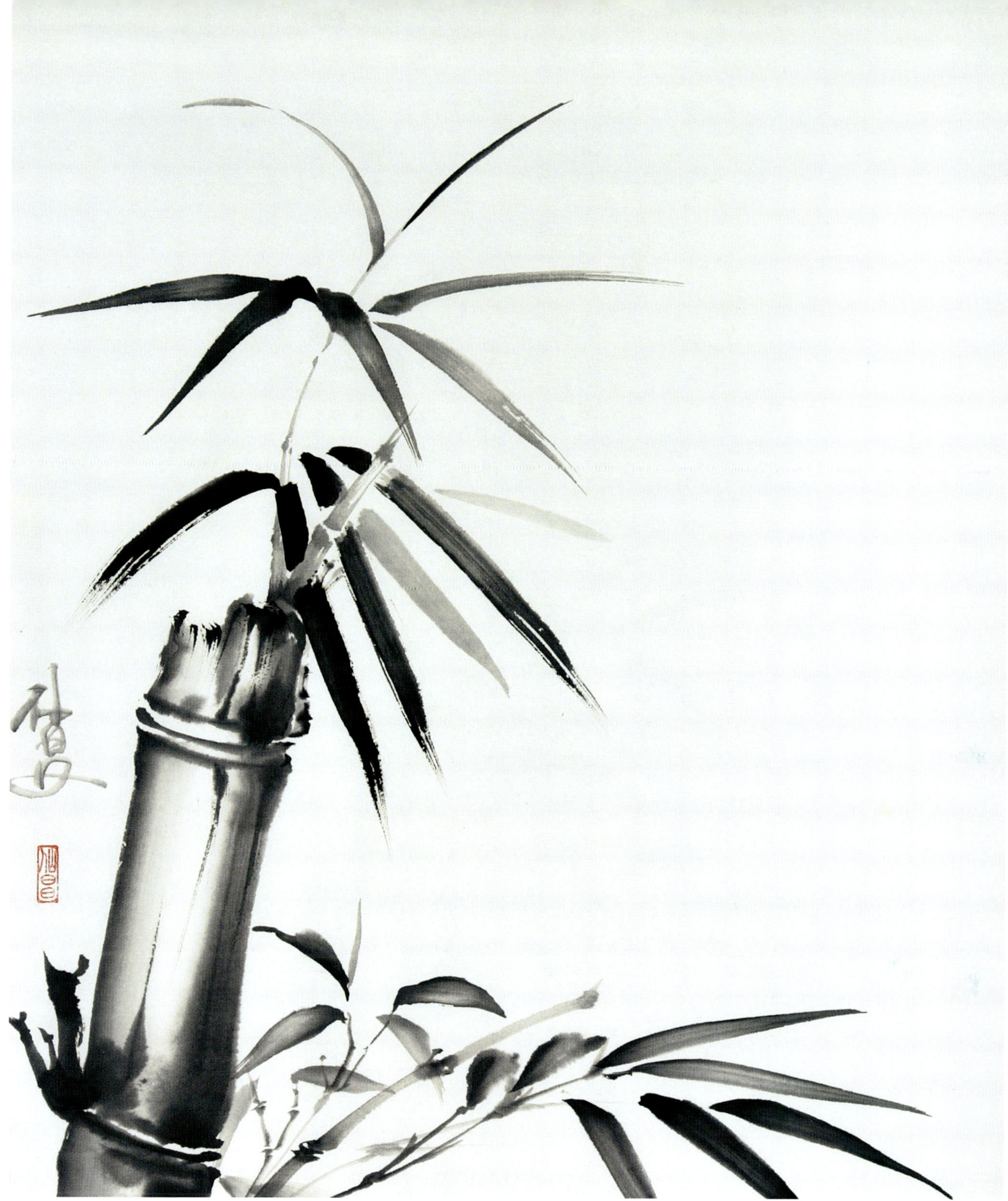

2. Hope

Size: H = 17.75"/45cm x W = 14.75"/38 cm
Paper: Shikishi board, unsized
Sumi Ink: Standard
Category: Sumi-e

Bamboo is so flexible and strong that it is almost impossible for one powerful person to break it. But I have seen a few broken bamboo stalks after a typhoon in Japan. From the break at the joint, new life in the branch will begin to grow.

In this painting, my attempt was to convey the vitality and strength of the bamboo, despite heavy damages due to the force of nature; therefore the leaves are quite secondary. The open space at the right top is reserved for the future new shoots.

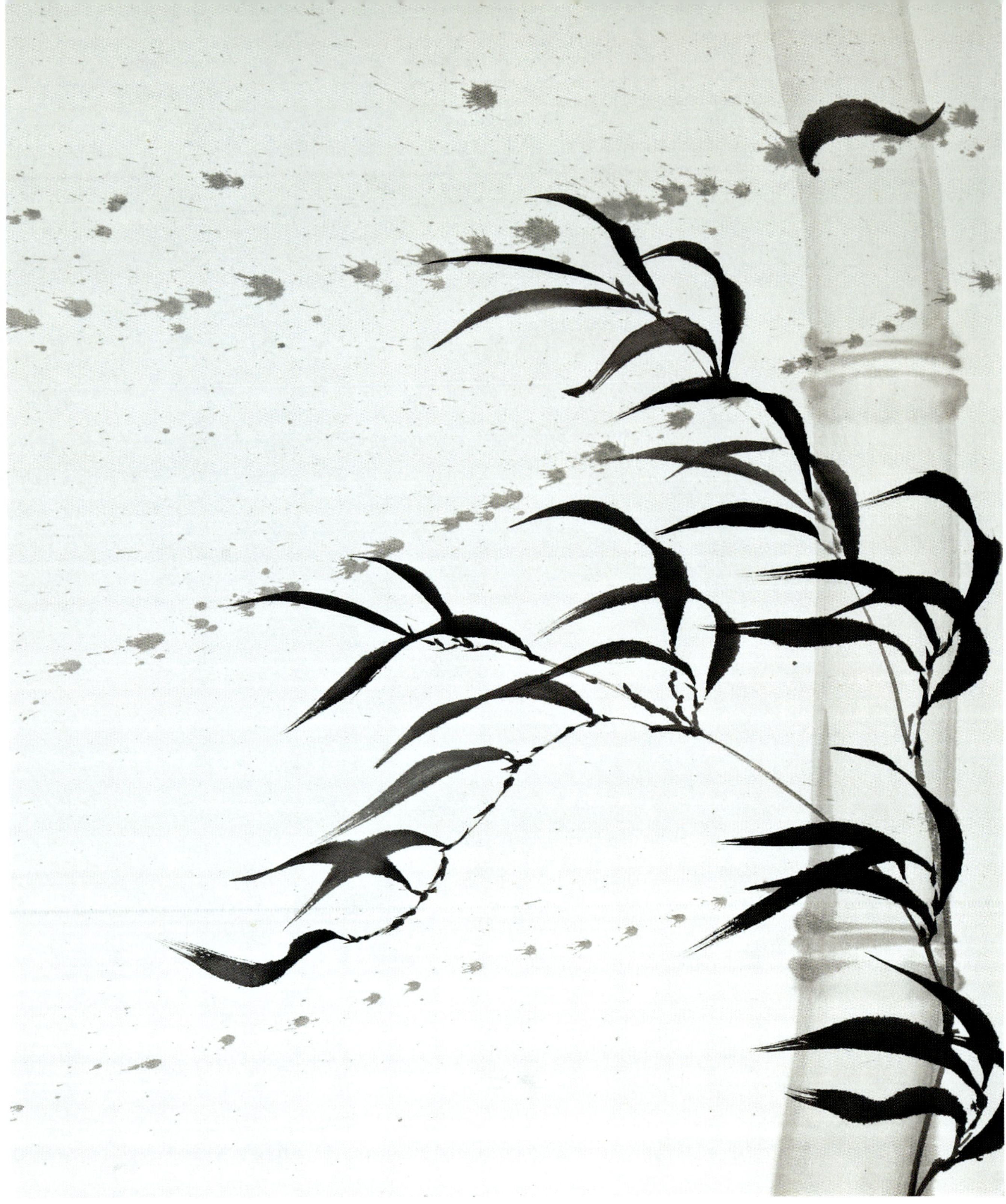

3. Gust of Wind and Rain

Size: 17.75"/45cm x W = 14.75"/38cm
Paper: Shikishi board, unsized
Sumi Ink: Standard
Category: Sumi-e

It is an accepted fact that nature is not always peaceful and tranquil. Our human emotions can also change as readily. This bamboo painting symbolically expresses such emotions as anger or distress. The branches are being blown to the left and the direction of the wind is enhanced with splashing of ink across the painting.

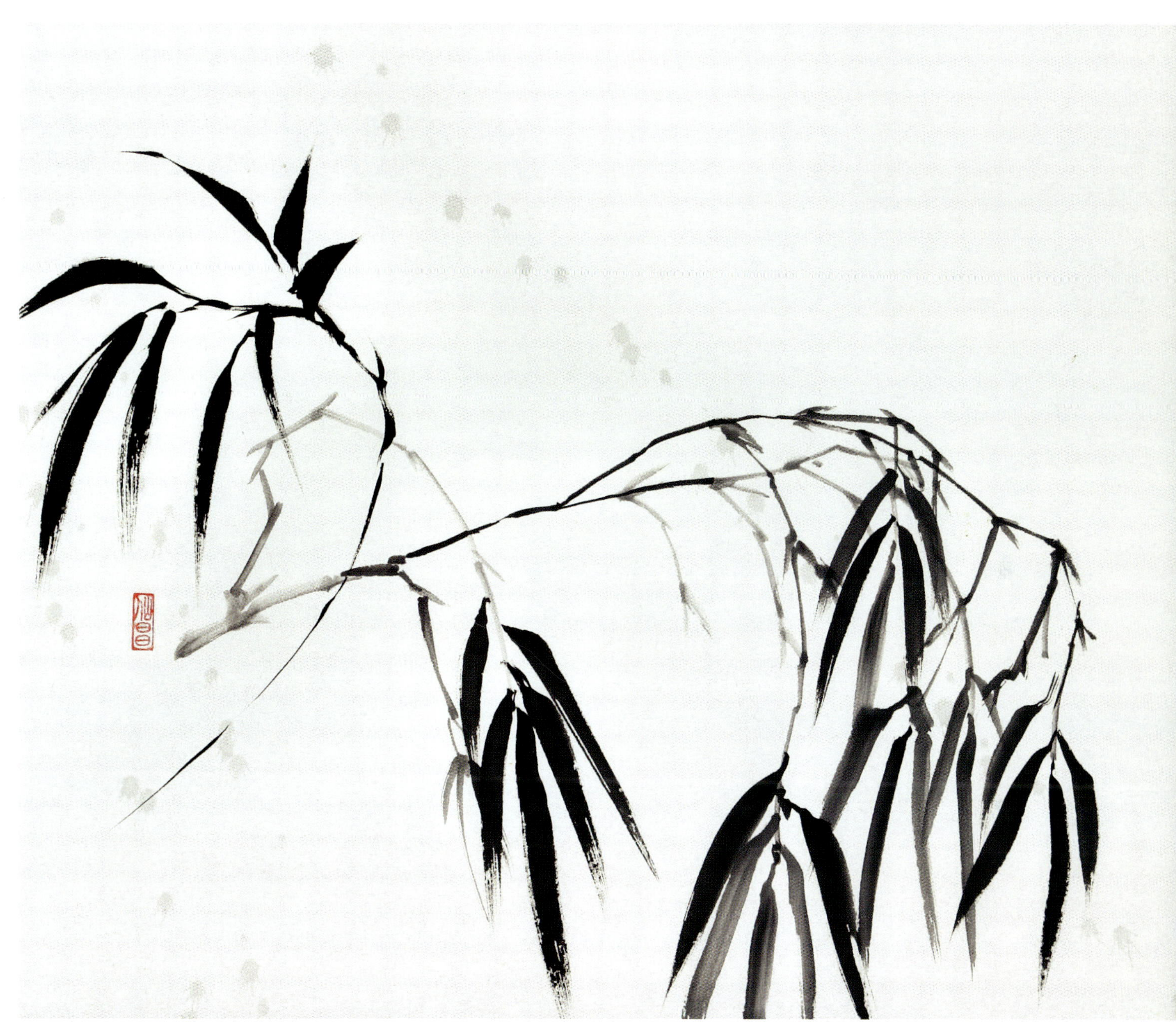

4. Summer Rain

Size: H = 17.75"/45cm x W = 14.75"/38 cm
Paper: Shikishi board, unsized
Sumi Ink: Standard
Category: Sumi-e

A summer thunderstorm beats the bamboo leaves down, but when the rain stops, the branches begin to spring back to their original positions. The complete range of emotions can be conveyed by borrowing bamboo as your visual vocabulary. This work and the others here are only a few examples; it is clear how an artist can spend many months and years using bamboo.

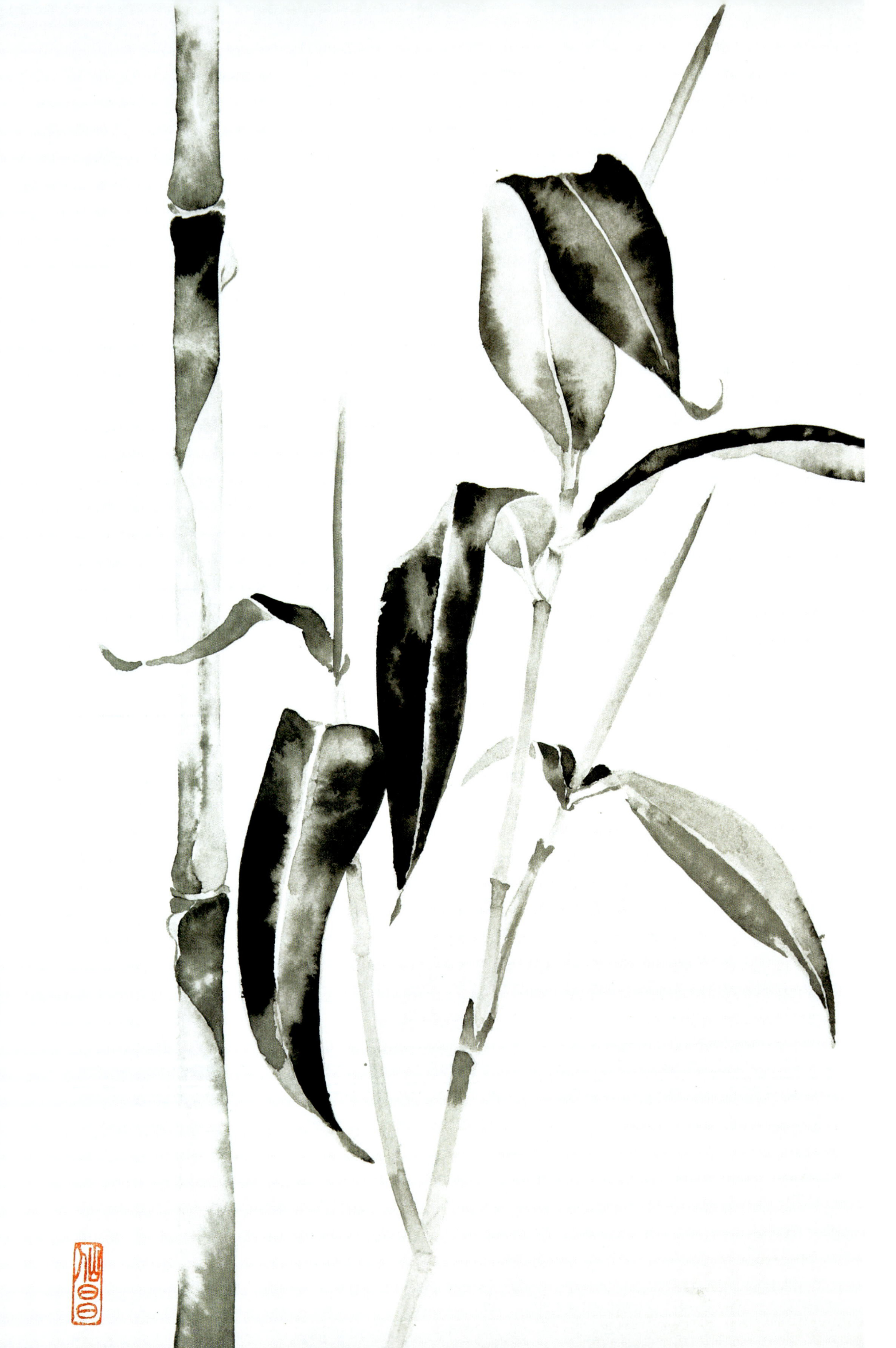

5. Tarashi Komi Bamboo

Size: H = 19"/48cm x W = 50"/127cm
Paper: Sized, pre-mounted on a board
Sumi Ink: Blue tone and standard sumi ink, and silver pigment
Category: Suiboku-ga (tarashi komi)

One unique characteristic of this species of bamboo is that each section grows about 0.75" (2cm) in diameter and about 3 feet (0.9m) in length. So from ancient times this species was important for archery because the length was ideal for constructing arrows. The leaves are much larger than those of most of the other bamboos, and the husk-like sheaths at the joints remain on the culms.

Up to this point we have used the basic technique, with common brush strokes. Painting bamboo in the tarashi komi technique is another kind of experience. It produces a very different effect in atmosphere from the previous examples. The tarashi komi technique works only when highly sized paper is used.

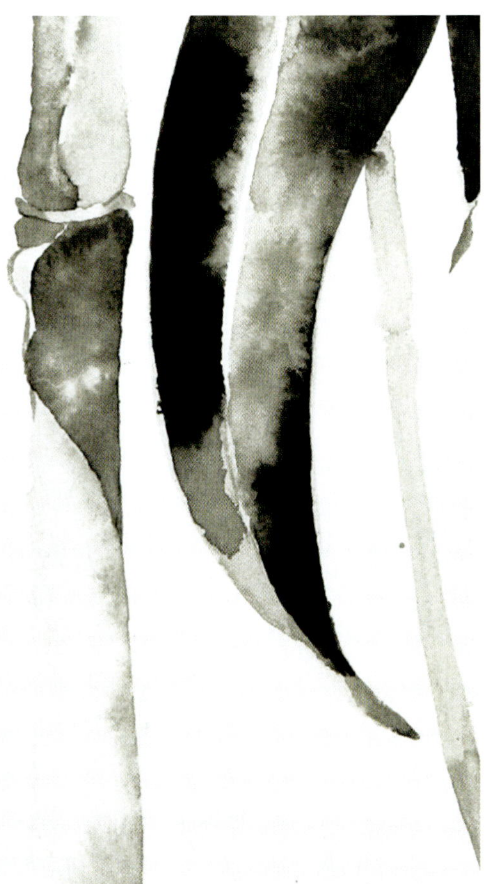

To paint using the tarashi komi technique, you must know exactly where to move your brush. Therefore doing a sketch of the painting beforehand, in very light charcoal, is necessary. Next, the outline of a form—a leaf or a stem—is painted with water or light ink to create and hold that form's edge. Then the inner surface is painted in light ink. Finally, darker ink is dropped on your form's wet surface, and guided to flow to the desired areas.

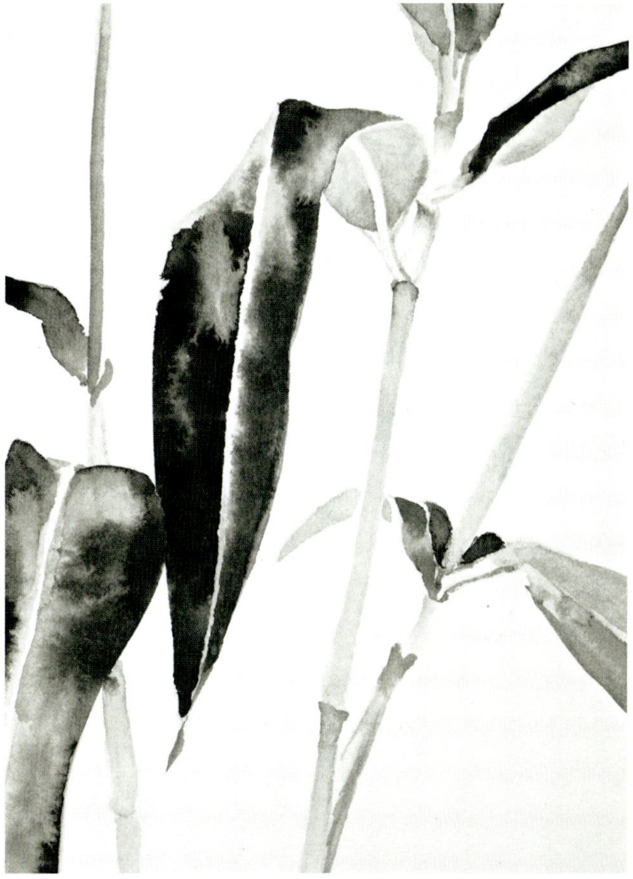

The leaf has a distinct vein in the center and care must be taken to keep it white. First prepare a small brush with dark ink. Paint the leaf with light ink, and while its surface is still very wet, touch the surface with the black-ink-loaded brush tip, almost as if you are tattooing. The black ink will immediately begin to spread on the wet surface. To control the area where the black is spreading, have another slightly moistened brush prepared to soak up the excess ink. And with another brush, gently guide the ink to the curve on top. Continuously add dark ink along the leaf's right edge, then the left edge. Make sure you do not wet the center vein, even with clear water, or it will be obliterated by the darker ink. Notice another example of where a white line must be maintained: on the back side of the this leaf, where the center vein connects to the bamboo stalk.

Painting Flowering Plum

The flowering plum has been known as one of the "Three Princes" in the paintings of China, Korea and Japan since ancient times. While it has been celebrated in countless paintings in the Far East, it also has symbolic meaning and has influenced these cultures in their poetry, literature and fabric design. Although botanically it is categorized as an apricot, "plum" has been the common terminology used for this flower for so many years that we will refer to it that way.

While the flowering plum tree's branches begin growing in straight lines, the aged trees have a tendency to develop gnarled and twisted shapes. It is a hardwood. The blossoms of five petals are simple in shape and come out before the leaves in early spring. They have a heady fragrance, which can spread out for miles from a grove of trees. While the petals are still in their prime, they fall making a carpet of perfumed beauty. These characteristics make the "plum" symbolic for masculine beauty especially during the age of the warriors. As a counterpart, the flowering peach which blooms after the leaves have come out later in the season have similar blossoms in dark pink and symbolic for feminine beauty.

Branches are different in curvature so the trees, while having similar looking blossoms, are treated very differently in symbolism for the arts: such as poetry, painting, ikebana and so on. In Ikebana, the art of arranging flowers, the flowering plum is masculine and the peach feminine so they are given distinctively different treatment in a creative work. The flowering plum has been featured in many masterpieces in the Far East. In Japan, artists in the decorative art of the Rimpa school have used the white and pink plum trees in blossom as a common theme on the gold background of a folding screen. For persons acquainted with reproductions of the highly decorative and stylized paintings of flowering plum on a gold background, comparisons with the monochrome paintings in suiboku-ga and sumi-e cannot be made. Therefore, each type of art whether Rimpa or monochrome should be evaluated differently, each on its own merit.

1. Pink and White Flowering Plum

Size: L = 31.5"/79cm x W = 21"/52cm
Paper: Unsized; pre-mounted
Sumi Ink: Standard
Category: Suiboku-ga

For centuries it has been said that "Sumi ink is black; yet it is not black." While it may seem that black ink has limited capabilities, there is a wide range in the ink tones and can give a sense of color. In the art of monochrome, the visual color has been eliminated, consequently it moves closer to abstraction. By stepping in the world of abstraction, the hidden awareness of the viewer is tapped. The color may be absent, but a sensitive viewer will discern the color. Tapping into human capability in awakening remembered sensory responses is unique to this art form. In a successful monochrome painting, a sensitive viewer becomes a participant and a totality of the emotional sensory experiences of the viewer must be awakened. That is the challenge that faces the creative artist in working with sumi ink.

In this first painting of the Flowering Plum, a corner of a grove is shown. From the dark close-up branches and blossoms in the foreground, successively the tree limbs and blossoms fade into the background to suggest the abundant proliferation of white and pink flowers in a grove. This leads to the suggestion of the fragrant scent such a grove provides for anyone who has experienced the luxury of being present just at the right time.

Collection of Jerry Proffit.

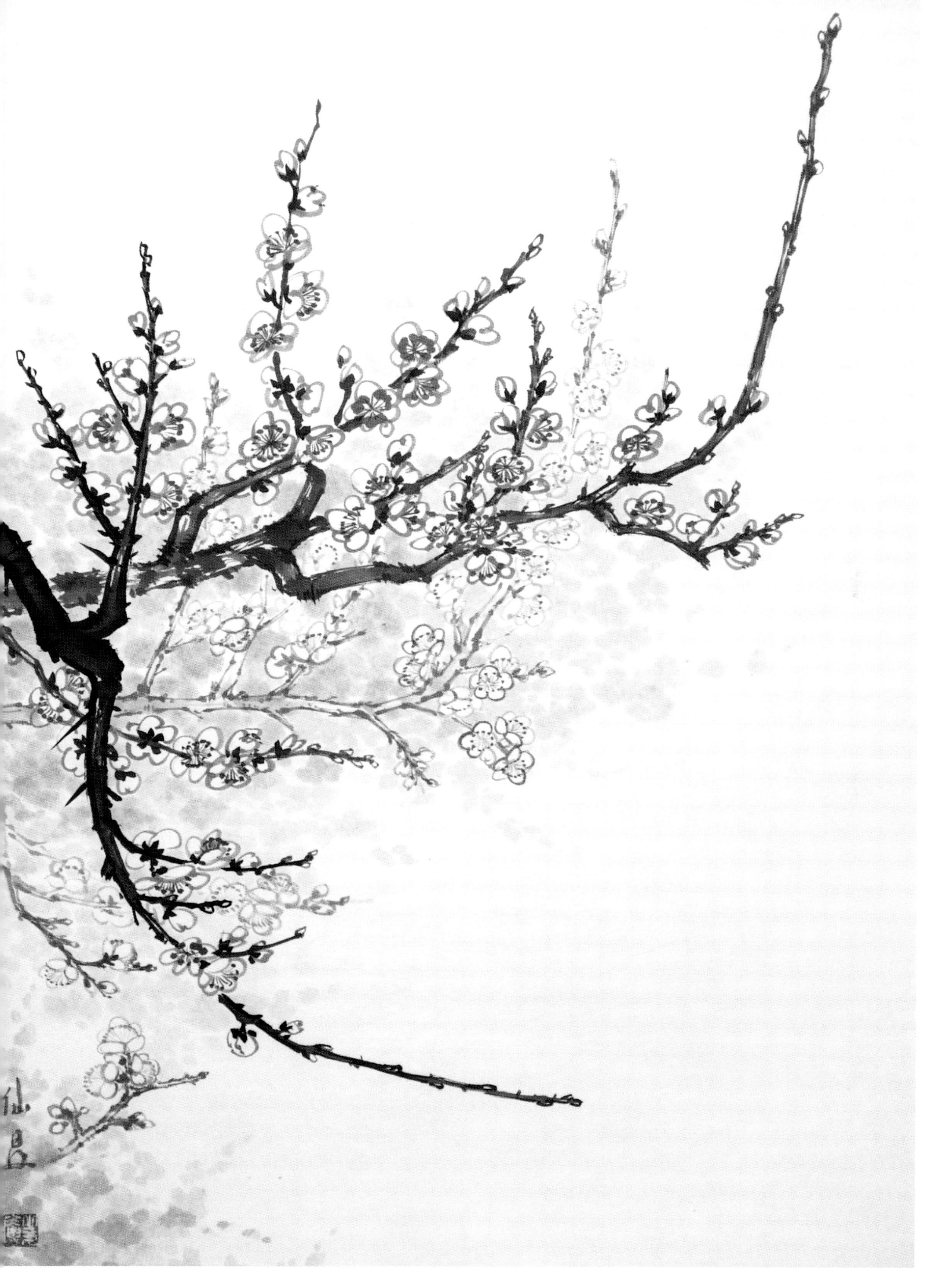

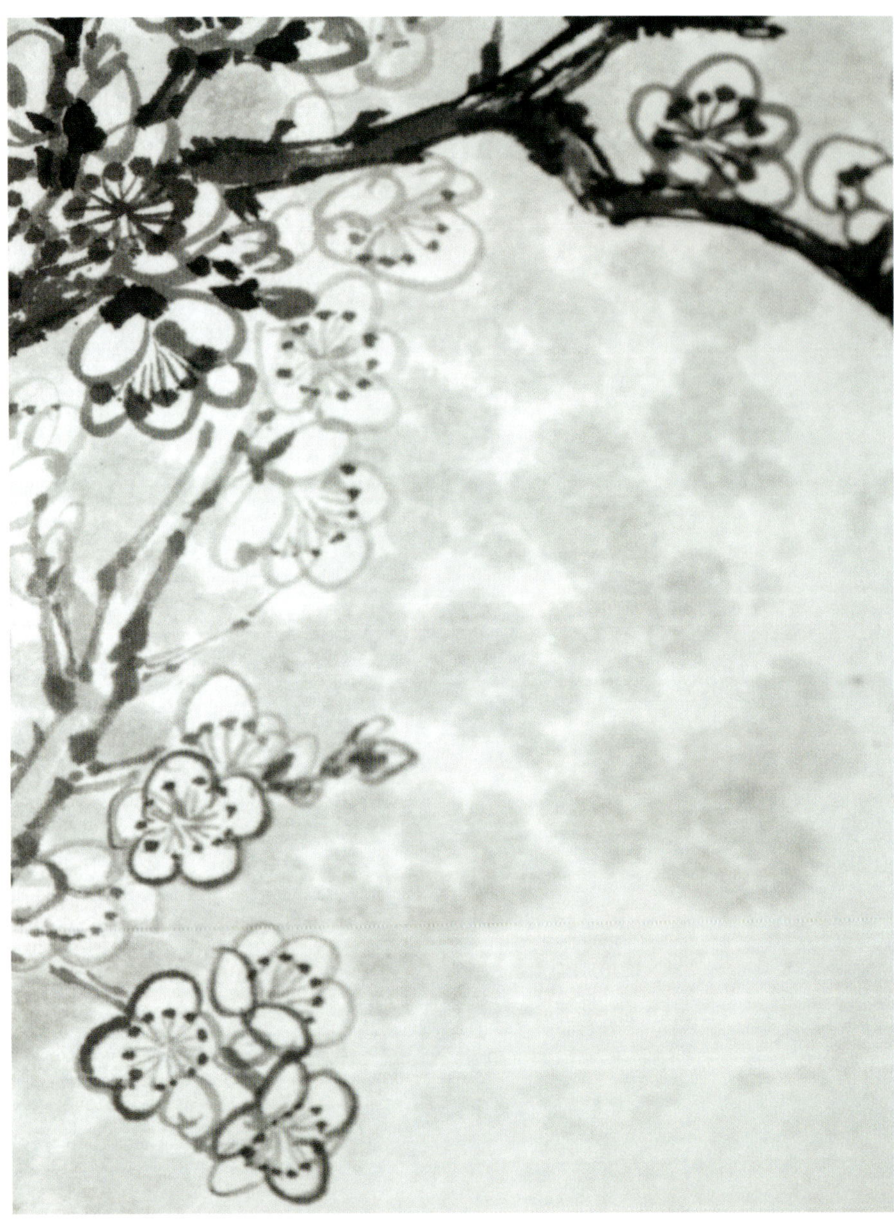

When flowering plum trees grow wild, the branches will generally grow straight; but, in an orchard with constant pruning, the branches eventually create unique formations. Masterpiece paintings of the flowering plum often show these gnarled branches, which are produced with dynamic calligraphic strokes. In this painting, the white blossoms are dominant and are the main focus so they are painted with dark outlines, and the pink blossoms are indicated by the grouped dots. If, in your own composition, you wish to suggest pink blossoms, paint the individual petals with darker ink. When absorbent paper is used, the spots will run (the nijimi effect) and have a soft outline, but on sized paper the five dots will be more rigid.

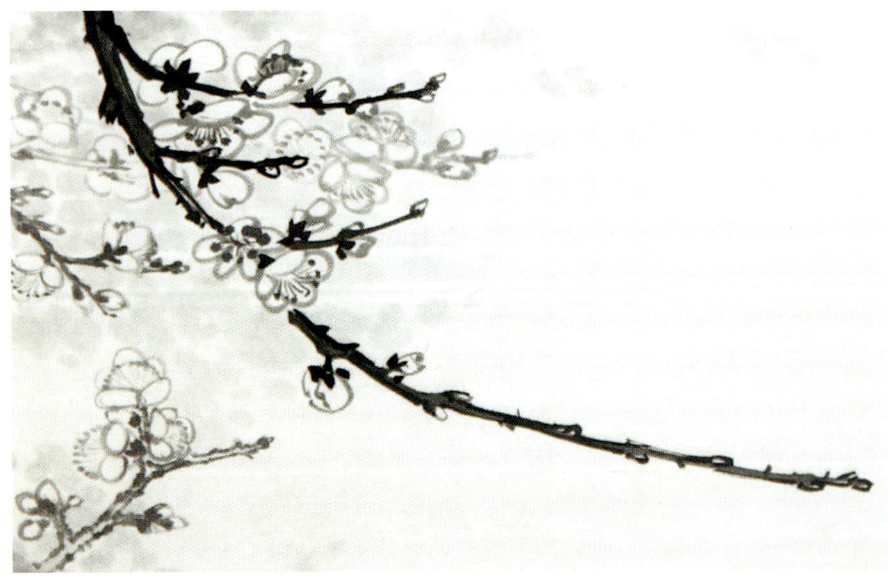

These blossoms are on a second year branch of the tree (the newest branches of the season do not bear blossoms). With sumi ink, dark tones come to the foreground and lighter ink recedes to the background, which helps in suggesting perspective. Here a darker outline was used for the foreground white blossoms and a lighter ink outline for the background white blossoms. The tip of this branch is very important for making the space beyond active; notice this aspect in the complete image on page 137.

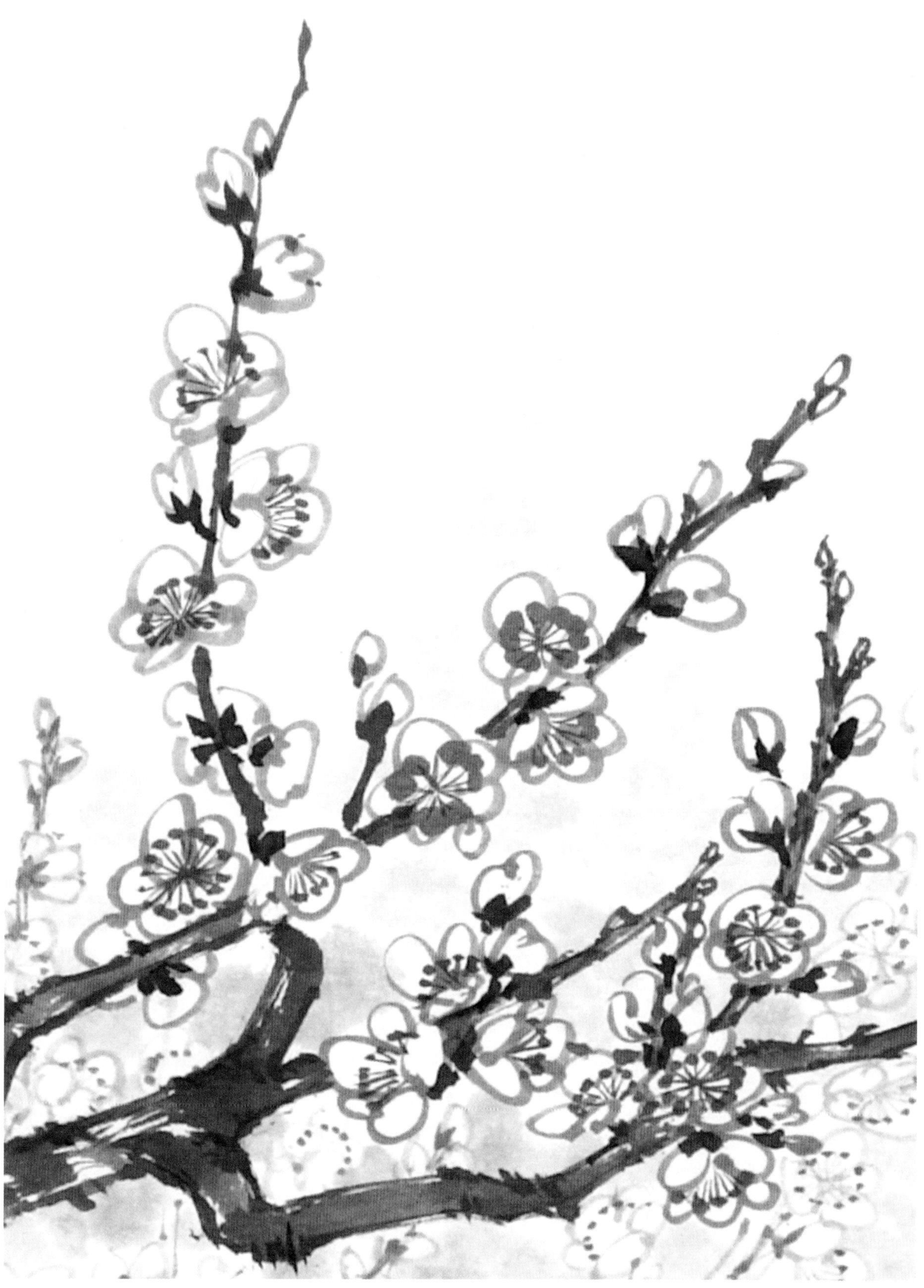

The direction of the blossoms should be varied, with some shown full face and others painted as side or back views. Also include buds, which help to create a sense of rhythm in the composition.

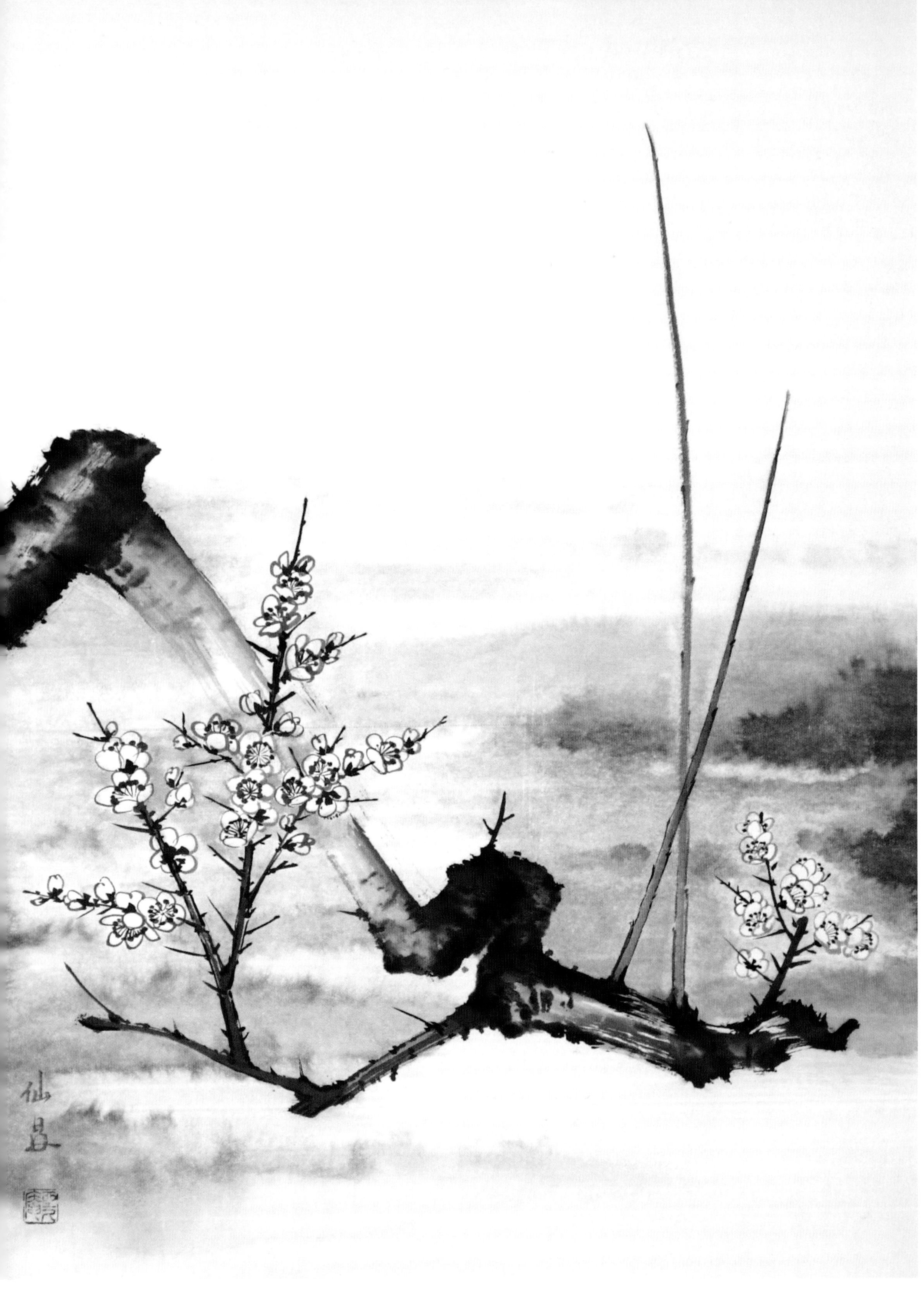

2. Aged Flowering Plum

Size: 31"/79cm x W = 20.75"/53cm
Paper: Unsized, pre-mounted on a board
Sumi Ink: Standard
Category: Suiboku-ga

The unusual composition for this painting came from a find in my sketchbook, an image which I had drawn years ago in a plum orchard in Japan. This amazing aged branch caught my attention as I noticed its gnarled scars from decades of struggle with the elements, with its two flowering branches and even new and tender young shoots in close proximity. The scene seemed to capture the trials and beauty of life.

Collection of Dr. and Mrs. Richard Morimoto.

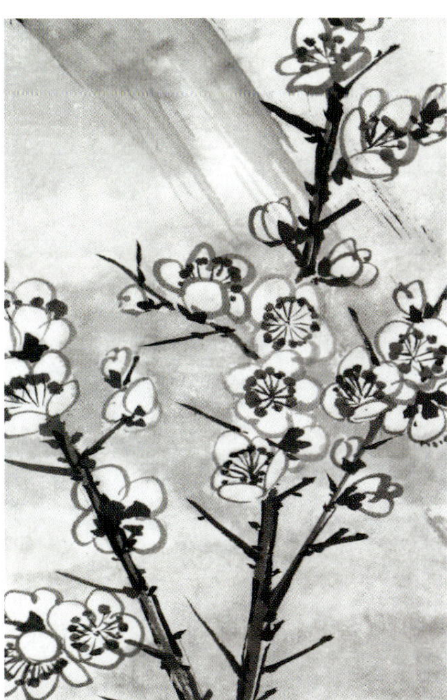

Close examination of older branches shows that they develop sharp thorn-like extensions. These extensions provide a wonderful visual contrast to the circular flowers.

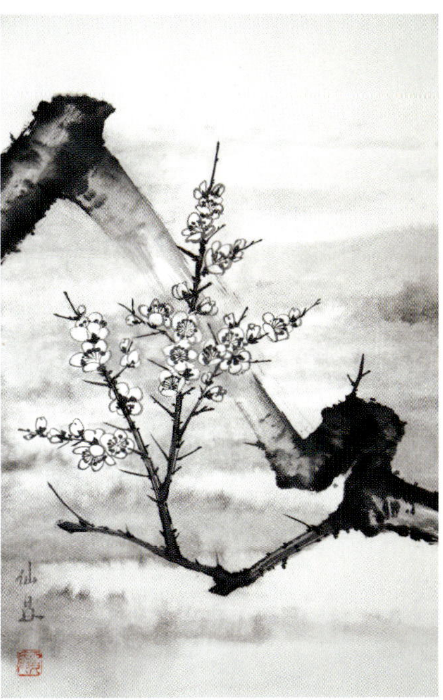

A dynamic calligraphy-like stroke is used to create the aged but living branch. When the background tree limb was formed, a space was left for the blossom cluster on the larger foreground branch.

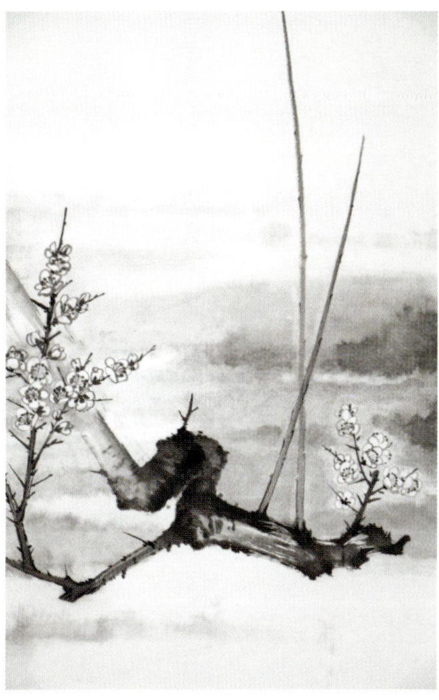

For the two young shoots, use darker ink for the shorter one in front and lighter ink for the taller one. After the lines are completed, use a thin brush with dark ink to add the supporting outlines, suggesting new leaf buds.

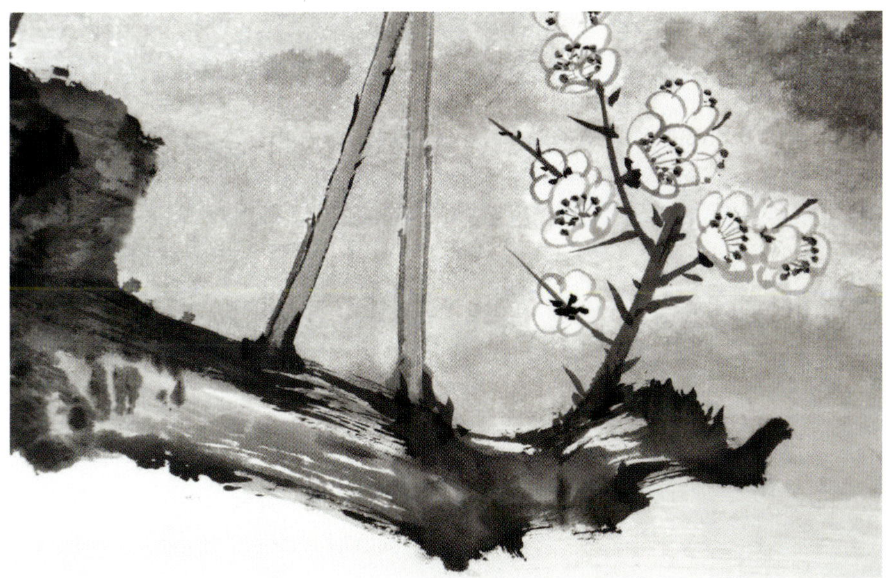

The toughness of the old branch is first painted with a drier brush to provide texture with each stroke. Yet it is from this brittle and seasoned limb that new shoots will break through the bark. So to enforce the compelling energy there, dark ink is added at the base of the new growth.

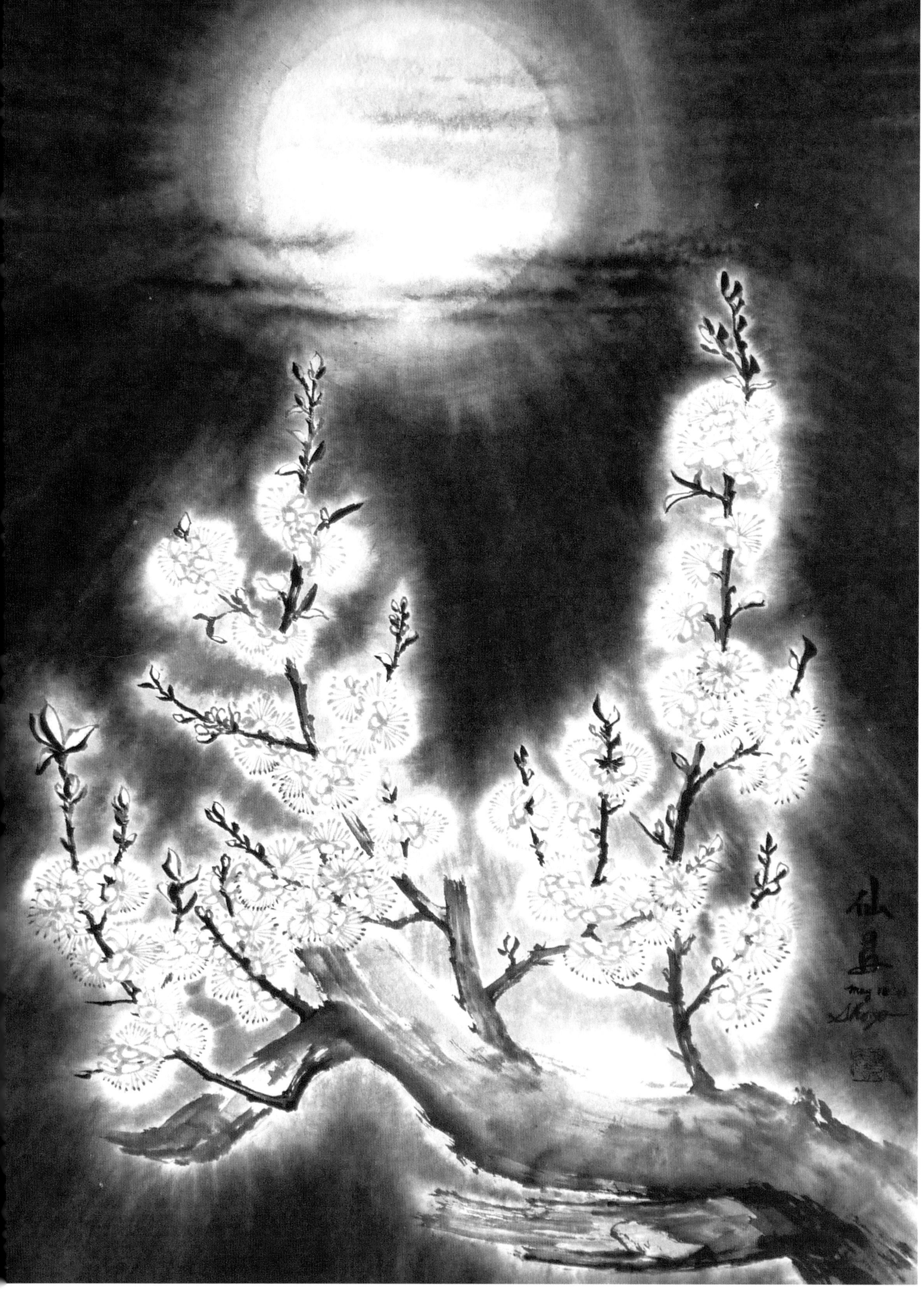

3. Fragrance of Plum under the Moonlight

Size: H = 31"/79 cm x W = 21"/53 cm
Paper: Unsized, pre-mounted on board
Sumi Ink: Blue tone
Category: Suiboku-ga

A mysterious force almost seems to beckon when the flowering plum is in full bloom, especially at night. Dew-covered and glistening in the stillness of moonlight with the higher humidity in cooler temperatures, the blossoms release a fragrance that permeates the atmosphere. Who can resist the call of such resplendence! This is the scene which enticed me out to a moonlit garden to sketch this painting. How does an artist capture and present all of these in black ink—the delicate moonlit beauty, the ambrosial scents and the depth of feeling that such a scene evokes?

Without the tool of color to create the depth that moonlight produces, a depth that almost seems to lift the flowers in the reflected sparkle of the dew, I used light ink to surround the flowers, then gradually intensified the darkness of ink, while at the same time remaining fully aware of direction of the moonbeams.

The moon that evening was full and the sky was clear, but I felt that mistiness and drifting clouds were a necessary addition to this scene. The traditional Japanese sensibility often defines "true beauty" as that which surpasses perfection. In the Zen-related arts this type of beauty is called *wabi-sabi*, a term that means imperfect or rustic beauty, including beauty in simplicity. Correspondingly, instead of the full moon being painted with clarity, here it is partially covered with drifting clouds and symbolically refers to the evanescence of all life.

Studies have shown that scent is one of the most vividly retained sensations in our memories. My intention was to have the profusion of the blossoms gradually fade in the background to expand their aura, and hint of their abundant fragrance.

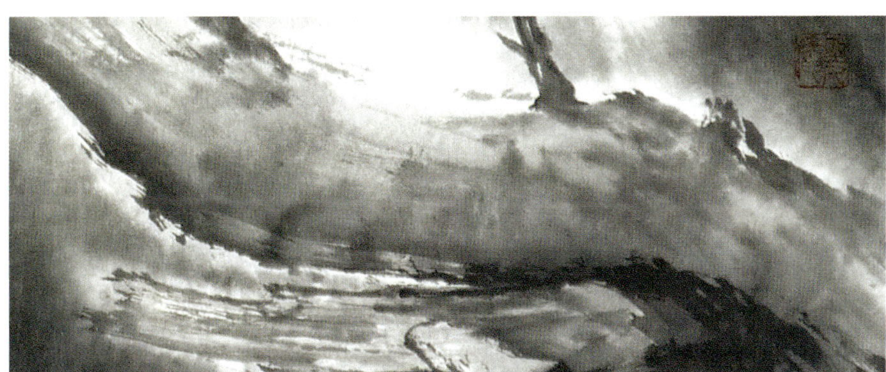

Because here the blossoms are painted more as a suggestion in formation, compared to the more detailed flowers in the previous flowering plum paintings, the tree trunk is given more emphasis in contrast, with the glow of the moonlight on the upper side and a darker shade underneath. The broken branch adds compositional contrast.

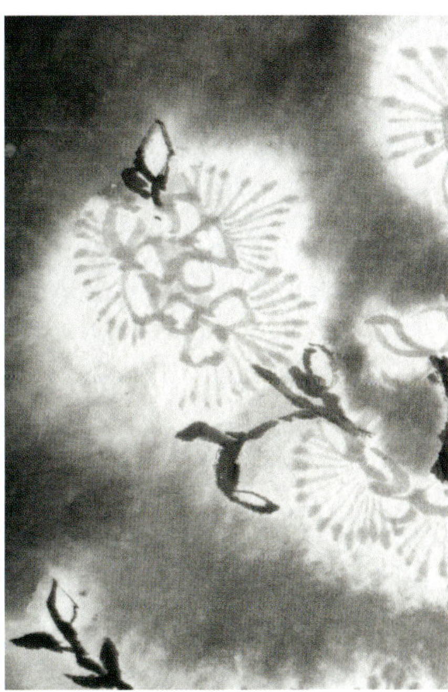

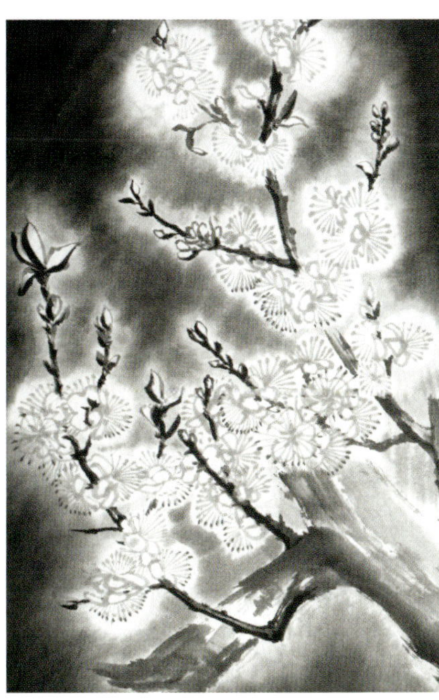

In order to evoke a sense of fragrance with this painting, each blossom is shown as fully opened, using very light ink. The length of the stamens and pistils signifies that these blossoms are clearly matured. Forming the blossoms themselves is less important in this work.

The *Mustard Seed Garden Manual,* first published in China during the seventeenth century, describes how to paint the form of a blossom from every angle. Knowing this level of detail about a subject is important, since it allows you to hold a clear image of your subject in your mind even if in your actual painting (as here) it will only be vaguely suggested. A total and clear understanding of the subject is important before moving on to simplicity and abstraction.

Painting Lilies

Beautiful flowers abound on this planet, but among them the stargazer lily is outstanding for its size, rich color and fragrance. The stargazer lily is a good subject for us to focus on to explore the age-old question: Color or monochrome? There are two schools of thought on how to approach the study of painting in the traditional arts of Japan.

An artist may spend a lifetime creating solely in one media or the other. However, if an artist should make a transition between the two, should he/she begin artistic activity in color first, then move over to sumi as the next stage in creativity? The reasoning behind this approach is that unless one has full capacity in sensitivity to color, it would be difficult to project or suggest color in monochrome painting. The other school of thought is that monochrome artists should begin with the use of sumi and should not be involved with color.

My own training began with the very traditional outline system and with using color; later I moved into the world of monochrome. It is for this reason that I am including some color painting in this book. The first example of the stargazer lily as subject, at right, is painted in traditional Japanese style. My Buddhist philosophical background is that all life is evanescent and all forms continue to change. The brief glory of the stargazer, too, passes in a few days and the black mist is the message that life and death are very much parts of a brief cycle.

1. Stargazer Lily in Gold Paint

Size: H = 19"/48.2cm x W = 19"/48.2cm
Paper: Sized, mounted on board
Sumi Ink: Standard, with Japanese color pigments and gold
          pigment
Category: Traditional Japanese painting

After painting this stargazer lily using the tarashi komi technique (see page 148), I was still haunted by the flower so this time I decided to focus on its color and the formation of the blossom. I used traditional color pigments, gold pigment and black ink. The background is painted with gold pigment, an aspect often seen in Japanese decorative art. The flowers were outlined in light ink, then filled in with color, which is a common technique for this art form. As a final touch the outline was reinforced.

As we explore the following pages, you will note a difference here in the fully opened flower on right bottom, compared to its depiction in the tarashi komi painting for instance. The individual petals in this painting are now beginning to reach maximum fullness with more curves. The blossom is now past its prime; the side view represents the present and the bud above is the future.

Collection of Don and Naida Disney.

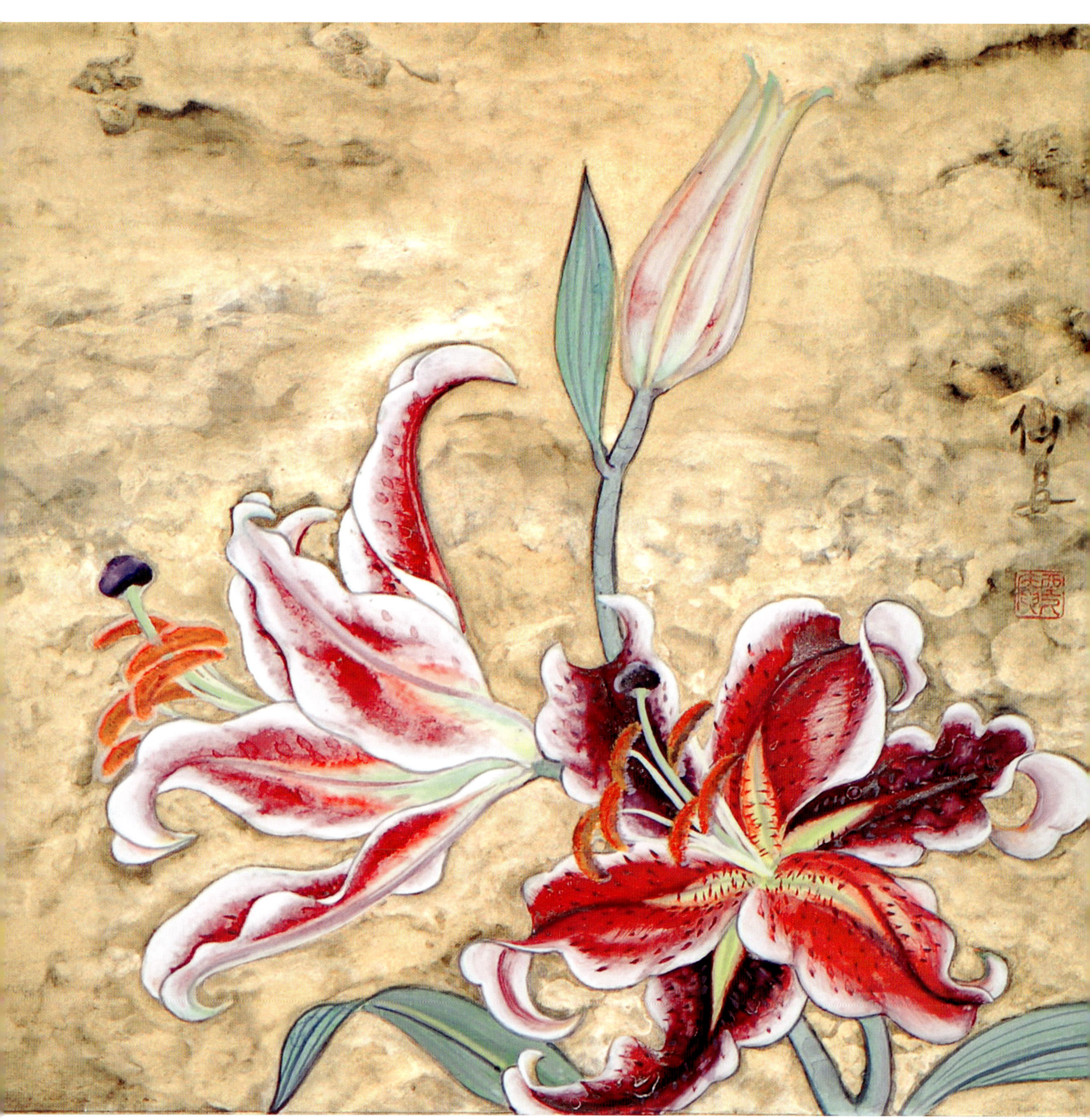

2. Stargazer Lily in Traditional Japanese Style

Size: H = 34"/88cm x W = 23.5"/60 cm
Paper: Special handmade paper stretched on board
Sumi Ink: Japanese traditional pigments, black ink and gold
           pigment
Category: Traditional Japanese painting

Like most artists working in color, during my initial training
in painting I was taught to use sumi techniques simply to
make outlines in my paintings. But in this painting, the influence of sumi techniques is obvious both in the foreground
and the background.

The black mist was created with traditional Japanese pigments, applied after the rest of the painting was completed.
Japanese pigments are made from natural materials of various
kinds, such as seashells and minerals, which are ground into
various grades from the roughest to the finest. By using pigments which are rough as sand, you can achieve effects of
transparency and layering. For this black mist, sand-like particles of obsidian were mixed with animal glue, and the
pigment was then painted over some areas. Sumi ink cannot
be used to create such overlapping effects; the result would
not be transparent.

This flower stem came from my garden, where it dominated
the scene with its rich beauty while its fragrance permeated
the entire area. As many as ten blossoms could be found on a
single stalk. The power of the stargazer seemed to urge me to
paint it, and I studiously began to sketch the formation, the
angles at which the blossoms faced and the stage in maturity
for each blossom. As I meticulously sketched, the flowers themselves became deeply ingrained in my memory system.

Relying upon a Japanese sense of beauty, I limited the number
of blossoms to cover the whole range of color that I found among
the stargazers. Because each flower itself is so rich in color, more
than one blossom in full color would be overwhelming. Therefore
only one flower actually faces the viewer. My philosophical belief
that a painting should express the concept of the past, present
and future creates the foundation for my composition. The tight
bud is the future, the half-opened flower is the present and the
fully opened blossom represents the past.

The fully-opened flower suggests the richness in color of the
stargazer; a few petals are in red so that the viewer's eyes will be
drawn toward the center of the blossom where they might sense
the remarkable fragrance of the stargazer. As described earlier
concerning *Fragrance of Plum under the Moonlight,* my challenge
was how to present the stargazer in totality so that even the fragrance was a part the painting.

My mentor always said: "Anyone can paint an apple, but a
true artist offers the taste of the apple as well. Anyone can
paint flowers, but can the artist capture the sense of fragrance?" This has been my challenge of a lifetime.

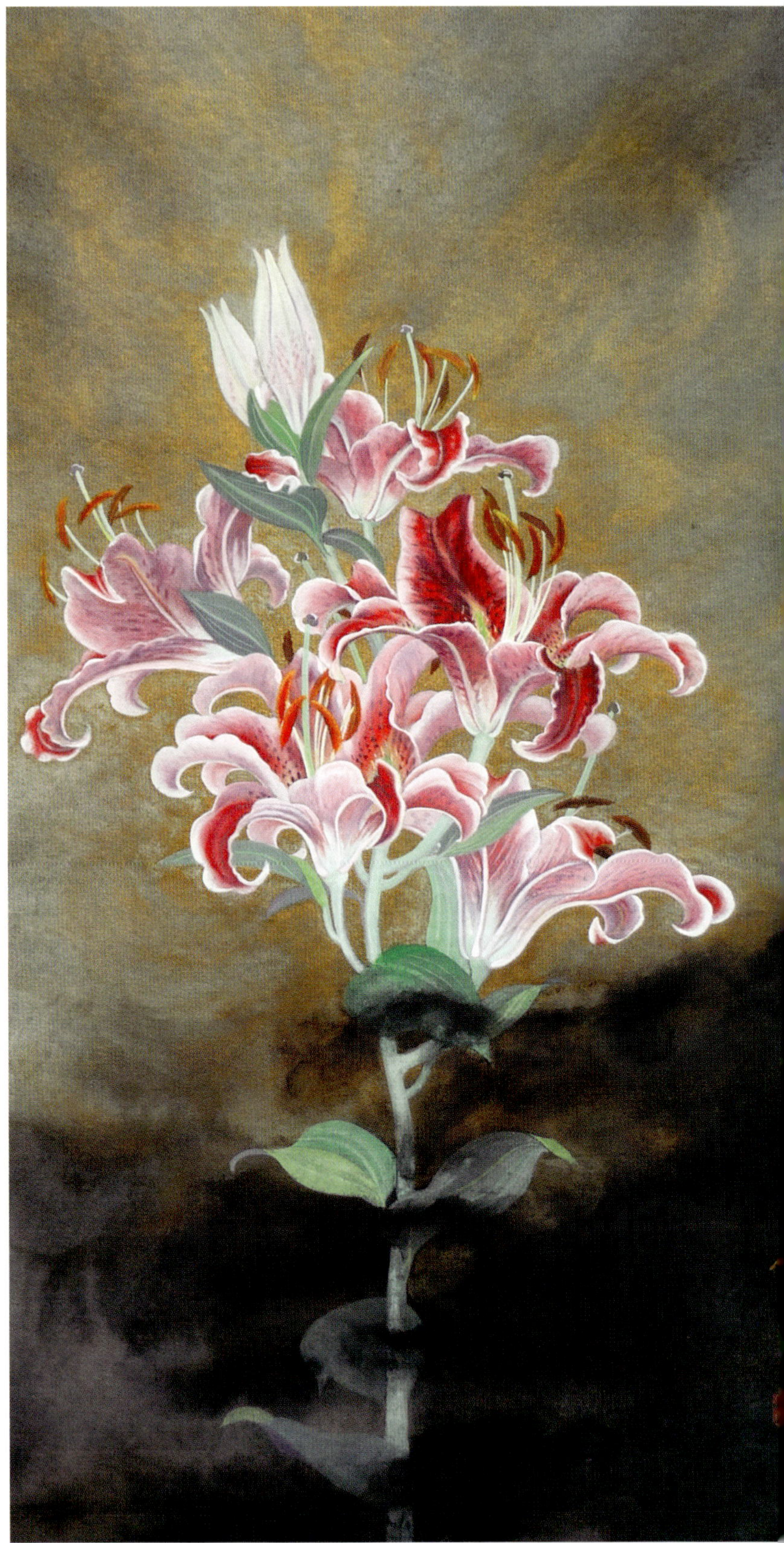

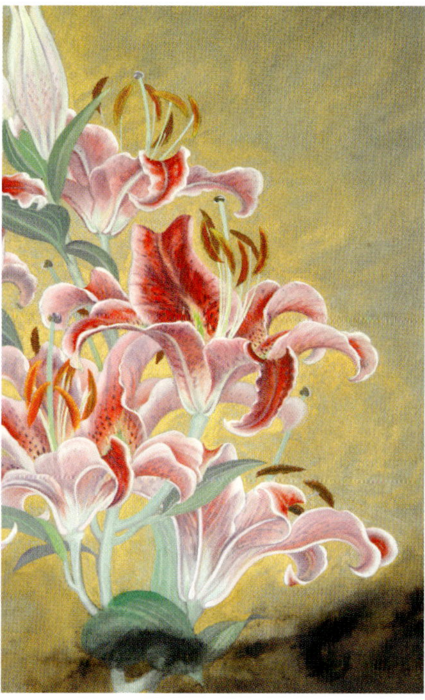 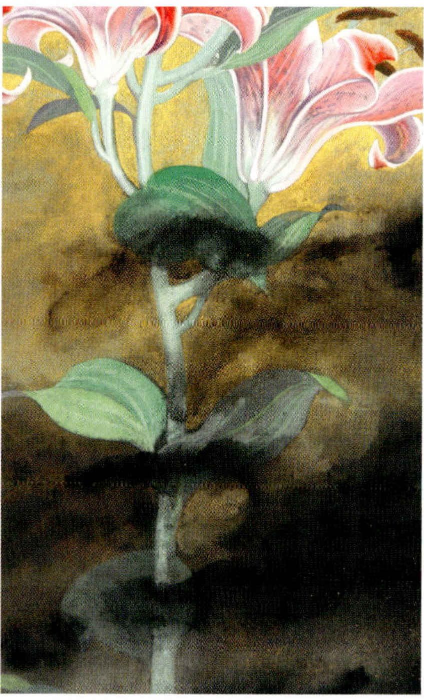 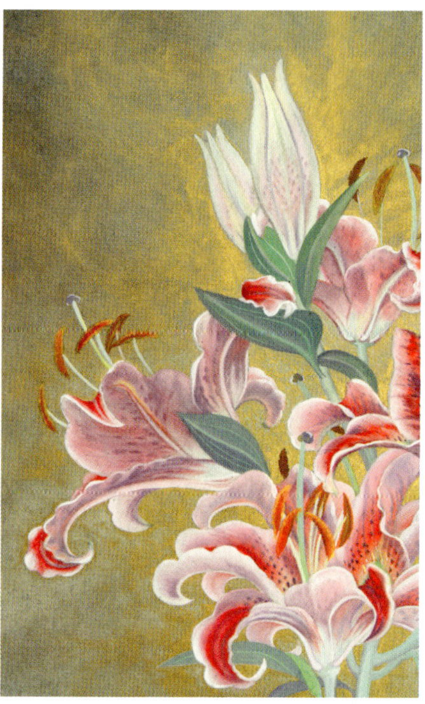

Sometimes the rich gold (or silver) of pigment creates a quiet background, until the source of the light or its angle changes, when it can suddenly dominate the painting. Here we see full light cast on the gold background.

In contrast to the full light on the blossoms, particles of fine obsidian pigment are used to cast the shadow of impermanency. The nature of the pigment allows for the creation of unique effects which cannot be obtained with sumi.

When you purchase lilies from the florist, their pollen-loaded anthers have likely already been removed. But in a painting on the subject of lilies, the stamen is an important source of information. The color of the anthers and the direction, length and angle of the stamen convey the age of the blossom.

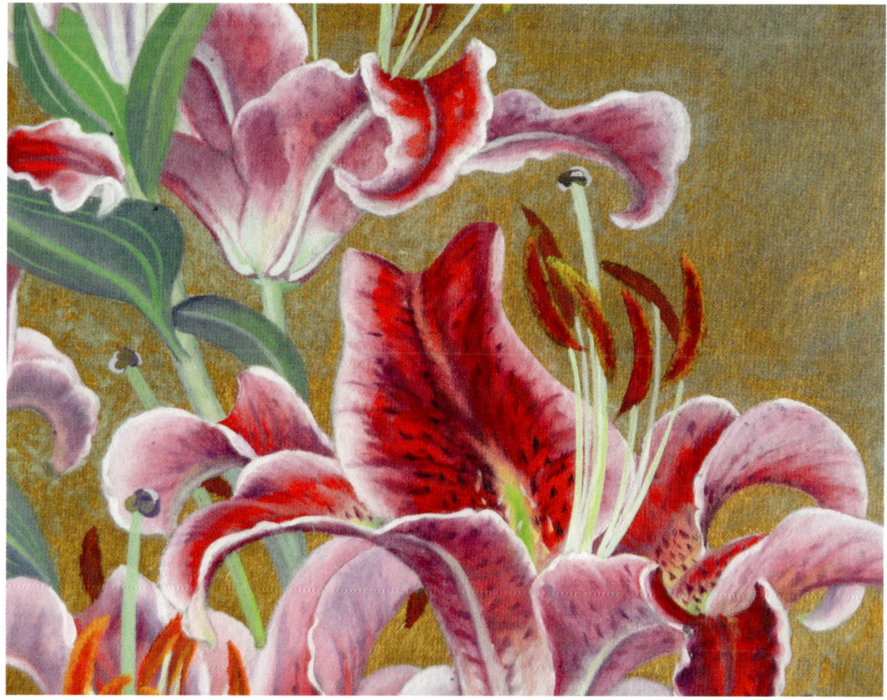

The surface of the stargazer's petal has a vivid and an almost bewitching color which seems to seep through to the back of the petal. As the flower matures and is fully opened, small "obtrusions" of black add to the color.

3. Stargazer Lily in Tarashi Komi Technique

Size: H = 18.5"/47cm x W = 13.5"/34cm
Paper: Sized, pre-mounted on board
Sumi Ink: Standard
Category: Suiboku-ga (tarashi komi)

After completing some works of the stargazer in
color, we now turn to monochrome, and this next
painting has fewer flowers on a stem. While this
painting is in monochrome, I again hoped to capture the full essence of the flower. My decision
was to use a combination of the traditional sumi
techniques with the tarashi komi technique.

The blossoms and buds were painted first in
the traditional manner. Then, to create the total
essence of the lily including scent I used the
tarashi komi technique for the background and
the leaves, hoping that the variations especially
in the leaves would add a very organic feel. I wet
the surface of each leaf, carefully avoiding the
white rib, and applied the darker ink to result in
tarashi komi's marbling effect. Then, for the
background, keeping the flower, buds, stems and
leaves from getting wet, I began by painting light
ink around the buds and blossom. Darker ink
was then gradually applied.

Without use of color, it is difficult to recreate a
sense of the vivid colors of the stargazer. Suiboku-
ga and sumi-e do have limitations and this
stargazer looks more like a white Casablanca lily.

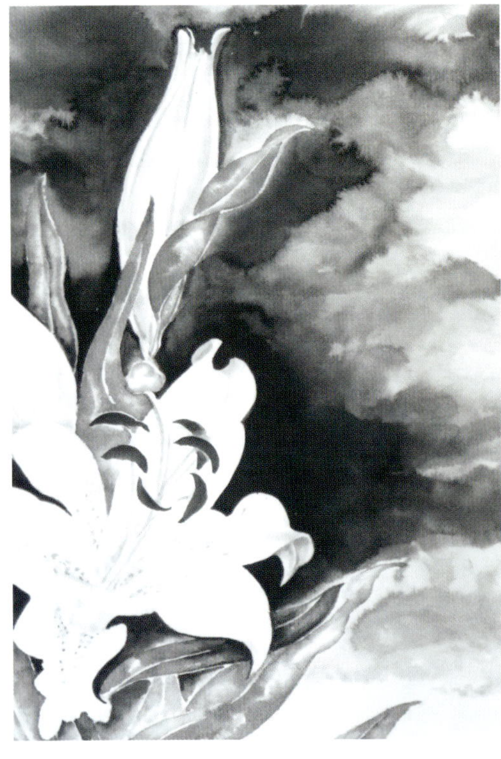

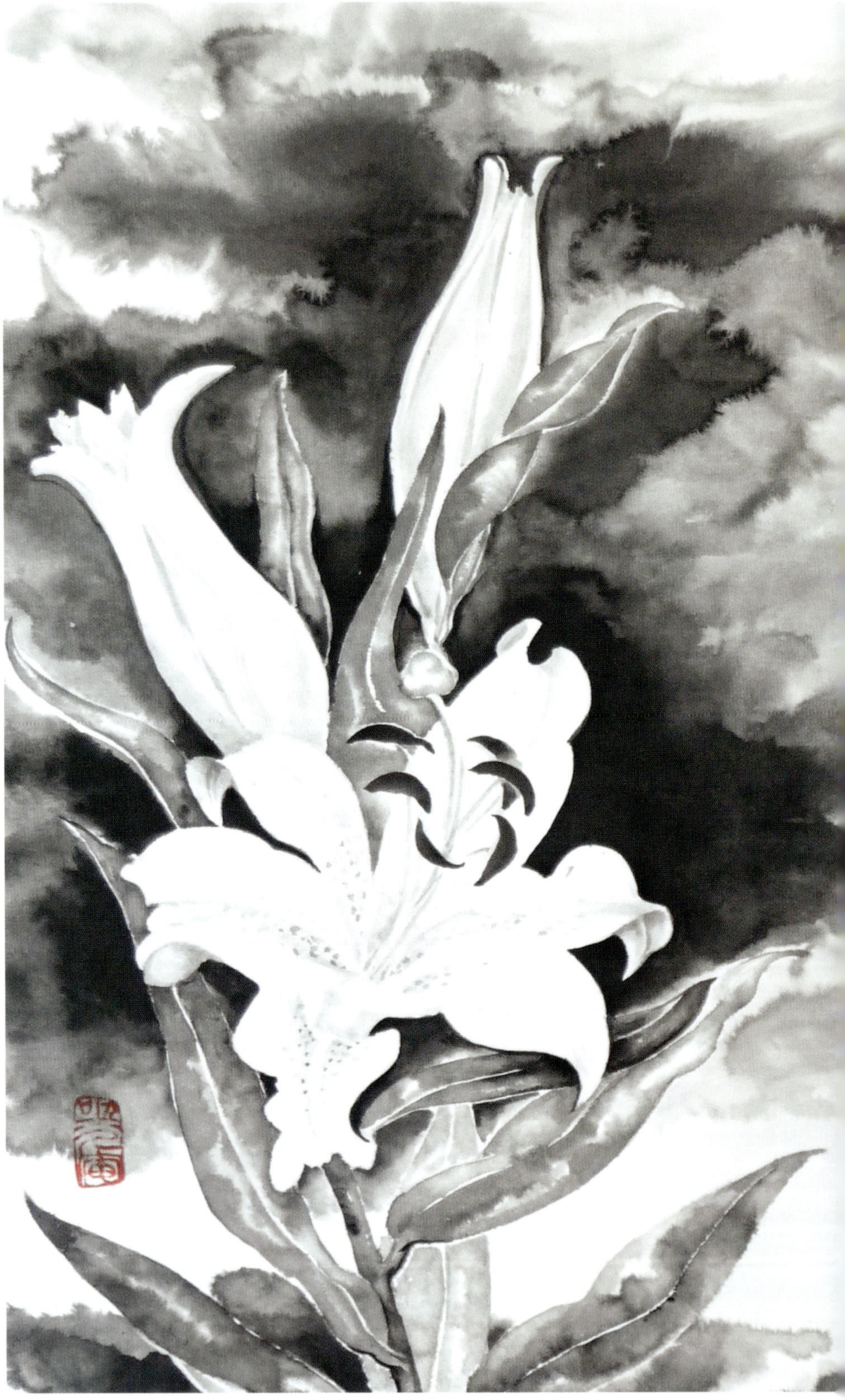

Collection of Harry and Diane Breen.

Left: To create the total essence of the lily including scent in black ink, I used the tarashi
komi technique, hoping that the variations especially in the leaves would add a very organic
feel.

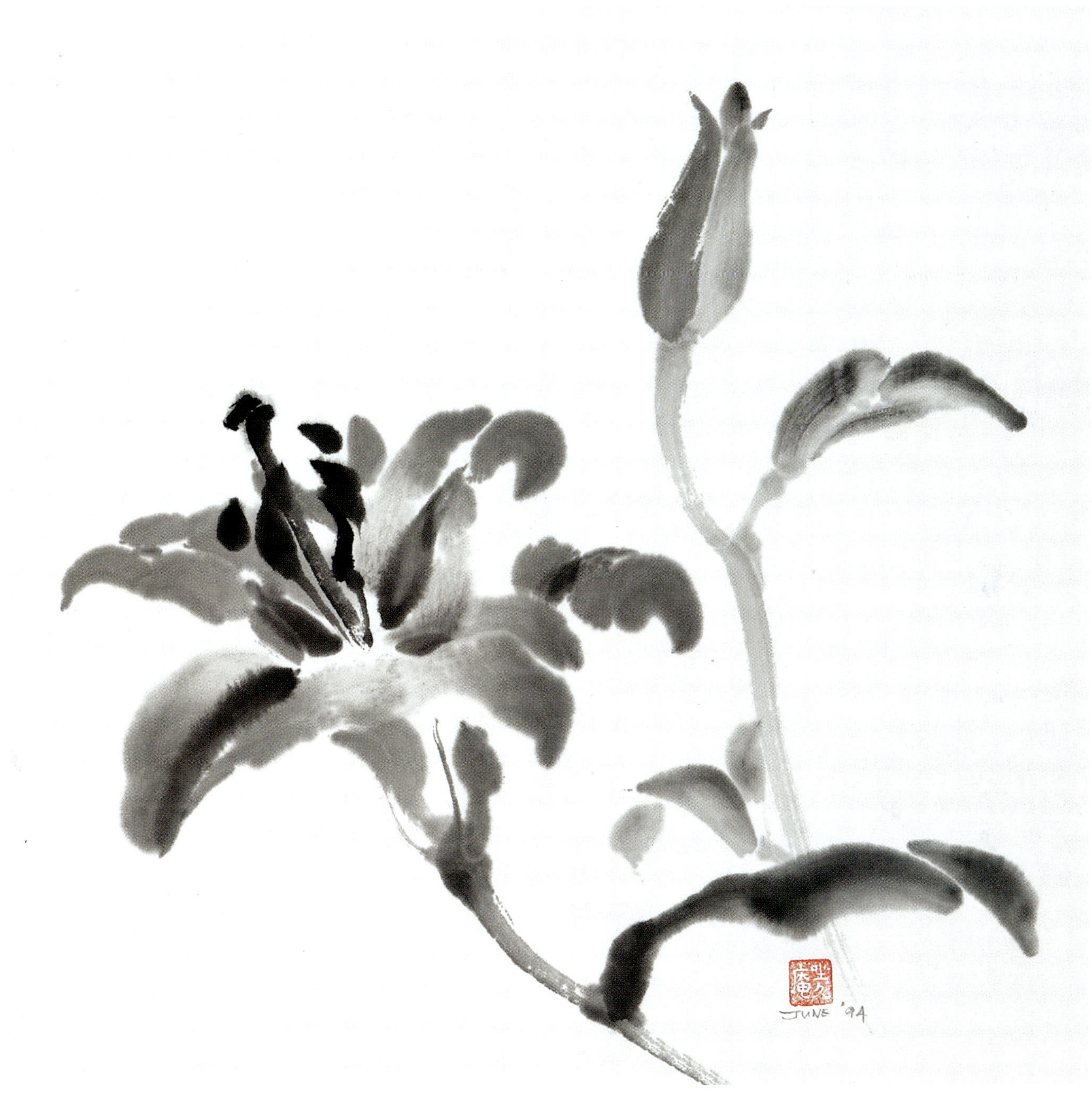

4. Stargazer Lily in Sumi-e

Size: H = 13.5"/34.5cm x W = 16.5"/42cm
Paper: Unsized
Sumi Ink: Blue tone
Category: Sumi-e

After completing the series of several stargazer paintings, I cleared the blossoms and the sketches from my studio. I also cleared my mind of all those images of the stargazer. This painting is my creative expression of the stargazer done in the minimal strokes of sumi-e. It took less than five minutes to complete, and serves as the summation of my artistic journey with the stargazer.

5. Calla Lily in Tarashi Komi Technique

Size: H = 14"/35 cm x W = 8.5"/21.5cm
Paper: Sized, pre-mounted on board
Sumi Ink: Standard, with gold dust
Category: Suiboku-ga (tarashi komi)

Calla lilies with thick petals in immaculate white are shaped like conch shells. A large yellow stamen protrudes from the center and the blossom is supported on a long succulent green stem. The curvaceous and irregular forms of the leaves provide a dramatic contrast to the flowers, making them an intriguing subject for painting.

This calla lily composition was first sketched onto the board. For the technique for transferring an outline of the final composition onto a mounted board, refer to Steps 1-3 on page 158.

Because the flower petal is so smooth and white, only a slight texture was added. (Be aware as you work to keep it slight.) Paint the leaves with water, then drop dark ink in the desired places. It is very important to control the spreading of dark ink so the white outlines of the flower will remain intact. The tarashi komi technique is marked by unexpectedness, and to use it to full advantage, you must have a clear vision when beginning on how you wish to compose the painting. If you have this solid foundation, you can enjoy and incorporate the unexpected results as enhancement.

When the flower and the leaves were completed and the painting was dry, the background was moistened with water and then painted with medium ink. This technique was used to make the whiteness of the calla stand out. Note the curved tip of the blossom. It is very important to carefully protect the tip from contact with any moisture during the process.

As the final touch, gold dust was applied to the petal tip and the veins of the leaf for an added accent. (See Chapter 3 for techniques for application of gold.) The gold for the stamen was applied using a dotting technique, to help suggest pollen, and it provides contrast with the smooth surface of the petal.

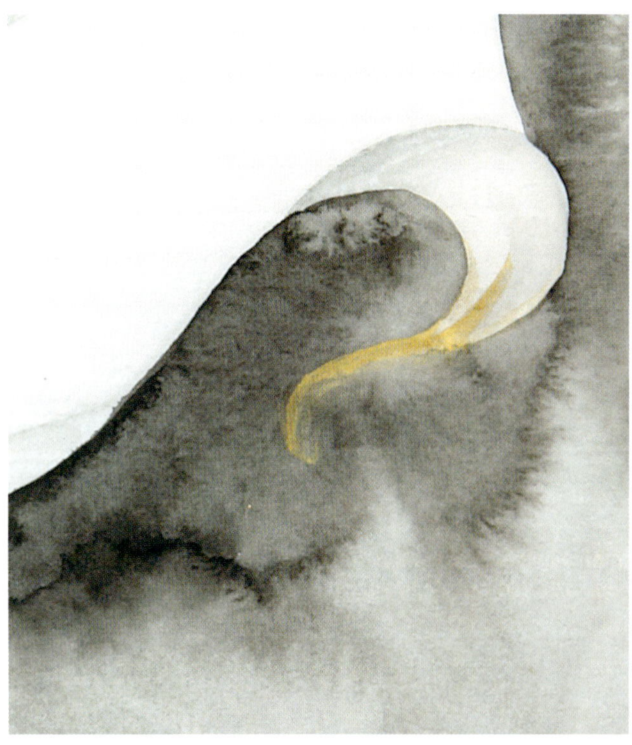

During the tarashi komi technique, it is important to ensure that crisp details, like the curved tip of the blossom, remain moisture-free.

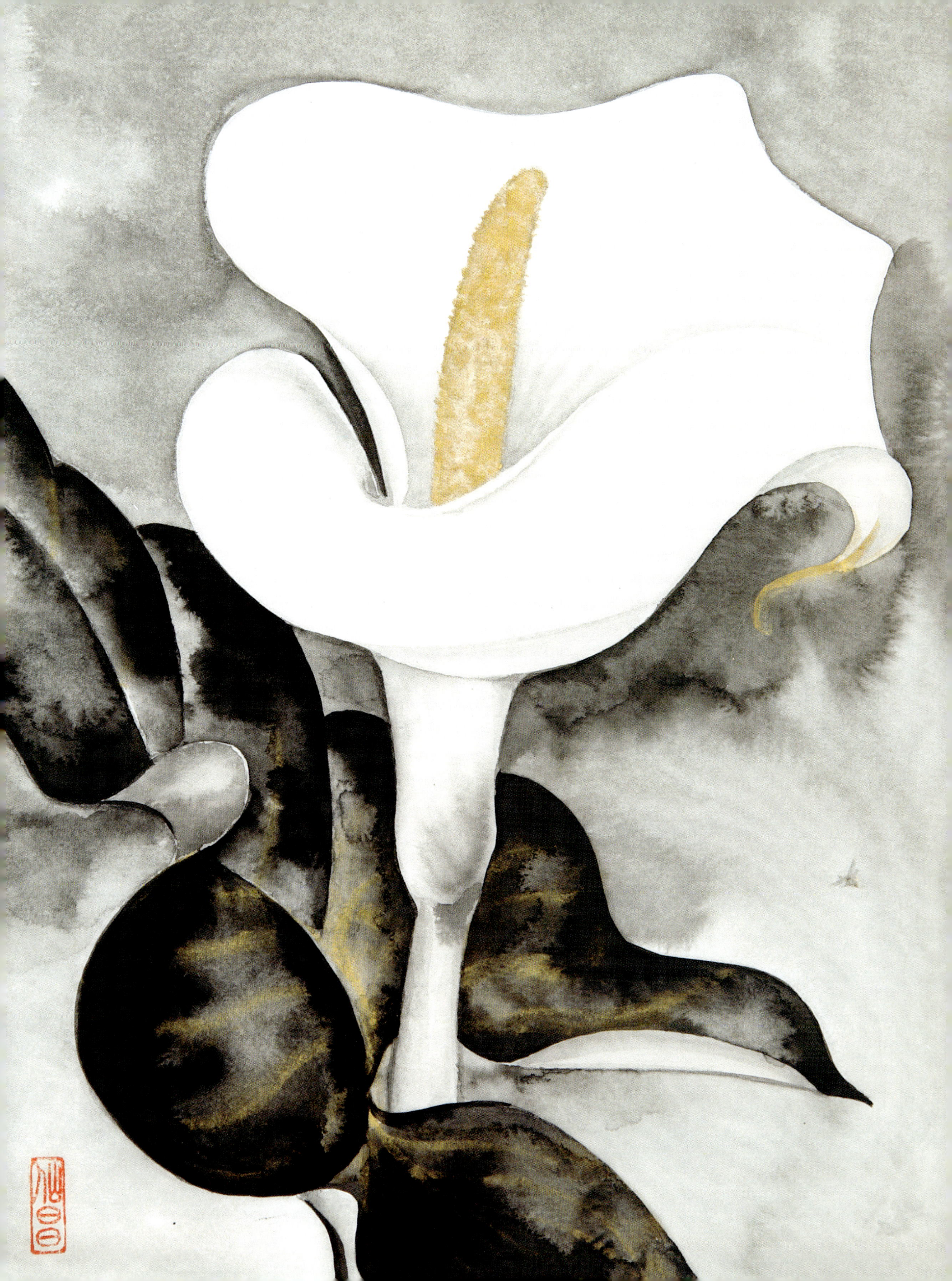

6. Calla Lily in Suiboku-ga

Size: W = 35.5"/91cm x W = 26"/66.5cm
Paper: Unsized, pre-mounted on board
Sumi Ink: Standard with gold pigment and gold dust
Category: Suiboku-ga

After completing a series of sketches of calla lilies, I reassembled different leaves, flowers and buds into a composition for this painting. I made a sketch of my composition in the size that the finished painting was to be. This was transferred to the unsized paper, mounted on a board since the added support would allow the brush to be moved more freely as I worked to capture the sense of the life force of the flower. (For the technique for transferring an outline of the final composition onto a mounted board, refer to Steps 1-3 on page 158.)

Begin with the lowest leaf on the right, using a large brush about an inch (2.5cm) in diameter. Apply ink to the brush in the traditional manner: rinse it in water, then apply light to medium ink at midpoint and dark ink at the tip. Using the tip of the brush, begin at the tip of the leaf, then gradually flatten the brush, moving to the left almost as if you were stamping the leaf pattern. Toward the end of the stroke, the dark ink will fade out and light ink and water take over.

Reapply dark ink on the bristles' tip and complete the lower part of the first leaf, again almost as if stamping. To finish the first curve, bring the tip of the brush up to complete the leaf. For the next leaf up, showing the side view, begin at the tip and complete it in one continuous stroke. In painting the leaf pattern, the brush moves up and down.

The leaf stems are created in much the same manner as painting bamboo. Wash the brush in water, flatten it, then apply dark ink on either side of the flattened tip; beginning at the bottom, move up and when reaching the leaf blade, lift one side of the brush so only one line shows the support for the leaf. While the ink is still wet, add the additional protrusions on the stem. If necessary, some of the outlines can be reinforced with a smaller brush. If the painted surface dries, it is important to add a little moisture by misting with a spray bottle, then removing the excess moisture with a paper towel before you make any additional strokes such as leaf veins.

The stems for the flowers are painted in a similar way to the leaf stems. The budding flower stems have side-view flower petals in front of them, so these must be covered with protective paper. (To see how this is done, refer to page 59.)

The outline technique is ideal for painting the single petal of the calla; I used a gray outline. Notice that the petal has been outlined with a line that varies in thickness to give a better sense of a three-dimensional effect.

After all of the leaves and flowers have been completed the gold centers are applied. (See Chapter 3 for techniques for application of gold.) Traditionally, color is avoided in sumi-e or suiboku-ga but gold or silver are acceptable. In this case gold dust is used to add richness in the painting.

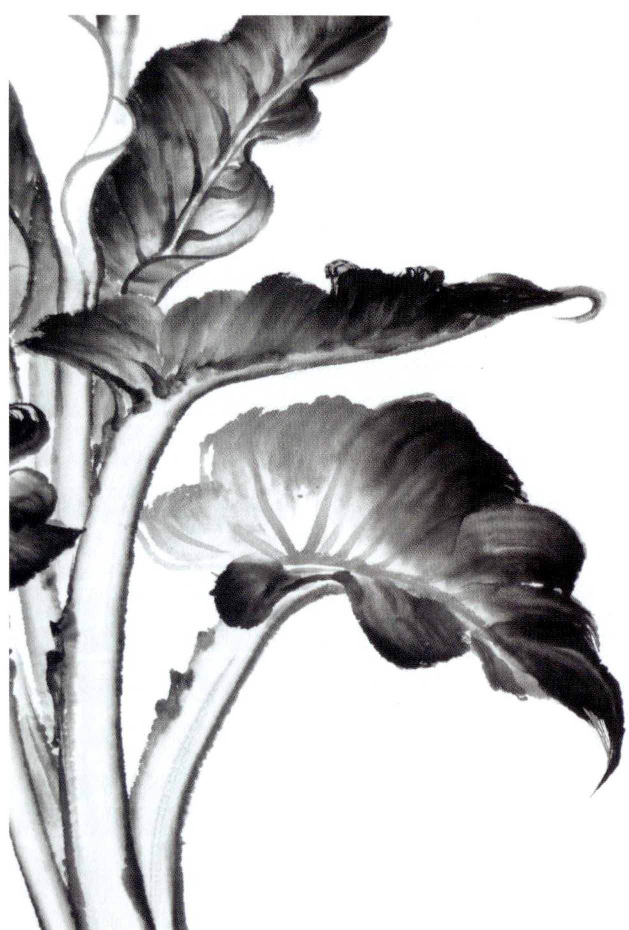

Calla lilies have broad succulent stems, so it is important to suggest that characteristic with sumi.

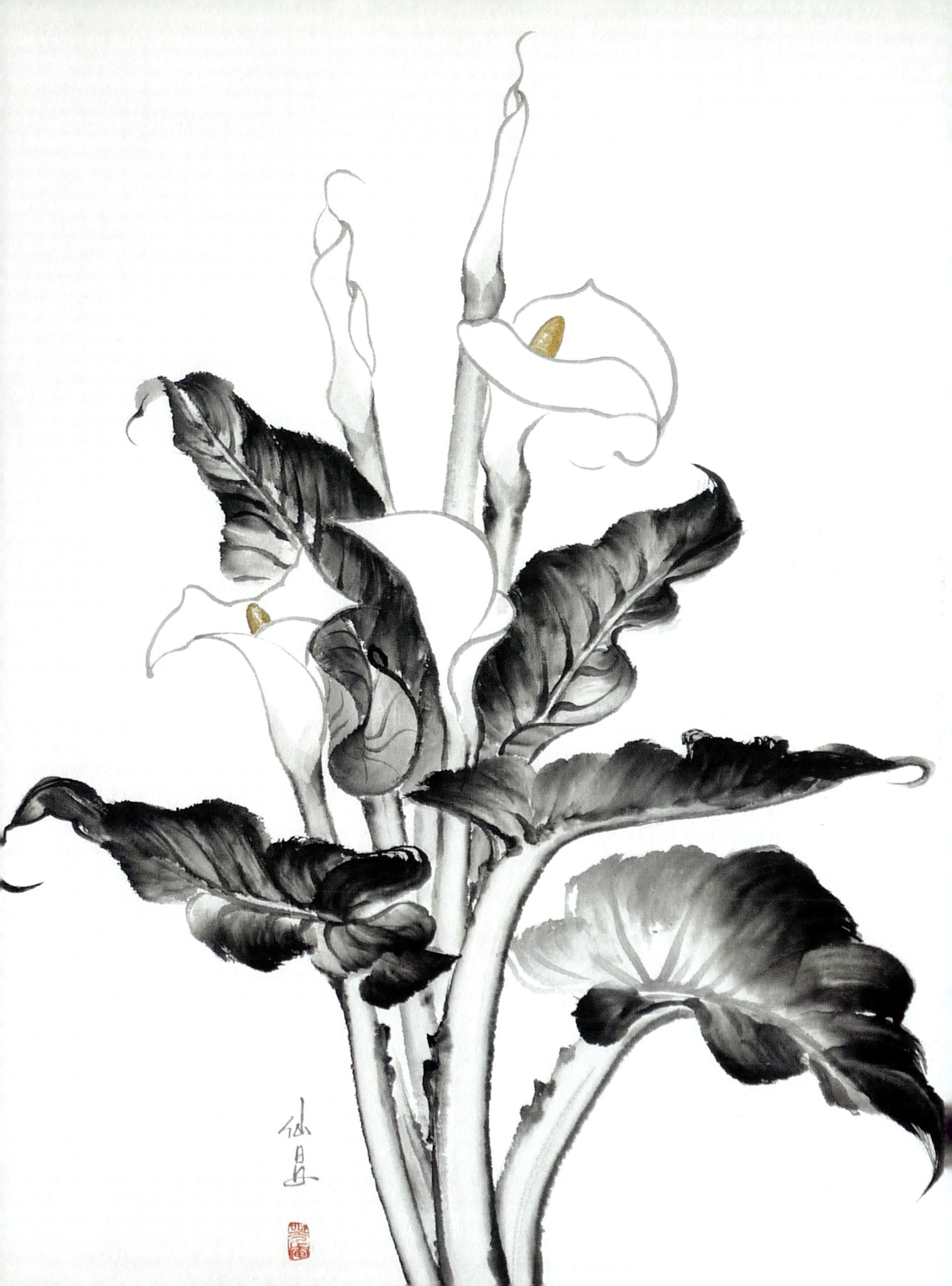

Painting the Shobu Iris

There are many species of iris in Japan, but the two species most commonly used in the arts are the ayame and the shobu. The ayame iris has smaller blossoms, between two and three inches (5 and 7.5cm) in diameter with a color range from deep to light purple. The leaf blades are wide, and are curved and short. The other frequently used iris is the shobu, which is often referred to as the Japanese iris. It is a tall iris with leaf blades and stems that are over three feet (1m) in height and it bears large flowers. Because the stiff leaf blade's form resembles a Japanese sword, the shobu iris is a traditional symbol for masculinity.

1. Shobu Iris in Sumi-e

Size: H = 10.75"/27cm x W = 8.5"/24cm
Paper: Unsized, on shikishi board
Sumi Ink: Standard
Category: Sumi-e

Most flowers in their bud stage have petals which are tightly overlapped. The shobu iris is unusual in that when it is in bud state the petals are crushed together within the sepals, and when the petals break out of the covering, similar to the wings of a cicada, the crinkled petals begin to unfold. Once they unfold, the petals become completely smooth. But the outline of each iris petal is not a smooth circular line (like a rose petal's for instance) until the flower is completely mature; until then jagged edges can be seen, so while the brush is moving, be sure to add vibrations to show this.

Load the brush with water first, then apply medium dark ink at the bristles' midpoint and dark ink at the tip. Each time the brush is loaded with the three tones, it is best to press the brush head on a plate or palette and vibrate it a little, so the tones within the bristles will blend.

Each petal should be painted in a two-stroke movement. Begin with one side of the petal, holding the brush with the water-loaded end in the center, and move down to create the first half of the petal. Vibrate the brush slightly as you move it, paying close attention to the tip of the bristle to see how it is forming the outline of the petal. Then, beginning on the right side, finish the petal by moving downward in a second stroke. Because the shikishi board for this painting is small and the blossom dominates, notice the way the leaf blades are not given emphasis.

This painting was completed in less than two minutes, formed from a crystallization of the shobu image held in my memory. Strokes were minimized so the active empty space could be enjoyed.

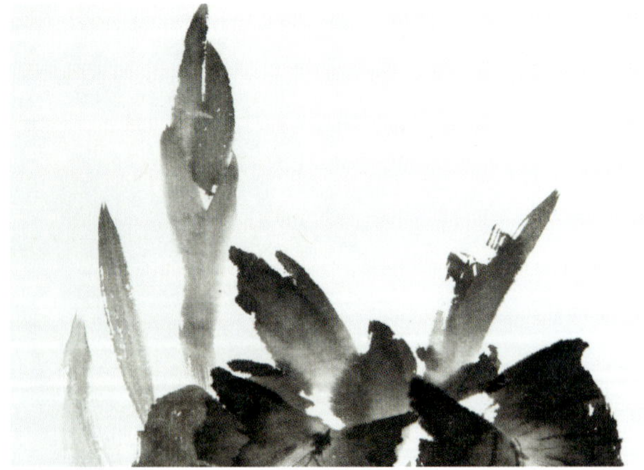

The crown petals are given additional strength and prominence by flattening the bristles and using them in a "pressing down" manner, so it is crucial to apply the proper amounts of water, light and dark ink.

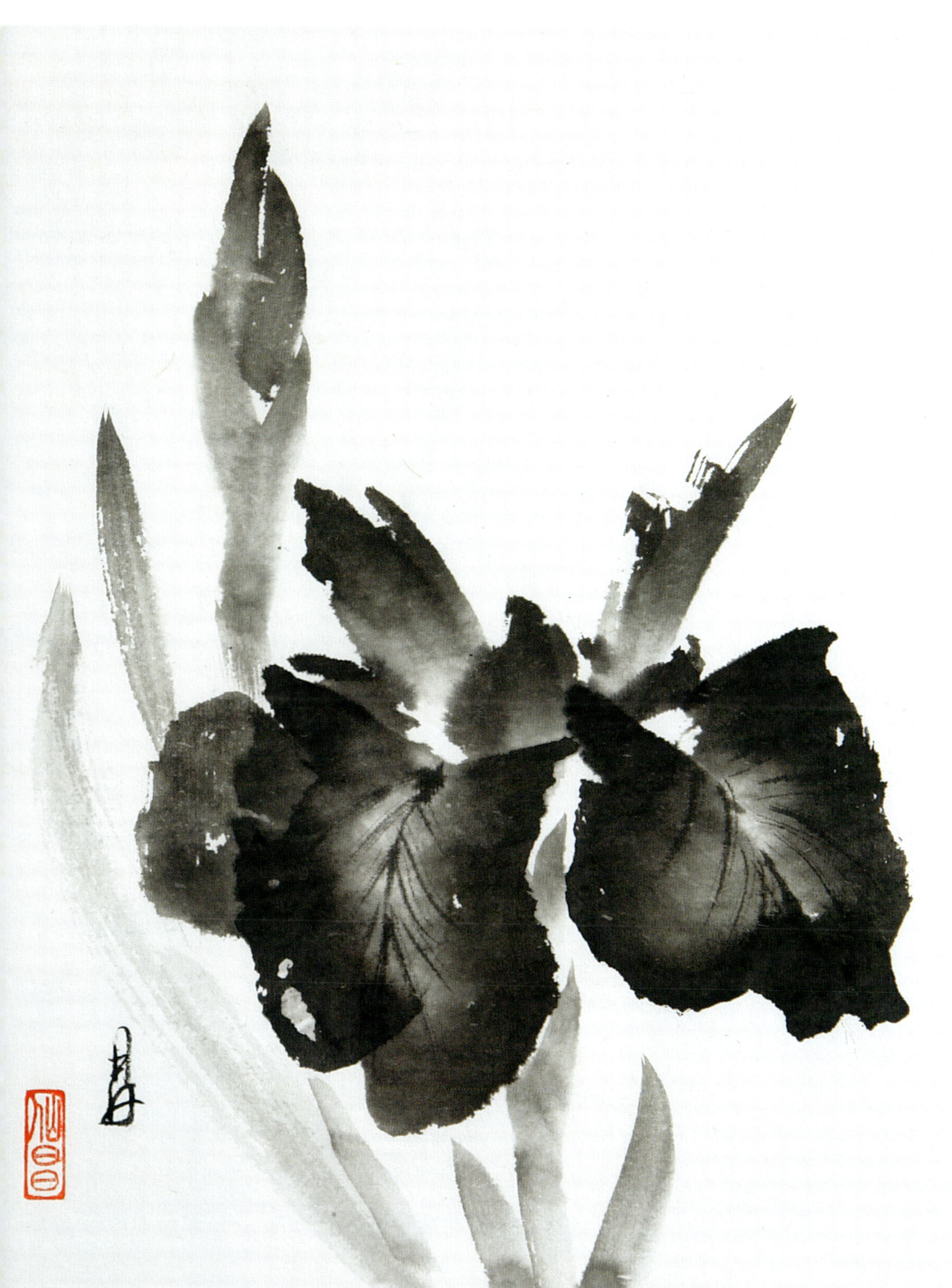

2. Shobu Iris with Silver Background

Size: W = 31"/79cm x L = 22"/55 cm
Paper: Unsized, pre-mounted on board
Sumi Ink: Traditional Japanese pigments, with standard sumi ink in background; silver paint sprayed on background
Category: Traditional Japanese painting

This painting of a shobu iris which grew in my pond symbolizes opulent masculinity.

Before the flower was painted, I used a hand sprayer with light sumi ink in blue tone to spray the background. Then I immediately remoistened the surface by spraying on clear water, thus creating the texture.

A spray of silver pigment was applied with the use of mesh and a toothbrush (see page 56). Gold or silver pigments require specific directional light rays for reflection, but when conditions are right, they can give unexpected pleasure. Under certain light conditions, horizontal lines in the lower part of this work suggest mist above the water surface.

The basic difference between western watercolors and traditional Japanese pigments is that the Japanese pigments have a more pastel effect in color. Western watercolors are transparent and are more vibrant. However, adding Chinese white to western watercolor paints makes them opaque, and more similar to traditional Japanese pigments.

Even though I was using very fine traditional Japanese pigments instead of black ink, the brush was loaded in the same way as for the previous sumi-e painting (page 154). Instead of water, white pigment was used; instead of black ink, purple pigment was used. With light purple at midpoint and dark purple at the tip, I painted the large center petal with two strokes, as described on page 154. All of the other petals were created by using one continuous stroke. After completing three of the major petals, I added the back sides of the petals with light purple. The crown petals were created by using a "pressing" technique. In creating the petals, remember after making contact with the paper to vibrate and jiggle the brush as you move, to create the petal patterns which are finely wrinkled just after opening.

After the petals are completed, add yellow to the bases. Finally, after the petals are dry, use opaque white to paint in the veins of the petals.

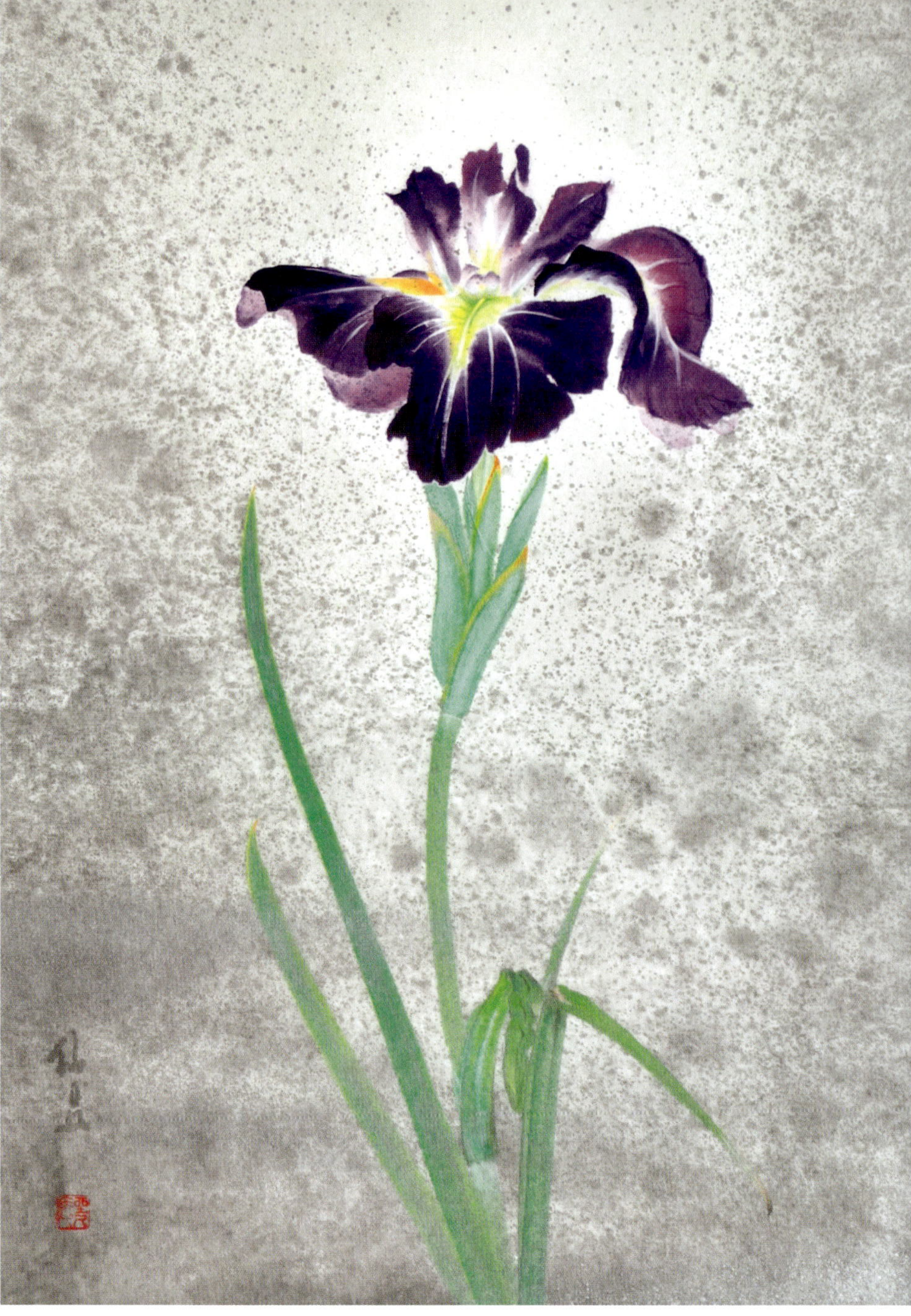

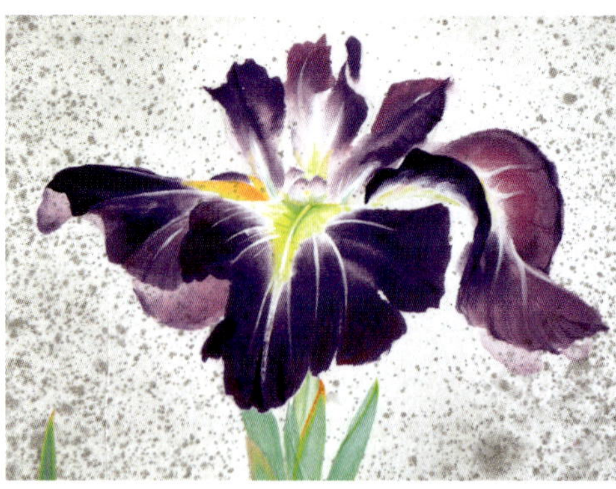

Above: A characteristic of the shobu iris is that the petals are very thin and the three outer petals drape out. The three center petals remain upright and are accompanied by three smaller "style" arms.

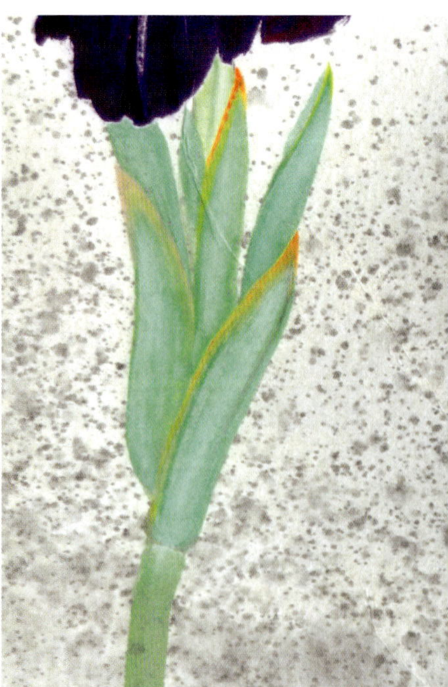

Right: The green buds and stems were created in basic sumi brush strokes. An orange tint was added to the edges of the leaf blades.

3. Shobu Iris in Tarashi Komi Technique

Size: H = 23"/58.5cm x W= 17.25"/43.5cm
Paper: Sized, pre-mounted on board
Sumi Ink: Blue tone with gold dust and gold leaf
Category: Suiboku-ga (tarashi komi)

As we have seen previously, the tarashi komi technique can give the effect of ornateness because it is not painted in a one-stroke style. It is as if the artist is "tattooing" a variety of tones of ink to the surface water floating on the paper. Plenty of time can be taken to contemplate the effect of the dark or light ink. This composition, similar to *Stargazer Lily in Traditional Japanese Style* (page 146), has blossoms that represent the past, present and the future. The center flower is semi-opened, so its crown is still undeveloped and the petals have not fully opened.

The fully opened blossom was accented with tarashi komi to enhance the sense of dark purple. After it was semi-dry, a few darker lines were added to the edges of the petal and in the center. On the back sides of the petals, light gray was added along with light gray lines. The tarashi komi technique provides interesting organic patterns in dark and light ink, so veins were omitted because they would disturb the patterns.

Standard ink gives a brown tone when diluted—not so suitable for an iris. One of the advantages in using high quality inks, whether in liquid or stick form, is that they are sold labeled with their special tones. This means that when very dark ink is used, the ink will convey a sense of, in this case, purple. The ink tone adds a new dimension to a painting in monochrome.

In this painting, the gold leaf and texture echoes the tarashi komi effect. (See Chapter 3 for techniques for application of gold.)

Right: The bud hints of growth day by day. This bud is just about ready to open up. Because the tarashi komi technique is used, the jagged lines of the folded texture become secondary here; thin lines simply suggest them.

Far right: Incorporating the natural formation of your subject is important. Shobu iris usually have a group of five or six leaf blades to form a base in the water, but the main blades are assembled three in a unit. These blades grow straight up to about three feet (1m) long and they have a claw-like tip that turns inward.

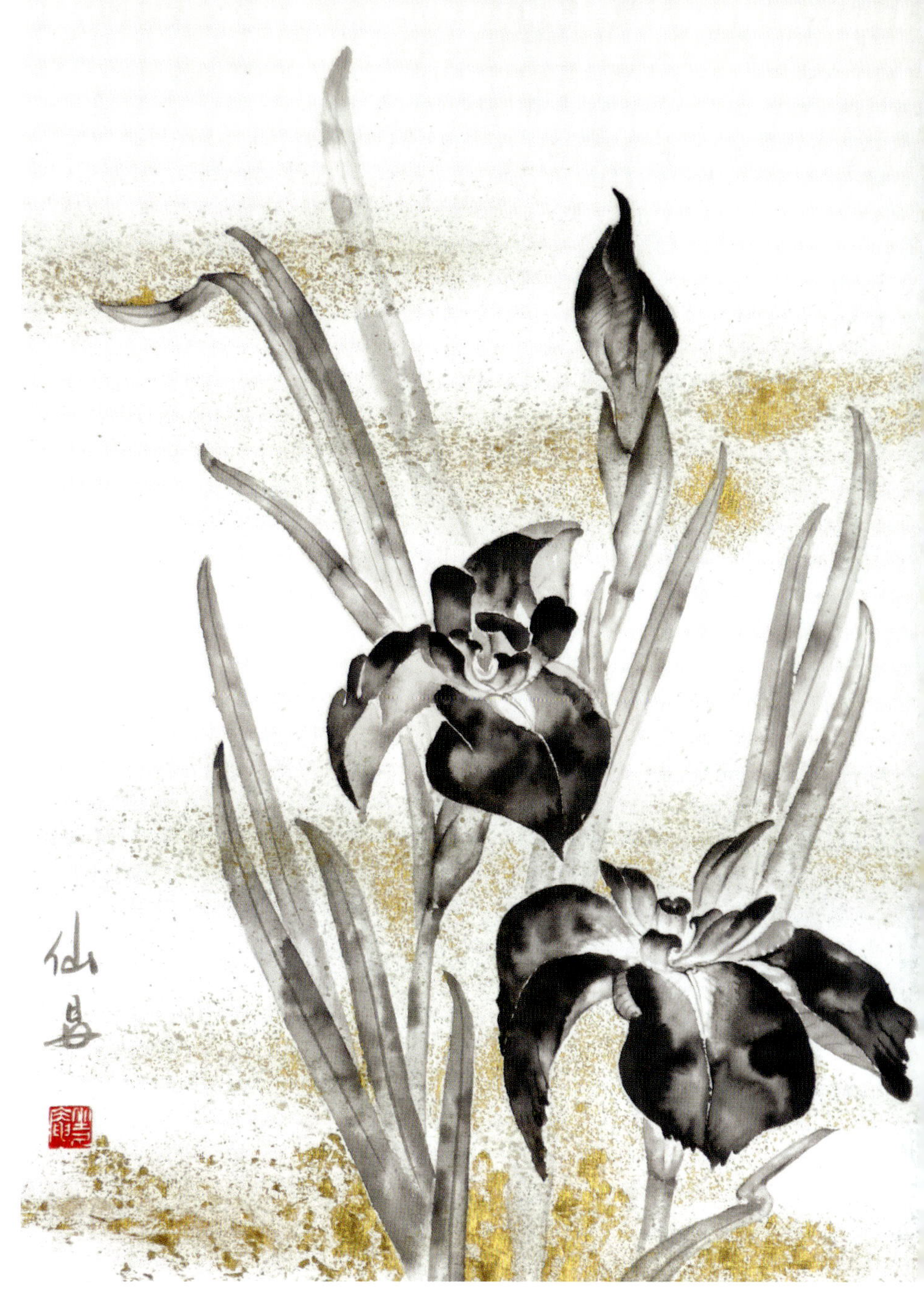

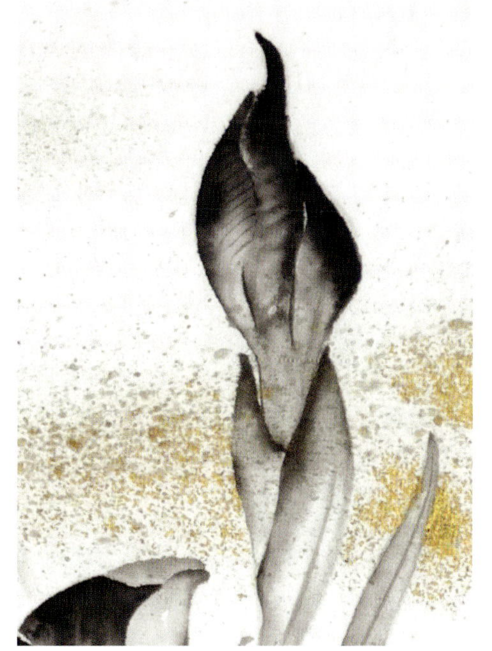

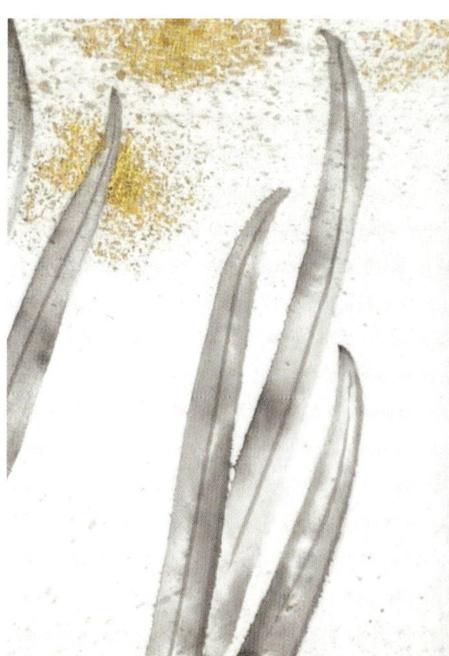

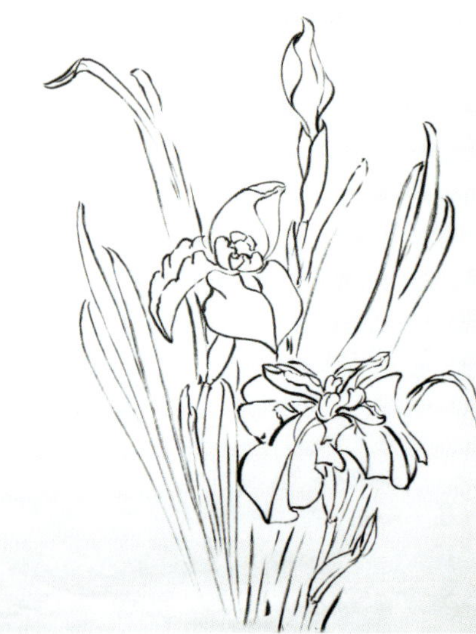

1. The first step is to make a sketch with your brush. Notice that here the crown petals of the lower blossom are already past their prime, while in my final sketch (see Step 3) the crown petals are upright—I switched to a younger blossom.

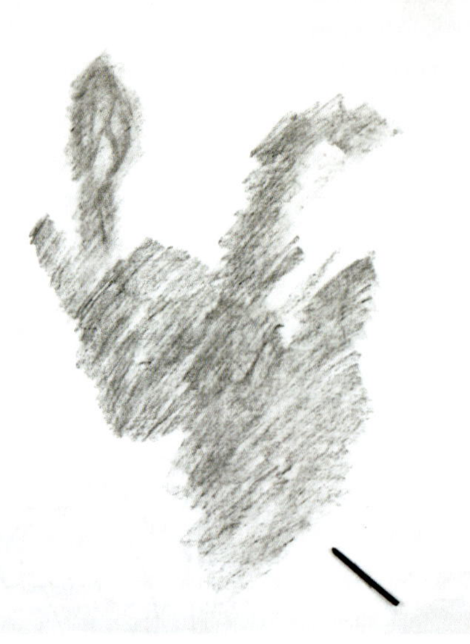

2. The back side of the original sketch is smeared with a stick of artist's charcoal so the sketch can be transferred. Place the sketch very carefully down on the pre-mounted paper with the charcoal side down.

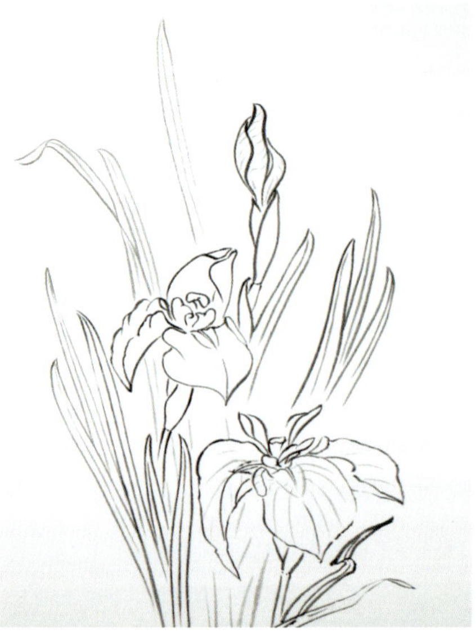

3. Then with a glass pen or a soft number 4-B pencil (do not use ballpoint pen because it might cut through the paper, and it also leaves a permanent mark) trace the entire sketch onto your prepared board. Once you have gone over the entire sketch with the glass pen, lift your sketch off the board: you will see your sketch marked in charcoal. Proceed to make a complete outline in light ink.

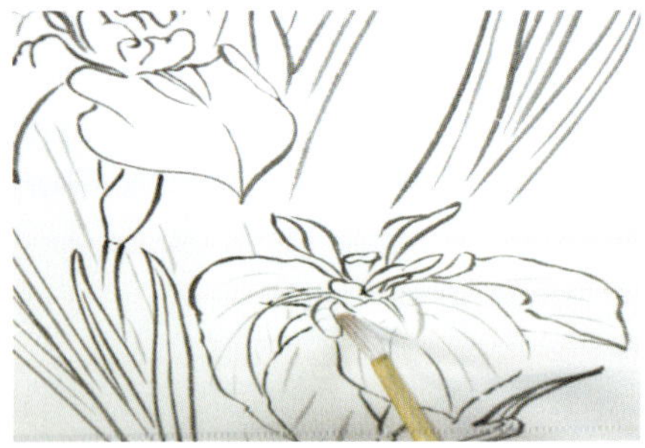

4. With water on the brush, wet the paper where you will paint with ink. Stay within the outline, leaving a small dry space between each section.

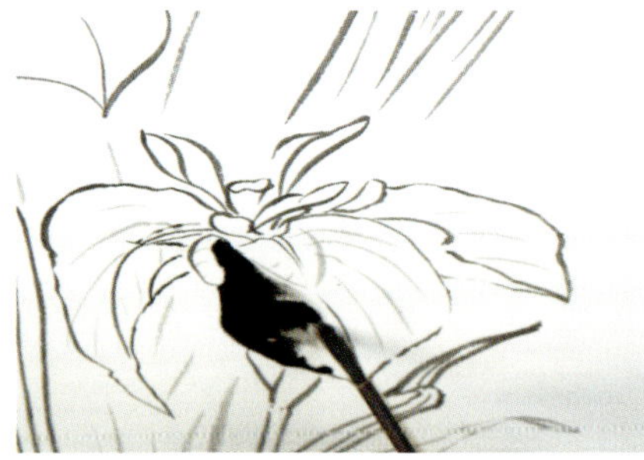

5. Immediately add the darker ink; it will start to run in any area where the paper is wet.

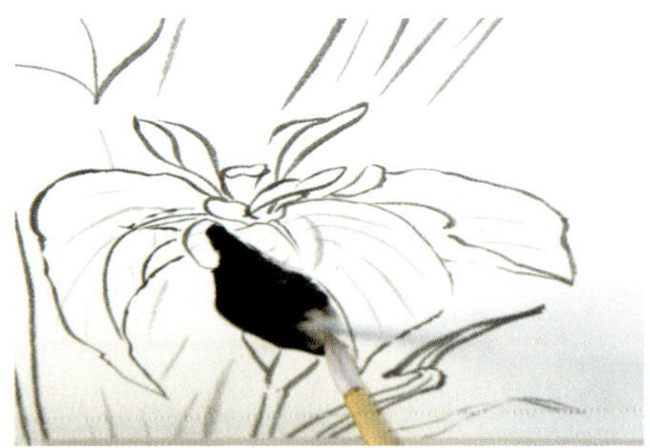

6. Add water to the dark ink section.

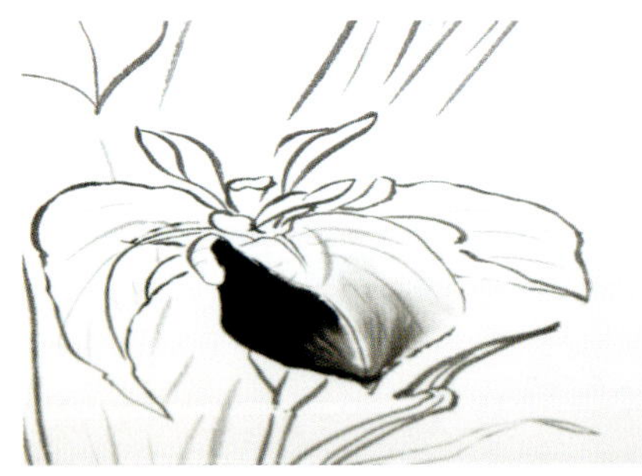

7. Notice the ink's flow into the wet area.

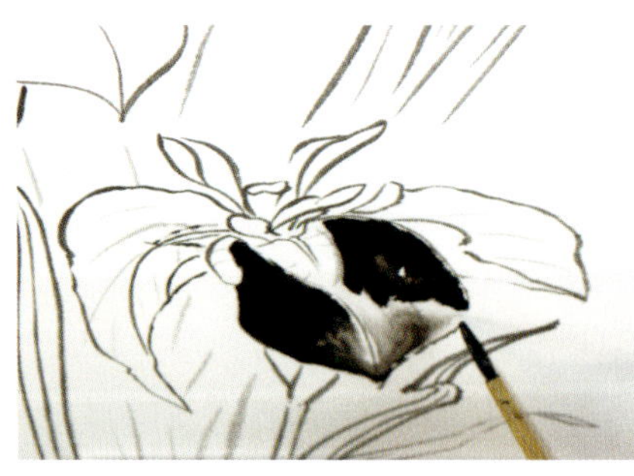

8. To the right side of the petal, add dark ink.

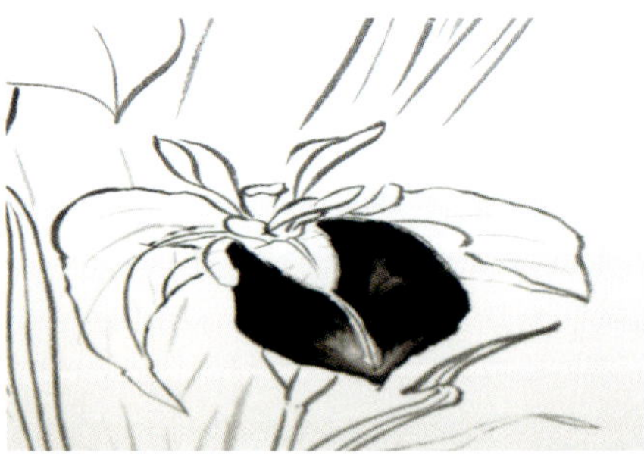

9. Dark ink has now spread over the entire right side of the petal.

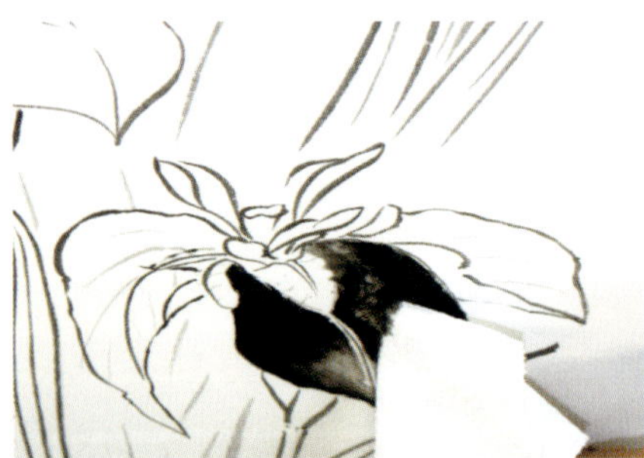

10. Extract unwanted dark ink with a paper towel. By touching the corner of the paper towel to the area, the ink will be soaked up.

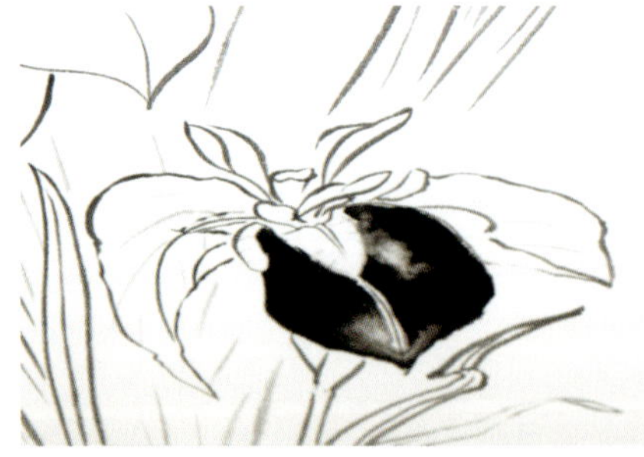

11. After the ink is extracted with a paper towel, the leaf will show highlights of the petal.

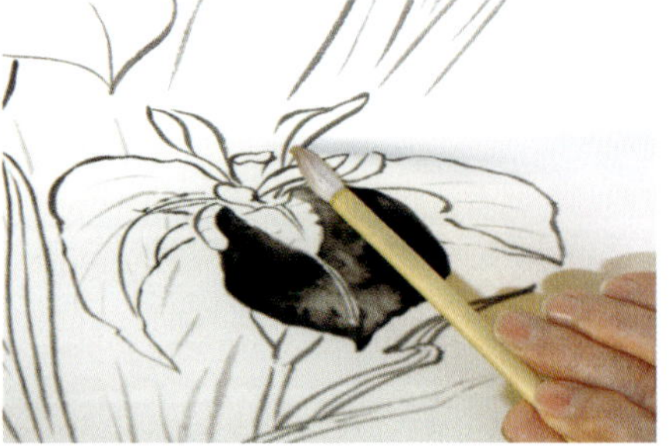

12. In that way, wherever it is needed, a brush or paper towel can be used to soak up unwanted ink. Continue by adding water to the crown petal.

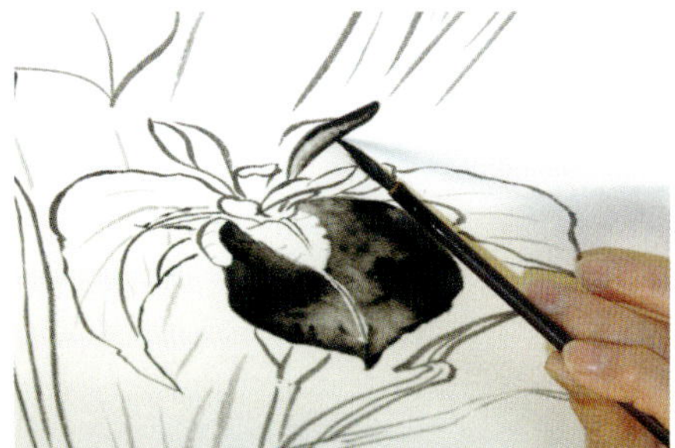

13. Dark ink is added from the outline side and the ink seeps in.

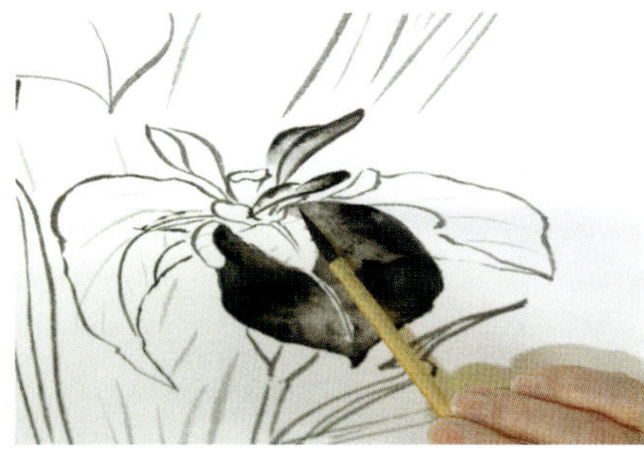

14. The other side of the crown petal is treated in the same way.

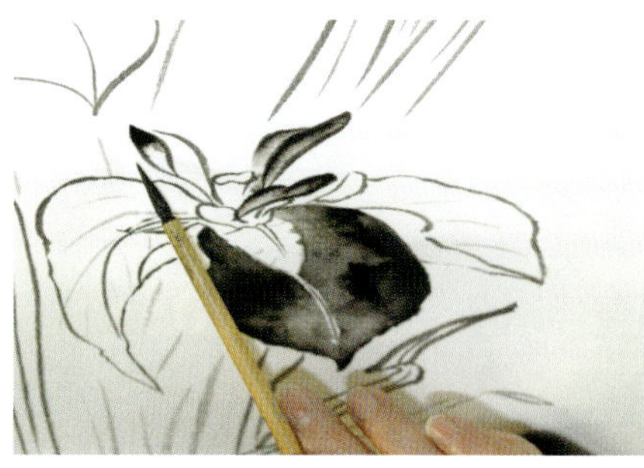

15. Continue the same process: water first, then dark ink on the crown petals.

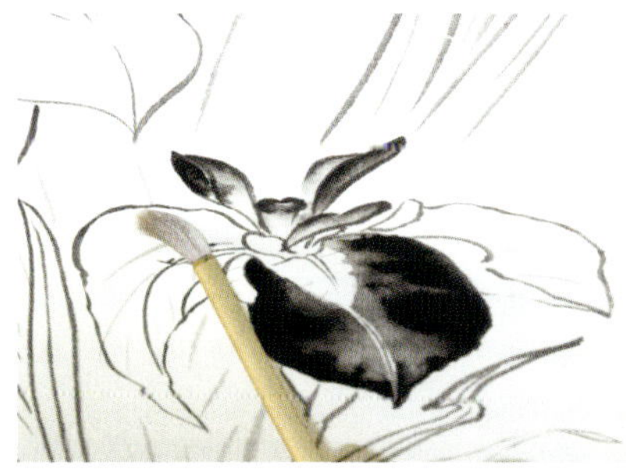

16. Paint the petal on the left with water. Remember to always leave a small dry space between each area.

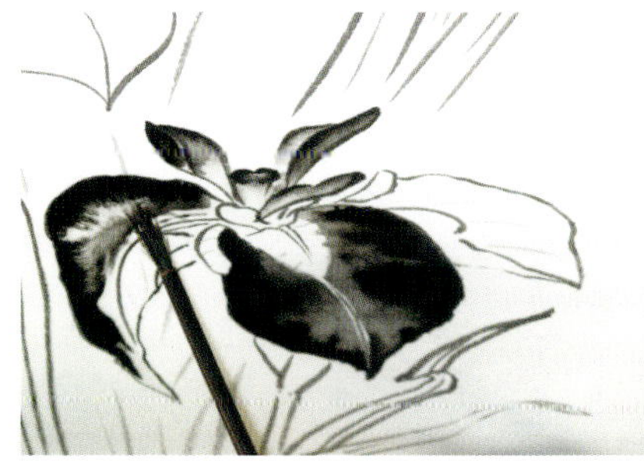

17. Add dark ink. A small and dry mountain horse hair brush with bristles spread apart is being used to guide the ink.

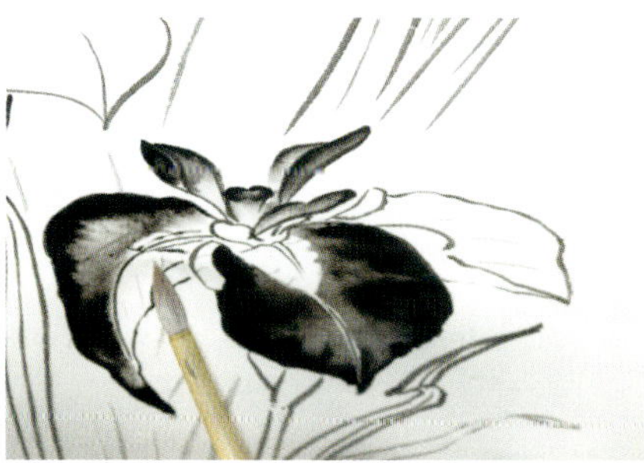

18. Add water to the underside of the petal on the left.

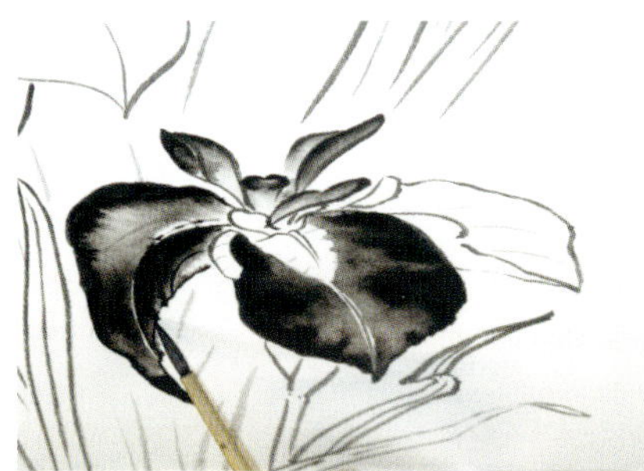

19. Repeat the same process with dark ink.

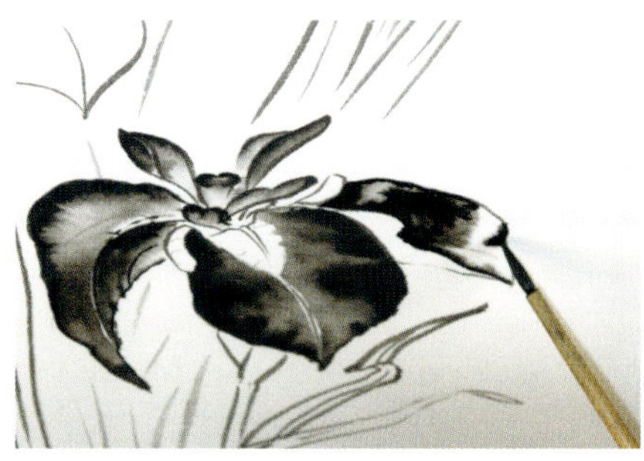

20. The petal to the right follows the same treatment in steps. Remember: the back side of the petal remains white until later. Because the back side will be done in light ink leave a thin dry strip along the border or the dark ink will seep into it.

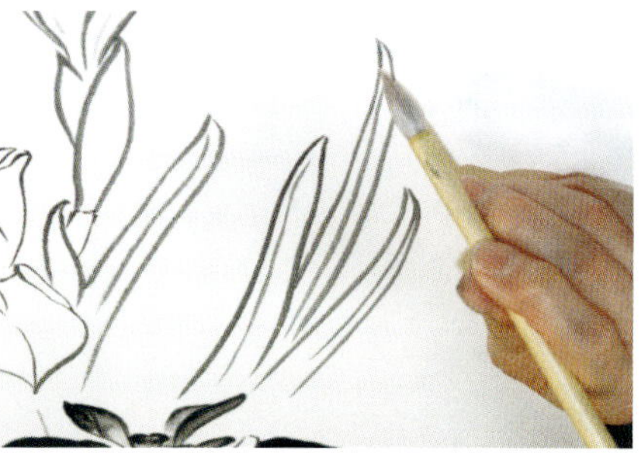

21. In the tarashi komi technique you are "enjoying" the interplay of water and ink and the effects that are spontaneously created, so you should not use a hair dryer to hurry the drying process. That may make the ink run in the wrong direction.

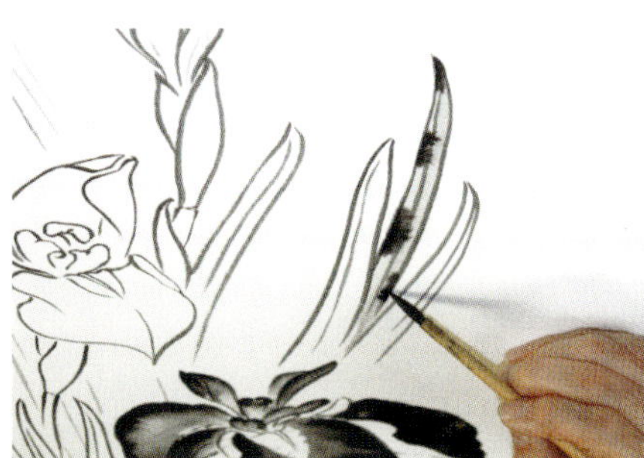

22. Instead, be patient. While waiting for one section to dry, begin working some other section, such as a leaf.

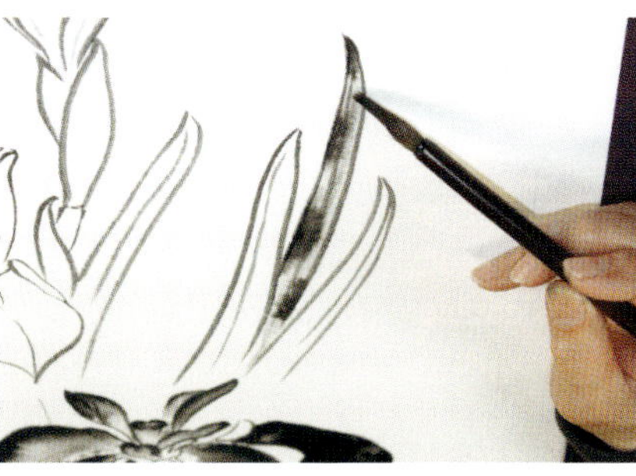

23. Once a leaf has been moistened, immediately drop dark ink in selected places. Guide the ink with another brush to create the effects you wish.

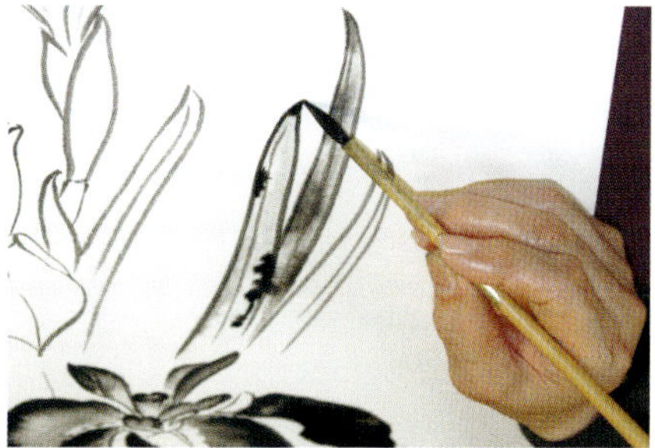

24. Repeat the same process on the next leaf.

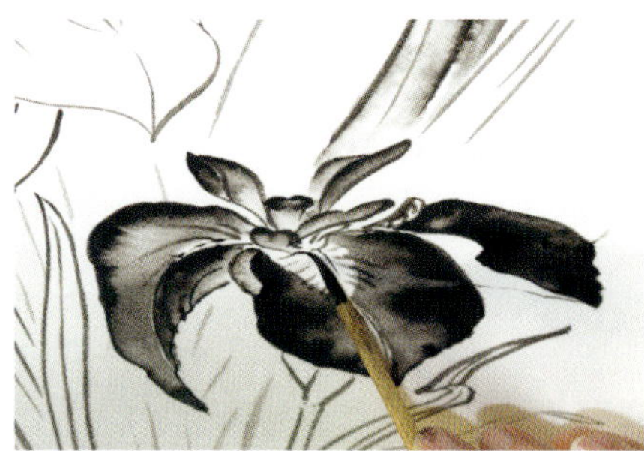

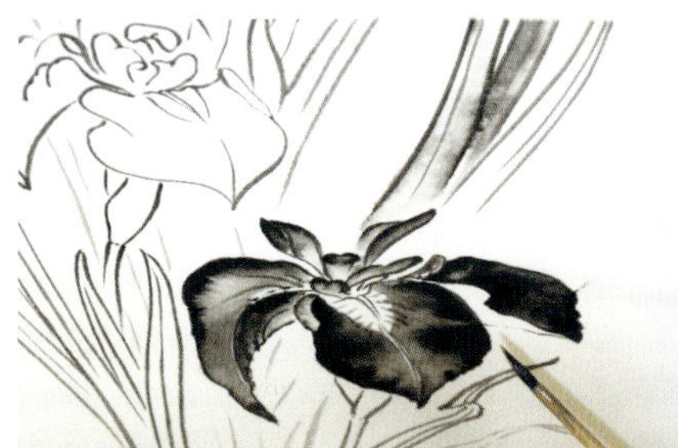

25. When the paper is dry, it will be safe to add dark lines to the petals to complete them. Add dark ink to identify the veins and the creases in the petals.

If your hands touch the surface of the paper, the oils left behind will affect the spreading ink. Always use protective paper wherever you place your hands on your work.

Continue the tarashi komi process, step by step, to complete the painting.

Painting Grasses

Unlike the usual subjects that are given dominant positions in paintings—trees, flowers, mountains, rocks, water—grasses most often are painted to give accent and flavor to a work. This project shows how to paint pampas grass in a simple way that suggests the gradual change of summer to autumn.

When painting narrow-wide lines for grasses, the length of the grass blade you plan will determine the amount of ink to load at the tip of your brush. As the brush moves down, the ink will become lighter; a very useful result, especially if the blades are overlapped at the base. Creating a leaf bend or twist (see page 128) is useful at times. You must use your discretion to avoid monotony.

This is a painting on a door with stainless steel handles. The top of the door shows a large sun low in the horizon as evening approaches. The rolling meadows at the bottom are made using three different tones of yellow-beige paper. Ornamentation with traditional gold leaf and dust was the final step for *A Setting Sun in Autumn*.

A Setting Sun in Autumn: Painted Door

Size: W = 36"/91.5cm x H = 80"/203cm
Paper: Sized, mounted on birch hollowcore door; beige papers
Sumi Ink: Standard, with gold dust and gold and silver leaf
Category: Sumi-e inspired

First, white butcher paper, which is sized, was glued on a regular door of birch wood with a hollow center, using wallpaper glue. (Unsized paper can also be used, but the glue will automatically size it, unless it is very thick paper such as double or triple weight. Then some of the effects of unsized paper will remain, such as nijimi.)

Before painting the foreground, a wash of very light gray was applied with a wide renpitsu brush (see Chapter 3, "Brushes") to provide a sense of depth. While the surface was still wet, the very light distant blades of grass were added to hint of mist in an autumnal sunset.

The two lighter yellow-beige background papers were glued on next: a "line in water" was created on the beige paper in the desired contour, and it was torn along the wet lines, then glued onto the door. After the paper dried completely, the foreground pampas grasses and the plume were painted. When the painting was completed, the final darker beige paper was glued on, to cover the base of the grasses.

The oldest blades in the foreground are the most mature, so they should portray toughness and strength. These are wide-narrow strokes. Brush movement begins at the bottom, with proper control of the ink. This control—of the amount of ink on the bristles based on the stroke length required—is very basic in the study of sumi-e.

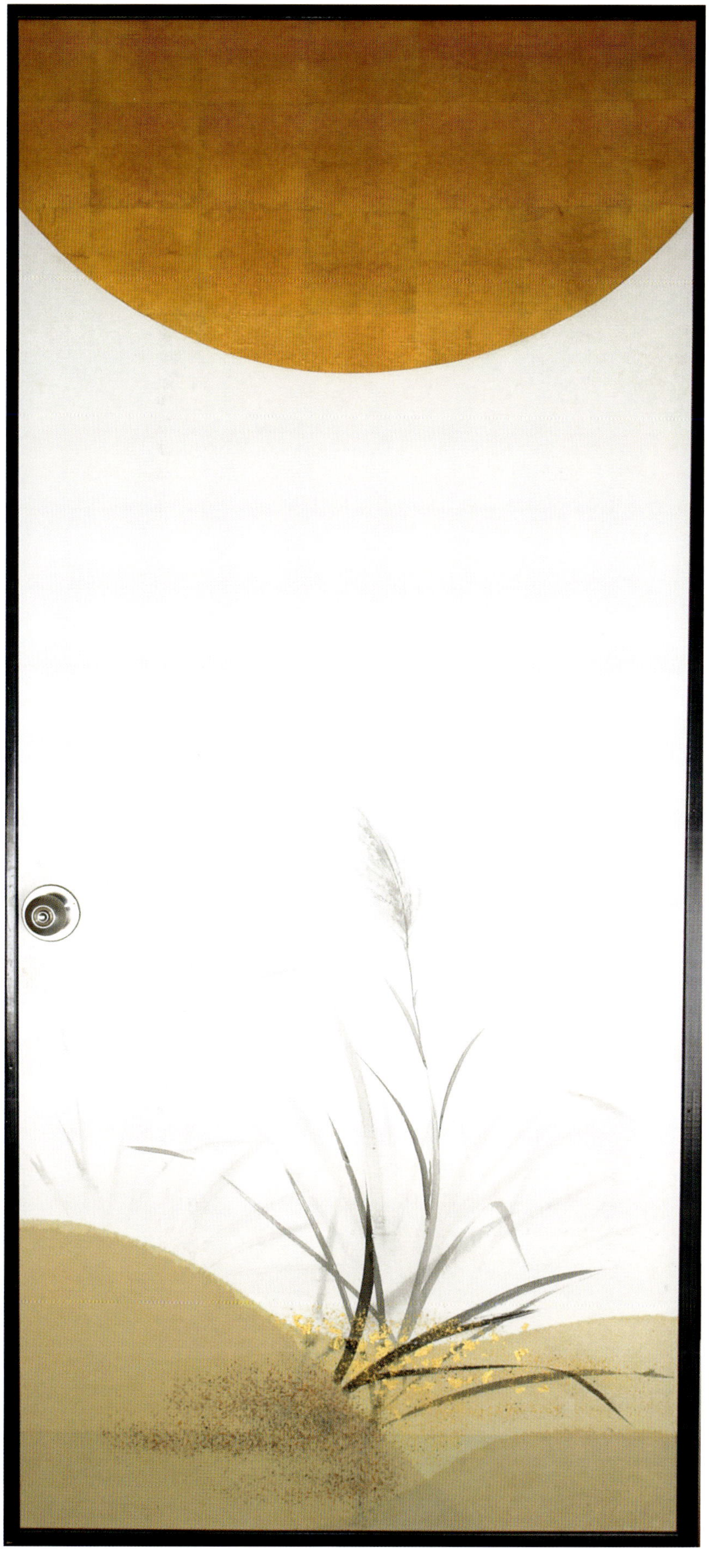

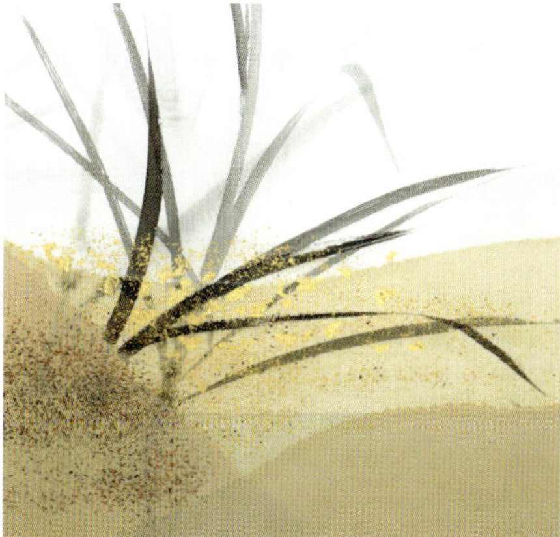

Gold dust was applied on the center right, and aged silver combined with aged gold leaves were used on the foreground paper to hint of the reflection of sunlight on the mist.

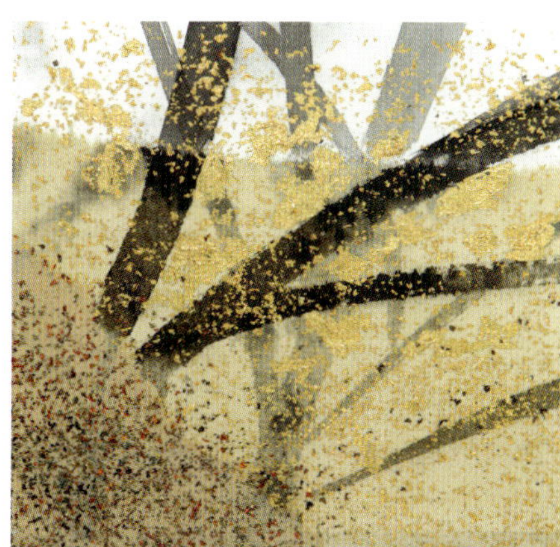

Because the gold dust is a suggestion of mist on the ground reflecting the sunlight, it is applied in horizontal strata. Darker gold and silver were used to suggest shade.

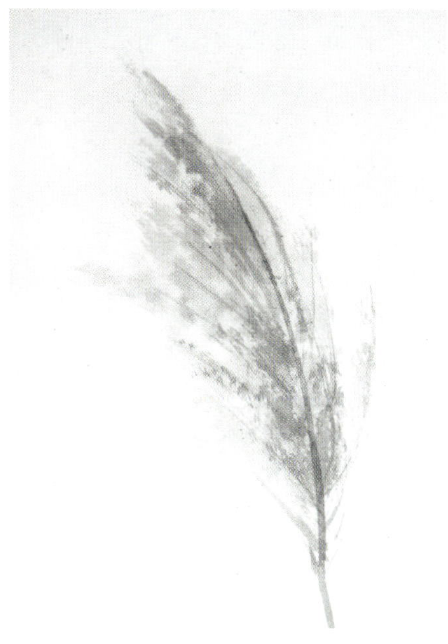

Since this is autumn, the plumes are feather-like and soft.

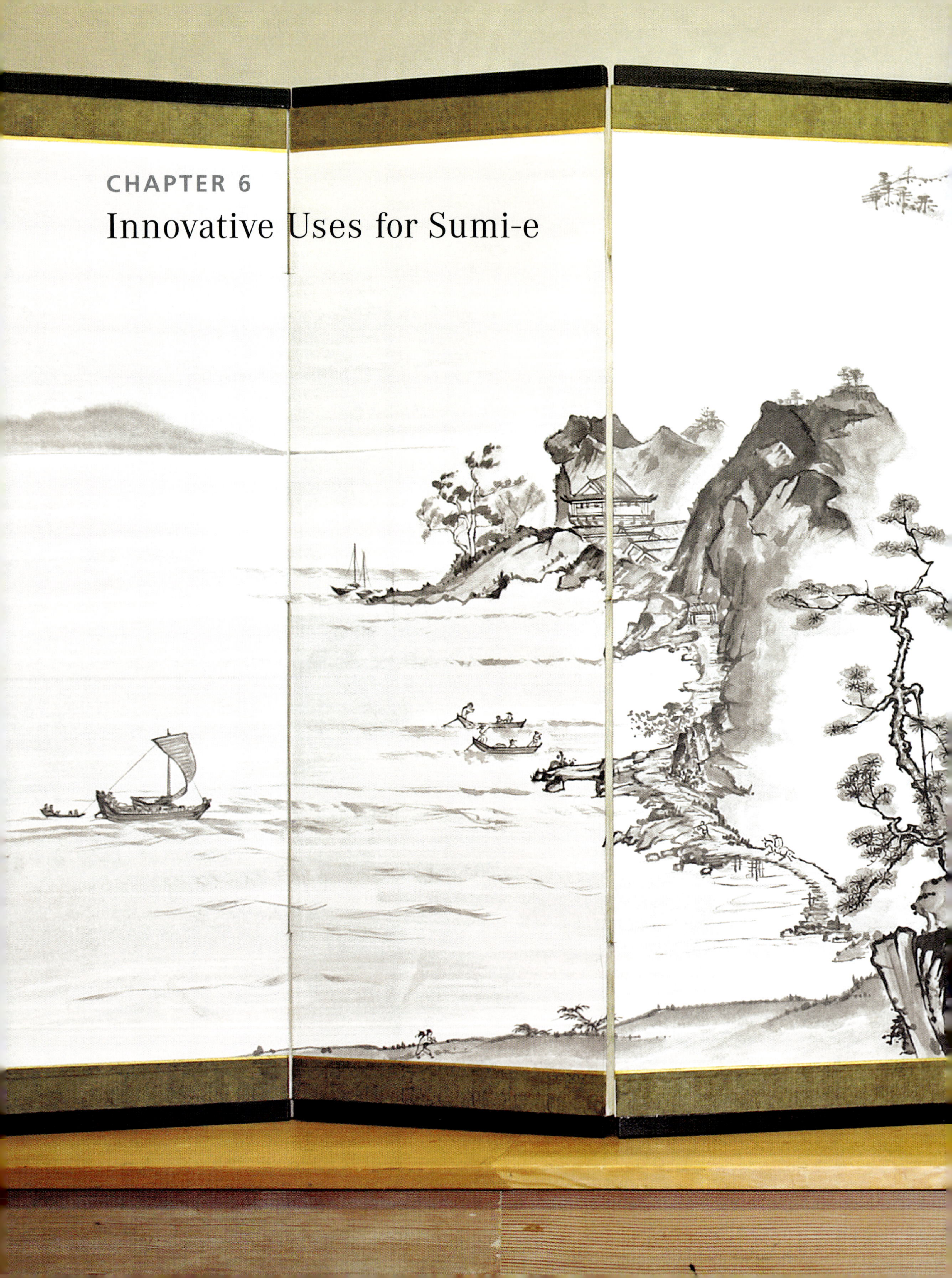

Innovative Uses for Sumi-e

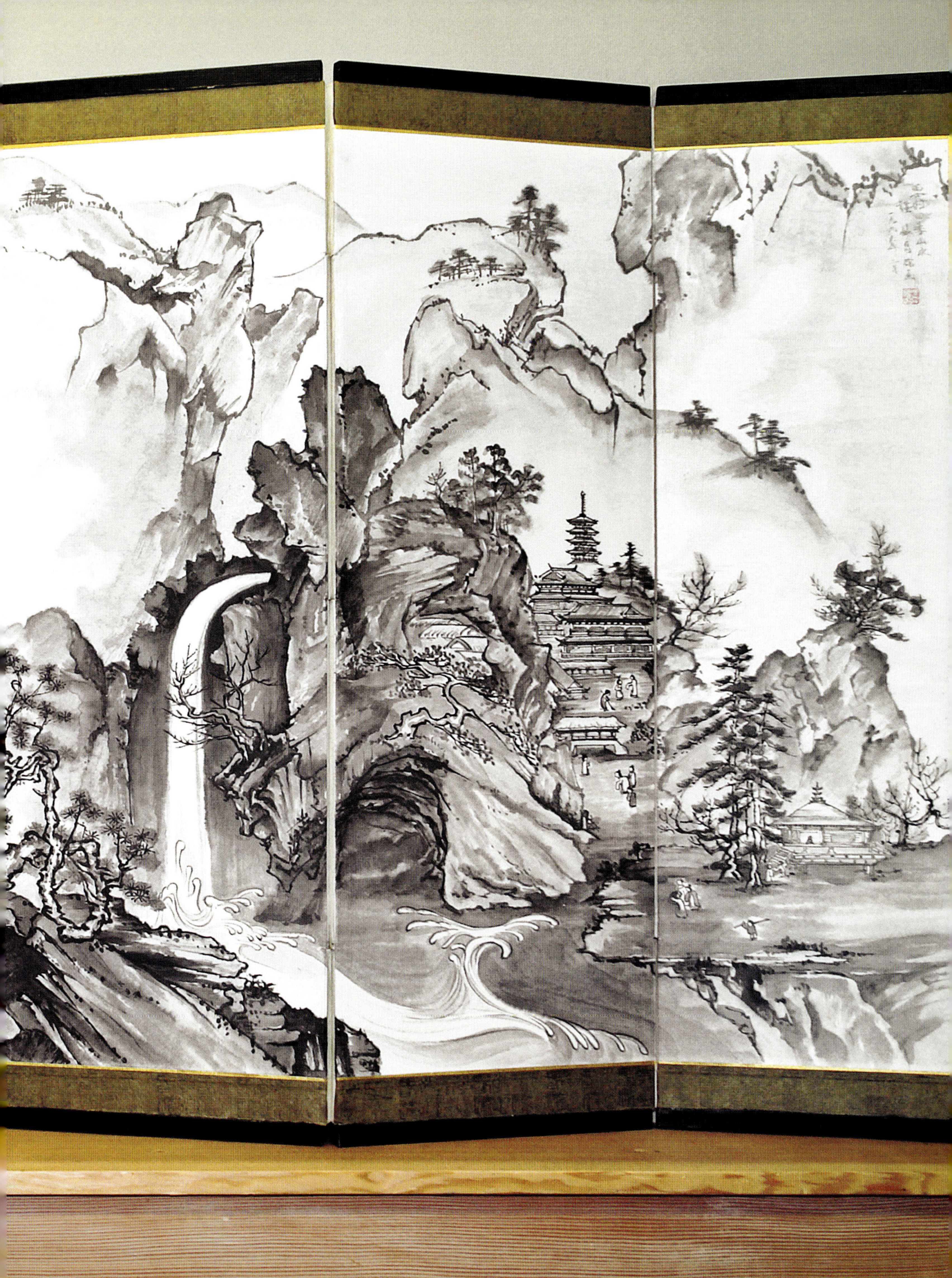

Using movable walls to provide a larger room when needed is an idea that stands the test of time. Many Victorian style homes in the U.S. also have sliding doors between rooms; however, they are usually made of heavy wood. The traditional Japanese screen, on the other hand, is a lightweight frame with a grille covered with paper. On occasion, these screens called *fusuma*, light in weight and large in size, may even be completely removed.

Throughout the centuries, it has been the custom to have paintings on the large surfaces that screens or sliding doors provide. Depending upon the tastes of the owner, the paintings might be in monochrome or color; they were sometimes gilded in gold or silver.

For creating adjustable space in a house, office or apartment, incorporating Japanese style screens or sliding doors might be an answer. Lightweight, sturdy sliding doors and screen surfaces can be made out of plywood backed with a frame to stabilize and strengthen them.

1. Creation of the Universe: Sliding Doors (*Fusuma*)

These sliding doors, or *fusuma*, were created for a tea ceremony room in which a table and chairs would be used instead of the traditional practice of sitting on the floor. Behind these sliding doors is a closet to hold tea ceremony equipment.

The main focus for the tea ceremony guests should be the equipment displayed on the table, like the tea bowl, the lacquered tea caddy, the porcelain water container, and so forth. Since the fusuma doors are to serve as a backdrop for the tea ceremony, a realistic painting of nature would pose a distraction. Instead, a more abstracted, nebulous image was created with the use of the tarashi komi technique. After the painting was completely dry, gold dust and crushed gold leaves were added to complete the work.

Sized paper in a light beige color was stretched on birch plywood upon which butcher paper was glued first as a base. Gold brocade acts as a border, framed in black lacquered wood. Ornate metal handles serve to open and close the doors.

The basic patterns of the entire work were completed in a few hours with water and sumi ink. It is highly important that the surface of the paper have a thin layer of water on it so that the movement of light ink can be manipulated in the desired directions. Also the panel must be completely level, flat horizontally, so that the ink will not move by itself in undesired directions.

Remember that the artistry of the tarashi komi technique is an attempt to control an uncontrollable situation. The test of your success is this: when the painting is completely dry, how natural does the effect appear to be? Although tarashi komi results from a random process of movement, the work is successful if it appears as if it was planned 100%. That is the Zen way of painting sumi art.

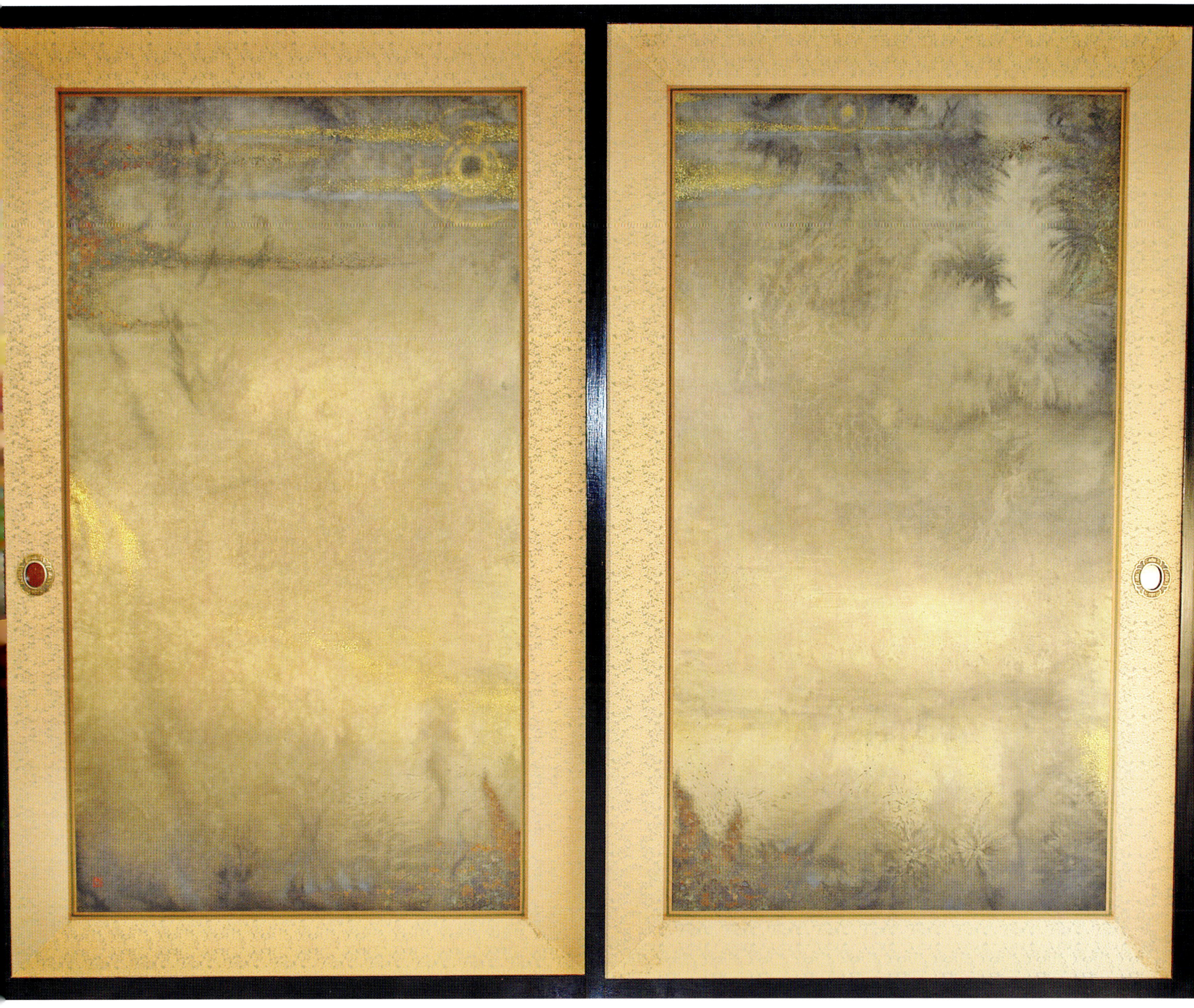

COMPOSITION OF LARGE WORKS

The large spaces that doors and folding screens offer—perhaps as large as seven feet (2.1m) in height and four feet (1.2m) in width—allow an artist to savor the challenge of creating large works of art. Just as with monochrome paintings of smaller size, planning the composition is essential. The function of the screen and the room should be a consideration in determining both the composition and subject matter for the painting. In this case, the screen was to serve as a backdrop to the tea ceremony. With the many tea equipment items on display in front of it, a realistic painting of nature, for instance, would be a distraction. This more nebulous composition serves the purpose well.

First a background of clouds and smoke-like atmosphere is created. Next the sun is painted with 24 karat gold powder mixed with animal glue, and after that, the golden mist of crushed gold leaf is added.

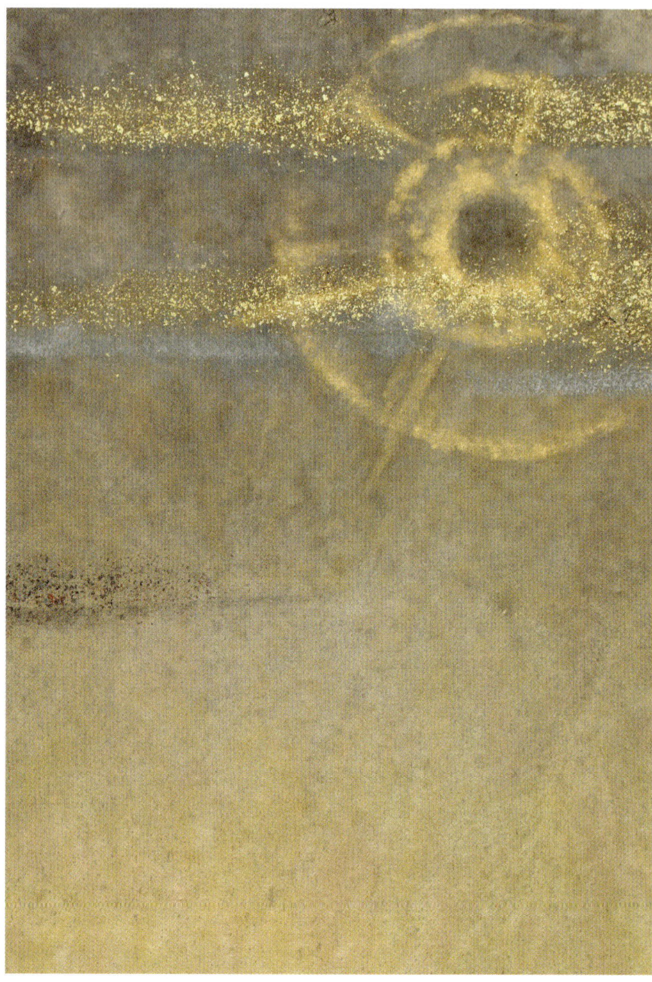

When the tarashi komi technique for the background has dried, horizontal patterns are created with the use of crushed metallic leaves, accented with red-gold leaf. (See Chapter 3 for gold dust and leaf application techniques.)

To create the effect of exploding gasses, light ink is sprinkled over the wet surface of the paper and a cool hair dryer is used to move the ink in the desired direction. If necessary the ink can be directed with a dry brush. Because the background paper has some color, the light ink, although gray, provides a completely different effect.

To create the lower part of the same scene which shows the nebulous clouds of exploding gasses, reddish metallic dust is applied to highlight the lower right side. Diluted Chinese white pigment is used with a touch of glue to bring emphasis to the lower section. The very dark ink floating on the surface of the water is guided with a dry brush to create patterns.

This is the very top center of the right panel. After the background is dry, the secondary sun is painted with gold powder mixed with animal glue. The horizontal clouds are created with gold dust and a touch of watery Chinese white.

This is a detail of the panel on the right. Motion of gasses is created by using tarashi komi.

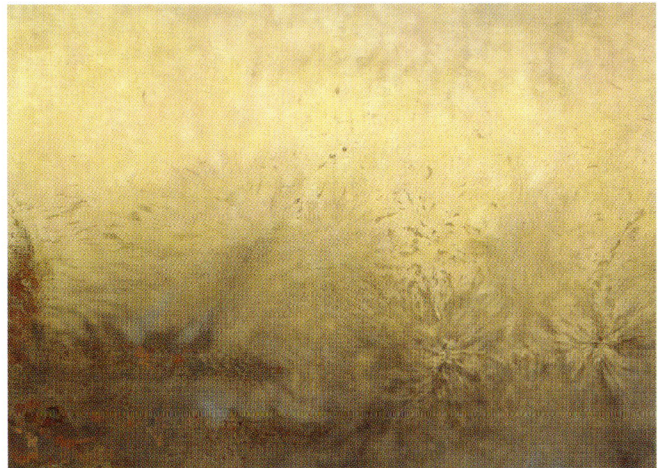

The nebulous atmosphere is created, while there is still water on the surface of the paper, by applying light sumi ink. Then dark ink is splashed down forcefully and the shock vibrates it to create the explosive effect. After the surface is completely dry, again use watery Chinese white with glue to give added accent.

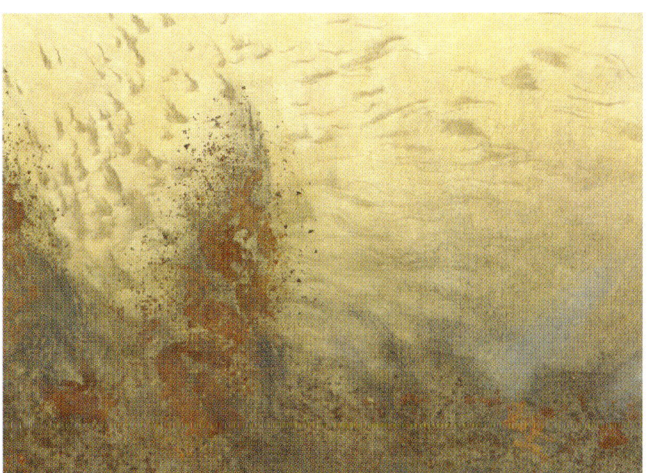

At the left bottom corner of the right-hand panel, on very wet paper, light sumi ink is splashed quickly; then a cool hair dryer is used to move the ink from right to left in one direction. After the motion of gasses is created, dark ink is added for gasses at the lower part. Metallic dust is then applied. Finally watery Chinese white mixed with glue is added.

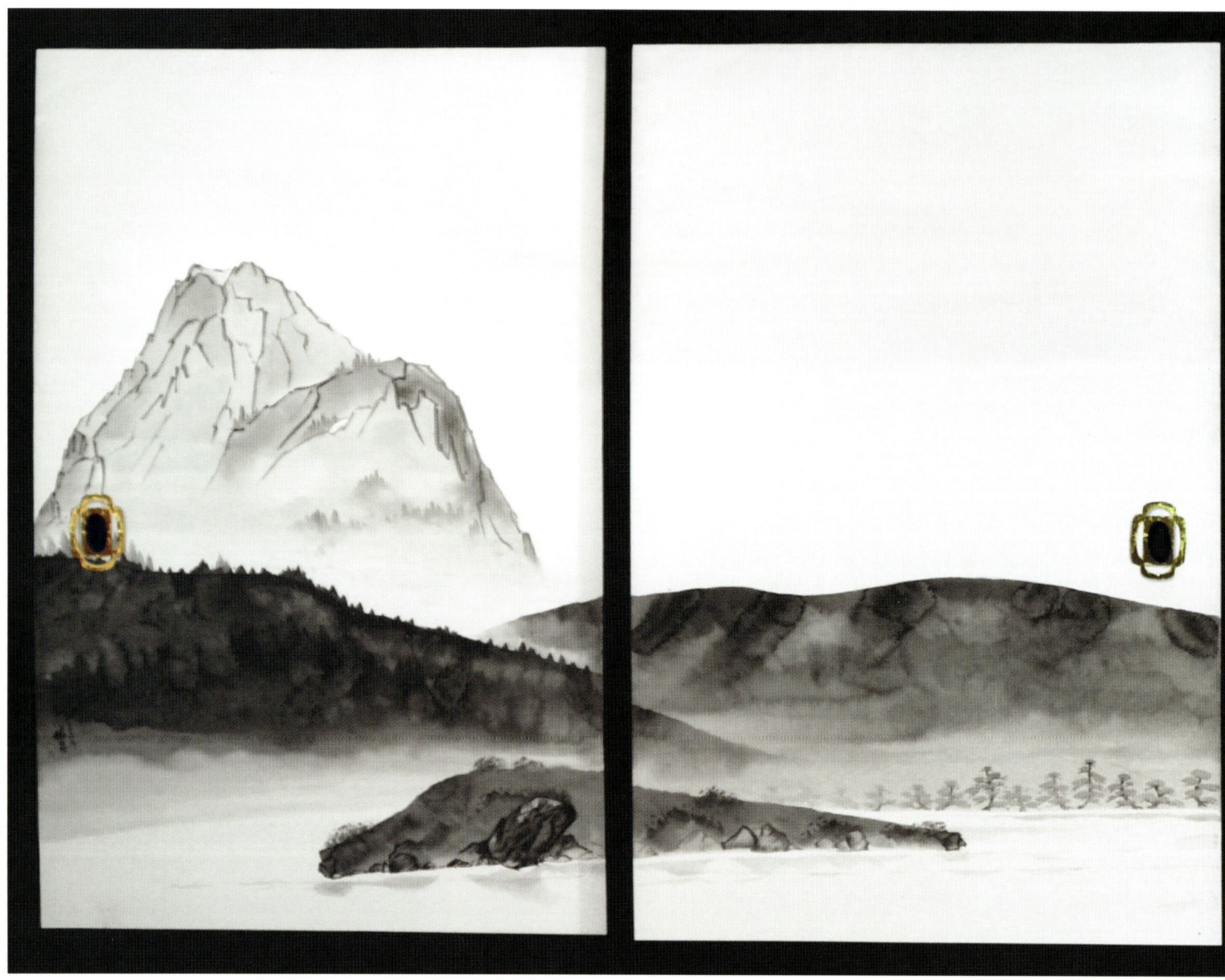

2. Flexibility in Composition: A Four-Panel Door

Space in traditional Japanese homes was divided into smaller standardized spaces with sliding walls. These convenient walls, or *fusuma*, provided an ideal "canvas" for paintings.

The four panels of the fusuma form a unit. Each panel has gold-rimmed handles to move the panel left or right. Usually the handle is placed lower than midway, so that it will slide more easily. The handle must be incorporated as part of the screen's overall composition.

The fundamental concept in composition is to have dominant, subdominant and subordinate components in a painting. This design concept must be honored in fusuma whether the panels are closed or open. When all panels are closed, as above, the spiritual mountain in center right is the dominant subject, the mountain on the left panel is subdominant and the pagoda is the subordinate subject. Normally the two center panels are the ones used for opening and closing.

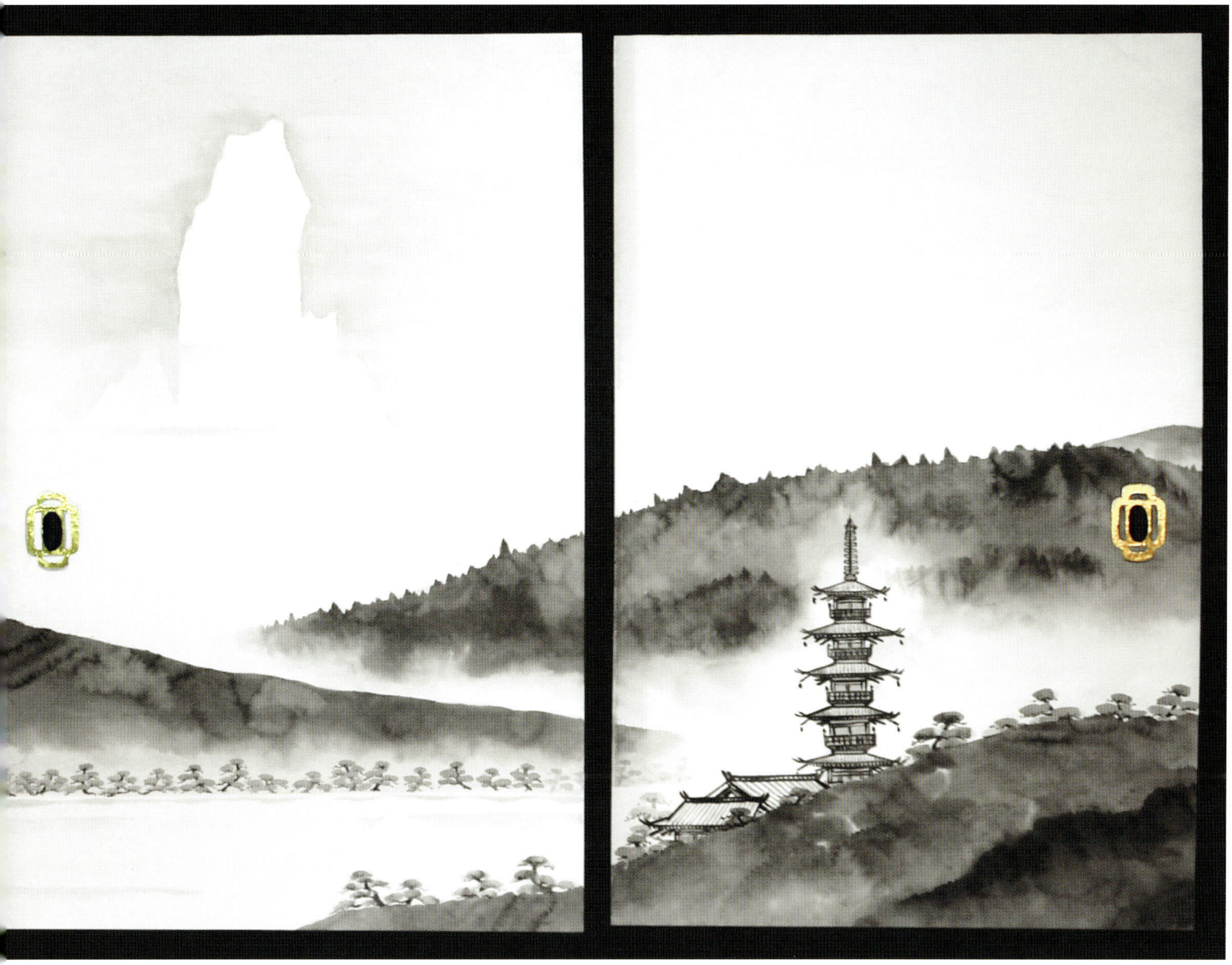

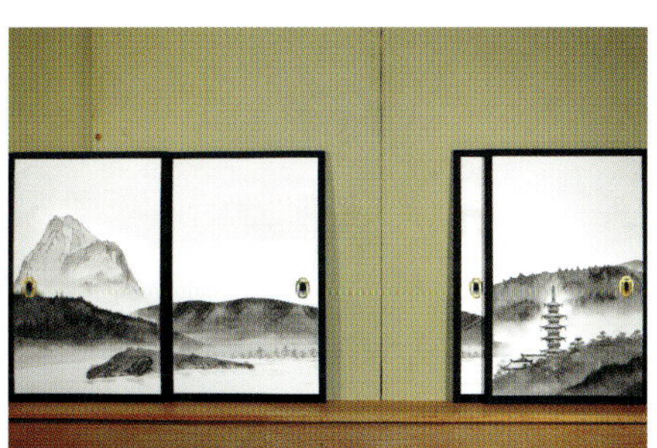

When the center right panel is opened and is hidden, the mountain becomes the dominant subject; the pagoda is subdominant and the rock island becomes the subordinate subject.

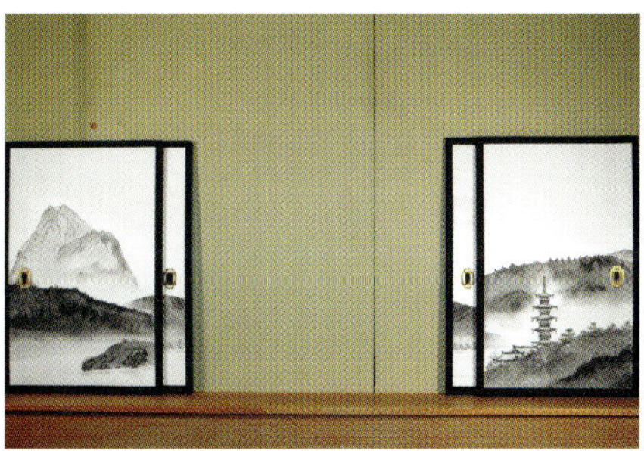

When both center panels have been opened, the composition remains the same as in the configuration we saw at left.

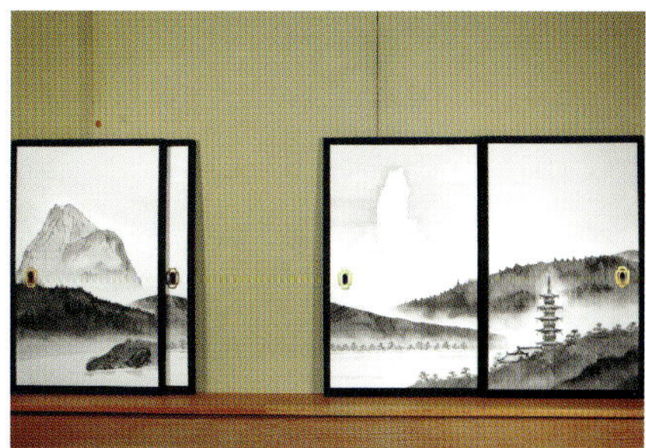

When the left center panel is opened, the mountain on the left is dominant because it is combined with a dark hill, the spiritual mountain is subdominant because it no longer has the supporting low-lying hill and the pagoda is subordinate.

3. Sliding Doors to Hide Utility Area

Because the utility area includes a sink and a washing
machine, the materials for this painting must be water-resistant; sumi will not do. In place of sumi ink, which is
water-based, a black lacquer paint in an oil base was used.
Turpentine was used to dilute the lacquer. The painting was
done not on paper, but directly on the white birch plywood.

First the plywood was treated with an off-white weathered
wood stain. Because the plywood has a beautiful grain, the
whitewash was used to stabilize the natural wood's color so it
would not turn to a darker color in a few years. The whitewash
is minimal enough to allow the beauty of the natural wood
grain to show. To give greater stability, the plywood was
mounted on frames with crossbars behind.

This three-panel sliding unit can pushed right or left
according to the need of the hour, so the composition was
designed to be interchangeable. Panel A is dominant, Panel C
is subdominant and B is subordinate. Usually, when seen from
the other room, it is Panel A that is in view.

The theme is one very traditional in Japanese paintings,
that of morning mist reflecting sunlight. The painting's subjects all came from sketches of plants growing in my garden:
bamboo, calla lilies, day lilies and astilbe. There is a skylight
in this small space and sunlight reflects on the gold leaves to
give vibrant energy to the painting depending upon the
weather and time of day.

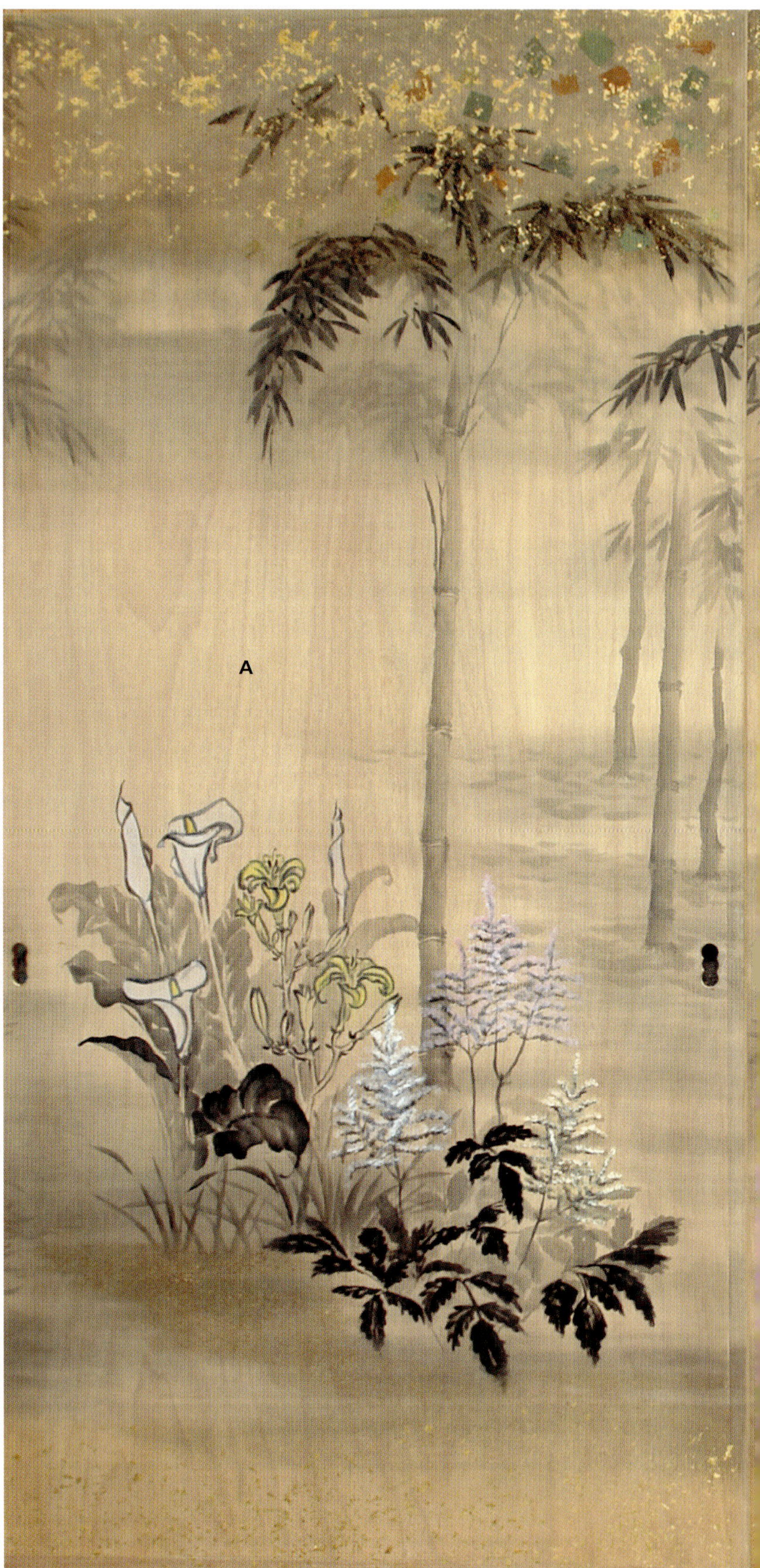

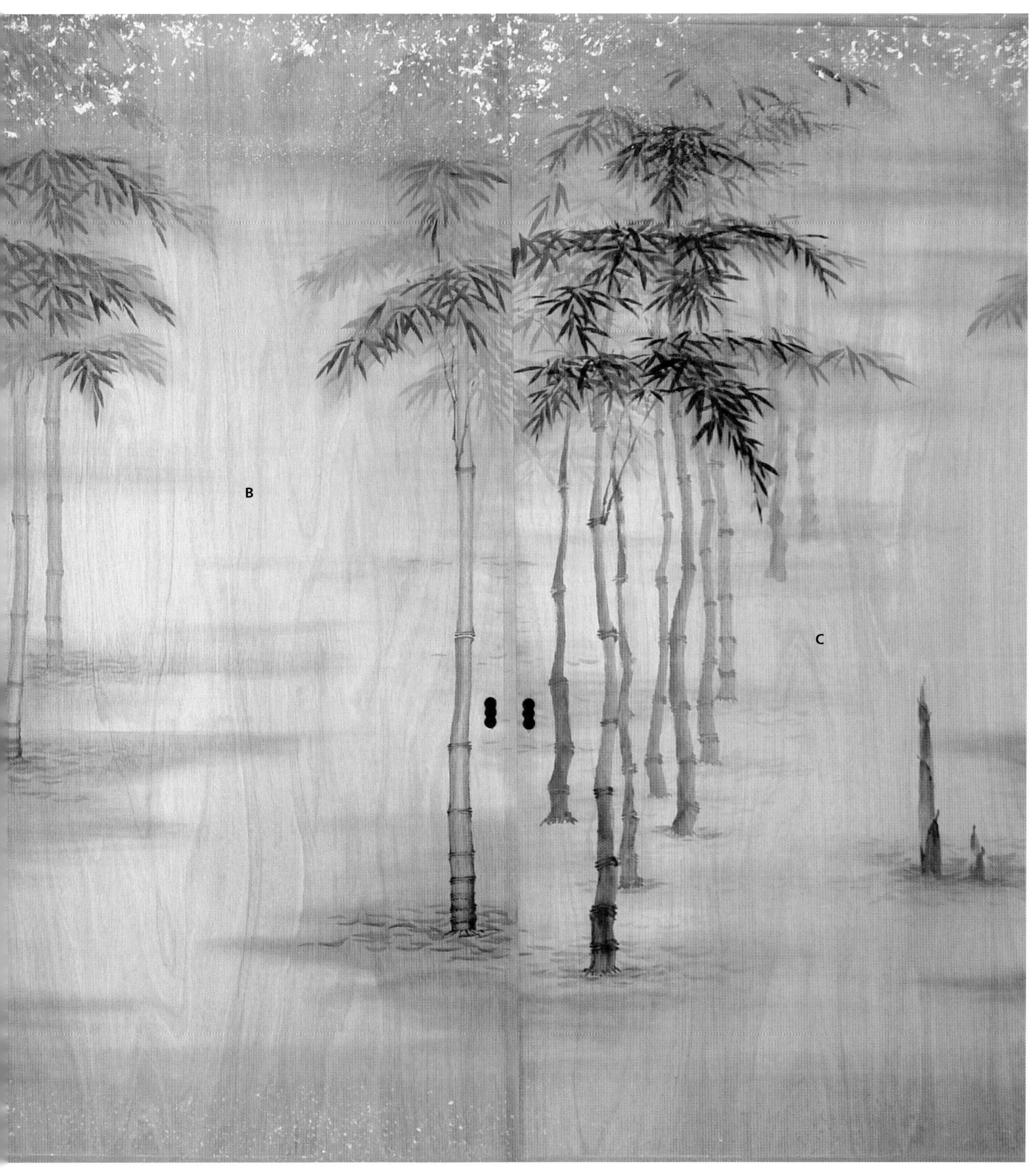

B
C

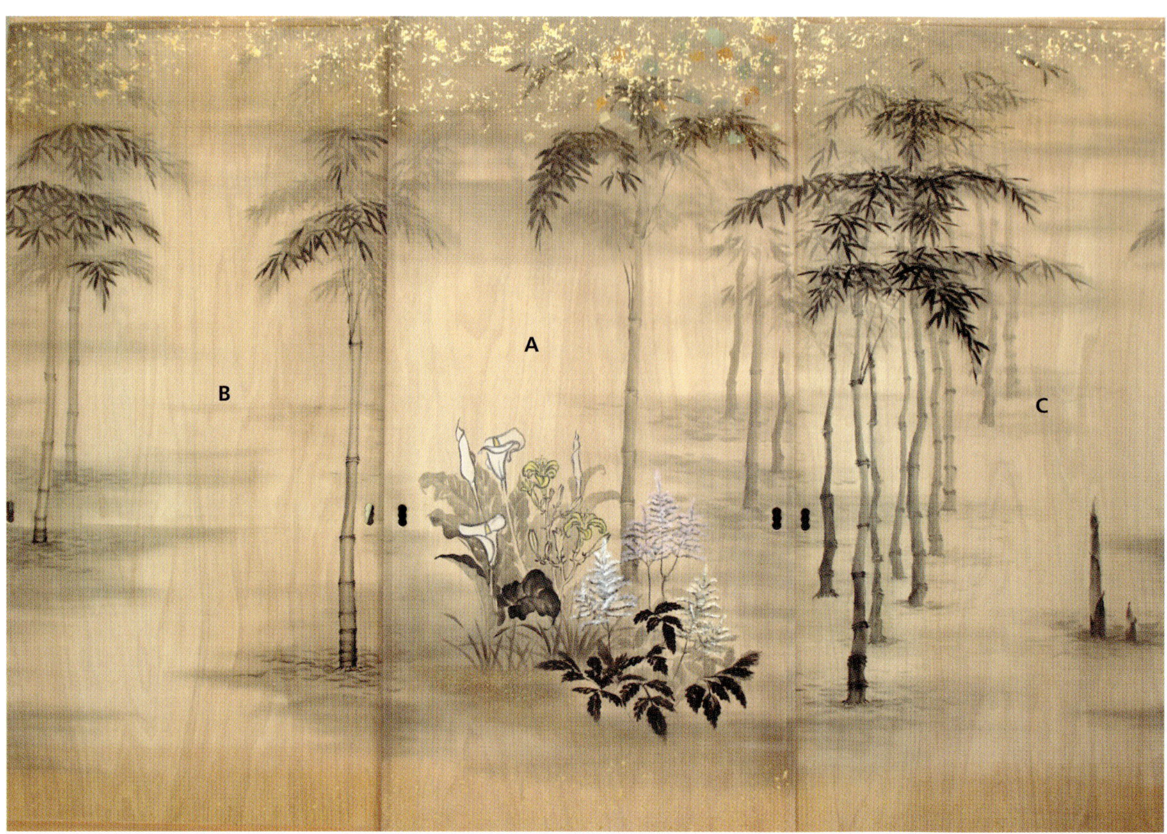

This three-panel sliding unit can pushed right or left, so the composition was designed to be interchangeable no matter what the relative position of the three panels is. Above is the second possible configuration of the panels.

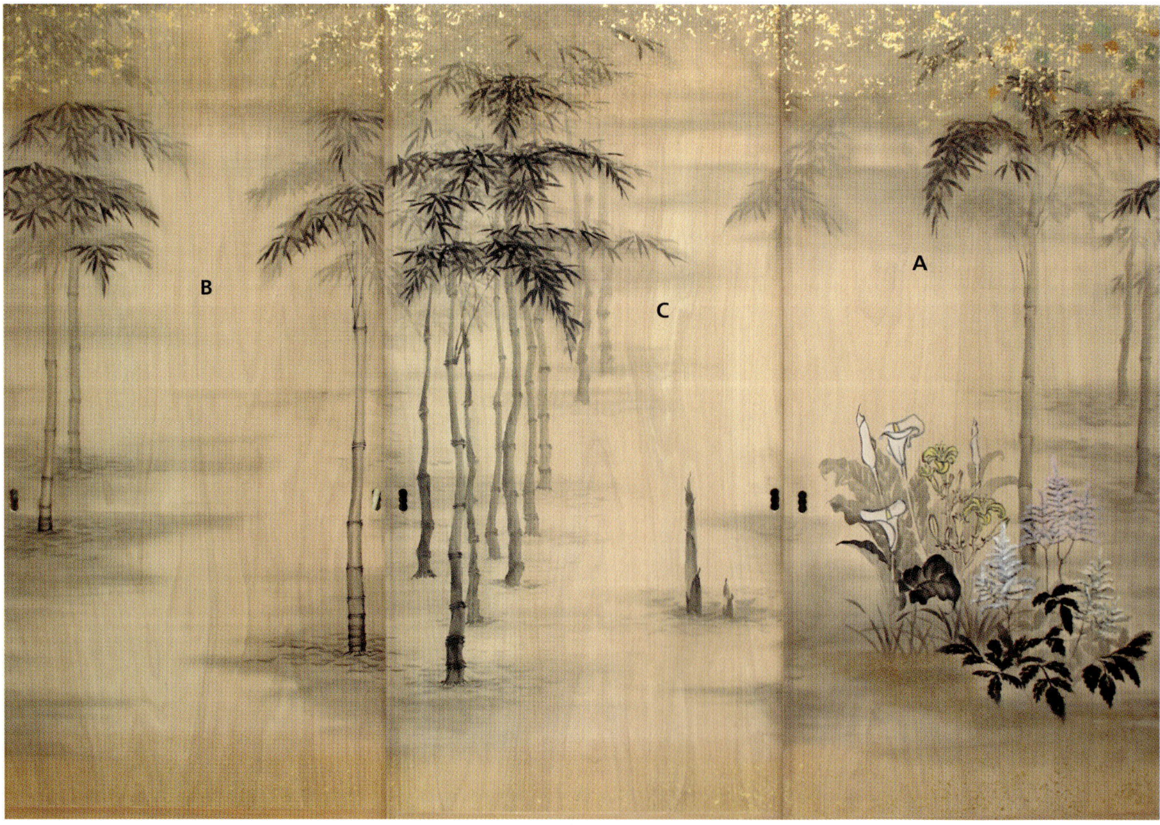

The panels in the third configuration. Notice that Panel A is dominant, Panel C is subdominant and Panel B is subordinate.

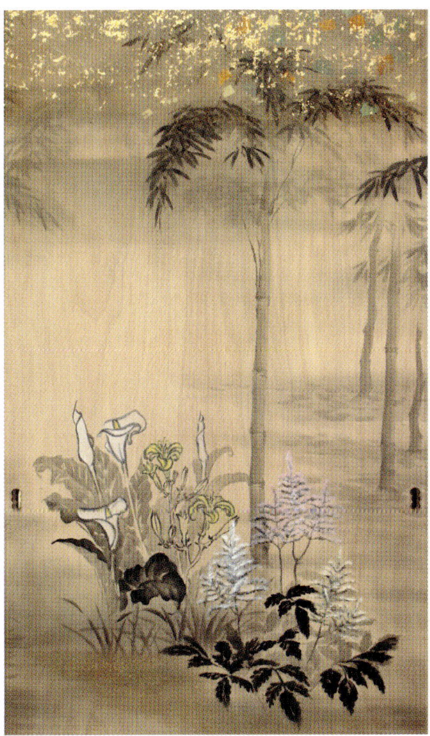

The sliding doors are for a utility area, so they must be waterproof. Plywood is the base, and rather than sumi, lacquer is used for the art.

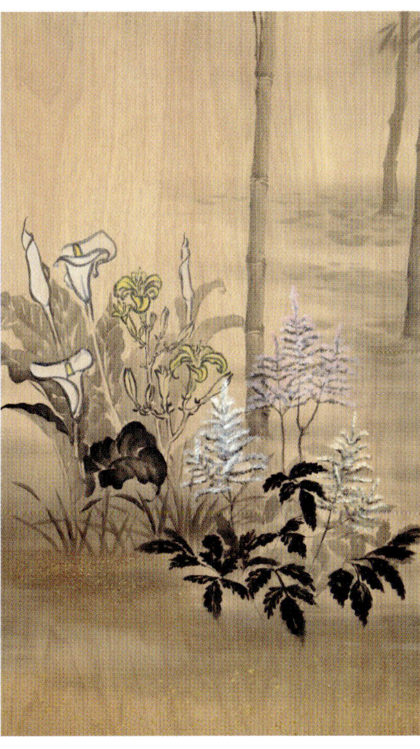

White lacquer colors the calla lilies and astilbe, and yellow lacquer is used for the day lilies.

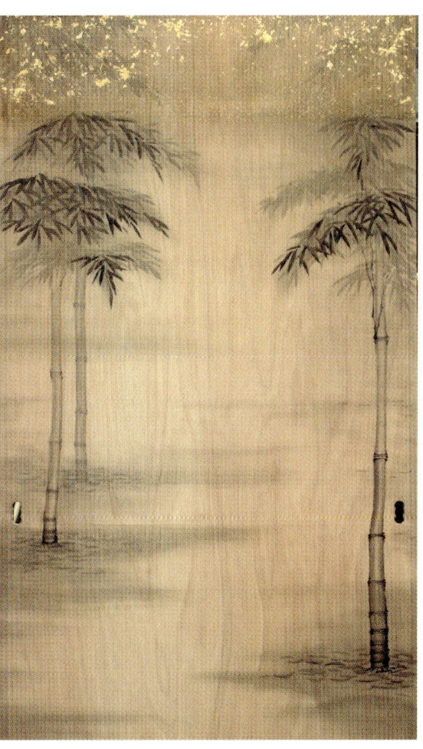

While the lower part of the bamboo is totally exposed, the upper part is covered with mist. Although bamboo is a popular subject for sumi work, rarely is the entire plant painted. If you wish to paint it in its entirety, note that bamboo is usually 15 to 20 feet (4.5 to 6m) tall.

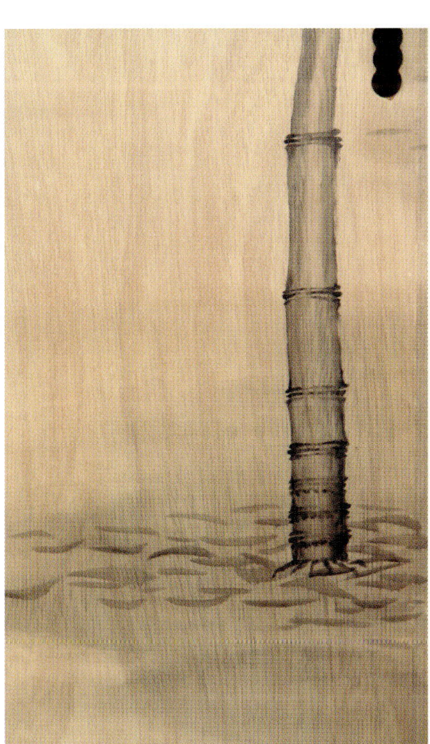

Each section at the base of the bamboo is much shorter; as the stalk grows, the sections grow longer. At the very bottom, notice the roots extending out into the ground. In the section above that you may not see roots, but will see the small beginnings of roots emerging. That is why the black dots are added. After five or six sections, each section becomes longer and more stable in length.

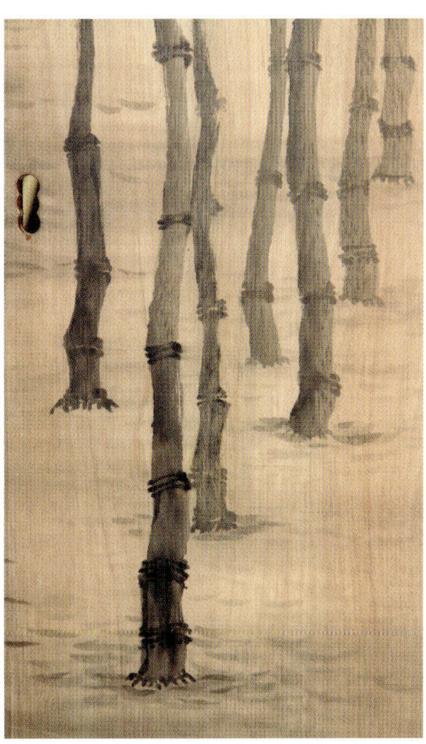

The bamboo were painted with the technique of using dark ink on both ends of the brush (see page 53). This close-up of the lower part of the bamboo is from Panel C. Instead of smooth upright lines for the bamboo culms, notice that many irregular joints in the stalk were made. If you visit a bamboo forest, this is quite a common sight. (See page 126 for basic techniques for painting bamboo.)

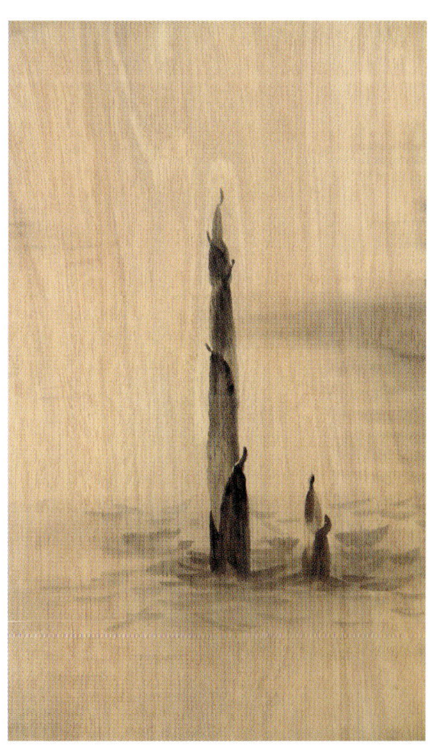

To paint bamboo shoots, begin at the very top; lower the bristles to gradually make the shoot wider. Use a brush prepared with dark ink at tip and lighter ink at the bristles' base. The very bottom husk is painted in the darkest ink to create a sense of stability in the shoot. For the final touch, use only the tip of your brush to create the very ends of the husks for each section.

4. A Folding Screen

Folding screens have been part of the traditional Japanese way of living for centuries. In earlier times, before the advent of central heating, large rooms in residences would often be cool and breezy. It was common practice to use screens to enclose a smaller, more intimate space, such as sleeping quarters. Screens were often covered with gold or silver because those metals would amplify the reflected light from oil lamps or candles. They were also used as decorative backgrounds for special occasions. This practice continues today in Japan; for governmental and public festive occasions, for instance, plain gold screens are used as a backdrop.

Folding screens, whether large or small, provide an ideal space to challenge the artist. This example of a folding screen is a copy of Shukei Sesson's original, which was painted in approximately 1560. Sesson lived from c. 1490 to after 1577, and his two folding screens titled *Landscape of the Four Seasons* belong to the collection of the Art Institute of Chicago. (One screen is a winter scene and the other is a summer scene. Each screen measures 36"/92cm x 74"/188cm.)

I painted this sample copy expressly for the special exhibition on Japanese folding screens held at the Art Institute of Chicago. For this show, in a room adjoining the main Exhibition Hall, I presented a workshop for the general public on how these folding screens were constructed, helping them to understand the special double hinge technique which allows the screen to fold in either direction; the concept in composition for folding screens; and the manner of display.

Often when I visit the homes of people who happen to own a Japanese folding screen, with great pride they show me their screen which is usually displayed as a centerpiece against a wall in their living room. However, the screen is usually displayed in the manner shown at the bottom of the facing page, where the left and right edges are toward the wall. (When I ask the reason, the reply is generally that it keeps pets from going behind the screen and it stays cleaner.) The composition of a screen's painting, however, is usually designed to show perspective with the foreground and the background carefully planned, so the placement of the screen is very important.

Folding screens are traditionally placed in the manner shown in the larger image here. In this screen's case, the waterfall, cave and tree are meant to be in the foreground and the distant mountains in the background.

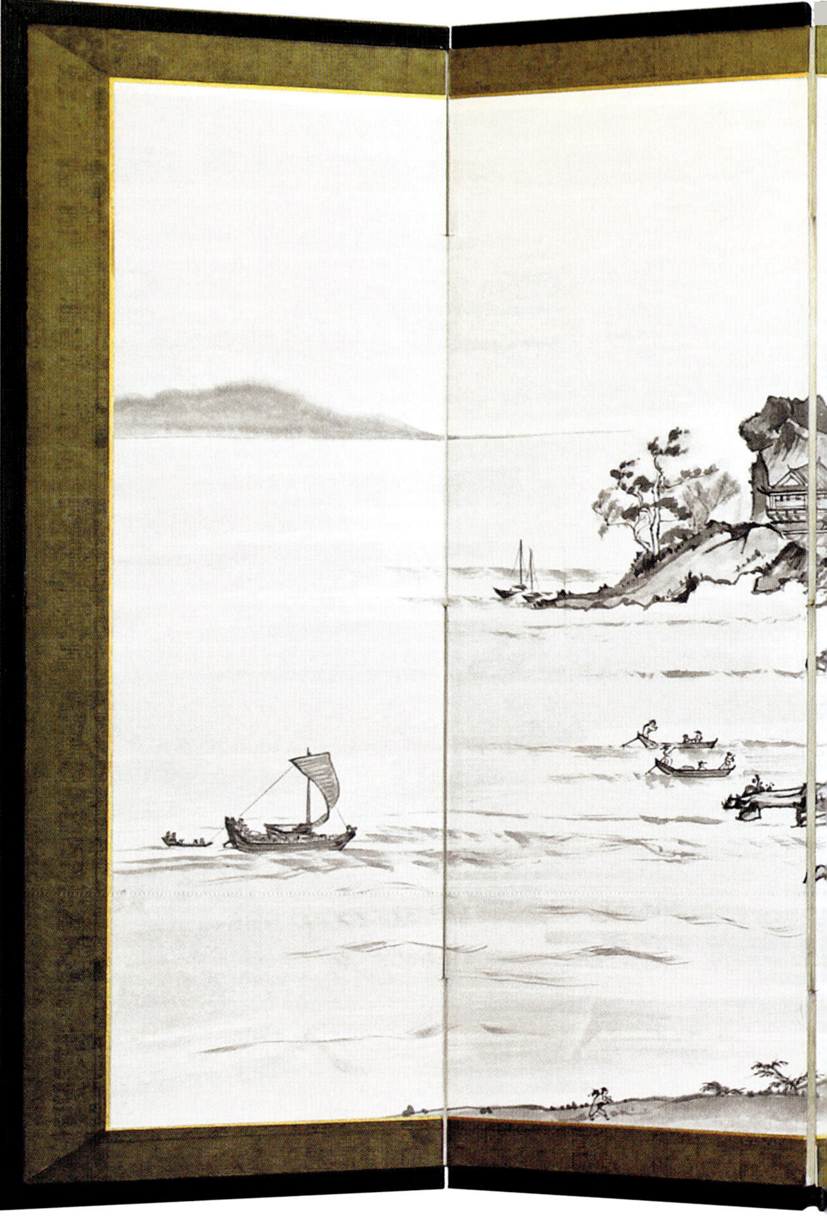

Right: This manner of displaying the screen, with the side edges bent back toward the wall, is incorrect. In all forms of ink painting, composition is vital, and this is true with folding screens. The waterfall, cave and tree should be in the foreground with the distant mountains in the background.

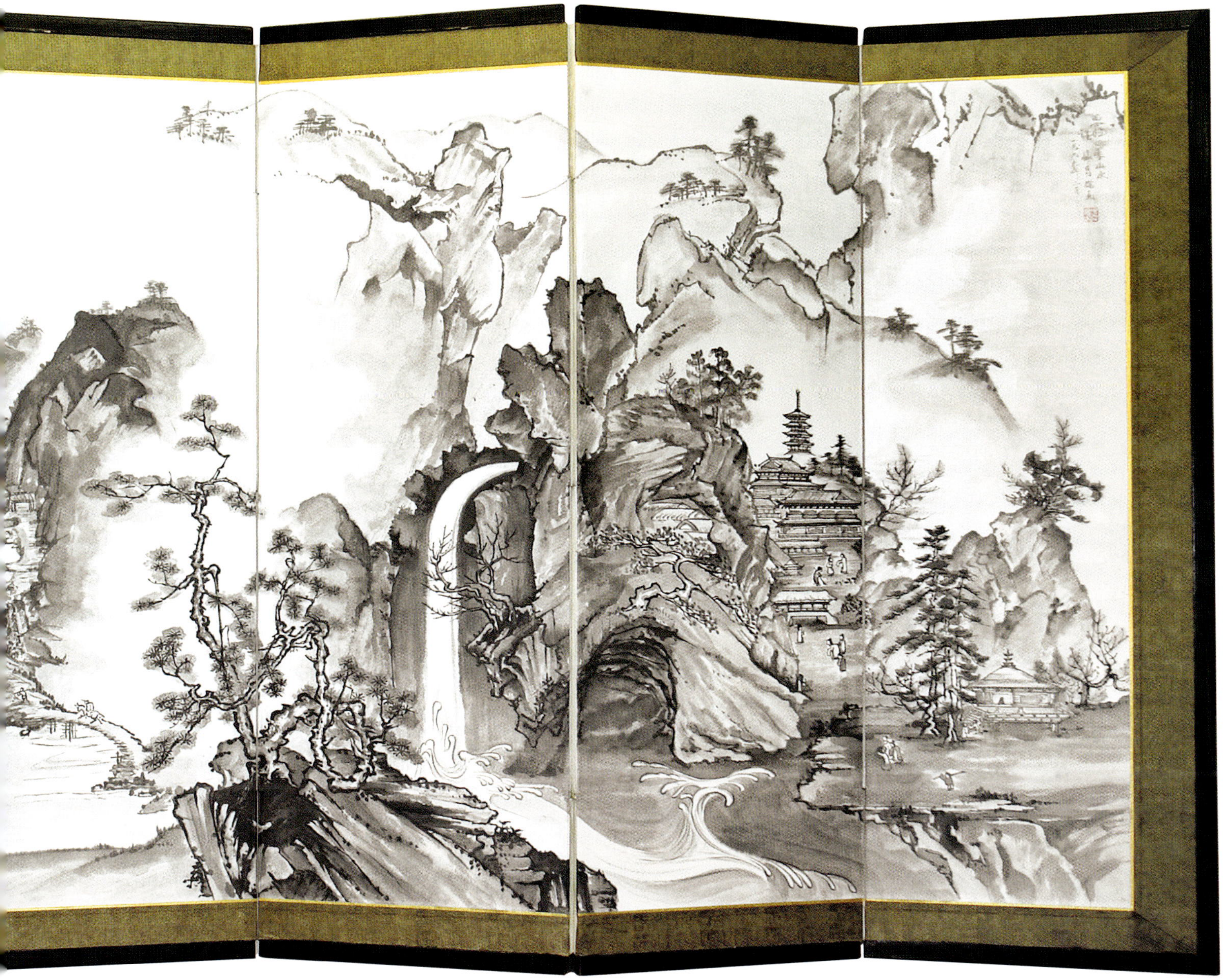

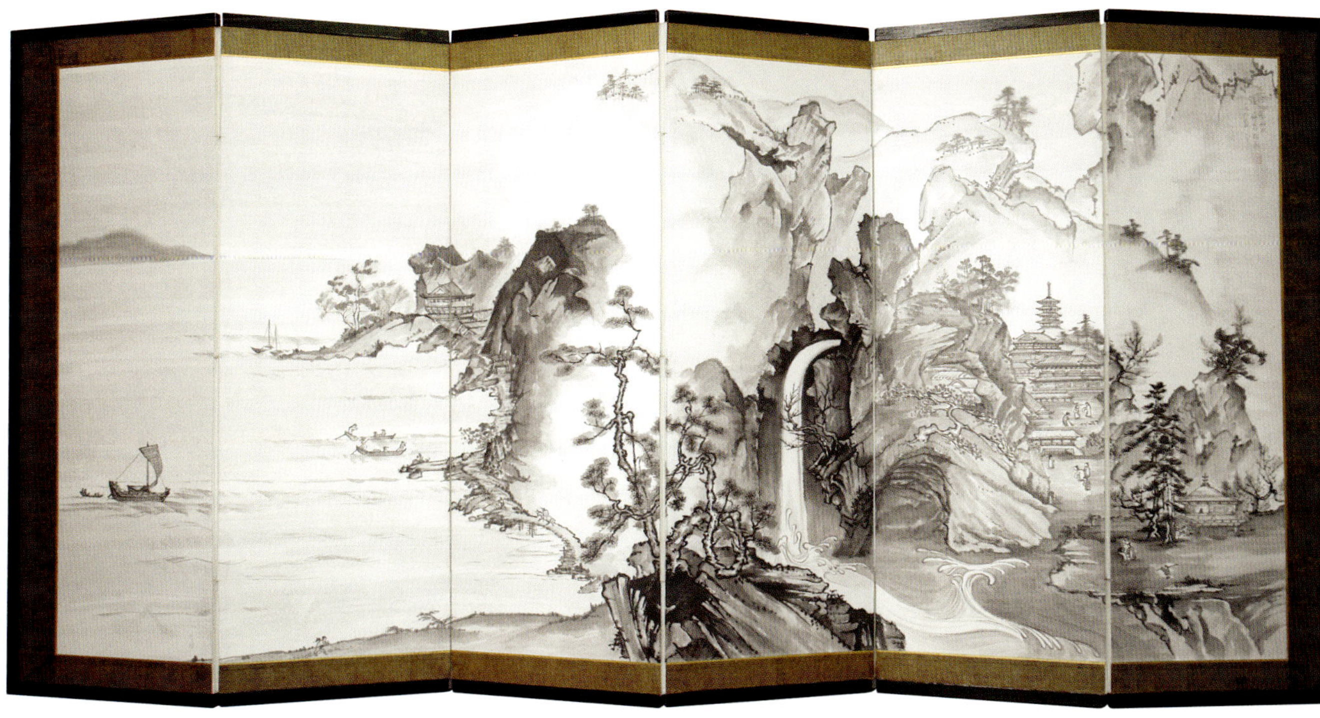

5. The Tokonoma: Mounting Your Paintings as Scrolls

Tokonoma alcoves have been regarded as the most honored space in traditional Japanese architecture. Alongside this space is a built-in desk and above it is a source of light through a shoji screen. On the desk is kept traditional writing equipment: a lacquered box with ink stick, a grinding stone, a brush and writing paper. On the tokonoma wall there are special nails to hang one, two or three hanging scrolls, and in the center of the wall is a retractable hook for hanging a flower arrangement when a scroll is not on display. The left corner also has a special hook for hanging a flower vases

The express purpose behind creating a tokonoma is to allow the appreciation of both hanging scrolls and flower arrangements. On display in the tokonoma on the facing page are scrolls which are reproductions of Sesshu's autumn and winter landscapes (see page 19). These are my freehand copies for study purposes, mounted in traditional style.

Notice that beneath the desk are cushions for use on the tatami-covered floors. The viewer will usually be seated on the floor about three feet away, and will look up at the artwork. For this reason, Japanese proportions in the placement of artwork and its relationship to the mat are different from the western concept of picture framing. For instance, as you can see in this display, the matting in the lower portion, below the painting, is shorter than the upper portion.

The art of mounting paintings as hanging scrolls developed in ancient China and the practice spread both to the east and west. To the west, paintings in the Tibetan Mandala style were on silk fabric without paper backing. To the east in Korea and Japan, the original Chinese methods were used. In Japan, influenced by tea ceremony aesthetics and the discerning tastes of the connoisseurs, every attempt was made to maximize the harmony and beauty of the artwork. Even today, when for example a scroll from the fourteenth century is being remounted, every effort will be made to match the patterns of that age to the greatest extent possible in contemporary fabrics. (It is almost impossible to find original fabrics of the age still in reasonable condition.)

There are rules to follow when mounting paintings: for instance, paintings of flowers should not be mounted on fabrics which have flower patterns, because that is redundant. When two hanging scrolls form a unit, commonly the two are mounted with the same fabric, or at least the colors are complementary. The hanging scrolls shown in this tokonoma (which, by the way, are usually displayed singly rather than as a unit) are mounted on the same kind of damask in two different colors to complement the scene: the winter landscape is mounted on dark blue and the autumn landscape is mounted on green. The colors support the paintings but the fabric pattern is the same.

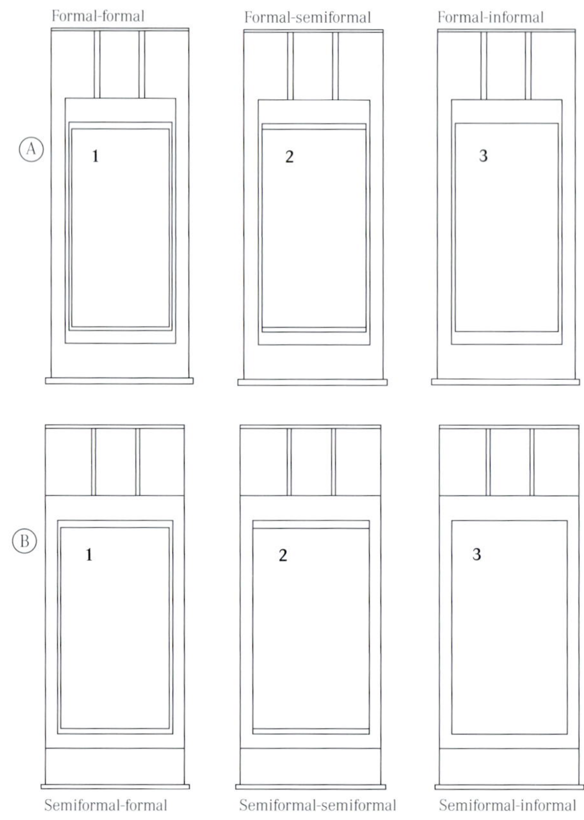

Rows A, B, and C show examples of Japan's system of traditional mounting styles for hanging scrolls. These very defined styles have existed for millennia. Today, contemporary scroll makers have begun to break with tradition, selecting colors, fabrics and designs in new ways.

Row A shows three categories for the formal style. In *A1, Formal-formal,* the work is completely surrounded with three different kinds of contrasting gold brocades (represented by the frame lines around the center painting's space). Examine the *A-2, Formal-semiformal* arrangement and notice how the brocades are used differently there, and finally how *A-3, Formal-informal,* varies from the others.

Row B's *B-1, Semiformal-formal,* looks very much like A-3; the major difference is that the top and bottom are plain without patterns, with the inner mat being gold brocade. *B-2, Semiformal-semiformal,* is more familiar because it is the most popular style. The hanging scrolls of Sesshu's copies are in the B-2 style. This style has thin strips of gold brocade immediately above and below the artwork.

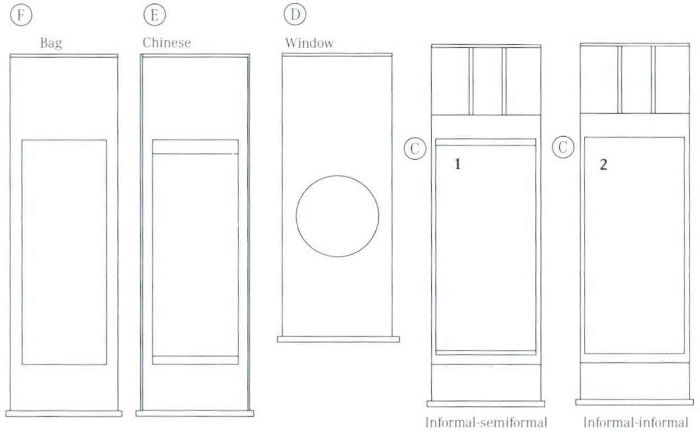

C-2 appears to be similar to B-2. The major difference is that formal and semiformal hanging scrolls have free-hanging wind belts. Commonly the wind belts are of the same fabric as the gold strip above and below. However, in C-1 wind belts are symbolically displayed by white paper glued on the proper place. D, E and F are more reflective of the Chinese style.

On display in the tokonoma are my Sesshu copies mounted in traditional style.

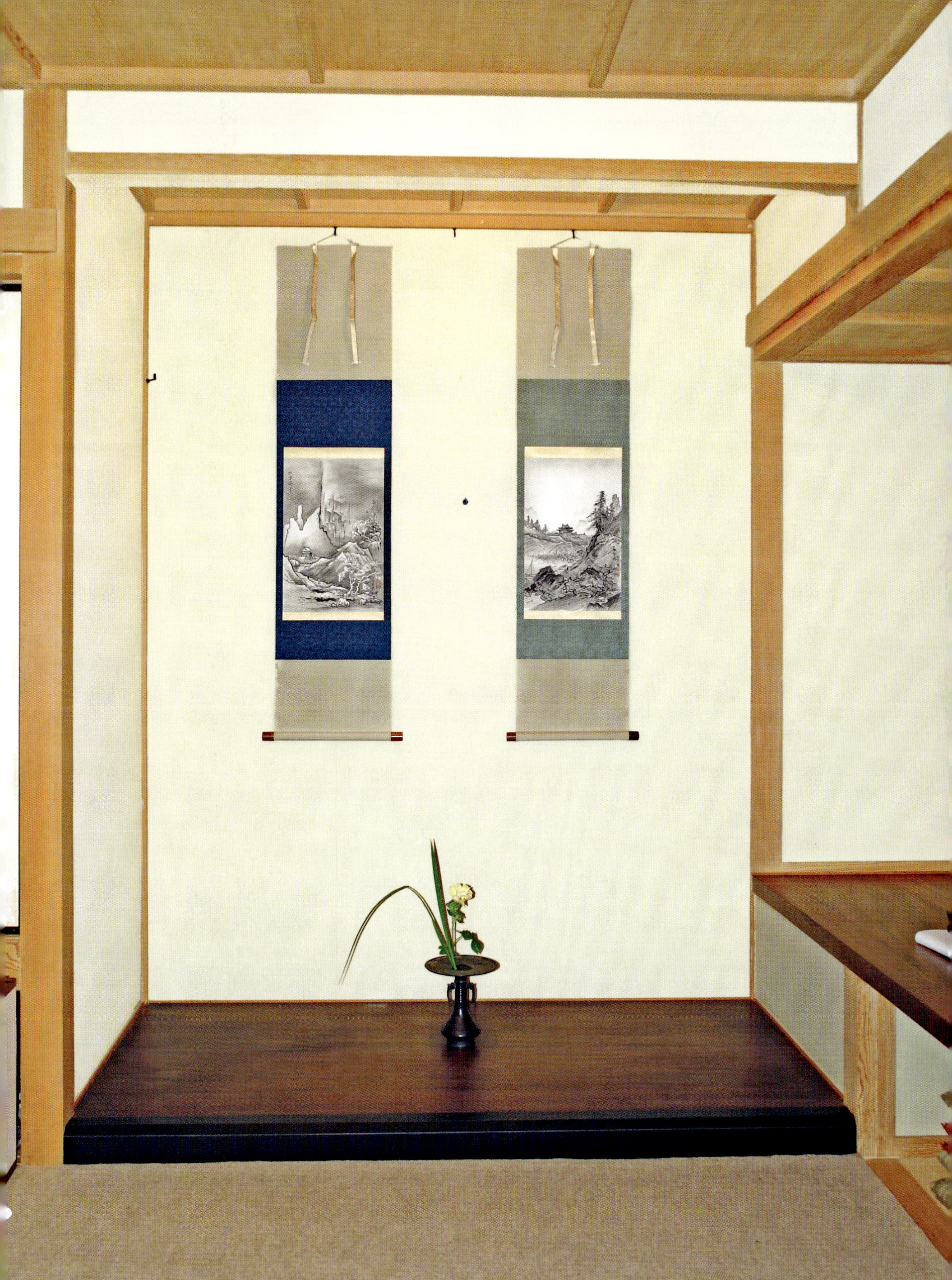

For both calligraphy and painting, hanging scrolls are still popular in Japan, simply because they save storage space. The work can be rolled up and stored compactly.

The kind of mounting used for a hanging scroll, whether it is of calligraphy or painting, depends upon the subject matter. If the painting or calligraphy is related to religion, then the mounting is usually more formal in style.

The system of categories shown on page 176 is based on traditional mounting styles, but contemporary artwork requires its own style. Today, contemporary scroll-making craftsmen have started to break with tradition. Their use of artistic and creative sense in selecting colors, fabrics, and styles for mounting is a new path in the long history of sumi painting.

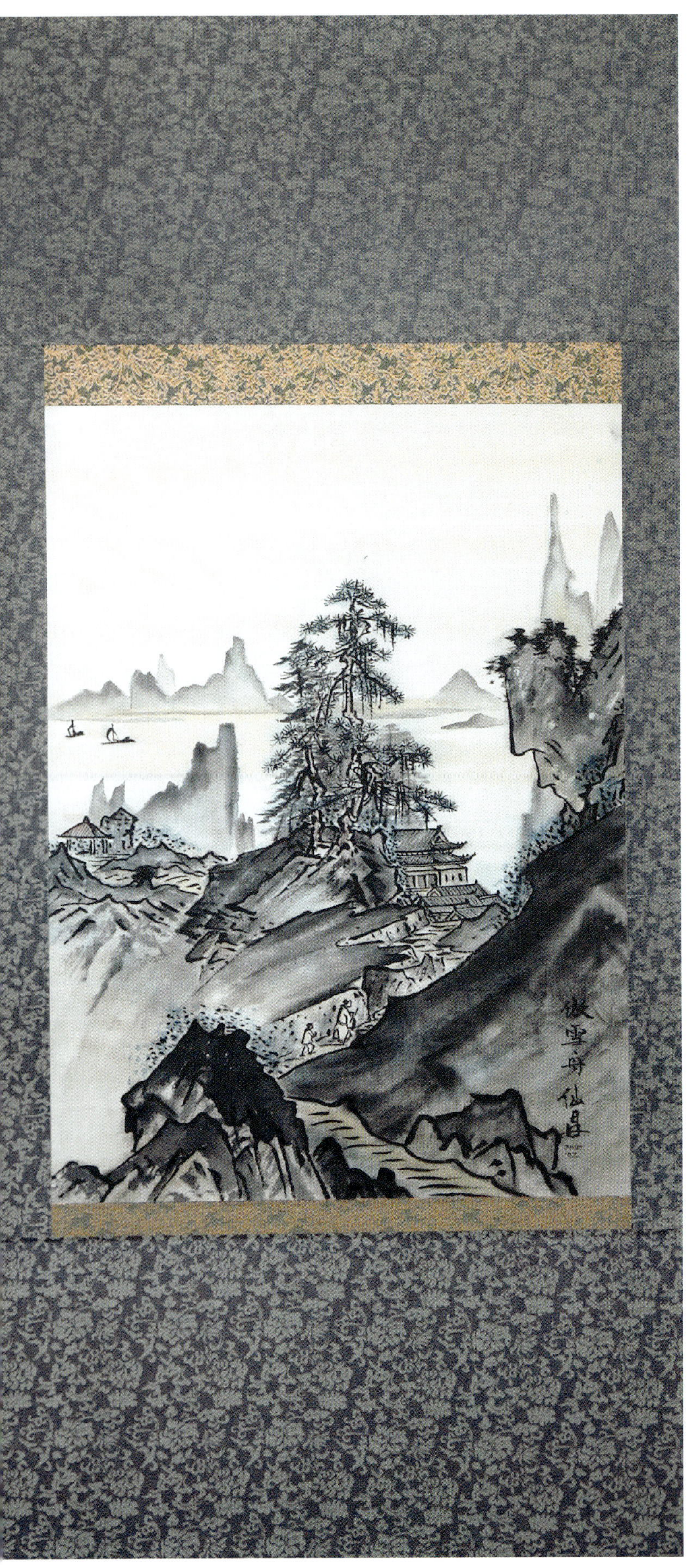

Paintings mounted on a board in the style of a hanging scroll. This painting, my study copy of a Sesshu landscape, is mounted on a board and matted in the style of a hanging scroll. When a scroll is unrolled under very dry weather conditions, often the paper cracks and remains in a half-circle shape until moisture relaxes the paper again. After years of rolling and re-rolling, the painting may also split horizontally. In such situations, museum staff will often soak the scroll in water to soften the glue; separate all the parts; and then reassemble the painting on a board and finish it in the style of a hanging scroll. It is then placed behind glass in a picture frame. This common practice protects the work and maintains a traditional effect.

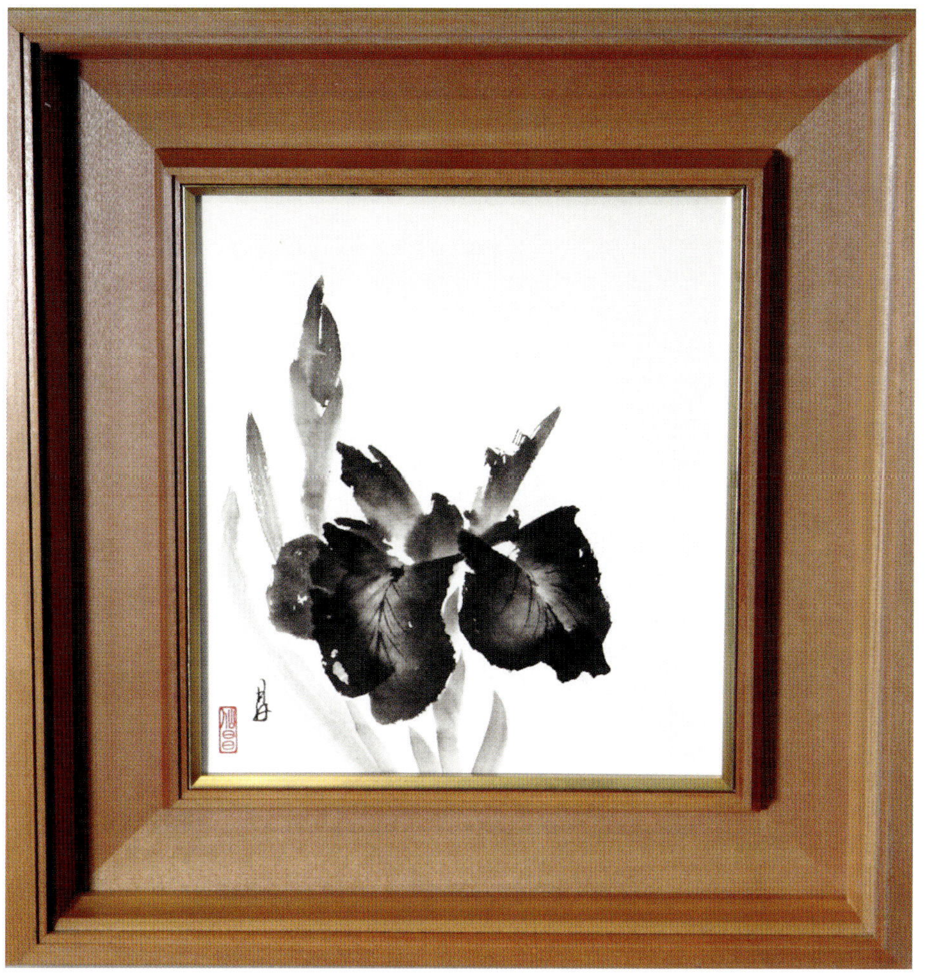

**Contemporary picture frames for tra-
ditional paintings**. *Shikishi* are commercially available art boards with pre-
mounted paper; they come in various
standard sizes. In Japan, commercial
frames are designed to hold a specific
size of shikishi. This is typical of such
frames. On the back are special clips to
release the backing so that the shikishi
can be interchanged. Paintings or calligraphy can be easily changed to complement
the season.

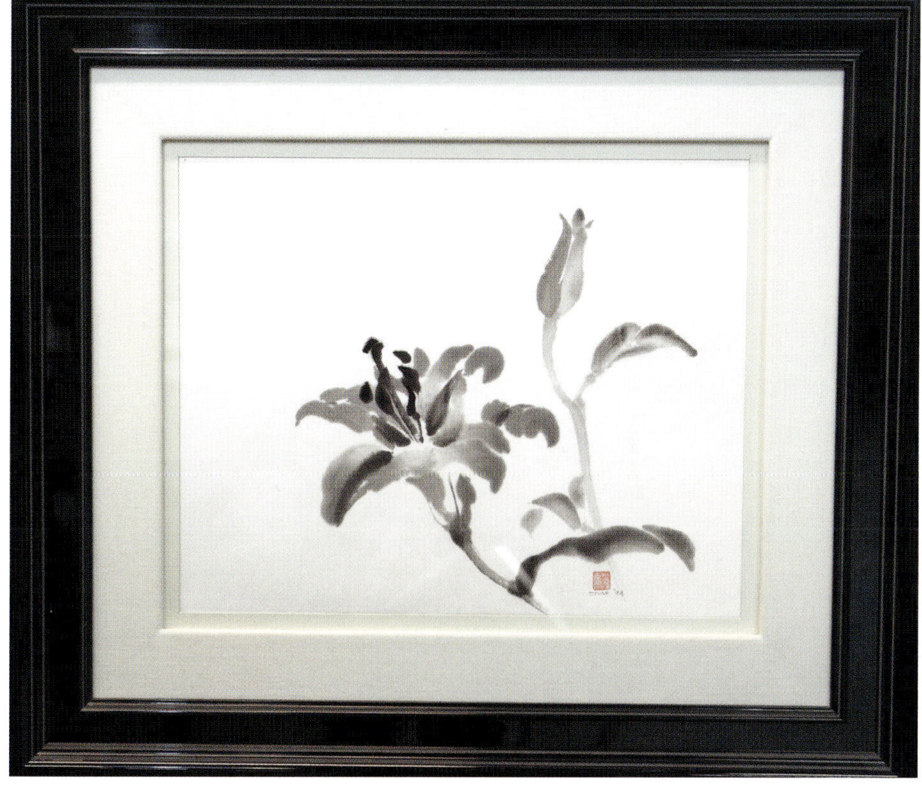

This is a custom-made frame from a
frame shop in the U.S. This frame also is
designed for changing the painting easily.

CHAPTER 7

Mounting Your Paintings

Most papers used for suiboku-ga or sumi-e are made from the natural fibers of plants, and therefore, they will react to humidity and moisture from sumi ink and water. When the painting is completed, the sections that were once wet will shrink and the areas which were untouched by moisture will maintain their original state.

The painting will be wavy and uneven. Usually, the painting is taken to a frame shop for mounting and framing. However, the staff in most frame shops generally are not accustomed to dealing with handmade paper of the sort used in sumi painting. So these framed sumi-e works, upon close examination, have fine spiderweb-like wrinkles because the hot press which is typically used by frame shops will not correctly stretch out the painting. A practitioner in sumi art should know the basic principles of how to make a work in sumi-e smooth again. There are several simple ways to do this quite easily at home.

The *mizubari* and *ura-uchi* techniques explained in this chapter will allow you to ensure that your works are properly prepared. Then, you will be ready to mount them yourself as scrolls if you wish, using the traditional *hyogu* technique. Another useful skill is to be able to make sizing formula and to size your own papers, and we will cover this also.

THE MIZUBARI TECHNIQUE

Since sumi ink is water-based and contains some animal glue as the adhesive material, once it is completely dried, the ink on the painted surface will not run when remoistened. It is very important to ensure that your work is completely dry and seasoned, before you apply moisture to carry out the stretching process. In Japan, professional *hyogu* craftsmen mount and repair scrolls, folding screens and sliding doors. A *hyogu* craftsman will always ask how much time has lapsed since the work was completed. Depending upon the elapsed time, he can determine the state, condition and stability of the ink.

In earlier days, before the convenience of electric hair dryers, the work was simply pinned up in the studio for a long period of time to dry and stabilize the ink. However, using a hair dryer will speed up the process.

The *mizubari* technique (*mizu* = water, *bari* = stretch) is done as follows:

Step 1: Use a very hot, but not scorching, hair dryer for a few minutes to completely dry the work.
Step 2: On a clean and smooth surface like a Formica tabletop, spray your work with water. Because handmade paper has a minute amount of glue incorporated to hold the fibers together, the paper will hold together. You will also need to spray a bare section of the tabletop, an area large enough for your work.
Step 3: Moist paper, especially single-weight paper, is very fragile, so handle it with care. On the moistened work lay a dry clean sheet of paper the same size or larger.
Step 4: With a dry soft *hake* or wide brush, gently brush the dry paper from the center out. This is very much the same technique you would use to hang wallpaper. The process will make your work very flat and smooth.

Step 5: Remove the protective paper, then move your work to the wet section of the surface that you sprayed earlier. Place a clean white paper over your work and brush it again to make sure your work is smooth and in full contact with the table. Remove the protective paper.
Step 6: Using any weight that is clean, straight and heavy, completely cover the work's edges on all four sides. Metal rulers or paper weights are ideal. The weights will help keep the paper from peeling off the table by itself during the drying process. Beware: The power of shrinkage in paper is unexpectedly strong, so your work should be heavily weighted for the best results.

Wait until the work is completely dry. Because no glue has been used, the painting will peel off from the Formica surface very easily. Now you are ready to take your *smooth* work to the frame shop.

A Variation

After your work has been moistened with the water spray and stretched, as described above, move it to a clean *dry* surface of the smooth (Formica) surface. Place strips of adhesive tape, such as transparent or masking tape, securely along the four edges and let it dry. Be very careful when you remove the tape, so that you will not end up by tearing your paper.

By giving moisture to the entire paper during the stretching process, the sumi ink section and the formerly-dry section of your work are now both in the same condition. Therefore, in the drying process when the tension of shrinkage is even (due to the tape), the paper becomes completely smooth. To view this process step by step, see page 189, "How to Size Paper"; the basic procedure is the same.

THE URA UCHI TECHNIQUE, CATEGORY A (FACE DOWN)

Ura uchi (*ura* = back, *uchi* = additional paper for support) is another basic technique for making your work in sumi-e smooth. In addition, if the work is on single-weight paper, the backing paper will add both support and strength to it.

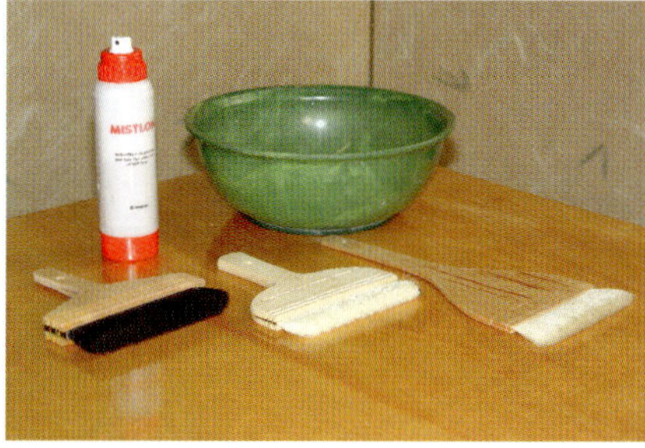

You will need:
Glue (rice glue, if available; wallpaper glue from a local hardware store will also work).
A large container of water.
A handheld compressor sprayer, if available.
Soft wide *hake* brushes. (Use separate brushes for glue, for water, and to brush the work.)

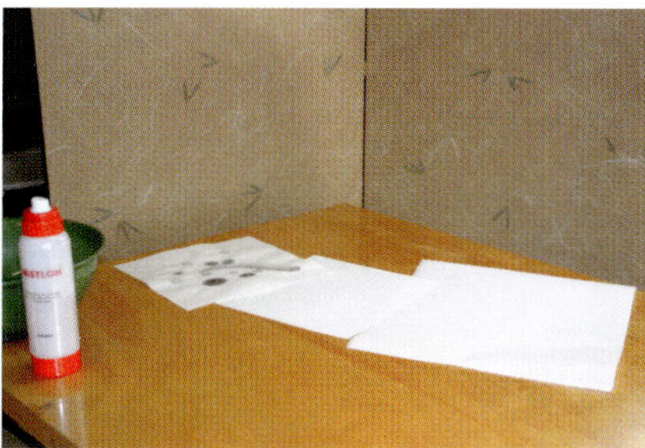

1. The work surface should be smooth. Formica works well. This work table is made from a tabletop which has had several coats of polyurethane applied to make it water-resistant.

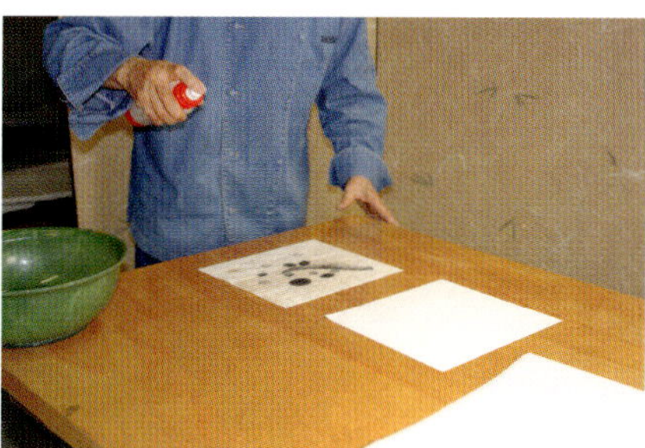

2. The paper on the far left is the work to be mounted. Next is highly absorbent paper cut the same size as the work; it is used to protect the paper by absorbing excess ink, in case any ink should run. The largest paper is for backing your work. Place the work on the highly absorbent paper, face down, and then spray the back with water.

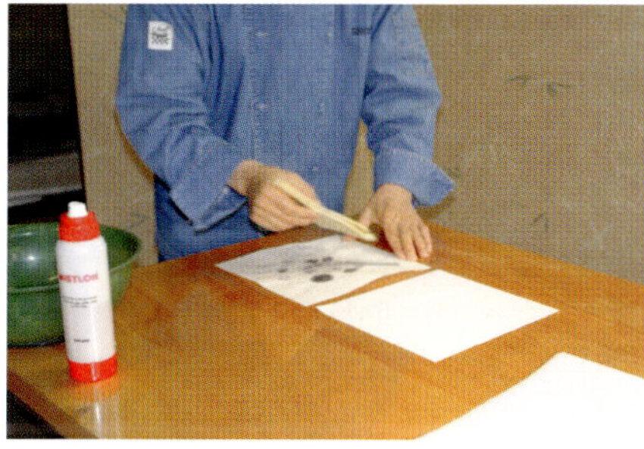

3. If a sprayer is not available, use a brush instead to moisten the work. (In this photo, the protective paper is not placed underneath. But remember that if the ink should happen to run, without a protective paper the work will be ruined.)

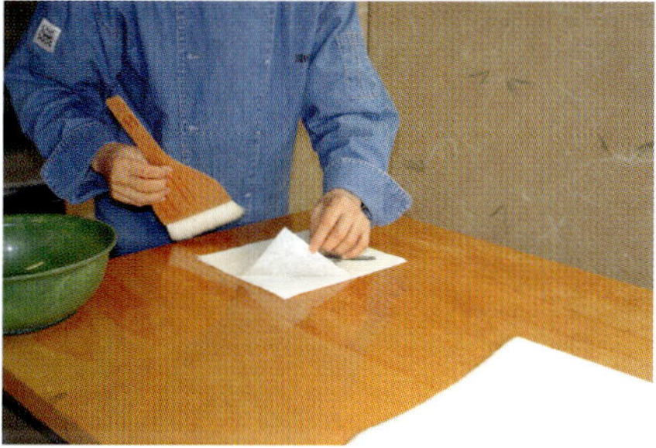

4. This is the proper method, with protective paper underneath. Your work should face down on the protective paper. It is difficult to apply moisture evenly with a brush, which makes the protective paper even more important.

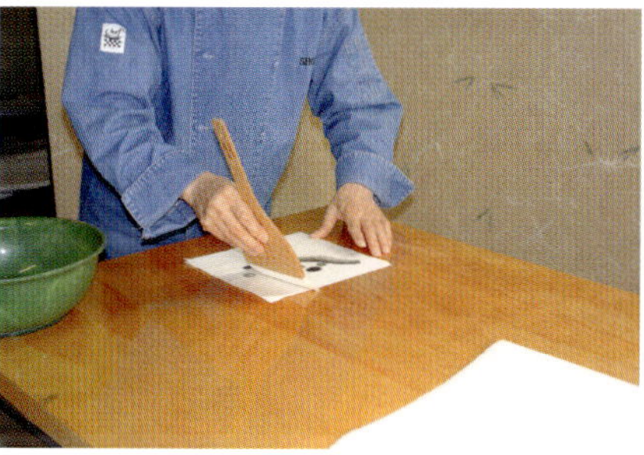

5. Next, use the other brush to begin to stretch your work.

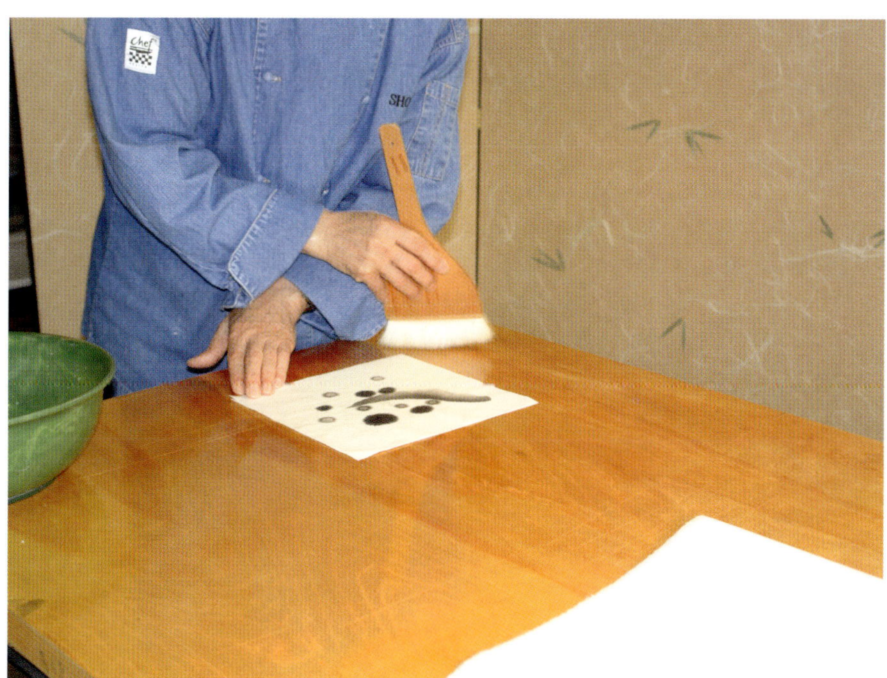

6. Gently stretch your work, brushing from the center toward the edges.

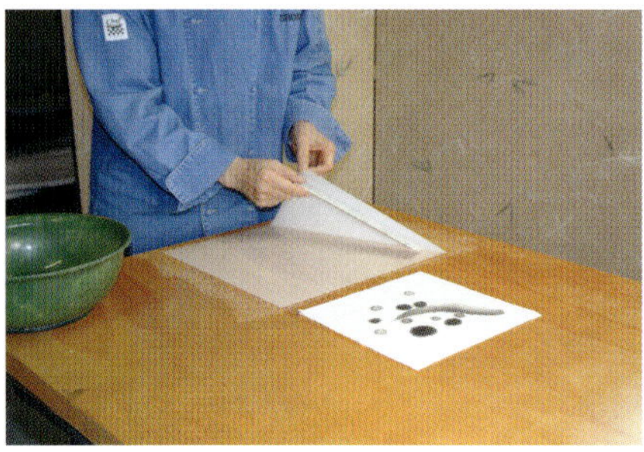

7. Now spread glue on the large backing paper, covering it evenly. Then, as shown above, use a ruler or similar "support bar" to pick up the far left edge of the backing paper and lift it up halfway.

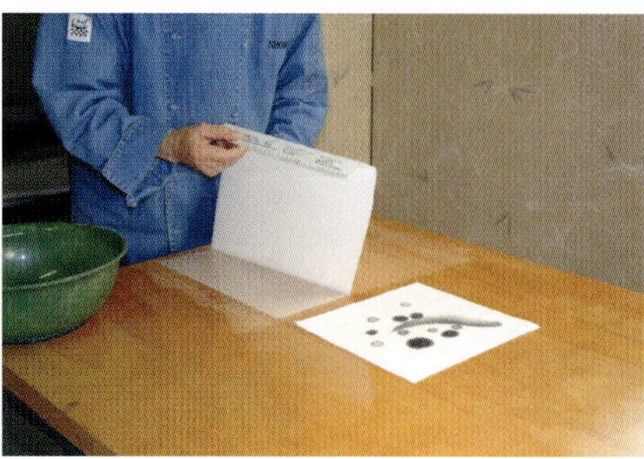

8. Place the edge of the paper evenly along the support bar. Use the bar to gently lift it. During this process, stay aware of the tension between table and paper. If you lift too quickly, it will tear.

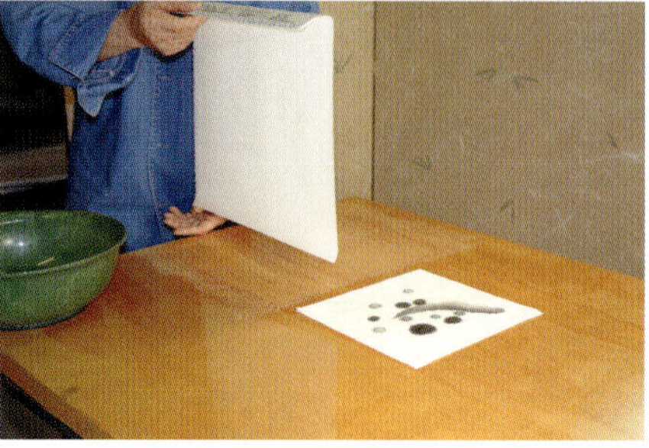

9. The wet, heavy backing paper has been successfully lifted off the table. At this point, pick up its bottom corner with your left hand.

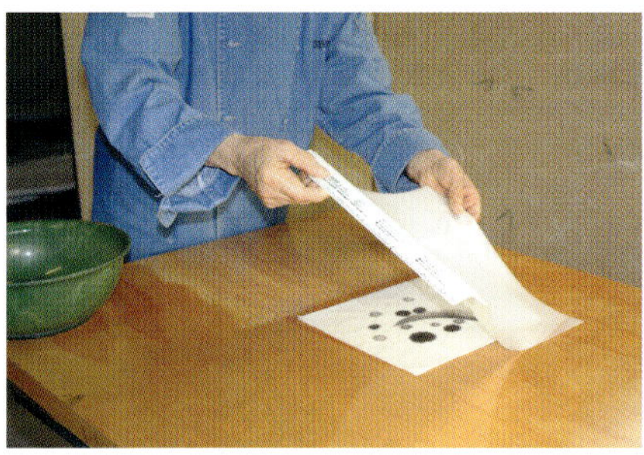

10. Make contact with the work surface at the backing paper's left top corner, positioning it over your work (which is still on the protective paper). Adjust the positioning, making sure the tension of the glue-wet backing paper is even and smooth. Here, the backing paper has been successfully placed over the work. It takes practice to learn how to adjust the timing and tension in lifting and moving the paper. Having an assistant will help immensely.

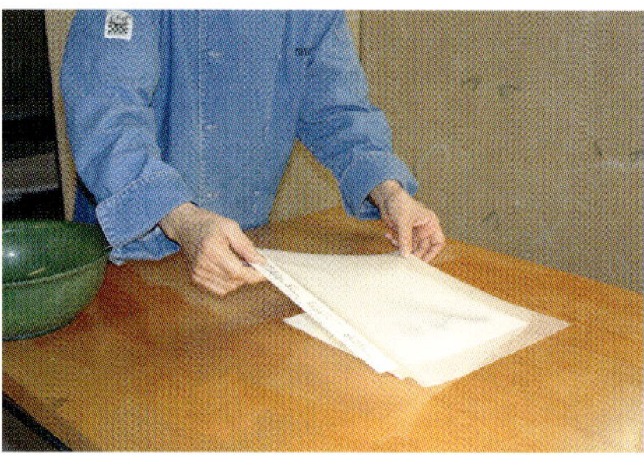

11. To remove the support bar, hold the corner of the paper down with your left thumb and rotate the support stick off in a counterclockwise motion. This process may require a few practice sessions; it is something that beginners often find difficult. The wet paper that has glue on it is heavy, but fragile in nature. Do not treat it, as many beginners do, as if it were a stiff board!

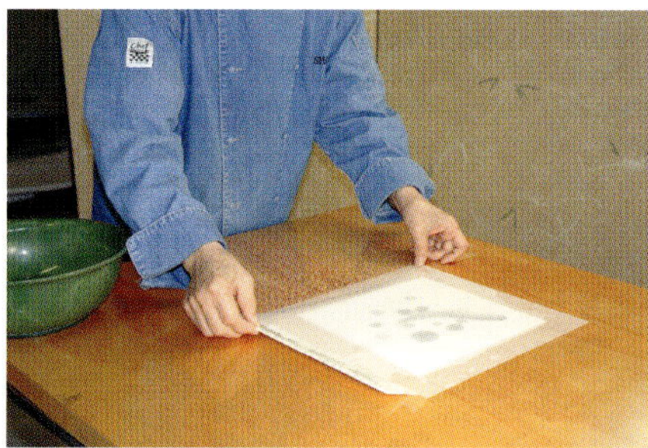

12. After the support bar is removed, lift the top paper again and carefully re-lay it across the painting. Because a backing paper must sometimes undergo moisture and repeated handling, it is best to use long-fibered handmade paper. *Kozo*, *gampi*, *mitsumata* or hemp are all long-fibered papers that are suitable. Short-fiber paper, on the other hand, would melt away at the halfway point of this process.

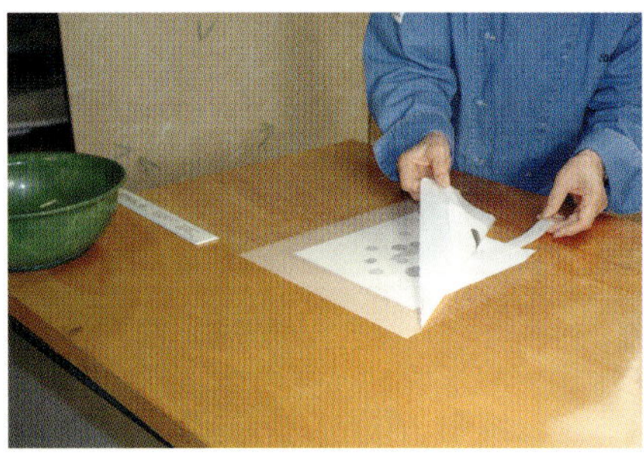

13. A half-inch-wide (1.2cm) slip of paper is placed between the bottommost absorbent paper and your work, then the backing paper is glued down again.

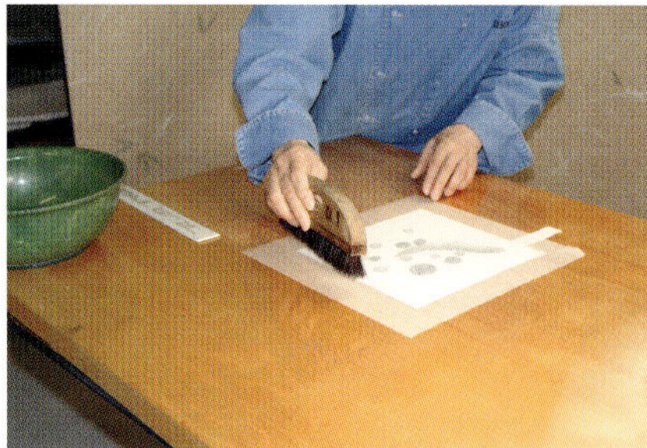

14. This hake with short coarse hair is designed specifically for use when backing a painting. With almost forceful pounding, begin from the center and with a staccato-like beat, pound all the way around with pressure. If the work is on double- or triple-weight paper the glue on the backing paper will not easily penetrate. In such a case, while it may appear to be a cruel handling of your work, extra pounding may be necessary to get the glue to penetrate the thickness. On a positive note, if you had a hairline wrinkle left in the work, the pounding will stretch it out. After the pounding is complete, inspect the surface to make sure the work and the backing paper are glued together.

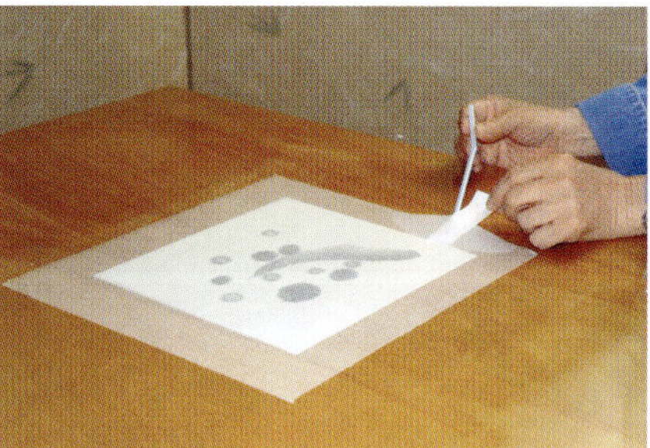

15. Whatever the thickness of the paper, during the pounding the glue may have seeped all the way through to the protective paper. It and your painting may now be glued together. To prevent a catastrophe, separate these two layers by blowing air through the space at the paper strip. It is convenient to use a straw. The air will create a small dome of separation between the two papers, enabling you to completely separate them. Too much air will lift up some of the outer edges, so after the straw is removed, press down to make certain all of the edges are securely glued to the table. If any paper fibers have been lifted up, use a brush to smooth the entire back surface.

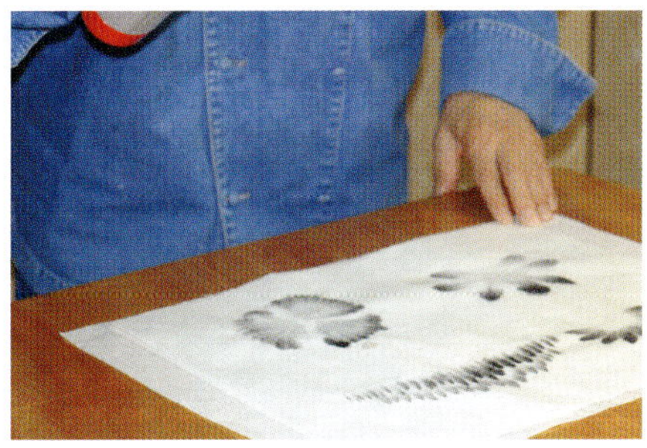

1. Ensure that your backing paper is of a larger size than your work, creating a margin of about 1 inch (2.5cm) all the way around your painting. You will also need another piece of protective paper (for instance, white butcher paper) the same size as the backing paper. Place your work on the protective paper face up, and spray it with a mist of water. Depending upon the atmospheric conditions of your work area—humid? dry? air conditioning? central heating?—you must adjust the amount of moisture accordingly. My terminology is "relaxing the paper."

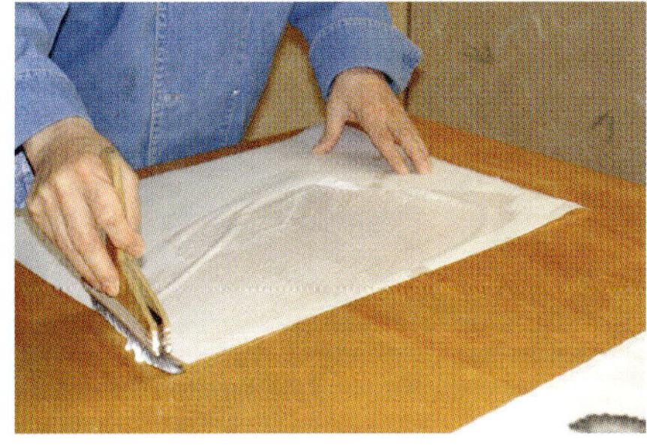

2. Now, use a brush to evenly apply the glue to the backing paper. When your thumbprint on the backing paper shows transparency, that means the glue has been evenly spread. The state of "relaxed paper" that you created in Step 1 must be consistently maintained in your painting, until the backing paper has glue on it and is ready for the painting. Often by the time the backing paper is ready the work has dried out; to help prevent that, you can place an additional sheet of butcher paper over the waiting, "relaxed" work.

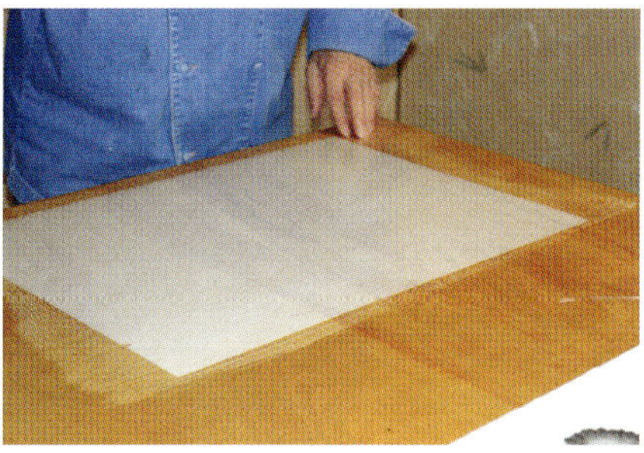

3. The application of glue on the backing paper is now completed. It is important that the glue is the right consistency, whether you use commercial rice glue, homemade rice glue or wallpaper glue. A consistency similar to crepe batter or soft and creamy yogurt is about right.

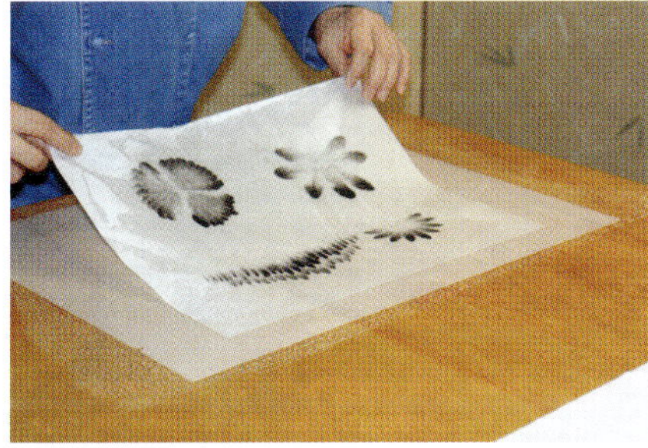

4. Lift your work from the protective paper and position it on the center of the backing paper. Take care that the work's edges are positioned so they will be evenly surrounded by a margin of backing paper, then gradually lower the painting.

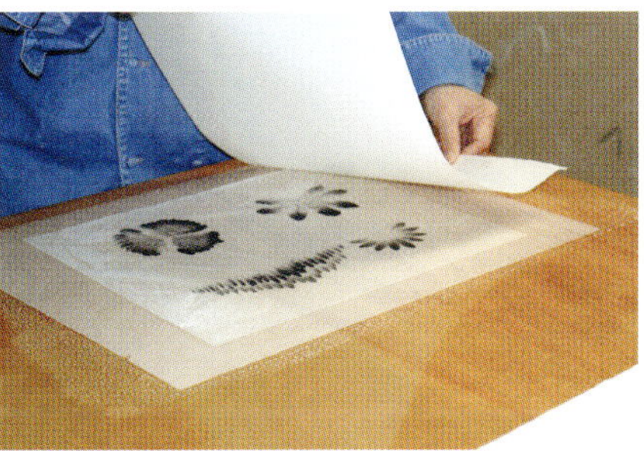

5. Lay the absorbent protective paper over the work and make sure it is flat. Check that there are no wrinkles. In the next step, the glue functions as a lubricant as you press and brush simultaneously over your entire painting.

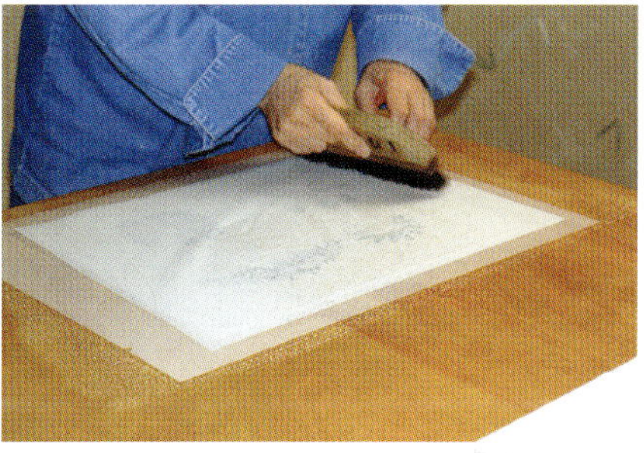

6. Using a sturdy horse-hair "backing hake," forcefully push down the brush and move it left to right and right to left. During this process, any hairline wrinkles will slide away.

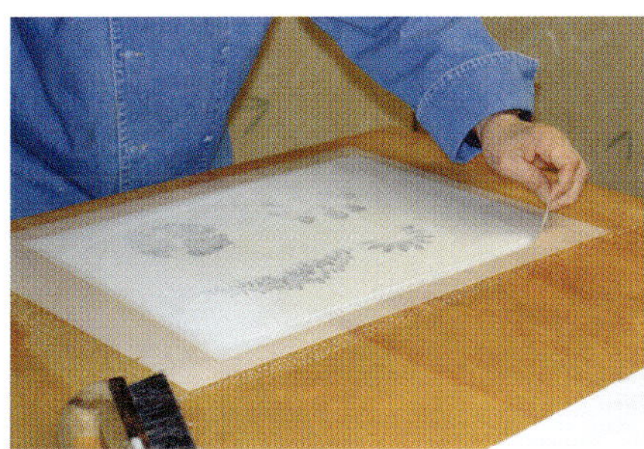

7. Gently lift up the protective paper, using a rolling motion.

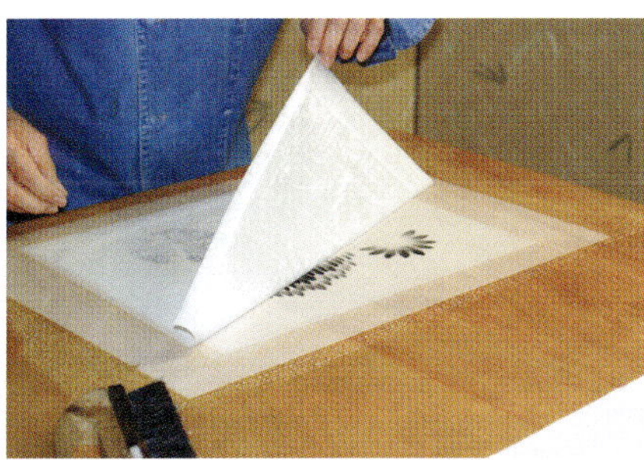

8. While removing the top protective paper, ensure that the painting does not lift away from the backing paper as well.

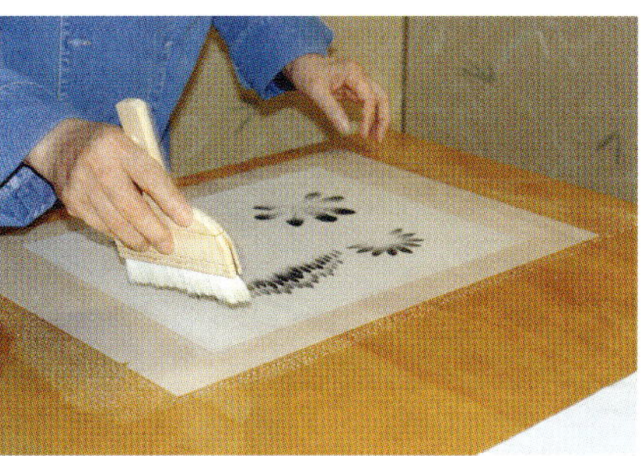

9. Doublecheck to see that the painting is securely glued to the backing paper and examine carefully to ensure there are no wrinkles. A hairline wrinkle can be smoothed out with a rounded smooth hard surface, such as your fingernail. Using a rolling motion will stretch and blend the fibers.

At this stage, if you have used thicker double- or triple-weight paper (which glue penetrates with more difficulty), you may want to add more glue under the outer edges, so that they will hold securely and will not pull free during the drying process. The power of shrinkage in paper is unexpectedly strong, and the edges must be able to withstand it and stay put.

The goal of the next steps is to eliminate any chance that the drying work will adhere to the table. You will create a cushion of air to separate the mounted work from the table surface.

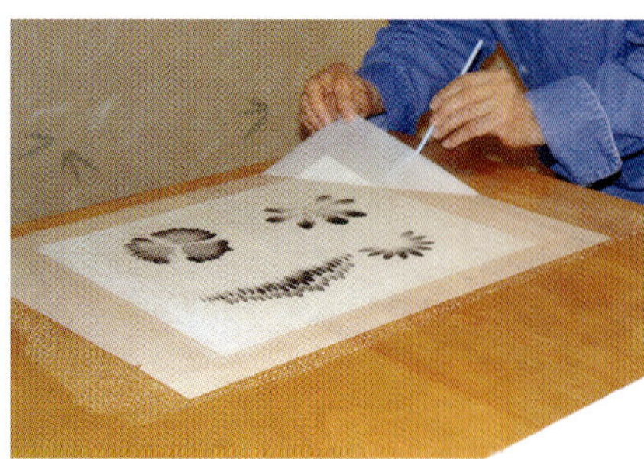

10. Blow air under the backing paper, using a drinking straw, to lift the work and separate it from the table. When the air has created a separation, slide out the straw and seal the border down. Make sure the backing paper is well sealed to the table around all edges, so that no air escapes. Be certain that you can see the air dome.

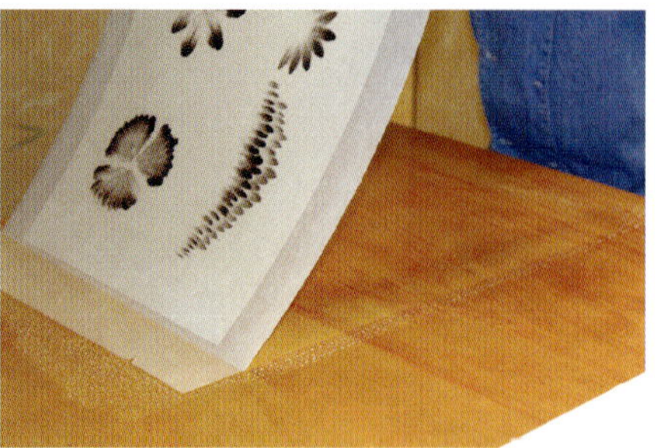

11. Alternatively, instead of blowing air in, you can lift your work off the table, clean the excess glue from the table and then carefully lay the work back down, capturing a cushion of air in that way.

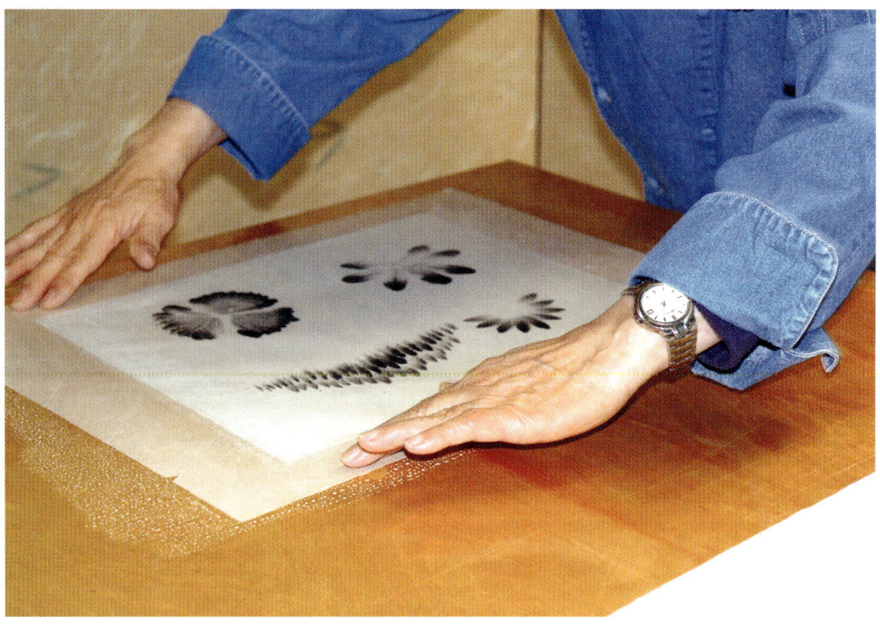

12. Now the mounted painting is back on the table with air captured underneath. Press the backing paper edges against the table again, possibly reinforcing them with more glue if that seems needed. Now allow the work to dry.

There are many other methods for backing your paintings. In this process, I did not include the use of additional protective papers during the drying process. A protective layer of air was sealed in, instead. But note that professional craftsmen will always use a protective shield, a highly absorbent paper that is almost felt-like, between the work and the table to eliminate any chance that the work will adhere to the table.

A Variation

In this variation, to keep the painting from adhering to the work surface as it dries, the protective barrier is a piece of paper instead of a cushion of air.

You will need a protective absorbent piece of paper that is exactly the size of your painting. Place it on a clean part of the table.

After removing the top paper in Step 8, and ensuring that the work is wrinkle-free in Step 9, next apply a quarter-inch-wide (0.6cm wide) strip of glue along the outer edges of the backing paper, all the way around. Then move the entire work to the clean part of the table. (It is definitely good to have an assistant for this.)

Turn the backed unit—work and backing paper—over so that the painting is facing down, and lower it onto the absorbent paper. The painting should be directly over the paper, aligned with its edges. Press the backing paper's glued edges securely down, sealing them to the table surface so that no part will release during the drying process. Allow the work to dry.

INTRODUCTION TO THE TRADITIONAL HYOGU TECHNIQUE

Some time ago, when I was still physically able to sit on a hard wooden floor for four to five hours at a time, I learned the ABCs of how to make wall hanging scrolls and folding screens. The work table was only six inches off the floor. My mentor was the Fourth Generation Master in Scroll Making, who lived in Tokyo. The experience was eye-opening.

Hyogu is the Japanese technique or craft of mounting. It has existed for more than 1,200 years, and today in Japan it holds the designation of a traditional handicraft. Good hyogu craftsmen are highly skilled.

On most hanging scrolls the main expanse of fabric that frames the art is of plain cloth, perhaps silk or damask, that has been woven especially for this purpose. The fabrics' threads are woven in arrangements of various patterns, so what appears at first glance to be plain fabric will show patterns when the light direction changes. In mounted scrolls, the fabrics appear thick and display richness; but actually they are very thinly woven, so thin that one can see through them. This is essential, because the fabric for a scroll, even after it is combined with several layers of paper, must remain flexible and easily rolled.

The narrow strips of cloth that are placed horizontally directly above and below the art are called *ichimonji*. Usually the best cloth, such as gold brocade, is reserved for the ichimonji. Although these brocades may be decoratively woven with various threads, colors and patterns, they are generally subdued. This cloth also is very thin.

Today, *hyogu* encompasses not only scrolls and fusuma (sliding panels) but also other practical kinds of ornamental pieces. Below, we will use the traditional hyogu technique for mounting scrolls. Instead of a scroll, however, our finished product will be a fabric-framed image mounted on stiff board, ready to hang.

Select the fabric of your choice. Thinness and silky smoothness are important; avoid fabrics that have any kind of nap, however scant. For the backing paper, choose a paper with long fibers, such as *kozo* or *mitsumata*, because it must be strong enough to carry the weight of glue without tearing.

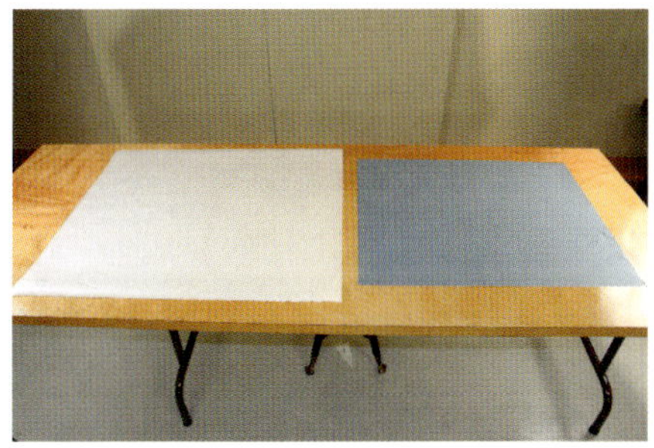

1. After the fabric is measured and cut to the proper size, cut the backing paper to a larger size to allow a margin of 1 to 2 inches (2.5 to 5 cm) all the way around. Later in the process, you will also need thick white glue; a knife; thin strips of silver paper for accent; foam board (I used half-inch-thick Gatorboard); a paper for the back; and cord.

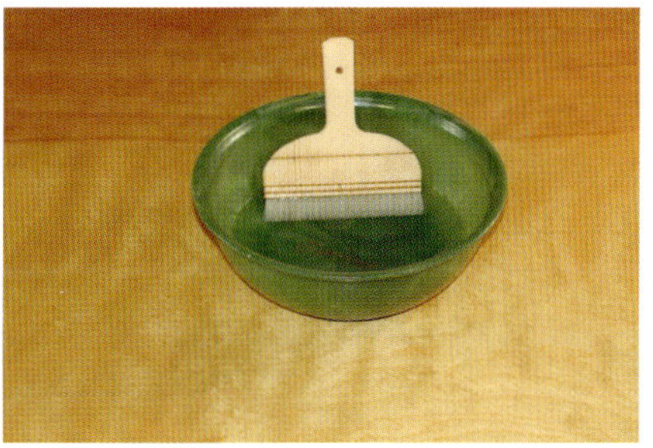

2. You will need a hake brush and a bowl of water. The water will serve as an adhesive to keep the fabric on the board, and also as a lubricant for moving the fabric when needed. Use a waterproof work surface; this surface is a door that has been treated with four layers of polyurethane. Formica with a slight "sandy" texture also works very well.

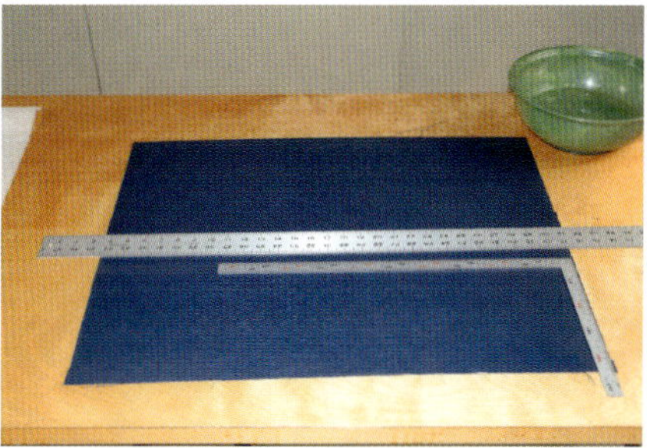

3. During the lesson in Tokyo, it was a surprise to learn that beautiful silk damask could be soaked in water. Here, the fabric has instead been brushed with water many times to soak it. Use measuring sticks to examine the fabric's woven lines. Adjust as needed; make certain they are absolutely straight, and run at a 90-degree angle.

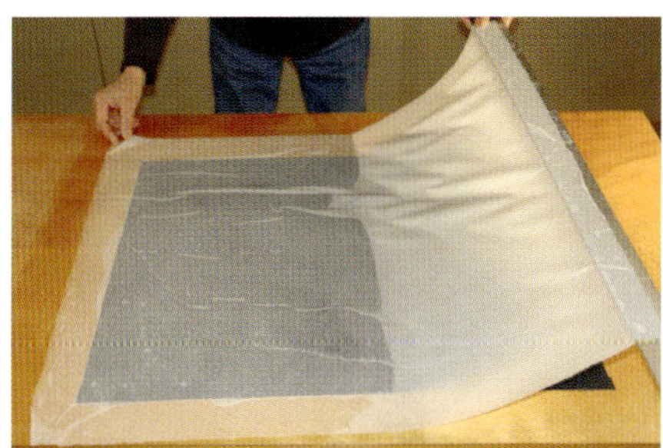

4. On a separate section of the board, brush glue onto the backing paper to completely cover it. Then, lift it using a stiff, lightweight slat or stick as a support bar: place the support bar along the paper's far left edge, and peel it up off the surface. Turn the paper over, so that the glue side faces the cloth. Position the paper over the fabric. Metal has a tendency to bend, so especially if your support bar is metal, it helps to have an assistant.

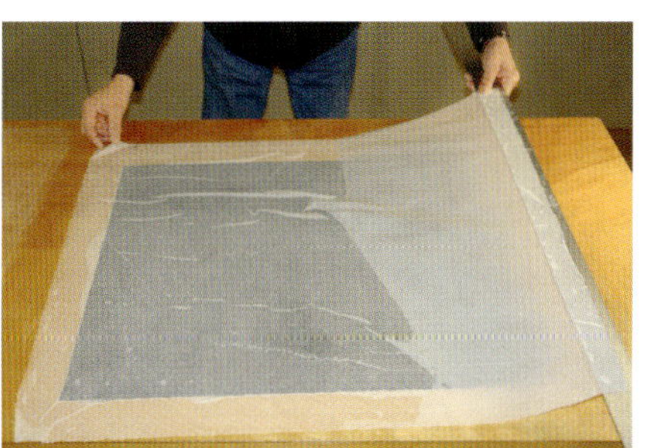

5. Ease the paper carefully over the cloth, glue side down. Then release the support bar from the paper's edge. As you can see here, there will be wrinkles in the center section.

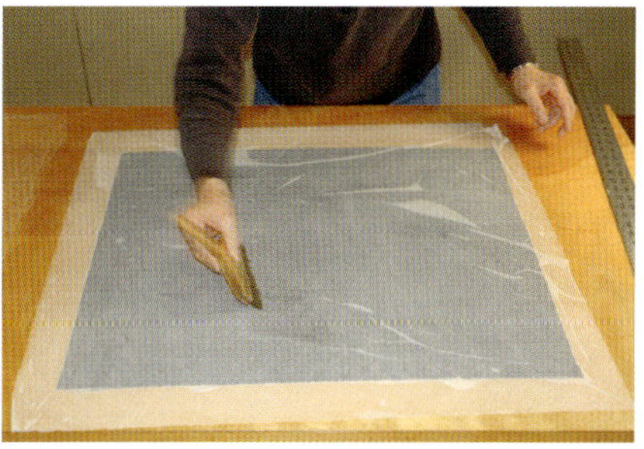

6. Small wrinkles can be stretched out using a hake brush with short stiff bristles. Glue between the two materials acts as a lubricant.

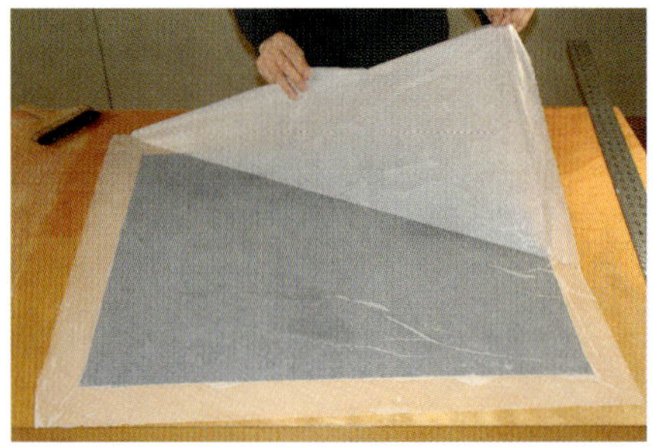

7. But if the wrinkles are large, it is best to pull up the backing paper and reposition it. The backing paper should be made of long fibers to help it withstand this arduous handling.

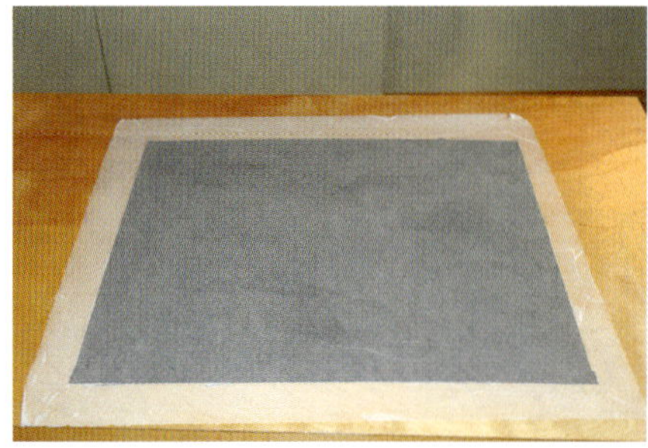

8. After you get the wrinkles out, make sure the margin of the paper is tightly attached to the table surface all the way around. During the drying process the wet section begins to shrink; if the outer support paper is not secure, it will peel off in certain places and the finished product will be irregular in shape.

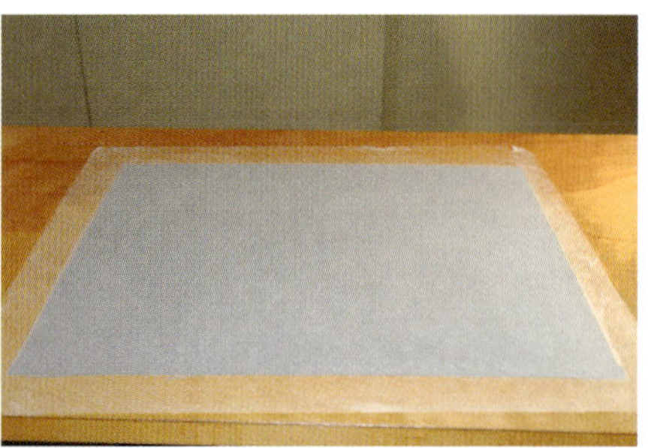

9. Soon after the smoothing out process has been completed, use wet towels to completely remove any glue left on the table. Allow the backed fabric to dry overnight.

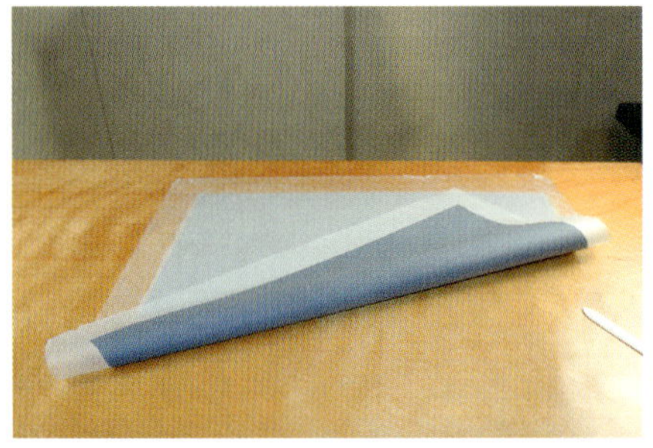

10. Insert a folding bone (if you have one; otherwise a table knife will work) under the backing paper margin, keeping it as flat as possible. Then push it forward, with the tip held at a 45-degree angle, in the direction that you are moving to release the paper from the table top. If the work surface is in good condition, the work can be simply peeled off. But if the work surface has absorbed the glue, then the whole unit is "stuck." It is impossible to peel off. If this should happen, cut the center fabric out with a razor blade. Re-soak the margin edge to remove the paper. Start again!

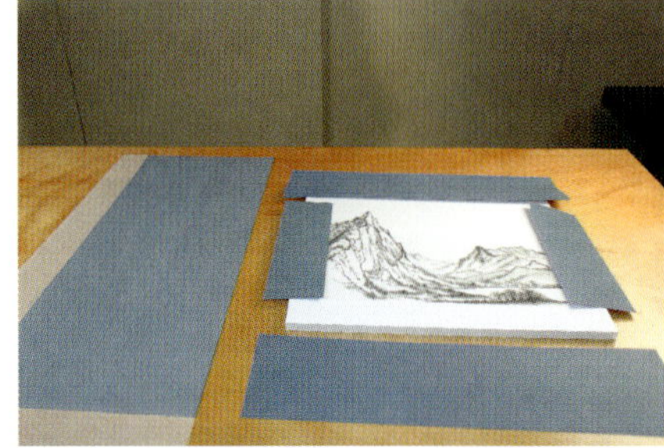

11. Carefully calculate the sizes of the four fabric pieces you will need, then cut them from your backed fabric. The backing will keep the cut edges from fraying. It is important to keep the direction of the fabric's weave consistent in your pieces, so that the weave pattern is running in the same direction on the top, bottom, left and right. If this is not done, when the work is displayed, the light reflections from the various pieces will differ almost to the point where it may appear that different fabrics have been used.

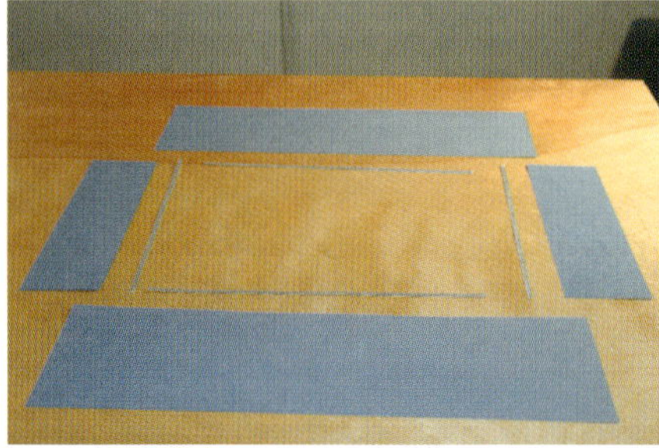

12. Four pieces of backed fabric and four paper strips in silver, which will act as accents between the art and the fabric, have been cut to size. Economy is important when cutting fabric which has been produced so carefully. During workshops I explain the need for care in planning the cuts, but often participants are so involved in their thoughts that they forget the economy part—they cut the sections they need, and their leftovers are useless. Calculate your cuts well. When the fabric is cut successfully, you will have a large piece left over for future use.

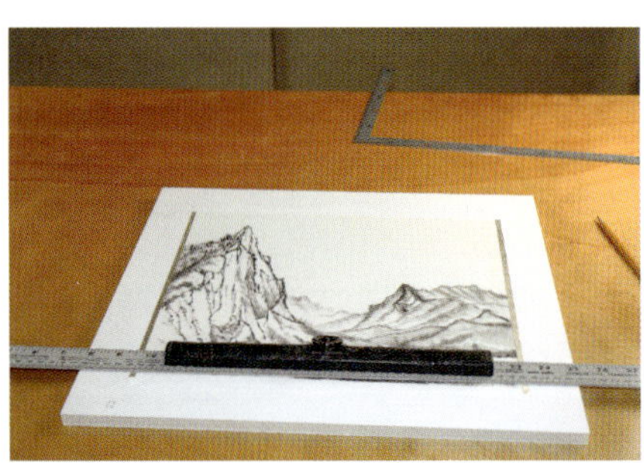

13. First you will apply the straight thin accent, which in this case is silver. Place a flat measuring stick along the edge where the silver line is to go, and put a paper weight on top for added stability.

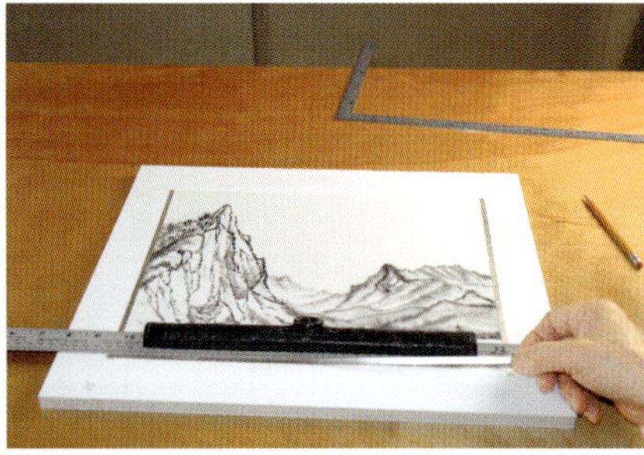

14. Apply glue to its back, then place the silver strip along the stick. It is very difficult to glue thin pieces of paper in a completely straight line; this *hyogu* method was developed generations ago.

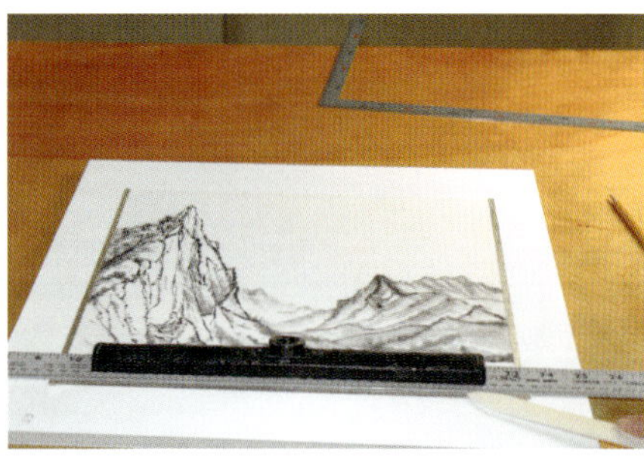

15. With fingertips, a bone folder, or a knife, gently push the silver strip into position so it is perfectly aligned with the ruler.

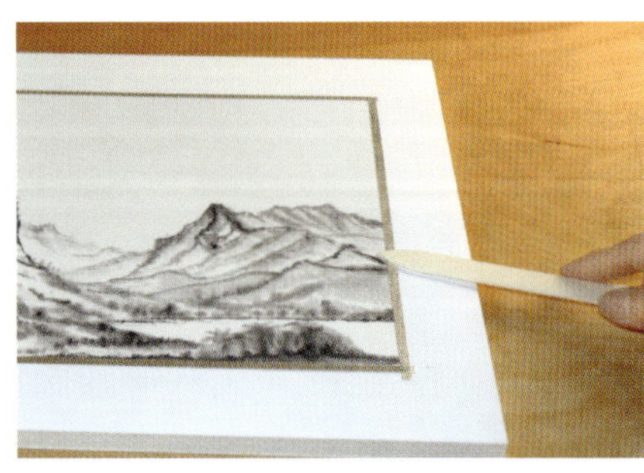

16. After gluing the silver accents to all four sides, use the flat side of the folding bone to make sure the strips are well-adhered to the painting. I usually use extra thick glue for this purpose.

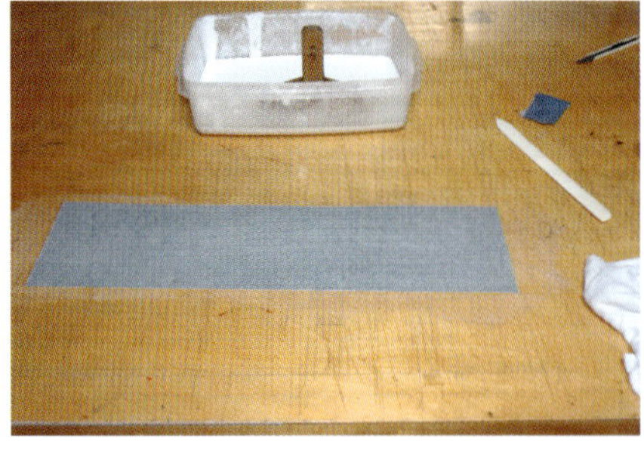

17. Apply glue to the backed fabric, using a brush. This glue is thicker than that used for ura uchi (page 181) which has a consistency more like crepe dough; this glue is more like paste. Shown at right are two handy prepared cloths, one wet and one dry.

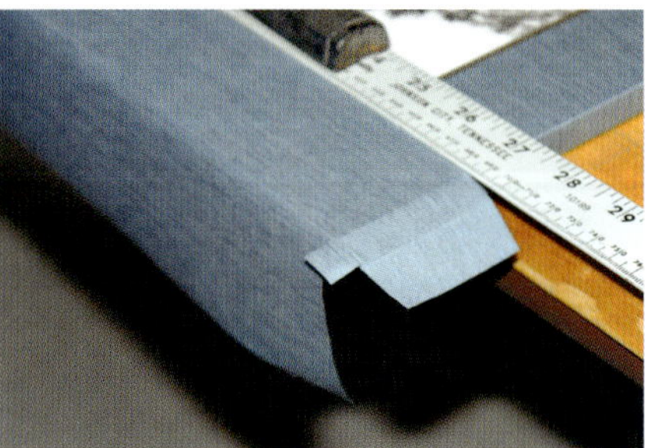

18. To align the fabric's edges on the front of the piece, against the silver strips, use the measuring stick and weight again as in Steps 13–15. Because this Gatorboard is thick, the fabric will need to be cut and folded at the corners.

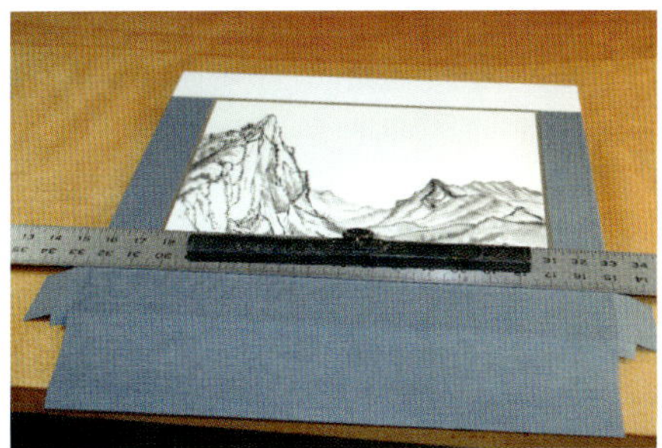 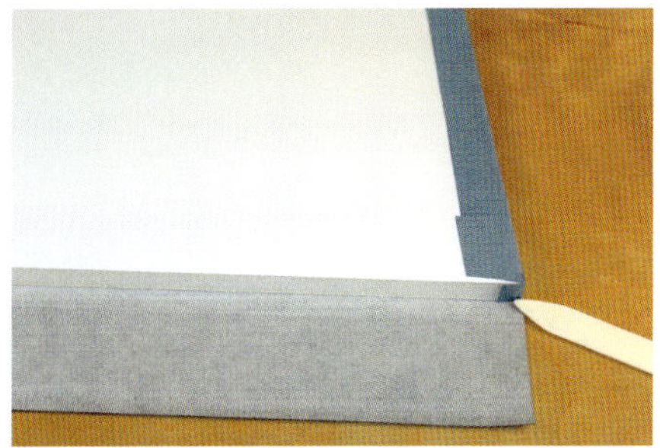 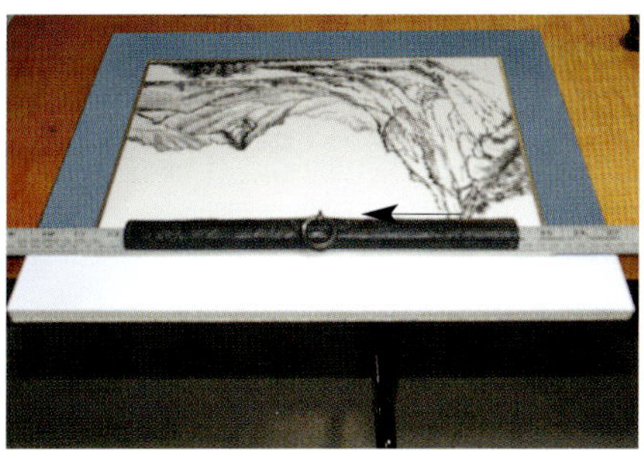

19. The two side pieces of fabric have now been securely glued on. Here the third, lowermost piece of fabric will be glued. After the fabric is in place, use both hands to wrap it smoothly around the board and crease it; then with scissors, eliminate unnecessary sections (see the fabric cuts shown in Step 18).

20. Make sure the fabric is firmly glued to the board. A bone folder or knife can be useful to firmly and precisely fold and press corners and smaller flaps of fabric.

21. The fourth piece of fabric, the top piece, is ready to be positioned. Here, the white Gatorboard extends beyond the edge of the table, for greater ease in wrapping the fabric.

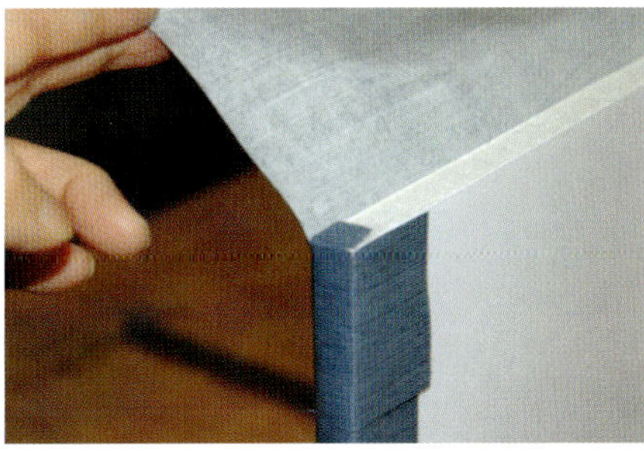 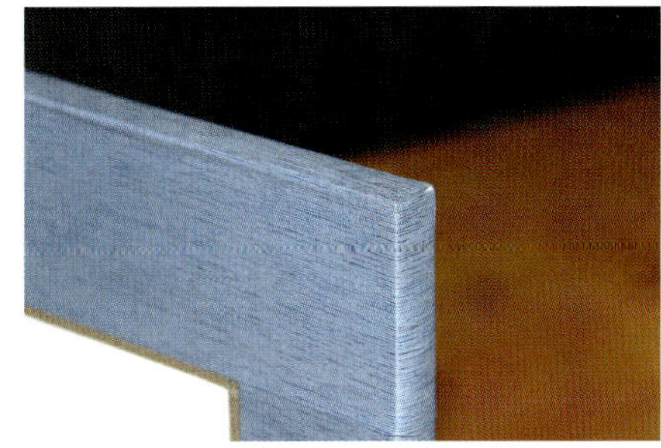 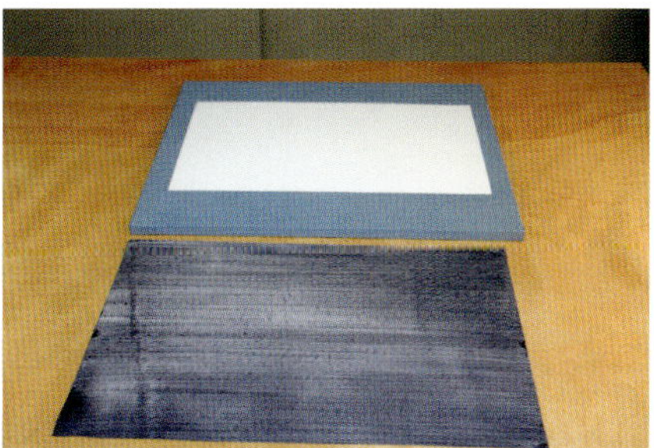

22. The final stage is to firmly glue the last flap down and around the back.

23. The fabric has been successfully and neatly attached to the board.

24. Now, cover the back of the board. Any type of paper can be used, but it should not be too thick. Brush it with glue, and center it on the board.

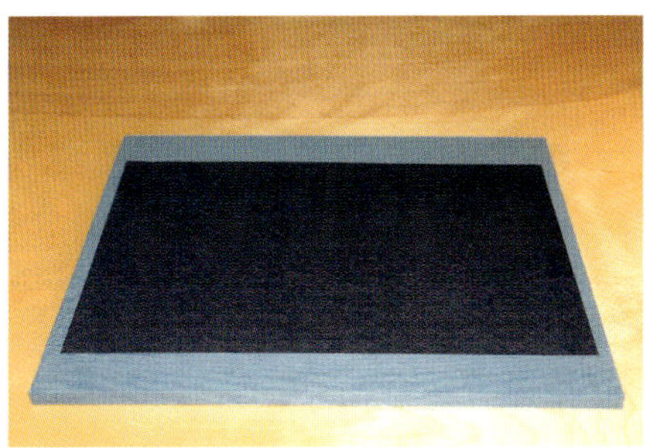 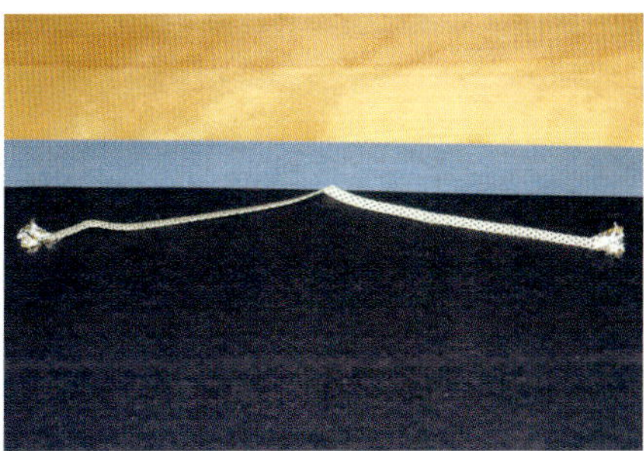 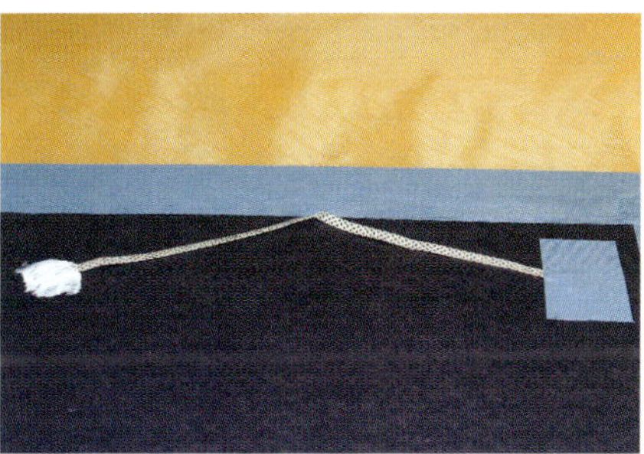

25. The back paper is now dry. The next step is to add a string or cord for hanging the painting. Measure the width of the painting to find the center, and place the midpoint of the cord there.

26. Note that both ends of this cord have been deliberately frayed so as to maximize the adhesive power of the glue.

27. On the left is undiluted glue covering the frayed end. Next, glue a square piece of leftover fabric over the glued end, as shown on the right.

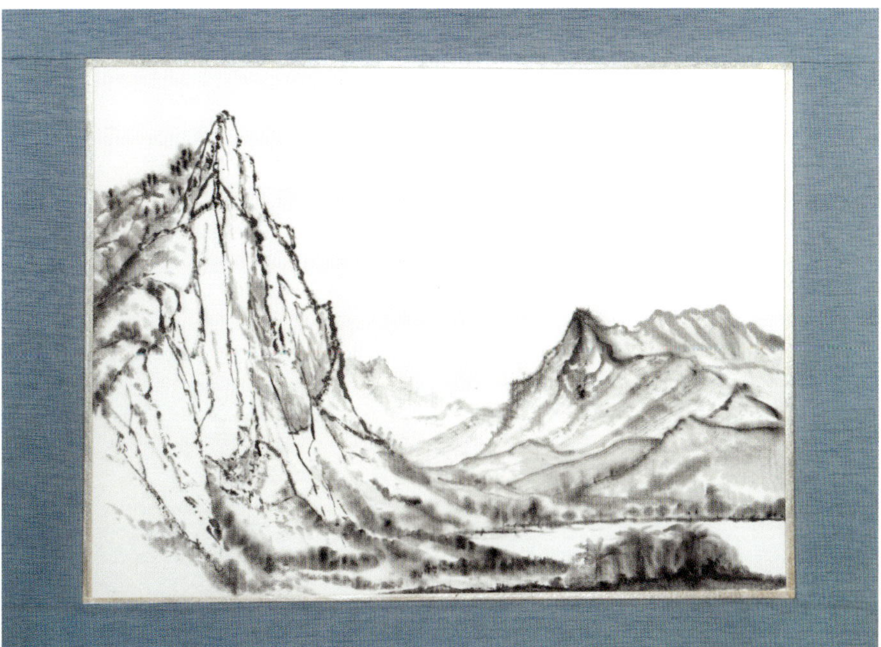

28. The finished piece. Let it dry overnight. Then your painting is ready to hang on the wall.

Take care in placing the cord. If it is attached too high, it will show when hung; and if it is attached too low, the picture will will jut out at an extreme angle. From experience, I have found that it is best to paste each cord end at a distance, measured in from the side, of one-fourth the mounted painting's total width.

HOW TO MAKE SIZING FORMULA

Most sumi-e artists enjoy the effects of nijimi when sumi ink is applied on unsized paper. But when you are painting certain subjects where a smooth transition from dark to light ink is required, or when using the tarashi komi technique, or when applying thick color components, it is necessary to use sized paper. If you are not able to obtain already sized paper, you may size your own paper using the following technique.

In the U.S. it may be difficult to find commercially prepared ready-to-use *dosa*, or sizing liquid. However, the components for making dosa are available. Gelatinized nikawa is available in stores that carry Asian art supplies. Rabbit skin glue, which will also work, can be found in arts and craft stores.

Recipe for Dosa (Sizing Liquid)

1 teaspoon gelatinized nikawa or rabbit skin glue
$1/_2$ teaspoon alum powder
5 Tablespoons hot water

Mix the above ingredients well, then microwave for about 10 seconds to completely dissolve. To use, mix 1 part of this liquid to 2 or 3 parts water. Apply the liquid to paper.

The thickness of the paper and its dimensions determine the amount of dosa you will need to use.

Seeing the *dosa* effect. The left side of the paper was sized with dosa, and the right side remained as natural unsized sumi-e paper.

Line A: In thick blue tone ink.
Line B: In blue tone ink diluted 30 times.
Line C: In common or standard liquid sumi ink.
Line D: In standard sumi ink diluted 30 times.

HOW TO SIZE PAPER

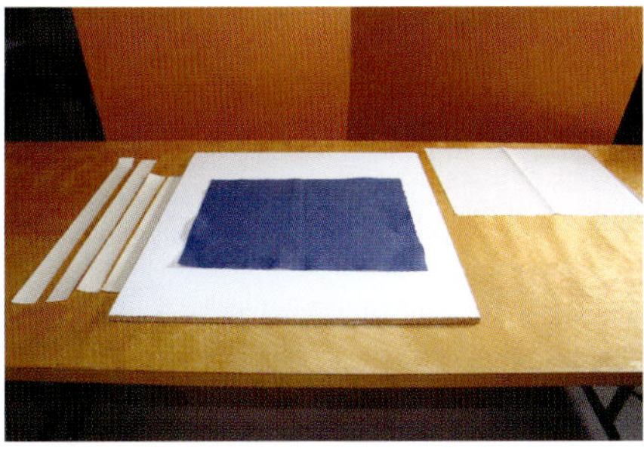

1. On a smooth Formica-type surface, place a piece of felt that has the same measurements as the paper you plan to size. Blue felt is used here only because it is easier to see; using white felt is best.

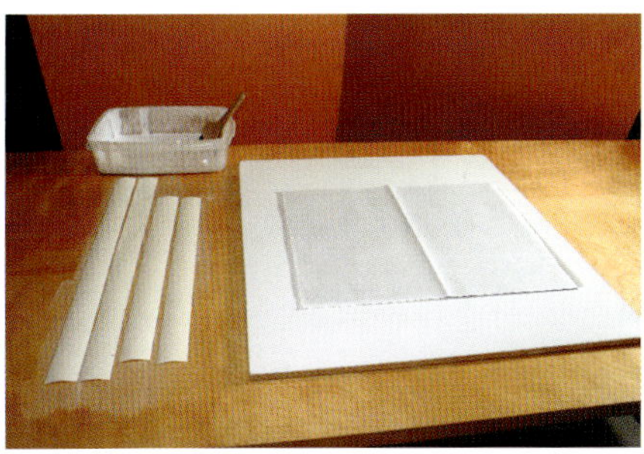

2. The four strips of paper, plus white paste, will be used as tape around the paper. (Regular packaging tape will not work: paper's "shrinkage power" is generally too great.)

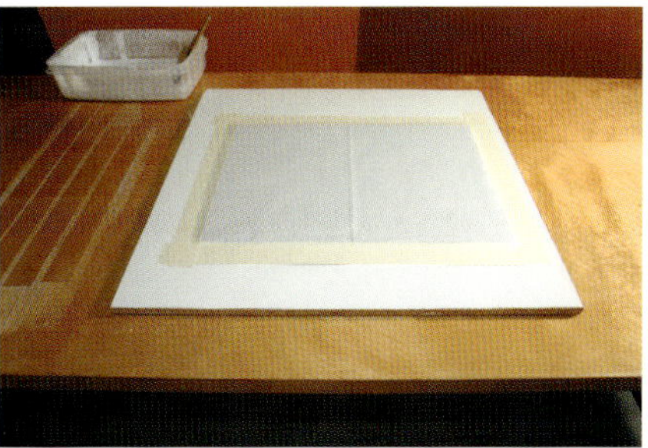

3. Place the sumi paper on the felt. Apply paste to the four strips of paper. Paste the strips along the paper's edges to hold it in place. Caution: Make sure the strips form a complete seal. Let it dry.

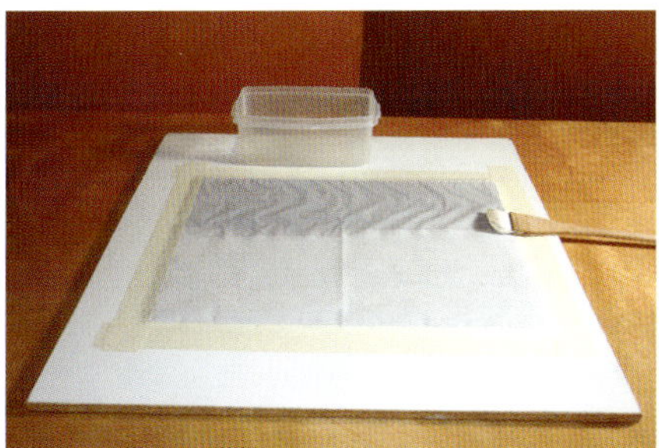

4. Paint dosa evenly on the paper.

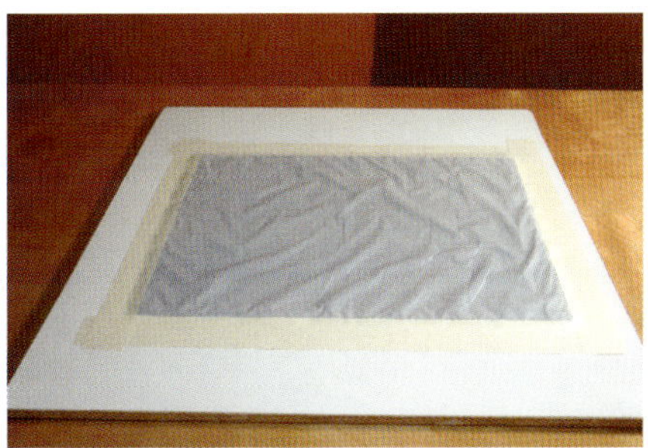

5. Dosa has now been evenly applied to the entire paper. Leave it overnight.

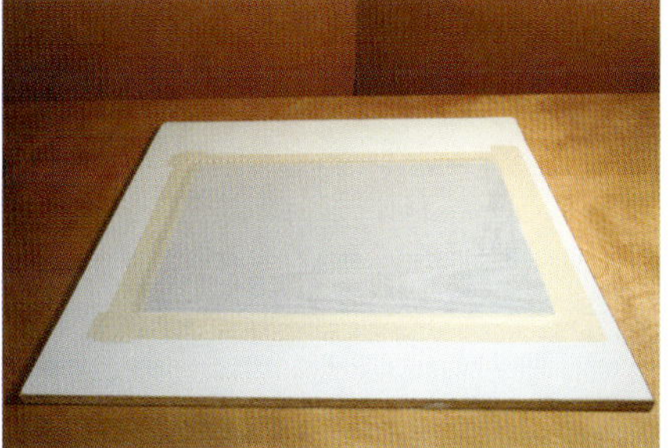

6. The paper will become smooth and tight. (Note that by using water in place of dosa, these same steps can also be used for stretching your paintings. See Variation of mizubari technique, p. 180.)

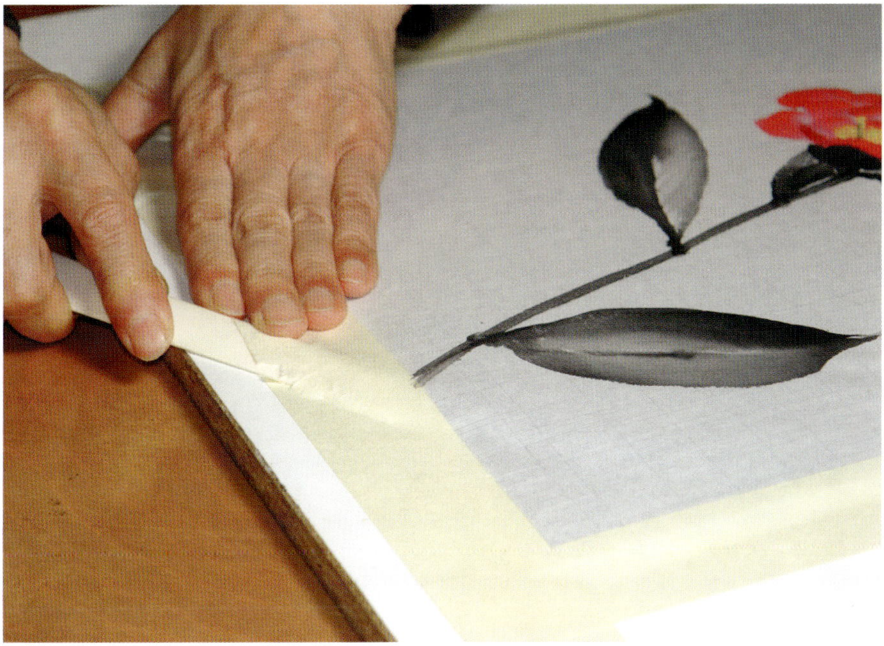

7. Use a folding bone or a table knife to carefully remove the paper from the board. It is important to become well-acquainted with how the paste used on the paper strips will react to the board. If the paste is too thick, it will be difficult to remove the paper strips. If the paste is too thin, the power of paper shrinkage will pull the paper strips loose. (Notice the painting: this photo depicts the use of the process for stretching, as mentioned above.)

Glossary

Bokkotsu 没骨: "bury the bones." In the bokkotsu technique, no outlines are used.

Boku 墨: "ink." This ideogram is also read as *sumi* in Japanese; see *Sumi*.

Bunjin-ga 文人画: Paintings by the bunjin (literati). The term has often mistakenly been used to mean the Southern Sung style of painting, but that is a misnomer.

Chi 気: Or *ki*. Concentrated energy tapped by "centered" willpower. Chi is utilized in the Asian fine arts, and in martial arts; in fact in all endeavors.

Choryu 長流: Type of brush basic to sumi painting; it offers flexibility and resilience.

Den sho 伝承: Traditional Asian method of teaching an art, in which knowledge is handed down from master to disciple forming a continuous system from one generation to the next.

Fusuma 襖: Traditional Japanese sliding panels which move horizontally to open to an adjoining room or create a larger space.

Gago 雅号: A painter's artistic name. These artistic or pen names may be retained for a lifetime, or may change from time to time.

Gampi 雁皮: A shrub (Wikstroemia spp.) used for paper making.

Gyosho 行書: Semi-formal or cursive writing style.

Hake 刷毛: A wide, flat brush. This category of flat brush includes many sizes and hair combinations.

Hyogu 表具: Traditional Japanese method for mounting fusuma, folding screens and hanging scrolls.

Ita hake 板刷毛: *ita* = board, *hake* = flat. Same as *Hake*.

Kaisho 楷書: Square or printed writing style. In this book it is called the "formal" style of writing.

Kano School 狩野派: Founded by Kano Eitoku (1543–1590). After he had studied the Northern Sung style of painting, the Shogun commissioned him to decorate the castle and official residence. The Kano style continued as the art used by the Shoguns, and influenced all later Japanese art.

Kan-ga 漢画: A name given to the Northern and Southern Sung Style of Chinese paintings, to differentiate them from the traditional Yamato-e Japanese style paintings.

Kobo Daishi 弘法大師・空海: (774–835) Respected as one of the three major calligraphers in Japanese history, the Buddhist monk Kukai was given the title of Kobo Daishi by the imperial court of Japan.

Kozo 楮 A species of mulberry used for papermaking.

Menso 面相筆 Type of brush for painting extremely thin lines.

Mitsumata 三つ又: A shrub (Edgeworthia papyrifera) used for papermaking.

Mizubari 水張り: A method of stretching a completed sumi painting to restore it to its original size and smoothness.

Nijimi 滲み: An effect in painting, caused by moisture from water and ink spreading or bleeding through the paper's fibers.

Nikawa 膠: *ni* = cook, *kawa* = skin. An adhesive used in painting and wood work. Animal skin is soaked in slaked lime water then cooked down, resulting in a brown jellylike substance, which is then refined.

Renpitsu 連筆: A type of brush made from individual smaller brushes fastened together to form a wider flat brush. Used in the same ways as a hake brush.

Rimpa School 琳派: A school of Japanese painting created in the seventeenth century by Honami Koetsu (1558–1637) and Tawaraya Sotatsu (d. c. 1643). Ogata Korin (d. 1716) consolidated the philosophy. The Rimpa school's refined style was appreciated by the public at large, whereas the Kano School was considered to be the governmental school of painting.

Sensho Zakyu-an 仙昌坐久庵: *sen* = sage, *sho* from "Shozo." *za* = seated, *kyu* = long, *an* = hut. Shozo Sato's gago.

Sesshu 雪舟: (1420–1506) Often called the "saint" of suiboku-ga. Buddhist monk who traveled to China and studied painting. In 1467 he returned to Japan and created masterpiece landscape paintings. His paintings have strongly influenced artists in succeeding generations. In 2002, a grand exhibition commemorating his 500th anniversary was celebrated in Japan.

Shikishi 色紙: Sized or unsized paper mounted on board and trimmed with a thin gold border. Used for calligraphy or painting. Shikishi come in many different sizes and shapes.

Shuniku 朱肉: *shu* = vermillion, *niku* = meat. Stamp pad, used with a seal to stamp an official signature upon a painting or a document.

Sosho 草書: Informal or "cursive" style of writing; sometimes called the running style or "grass style."

Suiboku-ga 水墨画: *sui* = water, *boku* = sumi ink, *ga* = painting. A word used to describe a sumi painting. Suiboku works generally use more strokes and require more time than do sumi-e works; see the Introduction for more about their differences.

Suiteki 水滴: *sui* = water, *teki* = drop. A specially created ceramic or metal container used to add water in small amounts to the ink as one grinds it on the suzuri.

Sumi 墨: "ink." This ideogram is also read as *boku* in Chinese. To create sumi/boku, oil is burned; the soot is then collected and combined with animal glue (nikawa). The resulting liquid is used for writing and painting.

Suzuri 硯: Grinding stone, used to prepare ink.

Tarashi komi たらし込み: *tarashi* = drip, *komi* = soak in. A technique involving dropping ink or water on wet portions of a painting to obtain special effects.

Tsuke tate 付けたて: A method using the placement of dark and light ink within a brush's bristles to obtain highlight-and-shadow effects.

Ura uchi 裏打ち: A method of stretching a completed sumi painting to restore it to its original size and smoothness.

Wabi-sabi 侘び・寂: In aesthetic terminology, *wabi* and *sabi* point in the direction of "beauty that is opposite from gorgeous and splendid" and indicate a simple, rustic and imperfect beauty.

Where to Purchase Asian Art Supplies

As sumi-e and monochrome art have become more mainstream, the sources for brushes, paper, ink, and the other tools you need have increased. Check your local art supply stores; many now carry sumi-e supplies. If you live near a large metropolis, try the local Chinatown, Japan Town, Korean or Vietnamese neighborhoods' shops. The Internet is also a convenient source, and today many fine-quality materials can be obtained from online vendors.

Below are a few of the many companies that carry a useful variety of Asian art supplies. Explore your local area to find others.

OAS Oriental Art Supply
www.orientalartsupply.com
info@orientalartsupply.com
Tel: 800-969-4471 or 714-969-4470
Shop located in Huntington Beach, CA 92646.

Man Luen Choon
www.manluenchoon.com
art@manluenchoon.com
Tel: (852) 25-44-69-65
Shop located at 2/F Harvest Bldg., 29-35 Wing Kut Street, Central Hong Kong.

Daniel Smith, Inc.
www.danielsmith.com
Tel: 800-426-6740
Shops located in Seattle, WA 98134 and Bellevue, WA 98052.

Dick Blick Art Materials
www.dickblick.com
Tel: 800-828-4548 (U.S.); 309-343-6181 (international)
Shops located in many states; check the website.

Published by Tuttle Publishing, an imprint of Periplus Editions (HK) Ltd., with editorial offices at 364 Innovation Drive, North Clarendon, Vermont 05759 USA and 61 Tai Seng Avenue, #02-12, Singapore 534167.

Library of Congress Cataloging-in-Publication Data

Sato, Shozo, 1933-
 Sumi-e : the art of Japanese ink painting / Shozo Sato.
 — 1st ed.
    p. cm.
  ISBN 978-4-8053-1096-0 (hardcover)
1. Sumie–Technique. I. Title. II. Title: Art of Japanese ink painting.
  ND2462.S26 2010
  751.4'252–dc22
                              2009045319
ISBN: 978-4-8053-1096-0

Distributed by:

North America, Latin America & Europe
Tuttle Publishing,
364 Innovation Drive, North Clarendon, VT 05759-9436
USA
Tel: 1 (802) 773-8930; Fax: 1 (802) 773-6993
info@tuttlepublishing.com
www.tuttlepublishing.com

Japan
Tuttle Publishing
Yaekari Building, 3rd Floor,
5-4-12 Osaki, Shinagawa-ku, Tokyo 141 0032
Tel: (81) 03 5437-0171; Fax: (81) 03 5437-0755
tuttle-sales@gol.com

Asia Pacific
Berkeley Books Pte. Ltd.
61 Tai Seng Avenue, #02-12, Singapore 534167
Tel: (65) 6280-1330; Fax: (65) 6280-6290
inquiries@periplus.com.sg
www.periplus.com

12 11 10   5 4 3 2 1

Printed in Singapore

Acknowledgments

For many years, all of my English publications have been edited by my wife, Alice Ogura Sato, and I take this opportunity to express my deepest appreciation for her dedication.

My great appreciation goes to Ms. Beth Corwin and Mr. Tom Wolsky, who readjusted their very busy schedules to help create the DVD. I am also grateful to Mrs. Betzi Robinson, past president of the Sumi-e Society of America, and to Mrs. Joan Lok, the current president of the Sumi-e Society of America, who both have provided information for this book; and to the members of Tuttle Publishing, especially senior editor Sandra Korinchak, editorial supervisor June Chong, and senior graphic designer Chan Sow Yun.

Finally, I would like to dedicate this book to the students who attended my intensive sumi-e workshops and eventually became my friends, who inspired me to take my creative energy to new heights in the constant search for a fresh way to create the art of black ink.

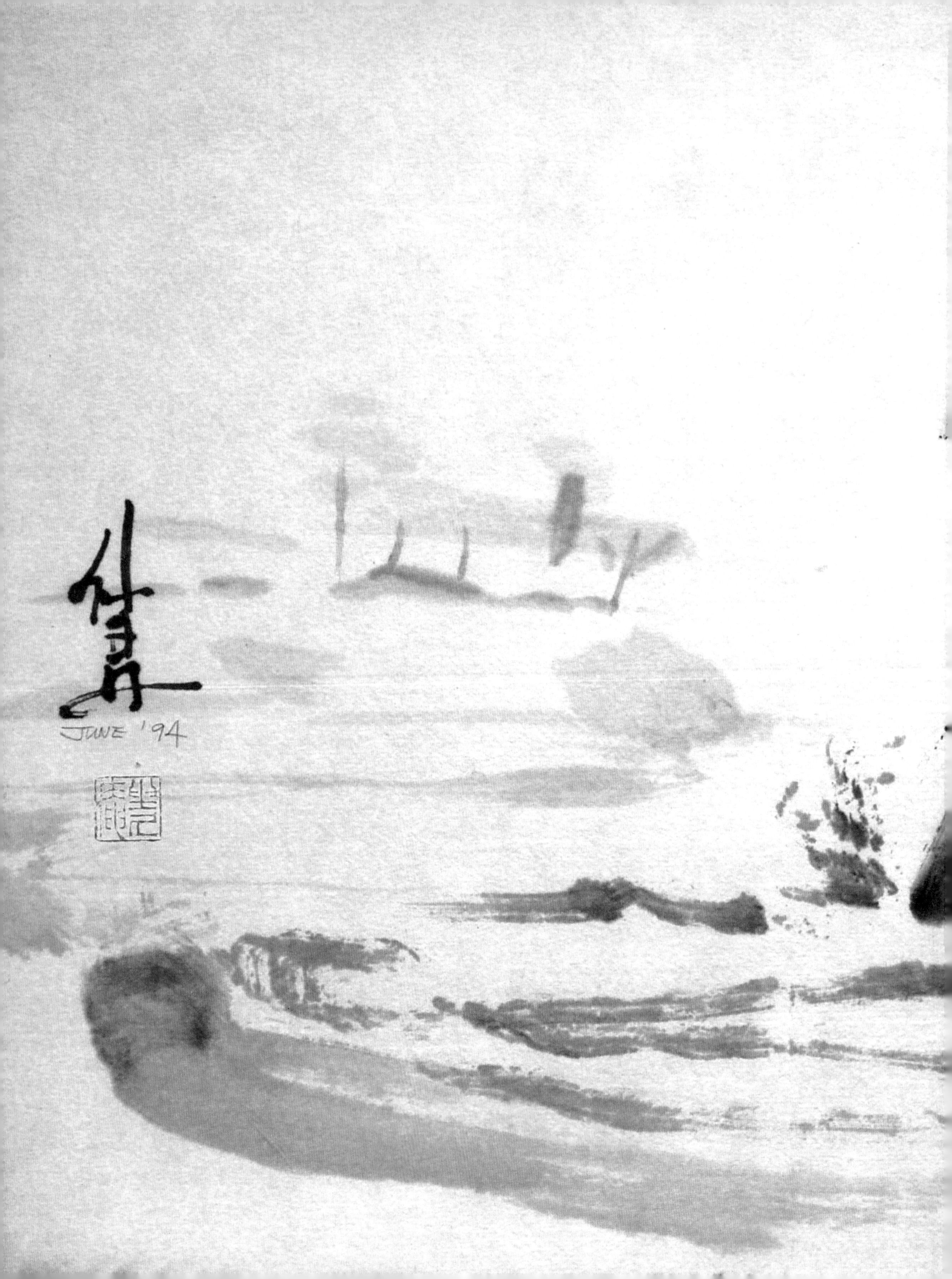

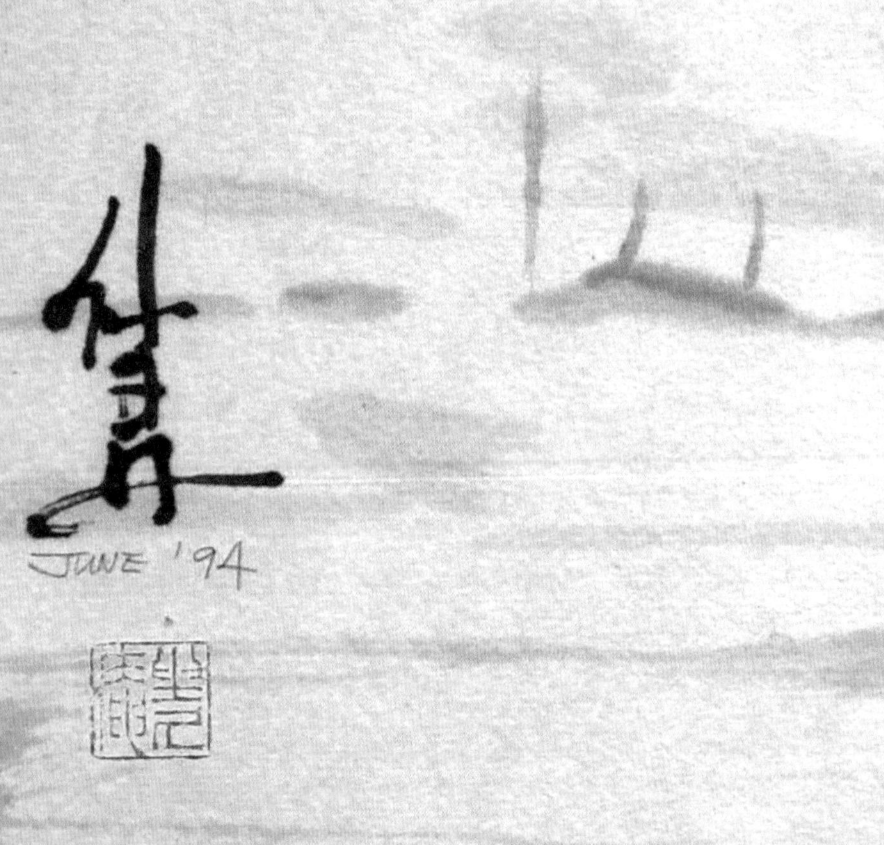

JUNE '94